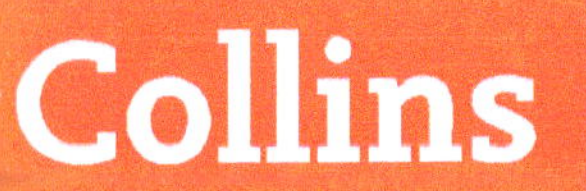

Cambridge International AS & A Level Art & Design

STUDENT'S BOOK

Alan Parsons, Liz Macfarlane,
Louise Arnould

William Collins' dream of knowledge for all began with the publication of his first book in 1819.
A self-educated mill worker, he not only enriched millions of lives, but also founded a flourishing publishing house. Today, staying true to this spirit, Collins books are packed with inspiration, innovation and practical expertise. They place you at the centre of a world of possibility and give you exactly what you need to explore it.

Collins. Freedom to teach.

Published by Collins
An imprint of HarperCollins*Publishers*
The News Building
1 London Bridge Street
London
SE1 9GF

HarperCollins*Publishers* Macken House
39/40 Mayor Street Upper
Dublin 1
DO1 C9W8
Ireland

10 9 8 7

ISBN 978-0-00-825099-7

British Library Cataloguing in Publication Data
A catalogue record for this publication is available from the British Library.

Authors: Alan Parsons, Liz Macfarlane, Louise Arnould
Commissioning editors: Joanna Ramsay and Lizzie Geldart
In-house editors: Hannah Dove, Caroline Green and Isabelle Sinclair
Development editors: Robert Anderson and Mo Dutton
Project managers: Hazel Geatches and Iolanda Steadman
Copy editors: Kim Vernon and Karen Williams
Proofreader: Nikky Twyman
Permissions researcher: Sophie Hartley
Cover designers: Kevin Robbins and Gordon MacGilp
Cover illustrator: Maria Herbert-Liew
Typesetter: Ken Vail Graphic Design Ltd
Production controller: Sarah Burke
Printed and bound by: Ashford Colour Press Ltd

We would like to thank the following students for giving us permission to reproduce their work:
Thomas Bailey
Jessica Bennett
Anna Buriak
Blaze Chapman
Naomi Flowers
Suki Fong
Jackie German
Eloise Groves
George Groves
Alison Page
Ashlea Philips
Julia Vila Rosell
Isabella Vanackere Castellano
Anna White
Christine Wiggil

We would also like to thank the following teachers and schools for their support:
Caroline Ferguson, Head of Art, Berkhamsted School, Laurie Pearsall, Palma College Mallorca and Becky Tough.

The publishers gratefully acknowledge the permission granted to reproduce the copyright material in this book. Every effort has been made to trace copyright holders and to obtain their permission for the use of copyright material. The publishers will gladly receive any information enabling them to rectify any error or omission at the first opportunity.

Contents

Introduction

The aims of this course

This book is written to support the teaching of the Cambridge Assessment International Education AS & A Level Art & Design syllabus (9479). It is a handbook for students that can also be used by teachers, covering the requirements of the Cambridge Assessment International Education syllabus. It presents information, ideas and activities that will enable students to develop their skills, and broaden their knowledge and understanding of the subject, while developing confidence and independence. This approach supports work towards all of the assessment components: coursework, externally set assignment and personal investigation.

This book makes reference to international contexts across the full range of art and design disciplines, and presents a wide range of practical activities and critical thinking tasks throughout. This will enable students to build a portfolio of evidence that can complement and supplement work undertaken during their teacher-taught course.

The course promotes six key concepts identified in the Cambridge International AS & A Level syllabus, which helps students to develop a deep understanding and make links across the whole subject. The six concepts are:

COMMUNICATION

Communication is fundamental to all art and design, from the simplest drawings to the most complex artworks. Communication is not just about what the artist or designer wants to convey. It is about the process and medium chosen as well as the relationship the work builds with the audience.

CREATIVITY

Creativity is at the heart of artists' or designers' practical processes and pushes them to produce work that truly connects and communicates with their audience. Creative thinkers question, investigate, experiment and take risks to produce effective outcomes and interesting and unique work. They use curiosity, imagination and innovation to solve art and design problems in new ways.

INTENTION

Intention is the starting point of a project that sets the artist or designer on their journey of exploration. An intention or purpose can come from a brief, proposal or research. At other times, it might begin as an idea or feeling, and develop as the artist or designer explores more deeply. It is important to identify the intention early in the process as well as to accept that it can change throughout a project.

MATERIALS AND PROCESSES

Experimenting with different materials and processes helps artists and designers to find their own personal style and build confidence. Skilful artists and designers select materials and apply processes that communicate their message effectively.

CRITICAL REFLECTION

The ability to reflect on work at all stages of the process is an essential skill. It helps artists and designers to learn from successes and mistakes and to make work more relevant. Receiving feedback from peers and teachers is a key part of this process.

RESEARCH AND CONTEXT

Independent research equips artists and designers with a broad view of the world. It also helps them to understand the context in which work is made and how it connects with its audience.

In this course, students will have the opportunity to develop the subject-based knowledge, skills and attributes they need to prepare them for the next stages of art and design education.

How to use this book

When using this book, you are encouraged to be open-minded and explore all **areas of study** and **disciplines**, as ideas and information can inform and influence practice no matter which area of study you may specialise in and promote breadth of thinking.

This book is in three parts:

1. Getting started
2. Modules (1–4)
3. Practical guidance.

1. GETTING STARTED

This will introduce you to the formal elements and basic **components** of art and design, and provide you with a framework to help you analyse works of art in a meaningful way. It will also give you brief introductions to each of the areas of study and disciplines.

2. THE MODULES

The main part of the book consists of four modules, each relating to the Cambridge Assessment International Education assessment objectives for the course:

- Module 1: Observation and intention relates to the assessment objective 'record'.
- Module 2: Contexts and concepts relates to the assessment objective 'explore'.
- Module 3: Development and refinement relates to the assessment objective 'develop'.
- Module 4: Audience and setting relates to the assessment objective 'present'.

The modules are colour-coded throughout the book as shown above.

Each module begins with a general introduction to the broad focus of the module as well as with a special feature on the Personal Investigation (see the boxed feature below). Each area of study is then covered within the context of each module, with the different disciplines within the area of study covered in the units. These units clearly state the learning objectives, outlining what you should know, understand or be able to do by the end of the module. The main text of each unit is accompanied by supporting practical activities as well as by opportunities to reflect on your work.

The Personal Investigation

The Personal Investigation is a key component of the Cambridge Assessment International Education A Level externally set assignment, providing 50 per cent of the final marks. It combines both practical work and written analysis of between 1000 and 1500 words on a related topic. If completing the A Level course over two years, you may not begin work on the Personal Investigation until your second year of study, but it is important to start gaining the skills you will need to carry out this component well.

area of study This term refers to one of the broad areas of art and design: fine arts; three-dimensional (3D) design; graphic communication; textiles and fashion.

component Part, quality or aspect.

discipline This term refers to a specific type of work within each area of study: for example, drawing and painting are both disciplines within the field of fine arts.

3. PRACTICAL GUIDANCE

The third part of the book provides practical guidance, covering advice on research for the coursework, how to select the best of your work and prepare supporting studies for assessment, and interpreting starting points for the supervised test. It also includes a selection of exemplar work by AS & A Level students that demonstrates how the assessment objectives can be met through varied approaches to coursework.

Other features of this book

There are a number of key features throughout this book that are designed to help you to get the most out of this course:

Activity boxes

Activity boxes provide a variety of practical activities, encouraging you to work with a range of media and techniques, to explore different contexts and respond to the work of other artists and designers. The practical work can contribute to your coursework portfolio. Activities are labelled A, B, and so on, within each unit.

Critical thinking:

Critical thinking boxes ask you to reflect on ideas and approaches and think about how you can apply what you learn to your own work. These boxes also help you to reflect on your own creative journey and develop the skill of recording your thoughts as annotations.

Materials and techniques:

Materials and techniques boxes introduce you to the media, processes and techniques that artists and designers use to make their work.

Artists and designers:

Artists and designers boxes explore the module themes through the practice of both historical and contemporary artists. This could perhaps provide inspiration for your own work.

Key terms boxes provide definitions of subject-specific terms as well as any other words you may have difficulty with if English is not your first language. In addition, there is a full glossary of terms for reference at the back of the book.

Tip:

Tip boxes provide suggestions and ideas to develop 'best practice' habits and study skills at AS & A Level.

Further research

Further research at the end of each section suggests links to websites, galleries and museums where you can find further information about artists and designers and their work, encouraging independent study.

Figures and captions

There is a rich variety of images throughout this book and each is referred to in the text using a numbered figure (for example, Figure 1.15).

The images are not intended to be just illustrations of the text, however. Sometimes the accompanying caption invites you to interact closely with what you are looking at, asking a question and encouraging you to look very carefully and reflect on what you see. Try to use the images as fully as possible, as inspiration for both thought and work.

Note that, where relevant, the first line of a caption gives you the following information about the image in order:

name of the artist, title of work (conventionally in italic for an artwork and in quotes for a design), date when it was made or completed, medium (what was used to make it).

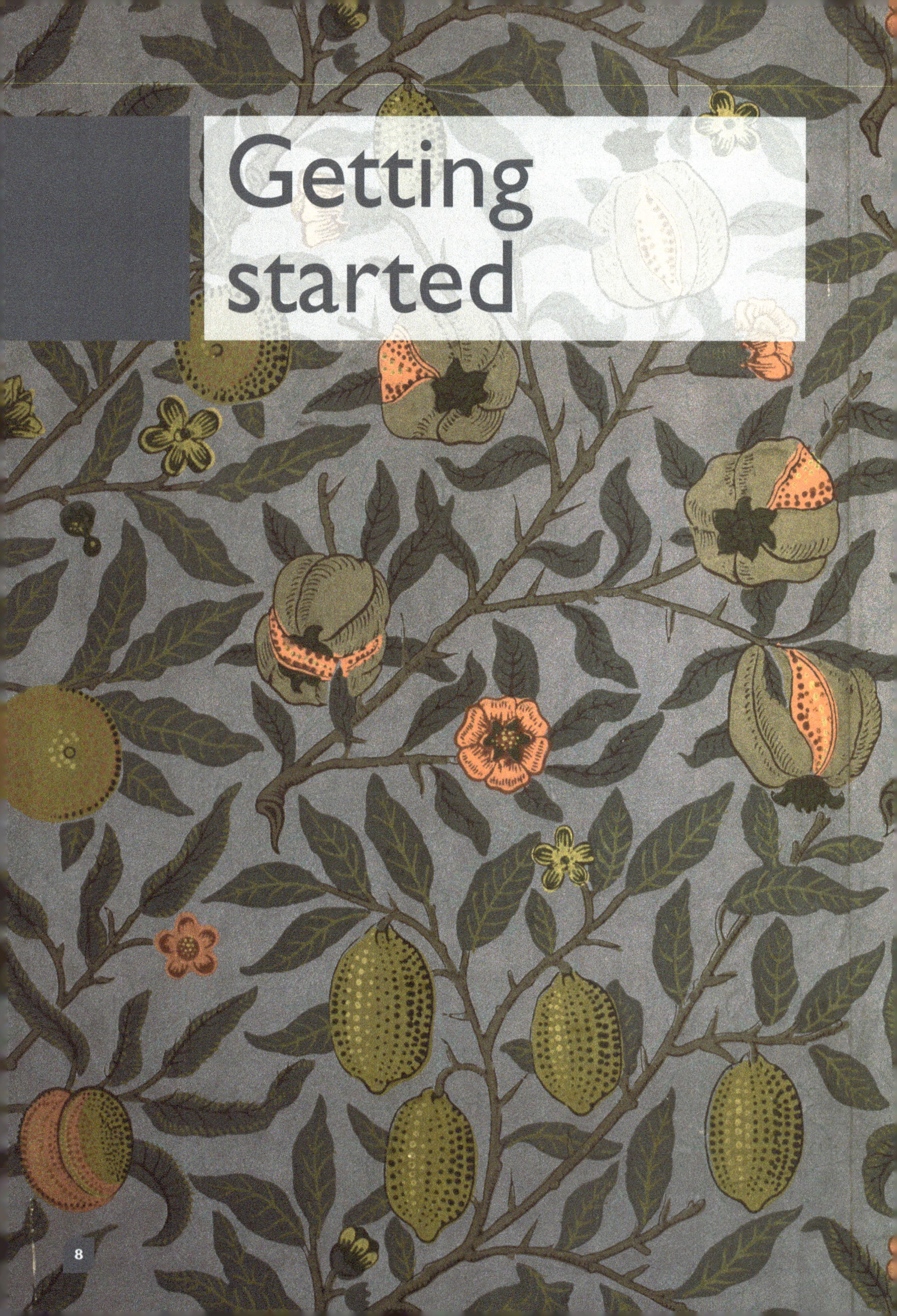

Getting started

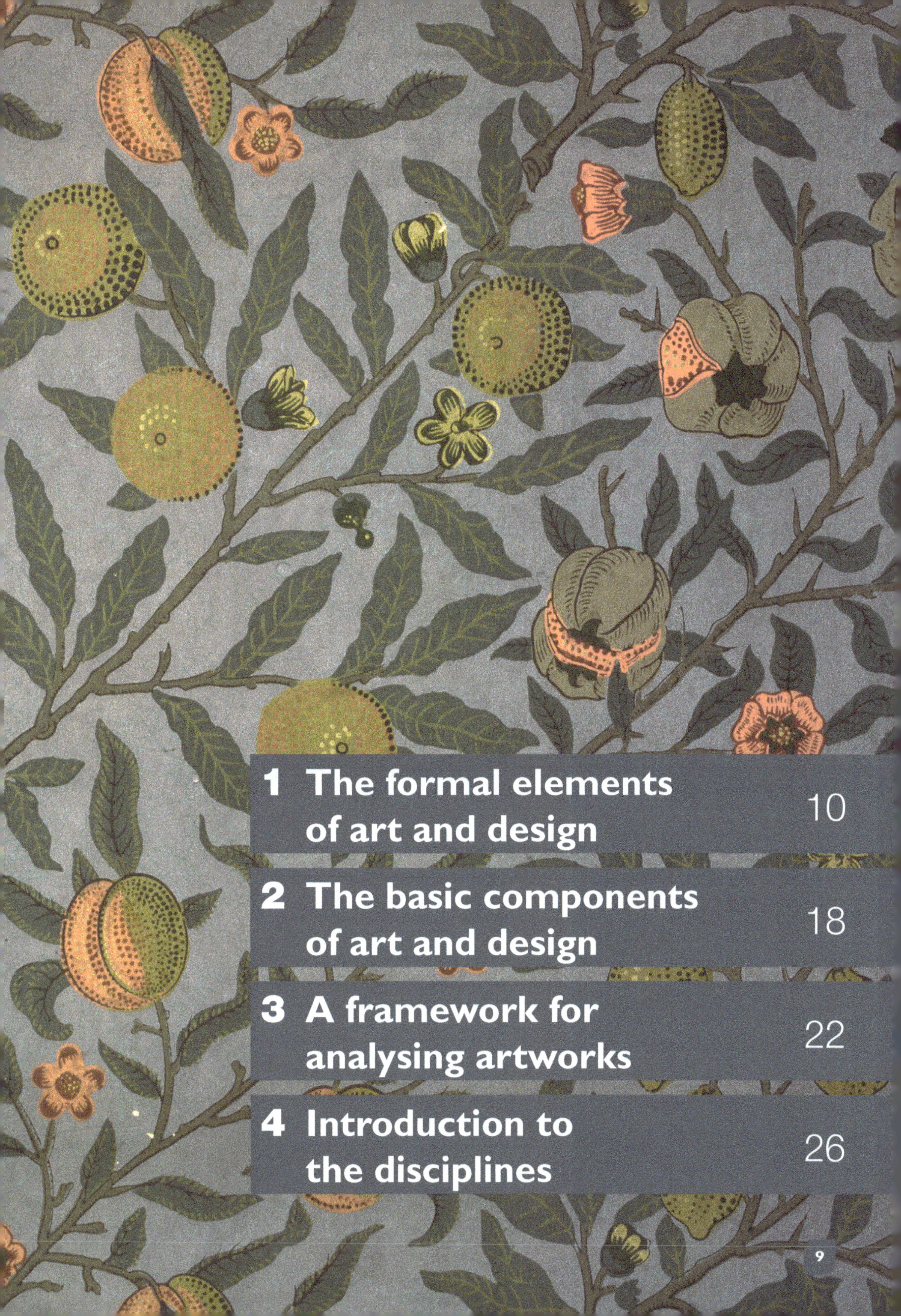

0.1 The formal elements of art and design

The formal elements of art and design are the fundamental components of any piece of work. The formal elements are line, tone (sometimes also known as **value**), colour, shape, form, texture and pattern. They are often used together, and how they are organised in a piece of art determines what the finished piece will look like.

LINE

Line is a narrow continuous mark, made by a pencil, pen or brush across a surface, or such a mark cut into or raised from a surface. Line can also be created when the edges of two surfaces meet in three-dimensional (3D) work. Line can describe different qualities – for example:

- Lines can show the shape and form of something, much as in the contour lines on maps and charts that join points of equal height or depth.
- Line can communicate feeling and emotion according to the way in which the mark is made: short, hard, solid lines can have a different feel to longer, soft, flowing lines.
- Line can suggest movement and speed (Figure 0.3).

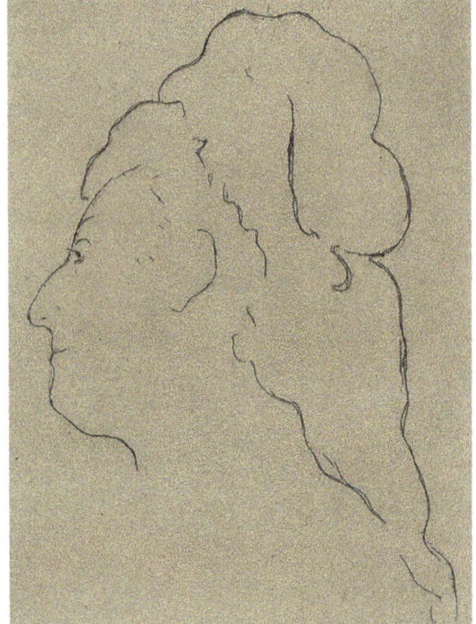

0.1 Édouard Manet, *Eva Gonzalès profile turned to the left*, 1870, **etching**, private collection.

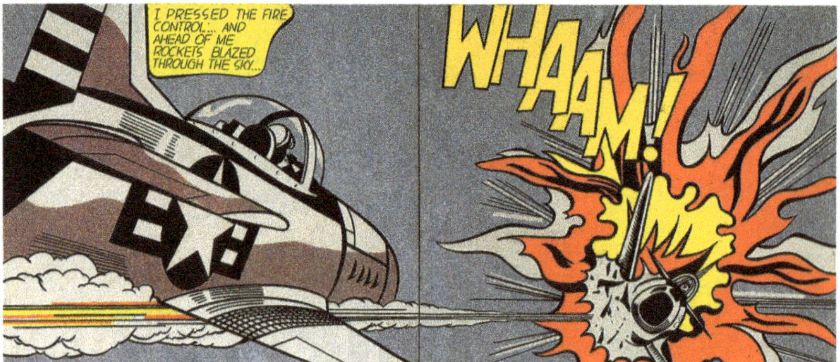

0.3 Roy Lichtenstein, *Whaam!*, 1963, acrylic paint and oil paint on canvas, Tate, London. The American artist Roy Lichtenstein has used simple bold lines to suggest the speed and movement of the exploding aircraft.

The type of line that is used can depend on the purpose of the drawing. Compare the quality of line used by the French artist Édouard Manet (1832–83) in an etched portrait of Eva Gonzalès (Figure 0.1) with a sketch for a furniture design (Figure 0.2) by the Scottish designer Charles Rennie Mackintosh (1868–1928). The line used in the portrait is flowing and soft. In the drawing of the dressing table, the quality of line is solid and hard, weighted to clearly show the difference between the outline shape and the detail of the decoration.

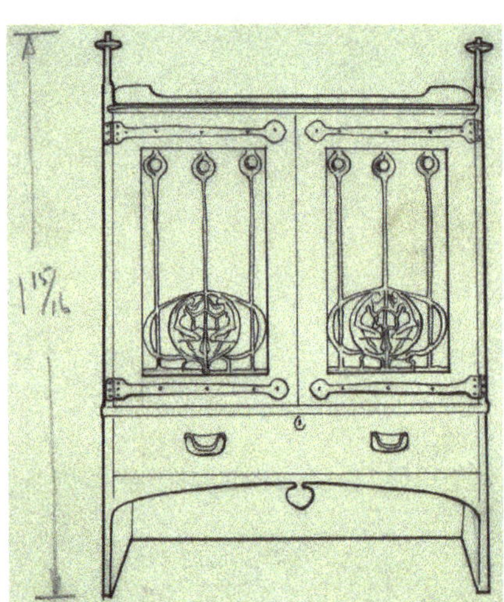

0.2 Charles Rennie Mackintosh, *Sketch for a furniture design (a dressing table)*, about 1910, ink on paper, private collection.

TONE

Tone refers to the lightness or darkness of something. It is also sometimes known as value. This could be a shade or how dark or light a colour appears. Tones are created by the way that light falls on an object (Figure 0.4). The part of an object that is closest to the light source will appear to be a lighter shade or brighter colour than other areas of the object, even though the colour of the object is in fact the same all over. The parts of the object that are in the strongest light are the highlights, and the darker areas are the shadows. There will be a range of tones in between the two.

You can see the effects created by light shining on a sphere in the drawing in Figure 0.5. Here, pencil shading has been used to capture the range of tones observed. Note how the direction of the pencil marks follows the outline shape of the sphere. This emphasises the round shape of the sphere and suggests a 3D form.

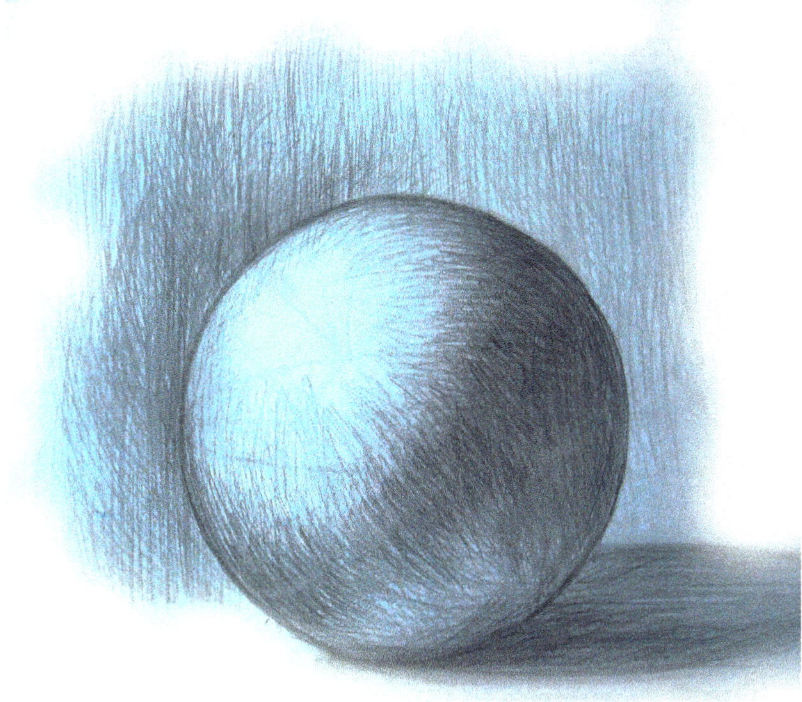

0.5 This pencil drawing captures the effects of light shining on a sphere. The drawing records the tonal variation, with the darkest shadowy areas furthest away from the light source.

0.4 The photograph illustrates how **tonal value** has been captured through the camera lens, with the darkest tones at the front and the lightest in the distance. This gives the image a sense of depth.

Tip:

You can focus on areas of light and shade more easily, and so better perceive tones, by half closing your eyes. Doing this reduces the amount of colour that you see and makes it easier to compare areas of similar tonal value in relation to each other.

etching Technique of intaglio engraving in which the image or design is engraved into the plate using acid.
tonal value The lightness or darkness of a shade.
value The lightness or darkness of a colour.

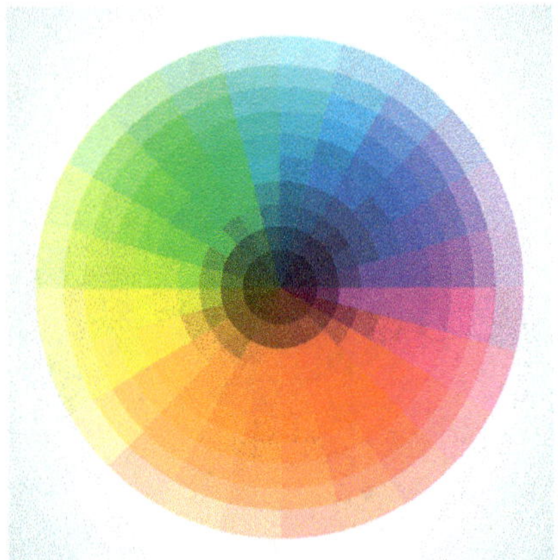

0.6 The colour wheel, or colour circle, shows how colours in the spectrum relate to one another. This example demonstrates the impact of different tonal value on the colours, from the lightest tints on the outer circles to the darker tones in the centre.

COLOUR

The colour (or hue) of something is the appearance that it has as a result of the way in which it reflects light. Colour and how we perceive it is closely linked to tonal value. When talking about colour and how dark or light it appears, we refer to the tone and **tint** (Figure 0.6). Tone usually refers to the addition of darker shades and tint to the addition of white to make lighter shades of the colour.

The colour in paints, pastels and other media are created by powdered **pigments**, mixed with oil, gum or other liquid. The colours red, blue and yellow are the traditional primary colours – that is, colours from which other colours can be made by mixing pigments. In theory, with the exception of white, all other colours can be made by mixing the primary colours together.

Mixing two primary colours together results in the creation of secondary colours. Red and yellow make orange, yellow and blue make green, and blue and red make purple. The secondary colours are **complementary** to the primary colour not used in their mix, and fall opposite each other in the colour wheel. When complementary colours are mixed together, they produce neutral grey, natural black and browns, known as tertiary colours (Figure 0.7).

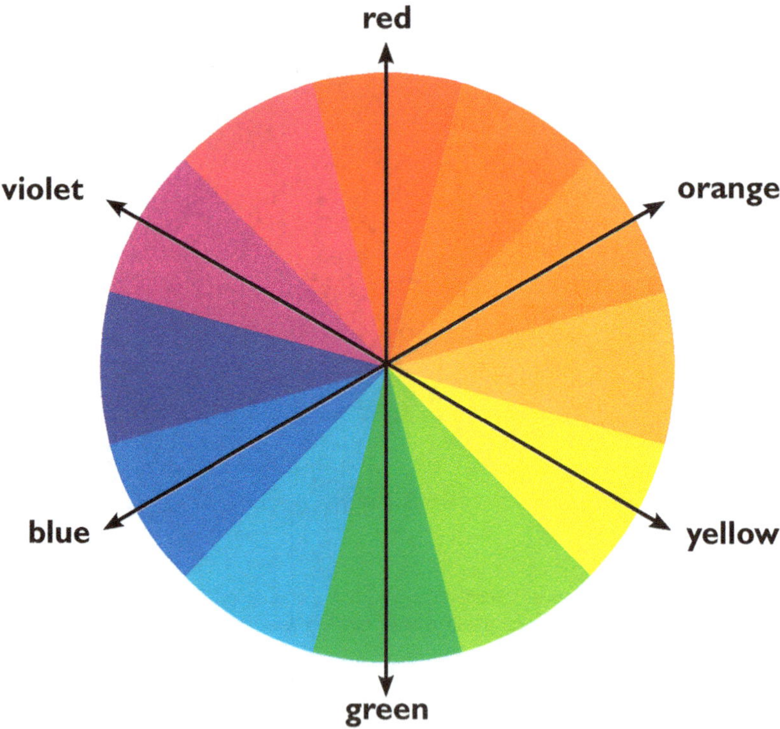

0.7 When mixed together, the complementary colours, opposite each other on the colour wheel, produce greys and browns.

Using complementary colours to make darker tones makes these appear more vivid and less flat looking, as can be seen in Figure 0.8.

Complementary colours create contrast, whereas colours that are next to each other on the colour wheel are harmonious. The use of harmonious colours or contrasting colours can affect the mood of an artwork and create areas of interest in an artwork.

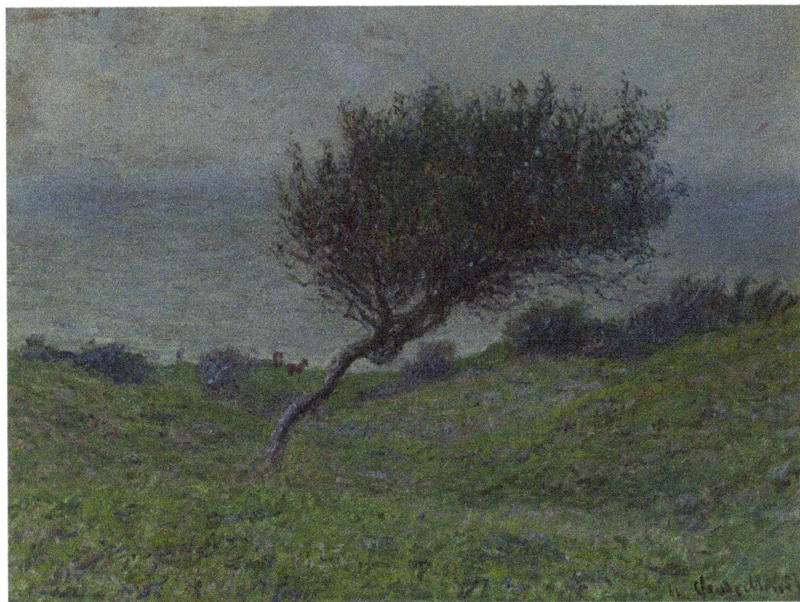

0.8 Claude Monet, *Seacoast at Trouville*, 1881, oil on canvas, Museum of Fine Arts, Boston. The French painter Claude Monet (1840–1926) has not used a pre-mixed black in this painting, instead, he has mixed primary and secondary colours to create the darker tones. This makes the darker colours look more vivid.

Activity A: **Practise mixing colours**

Using the type of paint of your choice, practise mixing secondary and tertiary (neutral) colours from primary colours. See how many different shades of the secondary and tertiary colours you can mix by subtly varying the amount of each primary colour you use. Compare the results if you vary the primary colours. For example, ultramarine blue is a different hue to cobalt blue, so you will achieve slightly different ranges of green when you mix each of them with the same yellow.

Next, try mixing colours using a different medium, for example, layering coloured pastels and blending them with your finger to achieve new secondary colours, or by overlaying layers of colour pencil.

Materials and techniques: **Colour in printing**

When talking about commercial or digital colour printing, we use the term 'four-colour process printing', or 'CMYK'. In this process, the colours of an image are separated out into four basic colours – the primary colours **c**yan (blue), **m**agenta (red) and **y**ellow, plus the '**k**ey' colour black – which are printed in layers, working from light to dark.

complementary A colour is described as complementary when it contrasts with and reinforces another colour. Green and red, for example, are complementary colours.

pigment A material often in the form of a dry powder that, after being mixed with oil, water and so on, is used for adding colour in artworks.

tint Another word for shade.

SHAPE AND FORM

A shape is an area enclosed by a line. It can remain just as an outline or it can be described through changes of colour or tone. Shapes can be **geometric**, such as a circle, triangle or square, or **organic** and free-flowing. The positioning of different shapes and a mix of different-sized shapes can help create unity and **balance** within an artwork (Figure 0.9).

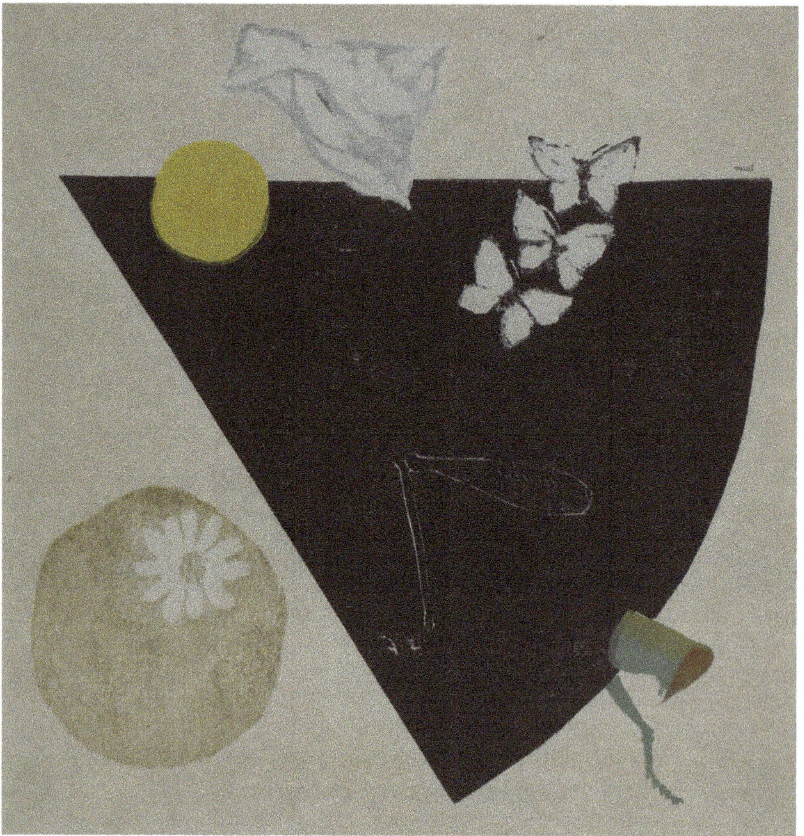

0.9 Kōshirō Onchi, *Family of the Field*, 1937, colour woodcut on Japanese paper. Dallas Museum of Art, Texas. The Japanese artist Kōshirō Onchi (1891–1955) has brought together both geometric and organic shapes and in different sizes to create a sense of balance within this image.

'Form' is the term used to describe a 3D shape, such as a sphere, cone or cube. It refers to the shape (including height, width, depth and volume) of real objects and artefacts, such as a sculpture, ceramic **vessel**, or structured **garment** or costume. Examples of 3D forms from different disciplines of art and design can be seen in Figures 0.10, 0.11 and 0.12.

'Form' can also be used to refer to a 3D quality in 2D artworks. For example, in Figure 0.5 the tonal pencil drawing of the sphere illustrates how a 2D circle is given form by adding shading to make it look 3D.

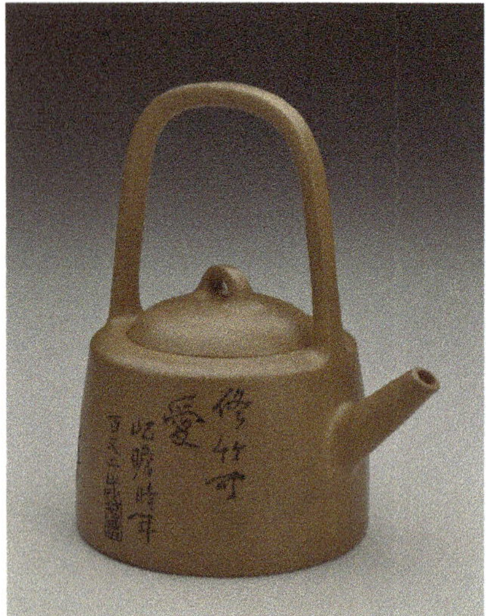

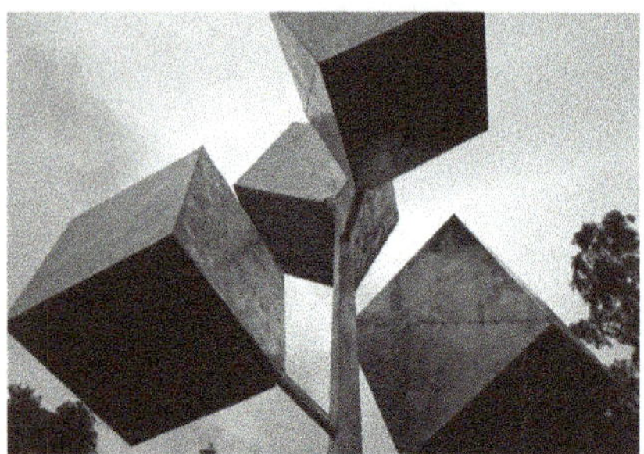

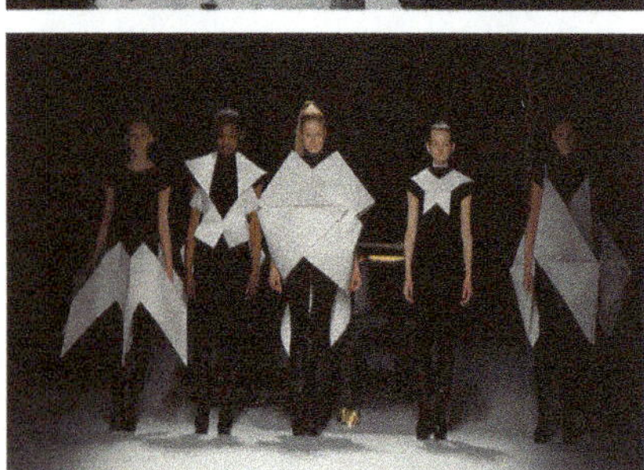

0.10, 0.11, and **0.12** Examples of 3D form: Unknown artist, *Chinese ceramic teapot with bamboo and rock image* (Yixing stoneware), 1993, Indianapolis Museum of Art at Newfields; George Rickey, detail from *Cluster of Four Cubes*, 1992, stainless steel, National Gallery of Art Sculpture Garden, Washington DC; garments by the Japanese fashion designer Issey Miyake, 2011. Write down some notes about the form of each object.

TEXTURE

Texture refers to the surface quality of something, the way something feels or looks like it feels. There are two types of texture: actual texture and implied, visual texture.

Actual texture refers to real textures that can be touched or felt. Texture is important in textiles, where you can create interest through the creation of different surface textures and by combining different fabrics (Figure 0.13). In 3D disciplines such as sculpture or ceramics, the surface finish can be varied through mark-making or use of processes such as glazing. In 2D disciplines, such as drawing or painting, using techniques such as **collage** or **impasto** can create interesting textures.

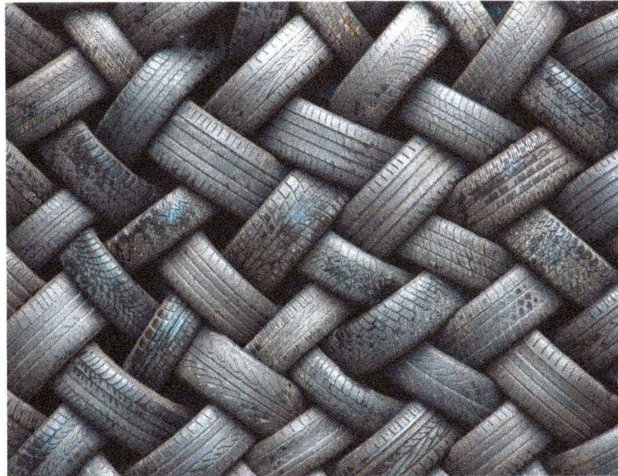

0.13 The image is of a wall where tyres have been joined together to give the appearance of being woven, creating the texture of fabric. Each tyre has its own unique texture (as well as pattern) created by the tread.

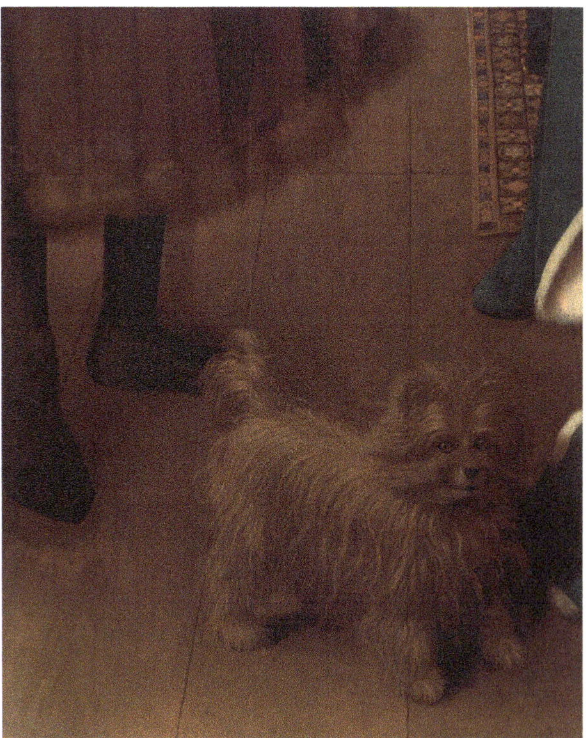

0.14 Jan van Eyck, detail from *The Arnolfini Portrait*, 1434, oil on oak **panel**, National Gallery, London. Here the artist has recorded the different textures of fabrics, fur, hair and wood with a remarkable **realism**. Find out more about this painting online at the National Gallery website.

Implied, or *visual, texture* is created using marks to represent real textures. It gives the illusion of a texture or surface, although, if you touched it, it would be smooth or at least smoother than it appears.

Implied texture can be created by experimenting with different mark-making and materials, using different qualities of line, tone and colour. Some artists are extremely adept at capturing different textural qualities. The Flemish artist Jan van Eyck (1390–1441) was famous in his time for creating the illusion of real textures in his oil paintings, as in the *Arnolfini Portrait* (Figure 0.14).

Activity B: **Collect and recreate textures**

1. Collect actual examples and photographs of a variety of different-textured surfaces and stick them into a sketchbook.
2. Next to each sample, try to recreate the texture by using any appropriate drawing or painting medium and mark-making technique.
3. Make a note about the media and techniques that you have used.

balance Harmony in the parts of a whole.
collage Artwork technique where a range of materials, such as newspaper, textiles, photographs and so on, are fixed or glued onto a surface (paper, canvas and so on).
garment An item of clothing.
geometric Patterns or shapes made up of regular lines.
impasto Where oil paint is applied very thickly to a surface (such as a canvas), often creating a dense, uneven texture.
organic Derived from nature.
panel Wooden board used as a surface for painting on.
realism Term used to describe art that captures very closely the look of real things. When used with a capital R (Realism), it refers to a specific art movement in 19th-century France.
vessel A container, especially for holding liquids.

PATTERN

Pattern is a design, or **motif**, created by repeating lines, shapes, tones or colours. Patterns can be made up of simple shapes, such as interlocking circles or a Greek key pattern, or formed from more complex arrangements of, for example, flowers and other natural forms (Figure 0.15). Patterns exist in nature, such as the markings on animal skin or fur, or they can be human-made and applied to a wide variety of surfaces, such as fabric, paper and stone.

Across all disciplines of art and design, motifs are used as decoration, for example:

- buildings, especially their **façades**
- ceramics, including tiles
- furniture
- textiles and wallpapers
- jewellery
- **decorative** art, such as tapestries or murals.

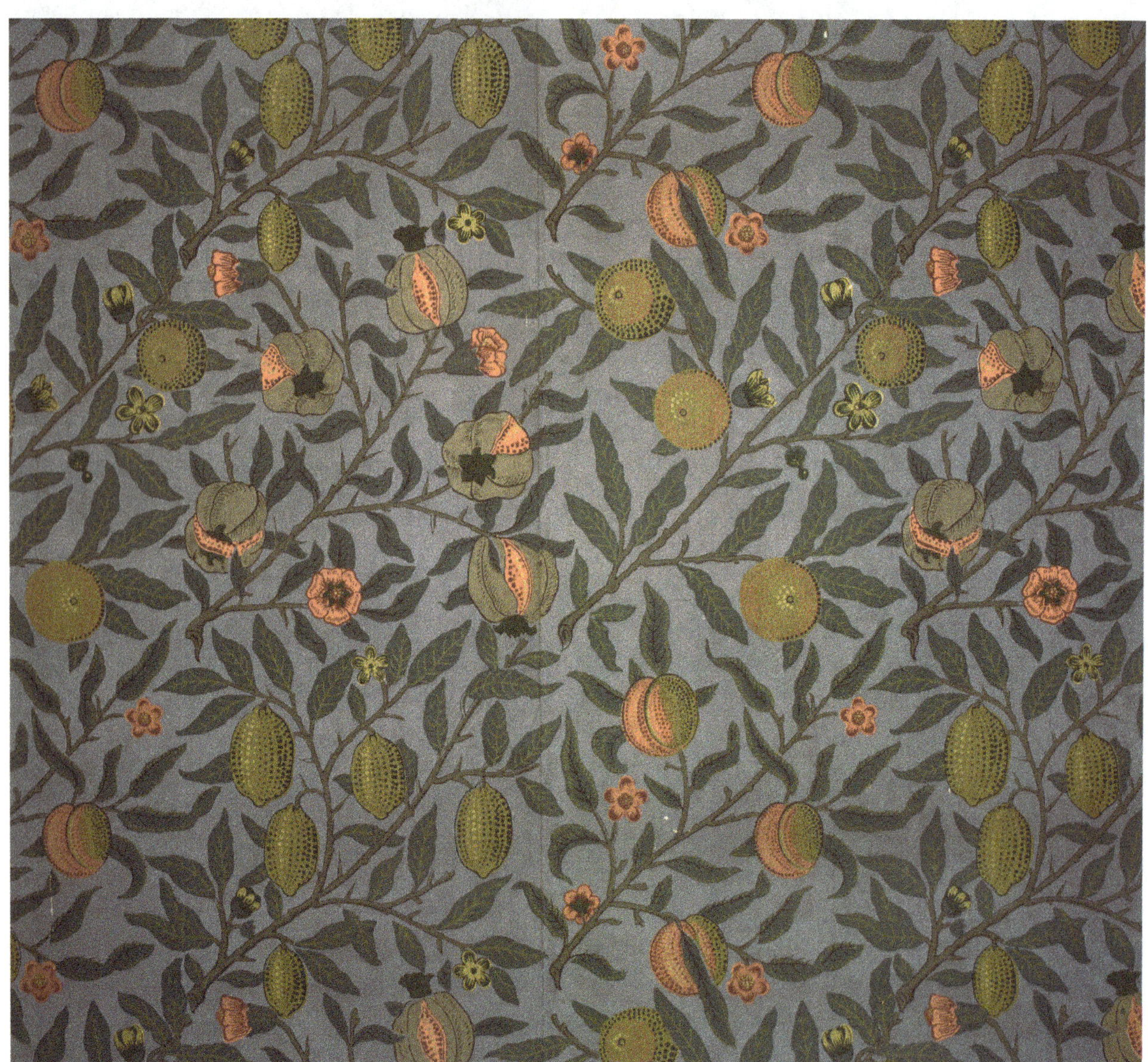

0.15 William Morris, 'Pomegranate' wallpaper, 1866. Can you work out the repeat pattern in this wallpaper by the English designer William Morris (1834–96)?

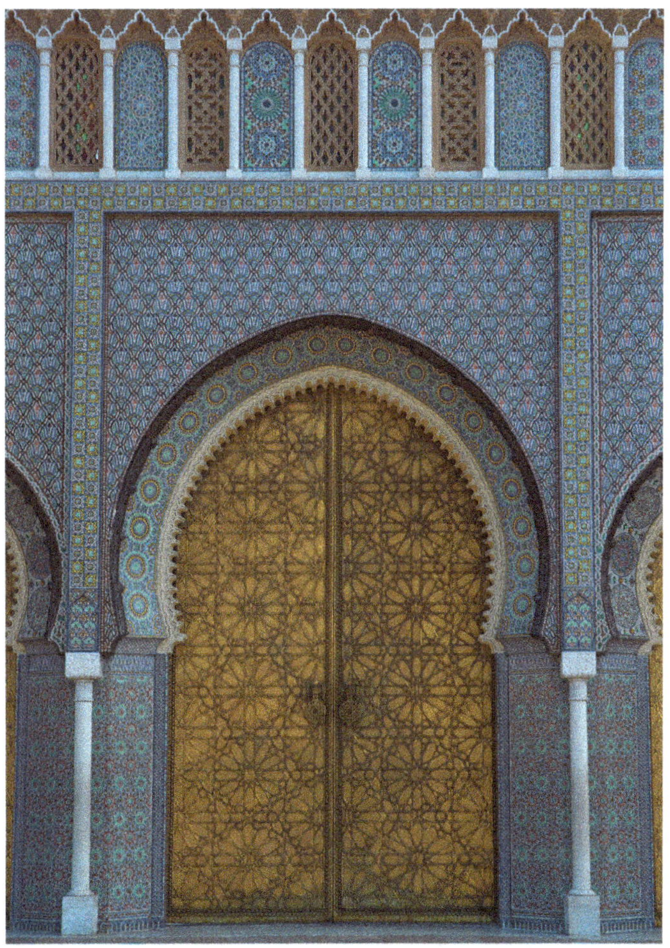

0.16 The entrance to the Royal Palace at Fez, Morocco, uses a wealth of vivid patterns.

Islamic art is often based around the use of geometric patterns. The designs often combine repeated squares and circles, which may overlap and interlace, forming intricate patterns. These patterns can form the entire decoration, or provide a framework for **floral** or **calligraphic** additions (Figure 0.16).

In many **cultures**, pattern has a **symbolic** meaning. For example, the textiles of the Quechua people of the Andes mountains in Peru feature a range of motifs, including the Sun (inti), river (mayu) and flower (t'ika), so each piece has its own complex meaning or story.

Activity C: **Record 10 patterns**

1. Consider how, and to what degree, pattern influences your own work.
2. Think about where you see patterns occurring in the natural and human-made world around you.
3. Take photographs or make sketches of patterns (five natural and five human-made) that you see.
4. Compare and contrast the patterns and make notes. How could you use these patterns in your work?
5. Keep the patterns and notes as a reference, perhaps as part of a pattern notebook, to use in your work later.

calligraphy Handwriting as an art, highly prized in many Eastern cultures.
culture A particular society or civilisation, considered especially in relation to its beliefs, way of life or art.
decorative Something that is intended to look pretty or attractive; ornamental.
façade The front or 'face' of a building.
floral Made up of flowers.
motif In the visual arts, a decorative image or design.
symbol An object that represents or stands in for an idea. The adjective is 'symbolic'.

0.2 The basic components of art and design

All works of art have a subject, form and content, and these are known as the components of art and design:

- The *subject* refers to the **theme** of the work.
- The *form* refers to how the work is made – the style and **composition** of the work, as well as its medium.
- The *content* is what the work is about and what it may mean.

SUBJECT

As part of your course, you will be given themes as starting points for your work. The externally set assignment comprises a selection of titles made up of a single word or short phrase, for example, 'Chairs' or 'In the workplace' – to which you must develop your personal response. The same title can be used no matter which area of study and discipline you have chosen to specialise in (Figures 0.17 and 0.18). This title forms the subject of the work.

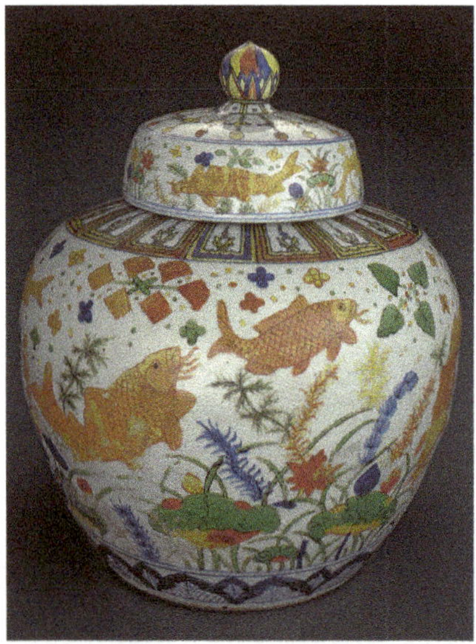

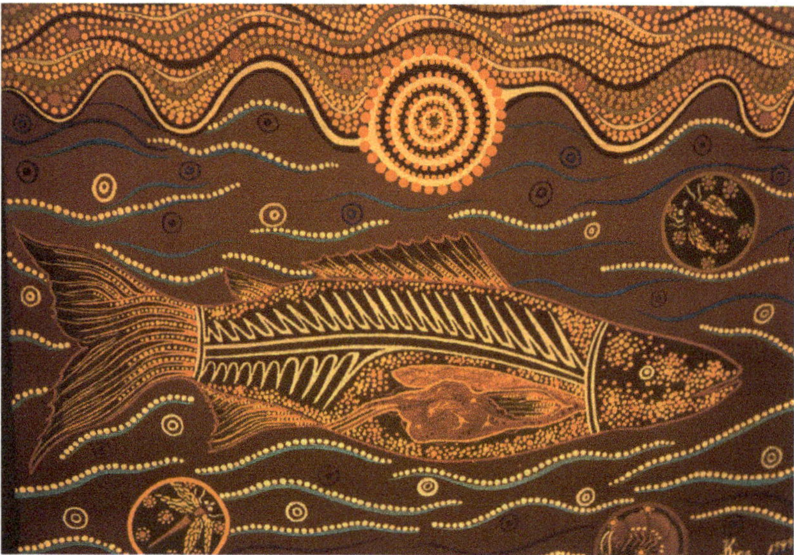

0.17 and **0.18** 'Fish' or 'Animals' could be used to describe the subject of both the Aboriginal Dreamtime painting and the Chinese covered jar from the Ming Dynasty (1368–1644), even though the works have a very different form and content.

Genre

As well as by subject, works of fine art can be categorised by **genre**. Genre literally means a kind or type of something (we often refer to films by their genre, such as horror or comedy). The genre describes what category the artwork belongs to, whereas the subject describes what the work of art depicts. The key genres are:

- *history* – showing a historical event or a scene from mythology
- *portraiture* – depicting an individual person
- *landscape* – depicting a scene of the countryside or a town or city
- *genre* – confusingly, in this instance, referring to art showing domestic scenes or incidents from everyday life
- *still life* – depicting ordinary everyday objects, such as fruit, flowers, vases and so on.

It is possible to have the same subject that can be categorised in more than one genre. For example, the subject of a chair could be categorised as being a still life, or it could be part of an everyday life scene, and so categorised as being genre. The subject can be the same in different genres, but the form and content can be very different.

FORM

The term 'form' here has a slightly different meaning from the meaning of the word 'form' as in 'formal elements'. When form is referred to as one of the basic components of art and design, it can refer to:

- the style of the work
- the media (materials), processes and techniques used to create the work
- the composition, as well as the other formal elements (see pages 10–17).

Style

When used to talk about art and design, the term 'style' means a characteristic of artworks from a specific period of time or group of people or by a specific individual. It describes the features or qualities that these artworks have in common.

Activity A: **Assess the features of a style**

The Memphis Group was a group of mostly Italian designers and architects who created furniture, fabrics, ceramics, and glass and metal household objects from 1981 to 1988. The style of their work was characterised by their use of **asymmetrical** geometric shapes and bright colours.

Look at the two examples of Memphis Group designs (Figures 0.19 and 0.20) and list the features of the style that the two designs have in common. Discuss your ideas with your classmates.

Media, processes and techniques

Media refers to the materials used to create the artwork. The medium an artist chooses to work with will have a powerful influence over the artwork. For example, a sculpture made out of bronze will have a very different effect than one made out of marble. The term 'mixed media' is used to refer to an artwork in which the artist has used several media, as often occurs in collage and **assemblage**.

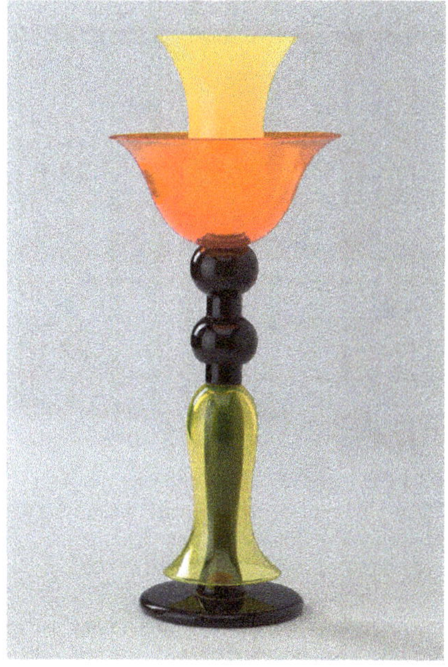

0.19 Ettore Sottsass II, *Malide Candlestick*, 1986, glass, Indianapolis Museum of Art at Newfields.

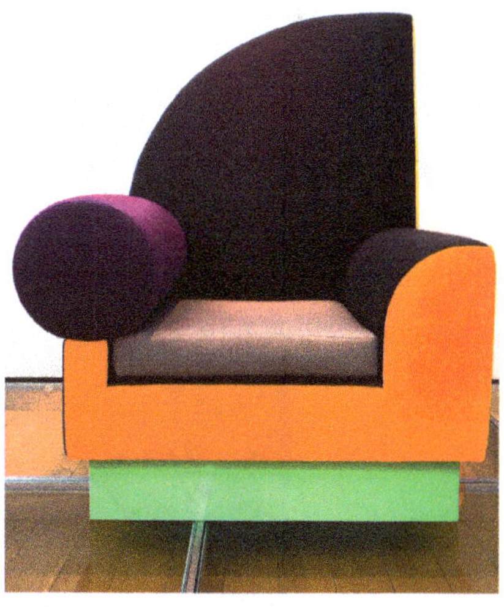

0.20 Peter Shire, *BelleAire Armchair*, 1982, Stedelijk Museum, Amsterdam.

assemblage Art technique involving the construction (assembling) of an artwork out of existing objects. It is like a 3D version of collage.
asymmetry Where the parts of an object are unequal and do not balance; the lack of symmetry.
composition The way something is put together.
genre Category – in film, for example, horror, comedy, romance, drama and so on; a type of art distinguished by subject, theme or style.
theme The underlying idea of a work of art.

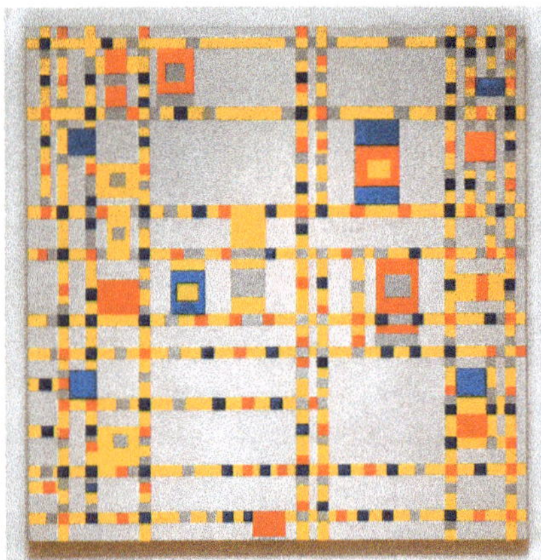

0.21 Piet Mondrian, *Broadway Boogie Woogie*, 1942–3, oil on canvas, Museum of Modern Art, New York. The Dutch artist Piet Mondrian has used repeated colours and shapes to create a rhythm for his composition. With reference to the elements of the title (both '**Broadway**' and '**boogie woogie**'), what does the painting make you think of?

Composition

When analysing the form of an artwork you need to refer to the formal elements of line, tone, colour, shape, form, texture and pattern (see pages 10–17). You also need to talk about the materials, processes and techniques that were used to create the work and the composition.

The composition is the way that all the visual components are put together. A successful composition will guide the viewer's eye around the work and lead it to the main **focal point**, or main point of interest.

Compositional elements include:

- *Space* – this refers to the positive (shapes or objects) and negative (spaces in between the shapes or objects) areas and to the sense of depth achieved in a work of art or design.
- *Scale* – this means the ratio between the size of something real and that of a model or representation of it.
- *Balance* – this refers to the arrangement of shapes or objects within the work. A symmetrical arrangement creates the sense of calm and harmony, while an asymmetrical arrangement feels more dynamic and unsettling.
- *Rhythm* – this is created by the **placement** of repeated colours or shapes within a work that creates a visual beat (Figure 0.21).
- *Movement* – a sense of movement can be created using lines, curved shapes and the position of objects within a work (Figure 0.22).
- *Contrast* – this is the effect of a striking difference, as in colour or tone, of **adjacent** parts of a painting, photograph, video-screen image and so on, or the size of components within a 3D work such as a sculpture.
- *Proportion* – this refers to how the size of the objects depicted relate to one another. We often refer to things being 'in' and 'out' of proportion.

With specific reference to architecture, structure, site or location, function and architectural features are also elements of composition to consider.

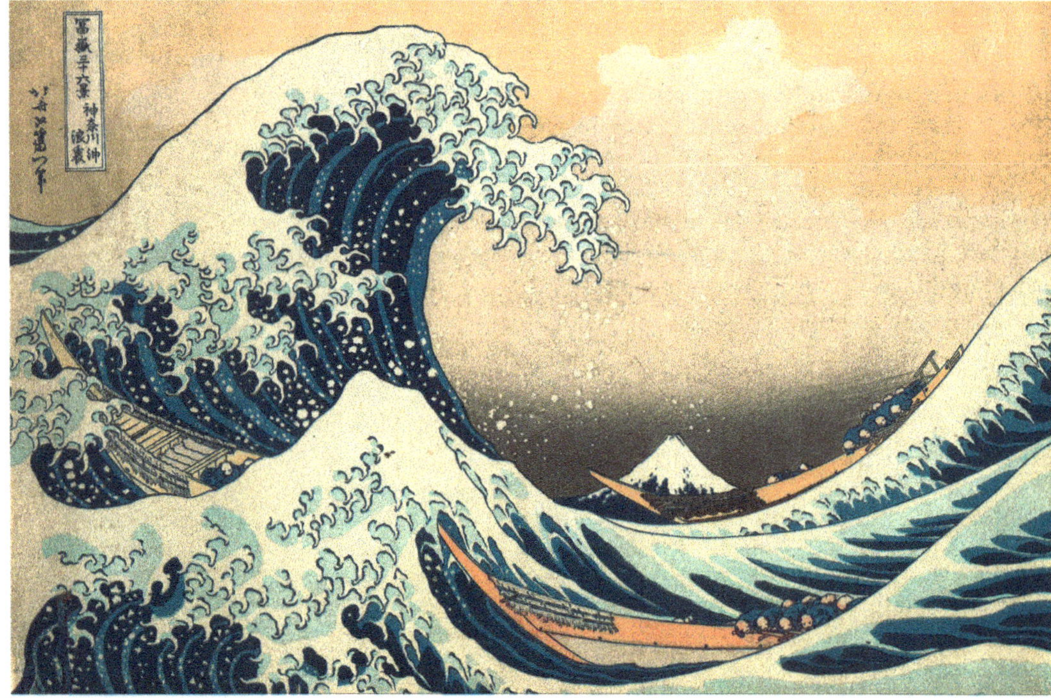

0.22 Katsushika Hokusai, *The Great Wave off Kanagawa*, from the series *Thirty-six Views of Mount Fuji*, c.1830–32, coloured woodblock print, The Metropolitan Museum of Art, New York. The Japanese artist Katsushika Hokusai (1760–1849) has created a sense of movement and energy through his use of line and curved shapes.

Activity B: **Analyse the compositional elements of a traditional Ndebele house**

Look again at the compositional elements. Selecting those applicable, write a 75-word paragraph about the compositional elements of the traditional **Ndebele** house in Figure 0.23.

CONTENT

Content refers to what is being depicted within an artwork, incorporating its **context** and meaning. It expands on the subject or theme of the work. The content can be **representational**, where the artist or designer attempts to show things as they really are. It can also be **abstract**, which makes use of shapes and patterns rather than showing people or things. When talking about the content, make sure that you consider the following:

- ***Aesthetics*** – this is a branch of philosophy that relates to beauty and taste. Making any judgement about a work of art in terms of its beauty is **subjective**, and dependent on personal taste.
- *Iconography* – this refers to the study of the symbolic meaning of images (the word 'icon' comes from the Greek word for 'image'). Different cultures and religions have developed their own iconography. For example, in Chinese art many animals and flowers have symbolic meanings – the lotus flower symbolises purity and the crane symbolises a long life.
- ***Ideology*** – this refers to a set of beliefs, especially the political beliefs on which people, parties or countries base their actions. The graphic arts of 20th-century communist Russia and China are good examples of art where the content is ideological (Figure 0.24).
- *Historic context* – this refers to how the work reflects the time in which it was made and how political, economic and cultural circumstances have influenced it.
- *Social context* – this refers to attitudes, beliefs and social conditions of a society. It can also relate to attitudes towards class and gender.

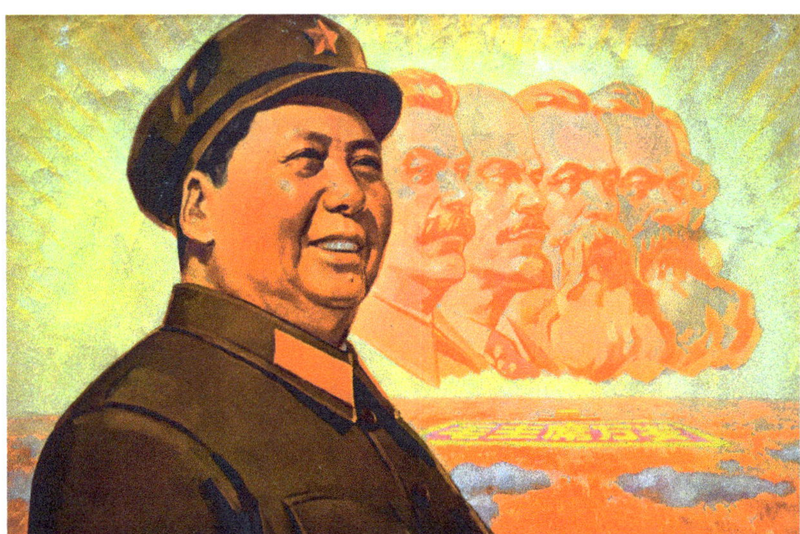

0.24 Chinese communist **propaganda** poster from the 1940s depicting the communist leader Mao Zedong alongside other communist leaders and thinkers such as Karl Marx and Vladimir Lenin. To understand the content of this poster, we need to know about the historic, social and ideological contexts in which its designer produced it.

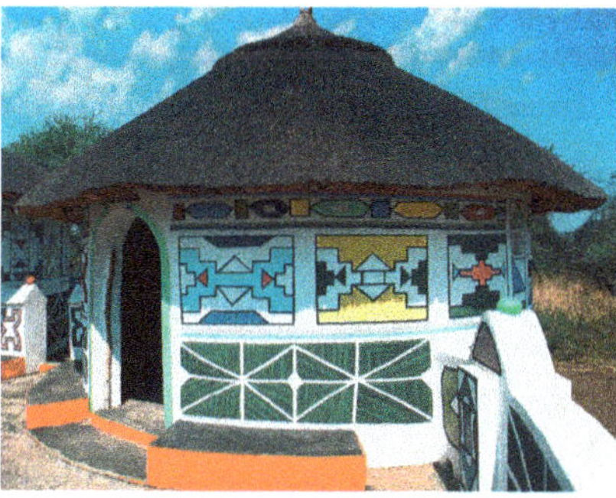

0.23 A traditional Ndebele house, South Africa.

Tip:

In art and design, it is often much easier to talk about the form rather than the content of the work, especially if the work that you are looking at is unfamiliar to you. Use the internet and books to help you research the content and the context of the time and place that the work was made, to understand it better.

abstract Work that uses formal elements such as shape and colour in ways not limited by reproducing visible subject matter.
adjacent Next to something.
aesthetics The study of beauty and of the human responses to beauty.
boogie woogie A style of piano jazz.
Broadway New York street famous for its theatres.
context The situation, background or environment in which an artwork is made.
focal point What the eye or interest is drawn to, the thing that people concentrate on or pay most attention to.
ideology A system of ideas.
Ndebele A native people of southern Africa.
placement Arrangement or position.
propaganda Information used to promote a political cause, often in the form of posters and leaflets.
representational Art that seeks to represent (i.e. depict) real things. Also known as figurative.
subjective Based on personal taste or opinion. The opposite is 'objective', meaning based on fact and unaffected by personal feelings and opinions.

0.3 A framework for analysing artworks

Throughout your course you will be expected to look at and research a wide range of work by different artists, craftspeople and designers, and make links between what you look at and the practical work that you produce. No matter what area of study you are specialising in, be open to the full range of **stimuli** that you can use to inform your work. This can be anything from visual stimuli, for example, sculpture, art, photography, architecture or film, to written stimuli, such as literature or prose, through to texture and music. This will help you to develop your ideas to become a more creative **practitioner**.

It is helpful to have a structure to follow when analysing pieces of art and design, whether you are writing formally about them, discussing them in class or annotating your own practical work. A structure will help you to consider the work in depth and is also very helpful if you want to compare two or more different works, as it ensures that you are comparing the same things. The structure below will also help you consider works of art and design using the appropriate language.

The framework outlined below takes you through the process of analysing an artwork by posing lots of questions or statements for you to respond to. Think in terms of five broad categories. The categories will have different degrees of importance and relevance depending on what type of artwork you are looking at.

Tip:

Other useful questions to ask include:

- Are you viewing the whole of the work or just a part of it?
- Has the work been altered in any way? Has it been cut down, destroyed or added to over time?

1. PHYSICAL PROPERTIES

This section refers to how the work is made and what it is made from:

1.1 *Size* – How big is it in relation to function, surroundings, the spectator and scale?

1.2 ***Support*** – In the case of 2D work, what surface has the work been created on? For example: canvas, paper, wood, metal, brick, …

1.3 *Media and materials* – Which media (materials) have been used?

1.4 *Execution* – What tools, processes and techniques were used to produce the work? For example: **chisel** and mallet, paintbrush and **palette**, needle and thread, … What techniques have been used to apply them or combine them?

Tip:

Always cover *four key areas* in your analysis:

- Description (Content)
- Analysis (Form)
- Interpretation (Meaning)
- Judgement (Merit).

The four key areas can be explored by asking four corresponding questions, which can be applied to analysing any piece of art, craft or design work:

1. *What* am I looking at?
2. *Why* was it created? What was the intention or purpose? Use any statements by the artist, craftsperson or designer, or your own ideas, to answer this.
3. *How* has it been produced?
4. *What* effect does it have on me?

2. COMPOSITION

This section refers to how the work has been put together visually.

2.1 *Preparation* – Are there **preparatory** sketches or drawings? How does the artist, craftsperson or designer work? What sort of relationship is there between the **concept** and execution, or between the raw visual material and the finished artwork? What is the balance between observation and imagination in the creative process?

2.2 *The formal elements* – How have the elements of line, tone, colour, shape, form, texture and space been used?

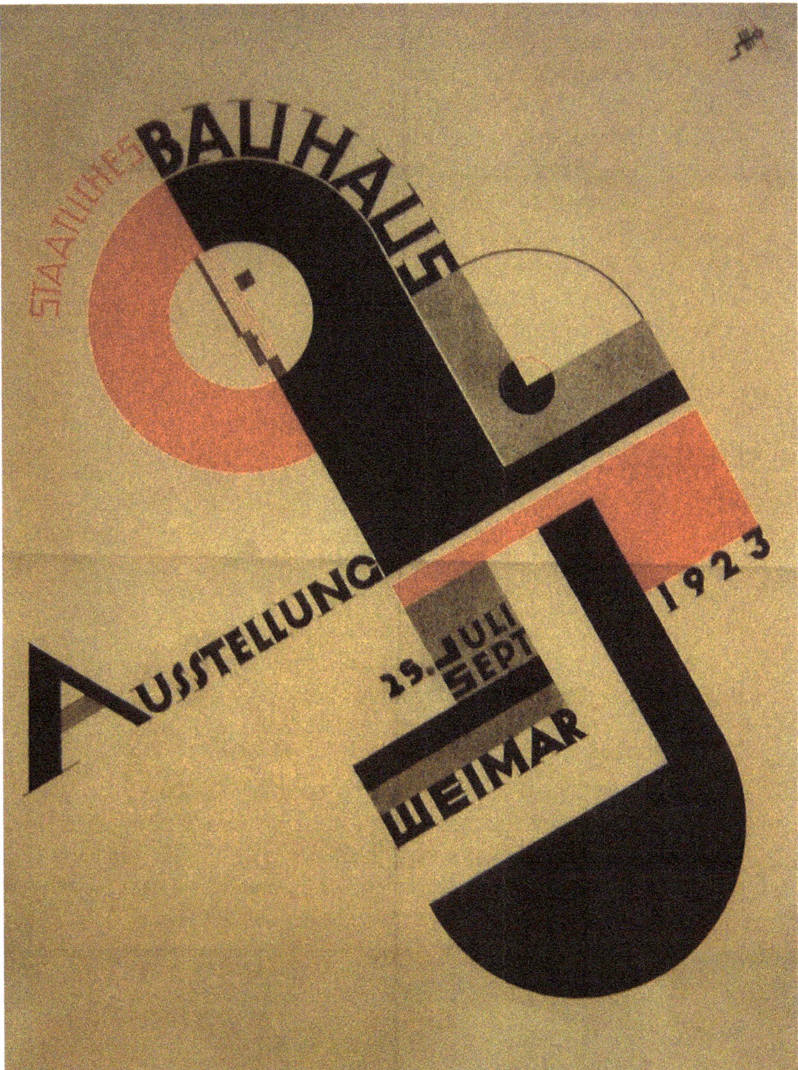

0.25 Joost Schmidt, poster advertising the Bauhaus Exhibition held in Weimar, Germany, in 1923.

Activity A: **Identify formal elements in a Bauhaus poster**

Identify the specific elements that you would need to refer to in order to describe the way that the German designer and typographer Joost Schmidt (1893–1948) has composed his 1923 poster advertising the 1923 **Bauhaus** Exhibition (Figure 0.25).

Tip:

Not all the formal elements will be present within every piece of work. It might be appropriate to refer to the use of light, movement and time, as well. For example, 'time' is an element that is appropriate to include if discussing the moving image or some web-based designs. You can discuss the formal elements separately and/or in combination; for example, colour and texture or space and form.

Bauhaus The architecture and design school founded by the German architect Walter Gropius (1883–1969) in Germany and which lasted from 1919 to 1933. The school's ethos, summed up in the statement 'Form follows function' (functionalism), was hugely influential on modern design.

chisel Tool that has a long metal blade with a sharp edge at the end. It is used for cutting and shaping wood and stone.

concept An idea or abstract principle.

palette In this context, the thin board used by painters to lay out and mix colours.

practitioner Catch-all term used to describe an artist, craftsperson or designer.

preparatory Term used to describe artworks that prepare for a final artwork. They represent an experimental phase in the artistic process.

stimulus Something that provides the inspiration or starting point for an artist's work. It could be, for example, something in nature, something glimpsed in a city street, another work of art, a piece of music, a poem or a personal experience. The plural is 'stimuli'.

support The surface that the artist uses to create artwork on, e.g. wall, canvas, paper.

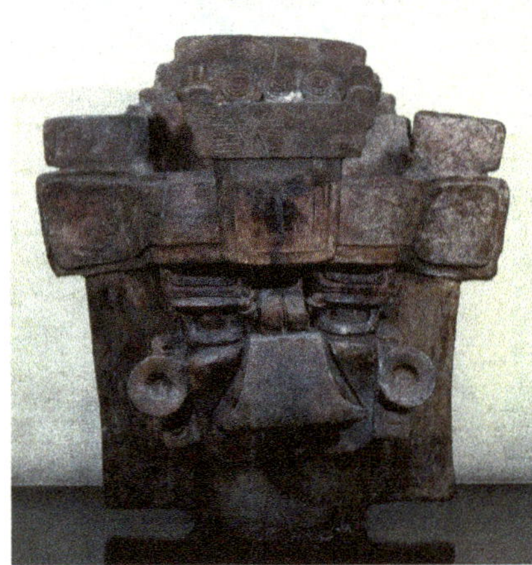

0.26 *Zapotec* *funeral* **urn** *from Monte Albán, Mexico*, 100–200 CE, ceramic, Museo Nacional de Antropología, Mexico City, Mexico. An example of an artwork where the historical context has great significance. In this context, do you think we can really talk about an 'artwork'?

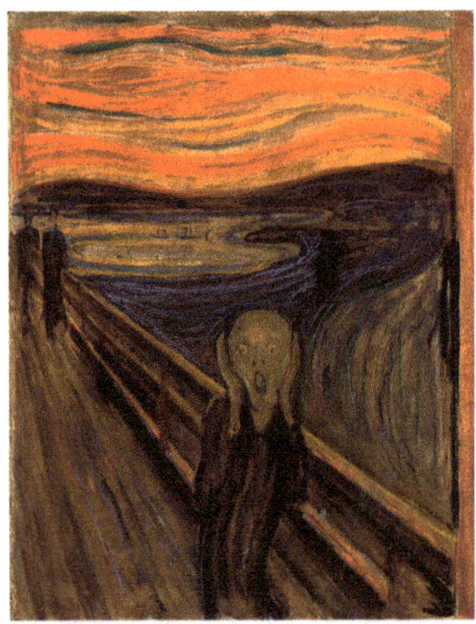

0.27 Edvard Munch, *The Scream*, 1893, oil, **tempera** and pastel on cardboard, National Gallery of Norway, Oslo. One of four versions of this famous image created by the Norwegian artist Edvard Munch (1863–1944). The image communicates a feeling of deep fear and unease.

3. HISTORICAL AND CULTURAL CONTEXTS

This section refers to when and where the work was created and what influence this had on the work.

3.1 *Place the artwork in its time and place* – When and where was it made? Note the century, decade, year, country and continent. Is it part of a **movement** or style that you recognise? Are there any important historical details connected with this time or place that are relevant? If the work can be placed as part of a movement or style, what qualities related to that movement or style does it show? Is it a key piece of work within that movement?

3.2 *Place the artwork within the artist's, craftsperson's or designer's career* – If relevant, state what the artist, craftsperson or designer was doing before and after creating the work. Is it an important piece within their career? If so, why? How representative is it of their style? What makes the work recognisable as their work?

3.3 *Identify any ethnic or cultural qualities* – In other words, can you recognise the work as being European, American, Chinese, South African and so on (Figure 0.26). If so, how?

3.4 *Evidence of influences* – What influenced the artist, craftsperson or designer? Influences can be literary, philosophical, religious, political, as well as visual. Is there direct evidence for suggesting an influence? How original is the work?

There is much more on context in Module 2: Contexts and concepts.

4. SUBJECT MATTER

This section refers to what the work looks like and what it is about.

4.1 *Give a brief description of the work.* Is it representational or abstract?

4.2 *Title* – Does the work have a title? Does the title explain anything about the work? If not, why might this be?

4.3 *Story* – Does the work tell a story? If so, is the story from history or mythology? Does the work communicate an idea or a feeling?

4.4 *Symbolism* – are symbols used within the work? Is the symbolism conscious or **unconscious**, personal or social, religious, political or national and so on?

4.5 *Other work by the artist, craftsperson or designer* – Is there other work around the same subject matter, either before or after this piece? If so, does this piece of artwork treat the subject matter differently from other pieces that they have made? Does the work express anything about its maker's emotional attitude to the subject (Figure 0.27)?

Critical thinking:

Look at Figure 0.28, which shows *C-Curve* by the British artist Anish Kapoor (born 1954) and answer the questions in the 'Relationship to the viewer/audience' section of the framework.

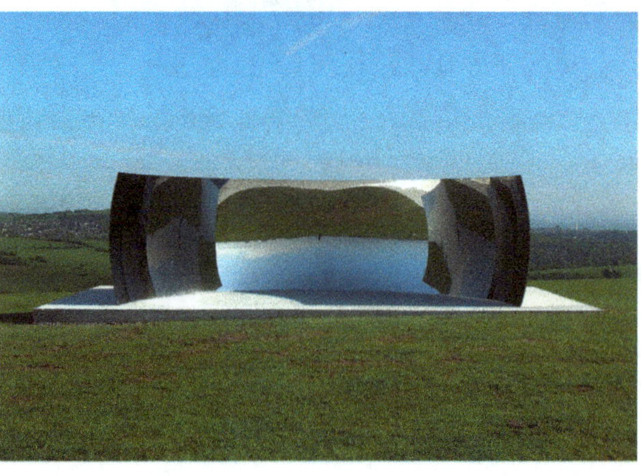

0.28 Anish Kapoor, *C-Curve*, 2007, concave stainless steel mirror, installation on the South Downs at the 2009 Brighton Festival.

5. RELATIONSHIP TO THE VIEWER/AUDIENCE

This section refers to how you respond to the work.

5.1 How does the spectator relate to the work physically? This could be in relation to sight, touch, sound or possibly even smell.

5.2 How does the spectator view or experience the work? Do you stand back to see it, view it up close, handle it, walk into it or around it?

5.3 Does the environment surrounding the work have an impact on it? Has the work been designed for a specific location or space?

5.4 Is the presentation of the work important? For example, is the way in which a painting has been mounted or framed an **integral** part of the work?

5.5 Does it require a set time to look at the work? Does the work change over time? If it is a film or moving image, does it need to be viewed from the start? Do you need to watch all of it?

5.6 What emotional reactions do you have when you look at the work? Do you engage with it? How does it make you feel? Does it create a mood or atmosphere?

5.7 Discuss your own personal reactions to the work. How does it make you feel and what you think about it?

There is much more on audience in Module 4: Audience and setting.

Activity B: **Analyse an image**

Look at this photograph by the American photographer Ansel Adams (1902–84) (Figure 0.29). The context to the photograph is as follows:

After Japan bombed Pearl Harbor in 1941, fear of a Japanese invasion and subversive acts by Japanese-Americans prompted the designation of the West Coast as a military zone from which 'any or all persons may be excluded'. Japanese-Americans were singled out for evacuation. More than 110000 people of Japanese ancestry were removed from their homes in California, southern Arizona, and western Washington and Oregon and sent to 10 relocation camps. Ansel Adams' series of photographs documents life at Manzanar War Relocation Center, Inyo County, California.

Use the framework to prepare a short presentation about the photograph to your class.

Activity C: **Create an analysis framework appropriate for different art forms**

For this activity, work in a group of three:

- *Person A* makes a list of the questions and statements that are applicable to analysing a 2D artwork, such as a painting or a graphic poster.
- *Person B* makes a list of the questions and statements that are applicable to analysing a video **installation**.
- *Person C* makes a list of the questions and statements that are applicable to analysing a piece of architecture.

Compare your lists and explain to one other why you have included some questions and statements and not others.

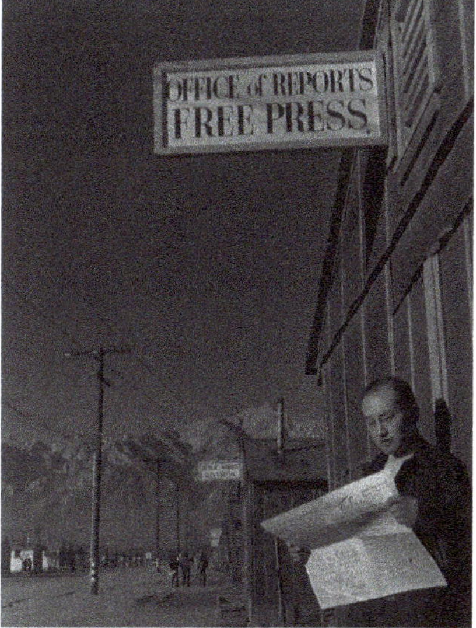

0.29 Ansel Adams, *Roy Takeno, editor of Manzanar Free Press, reading a copy in front of the newspaper office at the Manzanar War Relocation Center,* 1943, black and white photograph, Library of Congress, Washington, DC.

installation An artwork that is constructed in an interior space, such as a gallery; a work of art requiring construction or elaborate setting up at its exhibition site.

integral A part of something that is necessary to it or that cannot be removed without affecting its 'wholeness'.

movement In art, a group of practitioners who work with similar artistic goals.

tempera Fast-drying paint made up of a pigment and (traditionally) egg yolk. It was the form of paint used for artworks in European art until the rise of oil painting in the 15th century, though it was used by some Chinese and Indian artists many hundreds of years before.

unconscious Without realising something.

urn Vase-like container, often made out of ceramic and often designed to hold human ashes.

Zapotec Ancient civilisation of central Mexico that lasted from around 700 bce to 1521 ce

0.4 Introduction to the disciplines

The Cambridge Assessment International Education Art & Design syllabus is structured around the four areas of study:

- Fine art
- Graphic communication
- Three-dimensional (3D) design
- Textiles and fashion.

Within each area of study, there is a range of disciplines, each of which has its own distinct skills, techniques and knowledge. This section provides a brief introduction to each of the areas of study and disciplines within them.

There is considerable crossover between the areas of study: sculpture, for example, can be considered both as a fine art discipline and as an aspect of 3D design. Where this is the case, the introduction to the discipline can be found in the fine art section.

In the units, some key disciplines are given greater weight than others, and a few disciplines have been treated within the context of other disciplines.

FINE ART

The term 'fine art' refers to art created above all for its **aesthetic**, imaginative and intellectual content. For most students of art and design, the disciplines within this area of study will form the core of their study. Whatever their eventual chosen specialism – from painting to typography, and from illustration to set design – the disciplines provide them with many of the key skills they need. The value of drawing especially, across all disciplines, cannot be overstated.

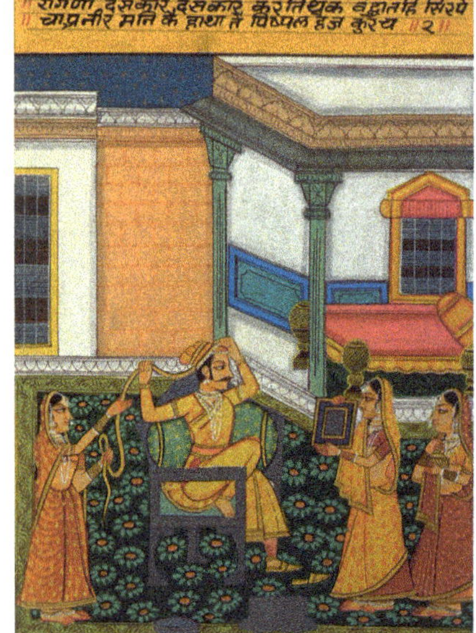

0.30 Unknown artist from the Nathdwara School, *Ragini Deshkar A King tying his turban*, unknown date, miniature painting on paper, private collection.

aesthetic Relating to beauty rather than other considerations.
non-linear Used to describe marks that are not lines.
wash A thin layer of paint; thinned paint applied in a layer over part of a canvas or support.

Painting

In East Asian art (see Figure 0.30), there is no distinction made between the disciplines of drawing and painting. However, in Western art painting is defined as the art or process of applying paints or other wet media to a support such as canvas, paper or board, using a brush, palette knife, airbrush or sponge, to make a picture or other artistic composition. So, it describes both the action and the outcome (result).

Painting has a rich history across the world, with the first known paintings dating from prehistoric times in the form of cave painting.

There is wide range of wet media for artists to work with. Traditionally, in the art of East Asia artists have used inks as the main medium in painting, whereas in the West oil paint and watercolours have been the dominant choice of media.

Paints and inks are made from pigments that have been mixed with a liquid, such as linseed oil, water and gum.

Drawing

Drawing is defined as the art of representing something by lines made on a surface with a pencil or pen. However, drawings can also include tonal areas such as **washes** of ink or watercolour and other **non-linear** marks. Like painting, the term 'drawing' also refers to the outcome as well as the process.

It is widely accepted that drawing is a skill that underpins all art and design activity. You are expected to draw, no matter which area of study you follow as part of the course. However, within the context of fine art the discipline of drawing is regarded as an art form in its own right, not just a preparatory stage for a painting or design.

The most commonly used materials for drawing are pencil, charcoal, chalk, pastel, crayon and ink. However, drawings can also be made with, or in combination with, paint and any other wet or dry media. Drawings can also be created digitally, using drawing software.

Sculpture

Sculpture covers 3D work made using one of four basic techniques:

- *Assembling* and *constructing* is where different materials are joined together to create a sculpture, using techniques such as welding, bolting, stitching or tying and balancing sections on top of each other (see Figure 0.31). They can include **found objects** as well as raw materials, such as sheet metal or stone.
- *Carving* is a **reductive** process and involves cutting or using a chisel to chip away material from a solid mass of material such as stone, wood or a plaster block (Figure 0.32).

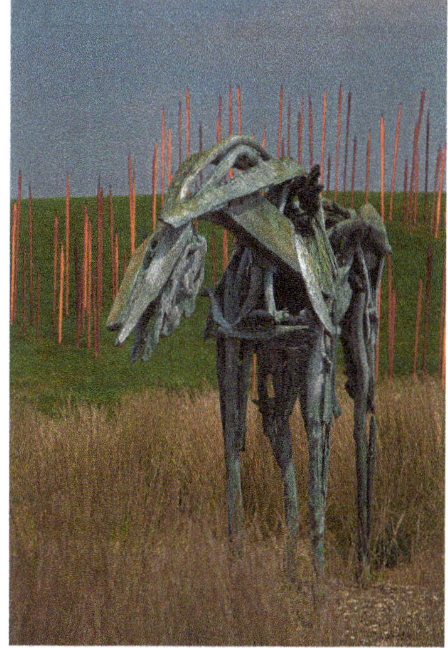

0.31 Deborah Butterfield, *Cabin Creek*, 1999, assembled sculpture, Frederick Meijer Sculpture Park, Grand Rapids, Michigan.

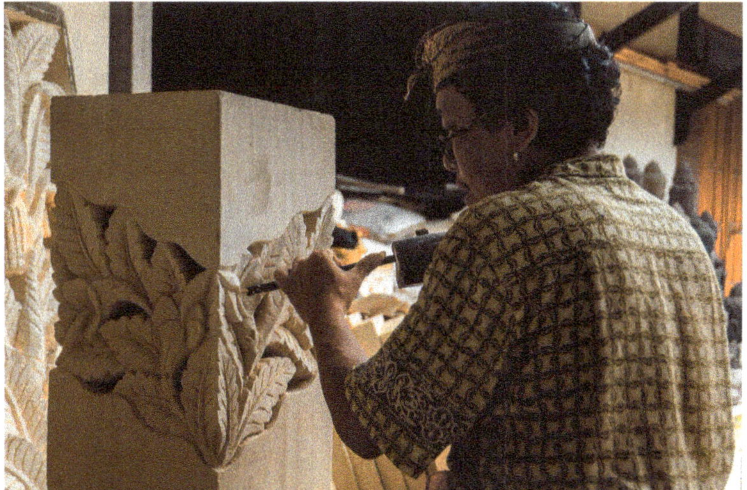

0.32 An example of stone carving in Bali, Indonesia.

- *Casting* involves creating a **mould** into which a liquid such as metal, plastic, fibreglass or rubber material is poured (Figure 0.33). When the liquid material sets, the mould is removed and the sculpted form (cast) revealed. It is often possible for an artist to use a mould more than once, thereby enabling several identical copies to be made.
- *Modelling* is an **additive** process that involves shaping soft, **malleable** materials such as clay or wax. Larger sculptures formed in this way are often built around an **armature**. Modelling is often used to create moulds from which sculptures are cast, or can be the finished piece.

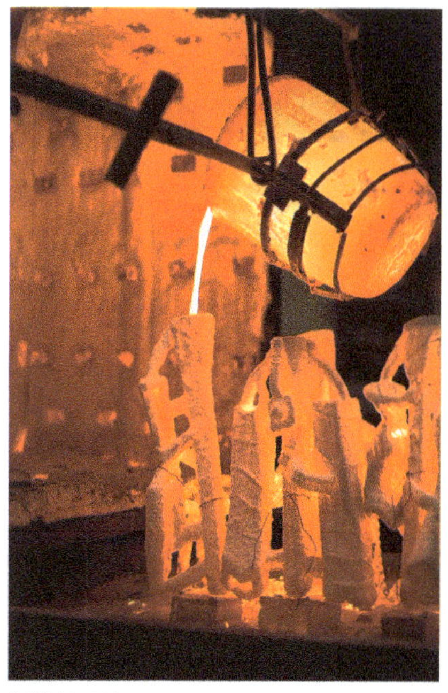

0.33 Liquid bronze is poured into a mould to create a cast sculpture.

additive Produced by adding material; compare reductive.
armature Framework to support the clay or other material used in modelling.
found objects Also known as *objets trouvés*, this means objects used for art that were not designed for an art purpose.
malleable A substance that is malleable is soft and can easily be made into different shapes.
mould A hollow container that you pour liquid into. When the liquid becomes solid, it takes the same shape as the mould.
reductive Produced by taking away material; compare with additive.

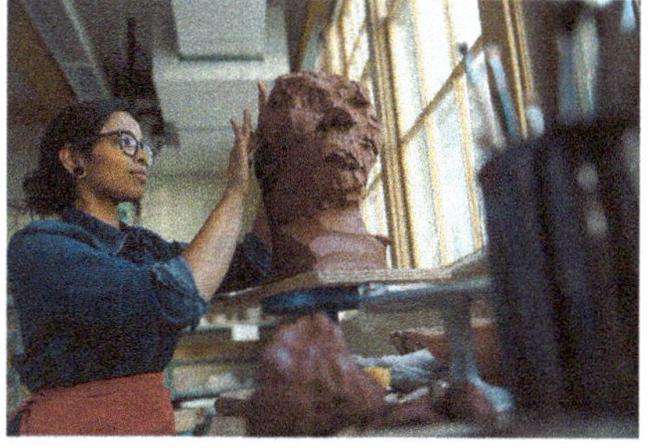

0.34 An example of modelling using clay.

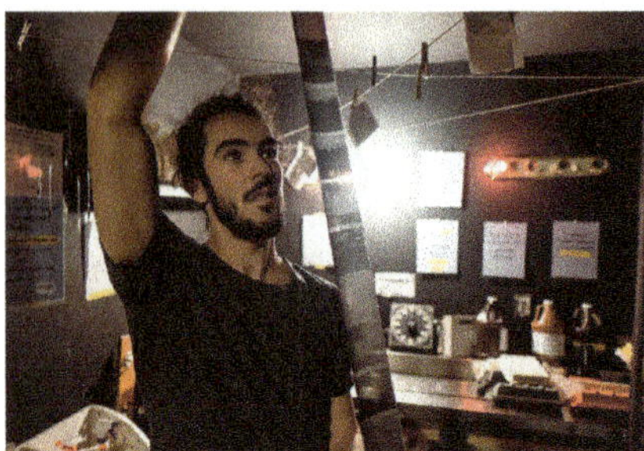

0.35 Non-digital photography darkroom processes transfer the negative into a positive print using a chemical process.

Photography

The word 'photography' originated in 1839 and comes from the Greek words *phos*, meaning 'light', and *graphê*, meaning 'drawing'. So, it literally means 'drawing with light'. It is the practice of using light to record images:

- by chemical action using a light-sensitive material such as film; or
- digitally using an image sensor.

In the non-digital process, photographs are made in two stages. First, when the camera takes a photograph, the light-sensitive film captures a negative image, where the colours and lights/darks are inverted. The negative is then transferred to photosensitive photographic paper in a darkroom, using chemicals to create a positive print (Figure 0.35).

In digital photography, the image is stored in the camera in a file format such as JPEG, TIFF or RAW. These can then be uploaded to a computer or directly to a printer.

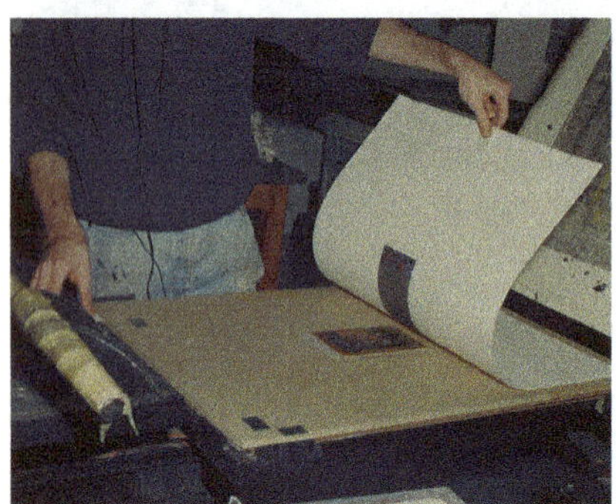

0.36 An artist creates a relief print from a woodcut using a printing press.

Printmaking

The term 'printmaking' covers many different techniques and processes, including **intaglio** and **relief plate** (see below). It consists of making a series of pictures from a specially prepared surface known as a plate and transferring the image onto another surface such as paper or textiles. Printmaking also includes screen printing and the use of **stencils**.

Intaglio is a term that refers to any of the various printing techniques using an etched or **engraved** plate, for example, etching and **drypoint**. The whole plate is smeared with ink, the surface wiped clean, and the ink in the cuts (incisions) is then transferred to the paper or other material.

Relief printing refers to techniques that create raised surfaces from which ink is transferred to the paper, such as woodcut (Figure 0.36) and **linocut**.

Screen printing is a technique that uses a stencil attached to a screen covered in a fine mesh. Ink is then forced through the mesh in the open areas of the stencil using a **squeegee** (Figure 0.37), printing onto the paper or textile beneath. Stencils can be very simply made from cut or torn paper, or can be drawn directly onto the mesh using a drawing fluid. A third method is to use photo stencils, which require the screen to be covered in photosensitive emulsion. The image can then be transferred to the screen via exposure to light.

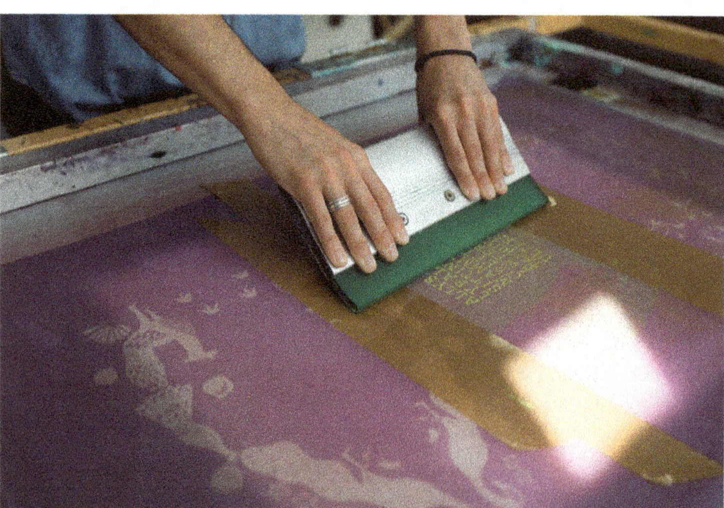

0.37 The screen-printing process: an artist uses a squeegee to force ink through a stencil applied to a mesh screen.

Mixed media

'Mixed media' is a term used to describe artworks that combine a variety of different art-based media or materials. It is different from multimedia artwork, as the latter usually refers to work that combines traditional art-based media with electronic media such as audio and video. Mixed media became accepted as an approach to making art during the early part of the 20th century, when the French artist Georges Braque (1882–1963) and Spanish artist Pablo Picasso (1881–1973) first introduced the use of collage into mainstream painting and drawing as part of the art movement known as **Cubism**. The use of newspaper and pre-printed wallpaper in the context of fine art was revolutionary at the time and challenged ideas about what art was.

Experimental – assemblage/construction

'Assemblage' and 'construction' are terms given to art involving the assembly and arrangement of unrelated found objects, parts and materials in a kind of sculpture-collage (Figure 0.38). It has its origins in the experimental work of the Cubist artists Picasso and Braque in the early 20th century.

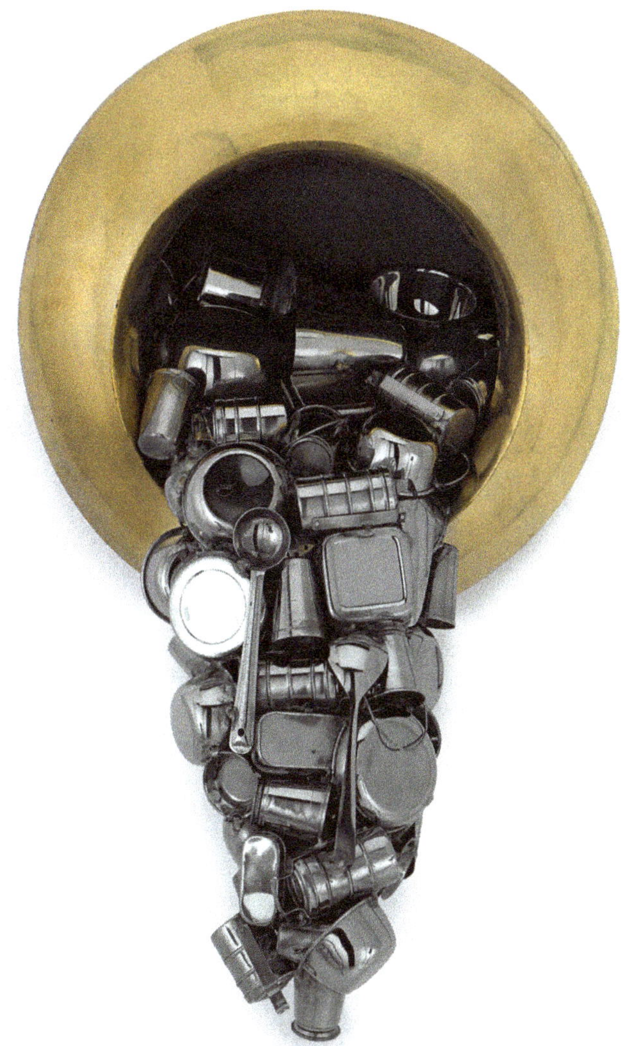

0.38 Subodh Gupta, *Melting Meteor*, 2010, brass and stainless steel, private collection. The Indian artist Subodh Gupta (born 1964) has created an assemblage using found objects.

Cubism An early 20th-century movement in modern art that represented the real world in an analytical way, often using multiple views of the same subject at the same time.
drypoint Technique of intaglio engraving using a hard steel needle, without acid, on a copper or acetate plate.
engrave To cut a design or image *into* a surface.
intaglio A printing technique using a carved or engraved surface to create a design in relief.
linocut Technique of relief printing, similar to a woodcut, where the design is created using a sheet of linoleum.
relief plate A printing plate where the parts to be printed are in relief (raised).
squeegee Tool with a rubber blade or roller used to remove and/or apply ink.
stencil Piece of paper, plastic or metal with a design cut out of it. You place the stencil on a surface and paint it so that paint goes through the holes and leaves a design on the surface.

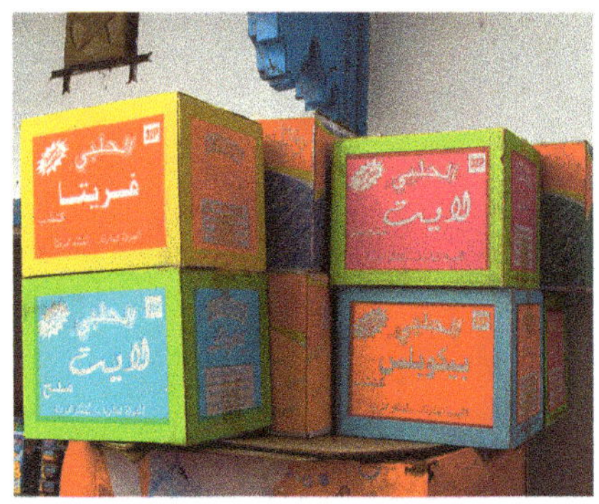

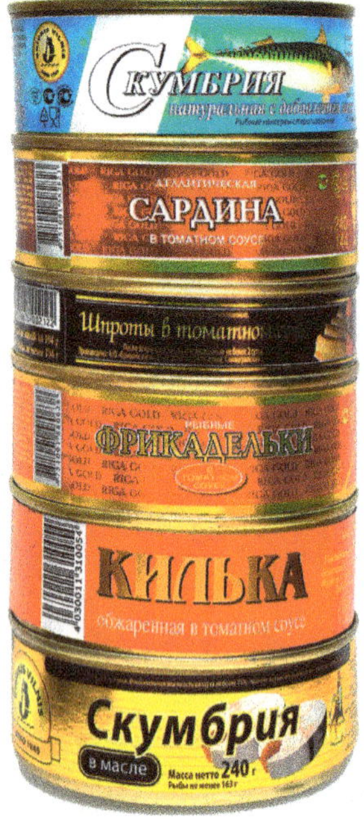

0.39 Colourful produce boxes in Arabic script. Taken in Essaouira, Morocco, 28 November 2008; canned fish from Eastern Europe with labels in Cyrillic script.

GRAPHIC COMMUNICATION

We live in a visual world, where stories, ideas and information are communicated primarily by visual means – whether through writing or images. The term 'graphic' derives from the Greek word for 'to write', but the field of graphic communication brings together a much wider set of disciplines: not only typography, but also illustration and disciplines closely associated with marketing – branding and advertising. As you will see, many of the disciplines are closely linked with one another; for example, advertising often brings in a range of graphic disciplines, such as typography and branding, to achieve its aims.

While graphic communication uses many of the formal elements and components of the fine arts, both process and outcome have a more commercial emphasis and flavour.

Typography

Typography is the design of **typefaces** (Figure 0.40) and **letterforms** and the use of these in printed or displayed texts – from books and magazines through motorway signs to packaging (Figure 0.39) and digital screens – to communicate information of every kind. Typography has different characteristics in specific languages and countries, such as in the flowing, organic strokes of Chinese characters or the geometric shapes of the Roman alphabet. Designers using typography have to understand both **legibility** and **readability**.

Aa Bb Cc Dd Ee Ff Gg Hh Ii Jj Kk Ll Mm Nn Oo Pp Qq Rr Ss Tt Uu Vv Ww Xx Yy Zz

Aa Bb Cc Dd Ee Ff Gg Hh Ii Jj Kk Ll Mm Nn Oo Pp Qq Rr Ss Tt Uu Vv Ww Xx Yy Zz

0.40 Two contrasting typefaces: Garamond and Reporter.

Illustration

Illustration is the making of images to help tell a story, usually in association with written texts. It has a long association with literature, but may also be used in magazines to support the meaning behind an article as well as in advertising. They are sometimes used to show the key stages and events in storybooks and comics. Illustration is key to the visual component of gaming. Illustrators use a wide range of traditional and digital media in their work.

Packaging design

Packaging is the design of materials whose purpose is to protect, present and market products. Often, packaging is designed to communicate a product's brand identity, as, for example, in the materials, printed surfaces and typography used in luxury perfume packaging.

Often, companies use packaging as a positive marketing point for their products. It can be used to communicate ideas about the product to the consumer.

Packaging can also use recycled materials as well as being itself recyclable.

Branding

Branding is the creation and communication of a company's or organisation's brand identity. Examples of branding can be found in many areas, from corporate logos and product design, through fashion, to websites and social media. The brand seeks to represent and communicate the organisation's or company's aims and values. It is sometimes called corporate identity (ID).

Branding is often closely linked to the target audience for a product and is therefore usually determined by market research. Some branding stays the same over a long time, especially in luxury brands where traditional values are seen as positive. Others change rapidly, especially if they are seeking to communicate the youthfulness and dynamic energy of the product or service.

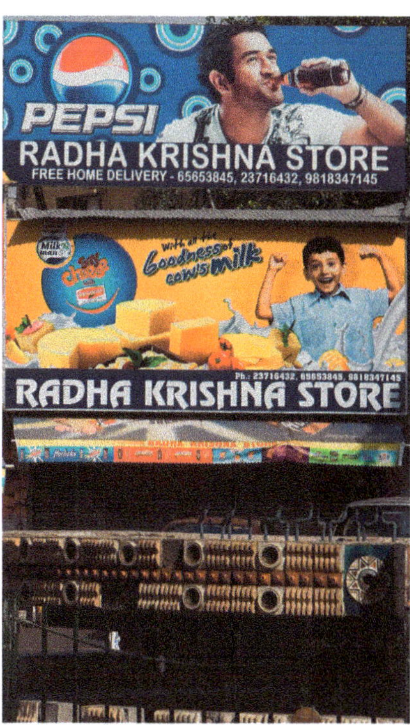

0.41 Advertising billboards in Delhi, India.

Advertising

Advertising communicates information about a product, service or event in order to maximise sales. It aims to promote the positive values of using the product/service or attending the event. Advertisers use market research to find out about the characteristics and **aspirations** of a particular audience. They then commission designers to produce graphic communications – advertisements, posters and so on – that will appeal to that audience. These can take either printed or digital form.

Advertising can link closely to branding, as the design of an advertisement can show a brand's values.

Signage

Signage is the visual communication of information – usually in the briefest form possible. It may use symbols and typography. Other signs can carry information designed for user interaction, such as traffic signage and digital signs at railway and bus stations. Signage can be universal or local, as in Figure 0.42.

Signage may include typography designed to reflect the meaning behind a sign, such as notices stating 'No parking or stopping'. These are 'ordering signs' and so use formal typography, often using **upper case** letters. Some signs use the universal language of symbols, as in hazard warning signs. Signage can include displays that change according to local conditions, as in motorway signage that controls speed along particular sections of road.

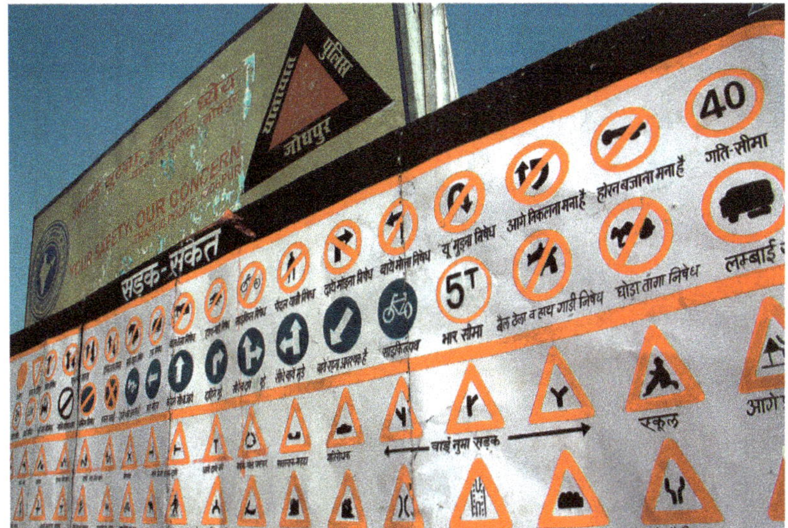

0.42 Hand-drawn road signs, Jodhpur, Rajasthan, India. Signs can reflect the cultures and places they are designed for.

aspirations The goals, values and lifestyle an individual or group of people aim to achieve.
legibility The clarity of a typeface, enabling the almost-instant communication of a message.
letterform The shape or design of an individual letter or character.
readability How easy a typeface is to read over a period of time; how easily a reader can read and understand a text as a whole.
typeface A designed 'family' or set of letters and numbers with a shared set of characteristics; for example, Bodoni, Futura, Caslon, Times New Roman.
upper case The capital letters of a typeface – A, B, C and so on.

THREE-DIMENSIONAL (3D) DESIGN

Three-dimensional (3D) design encompasses both design and fine art disciplines, although the outcomes usually have a more practical, everyday outcome than the disciplines traditionally associated with fine art. For example, in the field of architecture, as well as being aesthetically interesting in some way, a building must primarily provide shelter.

What may strike you above all in this area of study is the enormous diversity and **scope** of outcomes – from the design of the largest buildings to the smallest digital products. There is also usually a much bigger element of teamwork than in the field of fine arts, where the individuality of the artist is conventionally more highly prized.

Product design

Product design is the process of creating the things that people buy and use – from the generation of ideas to the point at which a product can be sold. It combines art, technology and marketing.

It is useful to approach product design as a process of problem solving. The designer identifies the need of a person or group of people – this is the 'problem' – and then works to respond to that need and solve the problem. For example, one problem could be that sufferers from arthritis in their hands find it difficult to open tin cans using a traditional tin opener. The designer's task is to create a tool that will overcome that problem, and the criteria for the success or failure of the design will be based on whether they achieve this.

Architecture

Architecture is the design and making of buildings. Architects work with planners, structural engineers, construction companies and project managers to make their buildings a reality. Architects must consider how their building will meet the needs of users, as well as being a statement of their own creative ideas and style (Figure 0.43).

Research, drawing, designing and model-making are all used as part of the **design process** in all aspects of architecture.

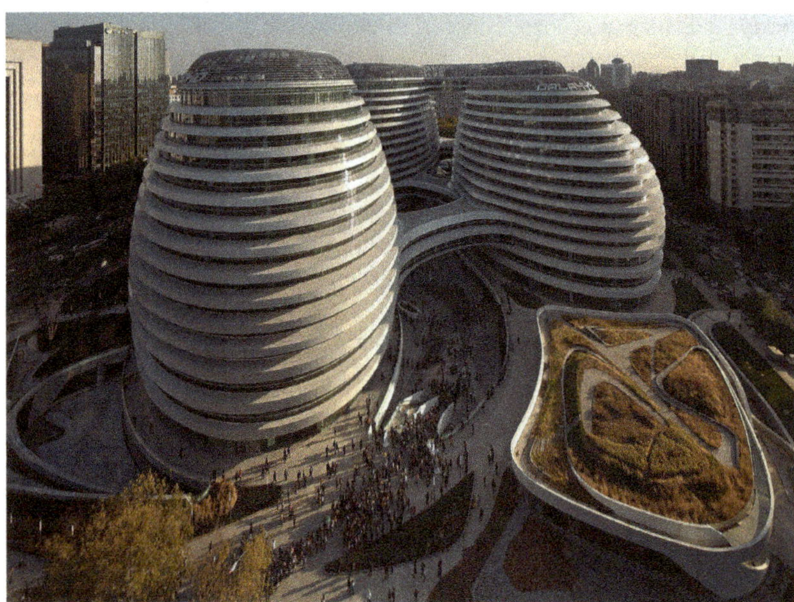

0.43 Zaha Hadid, Galaxy SOHO Building, Beijing, China, 2012. This retail and office complex by the Iranian-born British architect Zaha Hadid (1950–2016) serves a practical purpose as well as making a visually **dramatic** 'statement' in the cityscape of the Chinese capital.

Environmental design

Environmental design is concerned with how we interact with our environment. This includes how designers source materials for projects. Consumers have become more aware of the use of scarce resources. Designers have a responsibility to ensure that their projects are made with renewable or **sustainable** resources. Some designers are exploring how recycled materials can be used in design. You will find the issue of environmental design addressed in many units throughout this book: see, especially, pages 132–133.

Set design

Set design involves designing and making props, backdrops and costumes for film, TV, the theatre and special events such as fashion shows or product launches. Set designers have to address the key ideas and themes in the piece they are designing for. They use these as starting points.

The set designer works as part of a production team and has to communicate and present ideas (Figure 0.44). Ideas are often developed through drawings and layouts, using the storyline or scenes to be shown in the piece. Model-making is used to help create small-scale, 3D versions of sets for production teams to discuss and consider. Ideas can also be developed using **CAD** and 3D software.

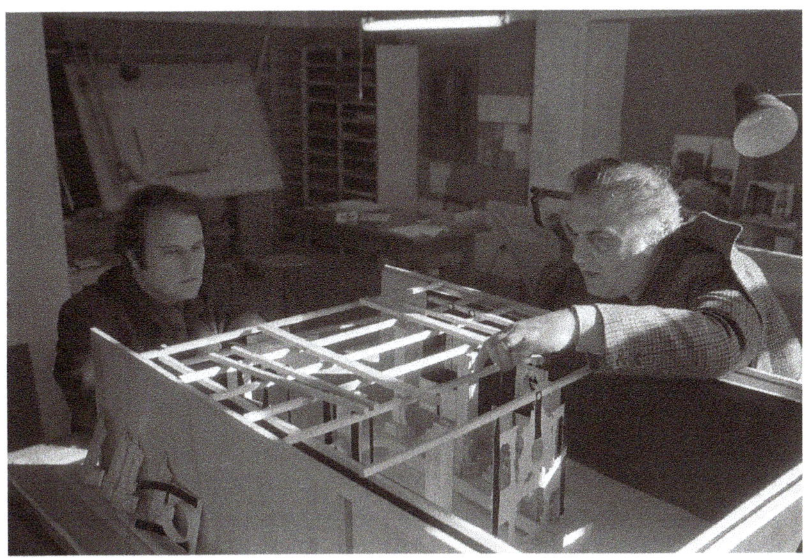

0.44 The Italian director Federico Fellini discussing a set design for a film in 1970. Communication skills are an important part of the process of set design.

Jewellery and fashion accessories

Jewellery and fashion accessories include body adornment, hats, handbags and footwear. Like clothes designers, designers have to respond to, predict and set trends in fashion, and use drawing and visual idea generation, **mood boards** and illustration to generate and communicate their designs. They apply formal elements to their design work – colour, shape, texture and so on – to achieve the end result.

CAD Computer-aided design – the use of computer technology in the creation of designs.
design process The act of creating a plan for the construction of something.
dramatic Filled with action, emotion or exciting qualities; vivid, striking and so on.
mood board An arrangement of images, materials and pieces of text on a board – used to explore and express a style or concept.
scope The area covered by an activity, topic and so on.
sustainable Careful use of natural resources so as to minimise damage to the environment and preserve them for the future.

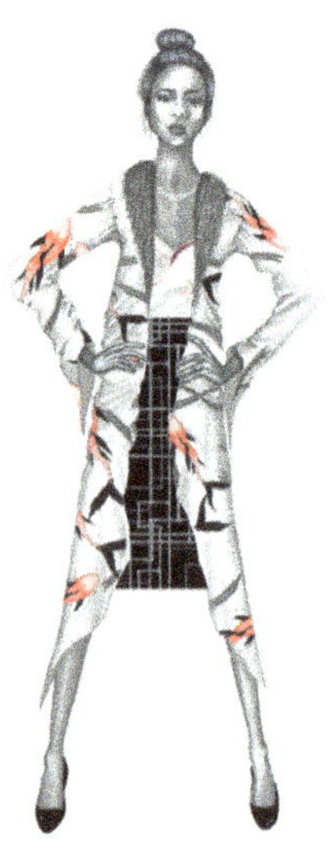

0.45 Katrina Kirk, fashion illustration, 2017, pencil and digital collage. Here the designer has communicated both the contrasting patterns and textures and a particular mood.

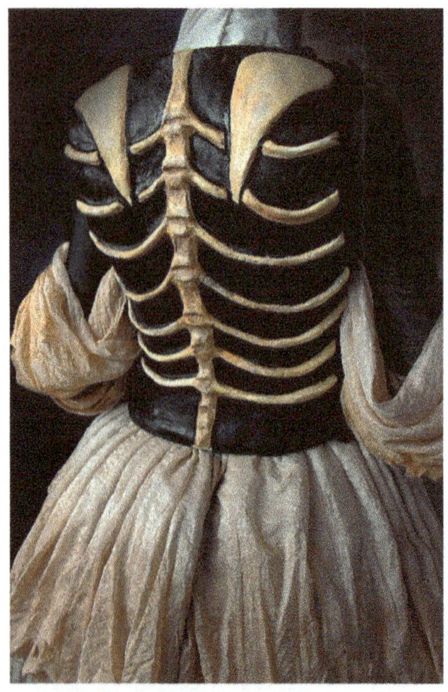

0.46 Kat Tunwell, costume design, 2017, silk. Here there is the dramatic contrast between the historical references suggested by the full silk skirt and scarf, and the nightmarish quality of the skeleton bodice.

TEXTILES AND FASHION

Textiles and fashion bring together the fine art world of colour, texture, surface, shape and pattern, and the commercial pressures of a fast-moving industry. You may be fascinated with how fabric is made and decorated, and enjoy experimenting using yarn, threads, stitches and dye. You may be interested in the construction of garments and how they drape on a body. The rich history of textiles and fashion and the contemporary dimensions of culture and sociology give this area of study a particular resonance and excitement.

Fashion illustration

Fashion illustration is an art form in itself and a creative way to communicate ideas (Figure 0.45). A successful illustration can easily translate the mood and sensibility of a designer's vision to an audience. Illustrations can be expressed using a range of mark-making and tools. Techniques such as drawing, collage and digital design can all be applied to a fashion illustration.

Costume design

Designing costumes for a stage or film production can be a highly creative and satisfying process involving collaborations with a production team and actors. A costume designer needs to have good research skills to carry out investigations into costume styles, designs and construction methods, using libraries, museums and the internet. The job of the costume designer is to help the characters come to life (Figure 0.46)!

Constructed textiles

Constructed textiles involve using fibres and sometimes other materials to create fabrics. Producing fabric from raw materials is an exciting process, as the designer has full control of how it is made. It is important to consider the function or purpose of the fabric, as this will determine how the fabric is constructed. The two main fabric constructions are *knit* – made up of interlocking loops of fibre or yarn and *weave* – a more compact fabric created by interlacing yarn, often using a loom.

Surface pattern

Once a fabric has been constructed, it can be **enhanced** with different techniques, including **embroidery** (Figure 0.47), print and **fabric manipulation**. It is important to consider how the fabric has been constructed, as this will affect what kinds of surface application are possible. For example, a fabric with pile cannot be easily printed onto, while a fabric with a loose weave is perfect for **deconstructing**, using the **drawn threads** technique. You can achieve some interesting results by manipulating fabric by changing its surface using techniques such as **appliqué** and **beading**.

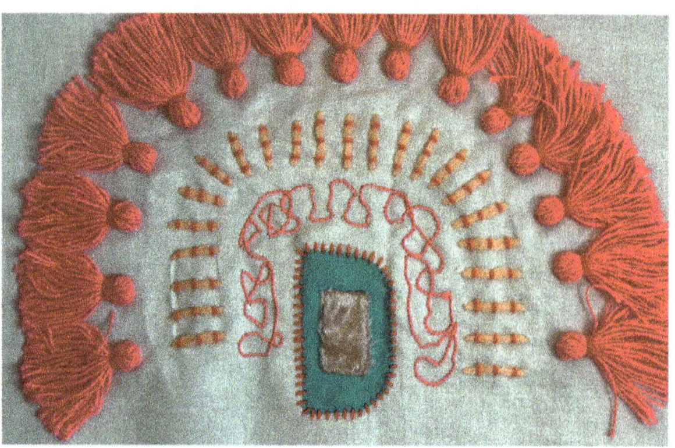

0.47 Emma Benson, embroidery on cotton, 2017.

Batik

Batik is a technique of dyeing textiles using wax resist and is over 2000 years old. Today, the best batik textiles are made on the island of Java in Indonesia. The process involves applying **hot wax** to fabric using a **tjanting tool** and then adding colour by dipping the cloth in a dye bath. The wax resists the dye, so only the unwaxed parts of the cloth are coloured. The process can be repeated so that new colours appear. This is a useful and enjoyable technique to explore how the colour wheel works.

Digital-printed textiles

Digital printing is a fast way to produce printed images onto cloth. You may have access to a sublimation printer. Your design is scanned and manipulated using software such as Adobe Photoshop and then transferred to the sublimation printer. The printed image is made up of special fabric inks that, when heated, transfer to fabric. You should practise screen printing alongside the digital method, so that you fully understand the 'wet' printing process.

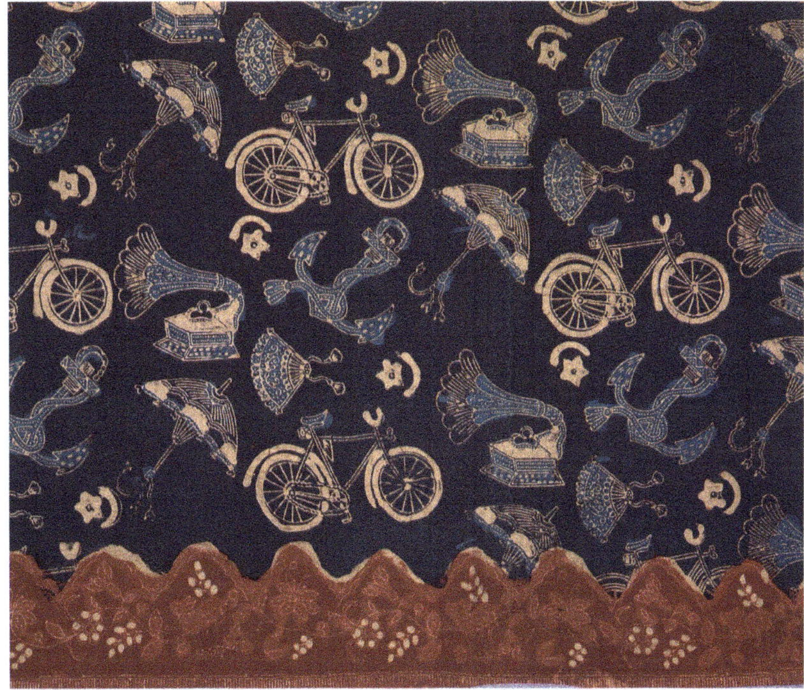

0.48 A detail of a batik sarong. The main motifs in the design are symbols of prestige and fashionable pastimes – bicycles, umbrellas, fans, gramophones and others.

appliqué Textile technique where one material is added to another by means of stitch or adhesive for decorative effect.
batik A process for printing designs on cloth. Wax is put on those areas of the cloth that you do not want to be coloured by dye.
beading Application of beads of varying sizes and weights to fabric, usually by stitching.
deconstruct To take apart.
drawn threads A technique involving the pulling out of threads in a fabric. The remaining threads are stitched into place with embroidery.
embroidery Technique to embellish fabric using a variety of threads and stitches, including French knots, chain stitch and cross stitch. This can be done by hand or by machine.
enhance To enrich; to add additional layers of meaning.
fabric manipulation Using different techniques to change the surface of a fabric.
hot wax Paraffin wax (or beeswax) used for sealing the parts of cloth to be protected from dye.
tjanting tool Pen-like tool used in batik for applying melted wax to fabric in order to draw pictures and patterns.

Module

1

Observation and intention

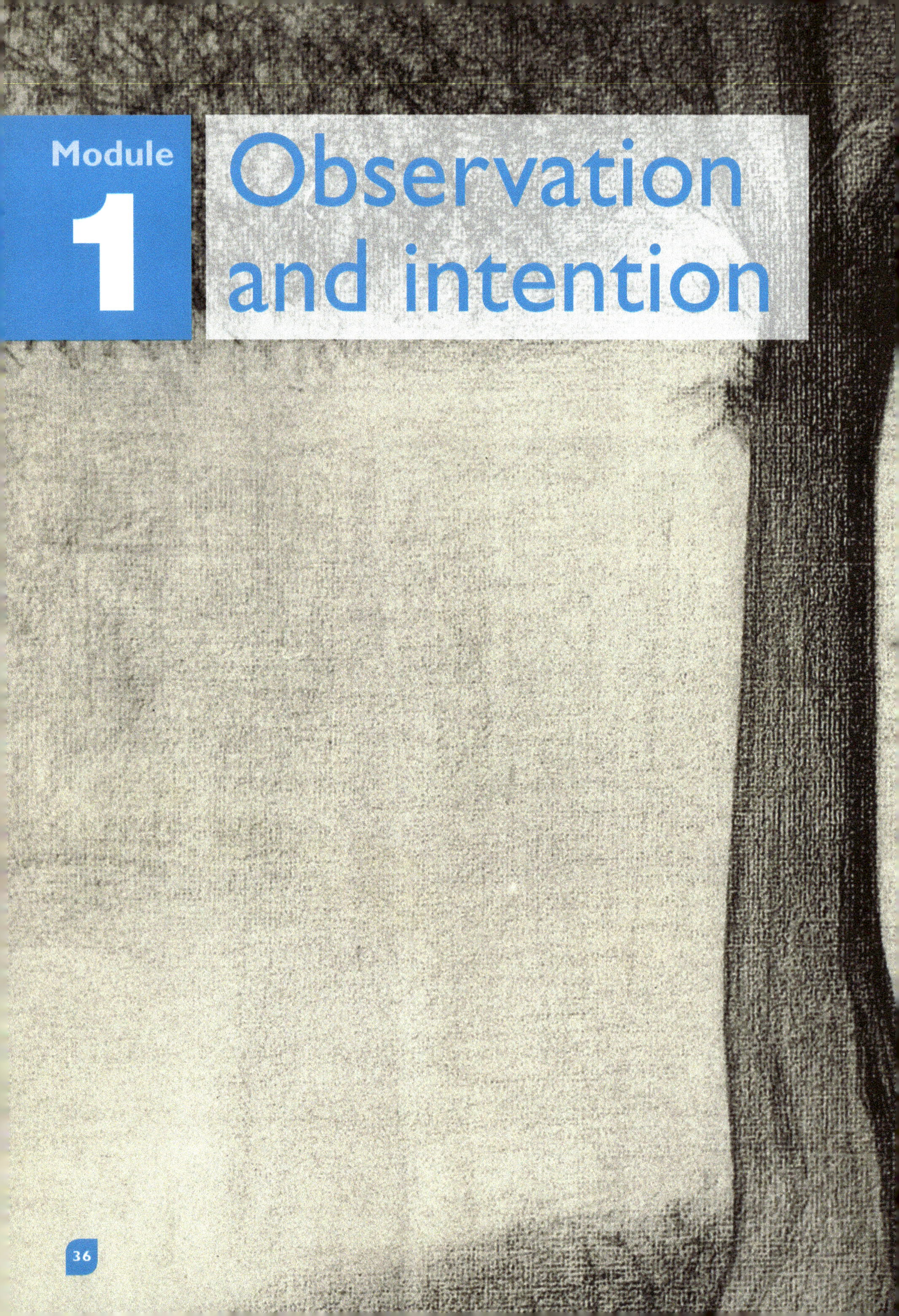

1.0 Introduction

This module introduces you to the different ways of beginning your journey as an artist, designer or craftsperson when responding to a given theme or stimulus. It aims to help you understand the different ways in which artists gather information that informs their work at the start of the creative process.

Artists, craftspeople and designers respond to the world around them. They are inspired by what they see, know and experience, and this helps them develop creative ideas in their work. The creative process begins with gathering stimuli in response to the chosen theme or **brief**. This is the same if the artist or designer is making a piece of jewellery, a painting, a ceramic pot, a design for packaging or an item of clothing.

STARTING POINTS

During your course, you will choose your own themes or starting points to respond to in a personal way. The theme and starting point will form part of a brief. This may also include other instructions, such as the materials and techniques you will need to use, the timeframe for completion, as well as evidence of your creative process; for example, annotations and photographs.

One way you can begin responding to a brief is to create a mind map. A mind map will help you relate to the theme in a personal way and explore your first ideas. It will help you see the relationships between different ideas in the form of a simple diagram.

The example of a mind map in Figure 1.1 uses the theme 'Contained'. This is typical of the type of starting point given on the question paper for the externally set assignment.

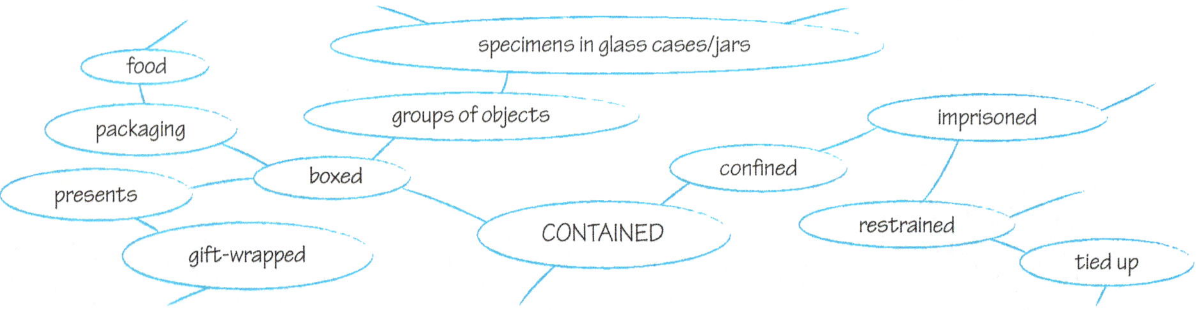

1.1 An example of a mind map using the theme 'Contained'.

Tip:

Don't decide exactly what your work will be or look like at the start of the project. You will miss opportunities to engage with the creative development of your ideas and limit what you can achieve.

Activity A: **Create a mind map on the theme 'Conflict'**

1. Write the theme or starting point in bold, capital letters in the centre of the page.
2. Add notes of all the ideas that you have relating to the theme. At this stage, explore *all* possibilities and avoid having a fixed sense of what you expect to produce as a final piece.
3. You might want to explore these ideas further, so add extra lines and notes for these too.

4. Finally, explore the relationships between your ideas, adding connecting lines and notes as necessary.

GATHERING VISUAL INFORMATION

In order to gather first-hand information, it is important to record from direct observation. This may be through drawing, but your investigations of visual processes can be in a variety of media:

First-hand information

- *Drawing/sketching/painting/collage*
  These are all different ways of making marks, using different media and materials, to explore formal elements (see Figure 1.2). Drawing is the key skill for recording observations and is the basis of every discipline, so we have looked at this more closely as part of this introduction (see pages 40–43).
- *Taking photographs*
  Photography provides a quick way of recording information. It is useful because it provides an accurate and realistic record of what something looks like. You will have all the detail exactly as it was at a given point in time, or as a sequence of time periods. You should think about the subject matter and composition of your image as well as the effect of different lighting and exposure. For more on using photography in this way, see pages 58–61, 248–250 and 316–317.
- *Making 3D models and maquettes*
  Respond to subject matter by working directly in three dimensions, for example, by 'drawing' with wire or modelling with clay to make a **maquette**. See the unit 'Sculpture', pages 238–240, for how to approach this.
- *Collecting objects*
  Always be on the lookout for interesting objects that might provide information and inspiration for your chosen project. For example, if working to the theme 'Journey', you might include tickets, maps and timetables as visual information. There is more about collecting objects in the unit 'Experimental/assemblage and construction', pages 62–63. Objects like this may even become part of the artwork.

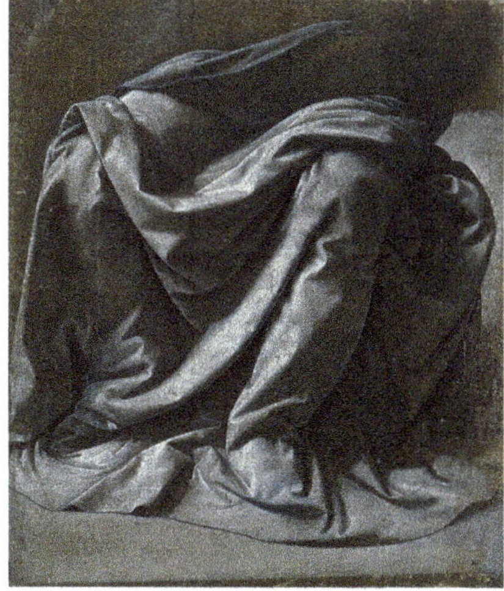

1.2 Leonardo da Vinci, *Study of Drapery of a Seated Figure*, c.1473, brush drawing, tempera on linen canvas, Musée du Louvre, Paris. Here the **Renaissance** artist explores the tone and form of draped fabric.

Secondary source information

Books, magazines, websites and online videos make it possible to quickly support your direct observation with visual investigations from a wide range of **second-hand sources**:

- *Making mood boards*
  Mood boards are created from secondary sources such as textures, patterns, colours and images from magazines or the internet. Apps such as *PicCollage* can be used to create digital mood boards. There is more on mood boards in relation to textiles and fashion on pages 99–100.
- *Collage and photomontage*
  Early ideas, compositions and new combinations of ideas can be quickly made using printed material of images collected from the internet. Scissors and a glue stick can create new starting points for development.

brief Outline of a task or project given to the artist or designer before they start work.

maquette A sculptor's small trial or experimental model – a kind of '3D sketch'.

Renaissance The 'rebirth' of culture and learning that took place in Europe during the 15th and 16th centuries. It took much of its inspiration from ancient ('Classical') Greece and Rome.

second-hand source A secondary source of information about an object or artefact created by someone at a later date; for example, a book, the internet.

> Materials and techniques:
> **Grades of pencil**
>
> The type of line and mark you get will depend on the grade of pencil you use. Pencils are given a letter label: Bs are softer and darker; Hs are harder and fainter. Pencil grades are also given a number: for example, a 6B is a lot darker and softer than a 1B, and works best for faster, softer drawing styles. Experiment with grades to develop your own personal style and preferences.

DRAWING AND MARK-MAKING

Practitioners use drawing across disciplines in art and design to observe and record from the visible world and to develop and refine ideas. It is also used as a means of **visual communication** in its own right (see pages 64–67). Drawing makes use of a wide range of materials, techniques and processes. A good material to start with is pencil, as it is useful and versatile.

Using pencil

Using pencil is one of the most basic techniques in drawing, yet can be applied to create extremely expressive **imagery**. It is also one way of starting a drawing by using construction lines or laying in basic shapes and simple outlines of an image. You can use it to describe outline or to develop controlled areas of tone.

Activity B: **Develop a series of A2 sheets of mark-marking**

The aim in this activity is to try out different ways of making marks using line, without having to worry about observing an object. In this way, you can enjoy seeing how the different lines work to create effects.

1. Divide your paper into boxes, or fold it to create a grid.
2. Using the example in Figure 1.3 as a guide, experiment with mark-making. Keep it simple – use only pencil for now.
3. Once you are confident with this way of working, change the technique and use tone – start with pencil, then go on to other materials, such as charcoal.

You can make as many sheets as you like – there is no limit. Aim to be creative in how you apply the materials, and to keep trying different ways of making marks.

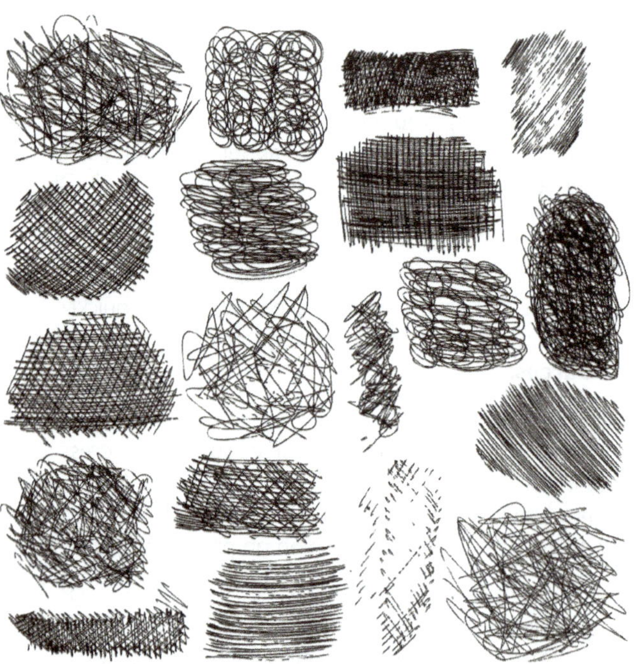

1.3 Example of mark-making. This example was made using digital drawing techniques – try this out yourself later on.

Activity C: **Explore different marks**

You can reinforce your learning by looking at examples of other artists' work.

1. Look carefully at Figure 1.4, which shows a drawing by the Dutch artist Vincent van Gogh (1853–90).
2. Make notes on all the different types of mark the artist has used.
3. Next, describe what the artist has used the different marks to represent; for example, the heavy **cross hatch** below indicates a shrub or small tree.
4. Finally, reproduce the marks yourself, using mark-making techniques. Try using materials such as pen and ink to see how they behave.

Critical thinking:

As you explore mark-making and develop your skills, allow regular opportunities for evaluation. This means stopping practical work, putting your sheets on a wall or surface and looking at them to see how far you have progressed. Use this time to make notes about your progress.

1.4 Vincent van Gogh, *The Corner of the Park*, 1888, ink and pencil on paper, private collection.

Activity D: **Make a drawing study in line from observation on A2 paper**

Choose one subject for your **study** from:

- the interior of a room – a fairly simple space
- a single object – neither overly simple nor complex, with enough interest to make you want to draw it
- any other object or subject of your own choice.

Allow up to 90 minutes. Try to use the mark-making you developed to help you realise any relevant details.

cross hatch Fine crossed lines used to suggest darker areas of tone.
imagery Visual images of a piece considered as a whole.
study A smaller or more quickly executed drawing or painting, made primarily as an aid in the production of a larger painting.
visual communication The communication of an idea, intention, message or theme to an audience using visual materials, techniques and processes.

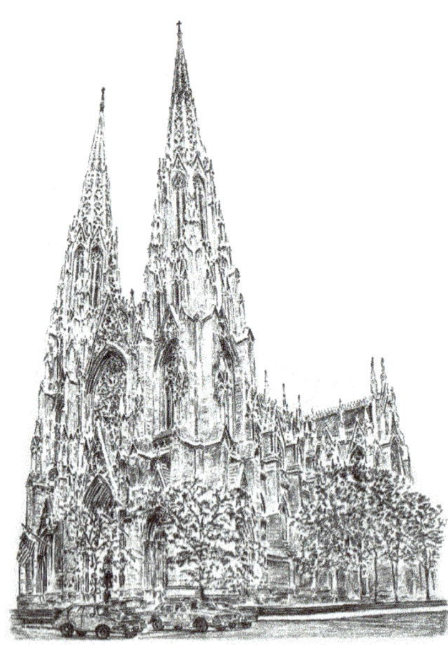

1.5 Anthony Butera, *St Patrick's Cathedral, Fifth Avenue, New York*, 2010, pencil, private collection.

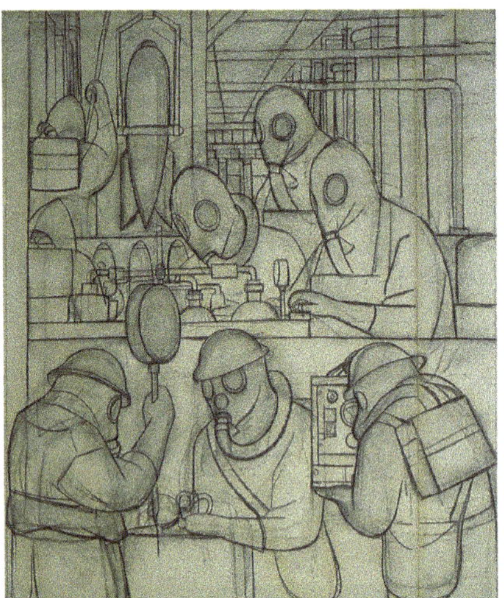

1.6 Diego Rivera, *Manufacture of Poisonous Gas Bombs*, preparatory drawing for *Detroit Industry*, fresco at the Detroit Institute of Art, 1932, charcoal on paper, Detroit Institute of Art.

Recording the world

The artworks shown in Figures 1.5 and 1.6 record and organise information about the world the artists have seen. The drawing by the American artist Anthony Butera records the detail of a complex structure – a cathedral – and celebrates this complexity. The drawing by the Mexican artist Diego Rivera (1886–1957) is a **cartoon** for a **fresco**, and uses line to arrange a composition and structure for the planned piece.

Activity E: **Evaluate how drawing has been used in an artwork**

1. Look at the image in Figure 1.7. What has the artist used drawing to record? How has he done this? Consider not just the objects in the drawing, but also the atmosphere.
2. Write a 100-word summary explaining your ideas and discoveries. (Refer to the section on formal elements on pages 10–17 to help you.)

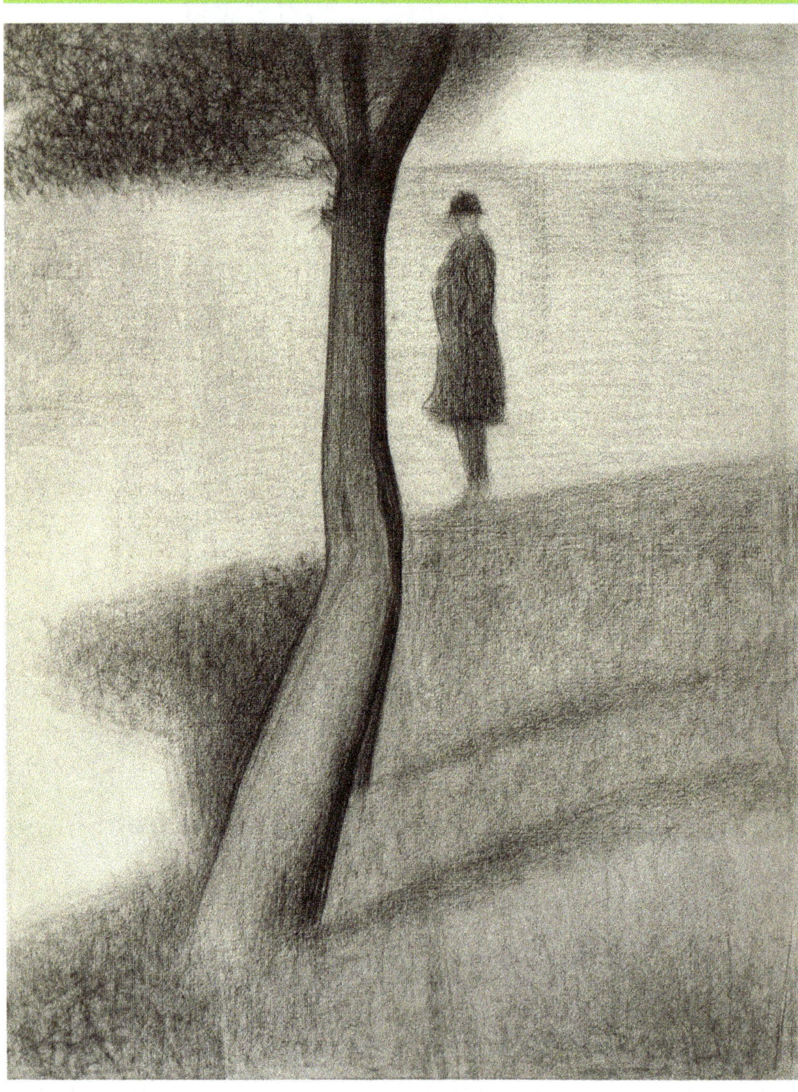

1.7 Georges Seurat, *Man Standing Next to Tree*, study for *La Grande Jatte*, 1884–5, pencil on paper, Von der Heydt Museum, Wuppertal.

Developing ideas

Practitioners use drawing as a way of developing and expressing their ideas, rather than recording the world around them. They not only use drawing to work out ideas for themselves – sorting things out and clarifying concepts in a visual way (Figure 1.8) – but they also use drawing to communicate their ideas and intentions to others.

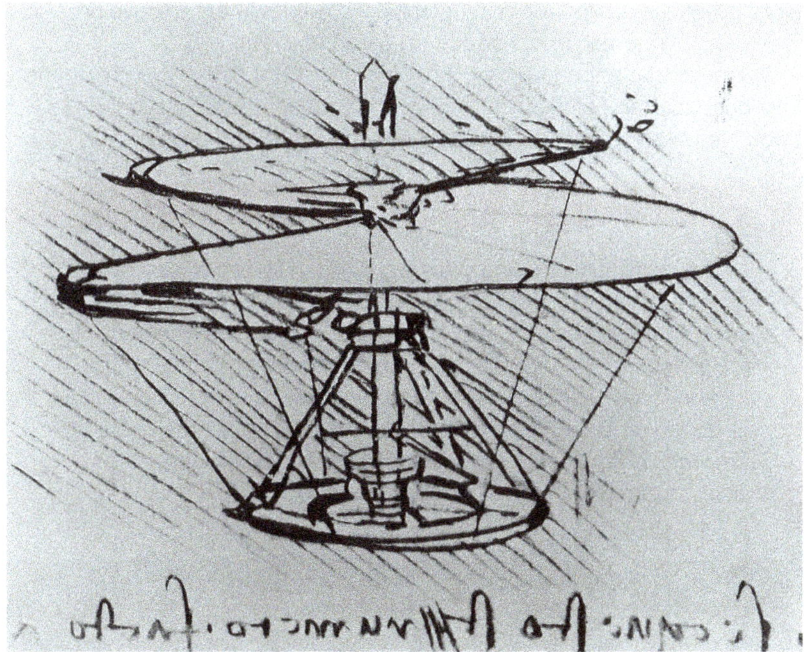

1.8 Leonardo da Vinci, *Detail of a design for a flying machine*, c.1488, pen and ink on paper, Bibliothèque de l'Institut de France, Paris.

Activity F: **Produce a drawing based on the theme 'Mystery'**

Using photographs as source materials, create a drawing that explores the potential to suggest an idea, atmosphere or tension, based on the theme 'Mystery'.

You can use existing photographs, or take some specifically for this task.

You can use a variety of pencils. If you want to develop the work, create further pieces using a wider range of drawing media, such as charcoal or conté.

Critical thinking:

Following on from **Activity F**, mount the original photographs and the drawing(s) on one or more sheets of card. Write a short explanation of how you used drawing to record and communicate your ideas and visual intention. Include notes on:

- your use of drawing materials, techniques and processes
- your interpretation of the theme 'Mystery'
- your planned creative intention, and how successfully you achieved this.

Materials and techniques: **Charcoal**

Charcoal is made by a controlled burning of wood, such as willow. The blackened sticks are suited to fast, expressive drawing and mark-making, as well as delicate tonal work.

cartoon In this context, a detailed study for a mural or fresco showing the final arrangement of the composition, tonal ranges, figures and design.

fresco Method of painting images onto freshly plastered walls. Fresco was often used to decorate the interiors of public buildings in medieval and Renaissance Italy and formed part of a decorative programme, or cycle, telling a story from the Bible or history.

Tip:

You can use a digital or a film camera for recording and observing. You can also use a video camera for moving-image-based recording.

PHOTOGRAPHY/LENS-BASED TECHNIQUES

Lens-based techniques offer artists and designers the ability to record quickly and in a wide range of conditions (indoors or outdoors, night or day, bright sunshine or in the rain and so on). Practitioners use lens-based techniques across many disciplines in art and design, to develop ideas or to record the progress of their work. They might take photographs of the different stages as work progresses, or include photographic techniques in the creative process – for example, in screen prints or pattern-based textiles.

Whatever the reason for using photographs, you should try to create the best ones you can. Follow the advice in the 'Getting started' section of this book. Here we focus on the key photographic skill of composition.

Materials and techniques: **Composition**

Using a camera involves choosing a (usually) rectangular area of the visible world that you want to record. This is done by selecting a subject to be photographed, and then looking through the **viewfinder** and carefully adjusting either the subject or your own position until the image in the viewfinder is what you want. The frame of the viewfinder will be the same as the frame of the image. This will be the image's composition. Some photographs explore composition by focusing the viewer's attention on specific details (see Figure 1.9).

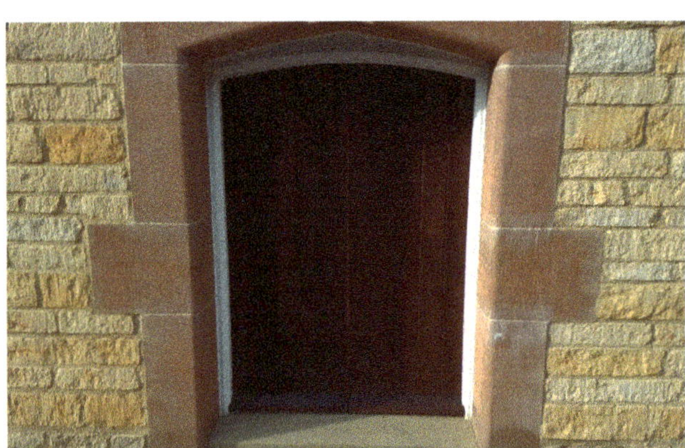

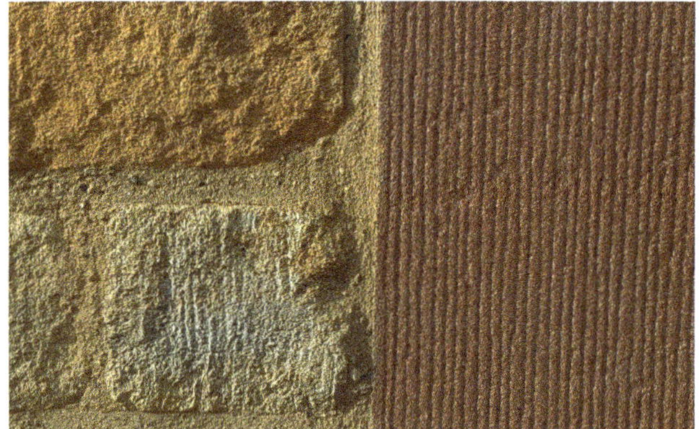

1.9 Alan Parsons, *Doorway*, 2017, photograph.

Activity G: **Produce a set of six photographs exploring composition, using the same subject**

1. Choose a subject that interests you, for example, this could be something you are working on in a current project.
2. Take your camera and record six different compositions – these will all be photographs of the same subject.
3. Consider what will be different each time about your position or viewpoint. To do this, you need to move around the subject, and consider the way you will crop your image in the viewfinder. You can also get creative here – try lying on the floor or standing on a chair or other high point (take care!) to find a less obvious viewpoint.
4. Which image do you prefer? Why?

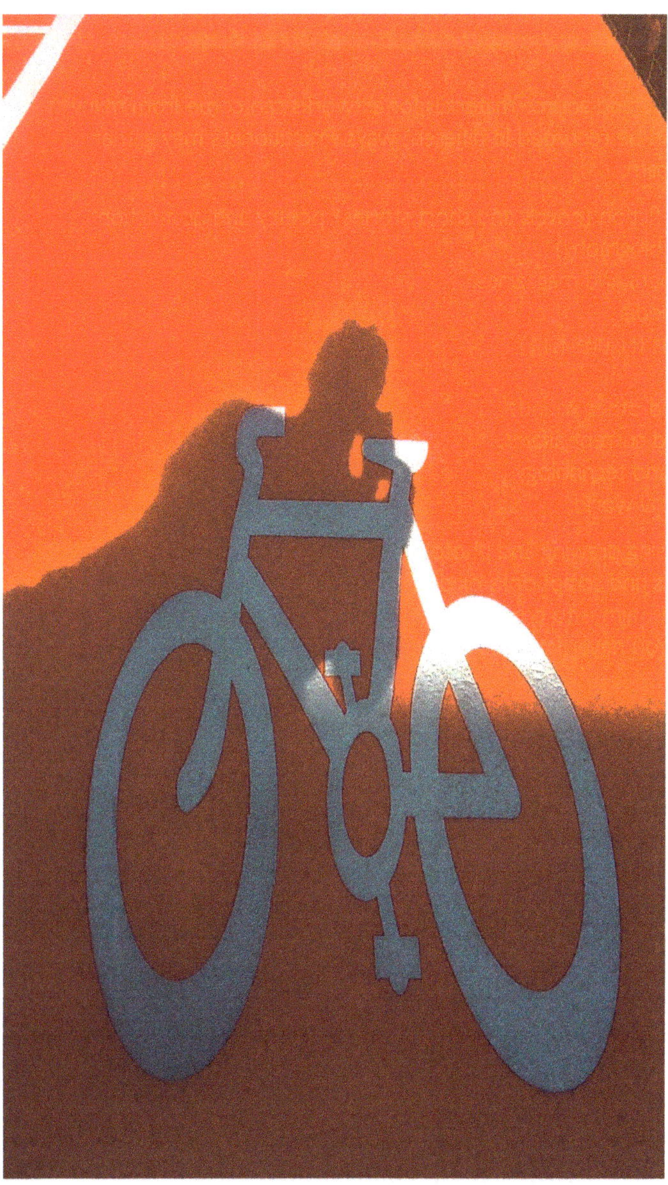

1.10 Alan Parsons, *Bike and Shadow,* 2014, photograph. You should learn how to recognise the visual potential in your surrounding environment.

Tip:

Think about a drawing class you have attended. Have you ever moved around the room to get a better viewpoint? If you have, you will know that the view you choose will influence the kind of composition you make. It is the same when you work with a camera.

Critical thinking:

Always spend time evaluating your images. Think about how successful they are in terms of your original intention:

- Do you understand how they can be used effectively as a recording tool?
- Have they helped you learn how to see things around you in a new way?
- Can you recognise the potential for developing your work using photographic images?

Then, write up a short summary based on this information, explaining your insights and views.

viewfinder Device on a camera showing the field of view of the lens.

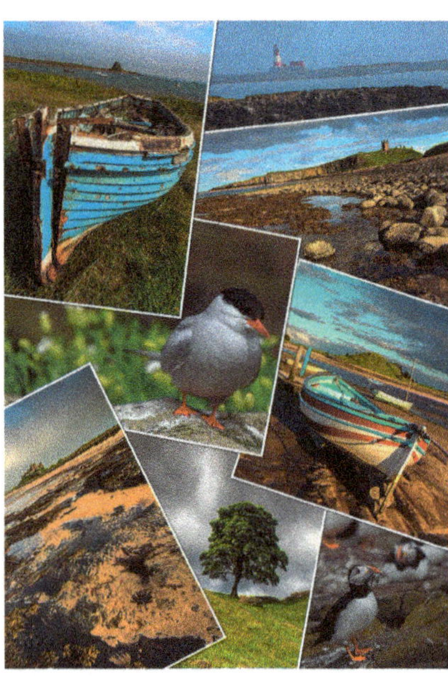

1.11 Collections of postcards can provide a rich resource for an artist.

OTHER FORMS OF GATHERING SOURCE MATERIALS

Starting points and source materials for artworks can come from many fields and can be recorded in different ways. Practitioners may gather inspiration from:

- books – fiction (novels and short stories), poetry and non-fiction (history, biography)
- newspapers and magazines
- online media
- postcards (Figure 1.11)
- films
- music and other sounds
- news and current affairs
- science and technology
- the natural world.

As well as using drawing and photography, you can record your inspirations in notebooks and scrapbooks or digital image-sharing platforms such as Pinterest. Your aim is to create a visual library that you can use to refer to and inspire you. You never know when a resource will be useful!

Materials and techniques: **Visual library**

A visual library is just that – a library of visual sources and references. Practitioners have different ways of storing information and retrieving it when needed. For example, the Scottish artist Peter Doig (born 1959) has a collection of postcards and always looks through the images before beginning painting as a way of focusing his visual sensitivity. Having your own visual library is helpful, as it can give you a head start when you begin a project or theme-based piece. Once you have got your library started, you can begin to use categories to organise the images. These could be by date as well as subject. You will be able to use these as starting points to get you thinking.

Activity H: **Start your visual library**

This activity is focused on the media and encourages you to get you started gathering images:

1. Over one week, collect as many images from the media (newspaper, magazines, online) as you can. These might be striking photographs of news events or combinations of text and image that you find graphically interesting. You can use **screenshots** from online media resources as well.
2. Store your images in an A4 folder or a portfolio.
3. After a week, spread your collection out and use some of the images to create a visual summary of the week. Use a collage technique. Add dates and written notes (annotations).
4. Consider your choice of images. How well do you think you have gathered your images? Is there a wide variety of subjects as well as sources? Are you already finding that your 'mini-library' is stimulating your work?

The resources you gather do not have to be visual. Some artists and designers respond to sound as part of their creative process and may collect **archives** of sound recordings. The Canadian artist Janet Cardiff (born 1957) uses sound in her work and creates installations that explore the relationship between the 'viewer' and sound. Part of her installation *The Forty Part Motet* is shown in Figure 1.12. These artists are still working with their own themes and ideas, but using different materials and techniques to record and make their work.

There is more on using music as inspiration for artwork in Module 2, pages 144–145 and 163.

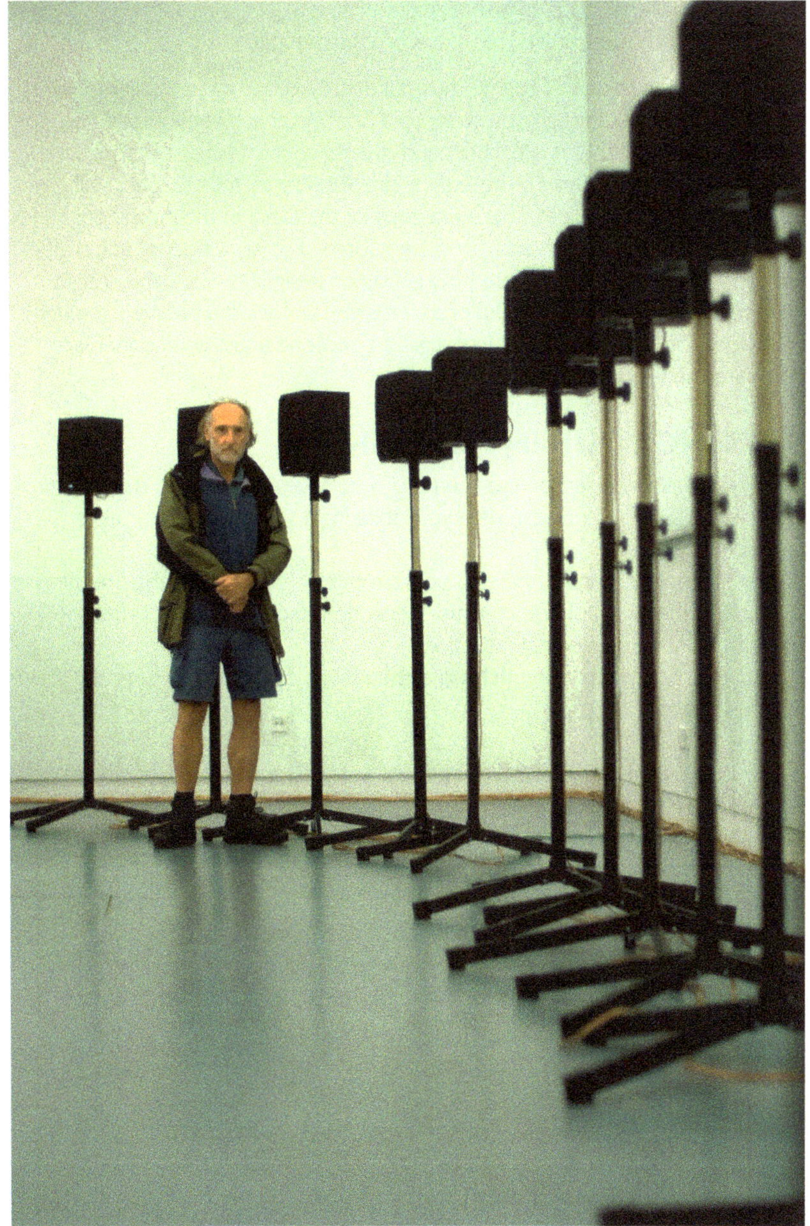

1.12 Janet Cardiff, *The Forty Part Motet (A reworking of 'Spem in Alium' by Thomas Tallis 1556)*, 2001, 40 loud speakers mounted on stands, placed in an oval, amplifiers, playback computer. Duration: 14 min. loop with 11 min. of music and 3 min. of intermission. Dimensions variable, Aberystwyth Arts Centre, Wales.

Activity 1: **Gather sample sound resources**

1. Using a sound-recording device, such as a smart phone, spend an hour gathering sounds in your local environment. Try to gather as many different kinds of sound as possible, both natural and human-made.
2. Listen back to your recordings carefully and choose *five* that you consider the most interesting and consider why. Do you think that any of the sounds could provide a stimulus for an artwork?

archive A collection of historical documents or artefacts.
screenshot Image of a screen-based operation, taken from the working screen and saved as a digital file.

INTRODUCTION

The Personal Investigation is the A Level component that combines both practical work and an extended written analysis of between 1000 and 1500 words in length.

As the title suggests, the Personal Investigation should be an aspect of art and design that has personal interest and relevance to you. This component requires you to include first-hand studies from **first-hand sources**:

- visits to galleries, studios or buildings
- contact with local artists, designers or craftspeople.

Therefore, your choice of theme must take into account your ability to meet this requirement. Although you work to a brief you have set yourself, you need to consult with your teachers and discuss your intentions before writing your statement of intent on the outline proposal form. Your teacher will give you the form to complete. There is a copy of the form in the Appendix.

The theme that you choose must be informed by an aspect of art, craft and design. You must investigate how artists or designers work; they might have responded to an issue, explored a theme, or solved a problem *through their work*. You can conduct an investigation into one artist or designer, or compare the work of two or more.

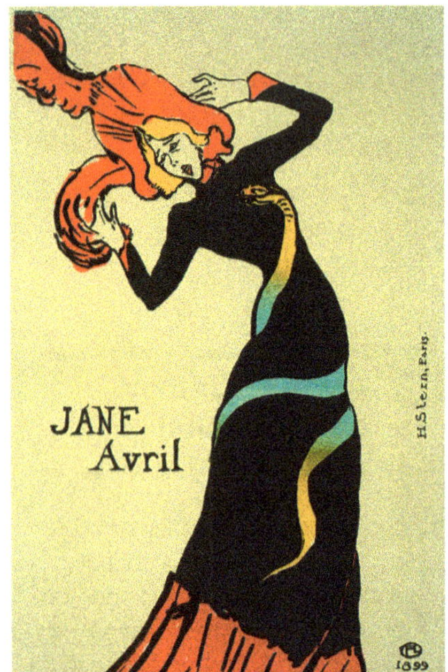

1.13 Henri de Toulouse-Lautrec, *Jane Avril*, 1899, lithographic poster, private collection. Is this a portrait or caricature of the French can-can dancer Jane Avril?

SETTING YOUR INTENTION

Once you have decided on the theme of your investigation, you must plan what you intend to do. It can help your thinking if you outline your aims and intentions.

For example, compare the two possible titles below where the intention is to explore the work of French artist Henri de Toulouse-Lautrec (1864–1901). Which title sets the clearest intention?

'An investigation into the **lithographic** prints of the artist Henri de Toulouse-Lautrec'

or

'Toulouse-Lautrec's lithographic portraits: does Lautrec's use of lithography turn portraiture into **caricature**?'

In the first example, the theme is very broad. Toulouse-Lautrec produced a very large number of lithographic prints and the scope of this title lacks focus. The second example provides a clear focus for the investigation. It sets **parameters**, as the intention is to look at *one* aspect of Lautrec's work and explore the impact of the print technique on the subject matter. It can then be linked directly to practical work that explores the theme 'Portraiture'.

PLANNING THE RESEARCH

Once you have clarified the focus of your investigation, begin to plan your research. At this stage, you need to keep your options open. Initially, your broad research for the written analysis might come from second-hand sources, such as books, published articles in magazines, newspapers and journals and on web pages. However, this component requires you to access at least one first-hand source. This can take the form of a visit to a gallery or museum, an interview with a practitioner or time spent at a local studio/workshop.

Remember that you can see original art and design work outside of galleries and museums too (Figure 1.14)! It could be artwork in public places, such as community art murals or sculptures, or billboard graphic advertising, architecture, religious buildings, or fashion, jewellery or products in a shop or retail outlet (Figure 1.15).

Wherever you go to see original work first-hand, always check to see whether you are permitted to take photographs. Remember that, even if you are allowed to take photographs, you might not be permitted to use a flash. Make sketches of the work and, if you are looking at three-dimensional (3D) work, make drawings from different viewpoints. Record details, as well as what the whole work looks like. For example, if looking at a garment, record what the fastenings look like, areas of embellishment, and details that show how it is constructed. This will help you when you analyse your research later.

Tip:

Try to plan visits and trips with classmates who might need to access the same first-hand sources as you. Always discuss your plans with your teacher, especially if you intend to interview an artist or designer where they work. For personal safety reasons, it is better to arrange an interview with someone that you do not know in a public place, or to take someone along with you.

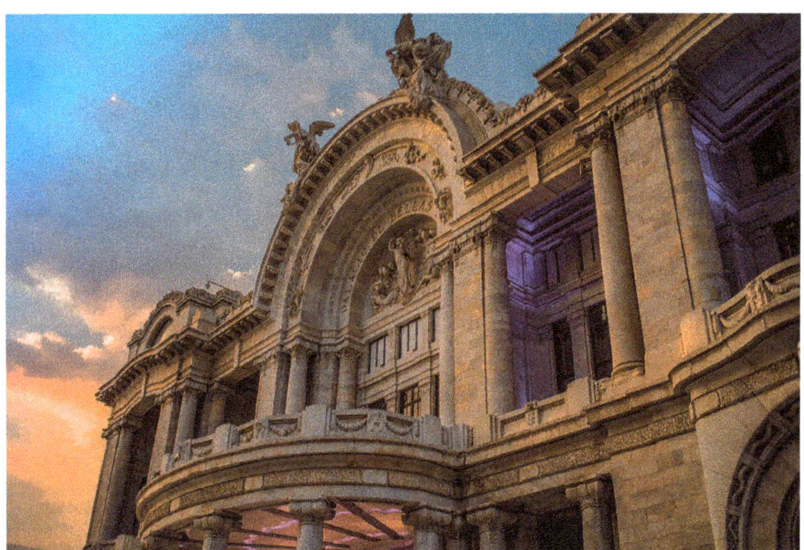

1.14 Fine Art museums, such as this one (Palacio de Bellas Artes) in Mexico City, are among the more obvious places to research your chosen theme.

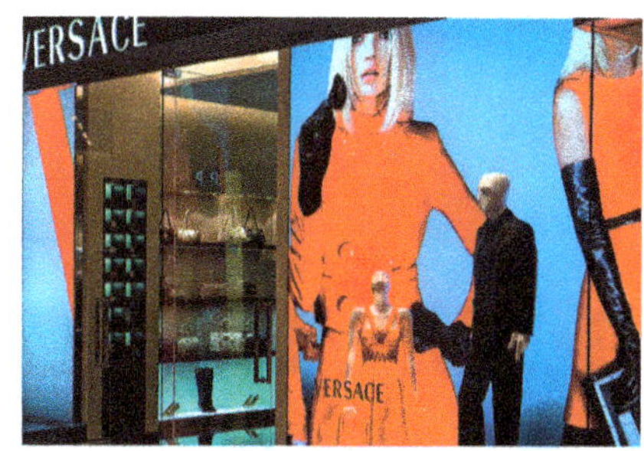

1.15 Remember that examples of original art and design work can be seen first-hand away from galleries and museums, as in this Hong Kong shopping mall.

Activity A: Plan local research

Make a list of all the places where you can access art, craft and design work where you live. It might help to share your thoughts with your classmates. Look at your list and identify the places that will provide you with first-hand sources of information for your chosen theme. Discuss with your teacher how best to structure your research.

caricature Image of an individual that focuses on and exaggerates their most obvious features.
first-hand source An object – for example, a painting or sculpture, that was created during the time period being studied.
lithography Printing technique invented at the end of the 18th century, originally using an etched stone plate.
parameters Limits.

PLANNING AN INTERVIEW

It is best if you can interview an artist or designer in person. In this case, the practitioner is likely to be a local one. However, you could also consider interviewing a practitioner by email. This will potentially open up the world to you, in terms of your choice.

Artists, craftspeople and designers can often be contacted either via their own websites or through galleries where their work is exhibited. You might not always receive a reply if you email or write to a practitioner directly, but it is always worth trying to contact them. If they do reply, it will add depth and breadth to your research and thinking.

When conducting any sort of interview, whether face-to-face or by email, you must make sure that you have thought through what you want to ask. This will usually be informed by your initial background research and the direction of your own practical work in this project.

For example, you might want to find out general information about the creative process that the artist, craftsperson or designer undertakes. Suitable questions include:

- What informs your work?
- Where do you seek inspiration?
- Who has been the most significant influence on your work?
- Do you use sketchbooks and take photographs to plan, or work directly in response to the theme or brief?

Alternatively, you might want to find out about specific techniques, media and processes that they use, their use of specific formal elements, or ask in detail about one or two pieces of their work that interest you. Whatever you want to find out, think carefully about your questions and the information that their responses will provide you with. It might not be possible to go back and interview the person again at a later stage.

If you can arrange a face-to-face interview with a local artist, check if you can take photographs (Figure 1.16) and, if possible and available, use a voice recorder. Make sure that you take plenty of notes throughout the interview. Record any details – such as titles – if they show you any of their work.

Tip:

Do not include full transcriptions of interviews within your written analysis, as the information that you acquire is only a part of what you will research. It helps to provide background information, gives you a unique context and demonstrates your ability to carry out independent research. However, you need to select the relevant information that develops your understanding and informs your subsequent analysis of selected pieces of art or design work.

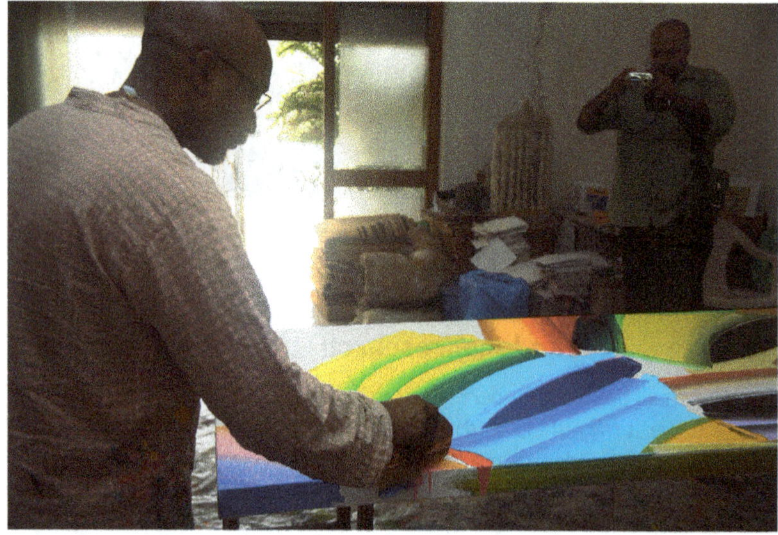

1.16 If possible, take photographs when interviewing local artists or visiting an artist's studio.

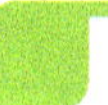

Activity B: **Plan a trial interview**

Imagine that you are interviewing a famous living artist, designer or craftsperson.

Research all you can about them in books and on the internet.

Now write a list of eight questions that you would ask them about their work. Try to create a structure for the questions so that they flow on from each other.

> **Tip:**
>
> Be realistic about your choice of theme and make sure that you have access to first-hand sources that relate to your theme.

SELECTING WORK TO ANALYSE

The main focus of the written analysis is an in-depth analysis of selected works. It is better to select one or two pieces to discuss in detail rather than several where your analysis is superficial. (Remember that you can reference other works more widely through annotations of your ongoing practical work.) You must view at least one artwork in person, although it is acceptable to analyse other images second-hand (for example, in a book or on the internet).

The key to being successful in this component is to make sure that the written analysis is your own analysis. However, your views must be supported by thorough research.

If you are researching the better-known artists, it can be very difficult to have original ideas about their work, as they have been written about so much. Likewise, if you do choose to look only at very well-known works, you will have to ensure that you write about your response to what you see and not be influenced by someone else's response.

It may be more interesting and rewarding to research and respond to pieces of work that are not well-known. However, in this case the information that is available to you might not be reliable or accurate.

To be able to achieve a balance, one solution might be for you to compare a less well-known artist or designer with a better-known one who uses the same themes or techniques. This will help you to form your own judgements and observations, supported by access to reliable and useful research material.

Remember that what you assimilate and learn from the written analysis will then inform, support and underpin the creative practical work that you go on to produce. The Personal Investigation section in Module 2 will provide more guidance on analysing your selected works.

1.1 Fine art

Painting

Learning objectives:

- To understand the potential for creative expression in different approaches to painting
- To explore painting created directly from observation
- To use photographic sources to support painting development

Painting is a rich and varied field and covers both **figurative** and abstract works, each involving varying degrees of observation and expression. It can also be incorporated into the creative process in other disciplines, such as illustration and hand-painted textiles.

As a discipline, painting is tens of thousands of years old. However, it has continued to evolve as artists extend ideas and techniques and respond to new technologies. Painting continues to allow painters to explore personal expression through mark-making and the size (scale) of their work.

Painters have worked from observation throughout history, and continue to do so today. They can:

- work directly from observation onto a **prepared canvas** or surface
- work on a set of observational studies that are brought into the studio and used as reference material for a larger painting
- record from observation using a camera or other lens-based resources if available, and work up paintings from these images/photographs.

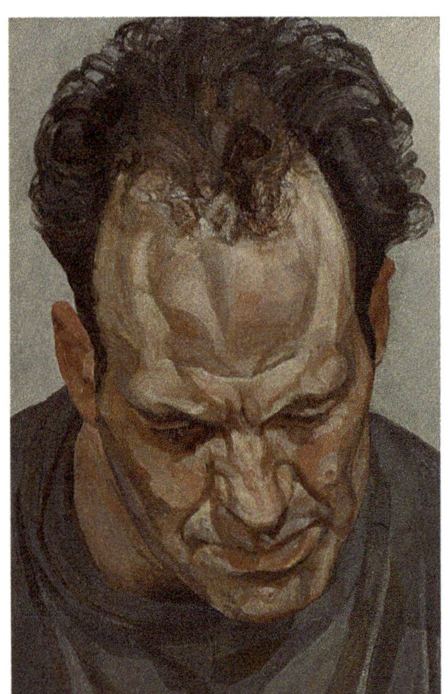

1.17 Lucien Freud, *Frank Auerbach*, 1975–6, oil on canvas, private collection. The artist painted this image working from direct observation of the sitter. What difference do you think it would have made if Freud had worked from, for example, a photograph?

WORKING DIRECTLY FROM OBSERVATION ONTO A PREPARED CANVAS OR SURFACE

The British painter Lucien Freud (1922–2011) is an example of an artist who worked directly from observation onto a prepared canvas. He worked on the portrait of his fellow artist Frank Auerbach during a series of **sittings**, responding directly to what he could see in front of him (see Figure 1.17).

This way of working on a portrait can create a dynamic between artist and sitter that can be revealed in the final image. Viewers find themselves asking questions: What is the person thinking? Why is his head bowed? What is the relationship between the artist and the sitter? This tension gives the portrait physiological depth and intensity.

Something similar can be achieved in paintings from subjects other than portraits, such as landscapes. Go online and have a look at some landscape paintings by Frank Auerbach.

Materials and techniques: **Painterly techniques**

Paintings made from direct observation may not look exactly like the scene or subject they are recording. The artist may use **painterly** techniques that both record the subject as well as communicate something about the paint itself. Brush marks are left visible and sometimes laid on very thickly (impasto), and colours can be blended while wet. Freud, for example, allowed the qualities of his medium, typically oil paint, to show through in his work as wet, slippery slabs of paint (see Figure 1.17).

Other artists might not let these qualities of paint show at all. In **Photorealist** work, for instance, the viewer may wonder whether the image is a photograph or a painting – there is no sign of the liquid quality of the paint showing (see Figure 1.19).

WORKING ON A SET OF STUDIES

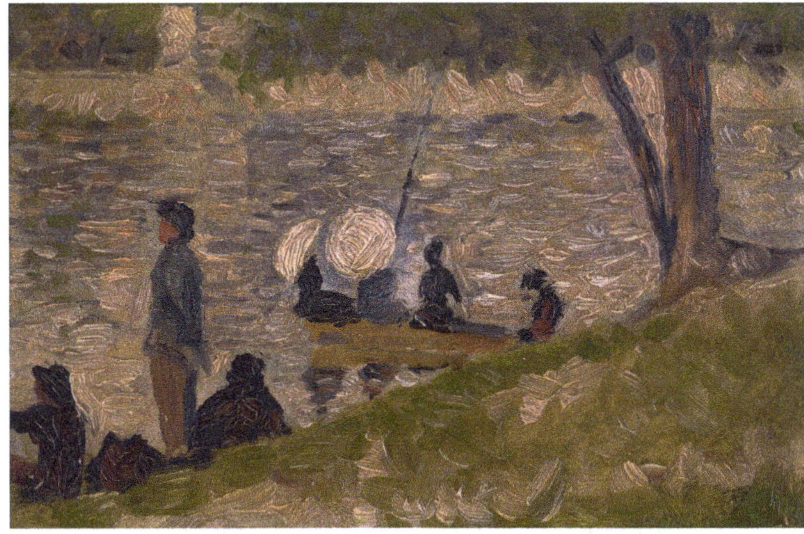

1.18 Georges Seurat, Study for *A Sunday Afternoon on the Island of La Grande Jatte*, 1884, oil, private collection. A study like this is both a record of a moment in time and source material for a larger work.

The French **Neo-Impressionist** painter Georges Seurat (1859–91) adopted the second approach: he first made **plein air** studies and used these to work up a much larger painting back in his studio. *A Sunday Afternoon on the Island of La Grande Jatte* is Seurat's most famous and largest work, more than 2 m × 3 m in size (look online for an image of this). Figure 1.18 shows a much smaller study Seurat painted in preparation for this work. He used such studies to record aspects of his subject – the interaction of light and shade or the postures that people adopt when relaxing, for example.

Materials and techniques: **Mixing paint**

Water-based paints are generally easier to handle when working in front of a subject, as they dry more quickly. They are also more portable. However, oil-based paints have a quality that some artists prefer. Mixing paint requires concentration and skill if you are trying to match colours to those you see in a subject.

figurative Art that directly represents the visible world.

Neo-Impressionism A movement of mainly French artists who in the 1880s and 1890s took the experiments of the Impressionist painters further. They especially used the technique known as pointillism – dots of painted colour on a canvas that appear to blend when seen from a distance.

painterly Method of painting that exploits and draws attention to the quality of the paint itself, so that brush strokes are visible in the final artwork.

Photorealism Extremely realistic style of painting that mimics the look of photographs.

plein air French term that means 'open air', used where an artist works outside directly from the subject.

prepared canvas A canvas made ready for painting with a layer of gesso.

sitting A painting session in the production of a portrait; the subject 'sits' for the artist even if the subject is not literally sitting down.

Tip:

It is easier to work from light to dark when mixing paint. This means using a blob of light colour first and adding very small amounts of a darker colour or colours to this, to get the right value. If you start with a dark colour, it can take a lot of a lighter colour to change it.

Activity A: **Produce a set of studies**

1. Select a subject to work from. You will be observing this subject directly, so you need to have access to it whenever you are planning to paint. The choice of subject is up to you. You can use this activity to begin work on a current project or theme. Make a set of brief notes explaining why you have chosen this subject.
2. Use a water-based paint to begin with – choose from watercolour, acrylic or gouache. Whichever type of paint you decide on, lay out a set of colours on a palette, starting with white and ending with black. This is where you will mix your colours.
3. Now look at the subject and try to identify the various colours within it. Next, mix your paints to see whether you can copy the colours you see. Once you have mixed the paints, apply them to your paper or canvas. Draw or set out the shapes of the composition before you apply the paint.

Activity B: **Make colour studies of an existing painting**

Practise mixing colours by making studies of areas of another artist's paintings. Try making small colour studies of areas of the face in the portrait by the American artist Chuck Close (born 1940) (see Figure 1.19).

Materials and techniques: **Applying paint**

Explore different ways of applying paint. Thickly applied paint is known as impasto and generally covers the support completely. (You can find more specific information on different supports on page 232 in Module 3.) Washes or **glazes** of paint are thinly applied and allow some of the colour underneath to show through. Try out different ways of applying paint as you work through the activities in this unit.

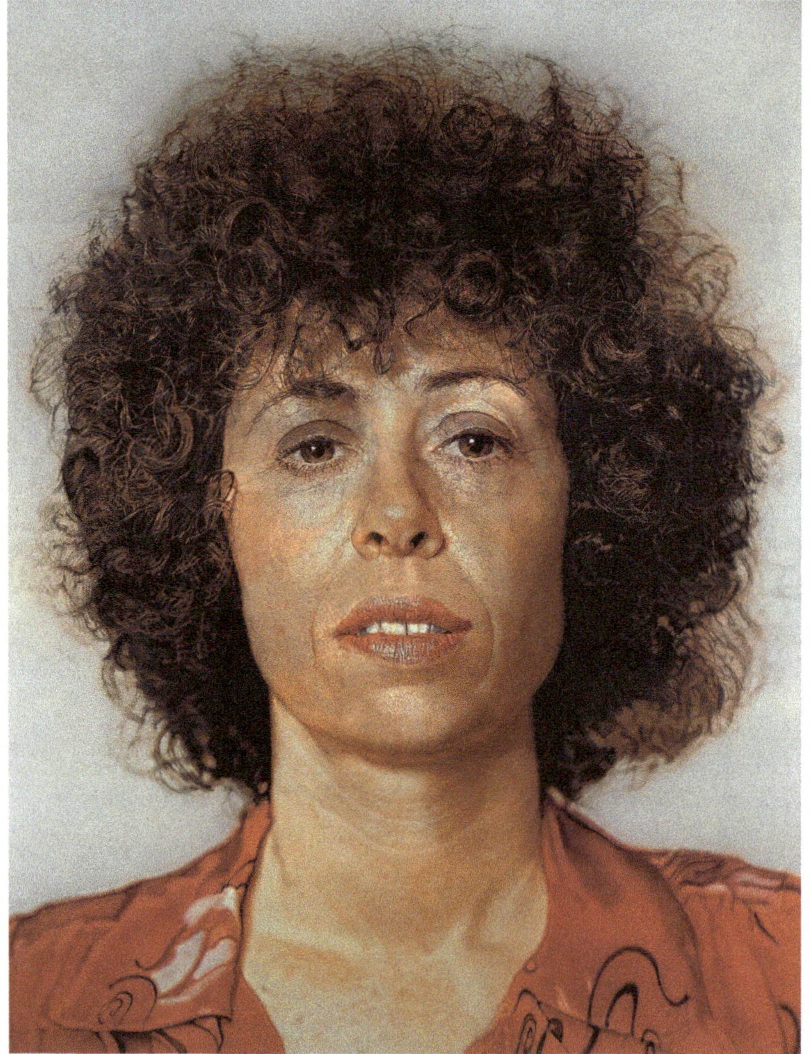

1.19 Chuck Close, *Linda*, 1975–6, acrylic on gessoed canvas, Akron Art Museum, Ohio.

RECORDING FROM OBSERVATION WITH CAMERAS/LENS-BASED RESOURCES

Many painters work with photography, incorporating photographic imagery directly into their work or using it as a source to paint from. Artworks created using this method have qualities that it would not be possible to obtain if working directly from the subject. A painting that explores photographic imagery is like a moment frozen in time. Details are captured by the **shutter** action that the human eye would struggle to see. The camera also offers artists the opportunity to redefine their compositions.

For example, compare the two paintings of horses and jockeys below: one by the British artist George Stubbs (1724–1806) (see Figure 1.20), the other by the French artist Edgar Degas (1834–1917) (see Figure 1.21). Stubbs's image is like a showcase for the horse: he has placed the horse in the middle of the foreground. Degas lived in a time after the birth of practical photography (1839) and often worked from photographs. Notice how the notion of the **viewfinder frame** has meant that Degas's horses are sometimes cut off by the edge of the canvas.

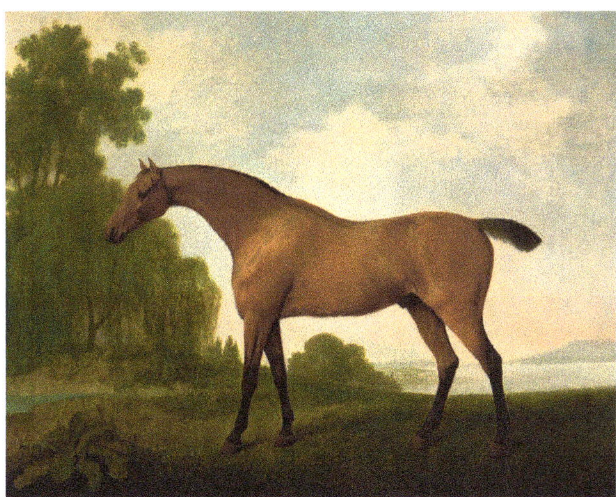

1.20 George Stubbs, *A Bay Thoroughbred in a Landscape*, 1801, oil on canvas, private collection. Describe the composition of this painting and compare it with the composition of the Degas painting (Figure 1.21).

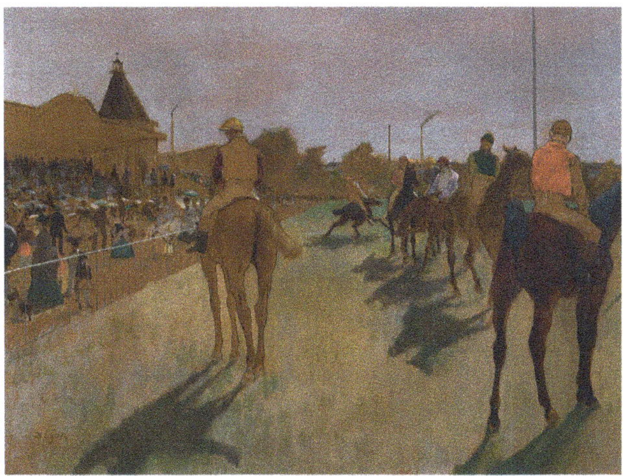

1.21 Edgar Degas, *The Parade, or Race Horses in front of the Stands*, c.1866–8, oil on paper, Musée d'Orsay, Paris.

glaze Thin washes of paint that allow areas of paint (underpainting) to show through – creating a sense of depth and effects of light and shade.
shutter A shield in a camera that, when tripped, allows light to pass onto the film or plate for a period of time, usually a fraction of a second.
viewfinder frame Open frame made from two L-shapes, used to view areas through – to decide on composition/selection of image for recording.

Tip:

Brushes wear out over time and with repeated use. However, old brushes can be used to provide very short and jagged marks, and can provide interesting effects. Keep your old brushes and explore the types of mark they make.

Activity C: **Make a painting based on a photograph**

In this activity, you will explore just what happens when you use photographs as a basis for working in paint.

1. Again, select a subject – this could be a theme or project you are currently working on.
2. Take photographs that explore the subject and your interpretation of it. Print these out and use them as a source for your painting. Select one image as your preferred image to work from. You can make a grid to help you to lay out the composition (see page 40 of the Introduction).
3. Before beginning work, think about how you can mix the different colours, and whether you want to adopt a painterly approach, for example, using impasto or allowing the paint to pool, drip or smudge.

Materials and techniques: **Paintbrushes**

Your paintbrushes are your tools, and you need to keep them in good condition if you want them to perform well. It is also really useful to get used to having your own set of brushes. Over time you will learn which types of brush you prefer, and what kinds of mark they make and effect they create. Clean them well after each session, and they will become an important piece of kit in your working practice.

Critical thinking:

Consider how your painting techniques were able to record your subject in **Activities A** and **B**. Ask questions such as:

- How closely did you look at the colours in the subject?
- How closely were you able to match those colours?
- What have you learned about paint and how to apply it?

Further research

Use the internet to research basic advice on mixing oil paints.

Discover more about Degas's use of photography in *Edgar Degas: Photographer* by Malcolm R. Daniel (Metropolitan Museum of Art, 1998).

Artists and designers: **Jean-Michel Basquiat and Kehinde Wiley – approaches to using paint**

Look at and compare and contrast the portraits in Figures 1.22 and 1.23 by the African-American artists Jean-Michel Basquiat (1960–88) and Kehinde Wiley (born 1977). Being able to undertake such comparisons is a vital skill in this course and will help enrich your own art practice.

Both artists have taken subject matter from their own lives, culture and environment and used it as a basis for their work:

- Basquiat has painted a self-portrait, something he did quite rarely during his short career. Many artists use the self-portrait to explore and assert their identity as an artist, especially in the early stage of their career.
- Wiley has created the portrait of someone he admires, one of the pioneers of hip-hop, LL Cool J. As in many of his works, the painter claims status for the musician by basing his portrait on European or American portraits of great white men from history. As an example, look online for a portrait of John D. Rockefeller (1917) by John Singer Sargent.

Each artist has used a technique that is suited to the intention and idea he wanted to communicate to his audience.

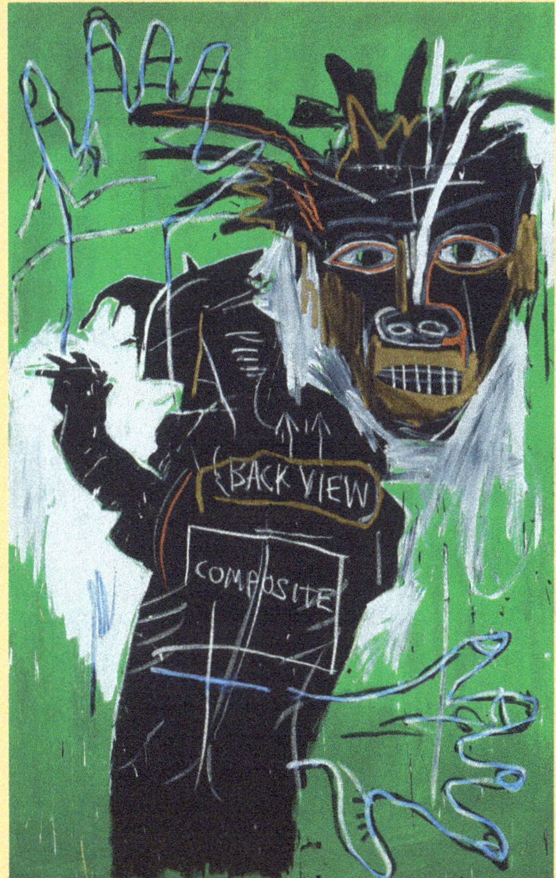

1.22 Jean-Michel Basquiat, *Self-Portrait as a Heel Part Two*, 1982, acrylic and oil paintstick on canvas, private collection.

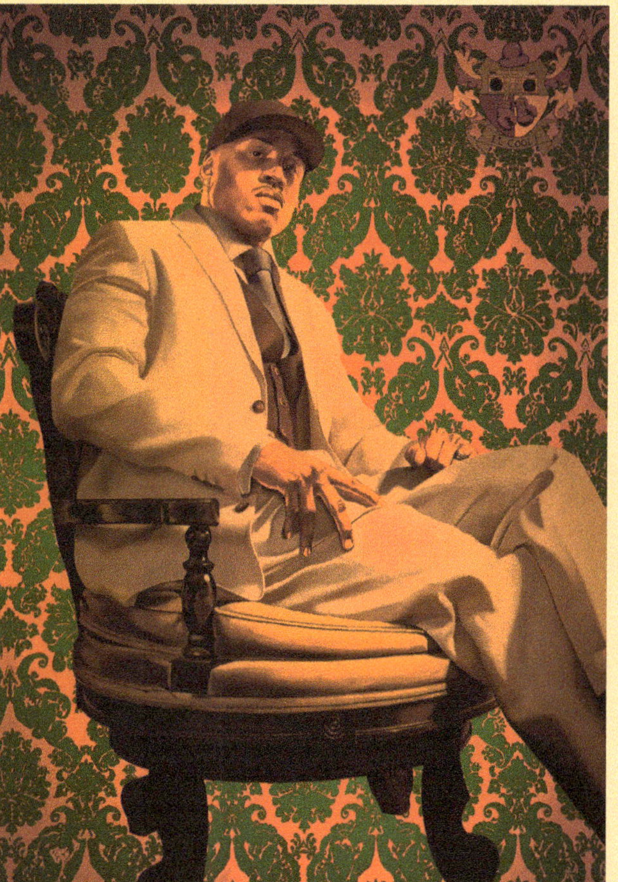

1.23 Kehinde Wiley, *LL Cool J*, 2005, oil on canvas, National Portrait Gallery, Smithsonian Institution, Washington, DC.

Photography

Learning objectives:

- To understand camera controls and their functions
- To understand the potential for creative work using photography

Photographers record the world in different ways, according to their intention. Fine art photographers tend to use the medium to communicate an idea or theme through the use of specific images. Photography is also used in many other art and design disciplines as an important stage in the recording process. Look at the Cambridge International AS & A Level Digital Media & Design syllabus 9481 if you would like to pursue the digital discipline. Note that any photography you submit as part of your general recording and/or within the fine art area of study must be submitted as prints, not as USB or digital files.

USING THE CAMERA CONTROLS

You can use a digital camera and/or a film camera to record. High-end smart phones are another possibility. However, if you want to develop your photographic skills, you need to use a digital single-lens reflex (DSLR) camera or single-lens reflex (SLR) camera if using film. The controls are very similar for both (see Figure 1.24).

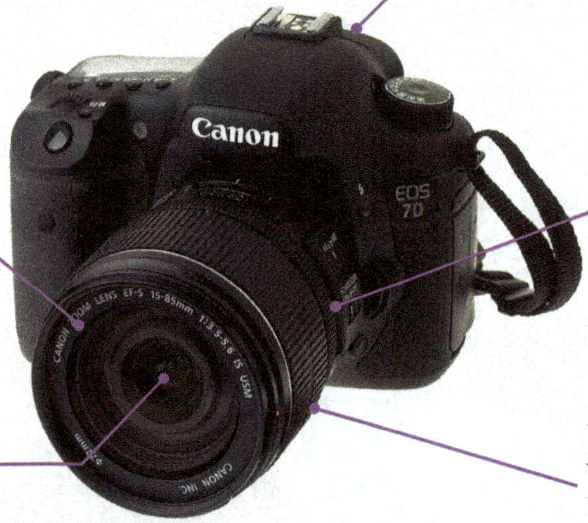

The lens – optical device that channels light onto sensor or film at back of camera

The shutter – small screen structure within camera that opens and shuts to allow light in for specific time, measured in fractions of a second upwards

The viewfinder – small screen allowing user to see composition of photograph being taken

The **aperture** ring – sets aperture size within lens section, measured in f-stops, controls the amount of light hitting sensor or film

The focusing ring – turned to focus on certain parts of image seen through the viewfinder

1.24 Get to know the main parts of a camera.

The controls on a DSLR have different shooting modes. You can start by shooting on Auto, where the camera makes a choice for you. However, you will soon want to develop your own way of using the camera, and you need to change the **shooting modes** to do this. In the instructions for your camera, look up the following:

- shooting modes: Aperture Priority and Shutter Priority
- **ISO** values
- **White Balance**.

Research how you can use each of these. You need to understand how these different modes work and what they affect.

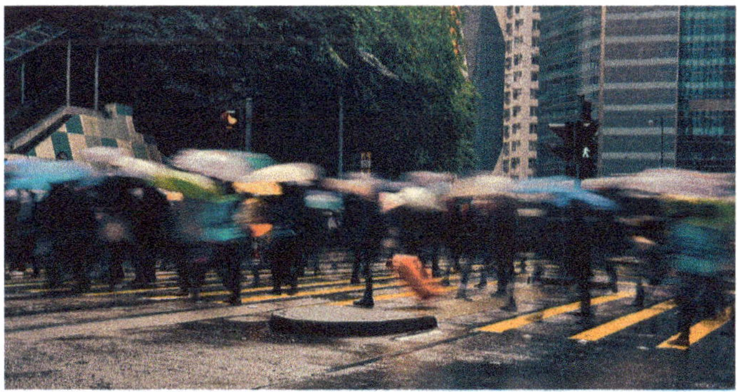

1.25 To make this image, the photographer set the camera controls to give a slower shutter speed, and so capture movement.

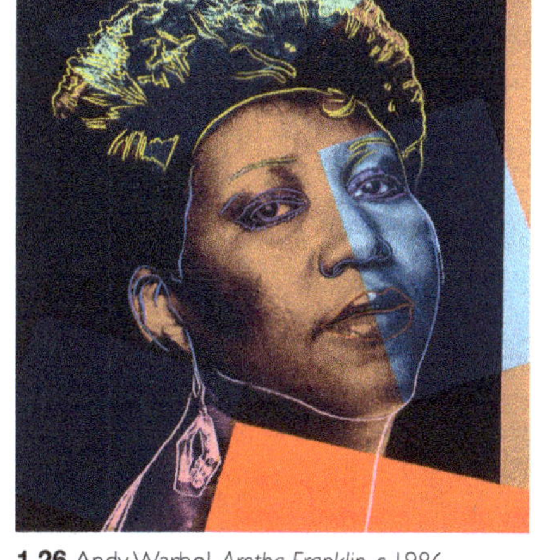

1.26 Andy Warhol, *Aretha Franklin*, c.1986, synthetic polymer paint and silkscreen ink on canvas, The Andy Warhol Foundation for the Visual Arts, Inc., New York.

Activity A: **Explore your camera controls**

Use a DSLR or SLR to explore how aperture and shutter speed work together, and the different effects that setting White Balance, ISO, Shutter and Aperture have on the images. You can use a smart phone if it has a Pro mode set of controls – you should find similar controls to those in a DSLR. Record the control settings and pair these with the resulting images.

PHOTOGRAPHY WITH PAINT AND PRINT

We have touched on this in the unit 'Painting' on pages 52–53. It is important to realise just how many fine artists have employed photography to create images that they then combine with paint or ink. The American artist Andy Warhol (1928–87) used the camera consistently as part of his work. He used photographic imagery as a basis for large-scale printed and painted work, exploring the differences between the two media by **juxtaposing** them in the same image. Warhol used this technique in his image of the American soul singer Aretha Franklin (see Figure 1.26).

Tip:

Using layers like this is similar to working with Layers in Photoshop. The same principles apply – you are using the software to place one layer on top of another, and changing the resulting image.

Activity B: **Combine photography and paint in an artwork**

In this activity, you will be developing your own piece of photography-inspired artwork.

1. Take a set of photographs of a recognisable subject, for example, a portrait or building.
2. At the same time, make a set of pencil studies of the same subject, making notes on the colours both in and around the subject. Record these with a camera if you prefer.
3. Next, capture the images and edit one of them, adjusting the Contrast to high contrast.
4. Print this image out onto A4 **acetate**.
5. Now refer back to the colour notes in your pencil drawings. Use these to create some painted surfaces on sheets of paper.
6. When these are dry, cut or tear them into shapes that relate to the photograph, and place these underneath the acetate – you should be able to explore different compositions in this way.

acetate A transparent sheet used in photocopying and printing.
aperture The hole through which light passes to reach the film or image sensor.
ISO This shows the level of light sensitivity a camera is set at – 'low ISO' means low sensitivity to light; 'high ISO' is high sensitivity to light. The acronym 'ISO' stands for 'International Organization of Standardization', which sets commercial and industrial standards worldwide.
juxtapose To set two contrasting objects side by side.
shooting mode A selection made to determine the way a camera functions, such as Aperture Priority shooting.
White Balance A feature many digital cameras and video cameras use to balance colour accurately.

INTENTION

Practitioners use photography to realise an intention:

- documenting and reporting on a significant event or situation that the photographer feels is important
- expressing personal artistic ideas, for example, emphasising imagery and/or the formal elements.

Look at the two photographs shown in Figures 1.27 and 1.28. Think what the intention of the artists might be.

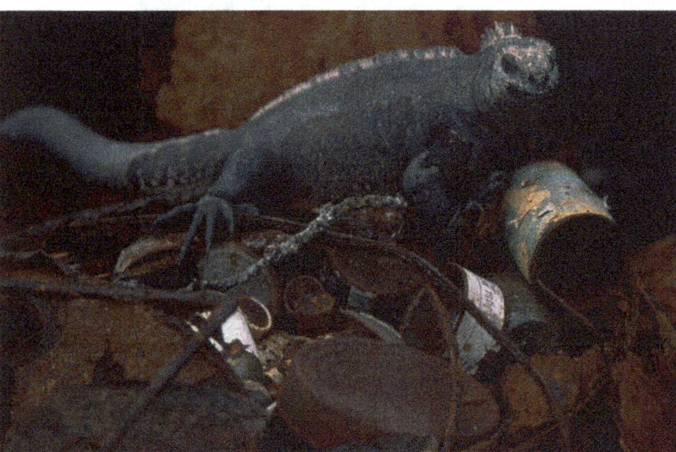

1.27 Stuart Franklin, *Galapagos, Marine Iguanas threatened by human development*, 1999, photograph. Photographer Stuart Franklin uses photography to highlight his concern about the environment; the texture and colour of the rusty objects provides an incongruous backdrop and harmful environment for the blue-coloured marine iguana.

British photographer Stuart Franklin (born 1956) has made photographic essays where he documents significant events in the Lebanon and Tiananmen Square, Beijing, China. Franklin uses photography to express his concerns for the planet, as when he travelled to Antarctica alongside Greenpeace in 1989. His work can highlight the negative effects of our relationship with the natural world, and the effect our activities are causing.

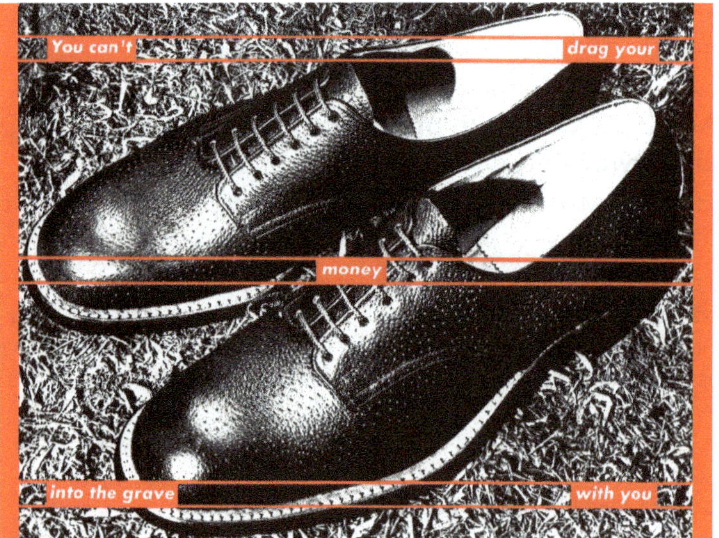

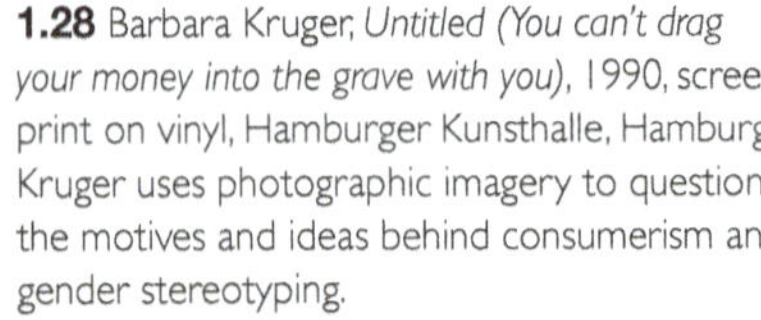

1.28 Barbara Kruger, *Untitled (You can't drag your money into the grave with you)*, 1990, screen print on vinyl, Hamburger Kunsthalle, Hamburg. Kruger uses photographic imagery to question the motives and ideas behind consumerism and gender stereotyping.

The American artist and collagist Barbara Kruger (born 1945) combines photographic imagery and text to produce images that have a clear, strong message. She uses imagery and text to make works that look like advertisements, but which in fact ask hard-hitting questions about **consumerism**.

Activity C: **Record your surroundings**

Figures 1.29, 1.30 and 1.31 show images from a set of photographs produced in the same location. They were based on a simple idea – recording the environment that surrounds people.

Using these as prompts, use your camera to record 40 images of your own surroundings – make sure that you consider the quality of each image as you take it.

Be creative with your camera. Once you are more confident with your camera, experiment with the controls. Figure 1.30 is deliberately out of focus, to create a sense of vagueness and dimmed light, almost like an **Impressionistic** view of the scene.

Tip:

Think about the formal elements of your chosen image (see pages 10–17). Your first task is to *recognise* them in your surroundings; your second task is to *record* them *appropriately* with the camera.

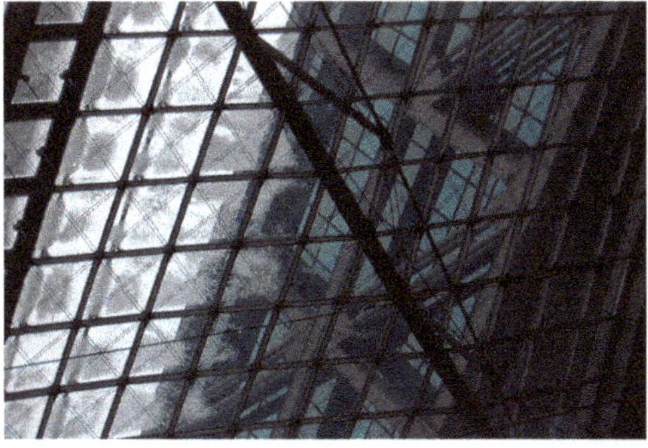

1.29 Alan Parsons, *Roof*, 2013, digital photograph. This image focuses on a small part of the overall structure, exploring the geometrical form and shapes.

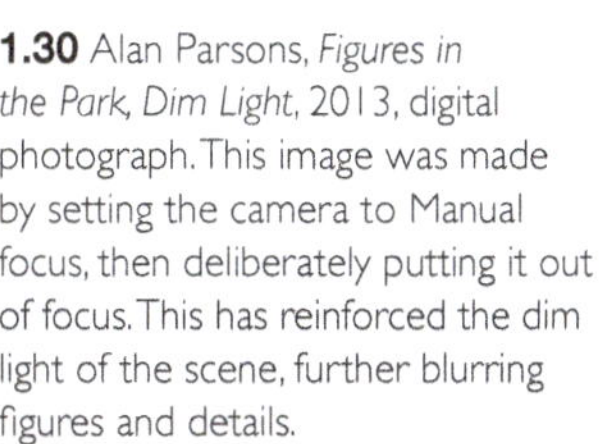

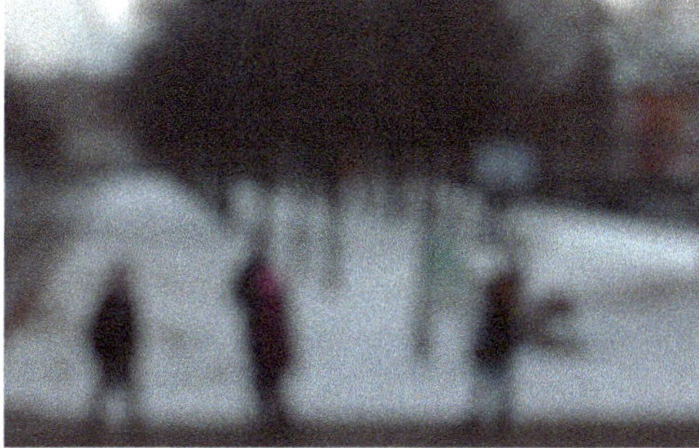

1.30 Alan Parsons, *Figures in the Park, Dim Light*, 2013, digital photograph. This image was made by setting the camera to Manual focus, then deliberately putting it out of focus. This has reinforced the dim light of the scene, further blurring figures and details.

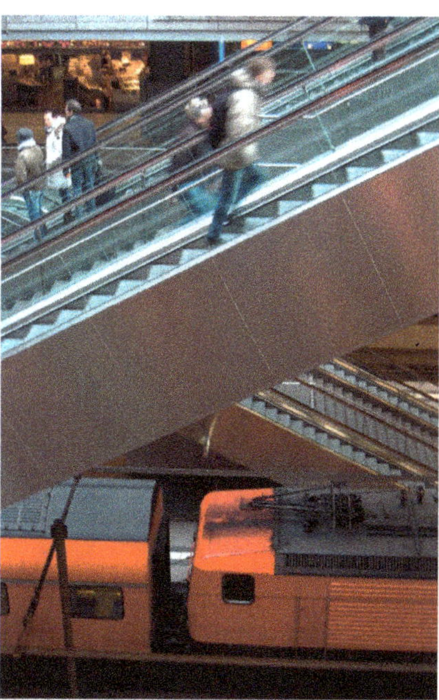

1.31 Alan Parsons, *Escalator and Trains*, 2013, digital photograph. This image has contrasting details and angles within its composition, leading the eye up and down the image. The people are moving in opposite directions, reinforcing the sense of transit. The image references paintings by Cubist artists that show figures in motion.

Critical thinking:

Consider the work you produced for **Activity C**:

1. Out of the 40 images, select the best five and display these as a set or series.
2. How successfully do you feel they have captured the **essence** of your surroundings?
3. What formal elements have you recognised and explored in the imagery?

If possible, discuss the outcomes for this activity as a class, showing appreciation and constructive criticism of other students' work.

Further research

For a good introduction to taking photographs, try *The Beginner's Photography Guide* (Dorling Kindersley, 2016).

consumerism An economic system (such as capitalism) that encourages people to buy goods beyond what they need.

essence The basic nature of something.

Impressonistic Something that is similar to the work of the Impressionist painters – not including every detail but suggesting the mood of a scene.

Experimental/assemblage and construction

Learning objectives:

- To understand how experimental fine art can explore ideas and themes
- To explore creative work by applying experimental fine art approaches

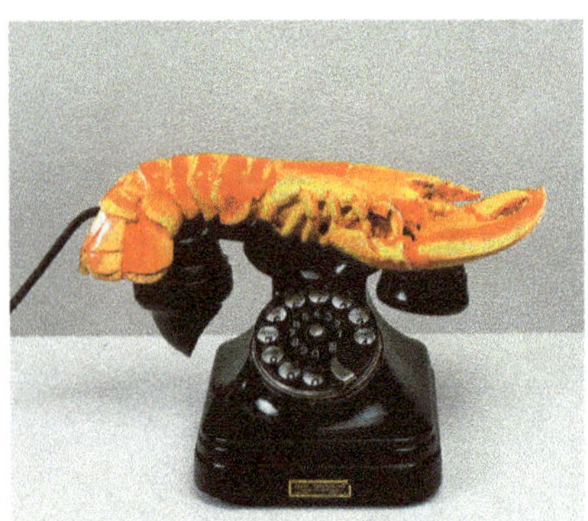

1.32 Salvador Dalí, *Lobster Telephone*, 1936, mixed media, including steel, plaster, rubber, resin and paper, Tate, London.

Artists have often used the potential in found objects to express their ideas. In the 1920s and 1930s, the **Surrealist** artists realised how objects could communicate with us through association – what we expect such objects to be like or how we expect them to be used.

The Surrealists created images that challenge, disturb and even frighten us by altering the context that objects were placed in. In *Lobster Telephone* (see Figure 1.32), the Spanish artist Salvador Dalí (1904–89) has replaced the receiver of a phone with a lobster. The shape of the lobster reminds us of a receiver, but we would, of course, not be able to use this telephone to make calls. If we did lift the lobster-receiver to our mouth and ear, the claws would hurt us, we imagine. The juxtaposition is unsettling.

These artists used objects to awaken our buried or forgotten fears and memories. In doing so, they communicated unsettling ideas about our lives and society. What do you think Dalí might be trying to communicate about *communication* with his *Lobster Telephone*?

The American artist Joseph Cornell (1903–72) took much of his inspiration from the Surrealists. He is best known for his collections of objects displayed in boxes with glass fronts (see Figure 1.33). He discovered many of the objects – old photographs and **bric-a-brac** – in second-hand shops. This kind of work of art is known as an assemblage (from 'assemble', or gather together) or construction.

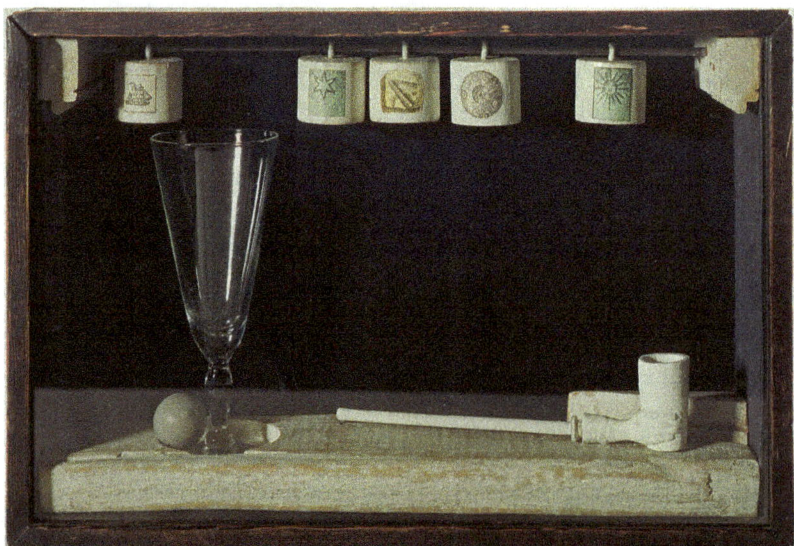

1.33 Joseph Cornell, *Untitled (Soap Bubble Set)*, 1949, mixed media, private collection. Cornell has arranged his objects carefully in a composition, almost like a still life. What associations would each of these objects usually create in you? How do they make you feel as a collection?

Materials and techniques: **Becoming a collector**

The best way to start creating your own assemblages/constructions is to collect anything that you find interesting. This can be literally anything – as long as it is safe, non-toxic and you are permitted to take it. Keep the items for future use. The items in your collection can be used as inspiration and starting points for new work, or physically collaged into works of art.

Activity A: **Memory piece**

The objects you collect can be very personal to you and can be used to create works of art that reflect and say something about your experiences.

1. Collect as many things as you can that define your life experiences so far. These can be things that reference personal aspects of your life, such as family photographs or keepsakes, or that reference the surroundings and society you live in.
2. Paint a large sturdy box white inside and out. You could use an old bathroom or display cabinet instead if you can find one. Then paint it white.
3. Construct your piece, placing the objects in an arrangement that is visually interesting.

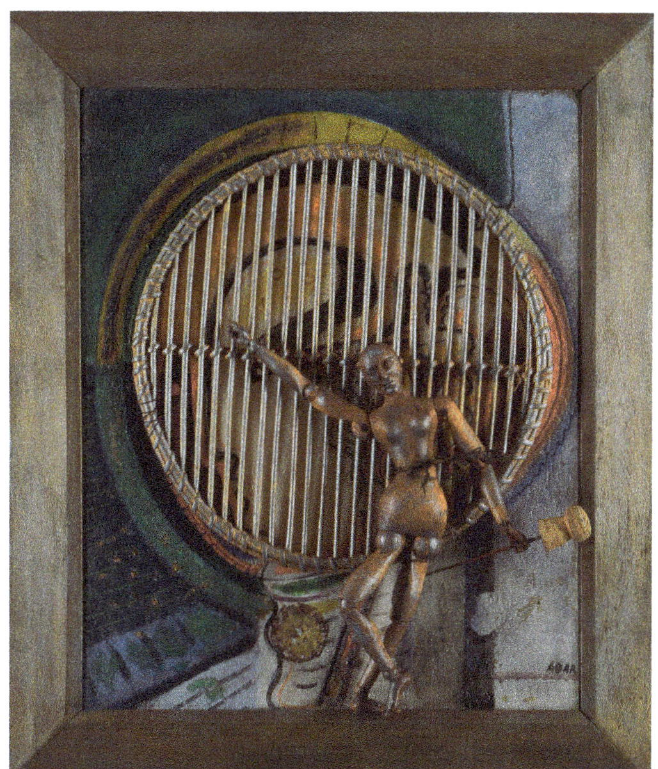

1.34 Eileen Agar, *The Object Lesson*, 1940, gouache and collage on soft board, Southampton City Art Gallery. Some artists, such as the British artist Eileen Agar (1899–1991), combine media to make images that explore the different characteristics of materials, as well as colour, texture and shape.

Tip:

In **Activity A**, try out a number of arrangements before you decide on the one you are happiest with. Take photographs as a record of your selection process.

Critical thinking:

Consider the work you produced for **Activity A**:

1. Does it work visually, as an interesting and well-considered piece?
2. What formal elements have you explored in the construction?
3. How successfully do you feel it communicates information and ideas about you and your experiences?

Further research

Go online to find out more about assemblage.

Explore the history of assemblage in *Collage, Assemblage, and Altered Art: Creating Unique Images and Objects* by Diane Maurer-Mathison (Watson-Guptill, 2008).

bric-a-brac Everyday household objects that people no longer need and have thrown away.

Surrealism Art and literary movement of the 1920s, 1930s and beyond that sought to explore the world of dreams and the unconscious mind through irrational, fantastic imagery. Surrealism took much of its inspiration from the ideas of the Austrian psychoanalyst Sigmund Freud (1856–1939). Key Surrealist artists include Salvador Dalí, Max Ernst and Hans Arp. There is more on Surrealism in Module 2: Introduction, and pages 166–169.

Drawing

Learning objective:

- To develop drawing skills by working from direct observation and personal experience

In the introduction to this module (pages 40–43), we looked at drawing as one of the fundamental tools of an artist as they observe, record and prepare as part of the process of making finished artworks in many disciplines. In this section, the focus is on drawing as an art form in its own right, not just a preparatory stage for a painting. A drawing of this type can be seen in the image of a runaway buffalo in Figure 1.35, an intricately worked **Mughal** drawing from the 18th century.

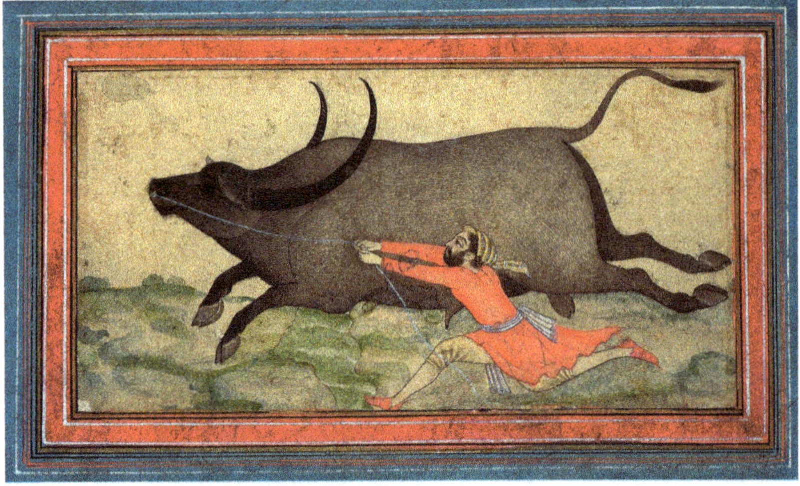

1.35 Anonymous artist, *Runaway Buffalo*, Johnson Album XIV, no. 11, verso, c.1700, coloured drawing on album leaf, British Library, London. The image is full of energy and humour, and the artist seems to have taken their inspiration from real life.

THE ART OF PERSPECTIVE

For many people, the challenge in recording real-life objects or landscapes is to make the drawing appear three-dimensional on a flat (that is, 2D) piece of paper. This is challenging, because you must deal with **perspective**. Perspective can be either **linear** or **atmospheric**.

Linear perspective

Figure 1.36 illustrates how linear perspective works: lines that in real life are parallel appear to **converge** in the distance at a point on the **horizon**, and objects nearest to the viewer are bigger than those further away. Reproduced in a drawing, these features give the illusion of depth.

The point at which parallel lines appear to meet in an artwork is referred to as the **vanishing point**. Where the horizon line is placed in a drawing depends on where the artist is sitting and will change if they move position.

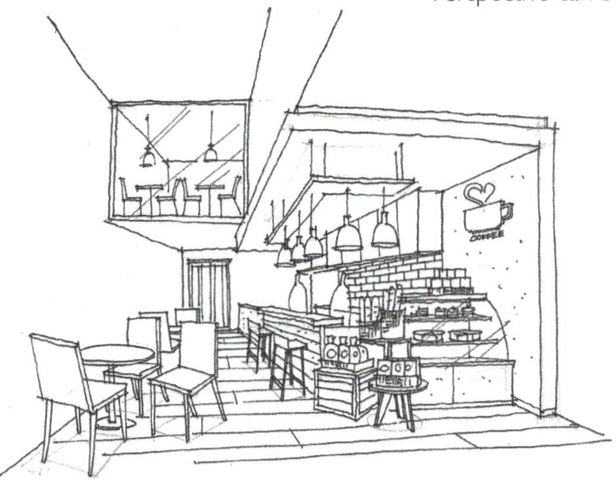

1.36 The sketch shows the use of linear perspective, with parallel lines appearing to come together at a point in the centre of the picture.

Activity A: **Practise linear perspective**

1. Sit at one end of a room or corridor with the back wall parallel to the bottom of your page.
2. Hold a pencil horizontally in front of your eyes. This is the level of your horizon line and the level at which the lines in your drawing will appear to converge. Draw a line faintly across your page, near the top edge, to represent this line.
3. Now, draw what you see. Make sure the parallel lines that exist in the room appear to come closer together in your drawing, meeting on the horizon line. Objects nearest to you will appear larger than those further away.

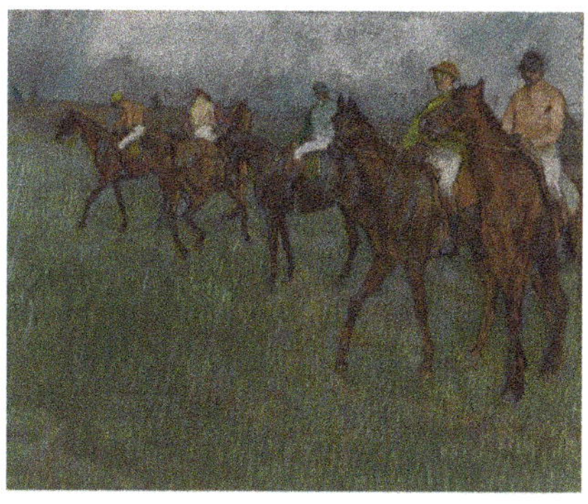

1.37 Edgar Degas, *Jockeys in the Rain*, c.1886, pastel on paper, Burrell Collection, Glasgow. In addition to using atmospheric perspective, in what other ways has Degas achieved a sense of perspective in this drawing?

Atmospheric perspective

Atmospheric perspective, sometimes also called aerial perspective, achieves a sense of depth by making objects in the foreground more detailed and clearer, or giving them a greater contrast in tonal value than those further back in the drawing, as seen in Figure 1.37, which shows a work by the French **Impressionist** artist Edgar Degas (1834–1917).

Other ways of suggesting perspective

Traditional Chinese artists treated perspective differently from post-Renaissance Western artists. They used an **oblique projection**: parallel lines remain parallel across the image, but are drawn at an angle of approximately 45 degrees to the horizontal (see Figure 1.38). From the 18th century onward, Chinese artists began to combine oblique projection with the use of scale to suggest distance: objects and figures get smaller the further away they are meant to be.

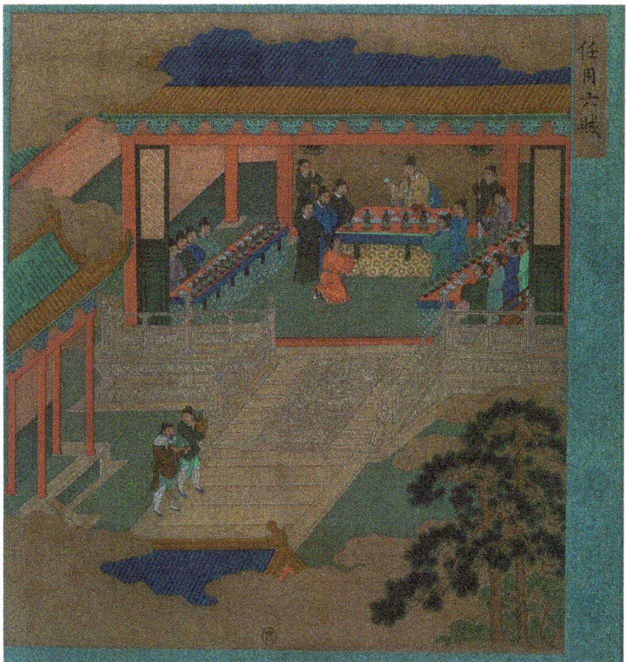

1.38 Anonymous artist, *Emperor Hui Tsung Taking Part in a Festival*, 17th century, colour drawing on silk, Bibliothèque Nationale, Paris. Oblique projection is used here as a means of showing three dimensions, but what do you notice about the figures?

atmospheric A way of indicating distance in gradation of clarity, tone and colour, especially blue.
converge To draw closer.
horizon In perspective, an imaginary line in a drawing or painting that would be level with the viewer's eyes if they were looking at a real scene.
Impressionism A style of painting developed in France from the late 1860s. It concentrated on showing the effects of light and colour rather than clear and exact detail, and on ordinary everyday life rather than on grand scenes from history or religious images. Key Impressionist painters include Claude Monet, Berthe Morisot, Camille Pissarro, Pierre-Auguste Renoir and Alfred Sisley.
linear Consisting of straight lines.
Mughal A period in the history of India from the 16th to 18th century when foreign Muslim emperors ruled much of South Asia, known for its flourishing arts.
oblique projection A simple way of making three-dimensional drawings from a front view of an object.
perspective The art of making some objects or figures in a picture look further away than others.
vanishing point The point in the distance where parallel lines seem to meet.

Artists and designers: **Two approaches to recording elephants in drawing**

Rembrandt Harmenszoon van Rijn (1606–69) was a Dutch artist who today is best known for self-portraits made throughout his adult life. He was also a great **draughtsman** who used drawings independently of his paintings to record his observations and feelings.

Look at Rembrandt's drawing of an elephant in Figure 1.39. He has used line very carefully – every mark helps to describe the form of the elephants. The outline is broken and the weight of the line varies. This helps to give a sense of perspective – the head of the elephant is drawn with heavier lines to bring it forward and the trunk seems almost to come out of the paper to touch us. Rembrandt's use of line also suggests the sense of the elephants being living creatures. The use of chalk lines on the body of the elephant helps to convey the texture of the skin.

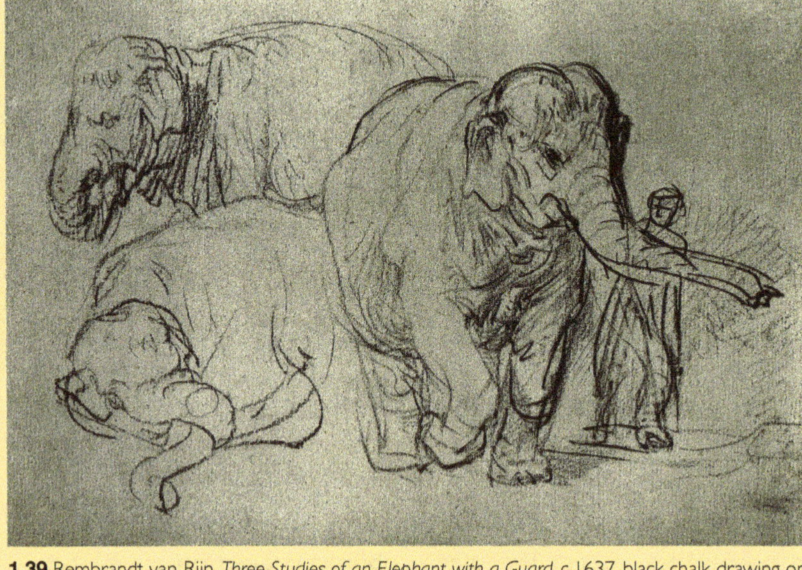

1.39 Rembrandt van Rijn, *Three Studies of an Elephant with a Guard*, c.1637, black chalk drawing on paper, Albertina, Vienna. The artist has used line **sparingly**, yet every mark helps to describe the form of the elephants.

The drawing style seen in the Indian drawing from the early 18th century shown in Figure 1.40 is very different from Rembrandt's drawing style. The elephant appears to be much flatter, as there is very little perspective in the picture. This is because the artist has drawn the elephant using an unbroken outline, which has the same weight (thickness) all round the animal. Lines have been blended together to build a fine texture around the head and the legs. This gives a very decorative feel to the drawing.

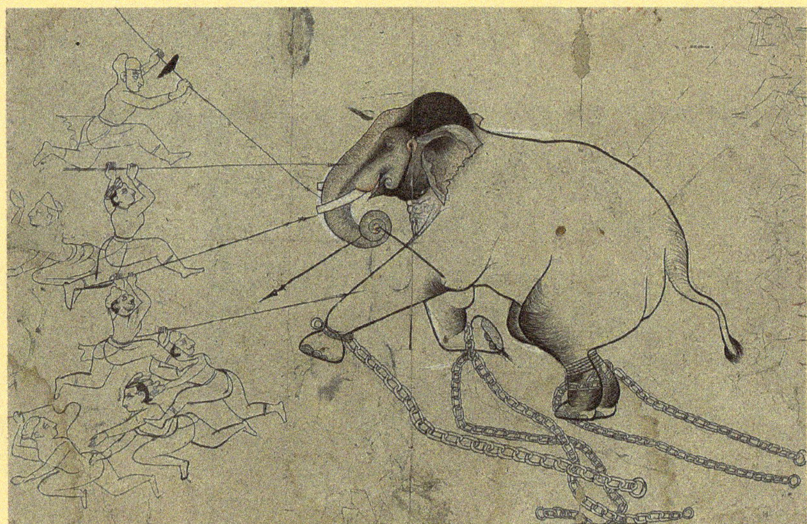

1.40 Anonymous artist, *Taming of an Elephant*, c.1720, ink and gouache on paper, private collection. This preparatory drawing of an elephant from India uses line very differently from the way that Rembrandt does. The unbroken solid outline and delicate use of tone give this drawing a much more decorative feel.

LOOKING CAREFULLY

Drawing is a skill that develops with practice. One of the key components within the skill of drawing is your ability to look carefully at your subject matter. Just as an athlete warms up at the start of a training session, you should start a drawing session with some quick warm-up exercises to help you sharpen your observational skills and make yourself familiar with the subject matter.

Activity B: **Two warm-up drawing exercises**

Try the following warm-up exercises to practise as much as possible:

1. Place a group of objects in front of you and look at them. Continue to look at them and spend five minutes drawing what you see without looking at your paper.
2. Use a pencil or ballpoint pen and draw the same group of objects without taking the pencil or pen tip off the paper, creating a continuous line (as in Figure 1.41). This will help you to consider the position of the objects in relation to one other and the space in between the objects.

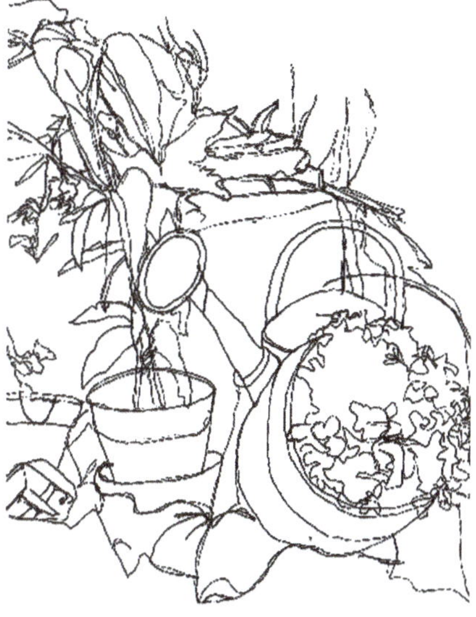

1.41 Example of a continuous line drawing.

DRAWING FROM TOUCH AND SOUND

Although we are likely to think of sight as the sense most closely associated with the activity of drawing, the discipline is not just about visual stimulus – it can be a reaction to the senses of touch and sound as well. The Russian artist Wassily Kandinsky (1866–1944) provides an excellent example of an artist who responded visually to music to produce his abstract '**Improvisations**', using different marks to express the moods and feelings suggested by the sounds (see Figure 1.42). There is more on responding to music in art in Module 2, pages 144–145.

Activity C: **Draw by touch and sound**

1. Take a small object linked to your starting point or theme. Hold it in your hand and, without looking at it, draw how it feels. Try to create a visual representation of the surface textures that you experience through touch.
2. Listen to a piece of music and respond visually to the sounds that you hear, as Kandinsky did in Figure 1.42. Repeat this exercise, this time listening to a very different style of music, and compare the resulting drawings.

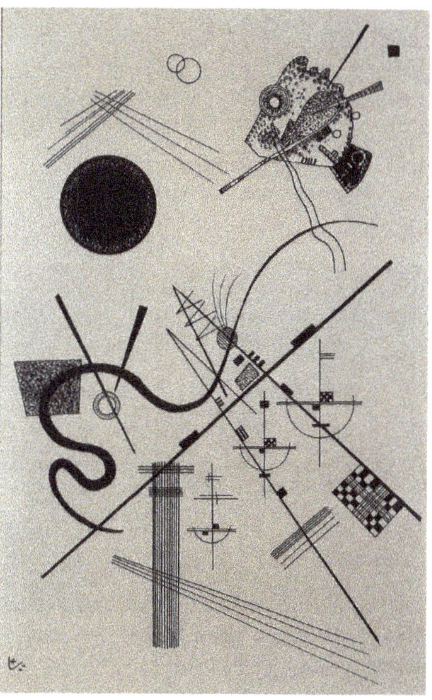

1.42 Wassily Kandinsky, *Untitled (Drawing 4)*, 1924, ink on paper, private collection. Kandinsky uses line and geometric forms to respond to the musical stimulus.

Further research

Go online to research how to develop your skill at drawing **one-point perspective**.

For more drawing exercises, try *The New Drawing on the Right Side of the Brain* by Betty Edwards (HarperCollins, 2001).

draughtsman/woman/person Someone who prepares detailed drawings.
improvisation Something carried out without a plan.
one-point perspective Method for creating perspective in a picture that uses a single vanishing point.
sparingly In a small quantity or economically.

Sculpture

Learning objective:

- To develop observation and recording skills for sculpture outcomes

When starting to make a piece of sculpture, it is important to gather resources that will prepare you to work in three dimensions. You should record observations to explore the formal elements of shape and form – these are the elements you will focus on during the process of making sculpture. You can also record information about pattern, texture, colour, line and tone.

You can record your observations in two ways:

- in drawing and paintings (or in other two-dimensional (2D) disciplines), from which you can develop three-dimensional (3D) work
- in three dimensions.

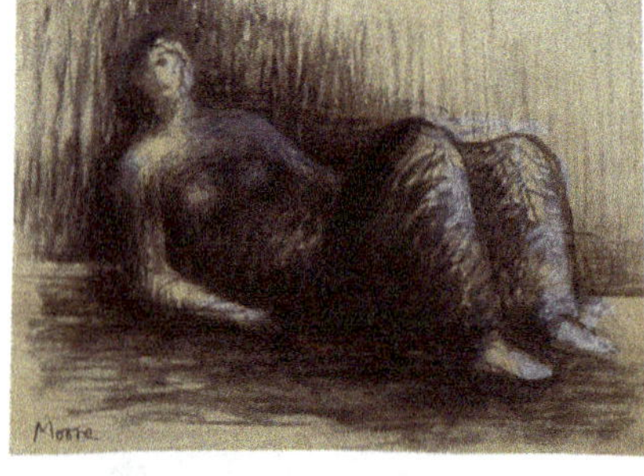

1.43 Henry Moore, *Reclining Woman*, 1982, charcoal, gouache and chalk on paper, private collection.

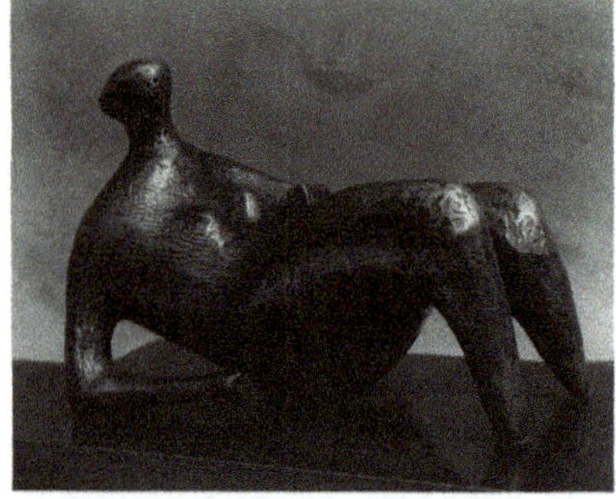

1.44 Henry Moore, *Reclining Figure*, 1983, cast bronze, private collection.

RECORDING FORM IN DRAWINGS AND PAINTINGS

The British sculptor Henry Moore (1898–1986) made many drawings in which he focused on recording form. For example, his drawing of *Reclining Woman* (Figure 1.43) depicts the figure as a solid object, without space or gaps between the arms and the body or between the legs. The marks he uses do not record **anatomical** details or textures, but describe the 3D outline shape of the figure. His use of dark tone conveys the mass of the form, and where he uses line he follows the **contours** of the body to also suggest the form. Compare the drawing with the finished sculpture – *Reclining Figure* (Figure 1.44). How has Henry Moore changed the sculpture from the drawing?

A different approach to recording form can be seen in the drawing of *Sir Robert Sainsbury* (1965) by the Swiss artist Alberto Giacometti (1901–66). The artist first applied flat grey washes to his background and then used outlines to describe the shape and features of the figure. Giacometti captured the sense of outline in the facial features of his sculptures by pulling and shaping the modelling clay that he used as if outlining the eyes and mouth, as seen in the example *Bust of a Man Seated (Lotar III)*, 1965. Look for these images online.

Tip:

Remember: if you are going to make a sculpture from your drawings, you will need to draw your subject matter from different viewpoints: from in front, the side and behind. This is because you will have to produce a finished 3D work that looks convincing from different viewpoints.

Activity A: **Record form in a drawing**

1. Look closely at the drawing style of both Henry Moore and Alberto Giacometti. Observe how each artist has used tone and line to suggest shape and form.
2. Work from observation and make a drawing of seated figures in the style of Moore, using heavy shading and lines that follow the contour of the body.
3. Then do the same, but this time in the style of Giacometti, using a flat grey wash and outlines.
4. Compare the outcomes of your work.

RECORDING IN THREE DIMENSIONS

You can also work directly with 3D media and techniques to record from observation. This can help you to consider and understand the 3D form of your source material from the very start of the creative process.

Try two different approaches to explore different qualities:

- by using modelling clay to explore form and mass
- by using wire to explore space and shape.

Activity B: **Record in three dimensions using clay**

Using clay, make a 3D study of a head.

1. Begin by walking round your subject and observing it from different viewpoints before modelling the basic shape.
2. Then pull and shape the clay to describe the facial features, turning your model frequently to see it from different angles.
3. Add clay where needed to build up features such as the nose and ears.

Activity C: **Record in three dimensions using wire**

This exercise relates to the continuous drawing exercise – **Activity B** (page 67). It extends the concept of looking as a key activity in any kind of drawing, whether 2D or 3D. Use the image of the wire head in Figure 1.45 as an example.

'Draw' in three dimensions using the wire. The wire is your line – use it to explore the elements of line, space and shape.

You can work by cutting and joining short lengths of wire, or by using one long piece, creating a continuous line effect.

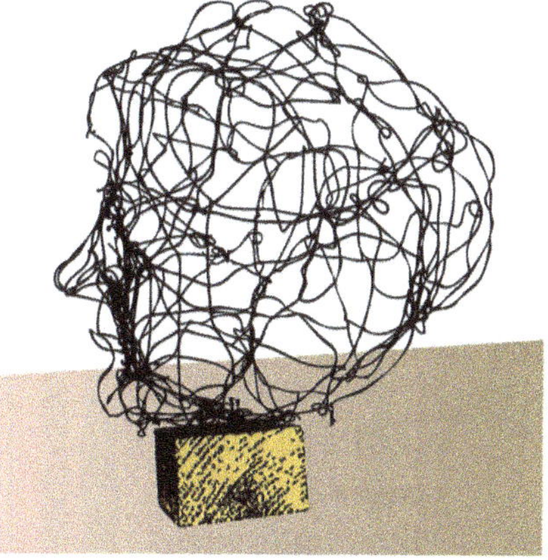

1.45 An example of a 3D head 'drawn' by joining wire together.

Critical thinking:

Think about the way that recording through drawing in preparation for a sculpture is different to drawing for a 2D outcome. Consider how the intention can impact on the approach to recording. Make notes about your intentions and how this has affected your decision about the type of recording that you decided on.

Further research

Go online and explore more sculptures by Henry Moore and Alberto Giacometti.

anatomical Relating to the structure of the body or an organism.

contours The shape or surface of a curving form.

Mixed media

Learning objective:

- To develop mixed-media skills by working from direct observation and personal experience

Using mixed media in an artwork can involve an almost limitless variety of materials. These can be both natural (for example, sand, pebbles, driftwood) and human-made (for example, newspaper, textiles, bric-a-brac). Using a variety of media in an artwork can help you to express ideas and emphasise textural qualities that using a single medium cannot achieve. One way of doing this is collage.

COLLAGE AS AN ART FORM

Collage is a way of working where the artist sticks materials such as paper and fabric onto paper or canvas to create images. The collage can then be drawn or painted over to give additional qualities to the piece.

Collage first became widely accepted as a fine art technique in the early 20th century after it was used by the French Cubist artist Georges Braque (1882–1963) (see page 166). *Bottle, Glass and Pipe (Violette de Parme)* (Figure 1.46) records information about a table top and the things on it, as well as the surrounding room. Braque has added various pieces of pre-printed paper to his drawing to represent some of the things, patterns and textures he sees – a newspaper, wooden panelling, a woodgrain pattern. He has then added further depth and complexity by drawing with charcoal over the collage.

Activity A: **Create a collage using paper and charcoal/pastel**

1. Find a variety of pre-printed materials, such as newspaper, magazine pages and wallpaper, and cut and tear them into different shapes and sizes.
2. Use your collection of papers as your palette and create a collage on a page in a sketchbook or on a sheet of plain paper or card. Don't use all your cut or torn pieces of paper – use a maximum of 10.
3. Arrange the pieces of paper until you are happy with the composition, then stick them down.
4. Draw on top of the collaged surface using charcoal or pastel.
5. Think about what qualities are added to your work by drawing on different surfaces. Note these in your annotations.

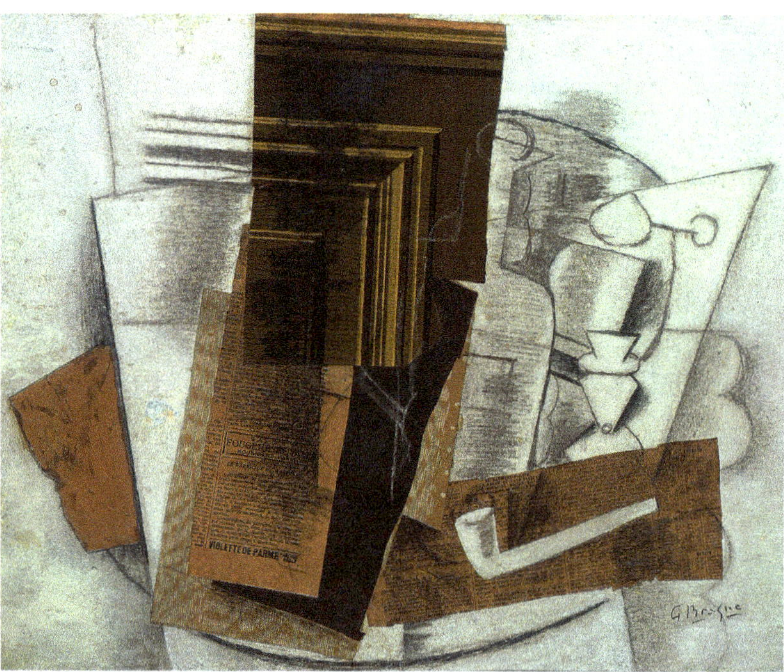

1.46 Georges Braque, *Bottle, Glass and Pipe (Violette de Parme)*, early 1913, cut-and-pasted newspaper, painted paper and wallpaper, charcoal, graphite, and gouache on paperboard, Metropolitan Museum of Art, New York.

ADDING TEXTURE

You can also add textural effects to your collage, using materials such as tissue paper, textured fabrics and sand mixed with **gesso** or an acrylic-based glue. You can apply texture in a very subtle way, as Liz Macfarlane has done (see Figure 1.47), or more boldly to produce more dramatic results, as can be seen in the work *Dadaville* (c.1924) by the German artist Max Ernst (1891–1976). You can find an image of this on the Tate Gallery website.

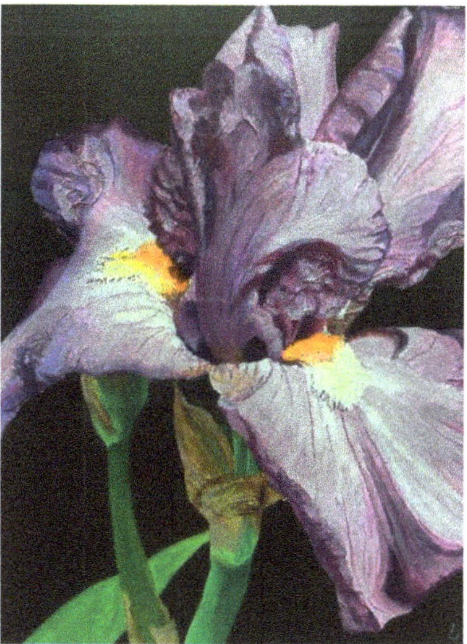

1.47 Liz Macfarlane, *Iris*, 2009, gesso, tissue paper and acrylic on paper. Here the British artist Liz Macfarlane (born 1963) has added tissue paper and gesso to selected areas of her painting of an iris to enhance the texture of the petals and the stamens.

2D/3D COLLAGE

Throughout the 20th century, artists continued to push the boundaries of art practice and adopted an increasingly open approach to working with mixed media. During the 1960s, the American artist Robert Rauschenberg (1925–2008) combined found objects and photographs in his work. ***Monogram*** (Figure 1.48) combines an extraordinary variety of 2D and 3D media. Rauschenberg called these works 'Combines'. This kind of collage is closely related to the Surrealist assemblage we looked at on page 62.

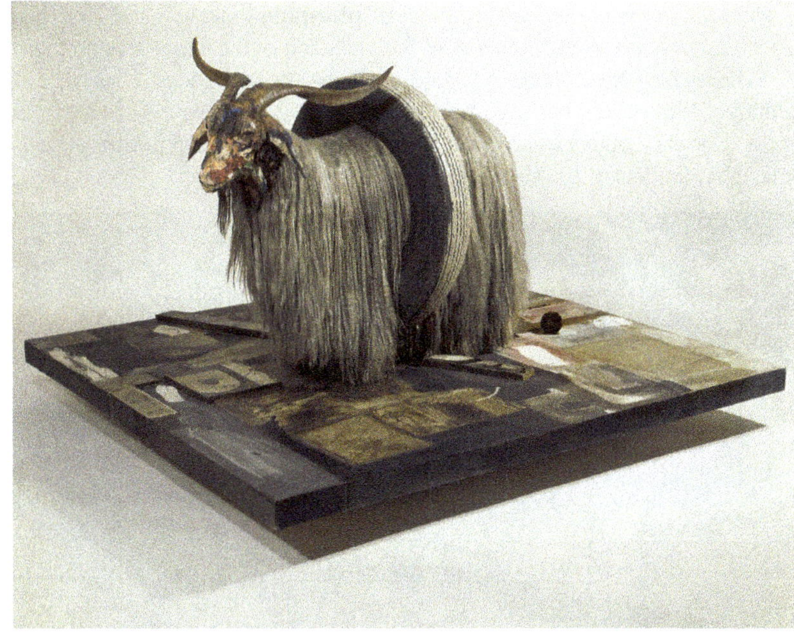

1.48 Robert Rauschenberg, *Monogram*, 1955–9, mixed media including oil paint, paper, fabric, printed paper, printed reproductions, metal, wood, rubber shoe heel and tennis ball on canvas with **taxidermied** Angora goat and rubber tyre on wood platform mounted on four castors, Moderna Museet, Stockholm. Rauschenberg has mounted his 'collage' on a wooden platform with wheels.

Activity B: **Create a 2D/3D collage**

1. Experiment with combining photographs and drawn and painted images. Take photographs of your subject matter and then draw on top of the photographs.
2. Include small found objects to introduce a 3D element to the work. You could use some of the objects from a collection of found or personal objects (see pages 62–63).

Critical thinking:

Think about how you have used the formal element of texture when experimenting with different mixed-media techniques. Which technique has enabled you to achieve the most interesting range of textures in your work? Why do you think this? Don't forget to annotate your work as you go.

Further research

Go online to research some of the leading artists who use/used collage.

gesso A mixture of glue, chalk and white paint.
monogram A motif made up of an individual's initials (a kind of logo).
taxidermy The craft of preserving an animal by stuffing and mounting it.

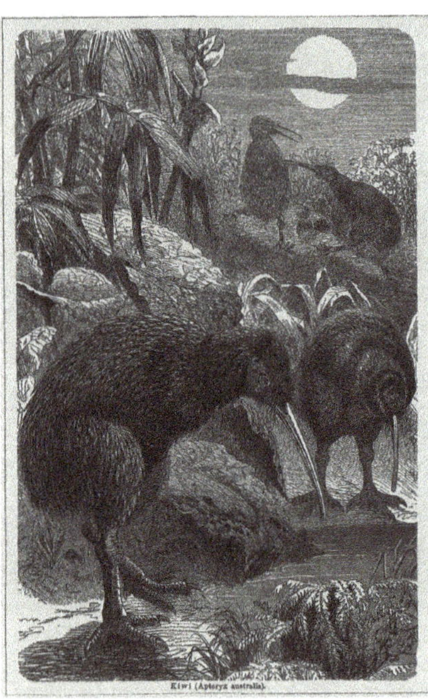

1.49 Anonymous artist, *Kiwi Birds*, 1877, wood engraving, private collection. The quality of the line in different parts of the print suggests different textures, for example, feathers and leaves.

Fine art printmaking

Learning objective:

- To understand how differing approaches to drawing can directly inform printmaking outcomes

Drawing and printmaking are closely related activities. Many forms of printmaking allow artists to draw or make marks directly onto the woodblock or printing plate. This can give the print the **immediacy** of a drawing.

USING LINE

Look at Figure 1.49, a 19th-century woodcut print made in New Zealand. The unknown artist has used line engraved into the woodblock to record birds in their habitat. To capture the elements of texture and tone, they have varied the direction and length of the lines, so the lines have been drawn closely together, and used different depths of lines to engrave on the woodblock. In the printed image, the birds' **plumage** looks soft and silky. This contrasts with the harder textures of their bills and of the leaves around them.

In his etching *Night Shadows* (Figure 1.50), the American artist Edward Hopper (1882–1967) has used **hatching** and cross hatching (where the lines cross over each other) to build dark tonal areas within his composition. The image has the feel of a lively sketch.

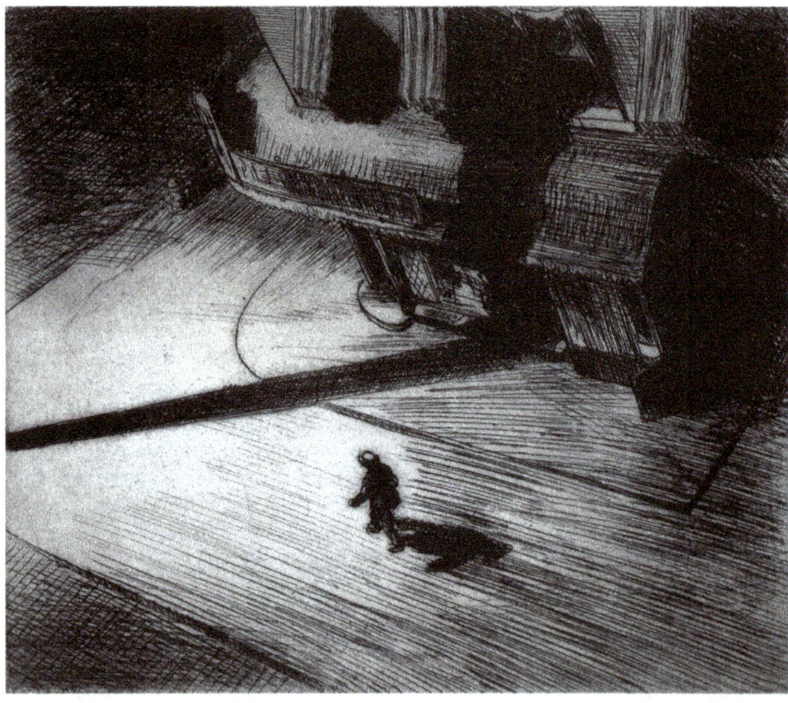

1.50 Edward Hopper, *Night Shadows*, 1921, wood engraving, San Diego Museum of Art, California. This print shows the use of cross hatching to build tone.

Activity A: **Analyse an artist's mark-making in a wood engraving or etching**

1. Research a wood engraving or etching online and print out an enlarged version.
2. Now choose a small section of the image you find particularly interesting in its use of line, hatching and other mark-making. Analyse the range of marks that the artist has used.
3. Draw your chosen section of the image, trying to imitate the marks that the artist has made.
4. Add annotations to your drawing, describing the formal qualities the artist has achieved..

MONOPRINTS

Monoprint is the simplest printmaking process – it allows you to draw and make marks directly onto a surface, which you then take a single print from. Two approaches to making monoprints are shown below. Once you have tried them, you can experiment with combining techniques as you explore your own approach to drawing and mark-making (Figure 1.51).

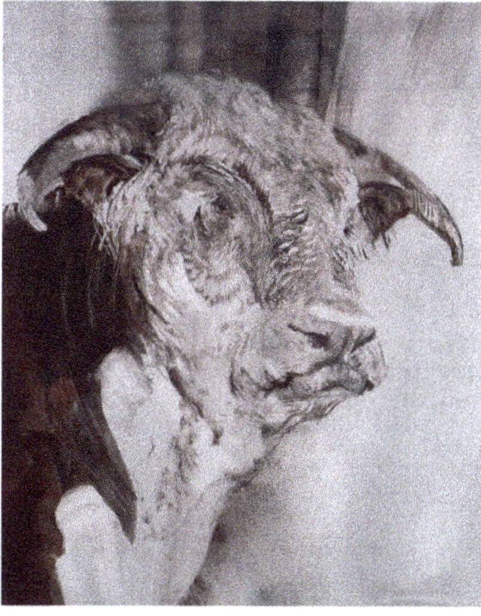

1.51 Paul Riley, *The Bull*, 1995, monoprint, private collection. This image shows the wide range of lines and marks that can be achieved by using monoprint techniques – from very broad areas of dark tone to fine lines.

Materials and techniques: **Two ways to create a monoprint**

The first way is as follows:

1. Find a smooth sheet of glass, metal or acetate to use as the printing surface.
2. Using a rubber roller, roll out a thin, even layer of relief printing ink over the printing surface.
3. Place a sheet of paper over the inked surface and then use a pencil to draw the image. Be careful not to lean on the paper!
4. Rub your finger across any areas of the drawing where you want to create tone.
5. Peel back the paper. Your monoprint will have distinctive line and tonal qualities.

A second way of creating a monoprint is:

1. Roll out the ink as before, but instead scrape and wipe marks and tonal areas directly from the inked surface.
2. Place the paper on top of the surface and roll over the back of the paper using a clean roller.
3. Apply enough pressure to transfer the image.
4. Peel back the paper to reveal the print.

You can also lay objects, such as leaves, torn paper, string or threads, directly onto the inked surface to create masked areas and enhance the range of mark-making.

Activity B: **Experiment with monoprints**

Experiment with making monoprints, drawing onto your plate from direct observation.

You can then **work into** your monoprint to further develop your image. For example, draw over the print with oil pastels to introduce different marks and colours.

Further research

Explore the history of monoprints in *The Painterly Print: Monotypes from the Seventeenth to the Twentieth Century* (The Metropolitan Museum of Art and the Museum of Fine Arts, Boston, 1980) and *Singular Impressions: The Monotype in America* by Joann Moser (The Smithsonian Institution Press, 1997).

hatching Fine parallel lines to create shading, used in drawing and engraving. Cross-hatching is when these lines cross over each other.
immediacy Spontaneity and freshness – brings and instant response.
monoprint Simple printmaking technique that produces a single print.
plumage The feathers of a bird.
work into To build on your first mark-making in an image, adding new media and ideas.

1.2 Three-dimensional (3D) design

Sculpture

Learning objectives:

- To understand how recording can be used as a starting point for three-dimensional (3D) sculpture
- To understand visual language used in 3D sculpture

Sculpture can exist in a variety of formats and you have already looked at this in a fine art context (see pages 68–69). In this unit, we will be looking at sculpture in public environments and spaces. We will also consider the way that practitioners think about placing sculpture.

MAKING LANDMARKS

Sculptures often provide a visual focus and landmark in a landscape or cityscape. This can be achieved by using a striking organic form, for example, or by using recycled materials (see Figures 1.52 and 1.53). This creates a space that viewers can walk through and around, and so experience the three-dimensionality of the sculpture and changes of texture close up.

Designers will sometimes use sculpture to both contrast with and reflect the environment. *Cloud Gate* (Figure 1.54) in Chicago by the British artist Anish Kapoor (born 1954) is an organic shape that seems at odds with its surroundings. However, at the same time, its mirror-like surface allows the surroundings to become part of the piece.

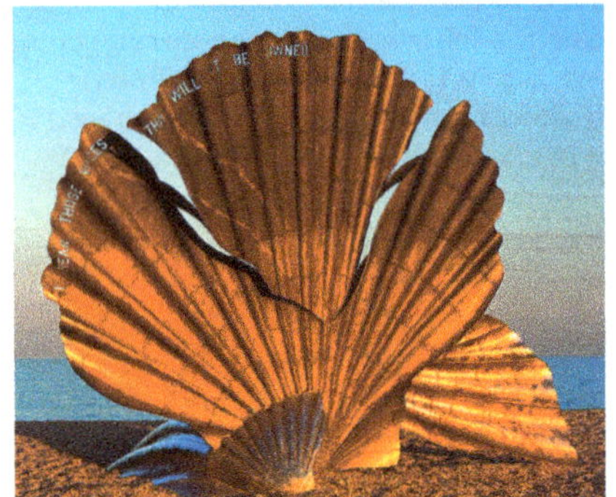

1.52 Maggi Hambling, *Scallop*, 2003, stainless steel, Aldeburgh beach, Suffolk, UK. This artwork is a tribute to the British composer Benjamin Britten.

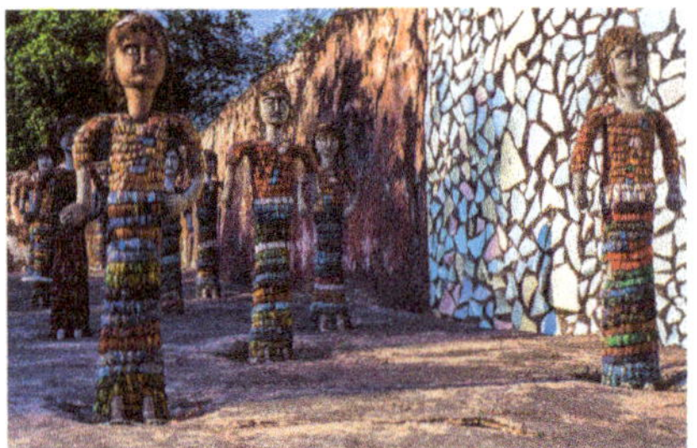

1.53 Recycled materials sculpture in Nek Chand's Rock Garden, Chandigarh, India.

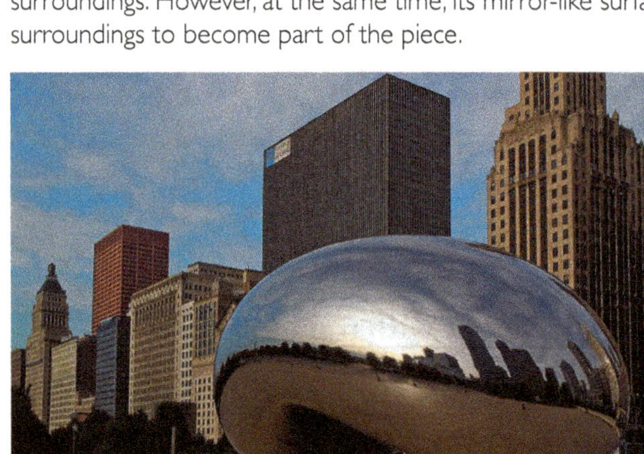

1.54 Anish Kapoor, *Cloud Gate*, 2004, stainless steel, Millennium Plaza, Chicago. There are clear reflections of the sky and high-rise skyline on the polished mirrored surface of Kapoor's sculpture, widely known as 'The Bean'.

Materials and techniques: **Researching materials and techniques used in sculpture**

As you learn about specific sculptures, try to research the production methods used to make them. This will often provide an insight into the various stages of the creative journey – from drawings, to maquettes, to scaled models and final production. This will help you to understand the discipline and consider how important these stages are in the process.

Activity A: **Write a report on a sculpture production method**

Research and write a short (300-word) report on one of the following methods used in the final production of a sculpture:

- bronze casting
- resin casting
- foam casting.

Present the report to your classmates, perhaps with accompanying images.

COMMEMORATION AND CELEBRATION

Some sculpture is designed to **commemorate** an event or celebrate an achievement. The designer or artist will incorporate visual elements that refer to the event or achievement, while at the same time maintaining the visual interest of the piece. The portrait-sculpture of Nelson Mandela in Figure 1.55 commemorates the 50th anniversary of his capture in 1962. The sculpture consists of 50 steel columns, like prison bars, that can be recognised as Mandela's portrait only from a particular angle and distance.

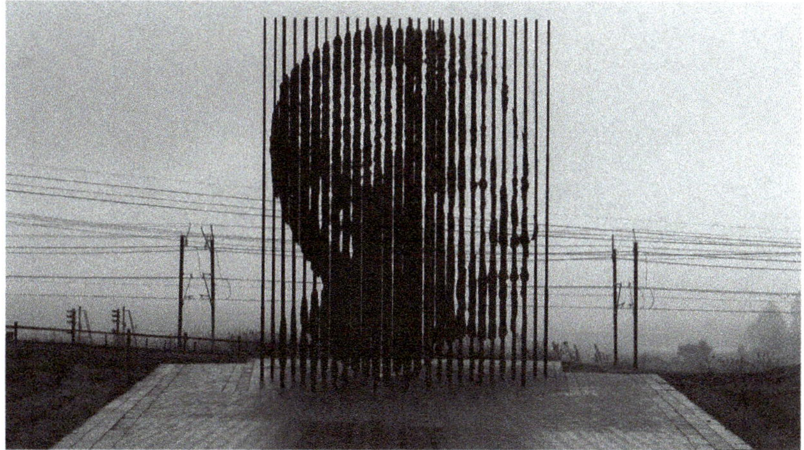

1.55 Marco Cianfanelli, *Release*, 2012, painted laser-cut mild steel and steel tube construction, painted black, Nelson Mandela Capture Site, near Howick, South Africa. This dramatic commemoration is a graphic image of the 27 years the leader of the African National Congress spent in prison.

Activity B: **Record from a sculpture in your local area**

Use a mixture of photographs and drawing to record from a sculpture in a public space within your local area. Make sure that you have permission to access the sculpture before beginning. Try to record the visual shapes that make up the piece. Make notes about the surroundings and how the piece relates to these, as well as notes about the purpose of the sculpture.

Critical thinking:

Consider the work you produced in **Activity B** and summarise your findings.

- How does the sculpture work within the environment in which it is placed?
- Is there any commemorative or meaning/intention in the piece?
- Are the materials used relevant to the site or purpose?

Further research

For a globe-trotting tour of some of the world's most impressive public sculptures, go to www.architecturaldigest.com

commemorate To remember and honour an event or person.

Ceramics

Learning objective:

- To understand how ceramics is used to communicate creative intentions

Ceramics is an exciting and varied discipline in the visual arts. It connects us with the remote past through the vessels that have been made and used from earliest times, and with cultures across the world, almost all of which have individual ceramic traditions (Figure 1.56).

Ceramic items can be put to practical use: they can be used to contain everyday food and drink, or sometimes as an **insulator** in industry. They can also have profoundly spiritual or symbolic meanings, for example, they may be used as part of a religious ritual. Finally, ceramics can also be purely aesthetic, as sculptural forms in their own right.

Materials and techniques: Ceramic

Ceramic is clay hardened by heat. The **malleability** of clay makes it an ideal vehicle for realising 3D forms. It yields to the maker's touch and can be built into any form desired. It can then be decorated and finished. It is a versatile material and can be used in experimental ways, provided it can survive the firing.

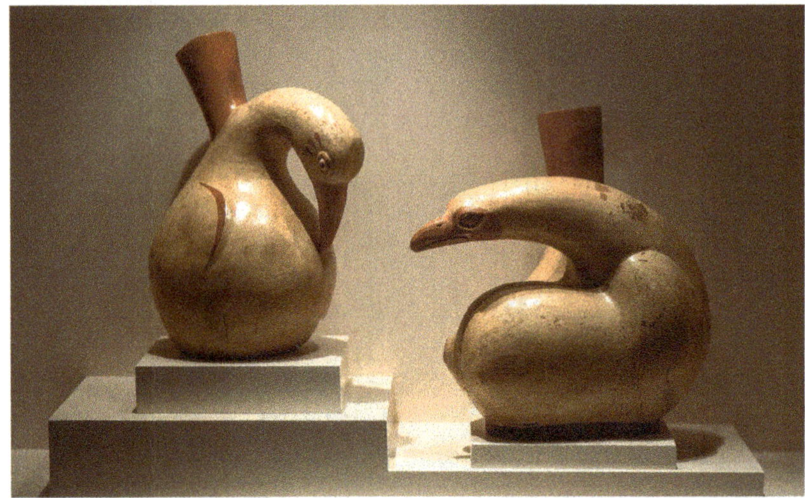

1.56 Huari Ceramics at Casa Cabrera, the Museum of **Pre-Columbian** Art, Cuzco, Peru. The ceramics of the Pre-Columbian Huari people are famous for their beautiful, richly coloured pots depicting gods, angels, plants and animals.

PRACTICAL AND EVERYDAY

Ceramics can have a functional use. These may be items that we use daily, such as plates, mugs, cups and pots. In some cultures, these are mass-produced. In other cultures, they may be made in small, local workshops, and some as individual sets of studio pottery. Some studio potters even dig their own local clay by hand to make their work. Ceramics are also used in industry, for instance as an insulator in the electrical industry, as well as in architecture (Figure 1.57).

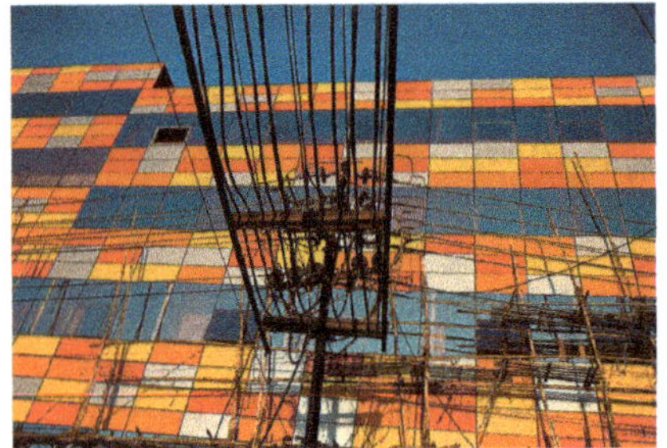

1.57 Colourful ceramic tiles cover a building at Haridwar, Uttarakhand, India. This example shows architectural ceramics – a colourful mosaic on a building's façade.

RITUAL OBJECTS

Ceramic figures and vessels have long played an important part in religious rituals, from **Neolithic** times onwards, for example:

- in figures depicting fertility
- as **receptacles** for human remains
- as ritual drinking vessels.

Shape and decoration were used to emphasise the objects' importance.

ART OBJECTS

Ceramics has belonged to both the craftsperson and the artist in varying degrees. Potters develop their craft through an exploration of materials and techniques. Artists, by contrast, have used ceramics as a medium to explore ideas or take imagery into a different market or field (see Figure 1.58). However, the distinction between the potter and artist who uses ceramics has become increasingly blurred.

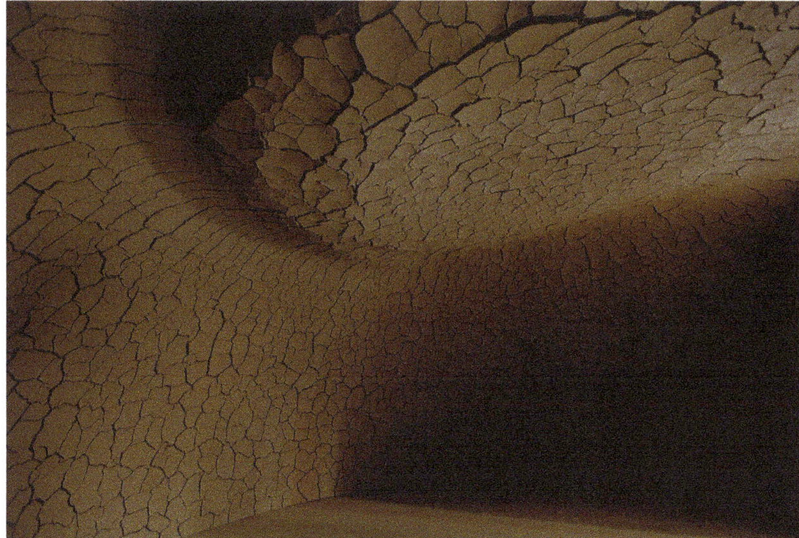

1.58 Andy Goldsworthy, *Domo de argila, Clay Dome*, 2012, Rio de Janeiro, Brazil. British artist Andy Goldsworthy (born 1956) has used raw clay to create a beautiful, atmospheric structure that will be allowed to crack and crumble over time.

Activity A: **Record shape and texture for ceramics**

In this activity, you are asked to record two sets of drawings:

- Set 1 – make at least two A2 pages based on recording shape. This could be from figures, animals and insects, buildings and so on.
- Set 2 – make at least two A2 pages based on recording texture. Apply some of the mark-making techniques shown on page 40 to help you, or use rubbing techniques (frottage) if you want to.

Record in black and white.

Complete the drawings and then display them.

Further research

Find out more about the history of ceramics since the earliest times in *The Pot Book* by Edmund de Waal (Phaidon, 2015).

Critical thinking

Consider the drawings you produced for **Activity A**. Evaluate them, thinking about:

- What shapes and subjects did you record?
- Would these drawings be useful as a basis for designing ceramic forms?
- Would the textures you recorded work as ideas for ceramic surface decoration?
- Based on your evaluation, how will you adapt your recording for designing ceramic forms in the future – what will you do next?

Huari (Wari) People and culture of Peru that flourished 500–1000 ce.

insulator A non-conductor of electricity or heat/cold.

malleability The ability of a material to be pressed into various shapes without breaking.

Neolithic 'New Stone Age' – period in the development of human cultures from about 10 000 bce to about 4000–2000 bce During this time both farming and the making of pottery became widespread.

Pre-Columbian Term used to describe the cultures of the Americas before the arrival of the explorer Christopher Columbus in 1492.

receptacle Another word for container.

Architecture

Learning objectives:

- To understand how architecture explores visual ideas
- To record examples of architecture
- To understand the characteristics of environmental design

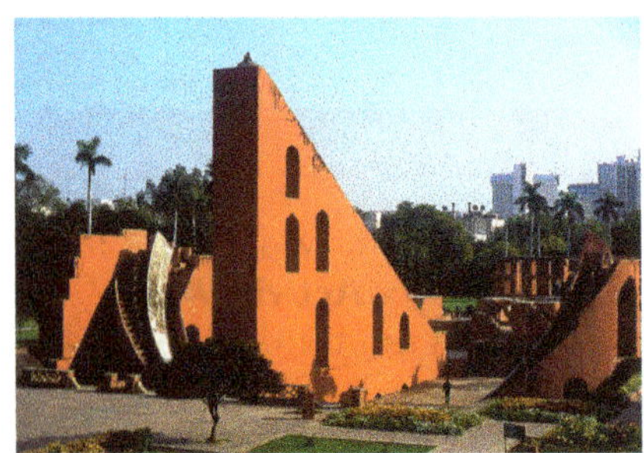

1.59 Jantar Mantar, Maharaja Jai Singh's 1724 astronomical observatory, near Connaught Place, New Delhi.

Architecture shapes our relationship with our environment, through our daily involvement with buildings and spaces. The range of architectural forms shows us the variety of creativity and approaches that are possible in buildings that provide us with shelter, warmth, rest and security.

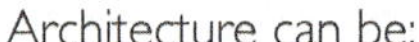

Architecture can be:

- **utilitarian**, as in some examples of Modernist architecture (see Module 2, pages 124–127),
  or
- sculptural and individual.

Architecture can:

- explore a variety of different materials in exciting ways
  or
- take a minimalist approach, using only a restricted palette of materials such as concrete, steel and glass.

Architects can design buildings that challenge us to look closely and experience their dynamic shapes and surfaces. This is all part of the aesthetic experience.

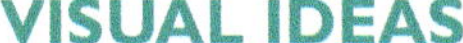

VISUAL IDEAS

Look at Figures 1.60 and 1.61 and consider how each of the buildings incorporates specific shapes. Some buildings are based mainly on shape and have limited surface variations, as they are made from a limited range of materials (for example, concrete and glass); others combine both form and texture using a wider range of materials.

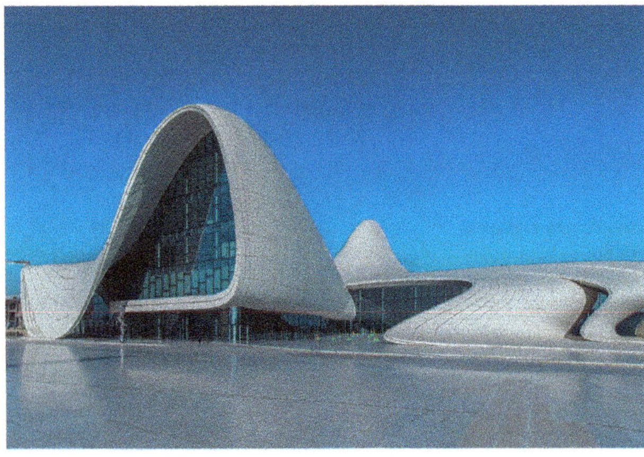

1.60 Zaha Hadid, Heydar Aliyev Center, 2012, Baku, Azerbaijan. Architecture can reference shapes and create dynamic environments for human interaction.

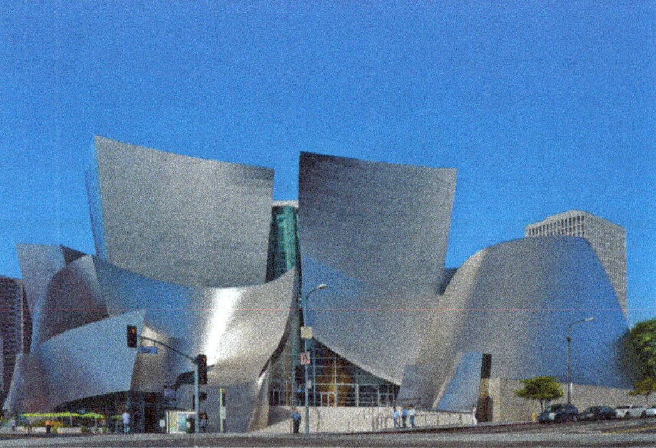

1.61 Frank Gehry, Walt Disney Concert Hall, completed 2003, Los Angeles, California. Some architecture is so distinctive that it becomes part of a city or town's identity.

RECORDING ARCHITECTURE

Be prepared to record examples of the buildings around you. Use your research skills to find out more about a building, such as the architect's name, its date, its purpose, and whether it is in a particular style. You should also get to know a building by recording and analysing its characteristics.

Activity A: **Record a piece of architecture**

Use either a camera or drawing, or both, to complete this task. Look at Figures 1.62–1.64, which record the Francis Crick Institute, in London, UK. Use these as a basis to carry out your own visual research into a building in your area. Be prepared to move around the building and get a variety of views, as well as details.

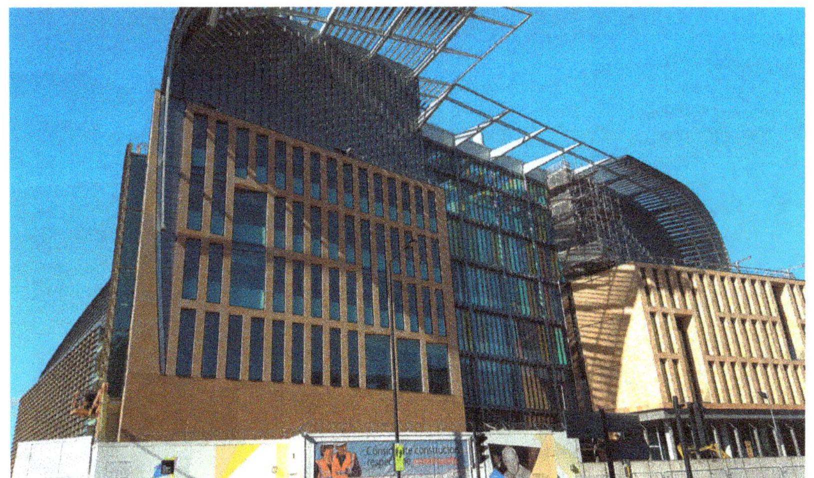

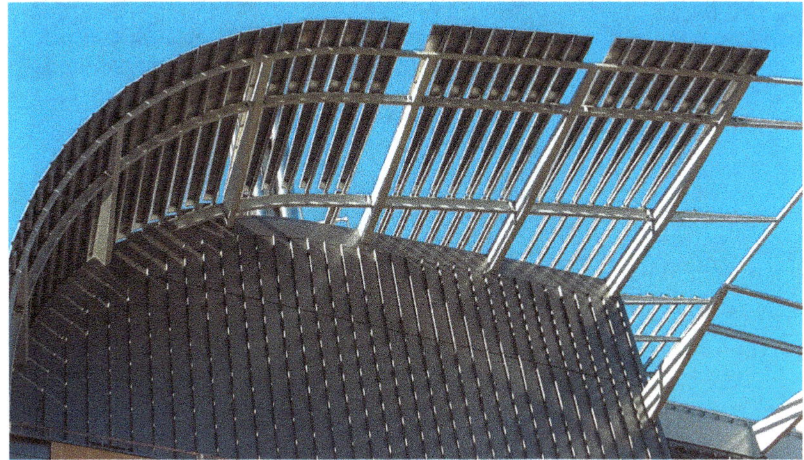

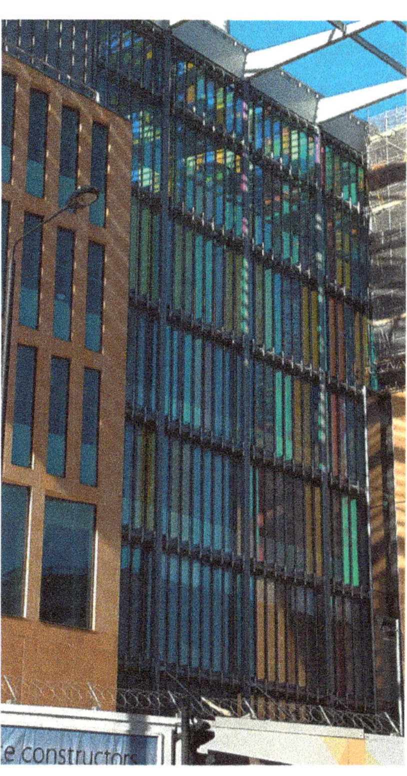

1.62–1.64 Alan Parsons, photographs of the Francis Crick Institute by architects HOK, London, 2016.

Critical thinking:

Pin up the examples of your recording from **Activity A.**

- How effectively did you control the camera/pencil?
- How well did you use different viewpoints and details to gain an understanding of the building you observed?

utilitarian Designed to be useful rather than attractive.

Artists and designers: **Zaha Hadid**

Zaha Hadid (1950–2016) was born in Baghdad, Iraq, but practised largely in the UK. She is known for her striking architectural ideas and buildings, which are often composed of expressive, sweeping lines and forms, together with stark geometric details. She said that her idea was 'not to have any 90 degree angles'. Her buildings can be found across the world and include:

- Guangzhou Opera House , Guangzhou, China (completed 2010)
- London Aquatlc Centre, London, UK (completed 2011)
- Eli & Edythe Broad Art Museum, East Lansing, USA (completed 2012)
- Heydar Aliyev Center, Baku, Azerbaijan (competed 2012) (see Figure 1.60)
- Dongdaemun Design Plaza, Seoul, South Korea (completed 2013)
- Jockey Club Innovation Tower, Hong Kong, China (completed 2014) (see Figure 1.65)

Research these buildings online and see whether you can define a single 'Zaha Hadid' style.

For Hadid, drawing and painting were key ingredients in her creative process. They enabled her to experiment with dynamic shapes and forms that might eventually be realised in her buildings (Figure 1.66). She was especially inspired by the work of early 20th-century abstract painters such as the Russian artist Kazimir Malevich (1879–1935).

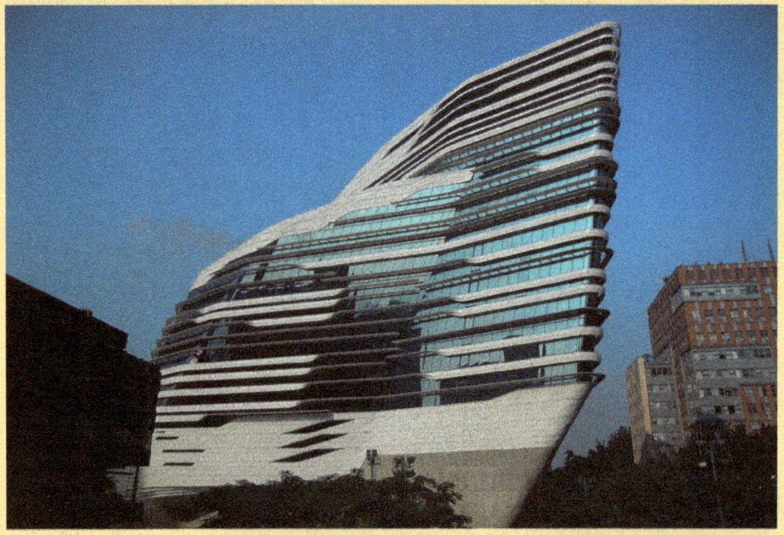

1.65 Zaha Hadid Architects, Jockey Club Innovation Tower, Hong Kong Polytechnic University, China. The strong, dynamic shape of this structure dominates the area around it.

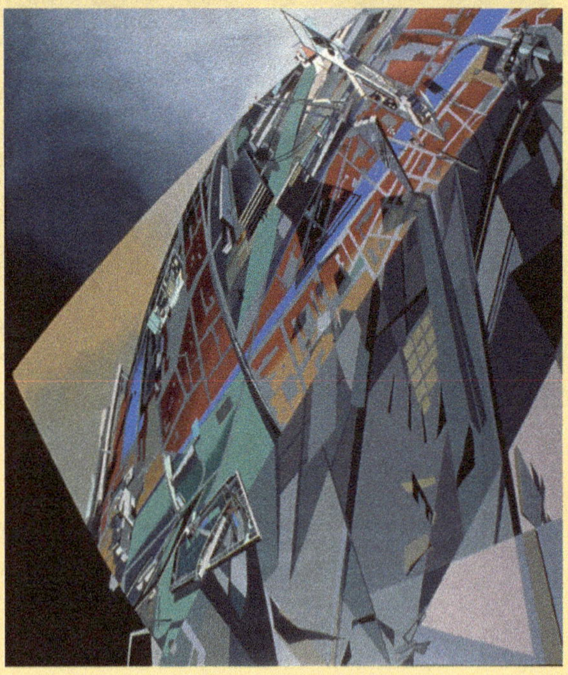

1.66 Zaha Hadid, *The World (89 Degrees)*, 1983, acrylic on canvas. Zaha Hadid Foundation, London. Hadid's exploration of form and abstraction in her drawings and paintings gave her the freedom to create new architectural forms.

DRAWING ARCHITECTURAL CONCEPTS

Architects use drawings that are often computer-aided to produce detailed plans for building projects, for example, floor plans, **elevations**. These are very **technical**, as they are used to communicate important details with other disciplines across the building industry, including engineering. However, architects also use drawing in a much more **spontaneous** way to come up with the initial concept or starting point. This is known as the concept sketch.

Materials and techniques: **The concept sketch**

A concept sketch allows you to record some of your ideas for a building in a very basic form. These are not technical drawings, so can be made quickly and quite loosely (see Figure 1.67). You can also annotate them as you go along.

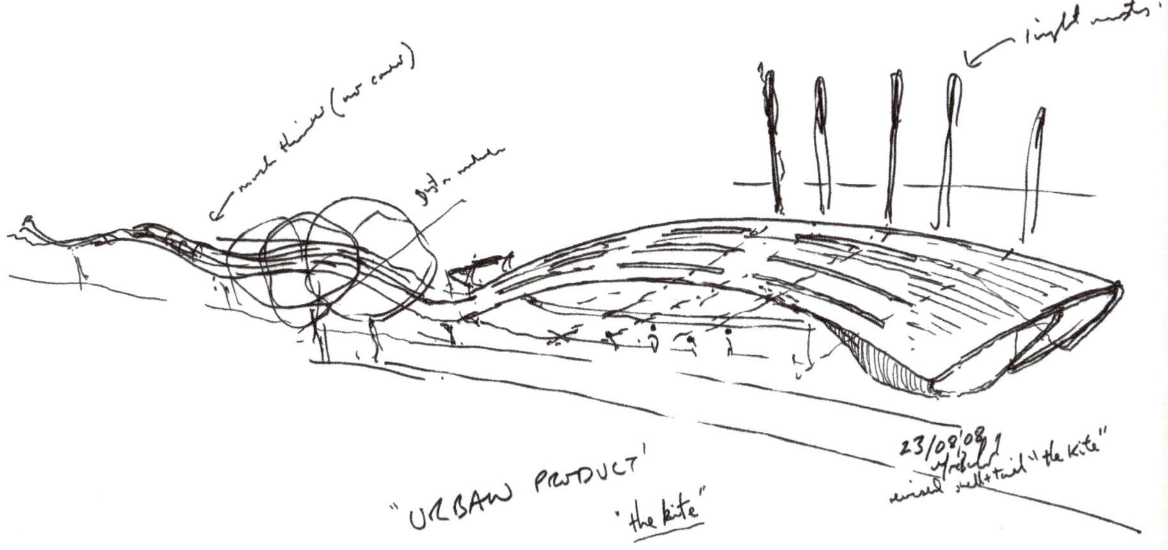

1.67 bblur architecture, concept drawing of Slough Bus Station, England, 2013. The architect, Matthew Bedward at the British firm bblur architecture, has used his sketch to express the basic shapes and feel of the structure.

Activity B: **Create a concept sketch**

Make a concept sketch for a small local theatre building based on the theme 'Waves'. The building should represent the theme in its shape and structure.

1. Research the theme 'Waves'.
2. Make studies of examples of waves using drawing, photography or film.
3. Using your understanding of the shapes made by waves, make at least three concept drawings exploring your initial concept for the building.

Further research

For a good survey of modern architecture, read *Modern Architecture A–Z* (Taschen, 2016).

Find out more about Zaha Hadid's work at her website.

elevation Technical drawing showing front, side or plan view of a structure.
spontaneous Unplanned.
technical Showing technique.

Set design

Learning objectives:

- To understand the importance of intention when working on set designs
- To understand how to record ideas for set designs

Any event or performance piece that uses scenery, props and lighting may need a set design. It could be for a theatre play, film, music event or fashion show, for example. It is important that the designer makes sure that they are fully aware of the purpose and intention of the event/piece, and that they design the set around this intention.

UNDERSTANDING INTENTIONS

Sometimes, designers are used to bring a concept to life – think of world-famous music artists where the stage set reflects a concept in their music, or reproduces visuals based on album artwork. The set usually is the first thing that an audience sees and provides the 'feel' – or sets the tone – of the event. The designer will therefore work closely with other professionals involved – musicians, sound technicians and so on.

This also applies to fashion shows where the set design is expected to **encapsulate** the concept and/or mood of the fashion collection (see Figure 1.68). Creating an impressive setting for a show helps draw attention to the collection at busy fashion weeks and can make or break its success.

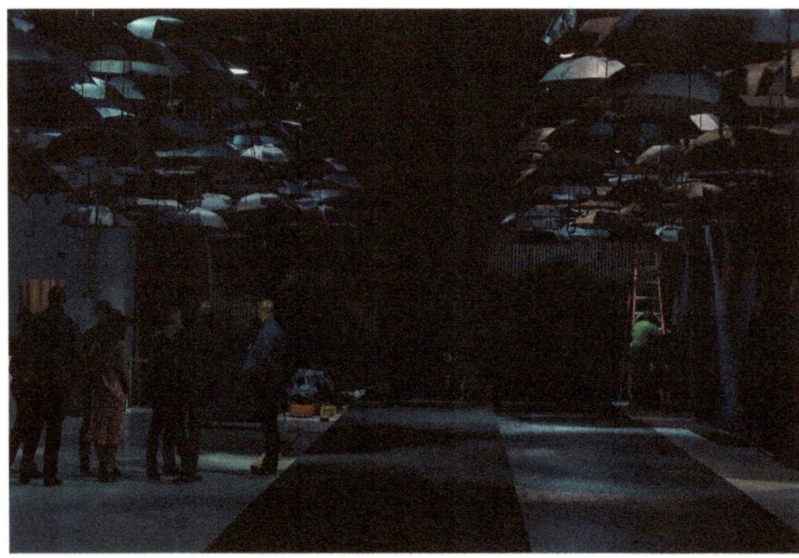

1.68 Fashion professionals put the finishing touches to a show in New York Fashion Week. Look at the visual clues on display. What do you think the concept of the collection might be?

Activity A: **Evaluate a set design**

Do this activity as part of a small group.

1. Arrange a visit to a local venue to look at and evaluate a set design – it could be a theatre or music venue, an exhibition space or a fashion show. Alternatively, you may be able to view an example of a set design online.
2. At the venue, take some photographs as a record. If possible, make some annotated drawings as well.
3. Your teacher may be able to arrange for you to meet the designers at the same time, to discuss their ideas.
4. Return to your classroom or centre and display your images.
5. In discussion with the rest of your group, think about the set design and how it relates to the theme of the show. How do you think it supported the intention of the piece?

VISUALISATIONS

The following section is supplementary. Look at the Cambridge International AS & A Level Digital Media & Design syllabus 9481 if you are interested in learning more about **visualisations**.

Set designs for films and theatre plays often begin with a series of concept drawings and visualisations. These allow ideas to be discussed at team meetings, where producers and directors can see the progress of the idea, from a script or screenplay on paper to a physical, visual thing or scene.

Figure 1.69 shows a visualisation of a vehicle to be used in the science fiction film *Blade Runner* (1982). You can see that this image also contains notes to explain the visuals.

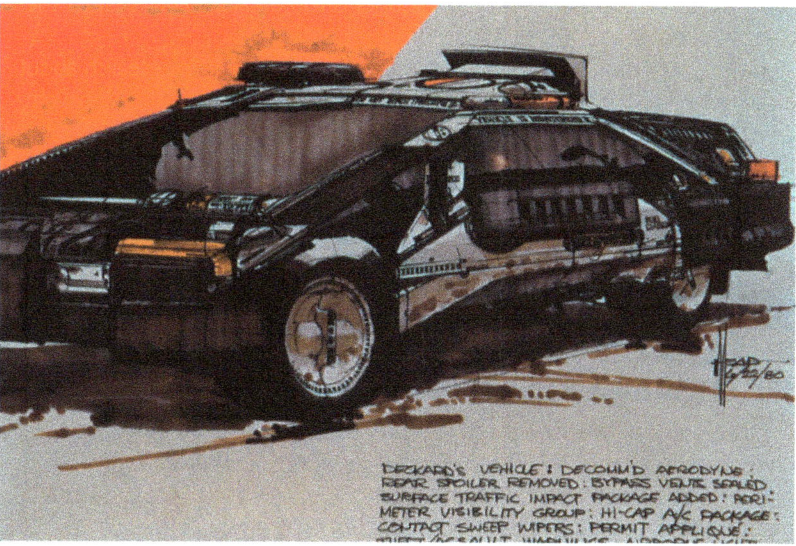

1.69 Syd Mead, set design artwork for *Blade Runner* (dir. Ridley Scott, 1982).

Activity B: **Reinterpret a set from a classic film**

1. Choose a classic film you enjoy watching. This can be from any genre, provided it is appropriate.
2. Take a set of still images from the film. (You can use screenshots from a PC or use a camera if you prefer.)
3. Using the set in the original film as a starting point, redesign the set by changing it to a modern-day setting or altering the location.
4. Use drawings to show how you have reinterpreted. You can include some drawings of the original design and then your new version.
5. Take your final idea, and produce a final screen-based design using digital art tools in appropriate software.

You can explore a range of different ideas and settings if you wish. You can also collage elements from the film into these new settings.

Further research

Keep up to date with recent developments in set design at the Prague Quadrennial website.

Materials and techniques: **Using screenshots**

You can use these to record any aspect of your work when working digitally. This could be a tool palette in editing software, or still images from a moving piece, or the progress of a digital design idea. Use a file-saving protocol to help clarify the details and sequence, such as date_name_version_number and so on.

encapsulate To sum up.
visualisation A drawing, painting or other artwork that communicates a concept in a visual way.

Product design

Learning objectives:

- To understand how designers work in response to a brief
- To understand how natural forms can inspire design ideas
- To understand how visualisation conveys intention to others

The starting point for a product design project is the brief. The brief will identify the need or problem that needs to be addressed by the design. The level of detail provided in the brief will determine the level of creative freedom the designer has. It is helpful to have some parameters, to give your work a clear direction. However, if the brief is too detailed it will restrict the creative process.

Once you know what is required, you can begin to gather research about existing or similar products that are on the market. You can do this through careful observation. Designers need to use a wide range of recording skills in their work and for various purposes:

- to observe and analyse existing products
- to find inspiration for new design ideas
- to visualise their intentions
- to convey their visions clearly to potential manufacturers and **end users**.

GATHERING RESEARCH

Undertaking a detailed visual analysis of existing products can help you understand how they have been constructed. Designers often work with marker pens to **render** their drawings and combine traditional hand-drawn methods with computer-aided design – CAD programs.

OBSERVATION AND VISUALISATION

One approach to take when looking for inspiration for a product design is to create fine art observational studies of source material, such as natural or mechanical forms. Look at the *Butterfly Stools* (Figure 1.70) by the Japanese designer Sori Yanagi (1915–2011), then look at an image of a butterfly. It is easy to see where he found inspiration.

Working from observation can also help you record information about how people use or interact with existing products. For example, in developing a product design for a chair, you might sketch or photograph the way people sit down in, use, move or stack chairs. This can help inform your design ideas in response to the brief.

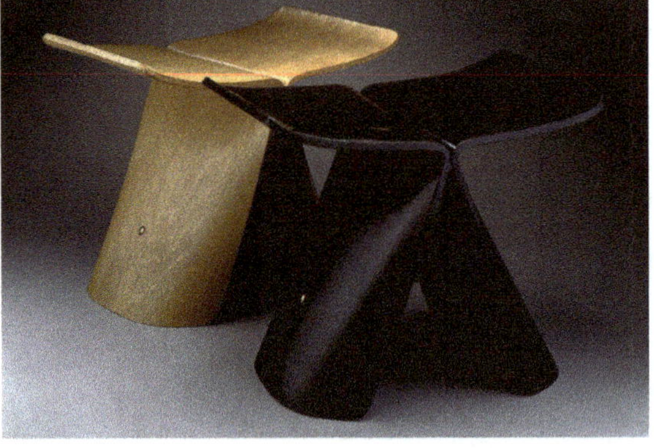

1.70 Sori Yanagi, *Butterfly Stools*, 1954, plywood and steel, Historic New England, Boston.

Materials and techniques: CAD

'Computer-aided design' (CAD) is a term that covers the three key aspects of product design:

1. drawing
2. modelling
3. visualisation.

There are a variety of 2D and 3D design packages available, and you will need to check which ones are available for you to use in your school or centre. CAD software enables designers to create and modify designs accurately and is often used in combination with computer-aided manufacture (CAM).

Activity A: Analyse a product

1. Choose a product and make analytical drawings of it from different angles. Record details to show how it fits together, or how it opens and closes. Begin with accurate line drawings and then render using marker pens.
2. Once you have done this, evaluate the product using annotations.

You can extend this activity by analysing another, similar product and then comparing them.

Activity B: **Drawing natural forms to inspire design ideas**

Make observational studies of natural forms and use your creative imagination to transform them into a product design. Sketch what you visualise and include drawings of people interacting with or using the product.

You can visualise your ideas using perspective or other representational drawing systems, such as **isometric projection** (see Figure 1.71). This is a method of three-dimensional drawing that is often used by designers. Drawings can be made on paper with a pre-printed **isometric** grid.

You will also need to master and use technical drawing techniques such as **orthographic projection** (see Figure 1.72). Such techniques need to be accurate in scale, dimensions and detail, as they are used to build **prototypes** of your product.

Together these isometric and **orthographic** projections demonstrate the range of visual information that product designers need to convey to their audiences – the manufacturer and the end user.

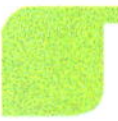

Activity C: **Write a brief**

1. Write a simple product brief and ask a classmate to respond to it. They should undertake initial research and present a visualisation of a solution to the brief. Ask them to set a brief for you to respond to.
2. Once you have both completed your research and visualisation, analyse and discuss how successfully each of you has responded to the other's brief.

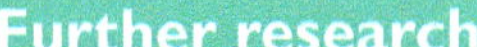

Further research

Explore some of the world's leading design museums at www.designmuseum.org, www.cooperhewitt.org and www. designmuseumdharavi.org.

end user The person who will ultimately use the product.
in situ In the original position.
isometric Technical drawing using 30° and 60° angles.
isometric projection Method for showing 3D objects in two dimensions, in which two of the three axes are drawn at 30° to the horizontal.
orthographic Technical drawing using 45° and 90° angles – the 90° plane is shown parallel to the picture plane.
orthographic projection Method for showing 3D objects as a flat view in two dimensions, in which the object is shown separately in two or more accurate, scaled-down views, as from the top, front and side. The views are typically displayed with the top view above and the side view alongside the front view.
prototype The product design in its first trial form; model of a product which is tested so that the design can be changed, if necessary, before the product is manufactured commercially.
render To add colour or shading to make an object look three-dimensional.

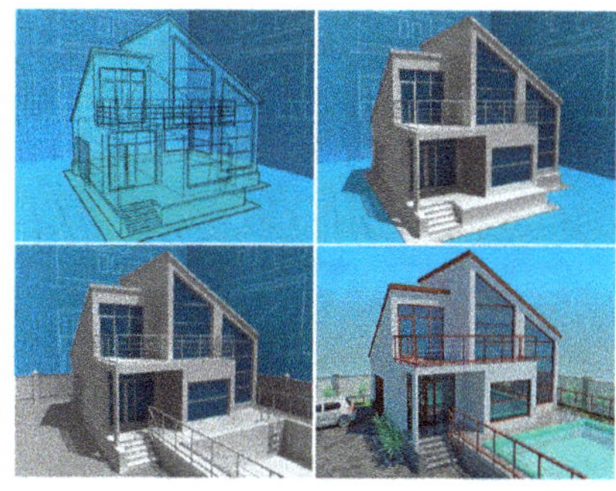

1.71 An example of a computer-generated isometric projection drawing.

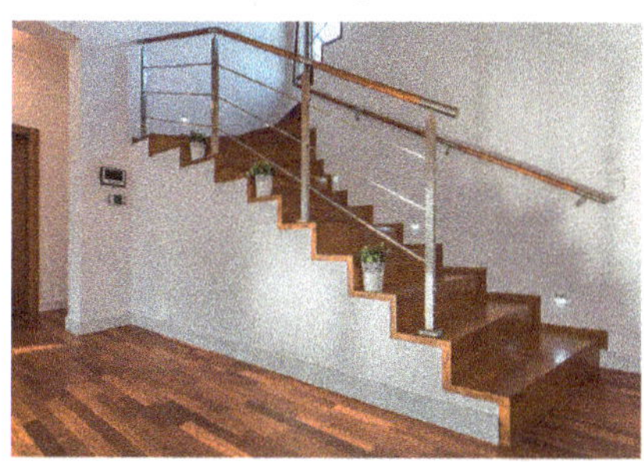

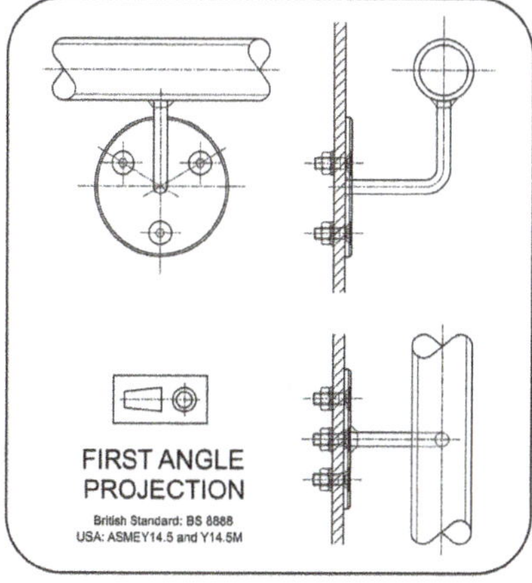

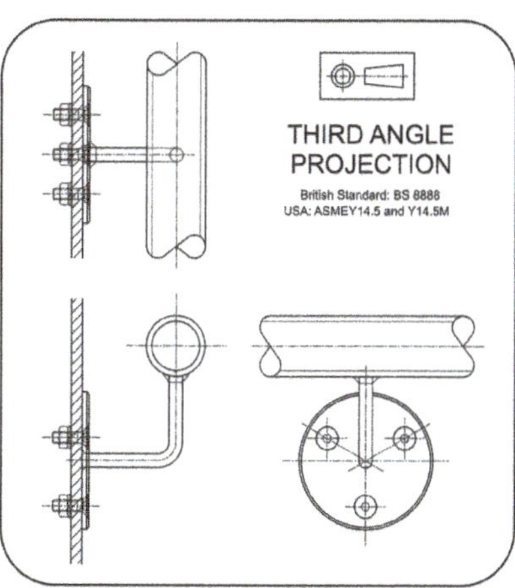

1.72 The image of the staircase with a handrail shows how the product looks **in situ**. The orthographic projection of a section of a handrail provides detail about size and scale, which will enable the design to be manufactured.

1.3 Graphic communication

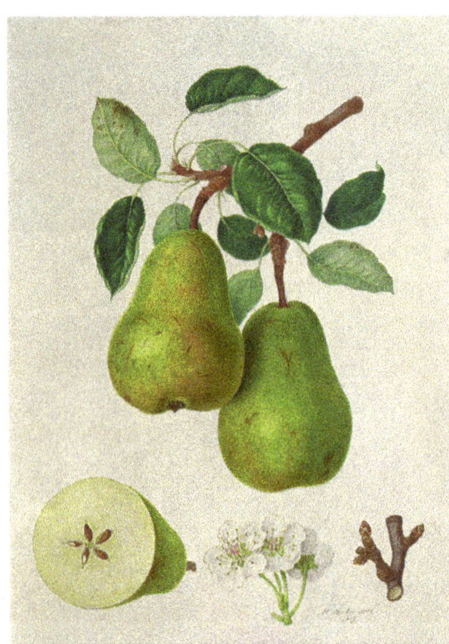

1.73 William Jackson Hooker, *The D'Auch Pear*, 1817, watercolour on paper, Lindley Library, Royal Horticultural Society, London. The British botanist and illustrator William Hooker (1779–1832) recorded his subjects in almost photographic detail in his watercolour studies.

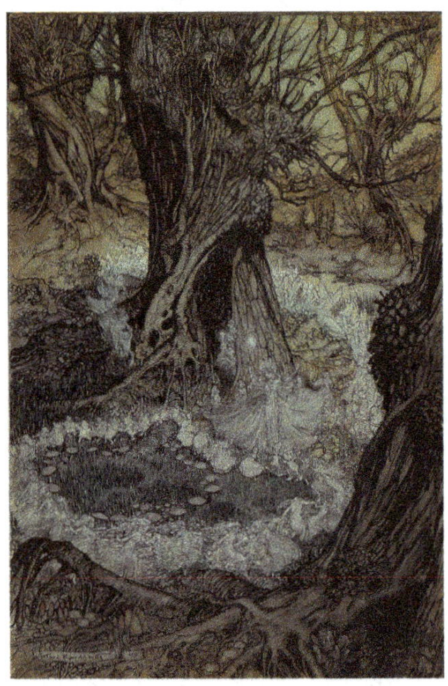

1.74 Arthur Rackham, *Come, Now a Roundel*, 1908, illustration, private collection. The British artist Arthur Rackham (1867–1939) was best known for his drawings of fairies and other fantasy creatures. This illustration was part of series illustrating William Shakespeare's play *A Midsummer Night's Dream*.

Illustration

Learning objectives:

- To understand how illustrators work in response to a brief by analysing texts
- To understand that an illustrator's work must reflect the intention of the author

Illustration is a visual interpretation, explanation or visualisation of a text, designed to accompany and enrich that text. The text could be a children's storybook, a botanical handbook (Figure 1.73), a cookery book or a classic play (Figure 1.74). For this reason, the most important thing an illustrator needs is a clear understanding of the text that they have been asked to illustrate, as well as the intention for the illustration.

ANALYSING A TEXT

As an illustrator, you will probably receive a brief. However, your starting point for any illustration project should always be to analyse the text in detail. You might, for example, have been commissioned to provide illustrations for a children's storybook. In this instance, you should read the text carefully to get ideas about what the characters look like and the key settings – for example, a lonely forest, a Gothic castle, a suburban street ... It may help to (indeed, you may be expected to) discuss your ideas with the author. Your work as an illustrator should reflect the *intention* of the author.

Illustrating children's fiction can provide you with creative scope. The type of illustrations that you produce might be colourful and help the story to flow from page to page. There may be opportunity for you to add amusing details of your own. However, if you are illustrating a non-fiction book, such as a scientific handbook, you will be expected to produce very accurate and detailed illustrations that have a particular function.

Activity A: **Analyse a text**

Take a short text (such as a short story or a poem) that you intend to illustrate, read it carefully and highlight any sections that describe when and where it is set, the characters involved and what action is happening. Make a list of the things you need to research visually to create your illustration.

EXPLORING MEDIA

As you can see by looking at the range of images in this section, illustrators produce work that is very detailed. They have highly refined analytical drawing and painting skills. It is important for you to develop your skills through practice and by exploring a wide range of mark-making techniques and styles.

When recording from observation, spend time looking carefully at what you are drawing, noting detail. Use the full range of drawing and painting media available to you. Many contemporary illustrators use digital tools to produce their work, often with specialist illustration or image manipulation software, such as Adobe Photoshop and Adobe Illustrator. However, digital illustration is about using the software as a tool, just as you would use a traditional brush and paint or pencil. Think about combining digital and traditionally drawn imagery in your illustration work, as the artist has done in Figure 1.75.

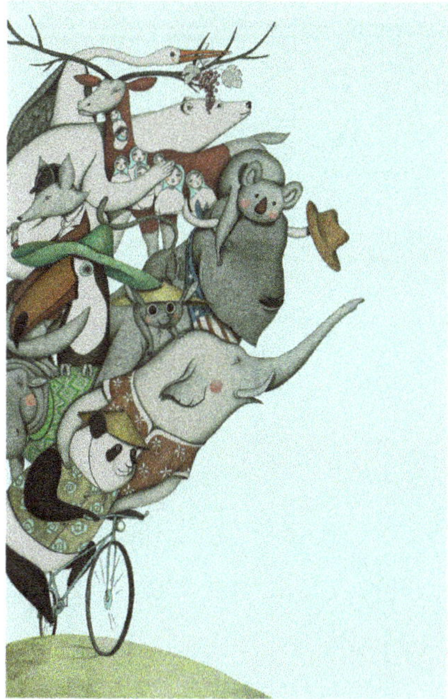

1.75 Alessandra Manfredi, *Let's go all together right now!*, 2014, lead, pencil and digital, private collection. This example of an illustration for a children's book combines digital and traditionally drawn imagery.

Activity B: **Recording with different media**

Using your analysis of a text from **Activity A**, make detailed studies of the subject matter. Use at least three different media within your work.

MANGA

A very different and popular style of illustration is manga (Figure 1.76). Manga comics take their inspiration from a style first developed in Japan in the late 19th century. The first manga magazine was published in 1874. 'Manga' is a term that literally translates from Japanese as 'whimsical pictures' and in Japan refers both to comics and cartoons.

Since the 1950s, manga has become a major part of the Japanese publishing industry. The illustration style, known for its **stylised** characters with large round eyes, has become a global art form. Manga illustrations have also been developed into animated films.

Activity C: **Create an image in the manga style**

First, research manga illustrations on the internet to get a feel for the style. Choose one of your studies from **Activity B** and recreate it in manga style, using a medium or media of your choice.

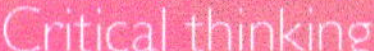

Critical thinking:

Ask a classmate to assess how successful your illustrations (**Activities A** and **B**) are in capturing the intentions of the author of your chosen text. Discuss how you could have improved the outcome.

Further research

For a more in-depth guide to creating manga, read *Manga in Theory and Practice: The Craft of Creating Manga* by Hirohiko Araki (VIZ Media LLC, 2017).

stylised Term used to describe an artwork that has a definite or non-realistic style.
yukata A casual summer kimono.

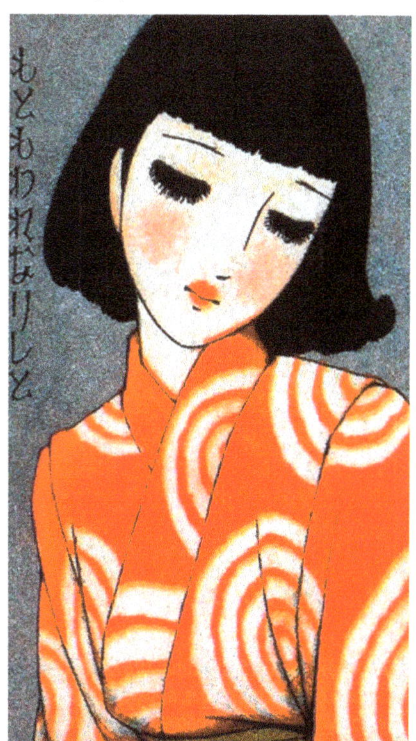

1.76 Junichi Nakahara, *Young Woman in a* ***Yukata***, c.1935, illustration, private collection.. The Japanese illustrator Junichi Nakahara (1913–83) was known for his work for fashion and girls' magazines and for drawing female characters with big eyes. His illustrations provided great inspiration to early manga cartoonists.

Printmaking

Learning objective:

- To understand how recording from observation using different approaches can directly inform print designs

A key technique used widely across fine art, graphic communication and textiles is screen printing (see page 28), sometimes known as **silkscreen** printing. Screen printing uses stencils and is ideally suited to creating imagery with bold colours and clear outlines. It can be used with either hand-drawn or photographic images, or a combination of the two. A separate stencil is required for each colour that you print, so when preparing images for a screen-printed outcome you need to think in terms of working in layers.

LAYERS OF COLOUR

Today, screen printing is widely used as a graphic medium and is particularly associated with poster and shop display design. It was the American artist Andy Warhol (1928–87) who popularised the use of screen printing as a general art form in the 1960s, bringing together fine art, advertising and popular culture in the movement known as **Pop art**. Looking at examples of his work (for example, at www.guggenheim.org), it is easy to see how Warhol has broken down images into separate layers of colours, printed on top of each other.

In *Self-Portrait* (Figure 1.77), Warhol has combined the use of simple cut stencil shapes for the blue, yellow and green areas of the print and combined these with a **photoscreen** technique to produce the final black layer.

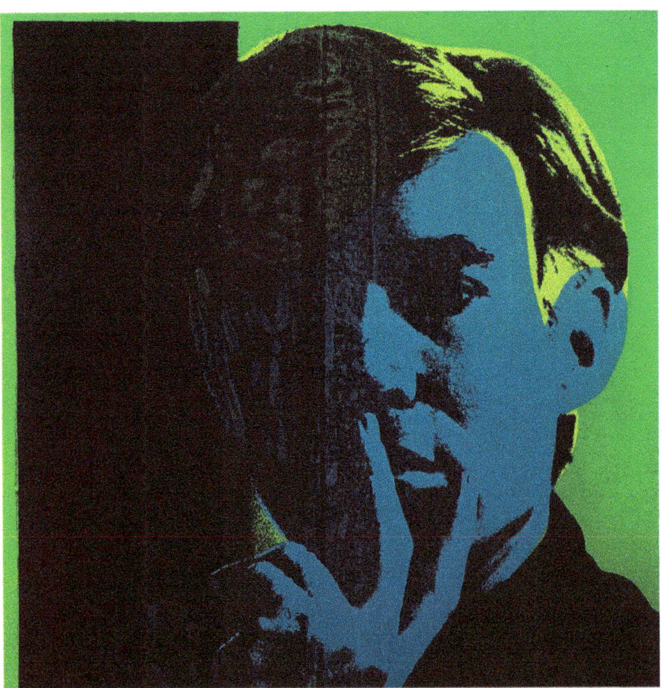

1.77 Andy Warhol, *Self-Portrait*, 1967, acrylic and silkscreen enamel on canvas, private collection. The colours have been printed as separate layers, with the black layer printed last to bring the image together.

As you have seen in the example by Warhol, each colour is a layer of the print. The following activity will help you think about building images using separate colour layers, from the point you begin to record ideas for your work from observation.

Activity A: **Create a paper cut-out**

In the 1940s, the French artist Henri Matisse (1869–1954) created a series of paper cut-out images in his series *Jazz* (1947), which were then taken into print format and published as a limited-edition book. Look at the example of one of the pages from *Jazz* entitled *The Codomas* (Figure 1.78) to see how Matisse has used the formal elements of colour and shape. The Codomas were a famous early 20th-century trapeze act.

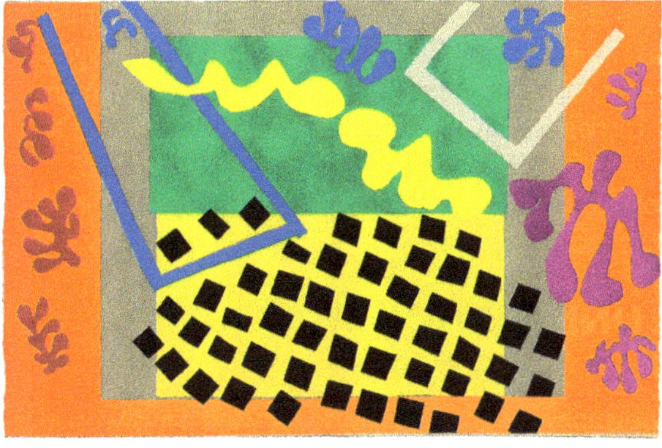

1.78 Henri Matisse, *The Codomas*, illustration from the portfolio *Jazz*, 1947, colour stencil print, Philadelphia Museum of Art, Pennsylvania.

Experiment with 'drawing with paper' by tearing and cutting sheets of flat coloured paper. Working in this way will require you to simplify your image into basic shapes and colours and work in layers. You can work in this way from direct observation of objects in front of you, or you can work from a photograph or drawing that you made earlier and simplify the shapes and colours that you see.

Tip:

In any printmaking process, the background colour of the surface you print onto provides an additional colour.

Figure 1.79 is a good example of how an image can be simplified when recording still-life objects, rather than Matisse's abstract forms. This is an anonymous American 1940 screen-printed poster, advertising a toy sale. The picture comprises four colours and the white of the paper, but it is still easy to identify all of the different toys that are depicted.

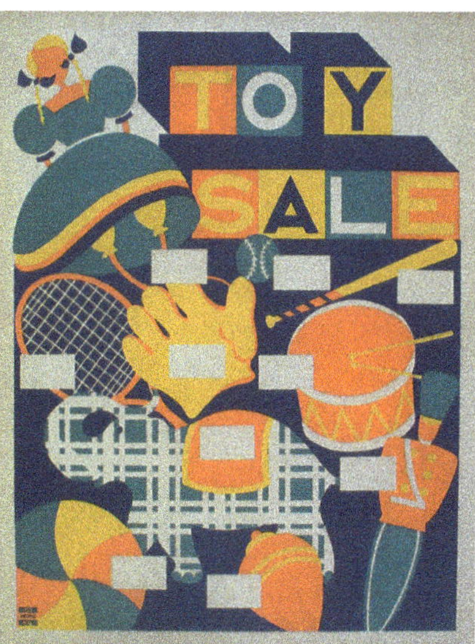

1.79 Unknown artist, *Poster Advertising a Toy Sale*, c.1940, silkscreen, private collection.

Activity B: **Create a simple poster design**

Using the image in Figure 1.79 as an example, produce a simple poster design to advertise a product or event. Use sketches and work in colour, using *four* colours in your design. Once you have the overall design, trace and redraw the image as four separate colour layers. Annotate your work to explain how you are using the elements of colour and shape within your work. You can then go on to cut the colour layer drawings to create stencils and use these to print your design.

How would you change your design if you had to limit your colour layers to three instead of four?

Further research

Go online to explore Warhol's screen prints.

Illustrations of many of Matisse's cut-outs can be found in *Henri Matisse: The Cut-Outs* (Museum of Modern Art, New York, 2014).

photoscreen A screen print where the stencil has been made using a light-sensitive process.

Pop art Art movement of the 1950s and 1960s that used popular culture for inspiration, from film stars to cartoons to household brands. Key figures include Andy Warhol and Roy Lichtenstein.

silkscreen Traditionally, the mesh used in the screen-printing process was made of silk (not polyester, as it usually is today), so you will sometimes still see the term 'silkscreen printing'.

Typography and signage

Learning objectives:

- To understand the visual characteristics of typography
- To use visual analysis to record examples of typography
- To record visual language used in signage

Typography is a key part of graphic communication. It carries the message and intention to the audience, alongside any visual information. Sometimes it is used to issue an order, as in 'NO ENTRY' signs; at other times, it might be gently coaxing the reader, such as in a list of meals on a restaurant menu. Whatever its purpose, it carries associations that designers have learned to exploit and apply.

In this unit, we will look more closely at the purpose of typography in graphic design, especially in relation to signage.

TYPOGRAPHY: UNDERSTANDING LETTERFORMS

It can be easy to take typography for granted – in some ways if it is working properly you will just read and absorb the message, without analysing the features of the typefaces used. However, as a graphic designer you need to look at typography in a different, more analytical, way. You can develop your understanding of different typefaces by collecting examples and then evaluating their design and how they are used.

Look at Figure 1.80, which shows the sign showing the entrance to the Paris Metro (underground railway) – the name of the station is on the other side. Analyse the individual letters, their shapes and how they work together as well as with the surrounding metal frame. The sign is useful – it tells passengers at street level where to go down into the station – but what mood is it creating?

ART NOUVEAU

ABCDEFG
HIJKLMN
OPQRSTU
VW XYZ

1.81 Look closely at the letterforms, especially the V, N and Y. Where do you think the designer took his inspiration from?

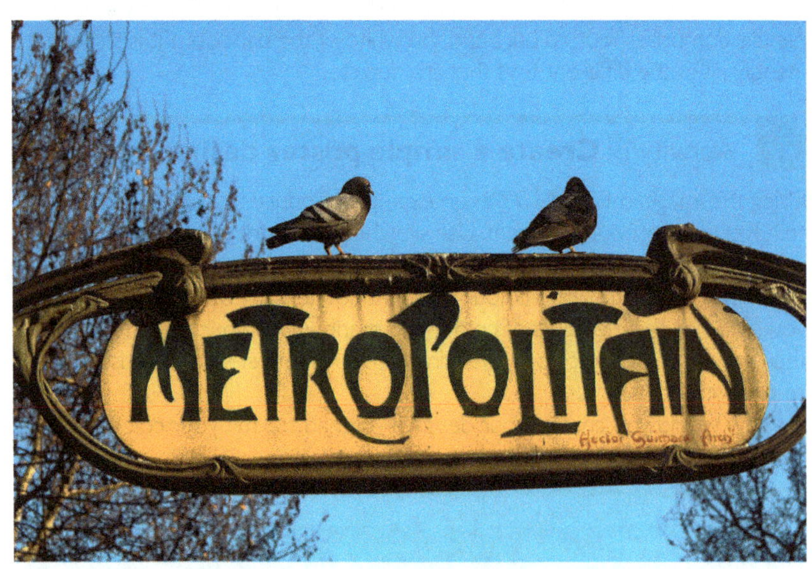

1.80 Hector Guimard, 'Metropolitain' sign for a Paris Metro station. The French **Art Nouveau** architect Hector Guimard (1867–1942) created his typeface specifically for the Metro. It is distinctive for its lack of straight lines and heavy contrast between thick and thin strokes, such as in the R.

Materials and techniques: Typefaces, fonts and letterforms

Typefaces are divided into serif and non-serif. Serifs are the little fine lines added to the main stroke of a letter and serif typefaces are especially used in small **point** sizes (for example, 12 point) in books and magazines. Non-serif typefaces are often used for short displayed pieces of text, as in signs, as they look bolder, cleaner and more eye-catching. A font is a particular size, weight and style of a typeface.

You should learn the names for different parts of letterforms, such as ascender, x-height and so on, as shown in Figure 1.82. This will help you better understand how typography is developed – and enable you to develop your own effective typography.

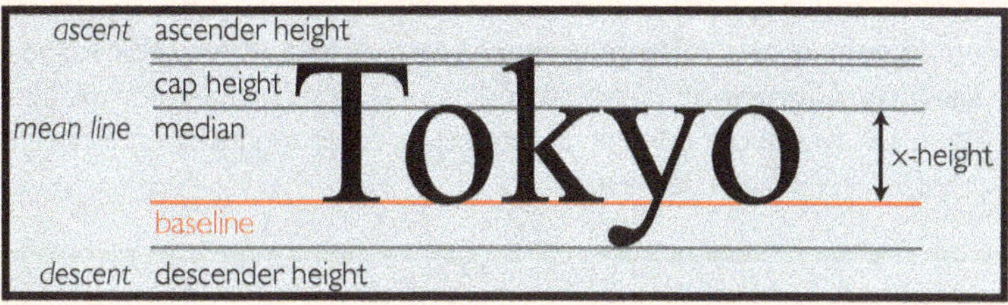

1.82 The main features of a typeface. The typeface here is Times New Roman.

Tip:

You can use examples of typography in your collection as starting points for your own design work. Practise drawing out different letterforms and typefaces – this will help you get to know their characteristics, and how designers have used shape and form within the letters.

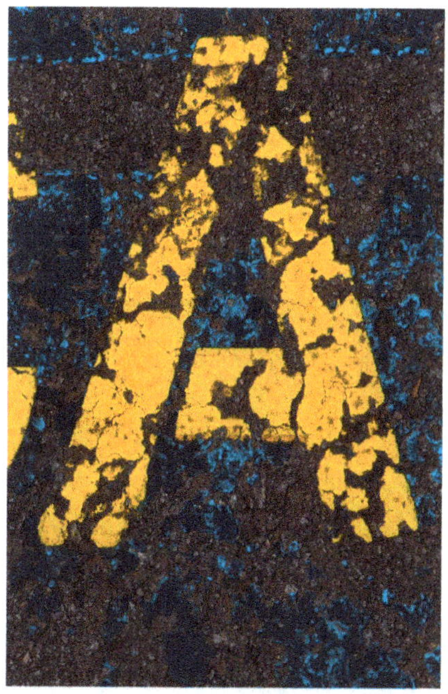

1.83 Letter A on a pavement in Barcelona, Spain.

Activity A: Look for 'found' typography

Artists sometimes use found objects in their artworks. A designer can use found typography.

Use a camera to carry out visual research in your school or centre. Look for anything that might look like a letterform – for example, a circular drain cover photographed from above could be an O.

Try to get examples where the objects or scenes suggest all the letters of the English (roman) alphabet if you can. (They may, of course, suggest the letters or characters from another alphabet or writing system.)

You can also find examples where the typography is fading or breaking down (see Figure 1.83).

You can develop this task by using drawing to help you understand the parts of the letterforms you have found. This can be further extended by drawing characters from other writing systems, such as Japanese **kanji** (Figure 1.84).

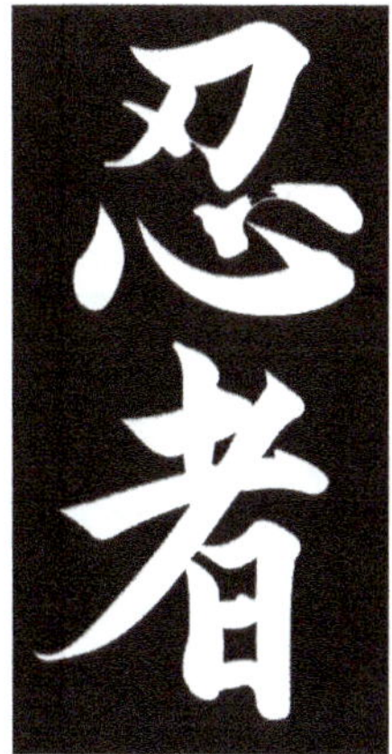

1.84 Japan: the word 'ninja' in kanji script (Chinese characters).

Art Nouveau ('new art') International style of art, architecture and decoration that flourished around 1890–1910 and took its inspiration from the natural world, especially plants.

kanji Characters used in the Japanese writing system that are borrowed from Chinese.

point Measurement used in printing and typography – in desktop publishing, 1 point equals 0.353 mm or 1/72 in.

Tip:

Remember: any experimentation in typography has to balance creative ideas with legibility.

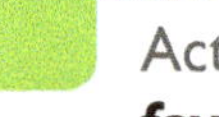

Activity B: **Remake a title page for your favourite book, using just typography**

1. Select a book of fiction you enjoy, and make a photocopy of its cover.
2. Think about the themes in the book, and what genre it belongs to – such as science fiction, action, romance.
3. Browse internet sources and select a free-for-use font that you feel matches the theme or genre of the book. There are many free sources available online.
4. Download the full alphabet in your selected font.
5. Print the alphabet out to scale for your remake of the book cover. Carefully cut the letterforms out. You may need more than one copy of the letters.
6. Explore different positions, layouts and arrangements of the letterforms, photographing the different versions you make. You can explore aspects of **kerning**, **alignment**, direction and so on. Think creatively, for example, if the book was about conflict of some sort, could the letterforms also be in 'conflict', colliding in some way?

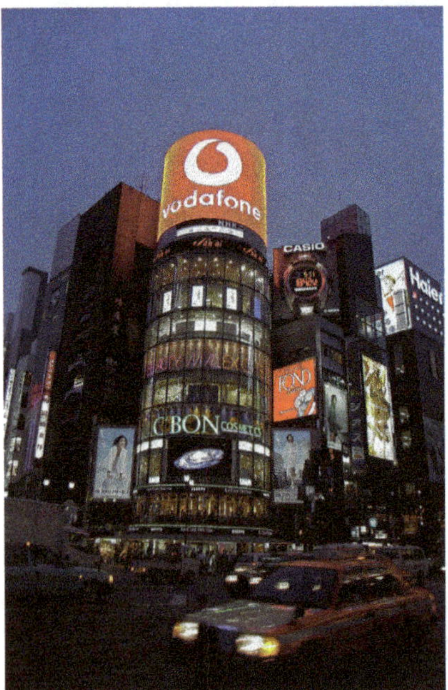

1.85 The Yon-chome crossing in the heart of Ginza, Tokyo, Japan.

SIGNAGE

Signage is all around us. If you take a journey into your nearest town or city, you may find yourself overwhelmed by the number of signs in different sizes and typefaces – from home-made signs, to the sleek signs of multinational companies (Figure 1.85). Signage has a number of functions, and this section aims to highlight these by introducing you to examples and tasks where you reach conclusions through analysis and evaluation.

Signs compete to be seen and stand out from one other, as well as display information such as the name of a store, product and so on. The designs have to be visually strong in order to stand out. They may use distinctive colour combinations, together with shape and scale. In many cases they use a simplicity that is deceptive – it may have taken a long time to arrive at that simplicity.

Activity C: **Review the signage in your local area**

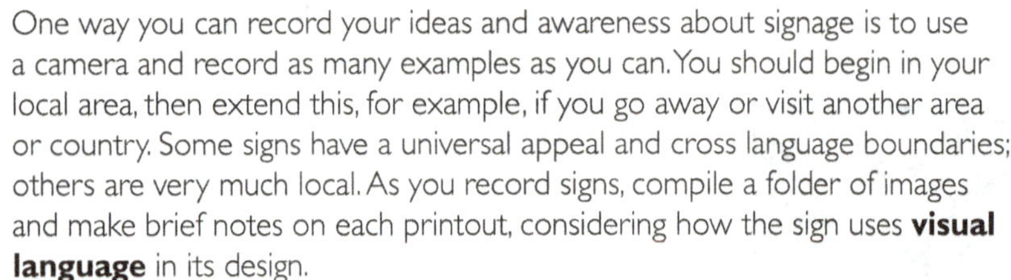

One way you can record your ideas and awareness about signage is to use a camera and record as many examples as you can. You should begin in your local area, then extend this, for example, if you go away or visit another area or country. Some signs have a universal appeal and cross language boundaries; others are very much local. As you record signs, compile a folder of images and make brief notes on each printout, considering how the sign uses **visual language** in its design.

Figure 1.86 uses a reduced set of visuals. The brand name is also suggestive of the type of product being served there. This sign uses a strong **visual device** in the way the arms and hands appear to be gripping a burger. The shape of this burger is actually the **negative space** between the hands, which just happens to be shaped like a burger. So the sign does a number of things at once: it tells us the name, it tells us the type of product and it attracts our attention by using a striking visual device.

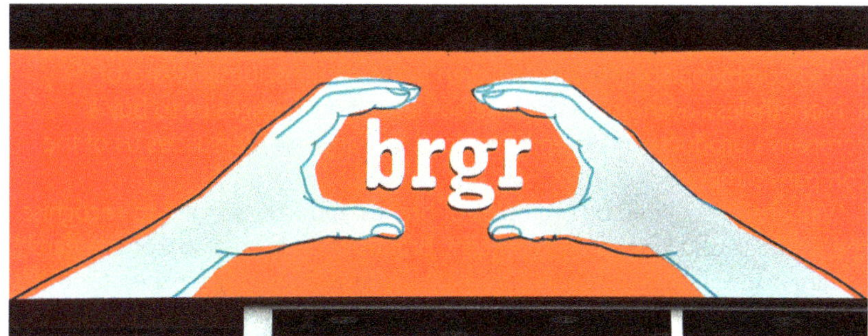

1.86 Shopfront sign, Manhattan, New York City, USA.

Activity D: **Create a design for a sign that uses a visual device**

In this activity, you will create a set of drawing-based ideas, not a finished item or design – this is about coming up with ideas.

1. Select an outlet you know.
2. Think about its range of products or services, and make notes on these, making sure that you define:
   a. the kind of product, service or organisation involved
   b. what physical shape the items associated with the company or organisation take. For example, for a car salesroom the most obvious example would be a car.
3. Now come up with a series of ideas on how you could use the item that relates to your chosen outlet, thinking about:
   a. how to translate the physical characteristics of the item into graphic form
   b. the use of typographic elements in your design.
4. Use the drawing skills you learned on pages 64–67.
5. Finalise your drawn design idea, including a logo as well if you want.

Critical thinking:

When you have completed **Activity D**, pair up with another student to discuss ideas. Consider the following questions when assessing your partner's work:

- How effective is the visual device in conveying the company's core product?
- Does the design make strong use of typography?
- How could the design be improved?

Further research

A classic manual of typographic design is *The New Typography* by Jan Tschichold, first published in 1928. Tschichold (1902–74) was one of the great typographers of the 20th century, famous for his book designs for Penguin.

alignment The setting of the text on the page or other background – common terms are 'flush left', 'flush right', 'centred' and 'justified'.
kerning The adjustment of space between the letters of words to improve the appearance of printed text, used especially in larger type.
negative space The space between objects in an image that have a value as a shape within the composition.
visual device A playful or eye-catching image that sums up an aspect of a brand or product.
visual language How formal elements are used to convey a sign or symbol, such as colour, shape, line and composition.

Branding and packaging design

Learning objectives:

- To understand the visual characteristics in branding and packaging
- To understand how designers work to a theme in response to a brief

In the contemporary world, branding is everywhere – on the internet, in our shopping malls, on our TV and cinema screens, and in sports stadia. It is so commonplace that we can even fail to be consciously aware of it. Nonetheless, even on an unconscious level, it encourages us to buy a company's products and, even if we don't buy anything, persuades us of the company's importance.

We are surrounded by examples of brands, and have learned to recognise the products and items they represent. Brands use information from research to target specific audiences, and develop a **visual identity** for their products that embodies the values their consumers hold dear. The key ingredients of branding include typography, colour and logo, all of which also play a key role in packaging design.

You can research examples of branding and look at how they work visually – their use of formal elements, and what makes them recognisable. You can use these examples as starting points for your own work and ideas development.

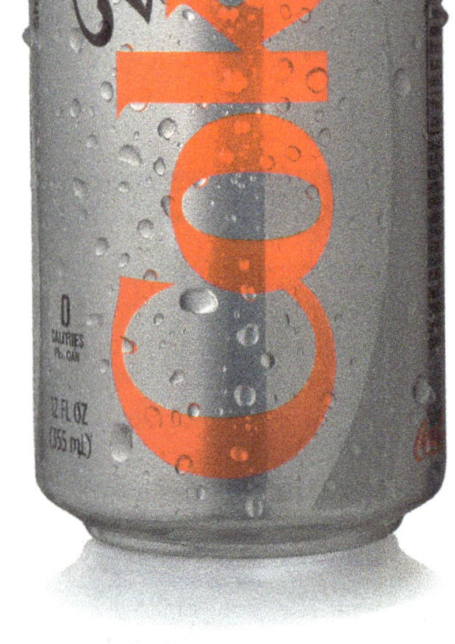

1.87 Can of Diet Coke.

MAKING BRANDS RECOGNISABLE

The Coke brand is instantly recognisable and has a universal presence (Figure 1.87). The brand identity and logo are simple and can be applied to different scenarios, such as magazines, screen-based platforms, billboards and so on. The typography, however, is very subtle. A close analysis shows the 'C' and 'o' are joined, as are the 'k' and 'e'. The brand generally uses the red version of this logo.

eBay also uses typography as its key branding element – its logo is formed by its name (see Figure 1.88, this design has now been superseded). The letterforms are slightly transparent and overlap. They are not lined up in a traditional way, and seem to float a little. They do not follow classic typographic rules. What, for example, do you notice about the kerning? What do you think the company was intending to communicate in its branding?

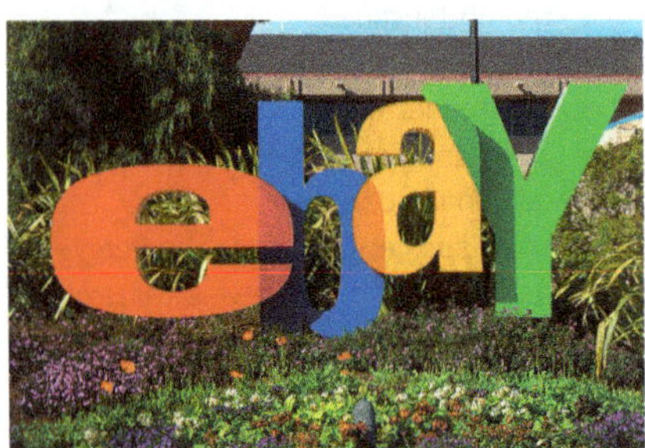

1.88 eBay logo.

Activity A: **Select and analyse 12 brands that are instantly recognisable**

Collect a range of brands that are instantly recognisable to you. Select 12 that you believe are the strongest. This may be because of their logo, typography or use of colour, or any combination of these. Make notes about which formal elements have been used, and how these work in making the brand recognisable.

LOGOS

Some brands use a graphic emblem or symbol – called a logo (short for 'logotype') – as well as, or instead of, words. A good logo can work internationally, as logos are not constrained by language. For example, the logo of Japanese car manufacturer Toyota features three linked **ellipses**, like planetary orbits or paths, giving it a futuristic or space-age feel.

A logo can also work in another way – conveying a set of values that the company wants to communicate to potential customers. The logo for the German car manufacturer Porsche is much more detailed than the Toyota one (see Figures 1.89 and 1.90). It features a **heraldic shield**, with a rearing horse, and antlers. This very traditional symbol relays messages about history, wealth, status and pedigree – values important to a luxury car brand like Porsche.

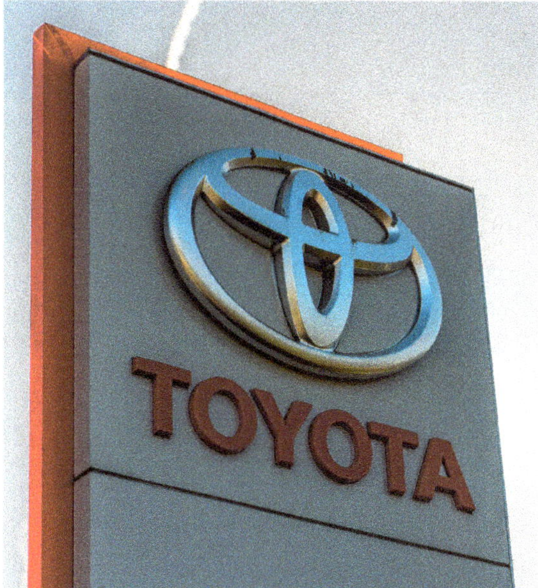

1.89 Toyota logo.

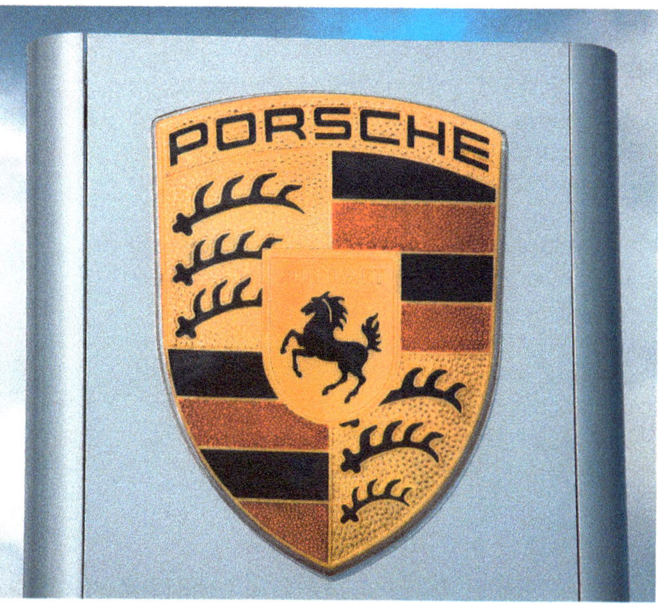

1.90 Porsche logo.

Activity B: **Analyse logos**

Find as many examples of logos as you can from one field or industry. Choose five of the most successful and draw a pencil study of each. Try to identify the shapes they are made from – think about the ellipses in the Toyota example. Record the information as closely as you can by drawing accurately. You can extend this task by looking at the way positive and negative space is used.

Critical thinking: **Summarise your findings**

Consider your studies of logos undertaken in **Activity B**:

- Can you identify any themes that consistently appear in the logos?
- Can you make links between the logos, such as those with a historical or luxury association or those with a modern/futuristic style?

ellipse Shape like the orbit of a planet around the Sun.
heraldic shield A traditional shield-shaped badge used by countries, cities and families, incorporating symbolic images and colours.
visual identity The look of a brand.

Artists and designers: **Rob Janoff**

The American graphic designer Rob Janoff was asked by Steve Jobs and Steve Wozniak to create a logo for their first Apple computer product. Jobs and Wozniak were working in their garage, and the year was 1977. Jobs had worked with Ronald Wayne on the first example of the logo for the brand, which shows an engraving-type image of the 17th-century scientist Sir Isaac Newton sitting under an apple tree, entirely in black and white. Janoff took a different approach to generating his ideas, and this was the beginning of the logo that has become instantly recognisable across the world, regardless of language boundaries (Figure 1.91).

Janoff developed his design ideas in the way that you are asked to do on some of the activities in this book. He presented his ideas as preliminary drawn sketches first. He based his original drawing ideas on examining and recording cross-sections of real apples. He wanted to create a silhouette of an apple, but needed to make it look like an apple rather than any round fruit. He knew Steve Jobs lived on a ranch with an apple orchard and that he thought that an apple was the perfect food. Janoff explains that he did what anyone would do when they get an apple, saying he 'took a bite out of it'.

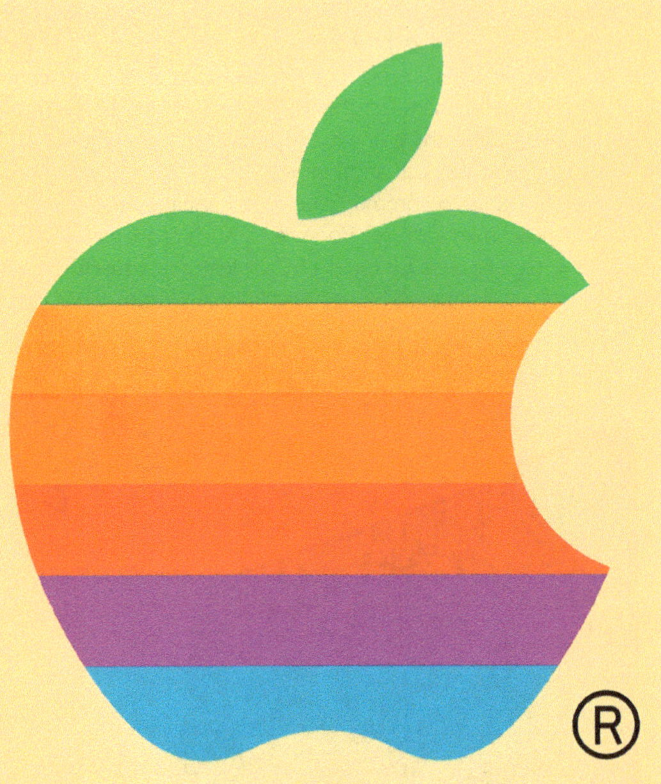

1.91 Rob Janoff, Apple logo, 1977. Bold, colourful, instantly recognisable all over the world.

PACKAGING DESIGN: RESPONDING TO A BRIEF

Branding plays the dominant role in packaging design, where a product must make itself distinctive and recognised in a crowded marketplace. Together, the branding and packaging design needs to reflect the market it's aimed at; for example, in terms of age and gender. It also needs to reflect the **brand image**, which means conveying a message about the lifestyle that people might aspire to if they buy the product.

When you start to design to a packaging brief, you need to understand who you are designing for and *what* the packaging functions are.

Who? You must identify the target market that your packaging design is aimed at, as this will help you to focus your research appropriately. Your starting point for recording visually might be very different if designing packaging for a video game specifically for 16- to 24-year-olds than if you are designing for a food product aimed at the general adult population.

What? The two main functions of packaging are to *protect* the contents and to *inform* the consumer about what is inside.

Your research will have two steps:

1. Collect and analyse examples of *existing designs* for a range of products. You might collect actual examples or find images of them on the internet or in books or magazines.
2. Research the *theme* that relates to the brief. For example, the designs in Figure 1.92 are examples of packaging design for fruit- and vegetable-based food products. So a starting point for the designers would have been to collect images of the varieties of fruits and vegetables featured in each range. In both examples, the designer has used the colour of the relevant fruit or vegetable as the colour scheme of their design.

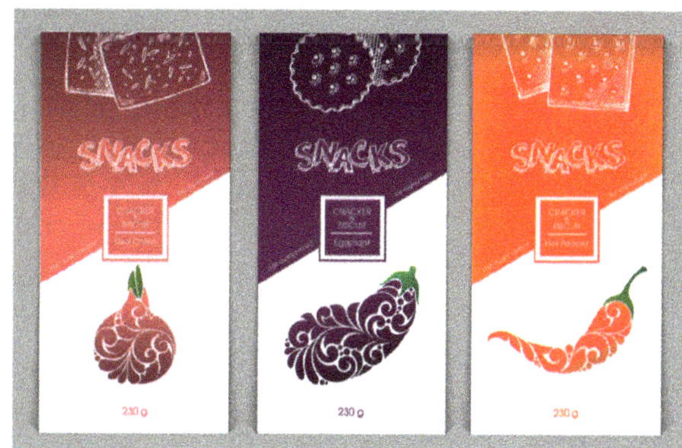

1.92 Packaging design for a brand called 'Snacks'.

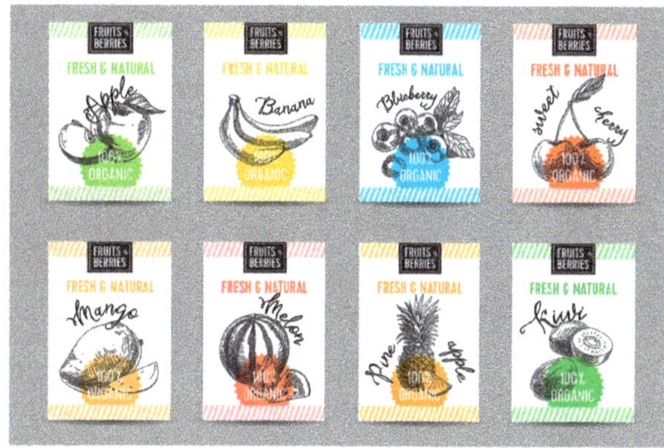

1.93 Packaging design for the brand 'Fruits & Berries'.

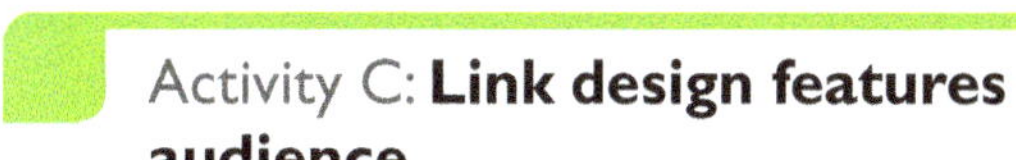

Activity C: **Link design features to target audience**

Look at the images in Figures 1.92 and 1.93. List the features common to both sets of designs. Who do you think the design of this packaging is aimed at? Give reasons. How easy is it to understand what the package contains by just looking at the visual images? As a designer, how could you make it clearer what the packaging contains?

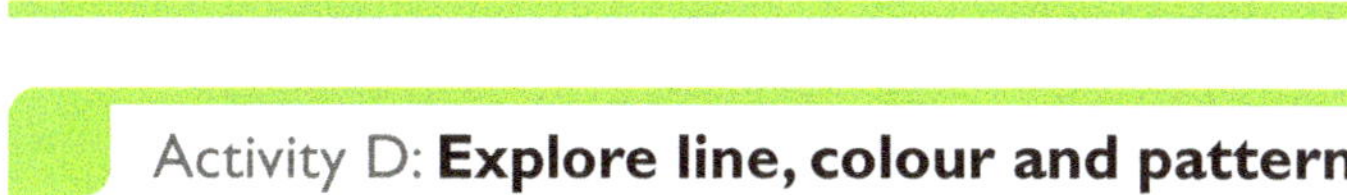

Activity D: **Explore line, colour and pattern in packaging**

Think about the formal elements used in each design and how they have been used in the representations of the different fruits and vegetables. Using your own brief and theme as a starting point, begin to make a series of drawings that focus on exploring the three elements of line, colour and pattern.

brand image The 'personality' of a brand built up over time. It should be consistent so that customers develop a relationship with, and loyalty towards, the brand.

PACKAGING DESIGN: SHAPE AND STRUCTURE

Designers must think about the shape and structure of the packaging from the outset, as well as the visual graphics. Figure 1.94 shows a partially opened package design that provides detail about how the parts fit together. Recording this type of detail from existing examples of packaging will provide information that will help you when you begin the process of designing your ideas.

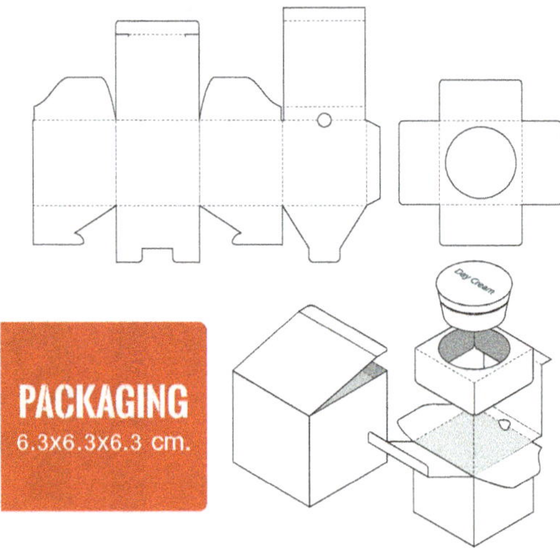

1.94 A partially opened package illustrating the opening and closing mechanism.

Activity E: **Analyse packaging structures and shapes**

Collect examples of different types and shapes of packaging, and record details, such as the opening and closing mechanism, by making accurate sketches and photographs. Add annotations to show how you are thinking critically about packaging design.

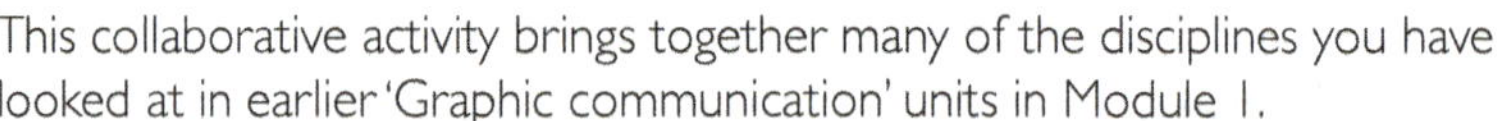

Activity F: **Create a new product design**

This collaborative activity brings together many of the disciplines you have looked at in earlier 'Graphic communication' units in Module 1.

Work with a small group of three or four to initiate ideas for a new healthy fruit-based energy drink to be targeted at the teenage market. Allocate roles within your group to undertake the following tasks:

- Write a clear, detailed brief, specifying the desired outcome and the tasks involved (see below), together with a timeline.
- Research the branding and packaging of existing products using sketches and photographs from first-hand and second-hand sources.
- Record, from observation, visual references to fruit and interesting typefaces that can inform your design ideas.
- Design ideas for a logo and suitable typefaces that will speak out to your target audience.
- Design imagery to be used across the packaging that relates to the contents. Consider the use of line, colour and pattern within the designs.
- As a group, present your ideas to other classmates and record their feedback.

Further research

The magazine *Design Week* has up-to-date news and articles on branding. Visit their website.

1.4 Textiles and fashion

Textiles

Learning objective:

- To explore different ways to refine and present research to support the creative process

Tip:

Use your own materials and photographs to set the mood of your board, to make it more personal.

Research is an essential part of a textile designer's creative process, as it helps them engage with their chosen topic or theme. It provides **key design elements** such as colour, fabric, texture and surface pattern. To broaden their research, they must also consider cultural, historical and current references, and market trends. Once a designer has collected and recorded this information, they can select and present their images. This process helps a designer define their intentions. One way to do this is by creating a mood board.

USING MOOD BOARDS

The example of a mood board in Figure 1.95 is by Azra Iqbal, a constructed textile designer specialising in knitwear. Here she presents us with a selected group of images inspired by fine web-like structures. Her board is made up of her own collaged images: she has experimented with a fine nylon fabric to produce ladder-like structures relating to a photograph she has taken, included in the mood board. At the bottom left of her board, she has made 3D multimedia structures that refer to her linear images.

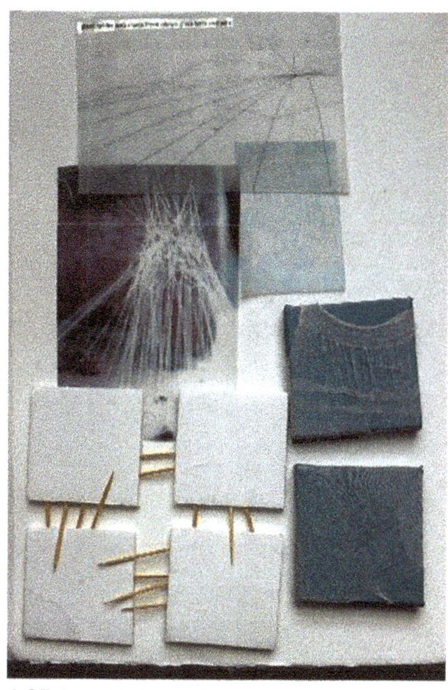

1.95 Azra Iqbal, mood board, 2017.

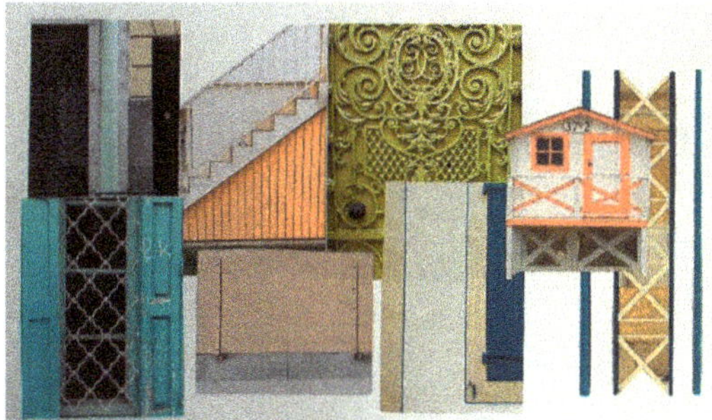

1.96 Ellamae Statham, mood board.

Activity A: **Define the story in this mood board**

For the mood board in Figure 1.96, designer Ellamae Statham has created a mood board using her own photographs of decorative façades of houses. She has formatted them into an abstract collage, playing with scale and colour.

1. Can you describe the mood of the images? Find some descriptive words that capture the essence of the **story**.
2. Next, create a colour palette. Can you identify the strongest colour? This colour is called the **accent colour** and tends to run through the whole collection of fabrics.

accent colour Small amounts of colour used to lift or to add impact to a colour scheme.
key design elements Parts that make up a textile outcome.
story The overall theme of a design.

Tip:

You can make mood boards either by hand, by cutting and sticking images using **adhesive spray mount** onto **mount board**, or by using a website storing system such as Pinterest, where you can select images and store them on an electronic device.

Activity B: **Create an A3 mood board**

Create a mood board that displays your personal ideas. Include a colour palette and images from both first-hand and second-hand sources.

- The first-hand sources can be in the form of photographs you have taken that represent your ideas best. For example, you may want to present a detailed pattern by creating close-up photographic images using a **macro lens** on the camera.
- The second-hand sources of images can be magazine cuttings or taken directly from the internet.

It is important that you choose carefully and show only what is relevant and clearly describes your intentions. For example, if your mood board is about a brightly coloured beadwork story, you could include images of the traditional costumes of Maasai warriors featuring intricate stitched beads. Limit your selection to 10 images on an A3 board.

Materials and techniques: **Using found objects**

Figures 1.97 and 1.98 show how a designer can also use found objects (see pages 62–63) to inspire their work. The designer has collected jewellery in interesting shapes. They are put on an overhead projector and projected onto a sheet of paper (where the image is seen in reverse). Only the silhouetted shapes are outlined with a pen. The result can be developed into a surface pattern textile. Find your own objects that have unusual shapes and do the same.

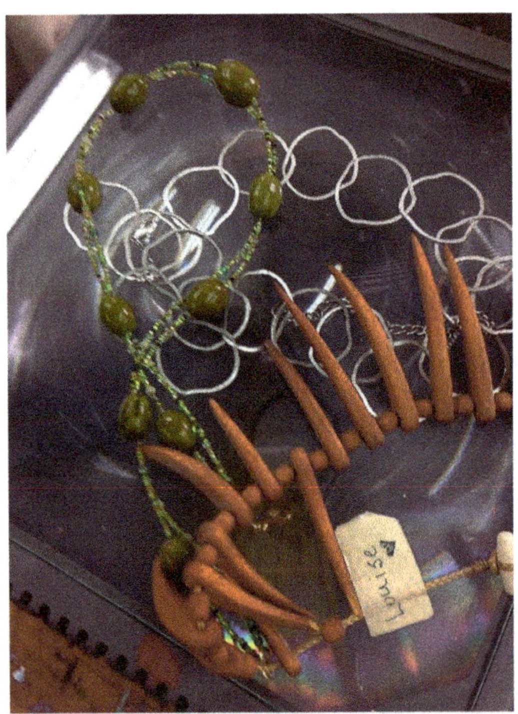

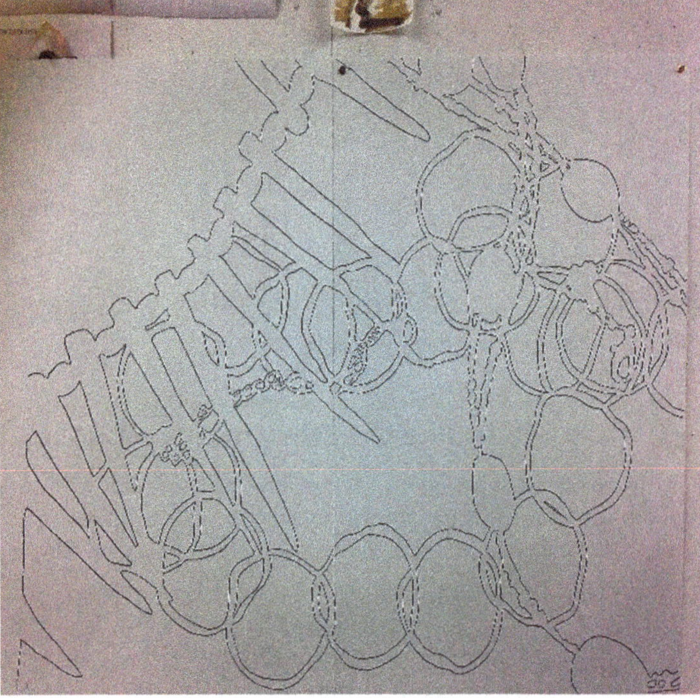

1.97 and **1.98** Use of found objects to create a surface pattern.

PRINTED AND DYED TEXTILES: MANIPULATING IMAGERY

Once designers have completed their research, next they need to make choices about colour and imagery. The designer will refine the research and begin to experiment with manipulating imagery, mixing inks and dyeing fabrics. The designer knows at this stage what the outcome will do – for example, whether the printed textile will be for fashion or an interior.

For printed textiles, a designer will need to decide on how the overall effect will look and how this will be achieved. For example, will the selected images work better as a single image on the fabric or repeated? If the image is to be repeated, it will go through a hand or digital formatting process. Will the imagery be abstract or realistic? If realistic, then a digital printing process may be more appropriate (see Figure 1.99).

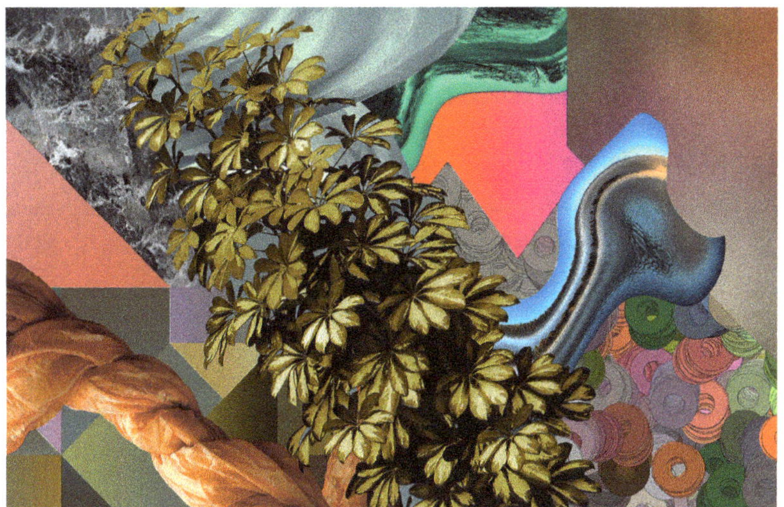

1.99 Basso & Brooke, *Vibrant Wilderness*, from the *Tropical Constructivist* collection, Spring/Summer 2012, digital print on fabric. If you look closely, you can just make out the distorted images of landscape and seascapes. The design plays with blocks of colour and pastel shades for a background, allowing the foreground to burst with colour and structure.

Activity C: **Collect imagery from second-hand sources for a digital print design idea**

1. Using the theme 'Abstract Seascape', collect and select secondary images (from magazines, books or the internet) of views of the sea. Your images do not have to be photographs but can be taken from a range of artistic sources. For example, you might like to use one of the brilliantly coloured seascapes by English painter J.M.W. Turner (1775–1851) or the iconic woodblock print *The Great Wave off Kanagawa* (1830–32) by Japanese artist Katsushika Hokusai, or both! Have fun experimenting with texture and scale.
2. Abstract these images by changing their original composition. This can be achieved by reducing or increasing the scale of the image, distorting it, or by cutting it up and placing it back together in a different direction.
3. Consider your colour palette carefully, so you present either a balance of subdued or of vibrant colours. Look again at the example design by fashion label Basso & Brooke (Figure 1.99) for ideas on layout.

Materials and techniques: **Distorting imagery**

Try distorting your images. Place the image onto a photocopier and, just as it prints, drag the image across the glass plate. Experiment with the speed at which you do this. Other ways to distort images include scrunching or folding an image on paper, keeping the creases in the paper and then redrawing what you see.

Tip:

The internet is a great source for gathering images. However, you must bear in mind the concept of **copyright**. Just because you can source an image from the internet does not mean that you can take it and claim it as your own.

Artists and designers can only use other artists' and designers' work in their own work if they transform it, by adding something new or different, or by adding a new insight. They can also use it if they want to make a comment about the original image or its context.

If you are in any doubt about your right to use an image, ask your teacher.

adhesive spray mount A spray glue that allows you to move and reposition your images.
copyright If someone has copyright on an image, piece of writing or music, it is illegal to reproduce or perform it without their permission.
macro lens Setting used for photographing close-up detail.
mount board Stiff paper card to mount work onto and display. Mount boards come in sizes A1, A2 or A3.

1.100 Peeling paint from a brick wall makes for an interesting surface.

CONSTRUCTED TEXTILES: CREATING SURFACE PATTERNS

For all textile designers, colour is basic. However, for makers of constructed textiles, it is the raw materials such as fibres and threads that are most important. Designers of constructed textiles use highly traditional skilled techniques such as knitting, weaving, felting, embroidery, tapestry, lacemaking and crocheting to make textured outcomes. It is the surface pattern that is most intriguing to the designer. They will begin by researching unusual surfaces to help visualise an idea.

Often the most interesting and revealing surfaces are the ones that go unnoticed. The example in Figure 1.100 shows a wall that has been distressed by age or weather.

It is observational images like this one that inspire designers, as such images have lots of interesting qualities for unique and exciting fabric surfaces. Figure 1.101 is a good example of how an outcome may have been inspired from initial research like the textured wall surface. The dress was created by Cypriot-Turk-born, British fashion designer Hussein Chalayan (born 1970) and is made up of stitched layers of fragmented pieces of fabric and appliquéd onto a partly transparent (opaque) cloth.

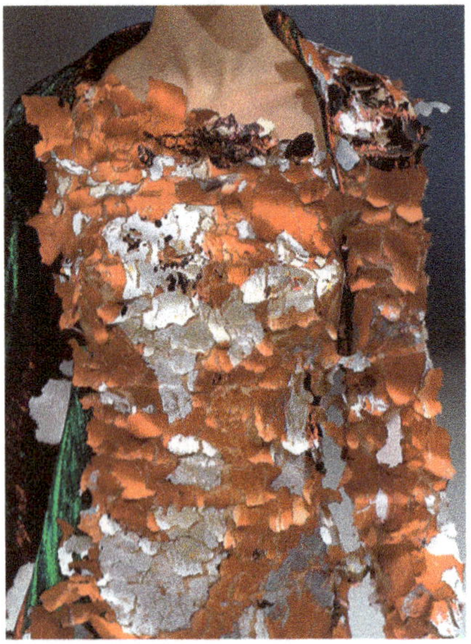

1.101 Hussein Chalayan, dress made from fabric stitched onto transparent cloth, Autumn 2014 collection.

Activity D: **Collect first-hand sources for surface pattern inspiration**

Use a camera to record 30 photographs of the *surfaces* of both natural and human-made structures. Take your time when looking for inspiration and look in unusual places (Figure 1.102). When selecting your surfaces to photograph, don't be too concerned at this stage about what the final outcome might be. It is important to have fun finding as many unusual surfaces as you can. You will begin to see things in a very different way!

Once you are back in your classroom or centre, begin to think about how the photographs might translate best into a textile technique.

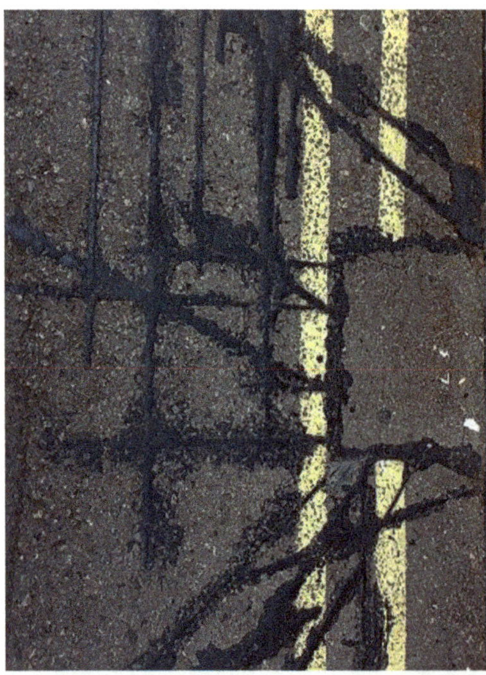

1.102 Photograph of a road with double yellow lines and signs of wear and tear.

Tip:

Keep the photographs you reject, as you might need them for future projects.

Artists and designers: **Dionne Swift – using observational research**

To see how textile artists use observational research to inspire their work, let's look at the British machine embroiderer Dionne Swift. Swift 'paints' with cloth and thread to create an emotional response to landscape. She builds up layers of texture and colour, mixing threads to create semi-abstract scenes.

She begins by recording landscapes in photographs. Once in the studio, she selects the best photographs, in terms of both colour and structure, that will work with her stitching technique.

Next, she makes quick drawings using oil bars and graphite. It is important for her to work in this spontaneous way, as it adds energy and freshness to her ultimate outcomes (Figure 1.103).

Once the drawings are finished, she begins translating these marks into stitch using a semi-industrial embroidery machine (Figure 1.104).

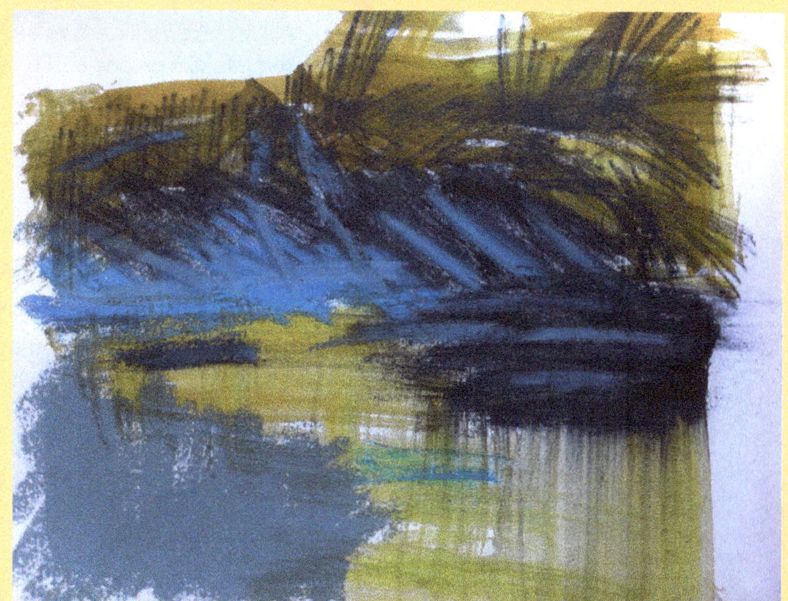

1.103 Dionne Swift, preparatory drawing, oil bars and graphite on paper. The designer adds texture to the drawing by scratching into the oil colour and overlaying graphite to give the added depth and layers.

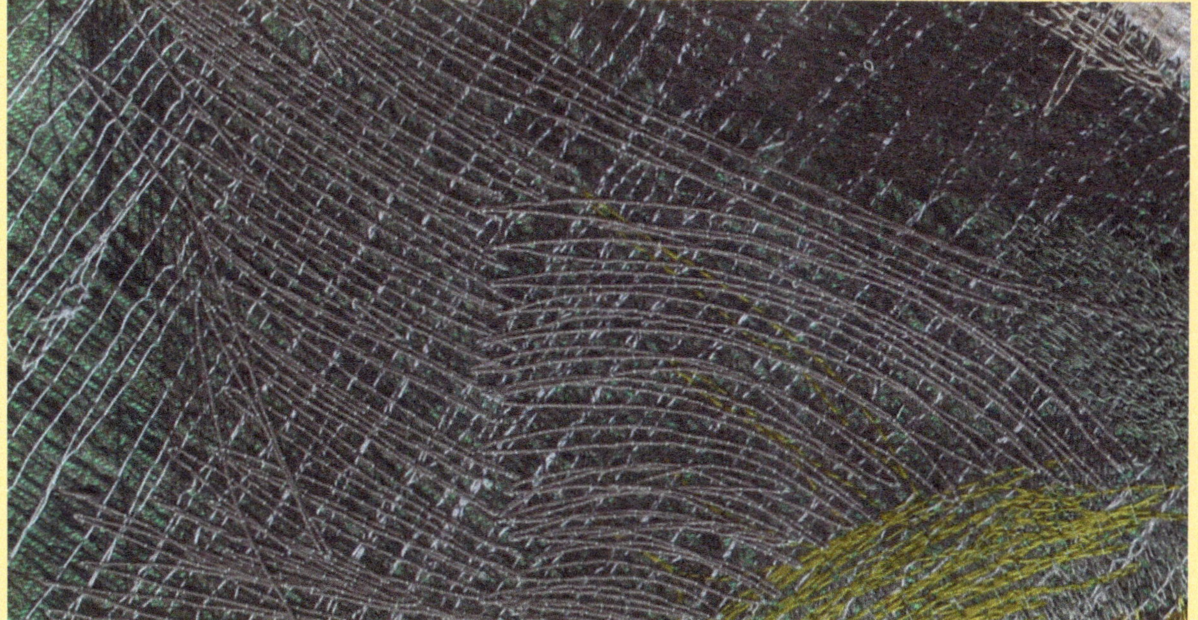

1.104 Dionne Swift, machine-embroidered fabric (close-up). Through her process of photographing, drawing and stitching, the artist is able to recapture the movement of foliage and water in the landscape.

Try **Activity E** , which uses a similar process.

Tip:

Make a viewfinder out of black card. Place it over the parts of the drawing or photograph that you find the most interesting in terms of line, colour, surface pattern or texture. By isolating these areas, you will discover more information and another image will emerge.

Critical thinking:

Following on from **Activity D**, review and refine your collection of photographs as follows:

- Lay the photographs out in front of you and consider which ones have the most stimulating surface qualities or 'ingredients'.
- Now make your choices and put them into piles that would most suit a textile technique. For example, an image that depicts holes or transparency could be inspiration for a lace or laser technique, while an image of volcanic lava with rippling folds could be an inspiration for manipulating fabrics using **pleating**.

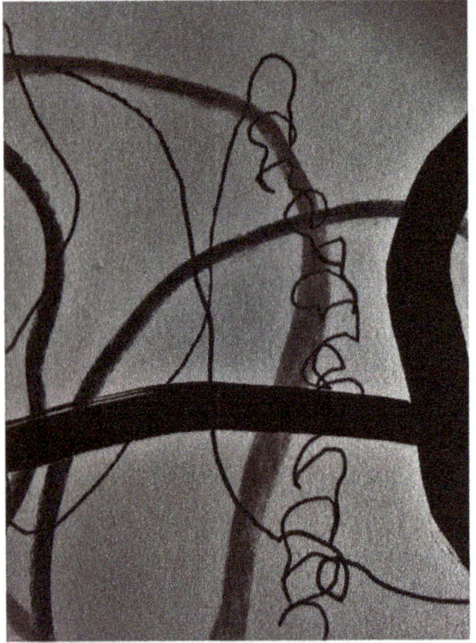

1.105 Louise Arnould, observational drawing, pencil, charcoal and pen on paper.

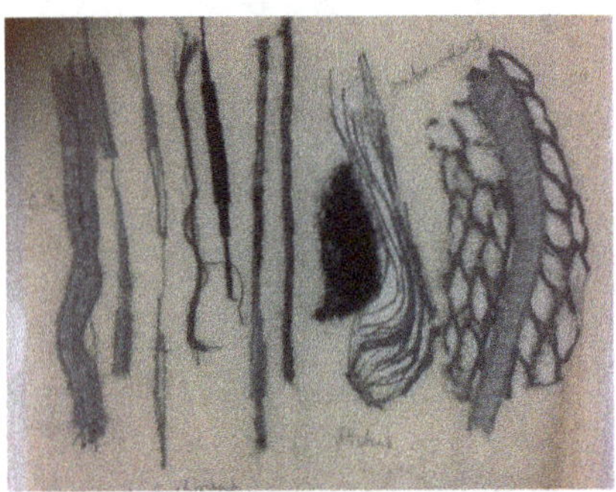

1.106 Louise Arnould, experimental machine embroidery stitches, threads and appliquéd fabric.

Activity E: Respond to observational drawing research through stitch work

The aim of this activity is respond to observational drawings and translate them into stitch work using a machine (see 'Artists and designers' feature on page 103). You can use hand stitching if you do not have a sewing machine.

Start by setting up a still life with three small objects that have unusual surfaces and shapes. Draw only the outline of the objects with a pencil. Do not look at the page you are drawing on. The result of the drawing will be a lively, spontaneous one with intersecting lines.

Select parts of your drawing that contain unusual and exciting mark-making (see Figure 1.105). Translate these marks onto fabric using a transfer method. Set the machine up with a free-motion embroidery attachment or **embroidery foot**. This will allow you to move around the fabric with ease. Stretch your fabric over an **embroidery frame** and thread your machine with black cotton. Use only black and grey tones, so that your samples focus primarily on the textures and lines, without the distraction of colour.

Practise using the machine until you feel confident that you can control the speed and follow the transferred lines. You could explore scale by reducing or enlarging the stitches using the stitch width and length settings on your machine.

Further research

Search YouTube to find a good demonstration of creating a mood board.

Explore Pinterest or other image-sharing websites for lots of creative ideas for dyed and constructed textiles.

embroidery foot An attachment for a sewing machine that makes free-motion stitching.

embroidery frame A metal or wooden ring, designed to keep fabric stretched while an embroiderer works on it.

pleating A permanent fold that is made in the cloth by folding one part over the other and sewing across the top end of the fold.

Fashion illustration

Learning objectives:

- To introduce mood to an illustration
- To explore and select appropriate materials
- To apply the collage technique to record and respond to visual information

Fashion illustration is an important part of a fashion designer's creative process. It is a way of communicating to an audience a fashion designer's vision and is also seen as an art form in its own right. A successful illustrator can capture the spirit of a designer's collection with only a few brush strokes. In the past, illustrations were either drawn or painted by hand. Today, fashion illustrators also use techniques such as collage, as well as digital software, to expand on their artistic vision. Here we compare two very different illustrations in terms of both style and technique.

CONTRASTING APPROACHES

In Figure 1.107, the Russian textile illustrator Nina Shirokova (born 1934) uses traditional painterly qualities in her work, using media such as fine felt-tipped pens, watercolour, oil bars and gouache. In this example, she explores negative space by leaving parts of the human figure out of the illustration, leaving the rest to our imagination. She makes little suggestion of how the garment is made or what it is made out of. The image is all about capturing the spirit of the garment and of the person wearing it.

The example in Figure 1.108, by the fashion illustrator Léon Benigni (1892–1948), shows a different approach. We can begin to see how the garment is constructed, as there is plenty of detail and a fabric example. Can you describe the mood or the style of this example compared with Figure 1.107?

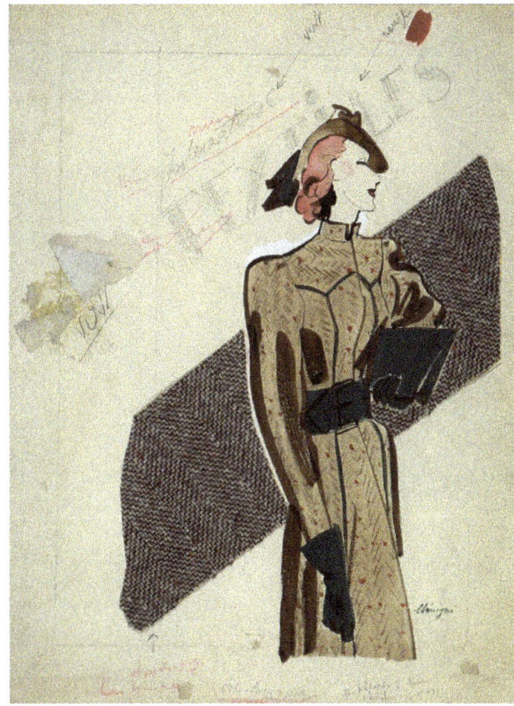

1.108 Léon Benigni, design for a winter coat, undated, gouache with fabric sample.

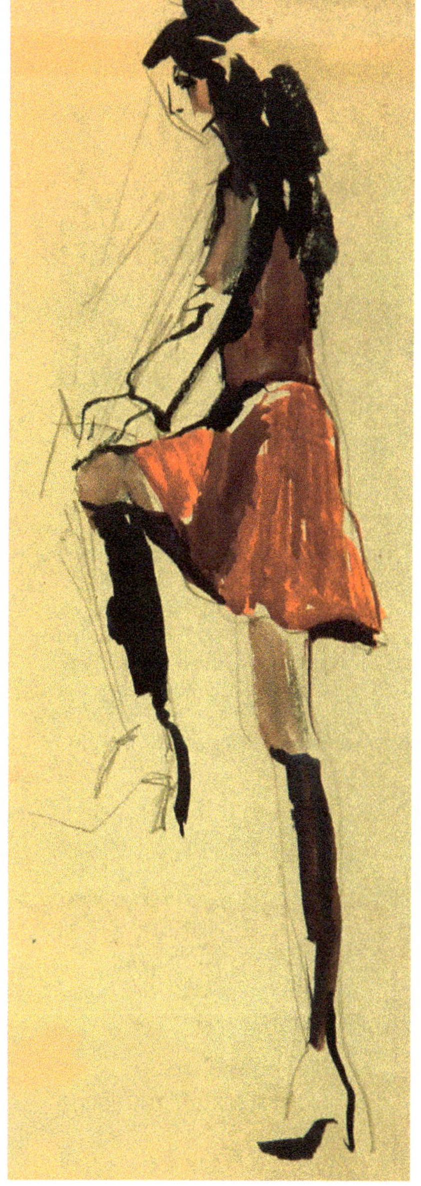

1.107 Nina Shirokova, *Fashion design*, 1970, watercolour on paper.

Tip:

Use your camera and/or a sketchbook to record people wearing different types of clothing. Try to capture what happens to the fabric as they move or the different types of silhouettes that clothes create. See whether you can get permission to attend a dance class and capture the movement of the dancers in their clothes.

Activity A: **Illustrate a choice of fabrics from your wardrobe**

1. Choose three or four items of clothing from your wardrobe. Make sure that they are made of different fabrics and show a variety of patterns and textures – for example, smooth surfaces such as **spandex**, or soft surfaces such as **faux fur**.
2. Arrange them on a table and create an image that recreates the fabrics in two dimensions.
3. Choose a range of media that you think best represents the fabrics. For example, you could use pencil or pen and ink for fine detail or experiment with mixing media. For faux fur, you could use charcoal overlaid with pastel, highlighted with white acrylic.

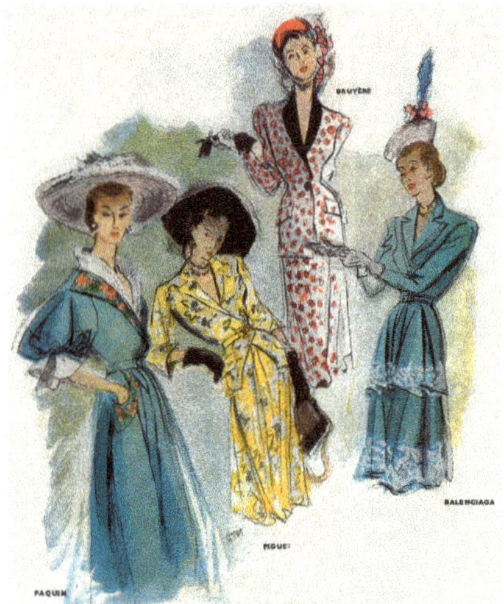

1.109 Pierre Pages, dresses by (left to right) Jeanne Paquin, Robert Piguet, Marie-Louise Bruyère and Cristóbal Balenciaga, Modes et travaux (July/August 1947). The illustration shows the silhouette that was fashionable at the time – slender, nipped-waisted and sharply tailored. It was soon to be swept away by Christian Dior's 'New Look', with its fuller, softer silhouette.

SILHOUETTE, MOVEMENT, MOOD

The **silhouette** is a key concept in fashion, and the fashion illustrator will often seek to convey this aspect in their work. Figure 1.109 shows the French artist and fashion illustrator Pierre Pages's impressions of the 1947 season's narrow, nipped-waist silhouette for a French magazine.

Clothes, however, are not just about cut and silhouette, pattern and texture, but also about how they work with the body in movement. Fashion illustrators, too, may also try to create a sense of movement in their work, recreating the flow of textiles through space and across the body (see Figure 1.110).

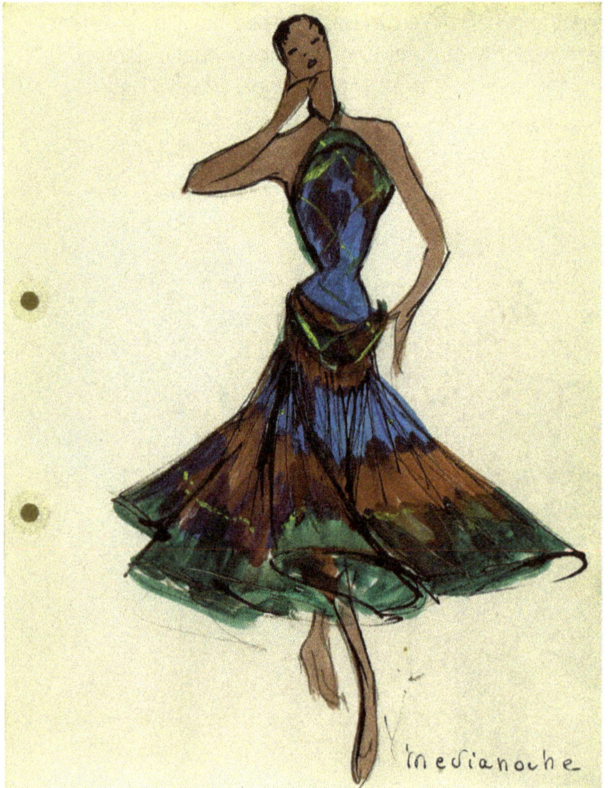

1.110 Crayon, ink and gouache on paper, fashion drawing for the Carven couture house summer collection, 1951, Musée de la Mode de la Ville de Paris.

Critical thinking:

Evaluate your work on **Activity A:**

- Did you find enough information to begin your costume design?
- Did you create a **cohesive** (unified) design?

Activity B: **Define a mood/pose**

1. Ask a classmate to dress in clothes that they think define their personality.
2. Ask them to strike a pose that also conveys their character: for example, if they are full of energy and outward-going, they may exaggerate their body, making bold shapes with their arms and legs. Ask them to try out different poses.
3. Make a series of sketches, working quickly and spending a maximum of two minutes on each sketch. This will help your images retain their freshness.
4. When you are confident, introduce colour using watered-down gouache paint.
5. Again, work quickly, filling in the areas with blocks of colour. Do not worry if the paint drips, as this will add to the mood of the illustration.

Tip:

Remember: nothing is wrong at this stage – you are exploring new techniques, so try to be confident, have fun and enjoy the process!

Activity C: **Create fashion illustrations using collage**

The aim in this activity is to create a collage from magazine cuttings (see Figure 1.111) that will form the outline of a human figure wearing garments. You will work from a life model – ask a fellow student or friend – so you can appreciate the 3D shapes and angle of the human body.

Start by selecting pages from magazines showing clothes with interesting surface patterns and textures. Now, ask your life model to make four poses (for example, two front views, a side and back) and create a collage to represent each one. Give yourself only three minutes for each pose – you will have to select, cut or tear, and paste very quickly.

Follow the contours of the figure and respond using similar paper shapes. For example, if the pose is very curvy, then highlight using long strips of wavy or linear pieces of paper. Aim to be creative and emphasise parts of the figure using bold colours or large-scale paper cut-outs.

Although challenging, this process will encourage you to work spontaneously and the results will be pleasingly unpredictable.

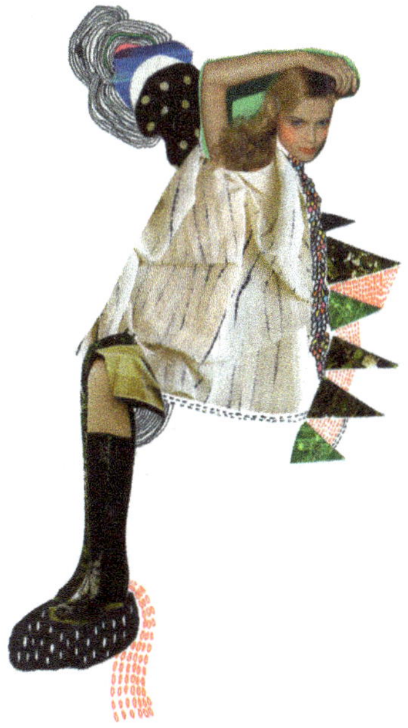

1.111 Example of a fashion illustration created using collage. Jackie Thomson, collage, mixed media.

Critical thinking:

When you have completed all four collages in **Activity C,** reflect on your results:

- Have you have used material from magazines in an inventive and unexpected way? In terms of composition, have you filled the page to make a bold statement?
- Does the result reflect the speed of working?
- Consider the mood you have created and how this was achieved.

Record your critical analysis next to your collages.

cohesive Consisting of parts that fit together well and form a united whole.
faux fur Synthetic fur-like material.
silhouette (in fashion) The outline or the shape of a body when clothed.
spandex Stretchy fabric often used in sports clothing.

Further research

Fashion Drawing: Illustration Techniques for Fashion Designers by Michele Wesen Bryant (Laurence King Publishing, 2016) provides an excellent introduction to this discipline.

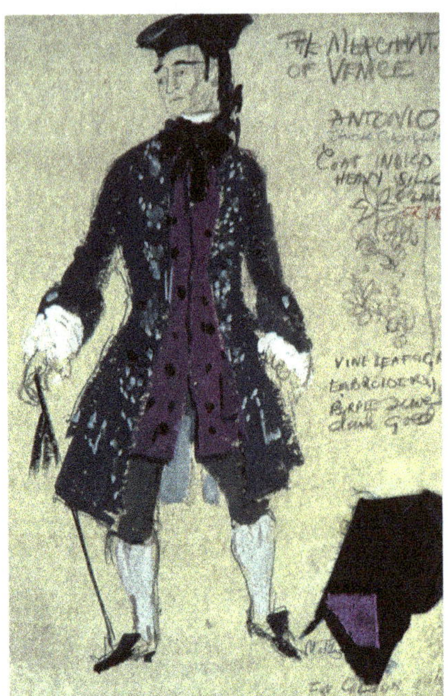

1.112 Working drawing for a character in an adaptation of William Shakespeare's play *The Merchant of Venice*.

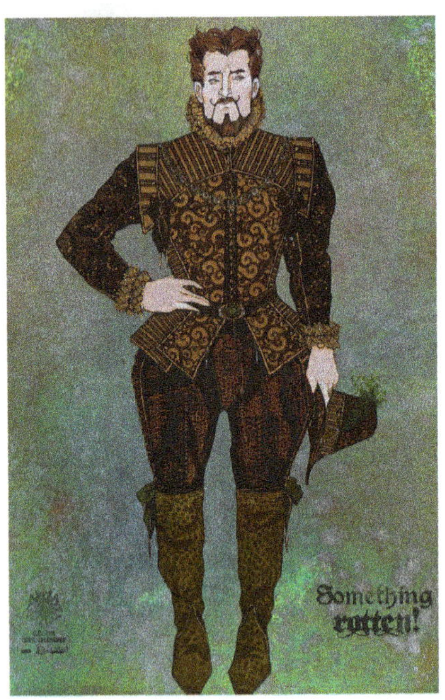

1.113 Gregg Barnes, costume designs for the musical *Something Rotten!*

Costume design

Learning objectives:

- To understand how costume designs explore sources for visual ideas
- To use second-hand imagery to refine intentions

The costume designer is responsible for visually bringing an actor's character to life. The designer will need to take into consideration the character's age, gender, profession and social class, the historical and cultural period to which they belong, and even the time of day and weather conditions. The costume designer has to be a historian, researcher and craftsperson. Like a fashion or textile designer, they will find inspiration from a diverse range of resources, including art, design, film, travel, architecture, photography, music, dance and literature.

A TEAM PROJECT

Costume designers will study a script and attend rehearsals to learn more about the story, setting and characters. They will also share ideas with the rest of the production team, such as the director, make-up artist, and set and lighting designers. This will help with the overall look of the character. Once the characters are fully realised, preliminary sketches and then **working drawings** are made, showing the style, silhouette, textures, accessories and unique features of each costume.

The example in Figure 1.112 displays a costume designer's vision for a character in a play. The page includes notes for detail and fabric swatches.

Figure 1.113 shows a fully rendered illustration by costume designer Gregg Barnes. The design is very detailed and shows everything that the **wardrobe master/mistress** needs to make up the costume for the production. Can you work out what medium and mark-making techniques Gregg Barnes has used to highlight the surfaces on the garments?

Materials and techniques: **Being practical**

A costume designer must consider different practicalities from a fashion designer to produce an effective design. For example, a costume for a dancer must provide comfort and flexibility as well as be hard-wearing. A costume for an actor on stage has to be seen from a distance and needs to be distinctive, so that the audience can easily tell the characters apart.

PAST INTO PRESENT

For a historical film production, it is important for the designers to be as true as possible to the period the story is set in – especially when there are lots of close-up camera shots. They visit galleries, historical fashion museums or study **fashion plates** for fabric and **embellishment** detail. The 18th-century costume in Figure 1.114 is a good example of second-hand research for a costume design – a silk court dress created by the Italian designer Milena Canonero (born 1946) for the film *Marie Antoinette*.

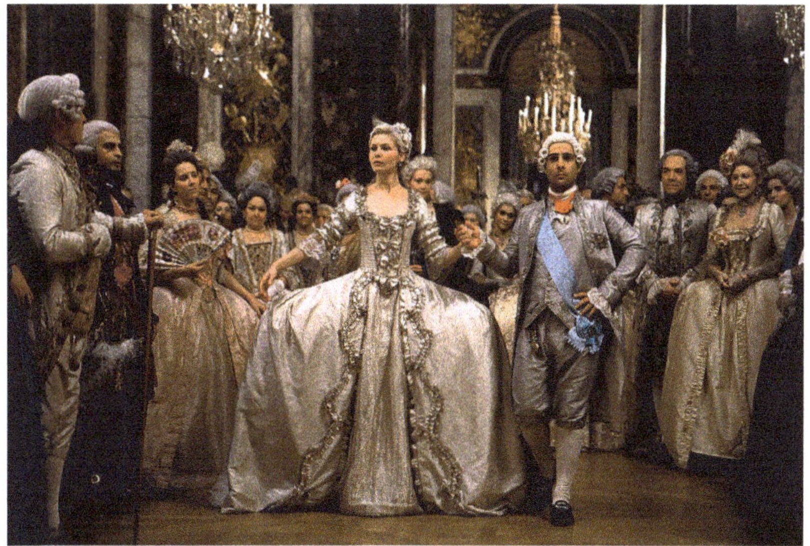

1.114 Milena Canonero, one of the queen's costumes in the film *Marie Antoinette*, 2006 (dir. Sofia Coppola).

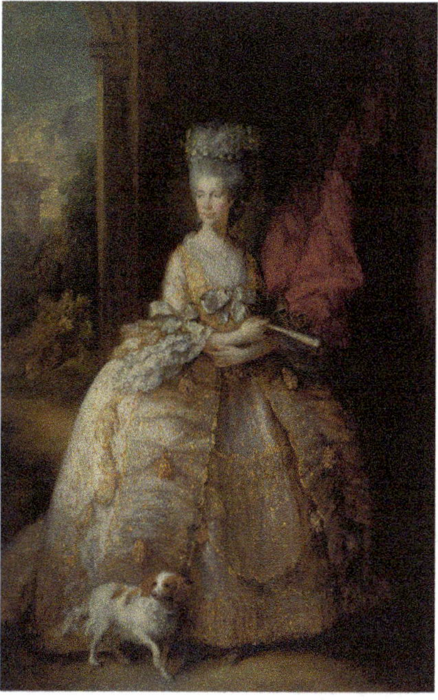

1.115 Thomas Gainsborough, *Queen Charlotte*, oil on canvas, 1781, Royal Collection Trust.

Activity A: **Create a unique costume**

The aim of this activity is to create a unique costume that is a mixture of historical and cultural inspirations.

1. Collect images of people wearing clothing from around 1700 to the present day. The images you choose do not have to be fashionable.
2. Make an A5 flip-book of 20 plain pages. You may have to scale your image up or down to fit the pages. Paste in your images and cut the pages into three equal-sized sections.
3. Experiment with the images and select what you think makes a pleasingly balanced garment. Use this as the inspiration to make some **preliminary drawings**. You will have to use your imagination and reinterpret your drawings many times until you are satisfied with the outcome.
4. Refine your ideas by making separate working drawings introducing colour.

Further research

Explore costume design using the Victoria and Albert Museum website. Better still, if you can, visit London's Victoria and Albert Museum to view its rich collection of costume designs. Many other design museums around the world have costume design collections.

embellishment (in fashion) A decorative detail added to an item of clothing to make it more beautiful – for example, a ribbon, button or trim.

fashion plate An illustration of a new fashion in a magazine.

preliminary drawing Rough unfinished drawing to show initial ideas; used to describe an artwork carried out in preparation for a final artwork – for example, a sketch.

wardrobe master/mistress In the theatre, the person charged with supervising the making of clothes for a production and then maintaining the costumes during the run.

working drawings Detailed drawings of design work highlighting the construction components of the garment, including seams, pockets, fastenings and topstitching.

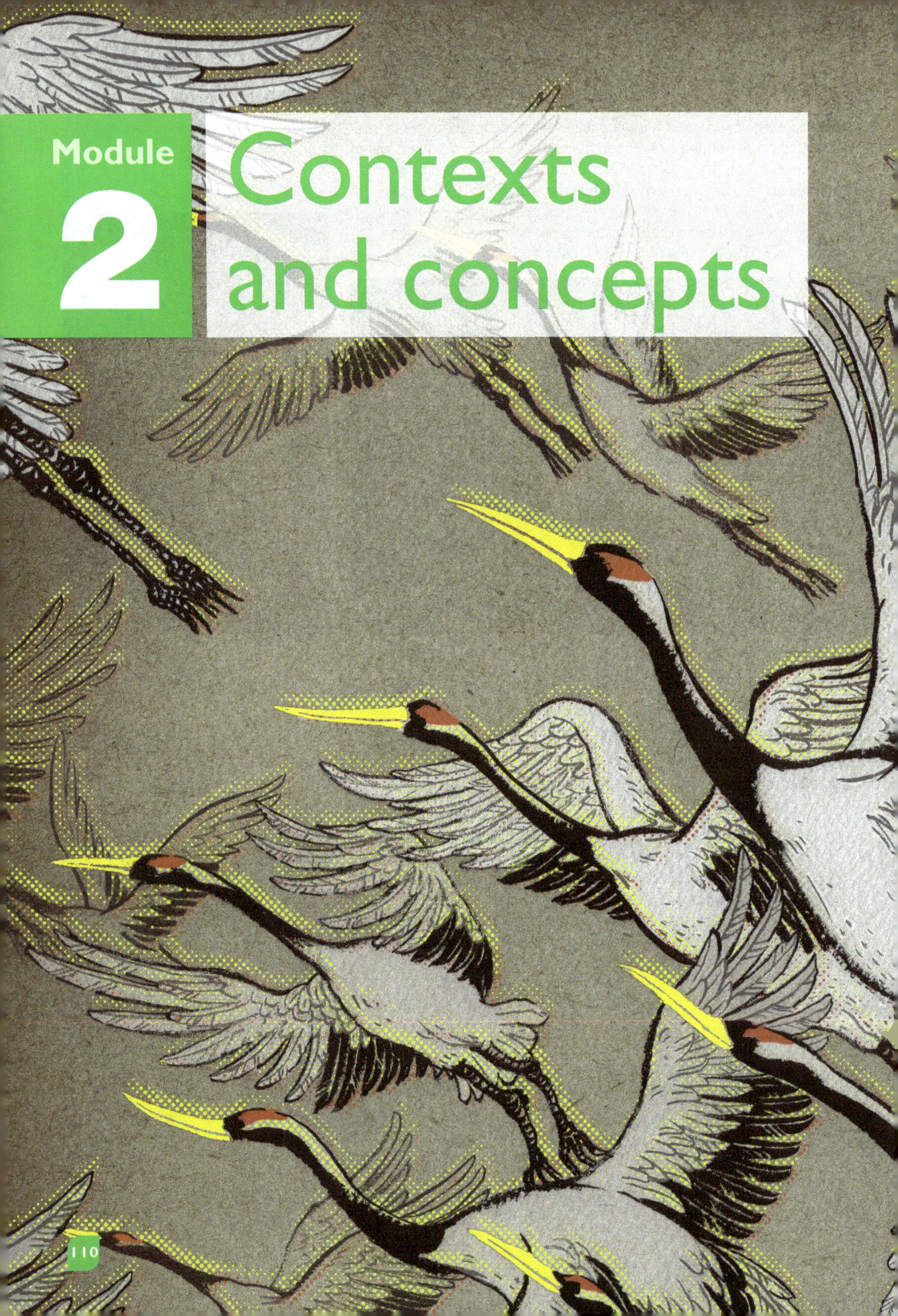

Module 2 Contexts and concepts

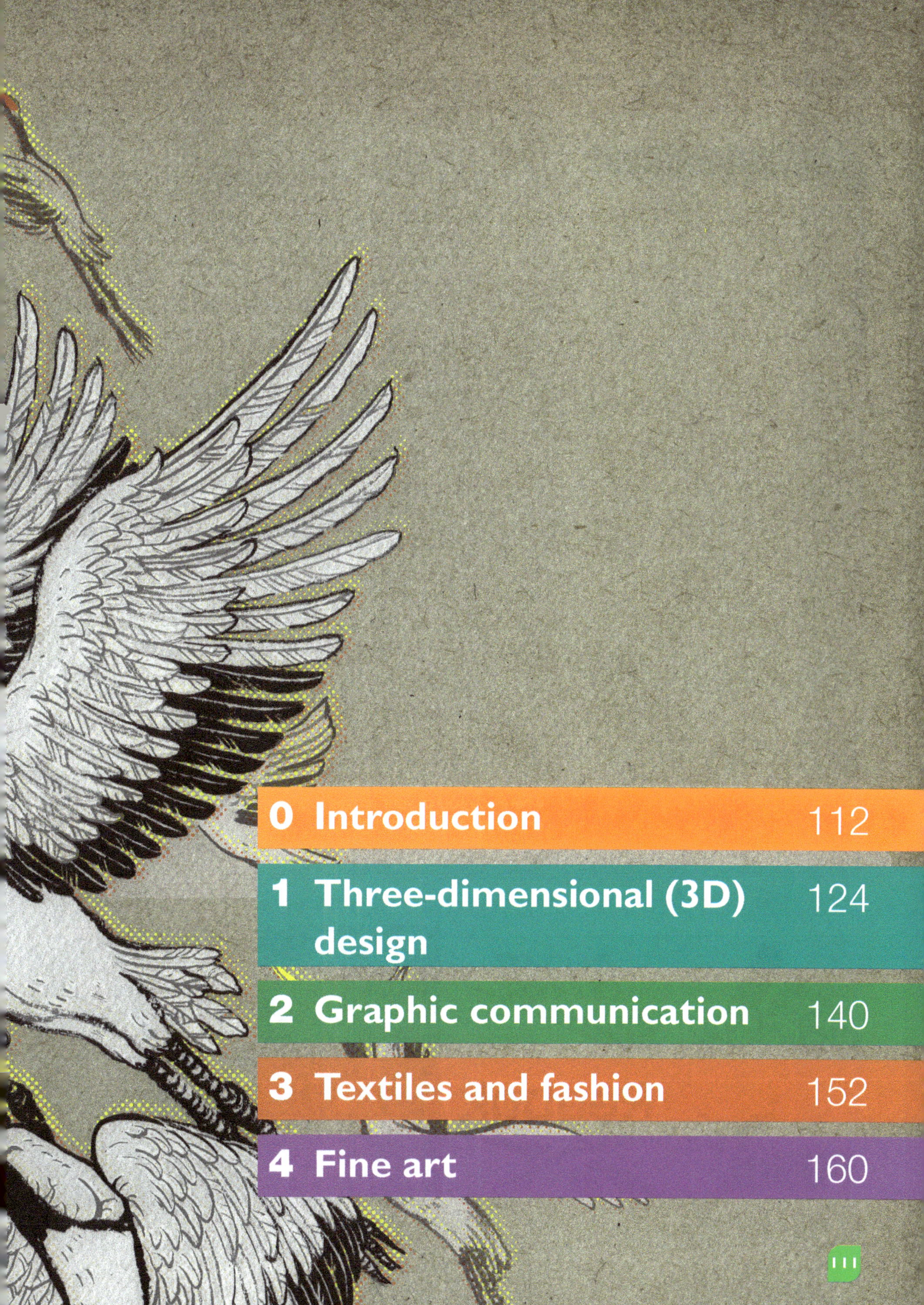

2.0 Introduction

> Tip:
>
> For this course, it is important that you make clear links between the work that you look at by other artists and designers and your own work, explaining what you have learned by doing so and what has influenced you.

This module introduces you to carrying out in-depth research into other artists and designers, ideas and cultural influences to inform the development of your work. It is about getting ideas or concepts for work and exploring the context in which ideas are developed.

Art and design are not created in a vacuum: artists, craftspeople and designers do not work in isolation. They are influenced, whether directly or subconsciously, by images and objects that they see around them.

Living in the 21st century, we are surrounded by images, brought to us through television, films and video games, printed in magazines, books and newspapers, billboard advertising and street signage, and, of course, on the internet. We can see a rich selection of art and design from around the globe at the press of a button and can make virtual visits to the world's greatest museums and galleries. What we see shapes how we think and respond visually.

CULTURAL CONTEXTS

During your course you are expected to look at a wide range of work by different artists, craftspeople and designers from different cultures and periods in time. This will inform you about different styles and ways of working, and give you ideas about how to approach your own work. Begin by reflecting on an aspect of culture that influences you.

Activity A: **Reflect on your personal culture**

1. Look at Figures 2.1 and 2.2. The sports logos and the photograph of teenagers breakdancing in the street are images that can be linked to youth culture. What do you learn about that culture from looking at the images? How do the logos relate to the breakdancers?
2. Select a maximum of *three* images that relate to a culture. Make a note of where you source your images. Your images could relate to music, sport, or perhaps to personal beliefs.
3. Now reflect on why you chose these images and briefly note how they convey your cultural identity.

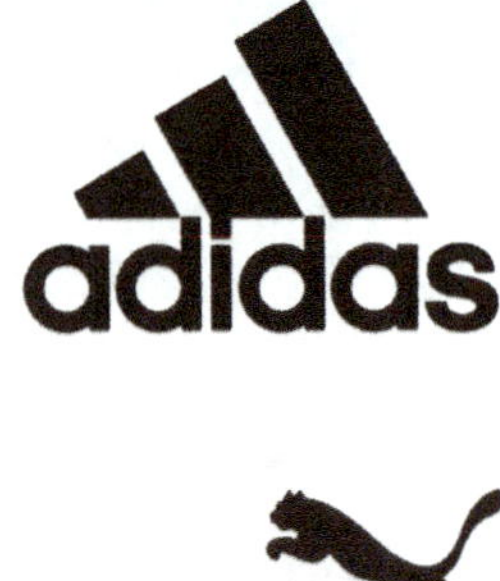

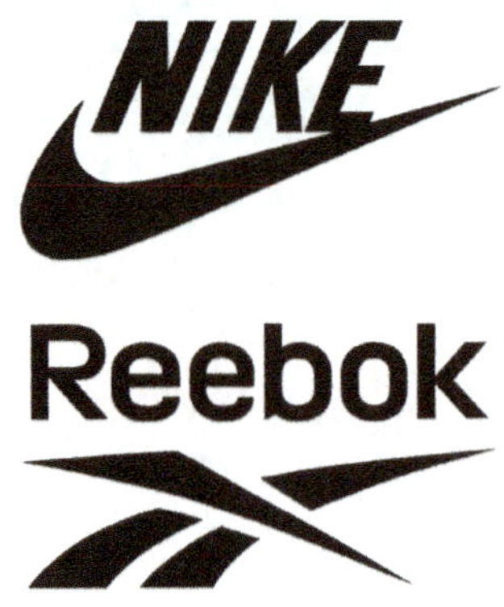

2.1 Sportswear logos.

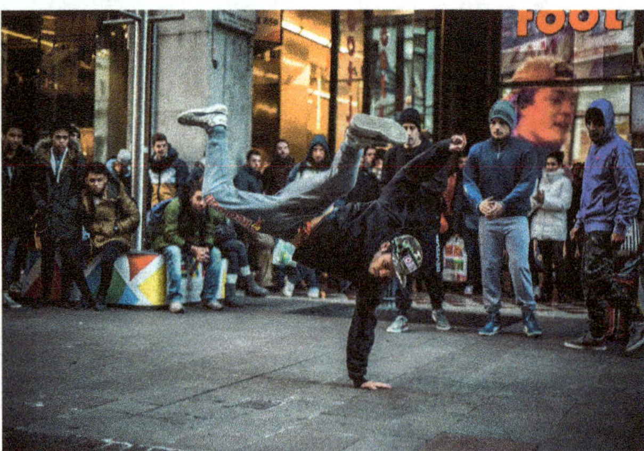

2.2 Breakdancers in Milan, Italy.

CULTURAL CONTEXTS: ARTIST TO ARTIST

Artists, craftspeople and designers take inspiration from other artists, craftspeople and designers around them. A traditional way of training to be an artist over the centuries has involved copying the work of other artists to learn how marks have been made, and colours mixed and applied. Japanese potters, for instance, traditionally learned their craft during very long apprenticeships under a master.

Artists and designers often work as part of a group or movement, alongside other artists and designers who work in similar ways or have a similar ideology. They look at the work of other earlier artists and designers, or they respond to social and cultural stimuli and incorporate what they see and learn in what they create, to develop their own concept.

It is important to recognise that artists, designers and craftspeople are influenced by work across all disciplines. An artist can have a profound influence on a designer and vice versa. For example, the French fashion designer Yves Saint-Laurent (1936–2008) looked to the distinctive abstract painting of Dutch painter Piet Mondrian (1872–1944) to inspire a collection of dresses from 1980.

Groups of artists, designers and craftspeople can be quite close-knit, as, for example, were the French Impressionist painters, who often exhibited together during the 1870s and early 1880s. Some movements can be much looser and almost global in reach, such as Surrealism.

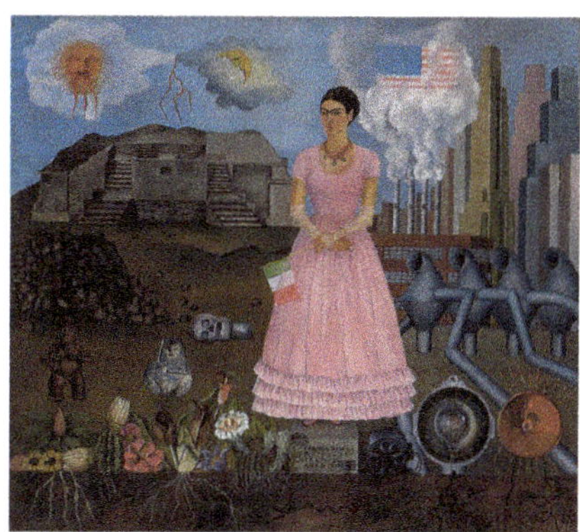

2.3 Frida Kahlo, *Self-Portrait on the Borderline between Mexico and the United States*, 1932, oil on metal, private collection.

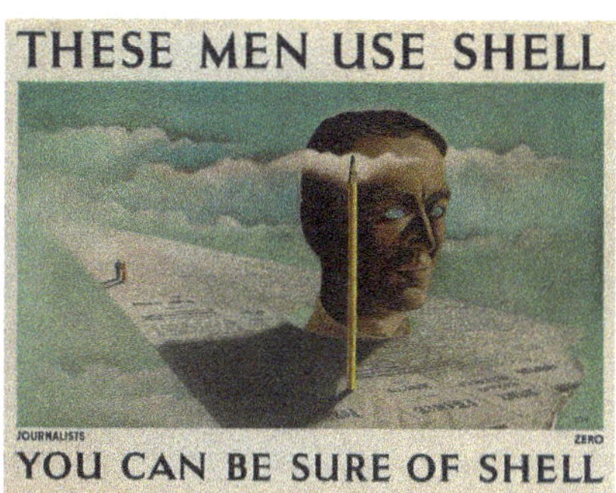

2.4 Hans Schleger, *These Men Use Shell*, advertising poster, colour lithograph, 1938, private collection. The German-born artist Hans Schleger (1898–1976), known as 'Zero', often used Surrealist imagery in his work.

Case study: Surrealism

The Surrealist movement took many of its ideas from the political ideology of Karl Marx (1818–83) and the psychoanalysis of Sigmund Freud (1856–1939), and is one of the most influential art movements of the 20th century. Many Surrealist artists used **automatic drawing** or writing to unlock ideas and images from their **unconscious minds**. They also sought to depict the worlds of dreams and the imagination. As well as being a fine art movement, Surrealism transformed theatre, film, design, fashion and advertising. Many Surrealist artists also worked as designers.

As a movement, Surrealism had a great impact on the cultural life of many countries and quickly became an international movement for artists, photographers, filmmakers, designers and writers. For example:

- The Spanish artist Salvador Dalí (1904–89) was not only one of the key figures in the Surrealist movement, but had a broad impact on film, fashion, design and advertising.
- The Mexican artist Frida Kahlo (1907–54) used a blend of Surrealism and folk art to explore her own identity as a woman caught between different worlds (see Figure 2.3).
- The Japanese artist Iwata Nakayama (1895–1949) met many of the Surrealist artists while travelling in Europe and the USA, returning home to develop his own kind of Surrealist photography, including photomontages.

Surrealism had a wide-ranging impact on graphic design and advertising. One of the key techniques used by the Surrealists was to place objects in unusual contexts. By adopting this technique, advertisers could make potential customers look at a product with fresh eyes (see the **Shell** advertising poster, Figure 2.4).

There is more on Surrealism on page 167.

automatic drawing A drawing made without the drawer thinking about it. Another word for this is 'doodle'.
Shell A British–Dutch oil and gas company.
unconscious mind According to Sigmund Freud, the part of the human mind (psyche) that is full of the anxieties and desires that are repressed (buried) in daily life.

CULTURAL CONTEXTS: CULTURE TO CULTURE

Since early times, cultures have influenced and shaped one another. Sometimes this has been through trade, as countries have exchanged goods (including artworks); at other times, it has been through conquest, as the culture of a stronger country shapes that of a weaker one. In today's globalised world, the internet and other means of mass communication are creating a complex web of **mutual** influences and **cross-fertilisation**. Whether this mass of influences will erode local cultures or create new **hybrid** cultures is a matter of ongoing debate.

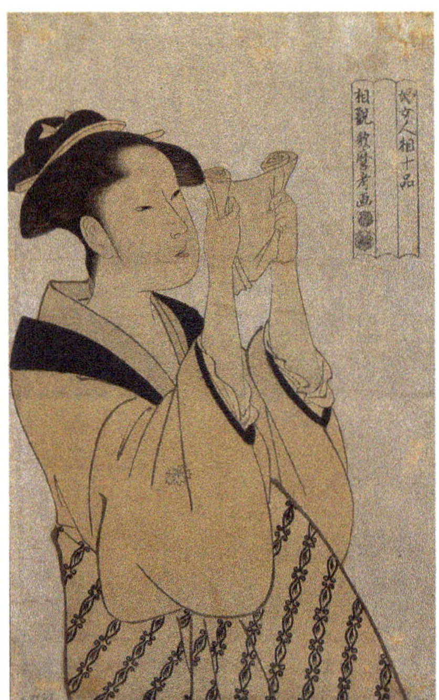

2.5 Kitagawa Utamaro, *Woman Reading a Letter*, late 18th century, woodblock print. Museo de Bellas Artes de Bilbao, Spain.

Case study A: Japan and Europe

The term 'Japonism' is applied to the influence of Japanese art and culture on Western culture towards the end of the 19th century. At this time, the relationship between Japan and the West was an unequal one: countries such as the USA, UK and France imposed their economic and political power on Japan. Japonism flourished after 1853, when the USA forced open the trade routes between the West and Japan. Imports of Japanese goods from ceramics to woodblock prints affected almost every area of the arts: performing arts and set design, decorative arts, ceramics, architecture and fashion, as well as fine arts. Japanese approaches to, for example, perspective, use of colour and pattern, and the natural world helped shape new art movements, such as Impressionism, **Post-Impressionism** and Art Nouveau.

Many of the Impressionist artists took some of their inspiration from Japanese woodblock prints. The prints introduced artists to new ideas about composition. Figures 2.5 and 2.6 show the influence of the Japanese print on the work of an American Impressionist living in Paris, Mary Cassatt (1844–1926).

The cultural exchange between Japan and Europe was two-way. After many years of isolation, during the Meiji Restoration period from 1868, Japanese artists began to study themes and techniques from Western art, culture and technology , including French Impressionist and Post-Impressionist painting and Art Nouveau art objects. Often, they were responding to work that showed the influence of Japanese culture (Figure 2.7)!

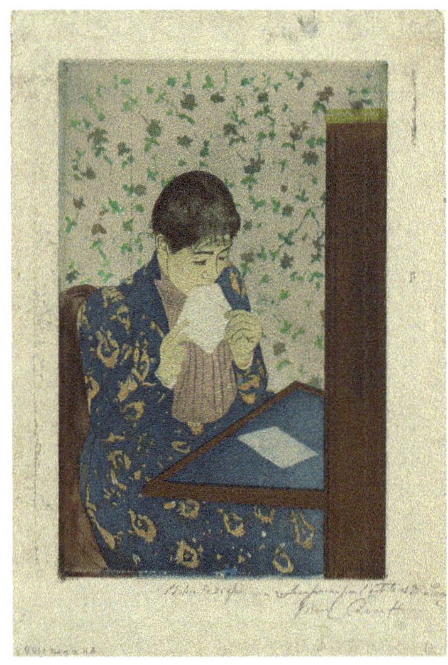

2.6 Mary Cassatt, *The Letter*, 1890–91, drypoint, softground etching and aquatint on laid paper, National Gallery of Art, Washington, DC. Cassatt admired Japanese woodblock prints for their use of flat planes, strong outlines, asymmetrical compositions and decorative character.

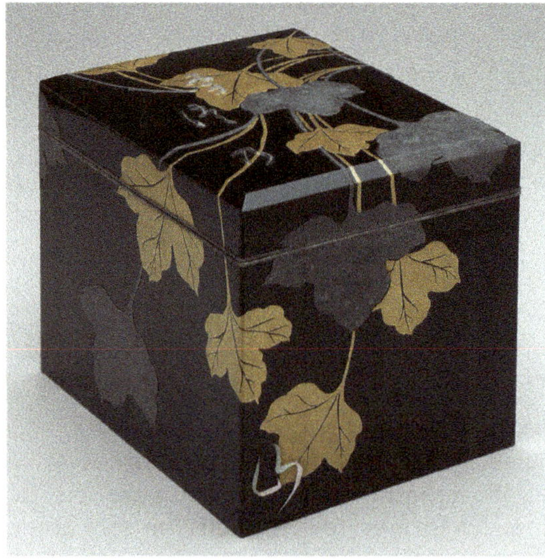

2.7 Kamisaka Sekka, Box, c.1925, wood covered in black lacquer with gold, shell, and lead decoration, Museum of Fine Arts, Boston. After a trip to Glasgow, Scotland, in 1901, Kamisaka Sekka (1866–1942) became heavily influenced by Art Nouveau. Art Nouveau was itself in part inspired by Japanese approaches to design.

Case study B: The influence of African art on European modern art

In the early 20th century, African artworks were brought to museums in Paris as the French empire expanded into Africa (Figure 2.8). Artists living and working in France, such as Henri Matisse (1869–1954) and Pablo Picasso (1881–1973), were introduced to African art through masks and carvings.

In May or June 1907, Picasso experienced a revelation while viewing African art. This experience revolutionised the style of his painting, as shown in *Les Demoiselles d'Avignon*; The Young Ladies of **Avignon** (you can search for this painting online). Picasso began the painting in May 1907 before seeing the African artworks and reworked it in July, *after* he had seen them. We can see two completely different styles at work.

Tip:

Remember that, as your art or design work progresses, you should demonstrate analysis and understanding of ideas by making connections between different images and between your ideas and the work of other artists and designers.

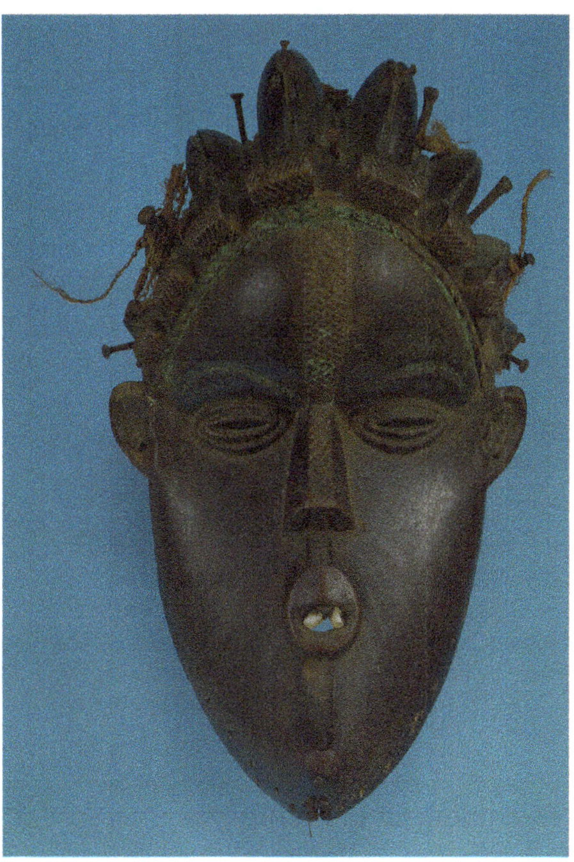

2.8 Unknown artist of the **Bassa** people, *Mask*, carved wood, Josef Herman Collection, London.

Activity B: **Analyse the influence of African art on Pablo Picasso**

African art continued to influence Picasso and his approach to representing the human form.

1. Research the following paintings either in books or online: *Head of a Man*, 1907, located in the Barnes Foundation, Philadelphia, and *Head of a Sleeping Woman*, 1907, located in the Museum of Modern Art, New York.
2. Read the section on how to analyse artworks (pages 118–123) and look carefully at the formal qualities of these paintings. Make notes about the influence of African carved masks on Picasso's painting and then discuss this with your fellow students.

Avignon City in south-east France.
Bassa A people of coastal West Africa.
cross-fertilisation Where two or more cultures enrich one another with new ideas.
hybrid Blended.
mutual Two-way.
Post-Impressionism Various styles of painting that took the experiments of the Impressionists further often using bold colours, clear outlines and flat, decorative compositions. Key Post-Impressionist painters include Henri de Toulouse-Lautrec, Paul Gauguin, Édouard Vuillard and Pierre Bonnard.

> Tip:
>
> Keep yourself informed about contemporary affairs. News events and issues can provide subject matter for future art projects.

SOCIAL AND POLITICAL CONTEXTS

Artists and designers respond to the societies they live in, as well as to key events and issues that have an impact on their society. Such events and issues may shape artists' work loosely, or artists may want to convey a specific message or criticism. For example, in Jan Asselijn's *The Threatened Swan* (c.1650), a swan fiercely defends its nest against a dog. In later centuries this scuffle was interpreted as a political allegory: the white swan was thought to symbolise the Dutch statesman Johan de Witt (assassinated in 1672) protecting the country from its enemies (Figure 2.9).

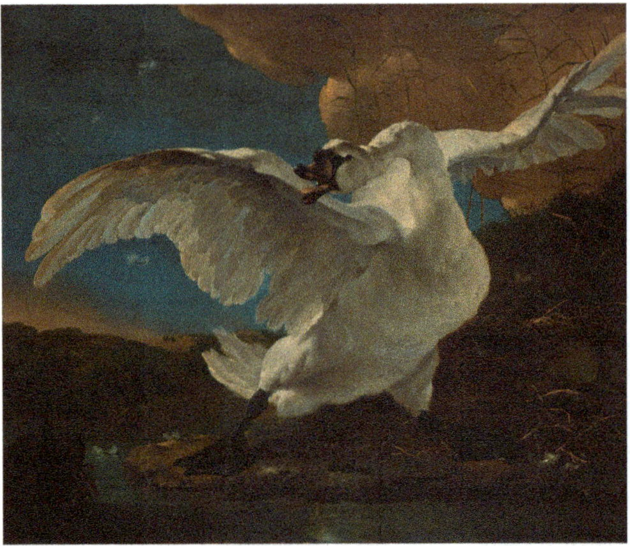

2.9 Jan Asselijn, *The Threatened Swan*, c.1650, oil on canvas, Rijksmuseum, Amsterdam.

While many artists and designers have used their work as a kind of political protest, others have used their skills to create propaganda for the state. For example, after the Russian Revolution of 1917, a civil war broke out between the 'Reds' (communists) and 'Whites' (anti-communists). The Russian Communist Party responded by commissioning designers to create propaganda posters as a way of delivering its messages to ordinary people (Figure 2.10).

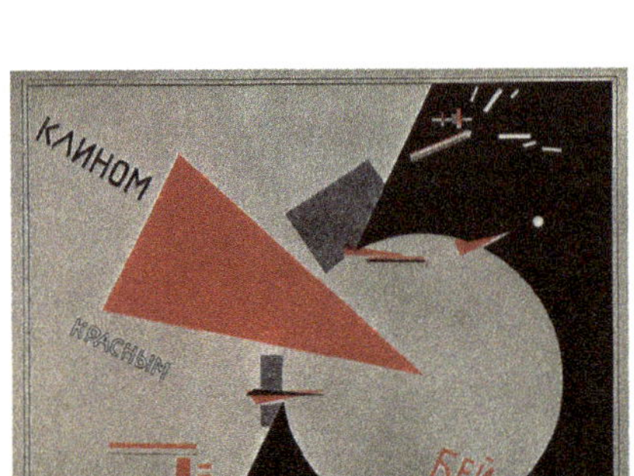

2.10 El Lissitzky, *Beat the Whites with the Red Wedge*, 1920, poster, private collection. El Lissitzky's (1890–1941) bold geometric design calls upon ordinary people to fight back against the anti-revolutionary forces. Why do you think this poster was so successful?

Activity C: **Responding to contemporary affairs**

Think about a social or political issue or concern that interests you – it can be local, national or global. Produce ideas for a piece of art or design that responds to the issue in a personal way.

TECHNOLOGY AND ART AND DESIGN

Artists and designers have always used technical innovations to help them to develop their work. For example, in the 16th century some painters in Europe used the **camera obscura** to capture greater detail and a sense of realism within their work, by projecting images onto their supports (Figure 2.11). In the 19th century, the invention of photography enabled artists to see in ways they had not been able to see before (see page 55). The relationship between technology and art and design has continued, and even intensified, in the contemporary world.

DIGITAL DRAWING AND IMAGE MANIPULATION

The following section is supplementary. Look at the Cambridge International AS & A Level Digital Media & Design syllabus 9481 if you are interested in learning more about digital drawing and image manipulation.

Case study A: Digital drawing and painting apps

In the first decades of the 21st century, the development of iPads and other tablet computers has enabled artists to have access to a kind of portable studio. The tools within the drawing and painting apps reproduce the mark-making range of traditional art materials, and the size of tablets means that they are as easy to carry around as a sketchbook. The British artist David Hockney (born 1937) is famous for using digital apps to create drawings and paintings made from direct observation. You can find out more about his work from his website.

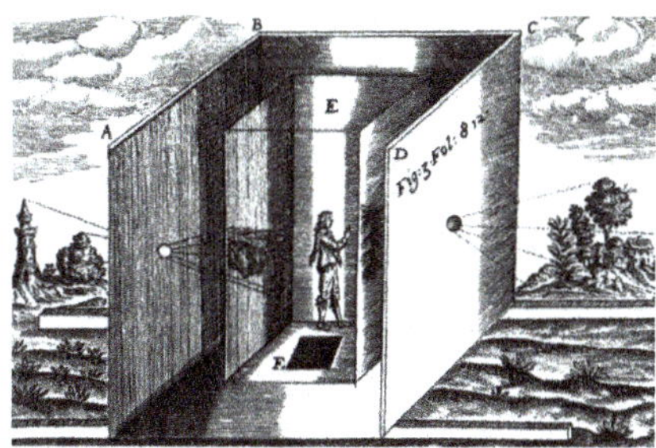

2.11 A Dutch illustration of an artist using a camera obscura to paint a landscape, 1671.

Case study B: Image manipulation software

In 1989, the introduction of image manipulation software, in the form of Adobe Photoshop, revolutionised digital technology in relation to art and design. Photoshop was originally designed as a tool to enable photographers to enhance and change digital photographs. However, graphic designers also began to use it combined with text editing, page layout and illustration software.

As software has developed, it has provided artists and designers with new opportunities to import hand-drawn images and combine them with digital techniques. The range of tools and effects that can be created has increased, as has the range of typefaces that graphic designers can select from.

Materials and techniques: **Digital images**

There are two types of digital images.

1. *Raster* images, or bitmaps, are made of **pixels**, and each pixel is a colour or a tone. If you have a low-resolution version of an image, it will be possible to see the pixels when you zoom in and enlarge the image. It will become pixilated.
2. *Vector* images are created by mathematical formulae that describe lines and shapes and do not lose quality even when they are enlarged. Vector images are widely used by graphic designers because they assure higher-quality outcomes, especially when crisp, clear text is required.

It is worth remembering that some digital art and design work is designed to be viewed on screen, while some is to be viewed printed out. While the software enables artists and designers to produce high-quality imagery, the quality of printouts also depends on the quality of the printer.

Critical thinking:

When you look at an artwork, think about what has influenced or inspired the artist to work in the way that they have. Can other people see what has influenced or inspired you when they look at your work? Make sure that you explain your inspiration and influences through your annotations as your work progresses.

camera obscura A darkened box with an aperture or lens that projects the image of an external object onto a screen inside the box.
pixel The smallest area on a computer screen that can be given a separate colour by the computer.

ANALYSING ARTWORKS

The main component of the written section of the Personal Investigation is an in-depth analysis of selected artwork. Some of this analysis must be based on first-hand research. How to undertake first-hand research is covered in the Module 1 Personal Investigation (pages 48–51). Here we explore ways in which you can analyse works of art and design and provide you with key vocabulary with which to analyse work. You will also need to refer to 'Getting started' (pages 10–25), which includes a very comprehensive framework for analysis that can be applied to any form of art, craft or design work. Read this section carefully and identify the prompts most relevant to the works that you have chosen.

Remember: the four key areas that you must discuss in your investigation of artworks are:

- Description (Content)
- Analysis (Form)
- Interpretation (Meaning)
- Judgement (Merit).

Before you start to write or draw anything, spend time looking at the work that you are going to analyse:

- Look at it from a distance and then look close up and in detail.
- If the work is three-dimensional, look at it from different angles.
- If it is something that you can handle or touch, then do so to experience it fully.

To analyse something means to examine it closely, and to look and touch are the most important ways of doing that.

When you analyse a piece of art or design work, check whether it is the final piece or a study or prototype for a final piece. If it is the final piece of work, find out what stages led up to the work being completed. If you are looking at work in a gallery or museum, there may be preliminary drawings and sketchbooks by the artist. If you are interviewing a practitioner, ask them about the stages of their creative process and how they shape their ideas and execute the final piece.

When analysing any work of art, craft or design, you need to do so in terms of three main aspects:

- You need to refer to and use the language of the formal elements – line, tone, colour, shape, space, form, texture and pattern. The formal elements comprise the aesthetic qualities of the work.
- You must also analyse the technical qualities of the work – how it has been created: the media, materials, processes and techniques used.
- You must refer to the context of the work – the stylistic, social, historic and cultural influences.

The balance of these aspects of analysis may depend on what the intention is within your investigation, but they must all be addressed, as they are all interlinked. Technical qualities will inform the aesthetic qualities, and the context can inform both how it is made and what it looks like.

Tip:

Whatever the focus of your analysis, make sure that your observations are your own – based on what you already know and what you can see. Give personal opinions, but always say exactly why you like or don't like something. Back up your opinions with evidence.

COMPARING WORKS OF ART

If you are exploring a theme within art and design, you will have to compare the work of more than one artist or designer, or work by one artist from different points in their career. You should compare and contrast the work.

Activity A: **Compare and contrast**

1. Look carefully at Figures 2.12, 2.13 and 2.14. They can all be categorised under the theme of 'Landscape'.
2. Make a list of what is the same or similar and what is different between the images.
3. Organise your list in terms of aesthetic, technical and contextual similarities and differences.
4. Reflect on what you have written and discuss with your classmates. Be prepared to justify your opinions.

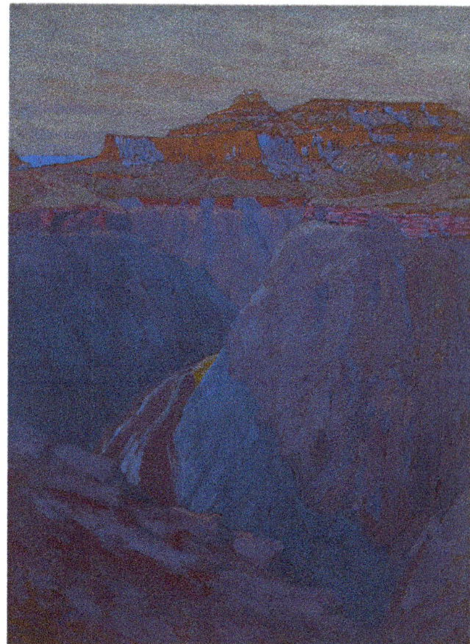

2.12 Arthur Wesley Dow, *The Destroyer*, c.1911–13, oil on canvas, Minneapolis Institute of Arts.

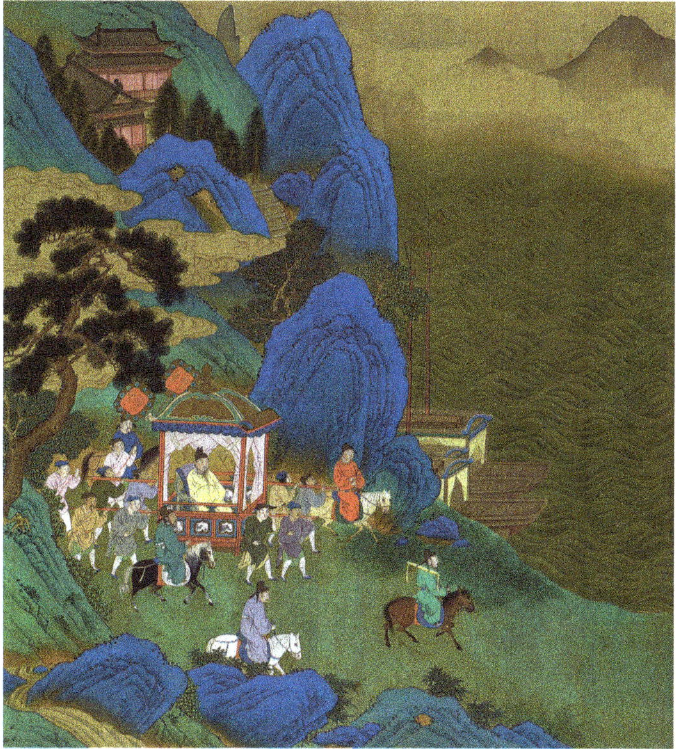

2.13 Unknown artist, *Emperor Ch'in Wang Ti travelling in a palanquin*, 17th century, colour on silk, Bibliothèque Nationale, Paris.

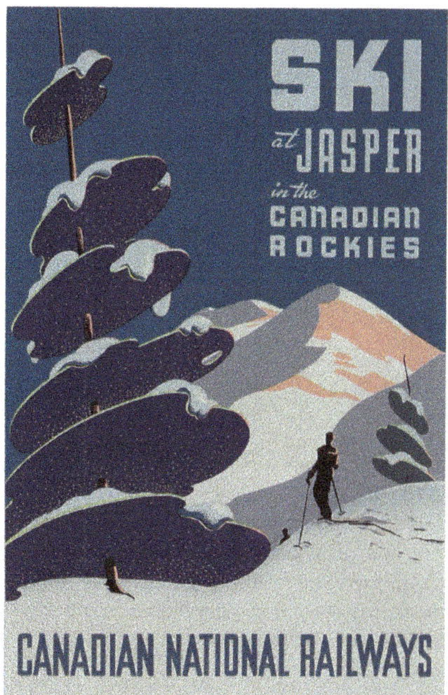

2.14 Unknown artist, *Ski at Jasper in the Canadian Rockies*, mid-20th century, colour lithographic poster, private collection.

Tip:

- Be clear about the focus of your analysis.
- Use appropriate aspects of the framework from the Introduction (pages 4–7) to help you to think and write about the key points.
- Make personal observations and judgements.

Tip:

If you are unsure about any of the meanings of the words listed, look them up in a good English language dictionary. We recommend *Collins COBUILD Advanced Learner's Dictionary* (Collins Cobuild, 2014) or that you use an online dictionary.

Activity B: **Describe a colour**

Look at Figure 2.15 and describe the quality of yellow that you can see in the painting.

2.15 Josef Albers, *Homage to the Square: Joy*, 1964, oil on board, private collection. The German-born American artist Josef Albers (1888–1976) painted abstract works of coloured squares in his 1960s series *Homage to the Square*. Albers was noted for his work about **colour theory.**

KEY VOCABULARY TO ANALYSE WORK

When writing your Personal Investigation, you are expected to use specialist vocabulary. This section will provide you with a bank of words to use when critically analysing pieces of art, craft and design work. It links to the formal elements and the basic components of art and design we looked at in 'Getting started' (pages 16–19).

Line

Lines can take many different forms and can be described in a variety of ways. When describing the use of line, you can refer to the 'quality' of line. They can be:

- straight, curved, wavy, diagonal, horizontal, parallel, contour
- controlled, freehand, ruled
- short, thick, thin, vertical, wide
- continuous, broken, dashed, solid, light, heavy, interrupted, meandering
- blurred, fuzzy, hatched.

Tone or value

Tone can refer to the value of colours as well as the overall tone of the piece of artwork:

- dark, light or mid (middle), multi-tonal
- graduated, contrasting
- flat, uniform, smooth, unvarying, varied
- constant, changing
- shade, tint.

Colour

A piece of art can be described as being **monochrome** if it contains shades of only one colour or is shades of black and white. When talking or writing about colour, think about the range of colour used and the overall impression that you have of the colours. How do they look and feel? Has the artist mixed the colours, or are they pure colours? They can be:

- warm, cool, hot, cold
- light, dark, dull, lively, bright, muted, loud, quiet, pale, pastel, soft, subdued, insipid, weak, strong, deep, intense
- flat, vibrant, luminous, glowing, saturated
- transparent, translucent, opaque
- mixed, muddy, pure, blended
- natural, clear, earthy, fluorescent, stimulating, distinctive
- complementary, harmonious, contrasting
- artificial, clashing, depressing, uplifting, discordant, garish, jarring, violent, soothing, calming
- primary, secondary, tertiary
- **monochromatic**, **polychromatic**.

Shape

Shape can relate to the actual shape of three-dimensional (3D) work or the depicted shape within two-dimensional (2D) work. Shape can be:

- three-dimensional, flat, one-dimensional
- regular, irregular, amorphous, nebular, geometric, elliptical, spherical
- balanced, asymmetrical, distorted, exaggerated, hard-edged, soft-edged
- overlapping, distinct, indistinct.

Form

Form relates specifically to 3D artworks. Form can be:

- natural, abstract, realistic, organic, geometric
- depth, height, width
- light, heavy
- imposing, ethereal.

Texture

If you are analysing a work from a photograph, it is not always easy to see textural qualities. This is particularly true if you are looking at a photograph of a large piece of work. Texture may exist, but refer to it only if you can see it. Texture can be:

- flat, raised, polished
- smooth, rough, coarse
- soft, hard
- shiny, glossy, reflective, **matt**, satin, silky, frosted
- furry, hairy, scratched, pitted, velvety.

In relation to mark-making, you can describe marks as:

- visible, smooth, blended, thin, thick, impasto, washes, glazes, stippled, splattered
- bold, timid, lively, vigorous
- layered, flat
- precise, defined, regular, systematic, regular, patterned
- sketchy, quick, uneven, irregular.

Activity C: **Describe 3D objects**

Look at the photographs of the ceramic vessel and the quilt (Figures 2.16 and 2.17) and write a short description of each. Refer to the formal elements that you can see.

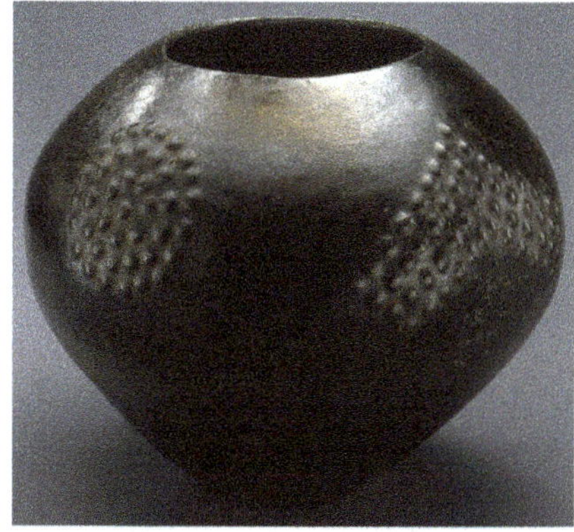

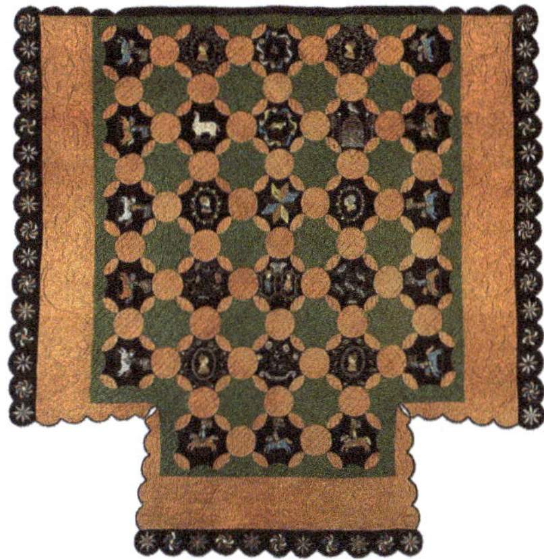

2.16 and **2.17** The words that you use to describe and analyse a ceramic vessel and a textile quilt will be different, because they have different qualities. This can be seen here in the 20th-century Zulu beer vessel and the 19th-century American quilt.

colour theory Practical guidance on colour mixing and colour combinations.
matt A non-shiny surface.
monochromatic Made up of one colour.
monochrome A design in one colour or values of one colour, usually black, grey or white.
polychromatic Made up of many colours, multi-coloured.

Lighting

Within a 2D work, the lighting will refer to how the artist or designer has used a light source, or not, within the composition to make objects appear 3D. If talking about a 3D work, you can comment about the lighting in the space where you view the work and the impact that has on the piece and the way that you relate to it. Lighting can be:

- natural, artificial
- directional, non-directional, back-lit, front-lit, spotlit, top-lit, side-lit
- cool, grey, blue, warm, yellow, white
- strong, dim, faint, gloomy, soft
- harsh, clear, bright, intense.

Viewpoint

This can refer to the position from which you view the work, or the angle or position that the artist or designer has used in depicting the subject matter within the work. This viewpoint can be:

- close-up, distant, bird's-eye (Figure 2.18), worm's-eye (Figure 2.19)
- front, side, three-quarters, profile, rear
- standing, sitting, bending, lying down, reclining
- single viewpoint, multi-viewpoint

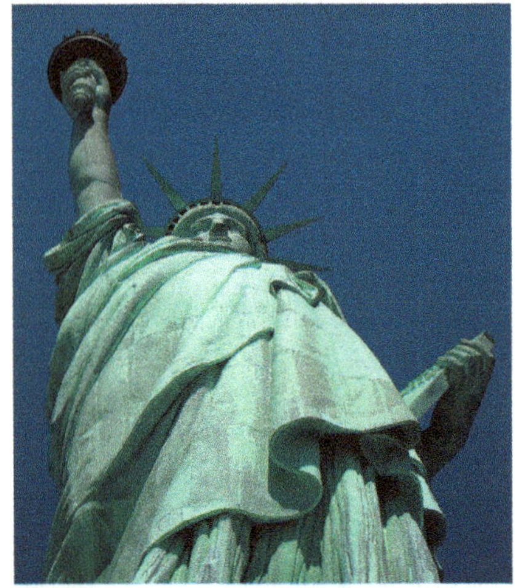

2.19 This photograph of the Statue of Liberty, New York, is taken from underneath and can be described as being a worm's-eye viewpoint.

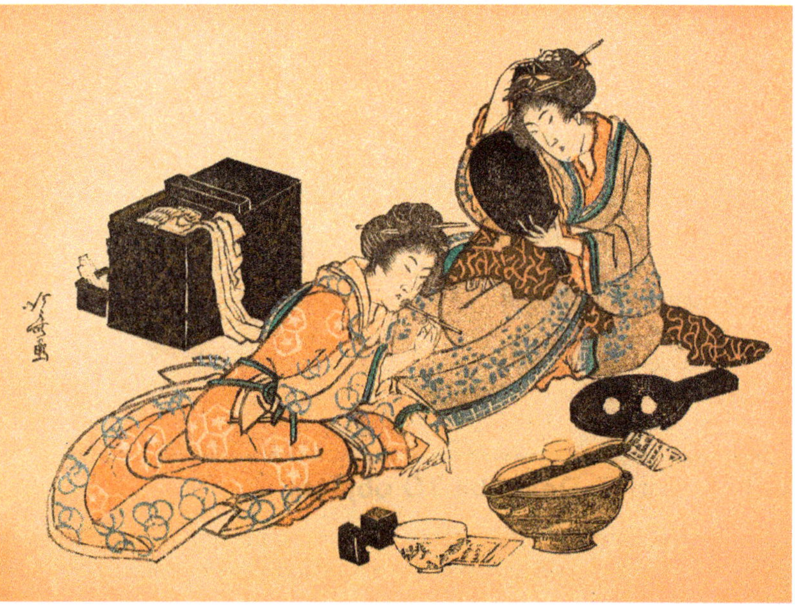

2.18 The print in this Japanese New Year card from 1913 shows use of a high, or bird's-eye, viewpoint, as we look down on the figures and the objects within the scene, as if we see them from above.

Composition

Composition can be:

- arrangement, structure, layout, position
- horizontal, vertical, diagonal
- foreground, background, middle ground
- formal, informal, relaxed, flowing, rigid, confined
- fragmented, chaotic, cluttered, overlapping
- organised, empty, spacious
- **positive space**, negative space
- landscape format, portrait format, circular, triangular, square.

Mood and atmosphere

Mood and atmosphere can be:

- calm, peaceful, relaxed, tranquil
- frantic, cheerful, light, happy
- gloomy, depressive, dark, moody, sombre, sad
- angry, aggressive, distressing
- stimulating, interesting
- boring, lifeless, dull.

Activity D: **Describe an artwork**

Look back at the Japanese New Year card in Figure 2.18. Write a 200-word description of the artwork, including subject matter, composition, colour and line. Compare your description with that of your classmates.

Critical thinking:

Review examples of any written work that you have done so far, both for the Personal Investigation and any annotations you have made, and introduce appropriate descriptive words to convey your points of view.

Further research

You may find the following book useful when analysing artworks: *A Short Guide to Writing about Art*, 9th edition (Prentice Hall, 2008). Find out more about colour theory in *Interaction of Color*, 50th anniversary edition, by Josef Albers (Yale University Press, 2013). This is also available as an iPad app, which allows you to carry out colour experiments.

positive space The main focus or subject of an image; negative space refers to the background.

2.1 Three-dimensional (3D) design

Architecture

Learning objective:

- To understand how architecture is influenced by contexts and concepts

Architects:

- must respond to the briefs of public and private clients
- must address constraints – budgets, location, materials and so on
- balance constraints with fitness for purpose – who will be using their buildings, and *how* will they use them?
- have their own ideas about shape and form, and how to apply these to architectural designs to make buildings interesting and memorable
- are influenced heavily by technology, exploring and applying new concepts and designs, construction method and materials.

In this unit, we will look at the two broad movements that have shaped architecture since the early 20th century – Modernism and Postmodernism.

MODERNISM

Modernism is a set of styles of architecture that developed in the first half of the 20th century. Modernism was in part a reaction against the decorative, **eclectic** styles of the 19th century. Modernist architects believed that these styles were backward-looking and that architecture should reflect a new age and be:

- functional
- embracing of technology – using glass, metal, reinforced concrete and steel frames
- visually **concise** – lacking ornamentation
- **rectilinear** with **plane** surfaces
- open and with light-filled interior spaces.

A pioneer of Modernism, US architect Louis Sullivan (1856–1924), summed up the **ethos** of the new architecture: 'Form follows function'. Only the features a building needed to have should be included in this architecture.

When used well, the concept created buildings that were functional and spacious, as well as beautiful (Figure 2.20). If used poorly, however, it could also create spaces that were cramped, oppressive and uninspiring to be in. Architecture influenced by Modernism became the norm in corporate and institutional buildings – in skyscrapers, office buildings and high-rise blocks. It was the first architectural style to have a global reach and became known as the International Style.

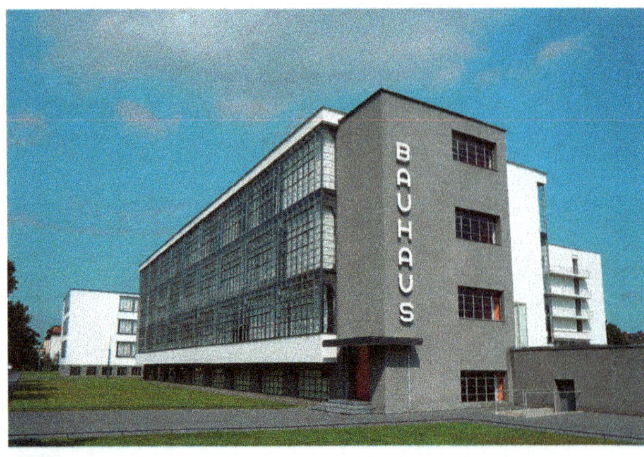

2.20 Walter Gropius, Bauhaus Building, Dessau, Germany, 1926. The Bauhaus Dessau by Walter Gropius (1883–1969) is a classic Modernist structure and was built to house the workshops and classrooms of the German art school Bauhaus. The curtain walls of glass allowed plenty of light in.

Activity A: **Research the work of a Modernist architect**

Choose one of the following architects:

- Lina Do Bardi, Italian-born Brazilian
- Alvar Aalto, Finnish
- Frank Lloyd Wright, American

Write a short report (500 words) on their careers and their contribution to Modernism.

If possible, present your report to your classmates using images.

POSTMODERNISM

From the 1960s, new architectural styles arose that were a reaction against the **austerity** of the International Style. Many architects began to see Modernism as too **prescriptive** – restricting their freedom to explore personal ideas, concepts and influences. Postmodernist architects borrowed architectural influences from a wide range of sources and often combined them in often surprising and playful ways. Postmodernist styles did not necessarily reject Modernism outright, but moved beyond it, allowing a richer, wider contextual framework (Figure 2.21).

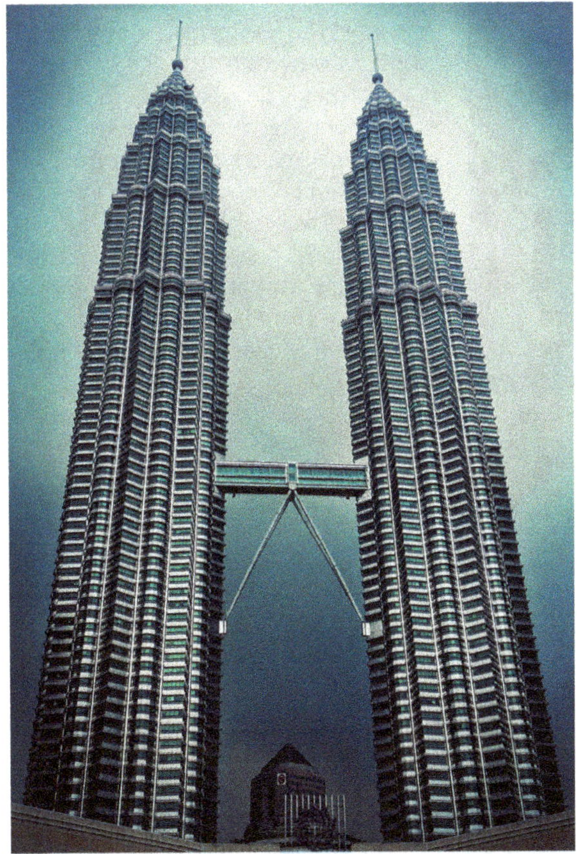

2.21 César Pelli, The Petronas Towers, Kuala Lumpur, Malaysia, 1997. The Argentine-born American architect César Pelli (born 1926) is a leading Postmodernist architect. The twin skyscrapers largely provide office space. However, in its form, the building reflects Malaysia's Islamic heritage – the pinnacles are like minarets and the cross-section is based on the **Rub el Hizb**.

austerity Strict simplicity.
concise Brief and to the point.
eclectic Showing a wide range of influences.
ethos Ideas and attitudes of a particular group or movement.
plane Flat and smooth.
prescriptive Laying down rules.
rectilinear With all lines at 90 degrees to one another.
Rub el Hizb Islamic symbol made up of two overlapping squares and used as a marker to divide up parts of the Qur'an.

Artists and designers: **Le Corbusier**

The Swiss-born French architect Le Corbusier (1887–1965) is often considered the most important figure in the Modernist movement in architecture. He had no formal architectural training but taught himself by studying books and journals and having discussions with other architects. Throughout his career, Le Corbusier believed that architecture and town planning played an important role in shaping society and human happiness. He developed a set of principles that he believed would fulfil his dream of making better housing, towns and cities.

Key to Le Corbusier's ideas was the 'Modulor' system. This used the mathematical proportions found in the human body to determine the living space needed by people. This in turn led to his interest in making urban plans for whole communities, indicating the type of buildings and density, recreational spaces and community/**municipal** buildings. He was also interested in the idea of 'Cities in the Sky' – buildings we commonly call skyscrapers.

Among Le Corbusier's most important buildings and urban plans are:

- Villa Savoye, Poissy, France (completed 1931) (Figure 2.22)
- the housing project Unité d'Habitation (the 'Cité Radieuse'), Marseille, France (1947–52)
- the church Notre Dame du Haut, Ronchamp, France (completed 1955)
- the town plan and key public buildings for Chandigarh, capital of Haryana and Punjab State, India (completed 1956, with some buildings finished later) (Figure 2.23).

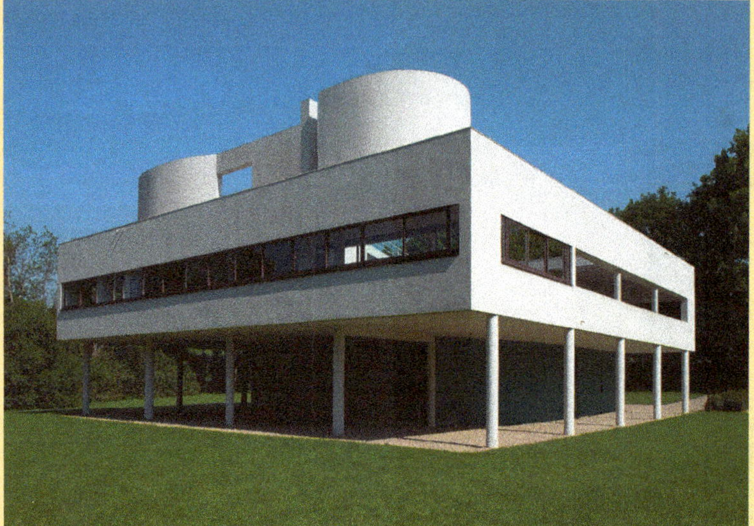

2.22 Le Corbusier, Villa Savoye, Poissy, France, completed 1931. This is one of Le Corbusier's most famous buildings and is typical of his Modernist style. It was built as a country home but is now open to the public.

All his buildings used smooth surfaces, minimal colour, little or no surface detail (other than that of the materials themselves) and simple geometric forms.

Le Corbusier's work has divided opinion. His achievements in designing buildings that were true to the spirit of their times is clear. He also used manufacturing techniques that were innovative. Some critics, however, have argued that Le Corbusier's ideas especially with regard to urban planning were too rigid. Today, people are much less comfortable in simply conforming to an overall plan about how they should live, especially when they have not had a say in this plan.

Can you think of examples in your town or city where urban areas have been planned with ideas similar to Le Corbusier's? Have they worked, in your opinion? Do some research to find out why the plan was successful or unsuccessful.

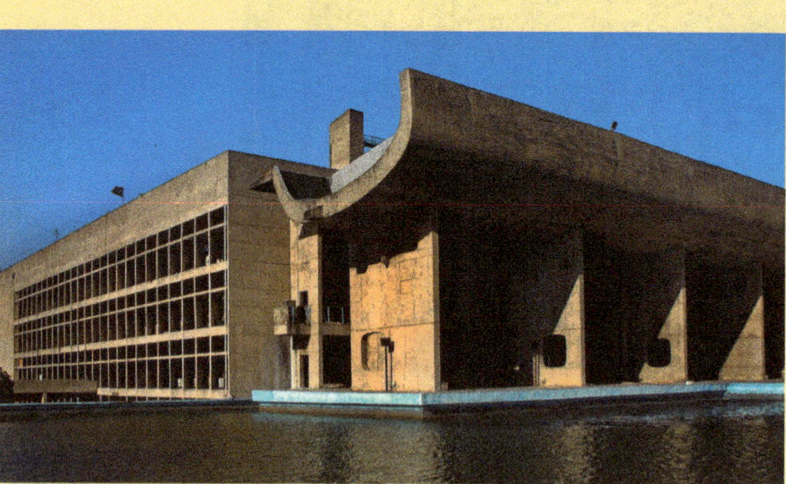

2.23 Le Corbusier, Palace of Assembly, Chandigarh, India, completed 1961. Here the Modernist style can be seen in the sweep of geometric curves and the regular spaces.

Activity B: **Record architectural forms that show a contextual influence**

Research a contemporary building in your area that draws on a wide range of influences. This can be in the way it borrows details from history in its forms, surface treatments or architectural details. Make a note of the influences and use drawing to make studies of specific architectural details. You can also use photos (see Figure 2.24).

Tip:

You are making drawing studies of sections of the building, not whole buildings. Concentrate on the details.

Activity C: **Create a concept sketch**

Your local area is looking for design ideas for a new community building. The building must have some links or references to local traditions – these could be:

- local cultures
- historical building types
- present-day industry and commerce
- geographical features or landmarks.

Make a drawing of a single front elevation of the building. This should be an artist's impression – not a detailed architectural drawing.

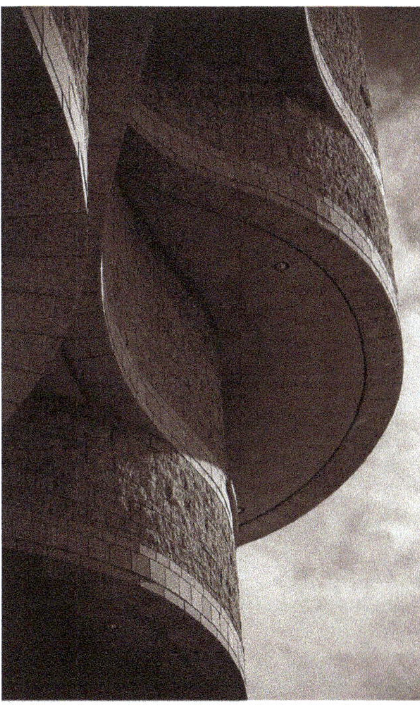

2.24 Detail of the exterior of the Canadian Museum of History (completed 1989), Gatineau, Quebec, Canada. The wave-like forms refer to the geological forms in the Canadian landscape.

Critical thinking:

Display your studies made for **Activity B**.
Evaluate these:

- Have you identified contextual influences and concepts in the architecture?
- What effect do they have on shape, form, colour, texture, materials and so on?
- How effectively did you use drawing techniques to record these influences?

Further research

Go online to explore the legacy of Louis Sullivan, pioneer of Modernism.

Then research some recent Postmodernist buildings online.

municipal Run or owned by local government.

Ceramics

Learning objectives:

- To understand how ceramics are influenced by context
- To explore ceramic design based on a concept

Ceramicists and artists using clay have responded to various influences depending on their location and the purpose of their ceramic work. Some ceramic work is purely functional. Other ceramic work challenges the notion of functional ceramics and explores, for example, sculptural qualities.

In this unit, we focus on functional ceramics – looking at forms, textures and glazes.

FORMS

Functional ceramics include plates, bowls and cups (for tableware) and vases (for flowers). To work well, these cannot depart far from the normal plate or cup form. The art of the potter lies in achieving a harmonious shape and pleasant feel or weight.

Traditional Japanese raku **ware** plays a key part in the ritual **tea ceremony** and usually takes the form of a tea bowl. Many raku bowls are designed to be simple and honest. They use simple shapes and glazes that reflect the purity of mind aimed at through the tea ceremony – their form reflects their purpose. The range of different glazes and **crackle** effects are highly valued.

The purity of raku and other Japanese kinds of pottery was very influential on Western pottery in the 20th century. The emphasis on simplicity fitted well with the Modernist movement. Shōji Hamada (1894–1978) was one of Japan's most important potters of the 20th century and inspired many potters in the West. He developed wood-fired **kilns** and lead glazes as part of his approach to a simple yet pure form of ceramics (see Figure 2.25).

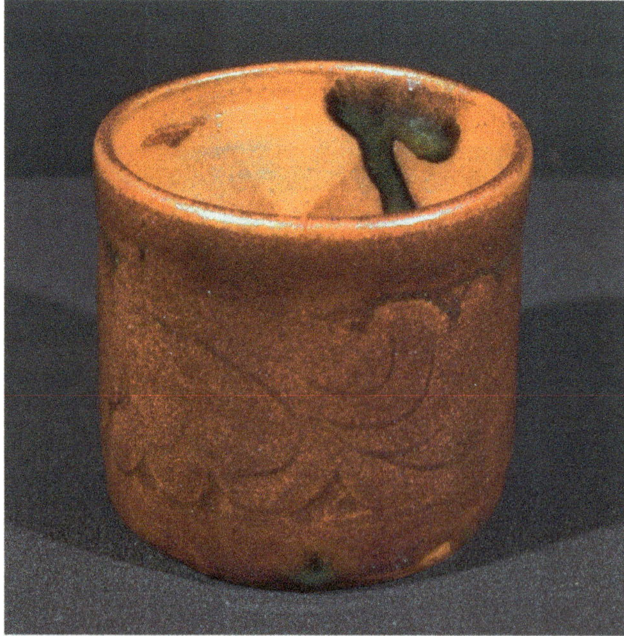

2.25 Shōji Hamada, *Tea bowl*, c.1923, **stoneware** with Japanese **tessha** iron glaze, The Royal Cornwall Museum, Truro.

Activity A: **Design a functional ceramic form to be used in the home**

The focus in this activity is on the *form* of the ceramic, not the texture or decoration.

1. Choose either a) a cup and saucer or b) a plate and bowl.
2. Draw a set of ideas that show how you are exploring different shapes – not just a single shape (for example, cups can be large or small, shallow and wide-brimmed, or more mug-like).
3. Make sure that each piece works with the other (for example, the cup with the saucer).
4. Make a set of drawings that show how you have developed your idea.

TEXTURES

Potters can include strong textural designs and features in their ceramics – grooves, holes, patterns and so on. Figure 2.26 shows some examples of pots made at Kpando in Ghana, Africa, in which the striking textures emphasise the overall shape. There is a balance between form and the surface decoration, such as in the grooved rings on the pots.

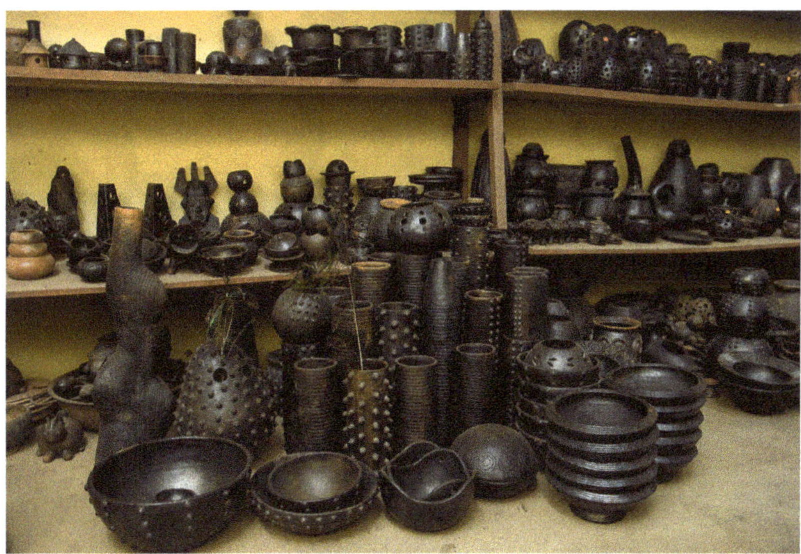

2.26 Pottery from Kpando in Ghana. The textures reinforce the organic, **monochrome** pottery shapes.

Tip:

Potters sometimes use stamps to make repeated texture patterns. You can try making stamps out of plaster for regular use in ceramic projects. You might like to make a stamp formed with your initials or a symbol, as your potter's mark. Search online for advice on making a simple plaster stamp.

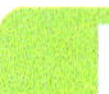

Activity B: **Experiment with textures in clay**

1. Collect a wide variety of objects with interesting textures – natural and human-made. These can include brushes, rubber car mats, bark, bricks, concrete blocks and so on.
2. Roll out a selection of clay slabs.
3. Use your collection of objects to make a series of texture slabs, exploring the potential in making textures from a variety of objects.

crackle Pottery surface covered with fine cracks.
kiln Oven or furnace used for firing pottery.
stoneware Non-porous clay body and glaze, capable of being fired at higher temperatures than earthenware (to around 1260°C).
tea ceremony Tea making and drinking ritual practised in Japan and other countries in the Far East for religious or spiritual reasons.
tessha A Japanese rust-coloured glaze.
ware Pottery type – for example, stoneware, Delftware.

GLAZES

Potters use glazes to add colour and decoration to their works and also to make them waterproof. Functional pots need to be able to hold water!

The following table shows some of the main types of glaze:

Glaze	Effect after firing	Example pottery type
lead	shiny, transparent	Chinese **sancai**; Japanese raku
tin	white, opaque	**faience**
ash glazes	dark brown or green, glassy	East Asian pottery types
salt	high gloss; sometimes uneven texture like orange peel	stoneware

Usually, potters add glazes to their work before it is fired.

Some glazes are added to the ceramic piece during the firing process, creating a mottled effect (see Figure 2.27).

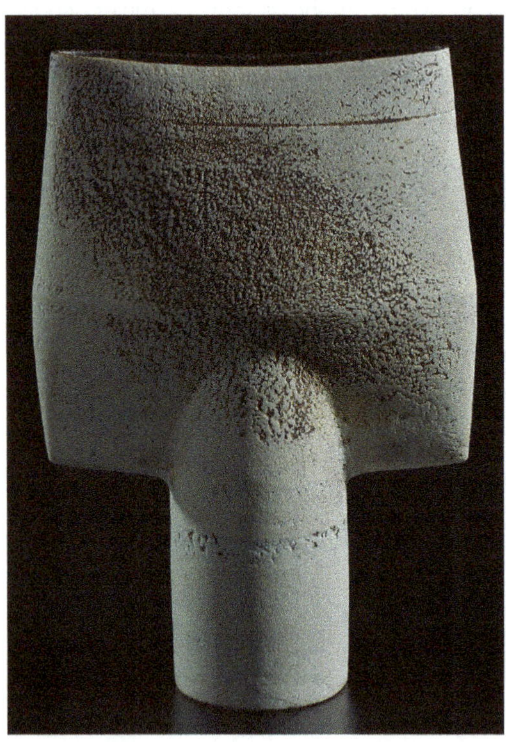

2.27 Hans Coper, *Vase*, c.1970, T-Material, porcelain slips and manganese, private collection. Hans Coper (1920–81) was a German-born British potter. Coper explored working his surfaces with brushed oxides and **slips**, and single firing techniques to create surfaces that look organic. This vase shows his signature 'spade' form.

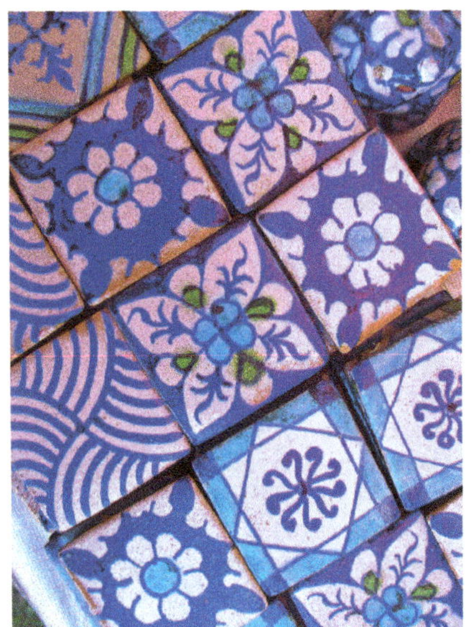

2.28 Beautifully made handicrafts from the south-eastern province of Sinch, Pakistan.

Activity C: **Experiment with glazes**

Experiment with as wide a range of glazes as possible, using clay slabs. You will need to ask your teacher's advice about kiln temperatures and firing times.

Take photographs of the results achieved and make notes about the process and effects.

FIRING

During firing, the clay is baked at very high temperatures and becomes hard. The firing process usually takes place in a kiln, but in some ceramic traditions a pit or mound is used instead. Most modern pottery is fired twice, with the glazes applied after the first firing. The final appearance of the pottery depends on various factors, including:

- the temperature of the kiln
- the length of firing
- the amount of air (oxygen) allowed into the kiln.

Always ask your teacher for advice on firing.

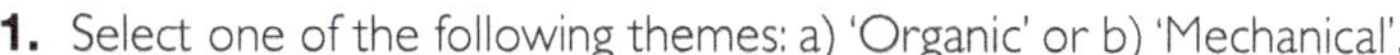

Activity D: **Create a functional ceramic form based on a theme**

1. Select one of the following themes: a) 'Organic' or b) 'Mechanical'.
2. Find a set of source materials that you can use as starting points – for example, a) shells, seeds, fruits, leaves, bark and so on, or b) small parts of cars, engines, computers and so on.
3. Consider how you will use the theme in your work. The piece must be functional.
4. Consider how you will explore the relationship between the form, texture and glaze in your designs.
5. Make a ceramic form based on your designs. You can use any combination of:
   a. coiling
   b. slabbing
   c. throwing.
6. Display the finished work together with your design ideas.
7. With a classmate, discuss your work as a pair.

Critical thinking:

When displaying and discussing your work on **Activity D**, think about:

- What was the concept behind your approach?
- How did your designs of both form and surface reflect the concept?
- Describe the ceramic building techniques you used – how successfully did you apply these?
- What can you learn from this task for future projects?

Further research

Go online to find out more about raku pottery.

Read more about Hans Coper in *Hans Coper* by Tony Birks (Stenlake, 2013).

Go online to find a detailed description of the firing process.

faience Tin-glazed earthenware.
sancai Chinese type of pottery decoration using slip or glaze and in three colours – brown, green and cream.
slip Mixture of clay and water used for decorating wares or joining parts.

Environmental design

Learning objective:

- To understand contextual influences and concepts in environmental design

We are becoming ever more aware of the limited number of resources on our planet and also of how much damage consumerism can cause. As designers, we need to ensure that we take account of the environment as part of the design and production process. We have a responsibility to use materials that are sustainable.

2.29 Emma O'Dare, *Vase*, 1998, crushed recycled glass mixed with ceramic oxides and wallpaper paste, The Geffrye Museum of the Home, London. This piece uses recycled material to create a new form.

WHAT CAN A DESIGNER DO?

Sustainable and responsible design aims to address these concerns by exploring how materials and production processes can be used sensitively and appropriately – to deliver high-quality products and experiences while reducing harm to the environment. As designers, we can:

- use recycled materials (Figure 2.29)
- **upcycle** and repurpose – that is, provide an existing object with an additional value, use or function
- create packaging solutions that use fewer materials
- improve energy efficiency throughout the product's life
- consider the product's 'end of life' and disposal.

Materials and techniques: **Life Cycle Assessment**

The Life Cycle Assessment (LCA) is a useful tool for designers when assessing the environmental impacts of a product, from cradle to grave or, best of all, **cradle to cradle**, as shown in the product life cycle diagram below (Figure 2.30). An LCA will:

- quantify or otherwise characterise all the inputs and outputs over a product's lifespan
- specify the potential environmental impacts of materials
- consider alternative approaches that change those impacts for the better.

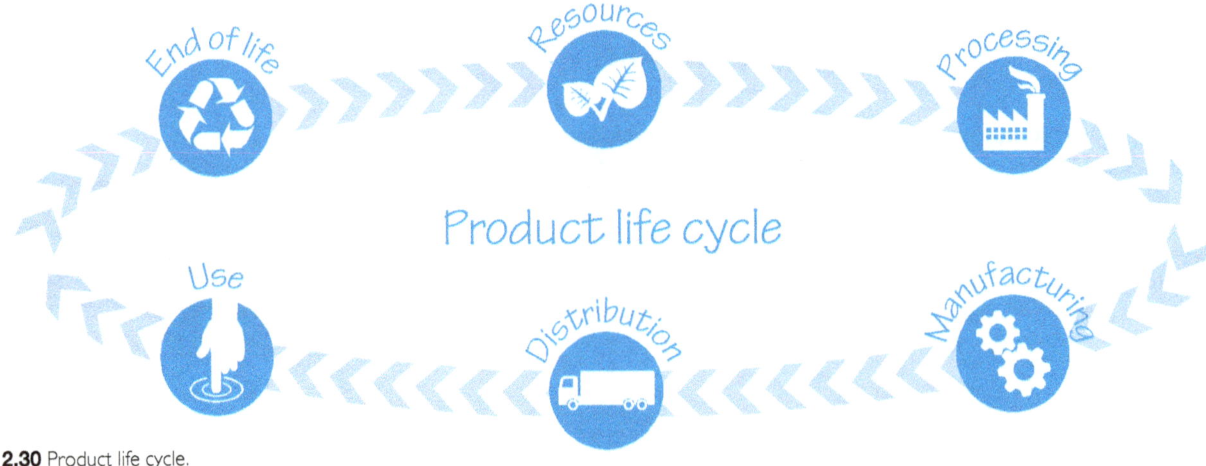

2.30 Product life cycle.

Case study: Using recycled cardboard

Cardboard is a versatile, low-cost recyclable material and has a wide range of uses. It is essentially heavy-duty strong paper, often built up in layers. You can get more out of working with cardboard by understanding how to apply different techniques. These include:

- *cutting safely* – work with a guard if possible, move the blade away from the body/fingers, and avoid pressing too hard, which may break or snap the blade
- *scoring* – making lines across the surface but not cutting. These are lines along which sections can be folded
- *gluing* – using contact and PVA-type glues
- *bending* – after scoring, or by gently forming around a shape
- *folding* – used in construction techniques, such as making boxes
- *using tabs and slots* – a way of joining shapes together securely where they are too complex to use simple folding
- *joining* – adding sections of parts together
- *layering* (***lamination***) – using multiple layers to create strength.

Figure 2.31 shows an example of a furniture design that uses recycled cardboard. Lamination has been used to create strength but is also part of the visual language of the piece.

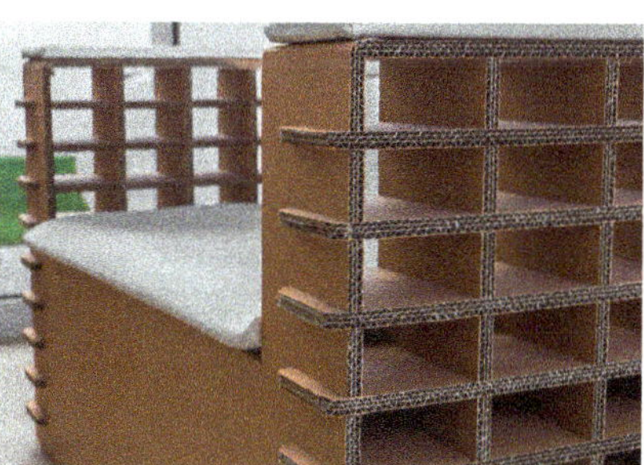

2.31 Nardi Cardboard Furniture, Italy, *Golliaz Armchair*, 2016, cardboard.

Activity A: **Transportation seating**

In this activity, you will design and make a model of a seat to be used on public transport, using recycled materials. You may find it useful to work with a classmate.

1. Take photos and make drawings of a range of seats and benches used on public transport.
2. Draw a concept sketch for your own design.
3. Analyse the main shapes that make up the bench:
    a. Some of these might be simple, such as squares, rectangles, cubes and ovals.
    b. Some might be more complex, such as the curved rectangle of the back of the seat.

These are the parts that you will cut from the cardboard and join together to make the bench.

4. Using your measurements and sizes from the existing seating as a guide, make a 1:2 scale model. Use recycled cardboard and associated construction techniques.

The cardboard should be visible. You are celebrating the fact that you are using this material, and you want everyone to know!

Critical thinking:

Display your work on **Activity A.** Evaluate your work, reflecting on:

- How well did you analyse the seats/benches in your drawing and photography?
- How many techniques did you use when working with the cardboard?
- How much did you need to simplify the shapes as you worked on the cardboard?
- How would using this seat or bench raise awareness of environmental design?

Further research

Go online for more on LCAs and to find out more about working with cardboard.

cradle to cradle From the 'birth' of a product to its 'rebirth' as a new one.
lamination Sheet materials glued or bonded together to form a strong construction material.
upcycle To recycle an object while adding value to it.

Set design

Learning objectives:

- To understand contextual influences and concepts in set design
- To produce a model of a stage prop using 3D making techniques

Set designers respond to ideas and concepts in any production they are working on. They can interpret concepts and themes using visual devices on the stage or in their use of colour, shape and lighting. They may borrow ideas from painting, sculpture and the arts in general in order to bring visual form to ideas on a page.

ART INFLUENCES IN SET DESIGN

Many set designs try to show real life – the classic set for a realist play is a sitting room, with 'real' armchairs, tables and other items of furniture. However, from the beginning of the 20th century especially, many set designers have introduced ideas from art and design movements into their work. This reflected the experimental art of the time, with movements such as Post-Impressionism, Cubism and Expressionism. Many set designers, of course, have also been artists in their own right.

In his work for the theatre, the Russian artist Léon Bakst (1866–1924) rebelled against the realistic, unimaginative stage sets of his time. He created stage sets full of bold colour and energy, borrowing ideas from the Impressionists and Post-Impressionists. His sets were like giant living paintings (Figure 2.32).

Activity A: **Research a Cubist set design and create your own Cubist set design**

1. The Cubist art movement also influenced set design. Research and write a short report with images (300 words) on the set designs for one of the following productions:
   - Pablo Picasso's set designs for the ballet *Parade* (1917)
   - Fernand Léger's set designs for the ballet *La Création du Monde* (1923).
2. Using your research as inspiration, make a sketch for a Cubist theatre set for a well-known play of your choice.

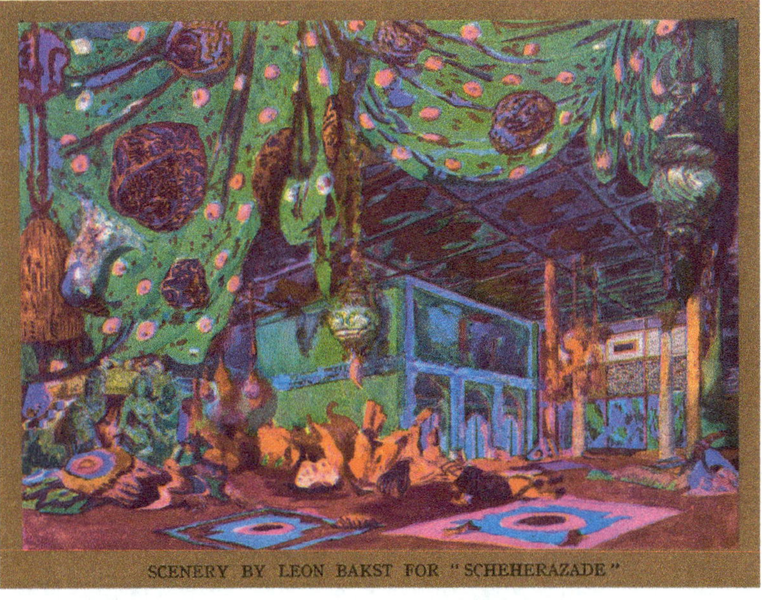

2.32 Léon Bakst, *Set Design for Scheherazade*, c.1911. Bakst often worked with the Russian ballet troupe Les Ballets Russes. *Scheherazade* was one of the troupe's most famous productions and Bakst produced sets full of 'Oriental' colour to match the ballet's story.

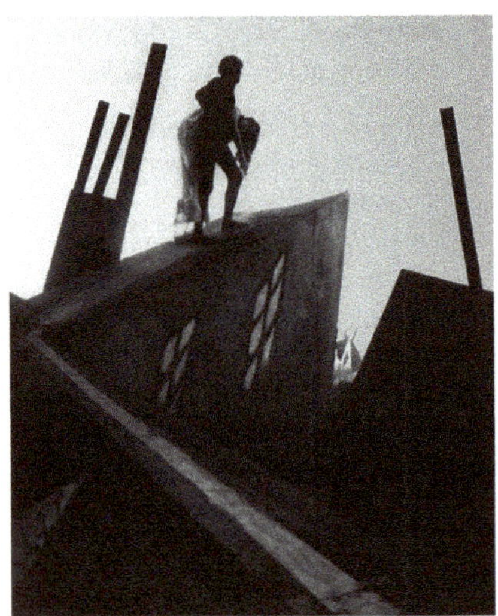

2.33 Walter Reimann and Walter Röhrig, film still from *The Cabinet of Dr Caligari*, 1920.

Expressionism also inspired set designers, both in the theatre and in films. For the German horror film *The Cabinet of Dr Caligari* (1920, directed by Robert Wiene), the German painters and designers Walter Reimann (1887–1936) and Walter Röhrig (1897–1945) created startlingly unreal sets full of menacing shadows and **zigzagging** shapes (Figure 2.33).

DEVELOPING PROPS

Set designers often develop **stage props**. 'Prop' is short for theatrical 'property' and describes anything that is portable and can be used on stage. Props are important on sets, as they can help the audience understand some of the themes in the piece as well as being representations of actual objects. Designers can explore ideas about different scales and visual effects in the ways they construct props.

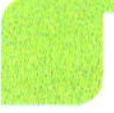

Activity B: **Make a prop using cardboard engineering**

You are going to produce a prop for a children's theatre production called *The Borrowers*. This is about tiny people who secretly live alongside normal-sized humans, and use human household items for their furniture and living areas. This scene is based on two of the 'Borrowers' going through a cupboard where the humans keep some household tools. They will be picking them up and wondering how they can use them.

For this activity, you are making a giant-sized version of an ordinary household tool, to be used in the set as a prop.

1. Select a simple household object. This should be a relatively simple form but have some detail, such as a screwdriver, metal measuring tape or torch.
2. Make a series of drawings where you analyse and simplify your chosen object's form. Think about the different shapes it is made from – for example, a screwdriver consists of a tube-like handle and a much thinner metal cylinder, ending on a flat point.
3. Measure the dimensions (length, width and breadth) of your household tool. Note these and enlarge them to the scale 1:10.
4. Develop a cardboard model of your household tool, using the enlarged measurements – this is scale model 10 times bigger than the original. Make sure that you have enough workspace!
5. Use a variety of construction techniques to work the cardboard into shape. (See page 133 for advice on how do this.)
6. Paint the piece carefully, avoiding letting the cardboard get too soft. Think about how it will look from a distance, and what colours would make children interested in it.
7. Photograph the final piece.

Critical thinking

Display your work on **Activity B**. Evaluate your work, reflecting on:

- How well did you analyse the shapes in your drawing?
- How many techniques did you use when working with the cardboard?
- How much did you need to simplify the shapes as you worked on the cardboard?
- How did you recreate and interpret any surface details and colours?

Further research

Go online to find out more about Léon Bakst.
Look at a copy of *The Prop Building Guidebook: For Theatre, Film, and TV* by Eric Hart (Focal Press, 2013).

zigzag Like the shape of a 'Z'.
stage props Short for 'stage properties' – anything portable used on stage, including ordinary items such as food, and constructed items such as light balsawood furniture.

Product design

Learning objective:

- To understand how and why the design of products evolves over time

The design of products evolves and changes all the time. This happens as materials change and technology develops.

The mobile phone is an excellent example of a product whose design has evolved significantly over time. There is a big difference between the mobile phones of the 1980s and the designs that we see today (Figure 2.34). What has enabled these radical changes to take place?

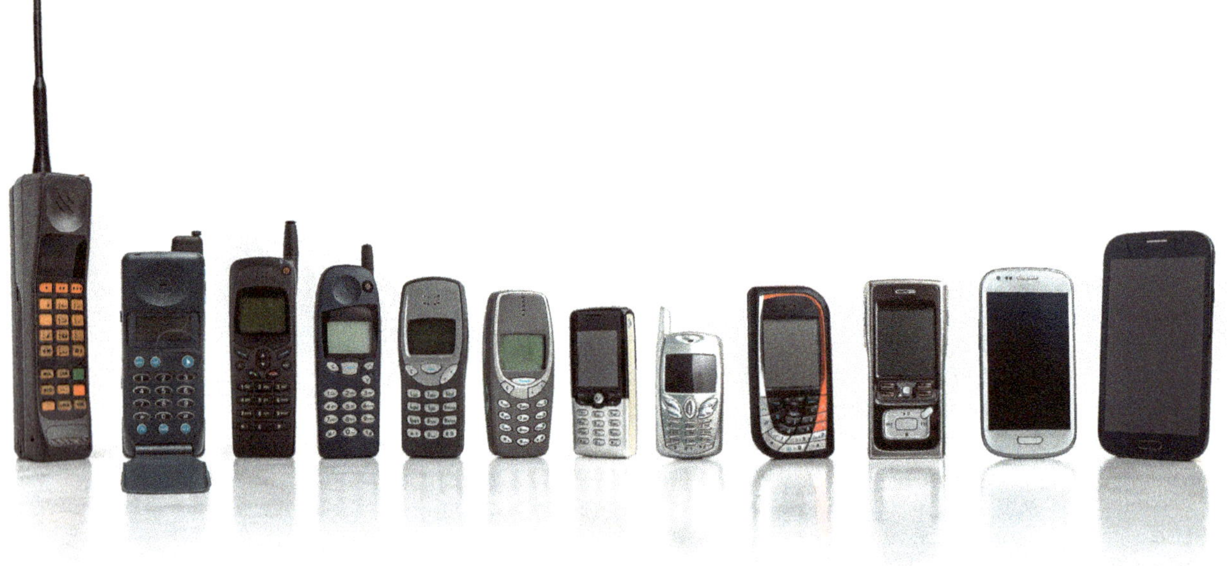

2.34 The development of mobile phone designs from the 1980s to the present day.

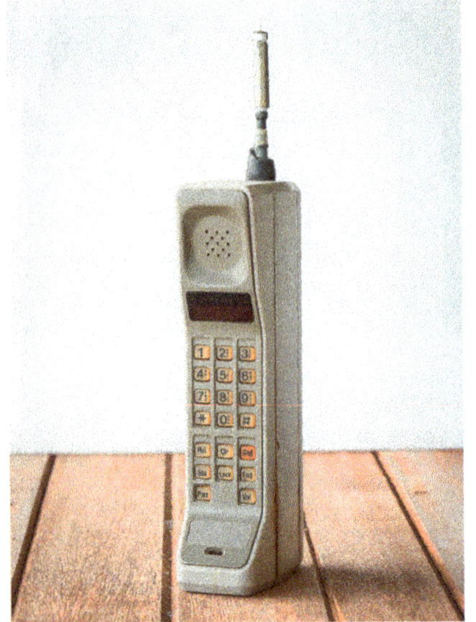

2.35 This example shows an early mobile phone handset design from the 1980s that resembles the shape of the handset of a traditional push button telephone from about the same time.

Mobile technology was developed in the 1970s and mobile phones first launched in the early 1980s. The original mobile phones look very different from those we see today. They were big and heavy because the technical components were less sophisticated than they are today. For example, they needed a large external aerial to receive a signal. The chunky shape resembles a more traditional telephone handset design. At this stage, the appearance of the phone was less important than the function (Figure 2.35).

As the technology changed, the design of the mobile phone changed, too. The handsets became smaller and the size of the aerial was reduced. Eventually, the need to have an external aerial disappeared altogether and the shape of the phone became more slimline. During the late 1990s and into the first decade of the 21st century, the mobile phone became very small and pocket-sized. The size of the screen started to become bigger in relation to the size of the buttons as the function of the phones changed to enable text messages to be sent and received.

Designers began to focus more on the look of the product and the shape of phones became more rounded and fitted into the human hand better. The flip phone was a design that became very popular, as the phone could fit easily into a pocket. The arrangement of the buttons became more **ergonomic**.

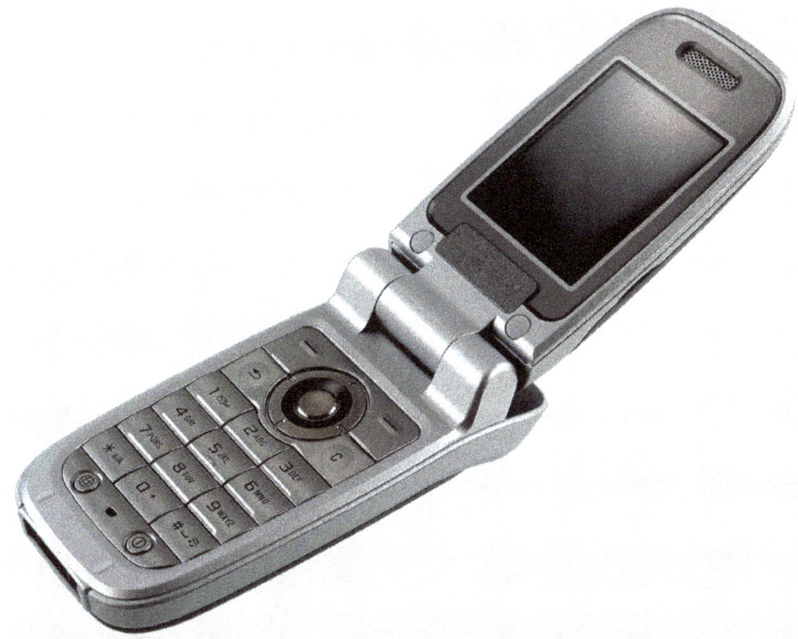

2.36 Phones became smaller and styles varied to include the flip-up designs that fitted easily into the human hand and pocket.

Now mobile phones have evolved again to become smart phones, incorporating mini-computers, high-quality cameras and the ability to transmit video calls. The buttons are now a technical feature within the screen, which has become big to enable touchscreen technology and a better display. The screen is now able to be wrapped around the side of the phone, as can be seen Figure 2.37. The phones also come in a wider variety of colours and finishes, making them more aesthetically pleasing.

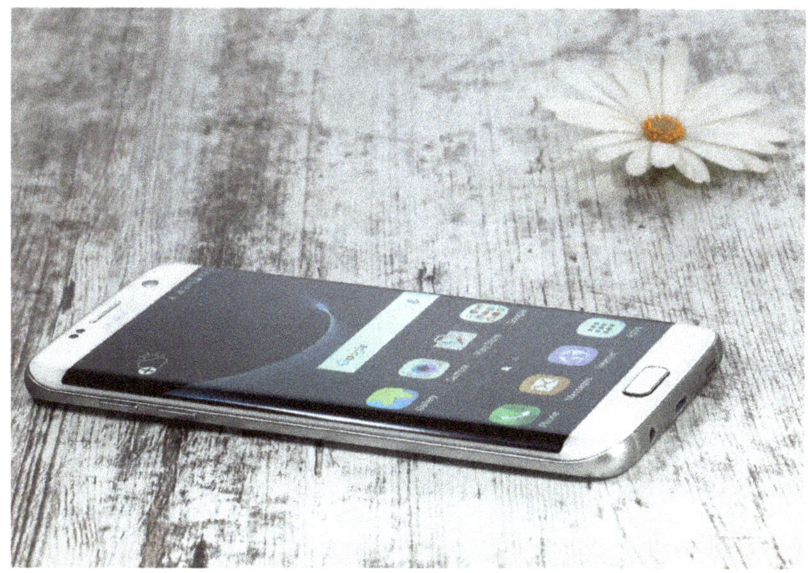

2.37 Samsung Galaxy S7 edge, 2016. Modern mobile phone designs have large screens that sometimes wrap around the edge of the phone.

Activity A: **Explore a design evolution**

1. Select a product that you are familiar with.
2. Using the internet and books, or by visiting local museums, look back at how the design of the product has evolved over time until the present day.
3. Note what design features have changed and suggest reasons why these changes have taken place.
4. Make a sequence of sketches of two key design features showing how they have altered over time. Add annotations.
5. Finally, sketch ideas of how you imagine the product might evolve in the future.

Critical thinking:

Think about who the main user groups of particular products are and how the design of a product could be changed slightly to make it either more appealing or easier to use by each group. For example, what differences could be included to make a mobile phone easier to use by a young child or an older person unfamiliar with technology?

Further research

Go to the Design Museum, London online to explore more design evolutions.

ergonomic Designed for comfort and efficiency.

Interior design

Learning objectives:

- To understand the historical development of interior design
- To understand the role of the interior designer
- To explore the key role played by colour in interior design

While architecture has always been held in high regard, the creation of the interiors of buildings has very often played a secondary role. Until the 19th century, the decoration of, for instance, the interior of a house was generally considered the responsibility of the owner. Although the house owner might have sought advice from, for example, a furniture maker or a house painter, there was rarely a thought-out plan or design.

From the 19th century onwards, increasingly more attention was paid to the interior as an important part of the overall design of a building. On the one hand, many architects began to design not just the structure of the building but also the fittings, furniture and lighting as well. This was especially the case with Modernist architects (see pages 124–127), who considered building and their interiors as **'total works of art'**.

For example, for his Sanatorium (tuberculosis hospital, completed in 1933) in Paimio, Finland, the Modernist Finnish architect Alvar Aalto (1898–1976) considered every detail of the interior carefully – from the beds and chairs to the washbasins and even the anti-glare paint used on the walls. The whole Sanatorium, inside and out, was designed with its function in mind – to help the patients rest and get better (Figure 2.38).

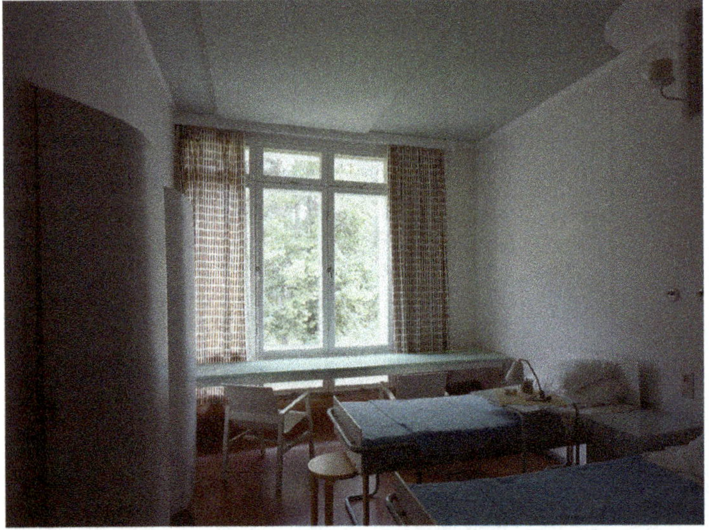

2.38 Patient room of the Paimio Sanatorium by Alvar Aalto 1929–1933. Aalto's approach to the interior design included use of restful colours, rational, clear use of space, and simple, ergonomic furniture. Many of the furniture designs, such as the 'Paimio chair' used on the balconies where patients rested during the daytime, are today design classics (see www.moma.org/collection/works/92879).

On the other hand, the profession of interior designer, separate from the role of the architect, also began to grow. The pioneering interior designers of the early 20th century were very often women, in part because the interior was traditionally considered to be part of the woman's 'sphere' or domain. Today this is increasingly no longer the case, and interior design, no matter what the gender of the designer, is given the respect this discipline deserves.

Activity A: **Research the work of an interior designer**

Choose one of the following interior designers/architects who also created interior designs:

- Owen Jones, English-born Welsh architect
- Otto Wagner, Austrian architect
- Candace Wheeler, American interior designer
- Kelly Wearstler, American interior designer
- Cherag and Roozmehr Bardolivala, Indian interior designers

Write a short report (300 words) on their careers and their approach to interior design.

If possible, present your report to your classmates using images, both sketches and photographs of the interiors.

Critical thinking:

Present your sketch from **Activity B** to a partner, as if they were your client. Explain your design and ask for feedback.

Whatever the project – a sitting room, restaurant, or office – the role of the interior designer includes some or all of the following:

- development of a concept – often in close partnership with the client and other professionals, such as the architect or building contractor
- consideration of the space – how will they use the available space to enhance its **functionality** (how it will be used), aesthetic appeal, and the well-being of its users?
- decoration – including the colour scheme and use of textiles and wallpapers
- lighting design – how will the lighting (lamps, concealed, uplighters and so on) contribute to the mood of the room?
- research, for example, into period styles
- sourcing and/or design of furniture, fabrics, carpets and so on
- project management of works.

Like the architect, the interior designer usually makes concept sketches: both to develop the project and to communicate the design to the client. The sketches include the use of colour, pattern, lighting and furniture. The designer may supplement these sketches with a mood board, much like that used by a fashion designer (see pages 99–100), including a colour palette (scheme) and fabric samples.

Materials and techniques: **Colour**

Colour is perhaps the most important tool in the interior designer's toolkit. Colour has a powerful influence on the look of a room as well as on the mood of those who use it (Figure 2.39). As a designer, you need to think carefully about how colour will contribute to the function of the room: warm, bright colours will create a lively space, perfect for a kitchen-diner; calm, soothing colours may be better for a bedroom. A good interior designer has a thorough understanding of the principles of the colour wheel (see page 12).

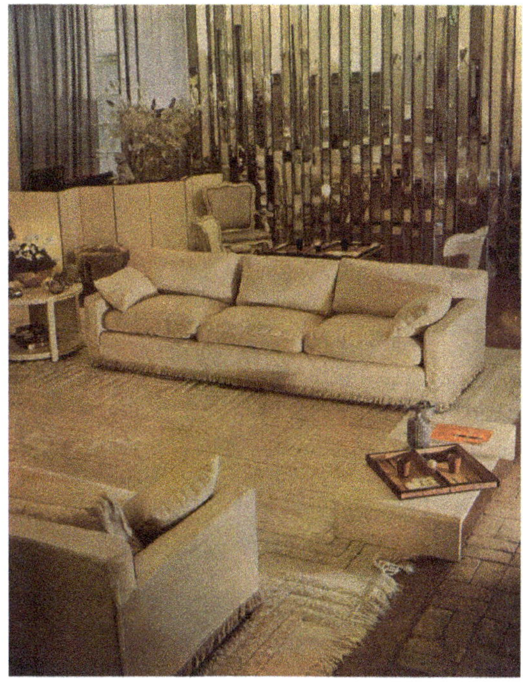

2.39 Syrie Maugham, Sitting room, Chelsea, London, 1920s. The English designer Syrie Maugham (1879–1955) was famous for her all-white interiors. The effect was both glamorous and relaxing.

Activity B: **Design an interior**

1. Choose one of the following interiors:
   - sitting room
   - child's playroom/bedroom
   - home office/study.
2. Now choose one of the following themes:
   - 'Seaside'
   - 'Forest'
   - 'Exotic'
   - 'Innocence'.
3. Next choose your colour scheme: begin with a 'lead' colour and then add no more than two other complementary colours.
4. Using drawing and colour, create a sketch of your design on an A3 sheet of paper.
5. Add annotations to your sketch, explaining key aspects of your design. If you have time, also consider creating a mood board.

functionality How well a building meets its function.
'total work of art' A translation of the German word *Gesamtkunstwerk*, used to describe creative projects that draw on a wide range of disciplines to create a unified aesthetic impression.

2.2 Graphic communication

Advertising

Learning objectives:

- To understand how advertising is influenced by contextual factors
- To understand how concepts are the basis of advertising campaigns

Advertising evolves to meet the needs of its audience. In doing so, it responds to a range of contextual stimuli, including technology, social trends and **demographics**, as well as to creative developments in the product field. Designers must respond to the briefs set by advertising companies, so it is important for us to understand the concepts behind advertising, so that we can apply this understanding to our own work.

THE CONTEXTS OF ADVERTISING

Technology

Technology plays a huge role in advertising and branding today. As consumers, we see images showing examples of products, services and goods every day. Advertisers are aware of this and compete to grab our attention and persuade us to engage with their product.

Technology is used in this process to create clear, well-defined images. Print-based graphic communication has evolved to include printing sharp, bright images at large scale. Designers also create advertising to be seen through the technology we use each day. This can be in digital screen ads on tablets and smart phones, and in larger versions in out-of-home advertising in urban areas (Figure 2.40).

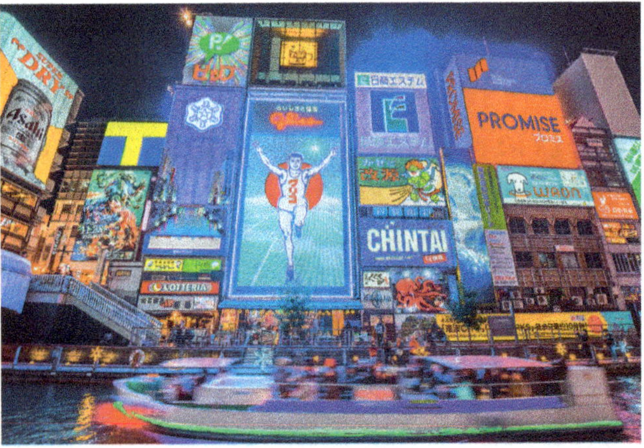

2.40 Advertising displays in Dōtonbori, Osaka, Japan, 2015. Here, technology has been used to create a collage of advertising imagery.

Social trends

Advertising also responds to social trends, as well as helping to reinforce them. In the United Kingdom in the 1950s, almost all advertising of household goods was aimed at women. This was a period of very conservative ideas about gender roles: women were supposed to be above all wives, mothers and homemakers, while men went out to work. The images in advertising therefore showed very traditional ideas about women, as we see in Figure 2.41.

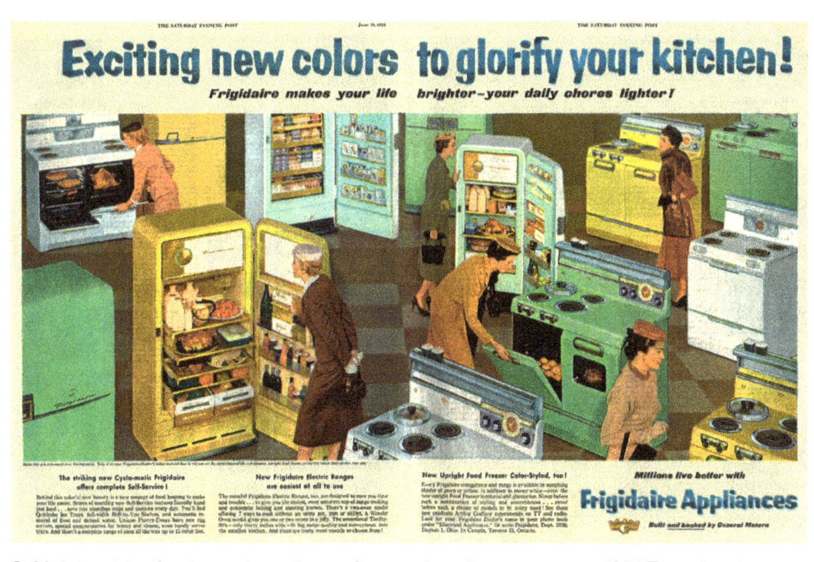

2.41 Advertising for domestic appliances from an American newspaper, 1954. The advertisement is clearly targeted at women, whose lives were supposed to be focused on the home, and especially on the kitchen.

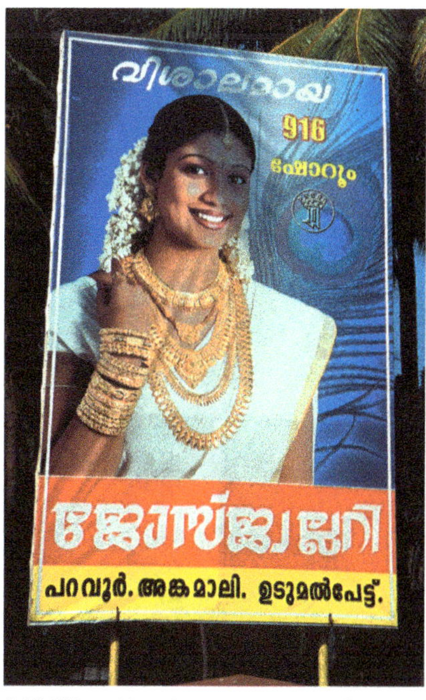

2.42 Billboard jewellery advertisement, Cherai Beach, Kochi, India.

Demographics

Closely related to social trends is demographics. Advertising companies use the insights provided by demographic research to match a **campaign** or brand to a target group. Target groups can be defined by gender, age group, ethnicity, class and **subculture**. They can be very broad (for example, sports cars may be targeted at men generally) or **niche** (for example, a toy aimed at teenage girls).

The advertiser and designer need to make the advertising and brand appeal to the targeted group in terms of:

- images
- language
- aspirations.

Activity A: **Consider changes in advertising**

1. Focus on a single well-established brand and collect information about how their designs and advertising have changed over the years. These can be:
   - magazine and/or printed advertisements
   - screenshots from television
   - web-based.
2. Keep the information you collect in a paper or digital folder, and make notes as you go along about the dates the adverts were produced, the design companies involved (if you can find them), and which country the adverts were designed for.
3. Research the dates the adverts were made, identifying any specific contextual factors that may have influenced the adverts.
4. Write up a short (300-word) summary. Make explicit links between the imagery and text used in the adverts and the contextual factors that had an impact on them.
5. Present your ideas to your classmates and discuss.

campaign A project undertaken by an advertising company for a product or brand.
demographics The study of a population based on factors such as age, race, sex and other characteristics.
niche A small target group with highly individual characteristics.
subculture Alternative ideas and art different from the rest of society.

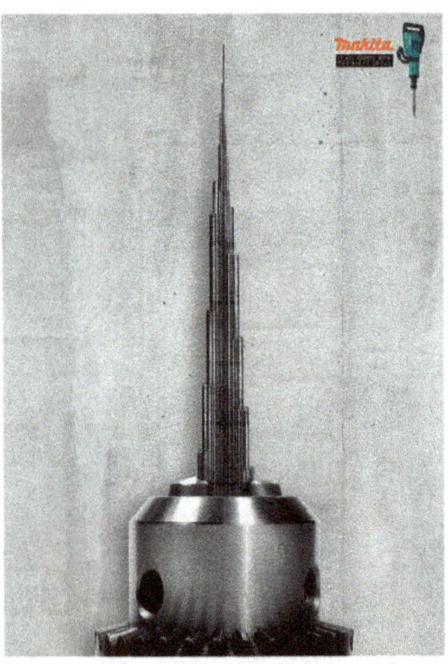

2.43 Leo Burnett, advert for the power-tool company Makita, 2013. In this image, the bit of a drill references the Burj Khalifa, the landmark tower in Dubai and the tallest building in the world. Note that the impact of the advert relies entirely on a visual pun. There is almost no text.

CONCEPTS

Concepts are the ideas and themes used in a piece of advertising. Some advertisements are concept-driven and are designed to be as memorable as possible, so an audience can easily identify a product. This will make potential customers more likely to buy the product in the future. An advertising concept could be:

- a visual pun or joke (Figure 2.43)
- a different way of looking at the world
- a visual device – often the juxtaposition of strikingly different visual elements, a concept developed by the Surrealist artists (see page 113)
- aspirational values – appealing to people's desire for a 'better' or more 'glamorous' life or to belong to a certain group of people (Figure 2.44).

Sometimes, the concepts can be more subtle or influence audiences unconsciously. While advertising may seem to appeal primarily to people's desires, it can also at the same time make a more hidden appeal to their fears and anxieties, for example, about not fitting in, not having the 'right' body shape or not being a good mother.

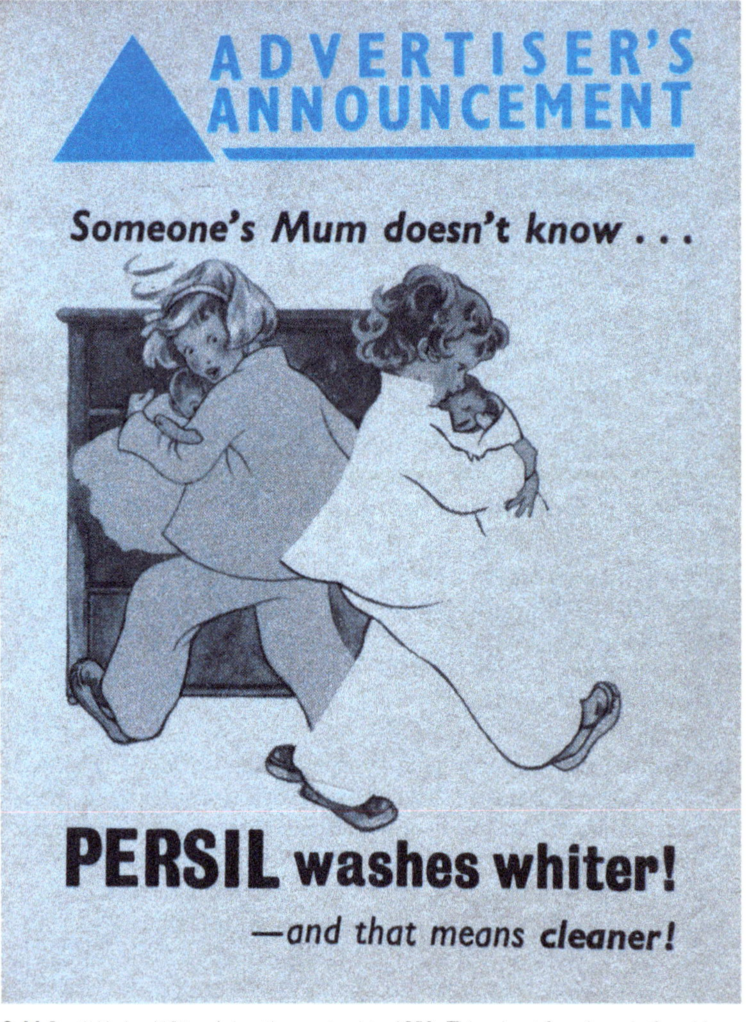

2.44 *Persil Washes Whiter*, Advertisement, c. late 1950s. This advert for a brand of washing detergent makes an appeal to the housewife's aspiration for a better quality of life – here brighter, cleaner clothes. At the same time, it also implies that a woman who does not buy the product might be considered uncaring as a mother.

Activity B: **Remake an advert**

In this activity, you will be making a new version of an existing advert.

- Working in pairs, select two advertisements that you both believe are effective – one each.
- Explain to your partner why you believe the advertisement you chose works, and get them to explain their choice.
- Take the visual components (what it shows) of your chosen advert and list these.
- Use a mixture of second-hand sources and first-hand observational drawing and photography to develop alternative designs for the advertisement.
  You must include at least *one* clear concept or idea in the piece. You can develop new concepts for the piece if you wish – you do not have to just copy what is there.
- Make a worked-up version and present this to your partner. Discuss how effectively you and they have used images and/or text.
- If you have time, swap advertisements and make alternative versions of these.

Critical thinking:

Review your work on **Activity B**, including any developmental work and rough versions. As you display this and discuss it with your classmates, consider:

- Did you identify the visual components in the original piece?
- Do you think you have communicated a concept that can be seen in the final piece?
- What was this concept?
- Is it the same as in the original version? If so, why?
- If not, how have you changed the concept, and why?
- Do your classmates agree?

Further research

Keep up to date with the fast-moving world of advertising by reading the magazine *Campaign*, which is available online.

For a guide to the modern advertising industry, read *The Advertising Concept Book: Think Now, Design Later*, 3rd edition, by Peter Barry (Thames & Hudson, 2016).

Illustration

Learning objectives:

- To understand how illustration can be used to reflect contemporary culture
- To develop illustration work combining illustration techniques

Illustrators may produce work for a range of media, including:

- advertising
- books
- newspapers and magazines
- music
- film
- comic books.

Each of these provides a particular context for the designer. In this unit, we look at music, film and comic books.

> Tip:
>
> Although streamed music has largely replaced albums, 'cover' artwork is still used online. Images need to be able to work on a small scale.

ILLUSTRATION AND MUSIC

Illustration has long been used to promote music, and in some cases has become nearly as important as the music itself, providing a visual expression of it. The clearest example of this is the album cover (for records and CDs). Here, the illustration becomes part of the product and its concept. Music and image reinforce one another. As in advertising (see pages 140–143), illustrators working in this field often need to appeal to a specific demographic group (Figure 2.45).

Practitioners can combine illustration with digital-based software platforms to create two-dimensional (2D) vector imagery that can be projected onto a very large screen. These play an important role in a musical performance, for example, as part of a backdrop (see Figure 2.46).

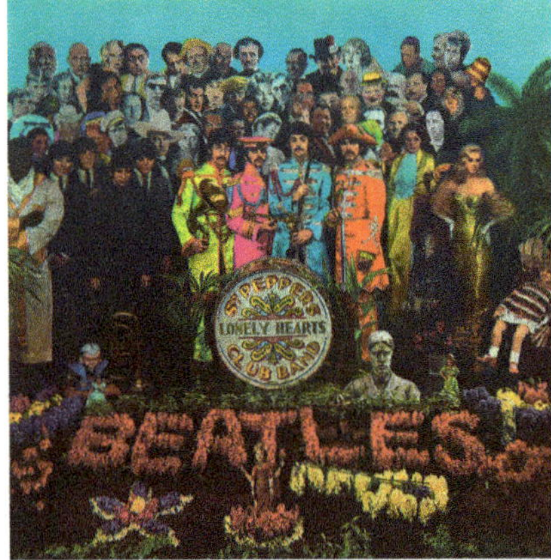

2.45 Peter Blake and Jann Haworth, *Sgt Pepper's Lonely Hearts Club Band*, album cover for The Beatles, 1967. For this classic album, the illustrators Peter Blake (born 1932) and Jann Haworth (born 1942) combined photography and illustration to produce a collage-type image that references the fashionable heroes and heroines of 1960s **counterculture**.

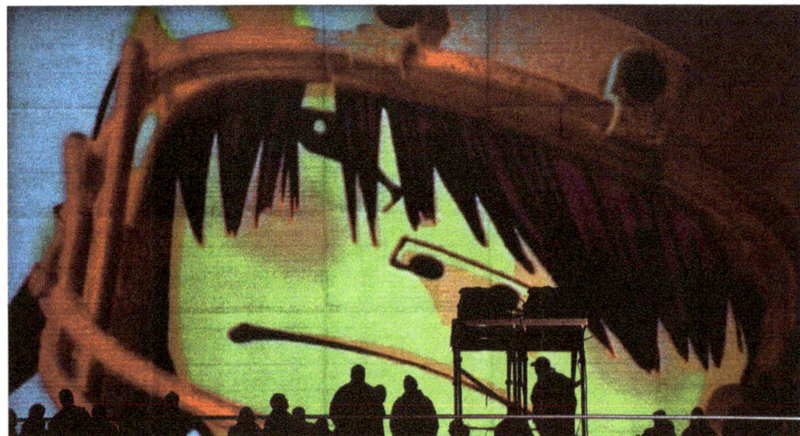

2.46 Jamie Hewlett, stage backdrop *Gorillaz*, 2006, London. Designer and comic book illustrator Jamie Hewlett's illustrated characters created for the band Gorillaz became as much a part of the group's identity as the actual musicians.

Activity A: **Create an illustration for an album cover**

1. As a class or individually, bring together a collection of album covers. Discuss/think about the illustration techniques that the designers have used to create them. How successfully do the covers 'marry with' the music?
2. Choose one of the album covers – perhaps one you thought was less successful – and create a new illustration to match the album. It will probably help to re-listen to the music, so that you get a feel for the concept or mood. For your illustration, you can use drawing and painting skills, collage or printmaking.

Further research

Research some classic album covers on the internet.

Materials and techniques: **Becoming a collector**

Printmaking typically produces 'clean' areas of flat colour and bold outlines and is the perfect means for creating crisp, eye-catching imagery for album covers. Printmaking can be used to create imagery for illustration in a variety of ways. Designers may use traditional relief printing techniques in illustrations, like engraving or etching (see page 28). They might combine traditional and digital printmaking techniques by scanning hand-printed imagery and using this in software-based illustrations. There are also software applications that allow illustrators to draw directly into digital formats with tablets and stylus, such as Wacom.

ILLUSTRATION AND FILM

Designers have long used illustration to promote films, especially in the form of the poster. Poster illustrators have traditionally presented a collaged 'snapshot' of all the film's key elements – genre, characters and settings – into a single image (see Figure 2.47). Some posters today combine stills from the film, edited and collaged using software. The principle is still the same: to present the key characters and portray a feel or taste of the film's subject and mood.

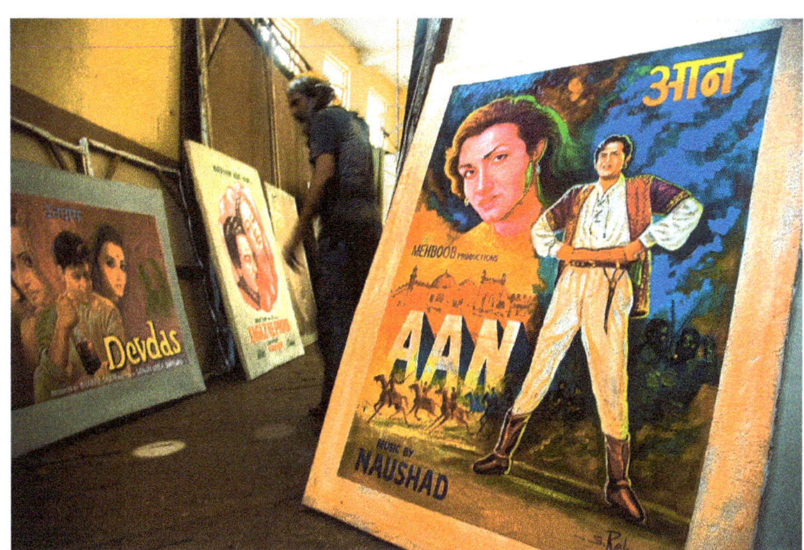

2.47 Poster for the **Bollywood** musical *Aan* (1952, dir. Mehboob Khan). *Aan* was India's first Technicolor film, so the bold colours of the poster gave the audience a preview of the visual style of the film.

Bollywood Name given to India's film industry.
counterculture Subculture that rebels against the conventions of the dominant culture.

Artists and designers: **Yuko Shimizu**

Yuko Shimizu (born 1946) is a Japanese illustrator. She is known for her cover work for the comic-book series *The Sandman: The Dream Hunters* (2008–9) and *The Unwritten* (2009–15). She has also produced work for magazines *Rolling Stone* and *Time*, book covers for publishers Scholastic and Penguin, and subway posters.

Shimizu's early influences were cartoons and comics in Japan from the 1960s and 1970s. Some images show limited perspective, with depth suggested by changes in tone and colour, rather than lines converging in the distance, as in some Western art. Her work also shows the influence of traditional Japanese woodblock printing in its use of flat colour, bold compositions and use of negative and positive space (Figures 2.48 and 2.49).

Shimizu works with a combination of traditional and digital techniques, exploring Japanese calligraphic materials such as specialist pens and nibs, alongside digital colouring.

Shimizu is able to adapt her style to suit her subject matter. Figure 2.50 shows an illustration for an article about the Chinese space programme. She has looked to Chinese propaganda posters for inspiration, mimicking the bold colours and dynamic composition.

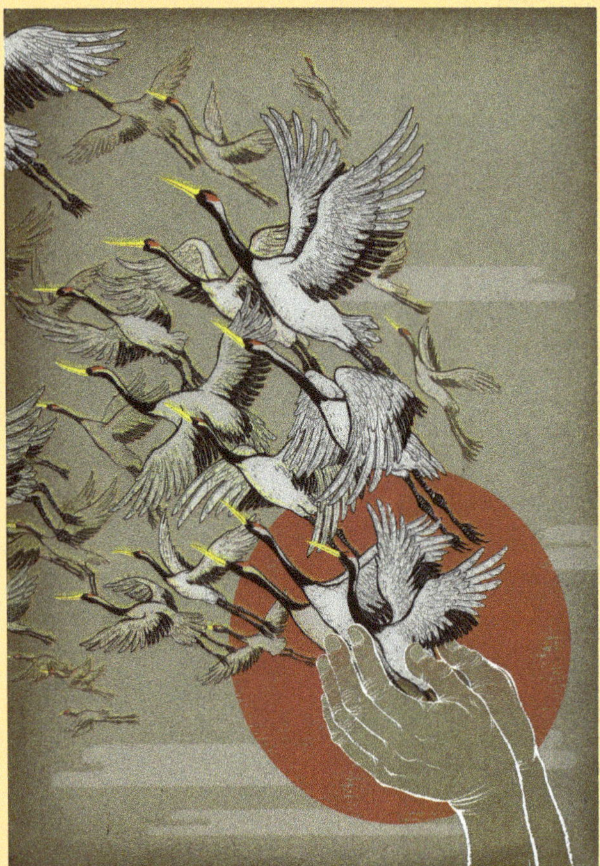

2.48 Yuko Shimizu, *Mitsui PR Committee poster*, a call for entries poster for the *Mitsui Golden Craftsmanship Awards*, 2015. Shimizu uses a mixture of traditional Japanese calligraphic techniques and digital colouring. The strong pattern formed by the **interplay** between positive and negative space is typical of Shimizu's illustration work.

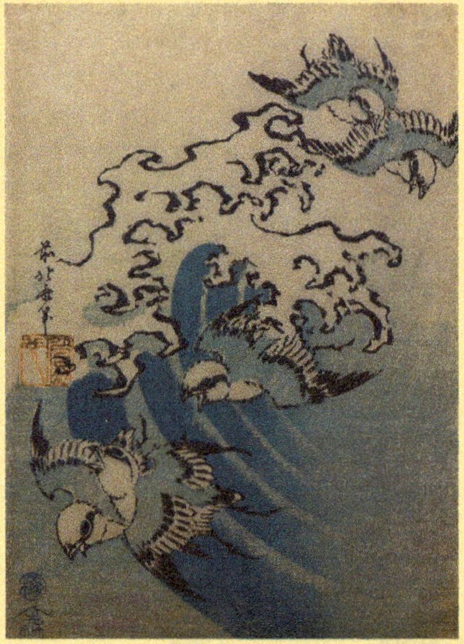

2.49 Katsushika Hokusai, *Waves and Birds*, c.1825, colour woodblock print, Victoria and Albert Museum, London. An example of traditional Japanese printmaking exploring movement through composition, line and simple colour. What similarities can you see with Shimizu's work? And what differences?

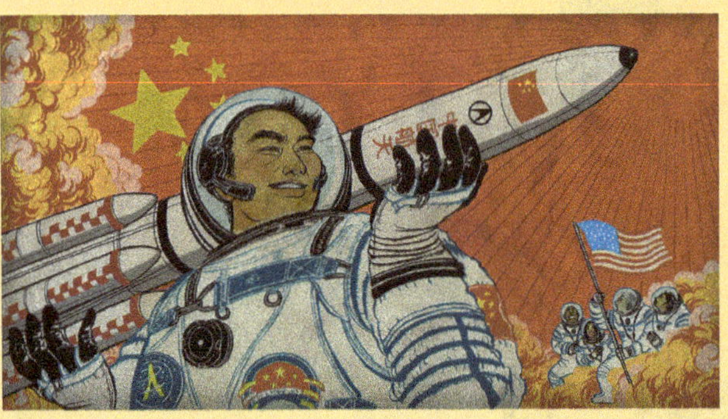

2.50 Yuko Shimizu, *China's Race to Space Domination*, opener illustration for *Popular Science Magazine*, October 2016.

ILLUSTRATION AND COMIC BOOKS

The comic book is one of the richest fields in contemporary illustration. There is a very wide range of comic-book styles for a designer to explore. These include:

- classic American styles (1940s) – often laid out in square grids and featuring bold drawing styles (for example, *Marvel* superhero comics)
- classic European schematic style (*ligne claire*) – clear outlines, geometric shapes, no shadows (for example, Hergé's *Tintin*)
- manga – Japanese styles often featuring characters with large eyes and small noses, **speed lines** and **screentones**
- American noir styles (1980s) – inspired by Hollywood **film noir**, featuring gloomy urban settings, night-time and/or rainy scenes and use of silhouettes.

There is also a very wide variety of genres, from children's comics, to adult graphic novels, to non-fiction. Whatever the genre, the combination of image, text and narrative can be extremely powerful.

Activity B: **Make a comic-book diary of your typical day**

The aim of this activity will be for you to create a simple comic-book page with six to eight **panels** of the same or various sizes, combining illustration techniques.

1. Divide your typical day up into segments – from waking up to going to bed.
2. Using drawing as a starting point, create a set of six to eight illustrations that tell the story of your day. Explore combining different techniques in the illustrations – for instance, by using pen to draw characters over backgrounds made from printed surfaces.
3. Bring the illustrations together on a comic-book page. Try to make sure that the page has its own visual rhythm.

Critical thinking:

Display and critically review the comic-book page you produced for **Activity B**.

- Does it successfully describe the different stages in your day?
- How well did your chosen illustration style(s) work with the material?
- How well did your illustrations work as a group?
- Ask your classmates for feedback as well – what do they think about your work?

Further research

For an introduction to illustrating comic books, see *Foundations in Comic Book Art* by John Paul Lowe (Watson-Guptill, 2014).

To find further examples, search online using a term such as 'comic book illustration'.

Tip:

You can create surfaces and textures before you start. Paint flat colour onto paper, let it dry and print textures over this using monoprinting, rollers or basic drypoint techniques. These can be experimental abstract surfaces or blends, to be used later to create interest in illustrations.

film noir From the French for 'black'. Genre of Hollywood crime films of the 1940s and 1950s featuring low-key lighting, gritty urban settings and dramatic use of shadow.
interplay Where two or more features work together.
panel Single image in a comic book.
screentone A dotted pattern applied as the backdrop of an illustration to create an overall shade or texture, using pre-printed sheets or computer graphics.
speed lines Parallel lines used in comic books to suggest movement.

Signage

Learning objective:

- To understand contextual factors and concepts in signage

Signage is used to communicate very specific messages. Signs provide information and directions that are **unambiguous** and direct. This unit looks at how signage is influenced by contextual factors, such as location and technology.

CONCEPTS IN SIGNAGE DESIGN

In creating signs, designers have to consider **semiotics** – how signs are communicated and received.

Sender →	Message →	Receiver
• Uses symbols and language to design the message • Understands the **conventions**	• In language understood by receiver • Must be made using conventions that can be understood	• Can read the language and symbols to understand the message

Activity A:
Assess the road signage in your neighbourhood

1. Using a camera, record a range of traffic signs in your neighbourhood. Make notes on the contexts in which the signs are used.
2. Assess the signs in terms of their use of formal elements, including typography, colour and shape.
3. How successful do you think the signs are in communicating their message? How do you think they could be improved?

TECHNOLOGY

Technology has enabled designers to make larger, more **durable**, brighter signage. For example, designs can be printed directly onto vinyls for banners to promote special events, or onto aluminium surfaces that have a long lifespan. Intricate designs that were once handmade can now be directly transferred from a computer screen to a surface material or shown on projection screens. Digital signage can change according to need to communicate varied messages, such as train departures in a station.

SIGNS AS SIGNALS – TRAFFIC SIGNALS

Traffic signage has to give instantly accessible directions and information. To achieve this immediate delivery of information, signs have to be *legible* and *readable*, especially as drivers must sometimes read them at speed. The manuals *Uniform Traffic Control Devices* and *Standard Highway Signs* are generally used to standardise road signage in the USA. Other countries have adopted versions of these, adapted for use with the local language (Figure 2.51). 'Smart' motorway signage can now change its message according to circumstances. For instance, speed limits can be altered on a stretch of road if it is busy.

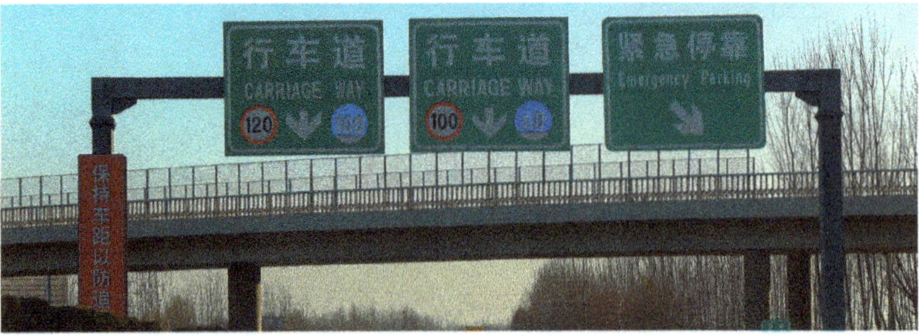

2.51 Chinese road signs on the Jinji Expressway, Tianjin, showing lane designations.

USING PICTOGRAMS AS SYMBOLS IN SIGNS

Signs are often used on packaging or in the workplace and are required by law. Some of these use **pictograms** to communicate their meaning or message rapidly, especially where there is danger to life or health. Such signs need to be universal: viewers must be able to read the imagery very quickly and interpret the signs' meaning whatever their native language (Figure 2.52).

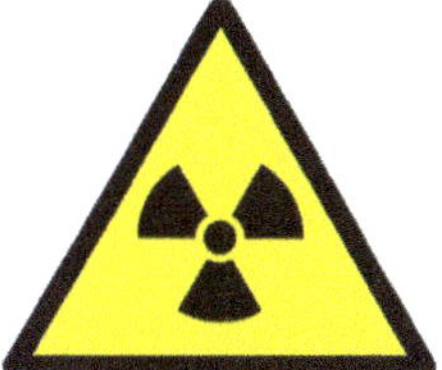

2.52 Universal hazard warning signs. How many of these do you recognise?

Activity B: **Create a design for a warning sign**

Design a warning sign for a specific situation, warning against either:

a. using a mobile phone while driving, *or*
b. sitting at a computer screen for too long.

You should:

1. Research existing signs relating to these warnings or uses.
2. Clarify what your message should be, based on facts you have found out about the hazard or danger.
3. Make drawings of source imagery from which you can develop designs.
4. Develop your source material to come up with a least two versions of your sign.

Critical thinking:

Display your work for **Activity B**. Review and evaluate this work with your classmates:

- How effectively does your design communicate the intention or message?
- How have you used visual language to communicate your message?
- How have you simplified details to achieve a simple, immediately readable sign?

Further research

For a thorough guide to designing signs, see *Signage Systems & Information Graphics: A Professional Sourcebook* by Andreas Uebele (Thames & Hudson, 2009).

conventions The use of shapes, colours and scale in signs to communicate – for example, using red as a colour in hazard signs.
durable Lasting.
pictograms A simple drawing, the earliest form of writing.
semiotics The study of signs and how they communicate and work.
unambiguous With one clear meaning.

De diſſectione partium corporis humani, Liber ſecundus.

Procemium.

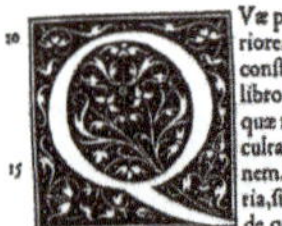

Væ partes in humano corpore ſolidiores & exteriores erant, quæ'q; ipſam machinam potiſſimum conſtituebant, ſatis iam explicatæ nobis videntur libro ſuperiore. Sequitur, vt internas percurramus quæ maximè pertinent ad vitam, & ad earum facultatum quibus incolumes viuimus conſeruationem. In quo (quemadmodũ inſtituimus) ſubſtantia, ſitus, forma, numerus, cõnexio, earum partium de quibus ſermo futurus eſt, breuiter exponenda. Ad quod munus ſtatim aggrediemur, ſi pauca prius de inſtituto ac de iudicio noſtro ſubiunxerimus. Quanq̃ enim hic noſter in ſcribendo ac diſſecando labor, complures non modo in anatomes cognitione, ſed etiam in Galeni ſententiæ interpretatione iuuare poterit: tamen interdũ veremur, ne quibuſdam nomen hoc anatomicum ſit inuiſum: mirentúrq; in ea diſſectione tantum nos operæ & temporis ponere: cum alioqui ab ijs qui nummorum potius quàm artis aucupio dant operam facile negligatur. Atq; ita nobis occurritur, dum quærunt: ſatiſne conſtanter facere videamur, qui cum corporis humani partiũ longiori indagationi ſtudemus, quæ magis ſunt vtilia, imprimiſq; neceſſaria prætermittimus: ſatius eſſe affirmantes, eius rei cognitionem ſicco (vt aiũt) pede percurrere, in qua alia certa, alia incerta eſſe dicunt: alia probabilia, alia minus probabilia inueniri. Quod certe dictum (ſi qui tamen inueniantur qui hoc dicant) hominum mihi videtur parũ conſyderate loquentium: atq; in maximis rebus errantium. Quibus vellem ſatis cognita eſſet noſtra ſententia. Non enim (vt inquit quidã) ſumus ij quorum vagetur animus errore: & incertis rebus demus operam, neque habeamus vnq̃ quod ſequamur. Quid enim eſt, per deos, abſoluta anatomes cognitione optabilius? quid præſtantius? quid Medico vtilius? quid Chirurgo dignius? quã qui expetunt & adſequuntur, tandemũ Medici ac Chirurgi dicendi ſunt: nec quicq̃ eſt aliud, quod Medicum aut Chirurgum magis commendet, quàm ipſa anatome. Cuius ſtudium qui vituperat, haud ſanè intelligo quidnam ſit quod laudãdum in huiuſmodi viris aut artibus putet. Nam ſiue oblectatio quæritur animi: quid æquè delectat, aut ingenuos animos afficit, atq; conditoris noſtri, in hoc microcoſmo procreando, diligenter perſcrutatum artificium? ſiue perfectio, & abſoluta quædam ars petitur: certe abſq; anatome, Medicina aut ars nõ erit, aut nulla omnino. Itaque neceſſe eſt, qui hæc omnia in quibus tantopere inſudamus, neglexerit: artem quoq;

Abbildung 139 Antiqua von Garamond (?) aus der Werkstatt von S. de Colines. 1545 137

2.53 A page from a book set in a typeface designed by Claude Garamond, 1454. Look closely at the letterforms and page layout. How would you describe them?

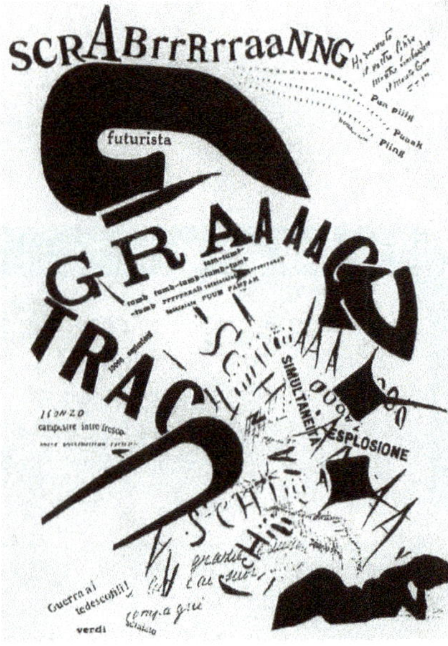

2.54 Filippo Tommaso Marinetti, a page from *Futurist Words in Freedom*, Edizioni futuriste di 'Poesia', Milan, 1919. The typographic layout of this poem expresses the conflict and confusion of the time, just after World War I (1914–18). Expressiveness is more important than legibility.

Typography

Learning objectives:

- To understand contextual influences in typography
- To develop a letterform based on a concept

Typography reflects the concerns and interests of particular times through its letterforms, compositions and applications. In this unit, we look at three examples, drawn from different times and places.

HUMANIST TYPE DESIGN

The introduction of mechanical printing in Europe in 1439 brought typography to the front of European culture. In the late 15th century, typefaces designed for the printing presses reflected and spread the ideals of the Renaissance, to which beauty, proportion and harmony were key. These ideals were collectively known as Humanism. In a period when new Humanist ideas were spread primarily through books and pamphlets, clarity in typography and page design was all-important.

Type designers designed both **roman** and **italic fonts**. The French type designer Claude Garamond (c.1490–1561), for example, created elegant roman and italic typefaces in which the focus was on legibility and readability (Figure 2.53). Descendants of Garamond's typefaces are still in use today, including as a screen font. Most serif typefaces used in books are still classified as 'Humanist'.

FUTURIST TYPOGRAPHY

At the beginning of the 20th century, the Futurists had a very different vision of the role of typography. Futurist artists, writers and designers believed that the speed of city life, technology, and even violence and war, were positive and necessary to the development of a modern world. Filippo Tommaso Marinetti (1876–1944) was an Italian poet and writer who argued that typography should express this new world. He called for an end to the harmonious pages of Humanist typography. Futurist books, he argued, should use lots of clashing typefaces and colours (Figure 2.54).

Activity A: **Draw different letterforms**

Drawing letterforms is a good way to get to know their characteristics.

1. Choose two of the following typefaces, one serif and one non-serif: Bembo, Gill Sans, Helvetica, Nagasaki, Nordic, Rockwell, Sabon.
2. Research the history and context of the typefaces.
3. Select and draw two of the same letterforms – for example, the letters A and R – from each typeface.
4. Compare their component parts, such as x-height, the **counter** and so on.
5. Can you identify any influences on the design of the letterforms?

CHINESE TYPOGRAPHY

Chinese writing is based on characters, rather than letters. Each character usually represents a syllable. The original characters, of which there were tens of thousands, were etched onto bone and shells. They have since gone through many changes to arrive at the modern versions. The biggest period of change was in the Qin Dynasty, around the 2nd century BCE, when the different variations of characters were brought together to form one writing system. In the 1950s the writing system was simplified even further, to make it more accessible.

To read a Chinese newspaper, a reader must be aware of some 2000 characters, each formed with a variety of strokes. Until recently, screen resolutions were too low to be able to show all of the curves and strokes in the characters. Advances in screen and smart phone technology mean that users are now able to use more defined characters, and the demand for new, personalised and modern typefaces is growing (Figure 2.55).

蒲松齡的《聊齋誌異》在成書之初，就受到人們的喜愛。 ← 11 pixels
蒲松齡的《聊齋誌異》在成書之初，就受到人們的喜愛。 ← 12 pixels
蒲松齡的《聊齋誌異》在成書之初，就受到人們的喜愛。 ← 13 pixels
蒲松齡的《聊齋誌異》在成書之初，就受到人們的喜愛。 ← 14 pixels
蒲松齡的《聊齋誌異》在成書之初，就受到人們的喜愛。 ← 15 pixels
蒲松齡的《聊齋誌異》在成書之初，就受到人們的喜愛。 ← 16 pixels
蒲松龄的《聊斋志异》在成书之初，就受到人们的喜爱。 ← 11 pixels
蒲松龄的《聊斋志异》在成书之初，就受到人们的喜爱。 ← 12 pixels
蒲松龄的《聊斋志异》在成书之初，就受到人们的喜爱。 ← 13 pixels
蒲松龄的《聊斋志异》在成书之初，就受到人们的喜爱。 ← 14 pixels
蒲松龄的《聊斋志异》在成书之初，就受到人们的喜爱。 ← 15 pixels
蒲松龄的《聊斋志异》在成书之初，就受到人们的喜爱。 ← 16 pixels

2.55 Firefly, an example of a low-resolution Chinese font.

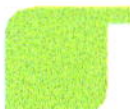

Activity B: **Design a typographic element for an event near your home**

1. Select an event that is happening near your home this year – for example, a festival, racing event or fair.
2. Take the name of the event and develop letterforms that you feel sum up the type of event. For instance, if it is a rural event, make your letterforms reflect this.
3. You need only create the letterforms in the title wording, not the complete alphabet.

Further research

Read *Type: A Visual History of Typefaces and Graphic Styles* by Cees W. De Jong and Alston W. Purvis (Taschen, 2017).

Critical thinking:

Review your practical work for **Activity B.**

- What event did you choose, and what characteristics did you associate with it?
- How did you decide your letterforms could reference the ideas or characteristics of the event?
- Did you use any source materials to support this, such as drawing-related objects?
- How well do you feel your letterforms communicate your intention?

counter The negative space within a letter, such as O, A, D, where the counter is fully enclosed. Some letterforms have non-enclosed negative space, such as G, U, C – these are also called counters.
italic font A sloping typeface.
roman font An upright typeface.

2.3 Textiles and fashion

Reconstructed textiles and fashion

Learning objective:

- To explore the concept of sustainability in textiles and fashion

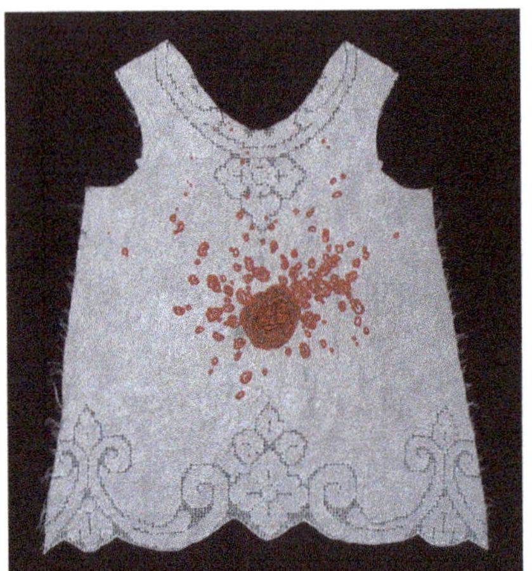

2.56 Erin Daniels, *Healing Sutra #10*, 2012, hand embroidery on antique table linen cut to the shape of a child's dress.

We are more and more concerned with our environment, and textile designers are finding creative ways to follow this trend. Environmental **sustainability** is a concept you will come across frequently during your A Level course and in the future if you choose a career in fashion and textiles. In this unit, we focus on textile designers who have a passion for recycling or reviving old and found textiles and objects.

The American designer Erin Daniels is a contemporary embroidery artist who stitches and draws onto found, second-hand fabrics and clothes in a very spontaneous way. In her work, she explores family issues and weaves them into her fabrics. Often, she reworks the stains in the second-hand fabrics so that they resemble the wounds or the hurt in family history and creates something new and beautiful (Figure 2.56).

The Nigerian artist El Anatsui (born 1944) makes large textile sculptures by stitching together recycled everyday objects such as bottle tops, copper wire and plastics. His pieces resemble draped fabrics with surface pattern designs that are similar to traditional Ghanaian dress. By using the **discarded** objects in this way, he makes an important statement about global waste. French designer Isagus Toche also uses recycled materials for his creations (Figure 2.57).

The work of both these practitioners deals with reconstruction and transformation and may be considered as examples of upcycling.

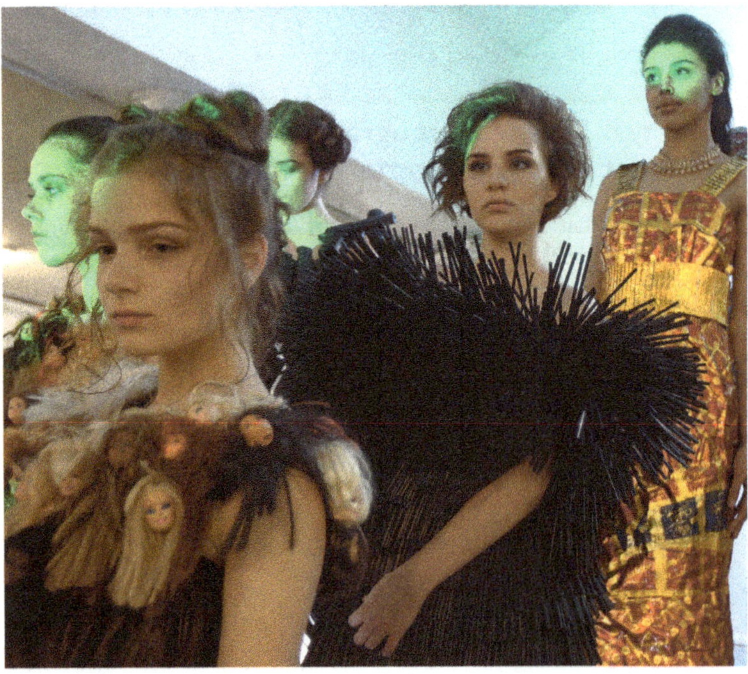

2.57 Models present creations made from recycled materials at a runway fashion show by French eco-designer Isagus Toche as a part of ecological forum, in Kiev, Ukraine, on 23 June, 2017.

Activity A: **Research a designer who uses upcycling in their work**

1. Choose one of the following fashion designers and research their use of found, vintage or recycled clothes in their work:
   - Belgian designer Martin Margiela (born 1957) (see Figure 2.58)
   - Dutch designers Viktor Horsting (born 1969) and Rolf Snoeren (born 1969) – known as Viktor & Rolf.
2. Write a short report (300 words) and present it to your classmates, with images if possible.
3. As a class, discuss the relationship between textiles, fashion and sustainability.

Activity B: **Explore reconstruction**

1. Begin by deconstructing an original piece of clothing so you have individual shapes.
2. Unpick the seams of the garment – avoid double-seam garments such as jeans.
3. Iron the individual fabric shapes.
4. Make paper patterns of each shape.
5. Place the fabric patterns on a **mannequin** and explore different ways to reconstruct the original shape.
6. Each time you make a new change, photograph it so that you have a record to present in your sketchbook, and make notes of the steps you took.

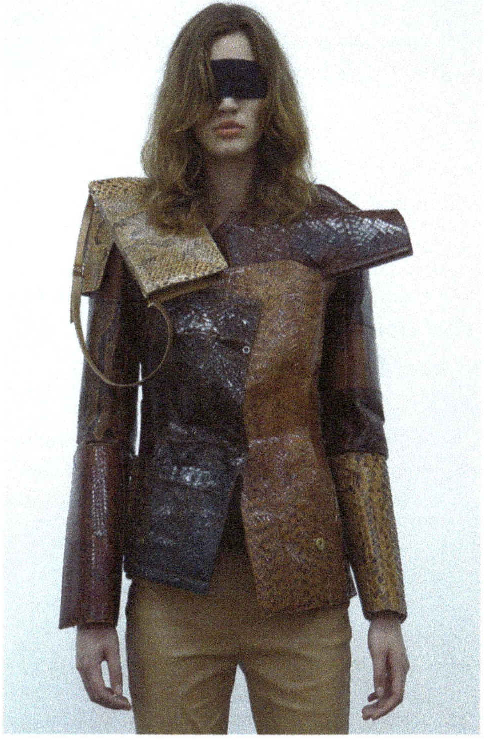

2.58 A model displays the creation of Maison Martin Margiela, made from deconstructed handbags, Paris Haute Couture Fashion Week, 2010.

Further research

Read *Sustainable Fashion and Textiles: Design Journeys* by Kate Fletcher (Routledge, 2014).

discarded Thrown away, forgotten or set aside.
mannequin A life-sized model of a person, usually used to display clothes.
sustainability Preserving natural resources to ensure the future of that industry as well as the planet.

Costume design

Learning objective:

- To use cultural contexts for research

Other cultures, as well as your own, are great sources of inspiration in costume design and fashion in general. If you have the opportunity to travel abroad or to a place that has a different culture from your own, take a sketchbook and camera to record what you find. You will find information in museums, galleries or on the street. Try to visit as much as you can to get first-hand research.

In this unit, we look at two examples of the use of cultural traditions to bring energy and colour to costume design.

ORIENTALISM

At the end of the 19th century and early 20th century, the countries of the West, especially in Western Europe, often turned to Asia in search of inspiration, vibrancy and bright colour. Art, literature, music and fashion were all inspired greatly by the reports, sketches and artworks brought home by Europeans travelling to places such as the Middle East. Often, Western people's ideas about the 'East' were coloured by a strong element of fantasy. Costume designers often took their inspiration from Western paintings of Eastern subjects (Figure 2.59), which mixed reality with the imagination. These kinds of works are today often known as **Orientalist**.

One costume designer who was deeply inspired by Orientalism was the Russian Léon Bakst (1866–1924), whose work we have also looked at in set design. In his costume designs for the ballet company Les Ballets Russes, he often used distinctive shapes, bold colours, rich embroidery and heavy appliqué, as well as accessories such as turbans, head-dresses and lavish jewellery.

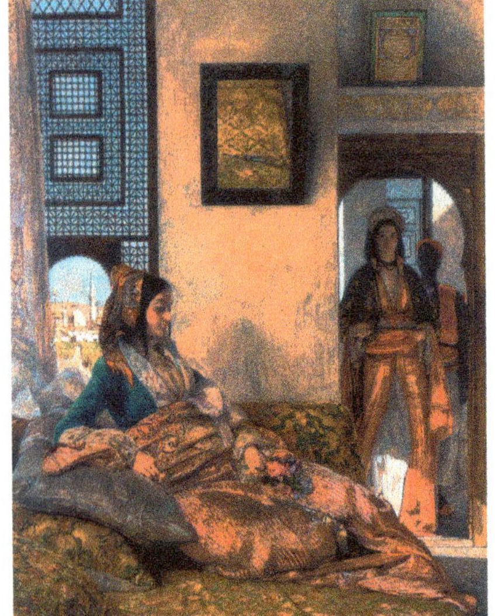

2.59 John Frederick Lewis, *Life in the Hareem, Cairo*, 1858, watercolour and bodycolour on paper, Victoria and Albert Museum, London. As a young man, the British artist John Frederick Lewis (1804–76) travelled widely in Turkey (then the Ottoman Empire). The experience influenced his artworks through his life.

Activity A: **Compare and contrast**

Compare and contrast Figures 2.59 and 2.60.

1. What similarities can you find? What differences?
2. Which do you think is more fantastic? Why?

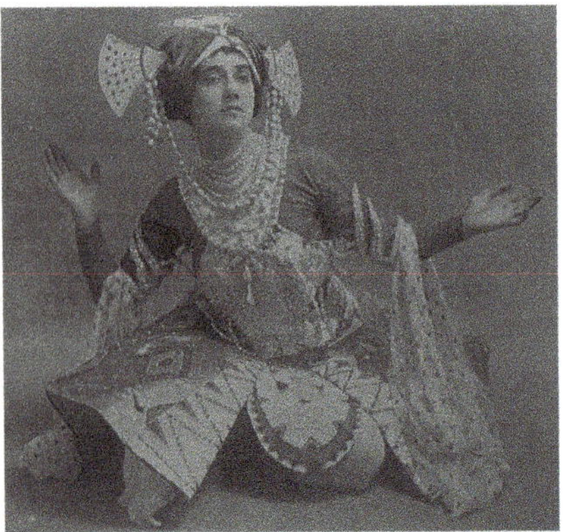

2.60 Léon Bakst, costume for Les Ballets Russes production of *Le Dieu Bleu*, 1912.

Activity B: **Discuss the use of other people's cultures in textiles and fashion**

Orientalism also influenced fashion. Research the work of the French fashion designer Paul Poiret (1879–1944). Use this research to have a class discussion about the ethics of using cultural influences in textiles and fashion. Think about:

1. Do designers have a right to take influences from other cultures?
2. Do you think that taking such influences demeans or celebrates the other culture?

MANISH MALHOTRA AND BOLLYWOOD

The Indian fashion designer Manish Malhotra (born 1966) often provides costume designs for Bollywood. In his fashion work, he often takes inspiration from his own cultural context and is known for his modern twists on traditional Indian clothing (see Figure 2.61). His silhouettes are an adaptation of the typical Indian garment known as the lehenga – a full-length skirt or gown often worn for traditional occasions. He often mixes in other cultural contexts as well – look online for examples of his work.

Bollywood films often celebrate traditional Indian culture and can feature lots of music and dance. For his Bollywood designs, Manish Malhotra keeps more closely to tradition but makes them spectacular by adding lots of detail such as **brocade** trims, and accessories such as jewel-studded collars (see Figure 2.62).

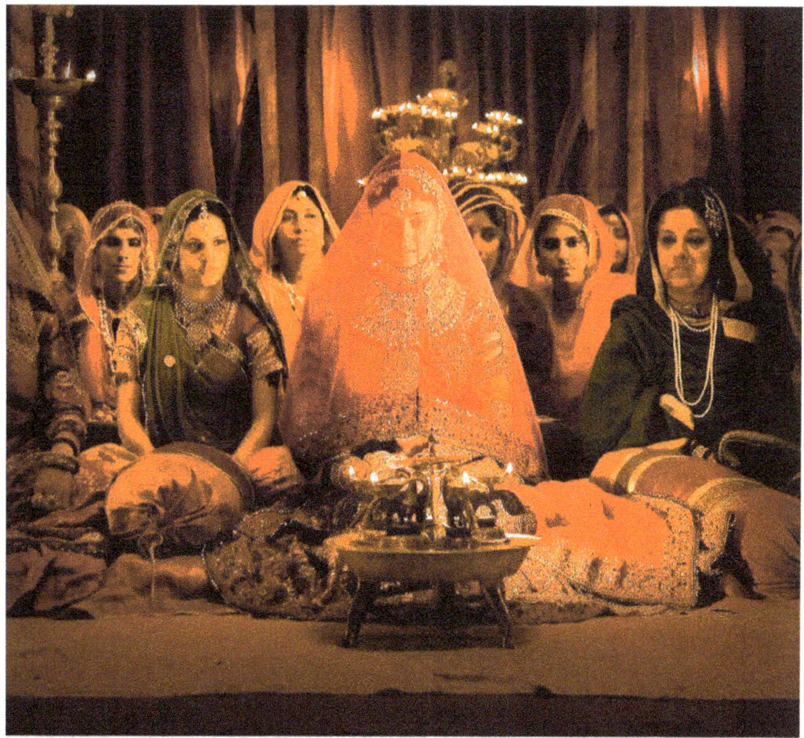

2.62 Manish Malhotra, embroidered sari for the film *Jodhaa Akbar* (2008, dir. Ashutosh Gowariker), worn by the actress Aishwarya Rai, seen in the centre of this still.

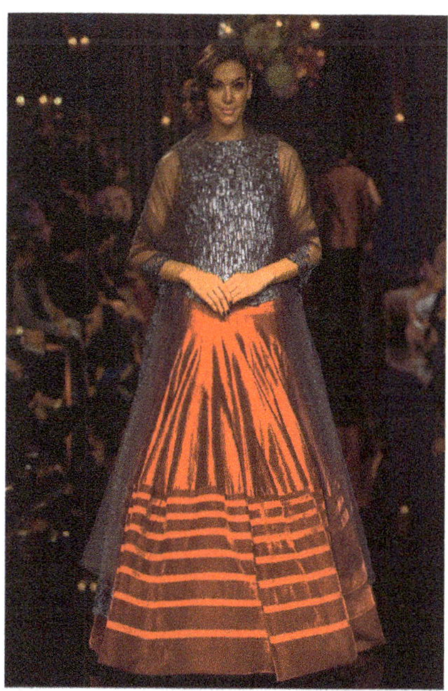

2.61 Manish Malhotra, 2014 catwalk collection,.

Further research

For the continued influence of Orientalism – especially Chinese art and culture – on global fashion, see *China: Through the Looking Glass* (Metropolitan Museum of Art, 2015).

Explore Manish Malhotra's designs on his website.

Activity C: **Explore cultural references and ways to use them for your own costume design ideas**

1. Take a character from a film or novel of your choice and reimagine the character set in a different culture or timeframe.
2. Find out as much information as you can about your chosen culture, by, for example, visiting galleries and studying paintings for costume details.
3. Create two or three coloured sketches for your character's new costume. Consider the personality of the character when creating your design.
4. Add annotations to explain your thinking and decisions.

brocade Richly decorated woven fabric.
Orientialism Term used to describe Western artworks, especially of the 19th and early 20th century, that took inspiration from many Asian cultures. Asian countries were loosely described at the time collectively as 'the Orient', meaning the East.

Fashion accessories

Learning objectives:

- To explore and understand traditional hat types/shapes
- To design a concept hat or 'head piece'

Hats have three main functions:

1. They often provide shelter and protection – for example, a broad-brimmed sunhat provides shade; a cycling helmet can prevent head injury in an accident.
2. They may show the person's role or status – a crown shows the wearer is a king or queen; a beret indicates that the wearer is perhaps a soldier.
3. They can have an aesthetic value – they can be beautiful, as objects in their own right and as accessories to complete or enhance an **ensemble**.

These functions can overlap. For example, we may expect a sunhat not just to keep light and heat away from the wearer's face, but also to look pretty and summery.

TRADITIONAL HAT SHAPES

It is this wide variety of functions that explains the large number and diversity of hat types and shapes that have evolved over history and across many cultures. Hat designers, of course, are usually most concerned with the aesthetic value of hats. However, they should have a good knowledge of more ordinary, practical hats, together with their meanings and associations. They should have an appreciation of their shapes and the materials they are traditionally made out of and also of who typically has worn them. Even quite ordinary hat types like the **tweed** flat cap – traditionally worn by working-class men in the UK – can provide rich inspiration for designers (Figures 2.63 and 2.64).

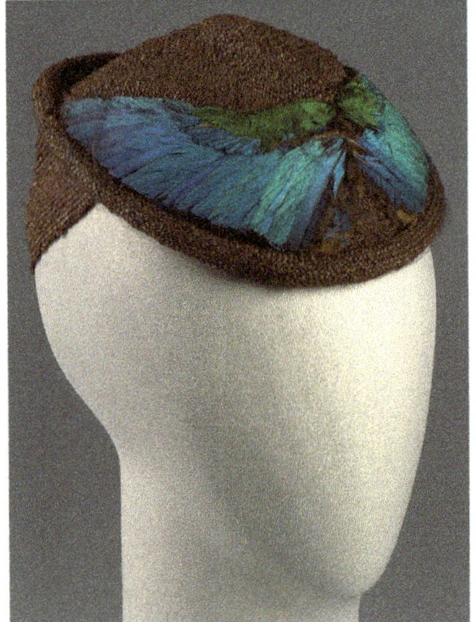

2.64 Lucienne Rabaté for Caroline Reboux, *Woman's hat*, c.1940, straw and feathers, The Metropolitan Museum of Art, New York. In her design, the French hat designer Lucienne Rabaté (1885–1960) has used elements of the masculine flat cap and added feminine embellishments in the form of brightly dyed feathers.

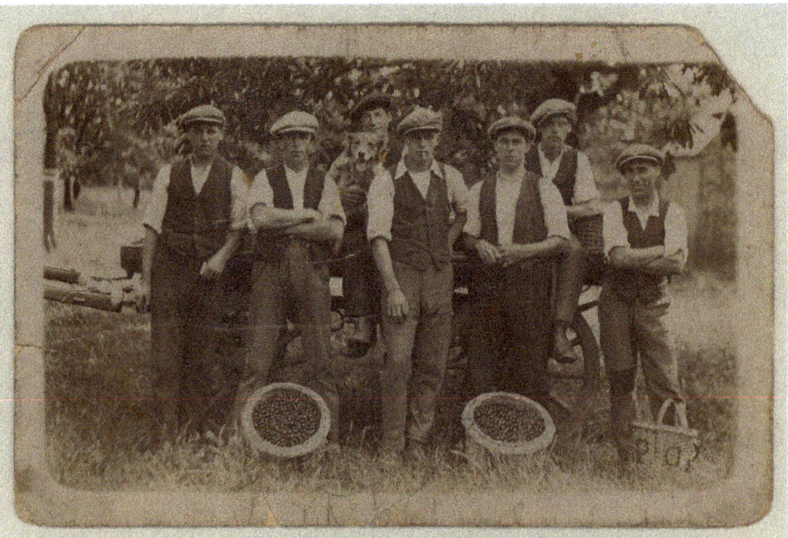

2.63 Farmworkers wear flat caps in this photograph taken in England in the 1900s.

Activity A: **Research and explore a hat type/shape**

1. Research one of the following hat types/shapes: baseball cap, bonnet, bowler hat, chef's toque, cloche hat, pork pie hat, top hat.
2. Find out about the hat's shape, the material it was traditionally made out of, and what kind of person wore the hat.
3. Make sketches from various angles, to gain an understanding of its 3D shape. Add annotations about the material, textures and any embellishments.
4. Using the basic shape as your starting point, make sketches for a new hat design. Your design should stay close to the original hat shape and should be practical, but add something new. You could change the function or material, for example.

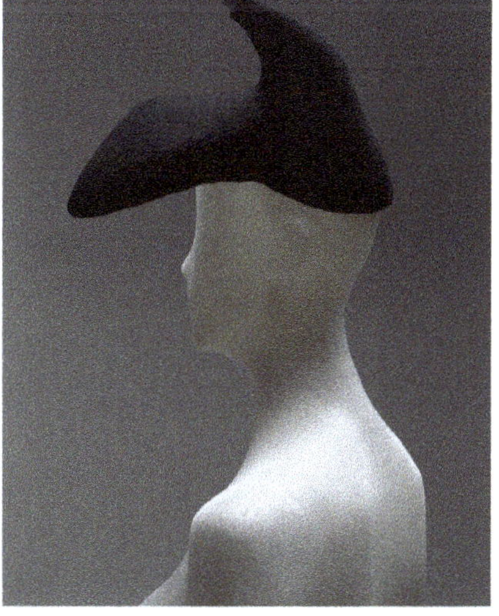

2.65 Elsa Schiaparelli, *Shoe Hat*, 1937–8, wool, The Metropolitan Museum of Art, New York. The hat was inspired by a photograph of Dalí wearing a shoe on his head.

CONCEPTUAL HATS

Hats are the most prominent of all fashion accessories, framing the head and face and adding a **flourish** that complements the rest of the wearer's clothes. For this reason, when creating for the fashion runway, a fashion designer quite often works closely with a hat designer. In this context, the hat not only can make an ensemble more memorable but it can make a statement about the concept or theme of the whole collection.

There is a long tradition of the 'concept' hat. The French queen Marie Antoinette (1775–93) wore lavish hats that sometimes made reference to contemporary events – for example, one hat took the shape of a ship to celebrate a recent French naval victory. One of the most famous hats ever made was the *Shoe Hat* (1937–8), made by Elsa Schiaparelli in collaboration with the Surrealist artist Salvador Dalí (Figure 2.65).

Fashion designers continue to experiment with conceptual, sculptural shapes. The focus is less on making a wearable, functional hat than making an object that sums up the designer's themes and intentions (Figure 2.66).

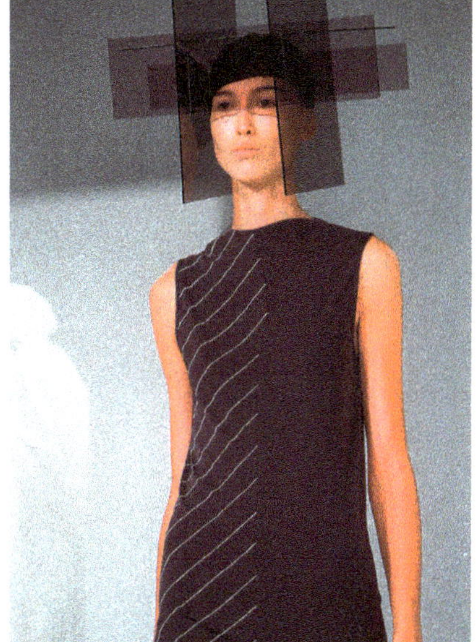

2.66 Scott Wilson for Hussein Chalayan, *Hat*, 1998. The Cypriot-born British designer Hussein Chalayan (born 1970) is well known for the conceptual 'head pieces' created for his fashion shows.

Activity B: **Create a concept hat or head piece**

In this activity, you should create a design for a hat on the theme 'Global Warming'. Consider how a hat might reflect this theme, perhaps in terms of its materials or shape.

Your design for a hat in **Activity A** was probably functional and wearable. This time your concept should play the lead role in defining your design.

Create a series of sketches exploring your idea and share them with your classmates for evaluation and discussion.

Further research

Explore the hat collection of London's Victoria and Albert Museum on their website.

For inspiration for contemporary hat design, read *Hats & Caps: Designing Fashion Accessories* by Gianna Pucci (Promopress, 2013).

ensemble Outfit.
flourish To do something with flowing, sweeping strokes.
tweed Rough woollen fabric made in Britain and Ireland, often with flecks of colour or a herringbone pattern. The material is associated with clothes designed for outdoor pastimes such as shooting and hunting.

Screen printing

Learning objectives:

- To use text and typography in textiles and fashion
- To use screen printing as a simple way of adding surface pattern and text to textiles and garments

Screen printing is one of the simplest ways of adding pattern and colour to textiles and garments. It is also an effective way of adding text or logos. Some designers use text on clothing, like T-shirts, to be playful, informative or sometimes rude. Other designers use text as a way of expressing a point of view or concern. A printed garment is like a message board and draws attention whether used on the street or on the fashion runway. Often, as designers, we do not just want to create beautiful things but feel passionate about an issue and want to integrate this into our work.

In the 1980s, the British fashion designer Katharine Hamnett (born 1947) introduced this simple technique into the world of high fashion (Figure 2.67). From 1983, she produced a series of oversized T-shirts on which were printed slogans relating to the politics of the time. Her first political slogan 'CHOOSE LIFE' was a protest against war and destruction. Hamnett's approach to typography, too, was big and bold – she used block capital letters, so that the T-shirts almost seemed to shout out their message.

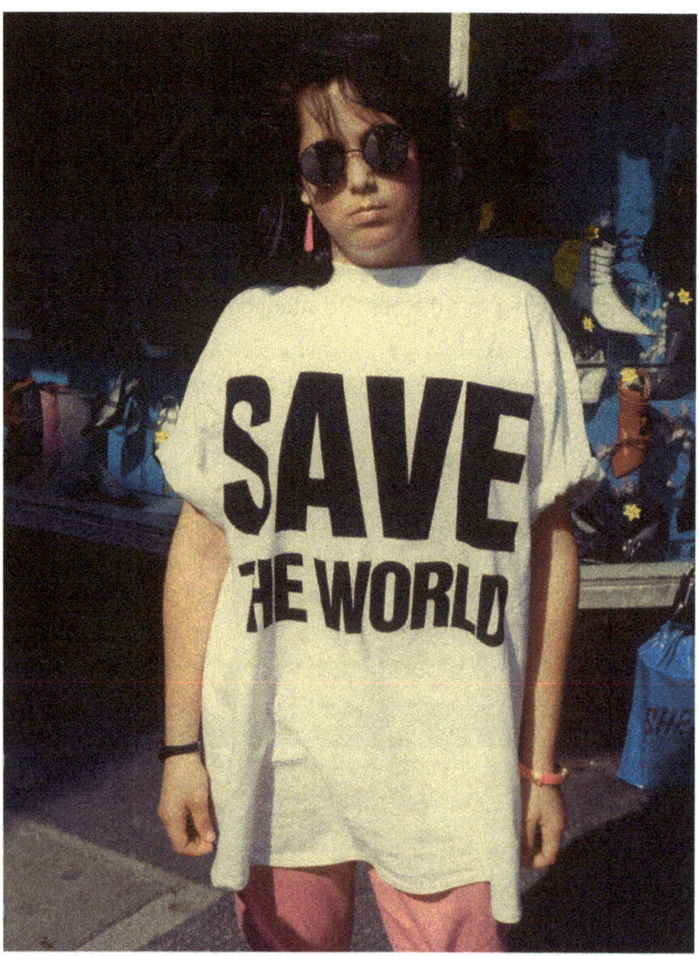

2.67 Katharine Hamnett, 1980s, oversized T-shirts with bold slogans.

Materials and techniques: **Simple screen printing**

To create your own simple screen prints, you will need:

- A4 screen (either ready-made or made by stretching 43T mesh over a canvas **stretcher** frame)
- washable screen-printing ink
- squeegee
- paper
- **craft knife**
- masking tape
- cotton T-shirt or textile

1. First create a stencil design. It needs to be one that you can easily cut out with the craft knife.
2. Cut out your design using the craft knife.
3. Use the masking tape to mask off the edges of the underneath of the screen. This is the side that will be in contact with the T-shirt or textile, so you want only the stencil design to come into contact with the ink.
4. Iron your T-shirt so it is smooth and flat.
5. Lay out your T-shirt and place the paper stencil on it where you want your design to appear. Place the screen on top.
6. Put a line of ink at the top edge of the screen.
7. Pull the squeegee firmly down across the screen, pushing the ink through the mesh. You need to use a lot of pressure. Repeat.
8. Hold the fabric down and lift the screen up and away.
9. When you have finished your print, wash the screen and leave to dry.

Activity A: **Use screen printing to add text to a T-shirt**

1. Choose a topic that is currently in the news and that you feel strongly about.
2. Create your slogan: it should be short and direct and use appropriate language.
3. Create a design that includes your slogan. You don't have to use the block capitals used by Hamnett. Research other typefaces and letterforms. Remember, though, that you will have to cut out the text with the craft knife, so the typeface should not be too detailed.
4. Use the stencil technique shown in the 'Materials and techniques' box to create your text.
5. Experiment with using multiple, different-coloured screen prints on the same garment.

Further research

For more on Katharine Hamnett's T-shirts, look at her website.

Search online for another method of screen printing T-shirts using photo emulsion.

craft knife A knife with a fine blade for cutting paper.
stretcher Wooden frame or support for canvas, which is stretched tightly across and stapled/pinned into place along the rear or edge.

2.4 Fine art

Painting

Learning objectives:

- To recognise different types of contextual influence and concepts in painting
- To understand how context can inform a concept
- To develop a painting response to a concept
- To explore making transcriptions of other artists' work

As we saw in the Introduction to this module, a wide range of factors influence painters and artists. These can include social, technological and scientific, environmental, political and spiritual influences. Artists can also be influenced by ideas and be inspired by the work of others. Influences can affect how artists select and use subject matter, themes and ideas in their work. They can also affect how they use materials, techniques and processes to develop their work.

Sometimes, painters work in groups or movements – sharing common ideas, goals and approaches. In this unit, we will look at some of the key movements in modern art, how these were shaped and how their ideas and approaches can continue to inspire and shape our artistic practice today.

We will also look at how the process of **transcription** can help us learn from the work of other artists.

REALISM

One approach or strategy to making art, and painting in particular, is for artists to record the world around them as closely as they can. This approach came to the fore in the 19th century. Realist painters such as the French artist Gustave Courbet tried to show life as it truly was (see Figure 2.68), not an **idealised** version of it.

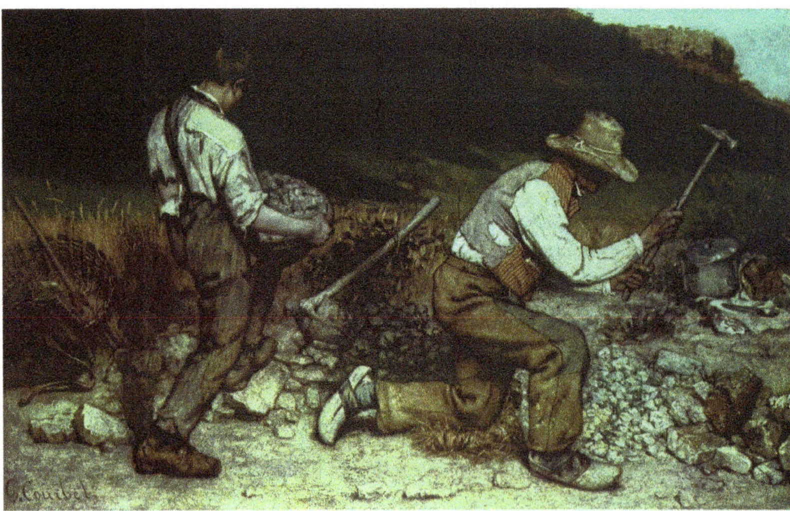

2.68 Gustave Courbet, *The Stone Breakers*, 1849, oil on canvas, Galerie Neue Meister, Dresden, destroyed 1945. Courbet's Realism is meant to be stark and unromantic. We can almost feel the backbreaking work of these two roughly dressed men as they break up stones in a harsh landscape.

Activity A: **Explore the theme 'Realism'**

Take the theme 'Realism' and research how you can make paintings based on it. Some artists respond to their surroundings, or use other people or themselves as subjects. Think about applying the skills that you have explored in drawing and painting techniques so far. Make notes about how you are interpreting the theme – is it an everyday scene or situation? Make at least two studies in paint that show your response to the theme.

The development of photography through the 19th century seemed to many people to undermine the Realist approach. What was the point of painting realistic images if photography could do this better and more easily?

Nonetheless, artists have continued to try to capture reality in their art. For example:

- In the early 20th century, Social Realists used painting (and other disciplines) to document the lives of ordinary working people. Their intention was often to draw attention to and criticise the conditions people lived in.
- In the 1960s and 1970s, a group of painters known as Photorealists used photographs as the basis to paint minutely accurate paintings of ordinary city scenes (see Figure 2.69).

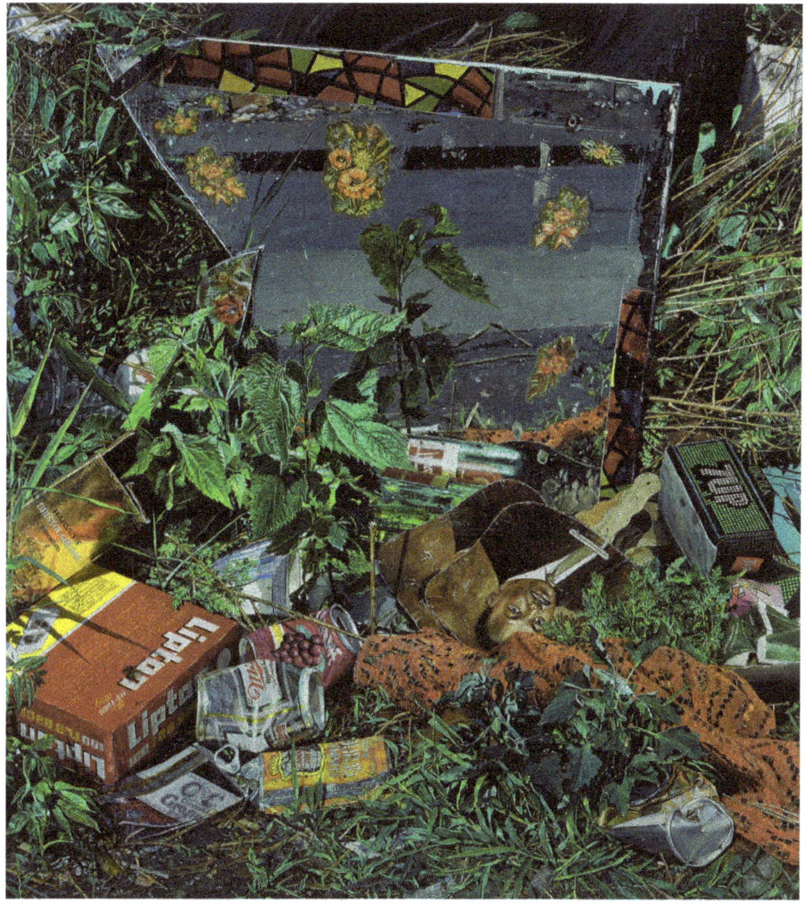

2.69 Idelle Weber, *126th Street, Harlem*, 1977, oil on linen, private collection. In this painting, Idelle Weber has presented a snapshot of litter on a street in Harlem, a district of New York City.

Critical thinking:

Display the studies from **Activity A** and evaluate: How successful is your representation of your theme? Which artists influenced you, and how?

Tip:

You can use drawings as a guide. Use them to work out the composition. You can also use them to add more detail on the painting if you need to.

Activity B: Develop your piece based on the theme 'Realism'

All the artists we have looked at in this section were reacting to things that influenced, inspired and even angered them. You can make your painting more meaningful by incorporating the influences around you.

1. Think about any other influences you may have:
   - List at least *three* key influences.
   - Briefly explain how each influences you.
2. Develop your studies from **Activity A** into a single artwork.

idealise To make something look better than it is in reality.

transcription In art, the reworking of the work of one artist by another. The verb is 'transcribe'.

Tip:

It is possible to view Impressionism as a development of Realism: it sought to capture reality.

IMPRESSIONISM

Art historians often consider Impressionism as the first modern art movement and the French painter Claude Monet as perhaps the archetypal Impressionist artist. From the late 1860s, Monet developed techniques for creating paintings out in the open air in front on his subjects. These were often the landscapes around Paris. He explored different atmospheric and light conditions, and used rapid brush marks to capture the fleeting effects of light and colour. *Impression, Sunrise* (Figure 2.70) is one of the best known of Monet's paintings. The title of this painting was used to sum up the art of these young **avant-garde** artists – Impressionism.

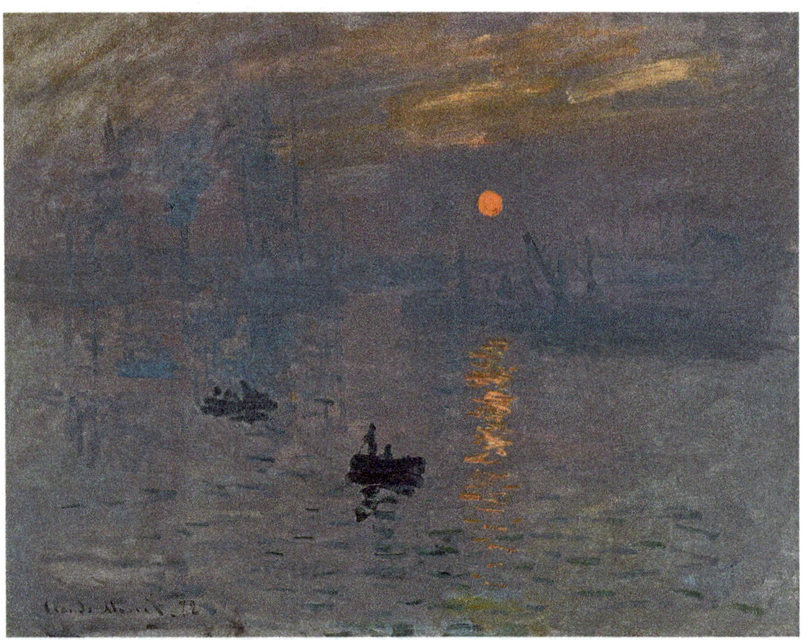

2.70 Claude Monet, *Impression: Sunrise*, 1873, oil on canvas, Musée Marmottan Monet, Paris.

Monet responded to many influences when making his paintings:

- Scientific: Monet was inspired by the scientific ideas of the French chemist Michel Eugène Chevreul, who had published works about light and the perception of colour.
- Themes and ideas in literature: He was influenced by the work of the writer Émile Zola, who wrote novels about contemporary life.
- Realism: He was inspired to seek out his version of truth or reality, and to do this he had to work outside, not in the studio.
- Technology: He was able to achieve this because oil paints had become available in tin tubes and were therefore portable.
- Modernity: He was inspired by the redevelopment of Paris, with new buildings and wide boulevards, and the development of a railway network, which enabled him to travel to the countryside.

Activity C:
Research the influences on a favourite artist

1. Choose a painting by an artist you admire.
2. Find at least three contextual influences on the work – more if you can. Say what kind of influence each is: scientific, technological and so on.
3. Briefly explain how the specific influences you found helped shape the artist's work.

ABSTRACTION

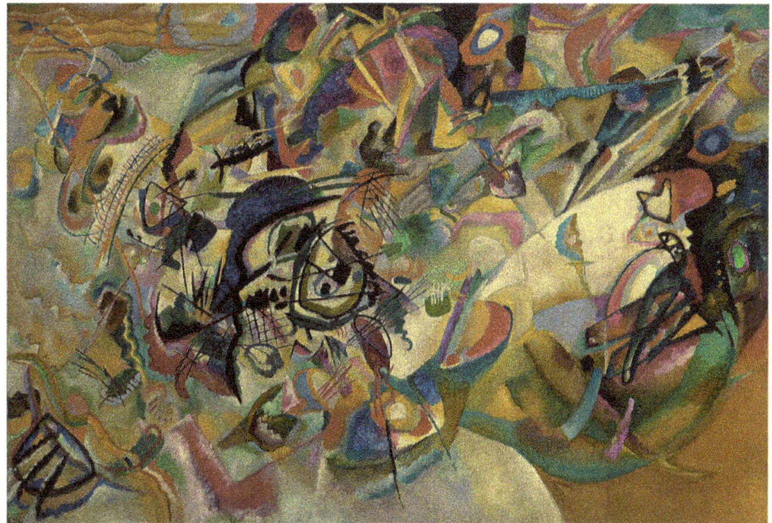

2.71 Wassily Kandinsky, *Composition No. 7*, 1913, oil on canvas, Tretyakov Gallery, Moscow. The Russian artist Wassily Kandinsky's (1866–1944) composition uses its own language of colour and forms.

Towards the end of the 19th century and at the beginning of the 20th century, new generations of avant-garde artists moved away from the Realist approach to art. They sought to depict an inner world of emotion and ideas. They used marks, shapes, colours and forms, not to reproduce real life, but for their own sake, as a kind internal visual language (see Figure 2.71). This development is known as 'abstraction'. Real things did not altogether disappear from the work of abstract artists, but they were simplified and transformed.

For some artists, such visual languages were like the language of music. A painting was seen as being like a piece of music. The harmonies between colours were like the harmonies between musical notes.

Activity D: **Explore the relation between sound and colour**

In this activity, you will explore the concept that paint can **equate with** sound. This kind of activity might not work at your first attempt; try it again. The piece of work at the end is less important than the experience of trying it.

1. Select a 30-second extract of music.
2. Listen to this extract *five* times. Each time you listen, make notes about what it reminds you of: 'a stormy sea', 'a dark and sinister street' and so on.
3. Now choose *four* colours to represent the emotional response you had to the music.
4. Draw a square onto a sheet of A2 paper and divide it into four smaller squares.
5. Paint the four colours as closely to how you imagined them.
6. You can develop this on another sheet if you feel more confident, such as using 16 squares in a 4 × 4 grid, and 16 colours.
7. Ask one of your classmates to spend some time looking at your work. Can they tell you roughly the kind of emotion or idea you were thinking about?

avant-garde People who work in a highly creative and experimental way.
equate with To be equivalent to; have the same effect as.

TRANSCRIPTION

To transcribe another artist's work of art means to recreate it in your own style or in another medium. It is not a copy, but a reinterpretation. Artists use transcription to:

- find out about others' work – how they have used colour, for example, or how they have expressed a particular idea
- pay tribute to another artist
- acknowledge the importance of a particular image or painting to their own work.

Look at Figures 2.72 and 2.73. The Dutch painter Vincent van Gogh here pays tribute to an artist he admires, the Frenchman Jean-François Millet, and whose work was important in his own development as an artist. Millet worked in a Realist style, showing the hard graft of a peasant as he scatters seed. Van Gogh has transcribed this image and made something new, using the brilliant, non-realistic colour harmonies of his own style – Post-Impressionism. Both artists were drawn to the theme because both respected the ordinary worker and believed they should be treated with dignity.

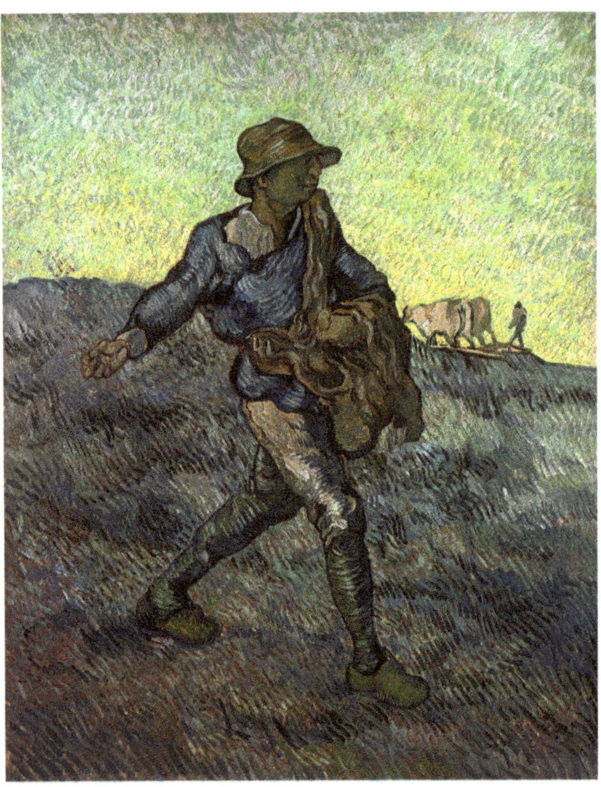

2.72 Vincent van Gogh, *The Sower (**after** Millet)*, 1890, oil on canvas, private collection.

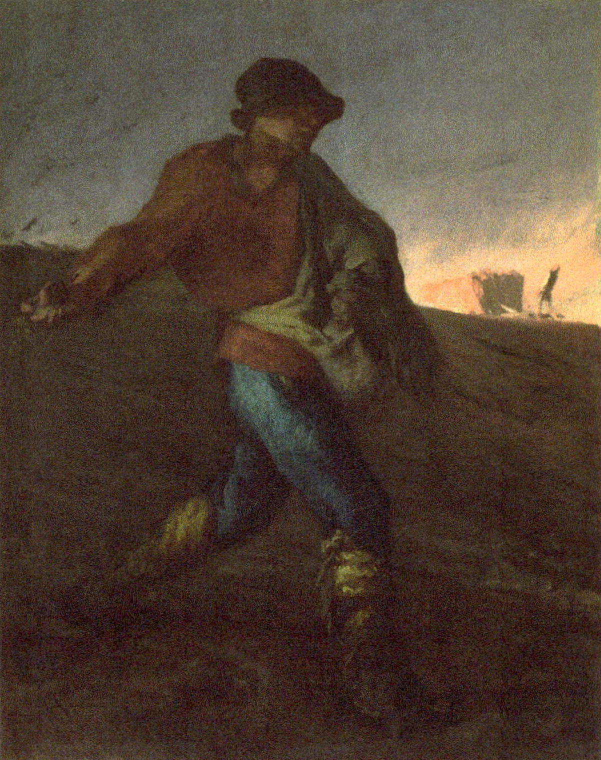

2.73 Jean-François Millet, *The Sower*, 1850, oil on canvas, Museum of Fine Arts, Boston.

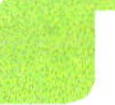

Activity E: **Make a transcription**

1. Select an image that is important to you. It might have a personal relevance to you, or be by an artist you admire, or show a subject or theme you often explore in your own work.
2. Write a short (75-word) justification for why you have chosen this image. Include a reference to any concepts and themes that the work contains.
3. Develop a transcription of the original that uses the image to explore a different approach to it.

BROADENING THE RANGE OF CONTEXTUAL FACTORS

As you develop your work, look for ideas and inspiration from non-art sources. Many artists have responded to ideas in literature in the past. Your work will have more relevance to you if you can include some of your own ideas about your surroundings, environment and situation. Think about which categories these might fall into – science, entertainment, religion, environment, technology, advertising and so on.

Critical thinking: **Evaluate your understanding of concepts and contextual factors**

As you complete the activities in this unit, think about how you have researched contextual factors:

- Can you describe 'contextual factors'?
- How might they influence artists' work?
- Can you identify any contextual factors that influence you?

Think about concepts:

- Do you understand how these are used by artists in their work – for example, as subject matter, to develop a series of pieces and so on?
- List at least two more ways artists used concepts in their work.

Think about making links between influences and ideas:

- Can you think of any examples in your work where one of your ideas has been directly influenced by a contextual factor?
- How was this influence shown or how did it physically affect the work?

Further research

Explore more of Claude Monet's Impressionist paintings at the Musée Marmottan Monet website.

Go to the Guggenheim museum website to find out more about Wassily Kandinsky in the development of abstraction.

A good survey of Photorealism is *Photorealism: Beginnings to Today* (Scala, 2014), while *The Music of Painting* by Peter Vergo (Phaidon, 2010) explores the relation between composers and artists.

'after' Used in an artwork title, this tells us that the image is based on another's work (for example, 'after Millet').

Drawing

Learning objectives:

- To become familiar with a range of artists and to make links with your own work as it develops
- To explore the medium of charcoal as a drawing material

Of all the fine art disciplines, drawing has one of the longest and richest histories. It is widely regarded as being the foundation of all artistic practice. However, artists have always used drawing in different ways to think about and explore their art practice. In this unit, we compare and contrast two approaches to drawing from the early 20th century – Cubist drawing and Surrealist automatic drawing.

The focus of this is on the portrait, so we also look at the portrait work of two contrasting contemporary artists, Frank Auerbach and Whitfield Lovell. As you work through this unit, consider how the approaches of all these movements and artists can enrich your own drawing practice.

CUBIST DRAWING

One of the most influential movements in art in the 20th century was Cubism. In Cubist artwork, the subject matter is analysed, broken up and reassembled in an abstract form. Instead of depicting objects from a single viewpoint, the artist depicts the subject from several different viewpoints to represent the subject in a greater context.

The first phase of the movement (c.1910–12) is known as **Analytical Cubism** and arose out of the experimental work of the French artist Georges Braque (1882–1963) and the Spanish artist Pablo Picasso (1881–1973). The charcoal drawing *Self-Portrait* (Figure 2.74) by another Cubist Spanish artist, Juan Gris (1887–1927), shows the Analytical Cubism approach.

In this work, Gris has broken down one-point perspective and instead used a geometric grid structure to create a multidimensional, fragmented image. He has applied the shading, used to give form to the face, in triangular blocks. The charcoal marks have all been applied in the same direction, and this has added to the angular quality of the drawing.

As a style of drawing, it is both abstract and representational at the same time.

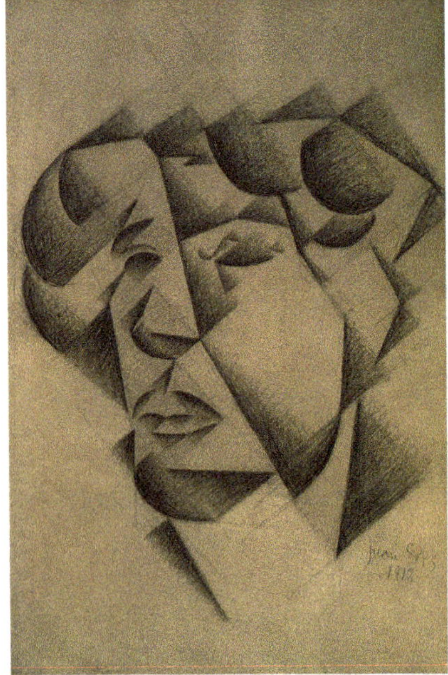

2.74 Juan Gris, *Self-Portrait*, 1912, charcoal on paper, private collection. Think about how light and shade have been used to create this multidimensional image.

Activity A: **Create a Cubist portrait**

1. Look closely at Juan Gris's *Self-Portrait* (Figure 2.74). Gris has produced a drawing that combines more than one view of his face.
2. Take two or three photographs, from slightly different viewpoints, of a classmate's face.
3. Using charcoal, create a portrait in a geometric Cubist style. Try not to mimic Gris's style too much, but bring your own interpretation.

SURREALIST AUTOMATIC DRAWING

As discussed in the introduction to this module, Surrealist artists used automatic drawing to unlock ideas and images from their unconscious minds, and to depict dream worlds. The pioneer of automatic drawing was the French artist André Masson (1896–1987), who made numerous automatic works in pen and ink (Figure 2.75).

In automatic drawing, the artist does not consciously think about what they are drawing. They draw by letting the pen or pencil move randomly across the paper. In this way, the drawing emerges by chance and, the Surrealists thought, from out of the artist's subconscious (that is, their non-rational) mind. Looking at the drawings that they had created, the artist might then try to see recognisable forms and develop the drawing into a more representational image.

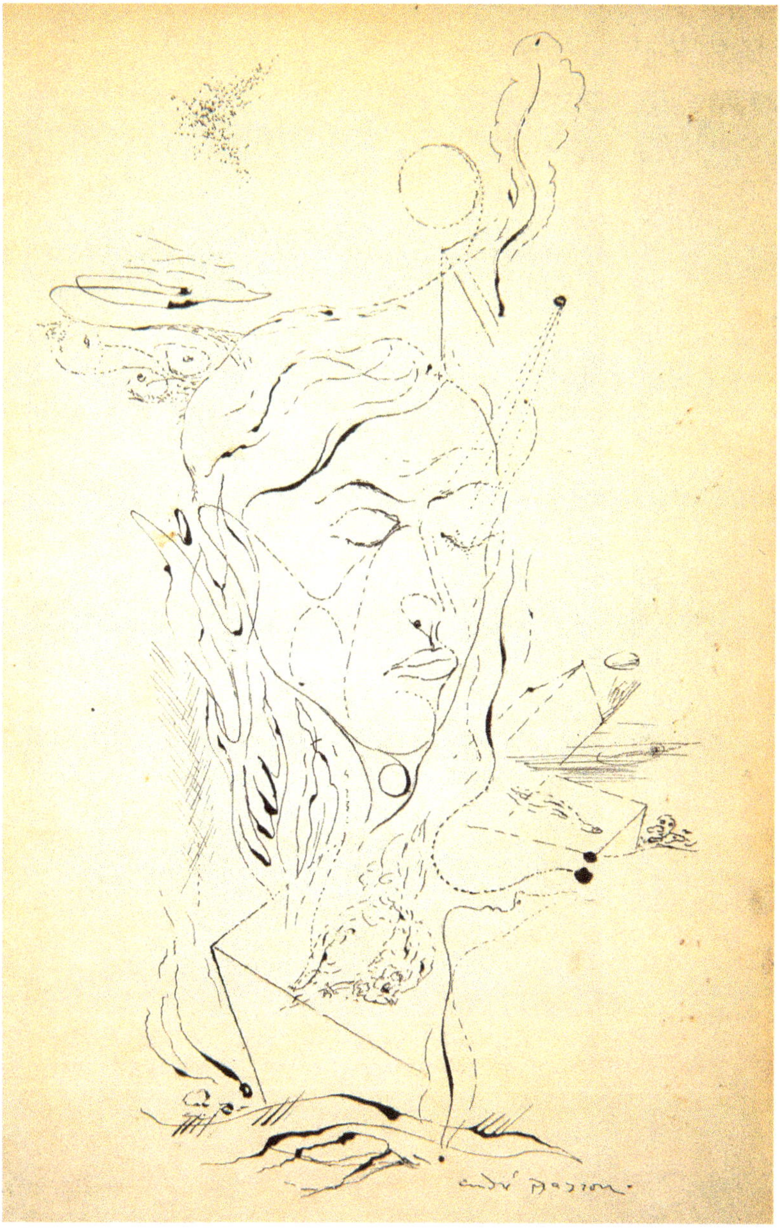

2.75 André Masson, *Automatic Portrait of Max Morise*, c.1925, ink on paper, San Diego Museum of Art. While Masson's drawings demonstrate the concept of automatic drawing, there is still a degree of realism. The rational mind never quite gives up control.

Activity B: **Create an automatic drawing**

1. On an A3 sheet of paper, create pencil marks while trying not to think about what you are doing. You could focus on another activity at the same time, such as listening to the radio or music.
2. When you have completed your drawing, look at it. Now begin to work into the shapes and lines that you have created using tone, with either pencil or charcoal, to create an abstract drawing. Think about the theme 'Portraits' when you draw into your doodle and see whether your conscious thoughts influence the outcome.

Critical thinking:

Look at the work that you have produced in **Activities A** and **B** above. Discuss the outcomes with a partner and what you have learned about different approaches to drawing.

Analytical Cubism The early phase of Cubism known for its geometric shapes and monochromatic use of colour.

Artists and designers: **Frank Auerbach, Whitfield Lovell and portrait drawing**

Artists make drawings on the same theme and using the same drawing materials, but can take very different approaches.

The British artist Frank Auerbach (born 1931) sees the role of the artist to bring order to the chaos of the world. He works, draws and paints the same small number of people repeatedly and has developed a strong, intense relationship with his subjects. He says that he is more engaged with his work when he knows the people he is drawing. He likes the fact that his models change over time as they get older and that his work reflects his feelings towards them (Figure 2.76).

The African-American artist Whitfield Lovell (born 1959) is known for his portraits of African-Americans from the first half of the 20th century – people he cannot have known. He works from photographs of his subjects, but states that the act of looking at the people makes his work become personal. The artist creates his drawings using charcoal or pencil on paper, wood or even directly onto walls. In some of his work, such as *Nkisi* (Figure 2.77), the drawings are paired with found objects that Lovell collects at flea markets and antique shops.

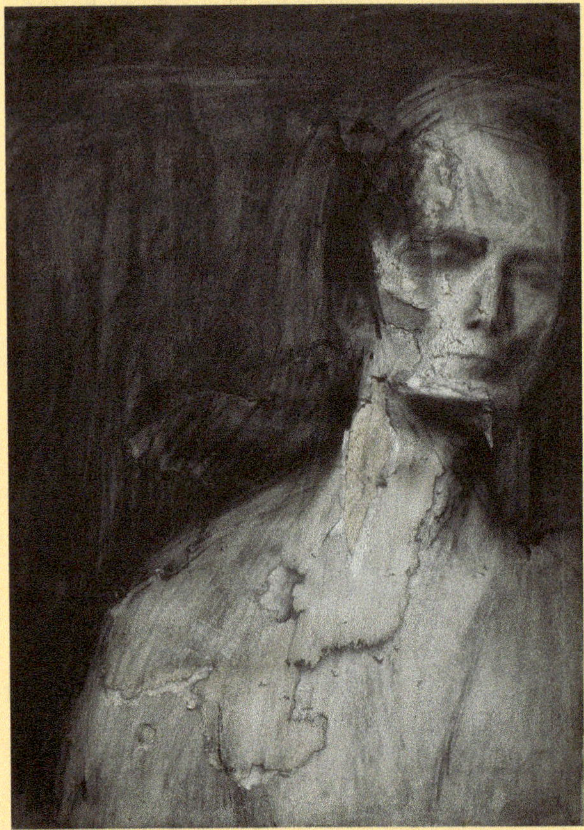

2.76 Frank Auerbach, *Head of E.O.W.* 1960, charcoal and chalk on paper, The Whitworth Art Gallery, The University of Manchester. The paper has a textured surface in parts – this adds to the expressive quality of the charcoal marks. Auerbach has highlighted some areas by the addition of chalk.

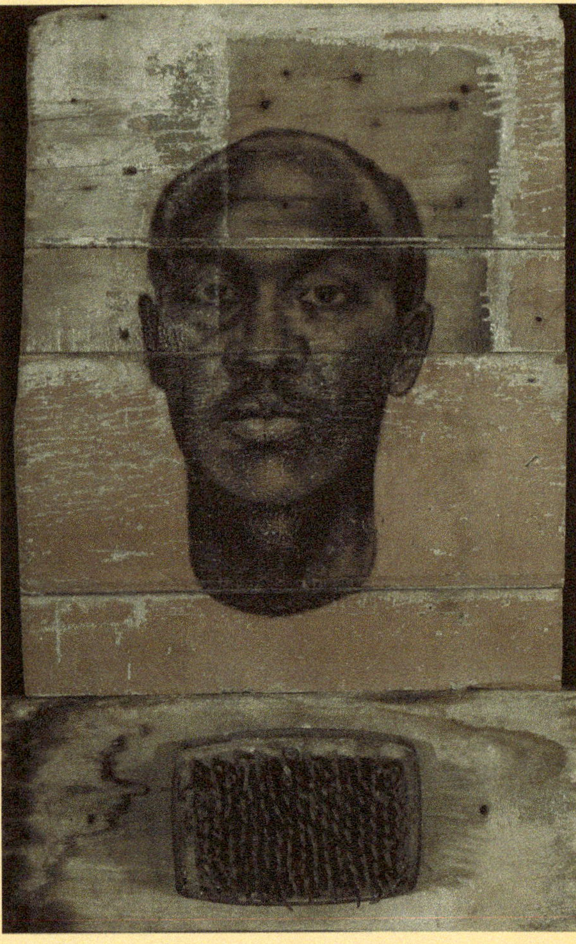

2.77 Whitfield Lovell, *Nkisi*, 2001, charcoal on wood with found object, Morris Museum of Art, Augusta, Georgia. The textured grain of the wood gives the drawing the quality of a **sepia** photograph.

Critical thinking:

Lovell draws portraits of people that he doesn't know and Auerbach draws people that he knows well, time and time again. Reflect on their different approaches to drawing a portrait, and discuss with a partner which you think is the most interesting way of working, and why.

Materials and techniques: **Charcoal**

Charcoal is a drawing material that dates back thousands of years. It is made from burnt wood, usually willow, and comes in variety of thicknesses, in both stick and pencil form. It can be sharpened to enable detailed work, or it can be applied on its edge to create broad areas of tone. It is easy to blend and is often used in conjunction with white chalk.

Gris's *Self-Portrait*, Auerbach's *Head of E.O.W.* and Lovell's *Nkisi* are all drawings where the main medium is charcoal. Look closely at the range of marks that the artists have used before starting Activity C.

Activity C: **Explore the use of charcoal**

1. On an A3 sheet of paper, explore the various marks that charcoal can make.
2. Experiment with the effects you can create.
3. Make a series of quick portrait drawings (three or four), either from life or from a photograph.
4. Compare the effects that you have achieved across the series, adding annotations. Is there any development? Which is the most successful?

Further research

Explore the work of Whitfield Lovell and Frank Auerbach online, and also research working with charcoal.

sepia Reddish-brown colour once used to add a warm tone to black and white photographs.

Fine art sculpture

Learning objectives:

- To become familiar with a range of sculptors and understand the context of their work
- To explore media and processes involved in creating sculpture

As seen in the introduction to this module, cultural heritage has been an important aspect of the work of many artists, both across cultures and the generations. In this module, we first look at the production of sculptures in sub-Saharan Africa. We then look at sculptors who take nature as their primary inspiration and medium.

Case study: Cultural contexts within sculpture

There is a strong tradition of sculpture in African art that dates back to prehistoric times and comes from across the African continent. We will focus here on sculpture from sub-Saharan Africa. Traditionally, the sculpture of sub-Saharan Africa, as in most cultures, had religious and ceremonial functions. The most common form of sculpture in Western Africa was masks, designed to be worn and used in ceremonial dances, in preparation for war and the harvest.

African sculptures have traditionally been made from a wide range of materials, using carving, assemblage and casting techniques. Statues are often crafted out of wood or ivory, and figurines made by bronze and brass casting, a process developed during the 9th century, in what is now Nigeria. In the 13th century, a group of more than 1000 metal **plaques** and sculptures known as the 'Benin Bronzes' were cast to decorate the royal palace of the **Kingdom of Benin**. The primary subject matter of African sculpture is the human figure.

The Nigerian artist Ben Enwonwu (1917–94) was inspired by his **Igbo** heritage. Enwonwu is today widely seen as a pioneer of modern African art and was the first contemporary artist from Nigeria to find international acclaim. His work has been described as 'a unique form of African modernism'. He developed a new kind of modern art rooted in an African tradition (Figures 2.78 and 2.79).

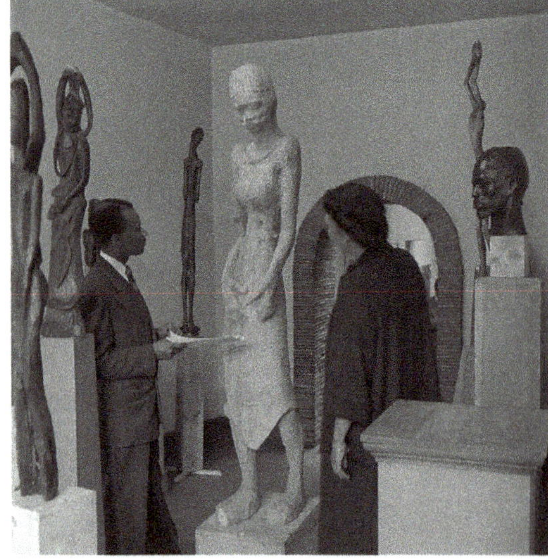

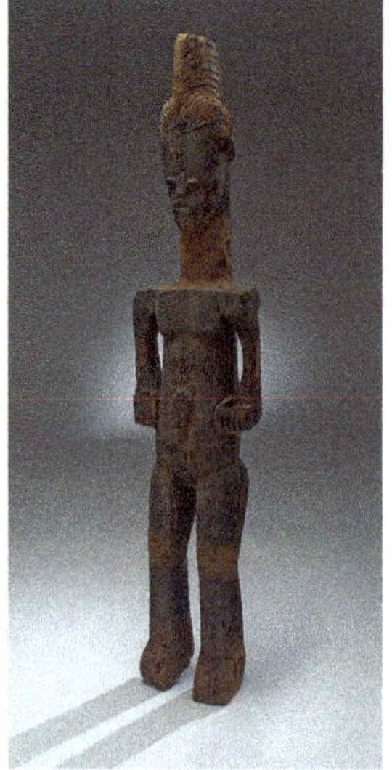

2.78 This photograph of Ben Enwonwu with his sculptures in a gallery shows his refined observation of human forms. The carved figures are long and elegant, but still keep the essence of traditional Igbo wooden carvings.

2.79 Unknown artist of the Igbo people, Nigeria, *Male figure*, mid-20th century, wood and pigment, Lowe Art Museum, University of Miami.

Traditional African carvings also had an important impact on the work of many Western artists during the early 20th century. Among them was the Italian painter and sculptor Amedeo Modigliani (1884–1920). What similarities can you see between Modigliani's *Head of a Woman* (Figure 2.80) and the typical carved wooded mask from Gabon (Figure 2.81)?

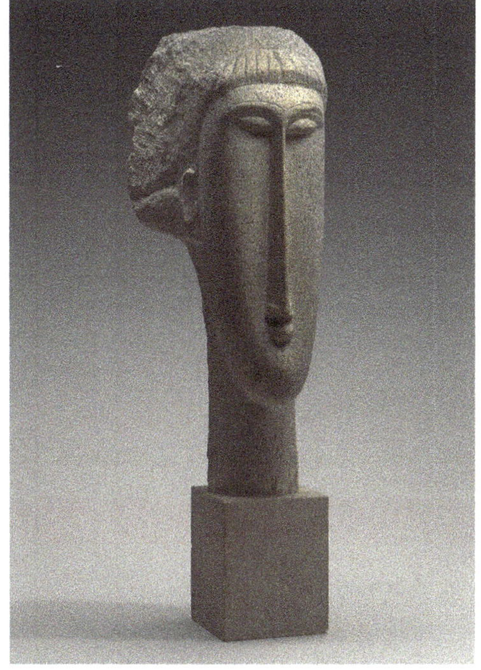

2.80 Amedeo Modigliani, *Head of a Woman*, 1910, carved stone, National Gallery of Art, Washington, DC.

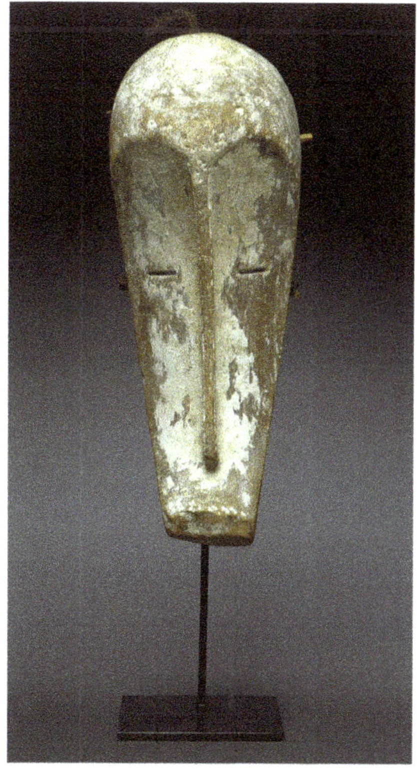

2.81 *Fang 'ngil' Mask from Gabon*, late 19th to early 20th century, wood, kaolin and paint, The Israel Museum, Jerusalem.

Activity A: **Explore the Benin bronzes**

1. Research and explore the Benin Bronzes.
2. Make a series of drawings to explore and study two or three pieces.
3. Add annotations on the main formal features. How did the Benin sculptors treat the human figure?

Materials and techniques: **Carving**

You can use a variety of materials to experiment with carving techniques, from easy-to-work material such as soap, to wood or breezeblock. Create your own blocks of plaster to carve by filling a hollow cube with liquid plaster, letting it set and then turning it out.

Experiment with different tools and explore the range of marks that you can make. For soft materials, such as soap, you can use ceramic modelling tools. For more durable material, such as wood, breezeblock or stone, you will need appropriate chisels and hammers.

Activity B: **Create a 'Benin' sculpture**

Following on from **Activity A**, create a piece of work out of soap or plaster inspired by the Benin Bronzes.

Kingdom of Benin Powerful kingdom of the Edo people of Western Africa that lasted from the 9th century to almost the end of the 19th century.

Igbo A people of Western Africa, in what is now south-east Nigeria.

plaque A tablet fixed to a wall as a way of remembering a person or event.

SCULPTURE IN THE CONTEXT OF THE NATURAL WORLD

As well as looking to cultural heritage to inspire them, many sculptors create their work in the context of the natural world. They use it both as a source of inspiration for subject matter and as a source of the materials that they work with. In the genre of art known as land art or Earth art, artists actually work in the landscape on **site-specific** pieces or bring nature into a gallery setting. See the 'Artists and designers' feature on the UK artist Andy Goldsworthy opposite.

Tip:

Your space in nature could be in the grounds of your school or home, in a city park or in the countryside. However, you *must* ask permission to use it first and clear your work away when you have finished.

Activity C: **Create a site-specific sculpture using natural materials**

1. Use a local outdoor space as a resource and produce site-specific work in response to the area. Work with a classmate if you want to.
2. Use natural materials, laying them next to one another or on top of one another.
3. Record the work that you produce by photographing it.

Critical thinking:

Reflect on how you approached **Activity C.**

- Did you have a preconceived idea about what your work would look like?
- Did the surroundings and materials available dictate the design?
- Compare this way of creating sculpture with others that you have tried. Record your thoughts about using natural materials and the outcomes you achieved.

Further research

Explore the National Museum of African Art – Smithsonian Institution, in Washington, DC online.

For contemporary African art, visit the website of the Zeitz Museum of Contemporary Art Africa, Cape Town, South Africa.

Find out more about Ben Enwonwu and Andy Goldsworthy on their websites.

ephemeral Lasting only a short while.
site-specific Artwork created to exist only in one place.

Artists and designers: **Andy Goldsworthy**

The British artist Andy Goldsworthy (born 1956) uses materials such as stones, mud, twigs, ice and snow within his work. He often balances the materials on top of each other, without the use of glue or other artificial materials to join them, or simply arranges them in a striking way (Figure 2.82). The nature of the work means that it is **ephemeral**: it is created and then decays naturally, back into the landscape from which it came. Many works of this kind are recorded only as photographs.

Some of Goldsworthy's work is made of more durable materials, such as slate and rock (Figure 2.83). These works remind us of very ancient ways in which humans marked the land, using cairns or standing stones, to show a boundary, a burial or pathway.

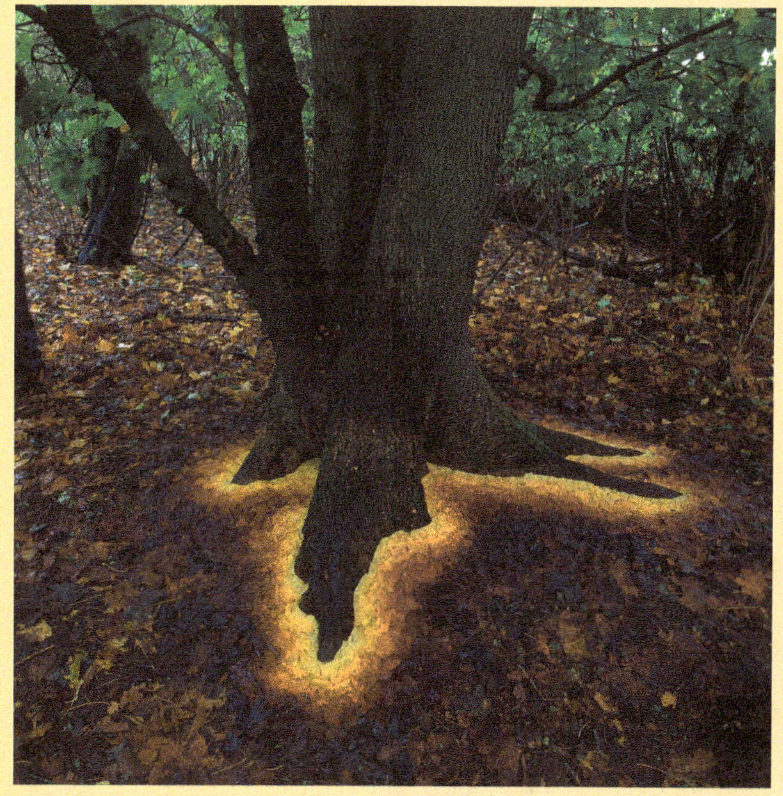

2.82 Andy Goldsworthy, *Sycamore leaves edging the roots of a sycamore tree*, 1 November 2013, Berrydown Foundation, Hampshire.

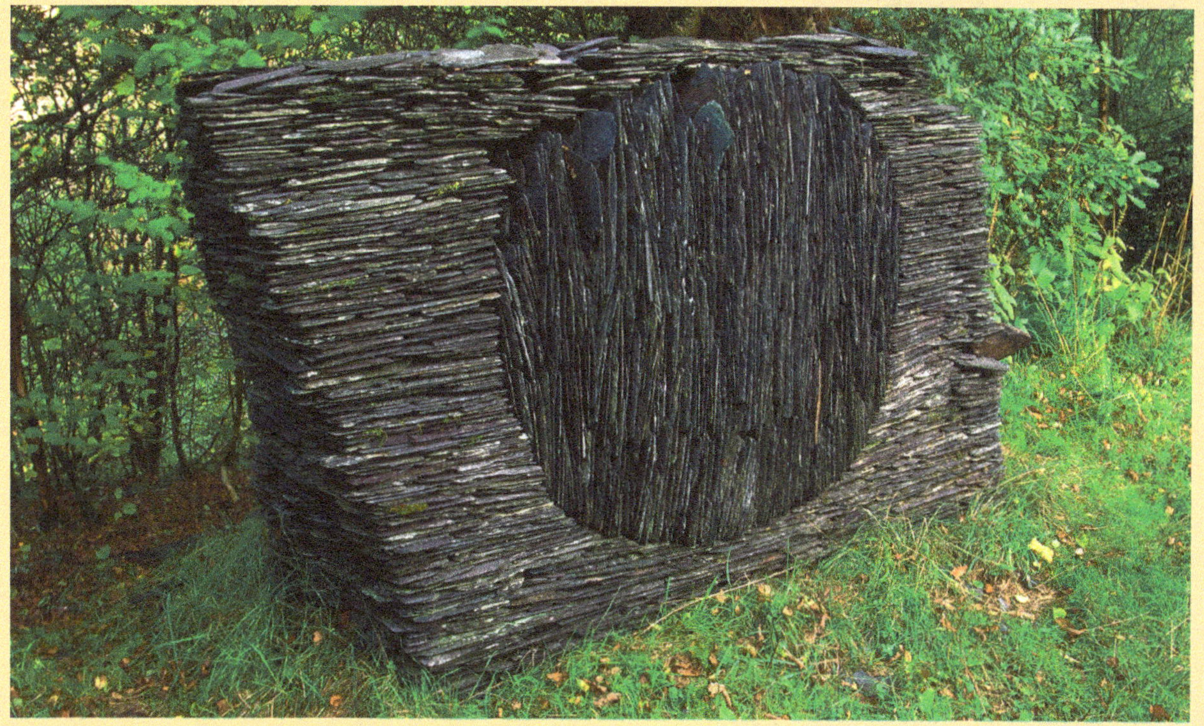

2.83 Andy Goldsworthy, sculpture in Scar Glen, Scotland.

Fine art printmaking

Learning objectives:

- To understand how printmakers have conveyed emotional and personal expression through their use of relief print techniques
- To understand how printmakers have used relief printing to communicate and question meaning about ideas and concepts

The art movement known as Expressionism refers to various groups of artists working in Europe in the early 20th century.

In this context, Expressionism has the following broad features:

- an overall simplified style
- bold, exaggerated use of line and colour
- a strong emotional impact, expressing the artist's inner feelings or ideas.

Expressionism continues to have a powerful influence on contemporary artwork – where self-expression is often considered to play a key role in artistic practice.

PERSONAL CONTEXTS IN PRINTMAKING

In Germany, Expressionism was closely associated with **relief printmaking** in the form of woodcuts – an ideal medium in which to convey direct, simplified, expressive marks. The raw and direct quality of the mark-making can be seen to reflect the artist's emotion. The woodgrain often contributed to the quality of the print.

There were two key groups of artists working within the German Expressionist movement – Die Brücke ('The Bridge') and Der Blaue Reiter ('The Blue Rider'). The artists of Die Brücke, such as Erich Heckel (1883–1970), were especially inspired by traditional African art. The expression of strong personal feeling can be seen in Heckel's woodcut print *Man on the Plain* (Figure 2.84) – a direct response to his experience during World War I (1914–18).

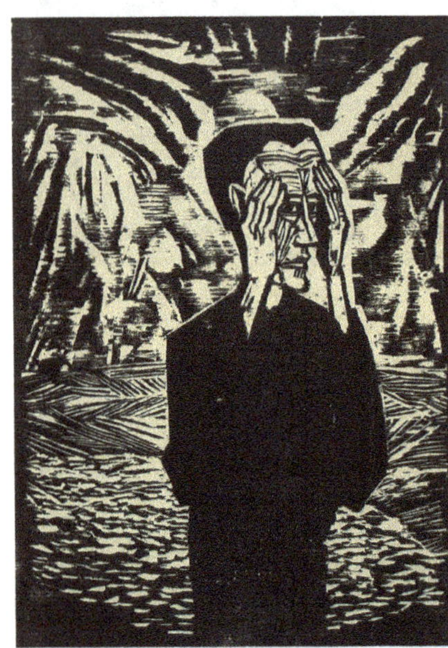

2.84 Erich Heckel, *Man on the Plain (Dube H 305 II)*, 1917, woodcut print, private collection. Heckel created this woodcut while serving in Flanders as a medical orderly. A lonely figure – clearly a self-portrait – stands in a barren landscape under a sky torn by **mortar** fire. The image expresses the despair felt by many who experienced the slaughter and destruction of World War I.

The contemporary American street artist Swoon (born 1977) was inspired by looking at the work of the German Expressionists, as well as by Indonesian shadow puppets. She creates realistic and life-size linocut prints depicting people, often her friends and family (Figure 2.85). She then pastes these onto the streets and onto walls of disused buildings. The marks that she makes in the **lino** have expressive qualities, and she puts her own twist on Expressionism through the exaggerated scale of the lino print medium.

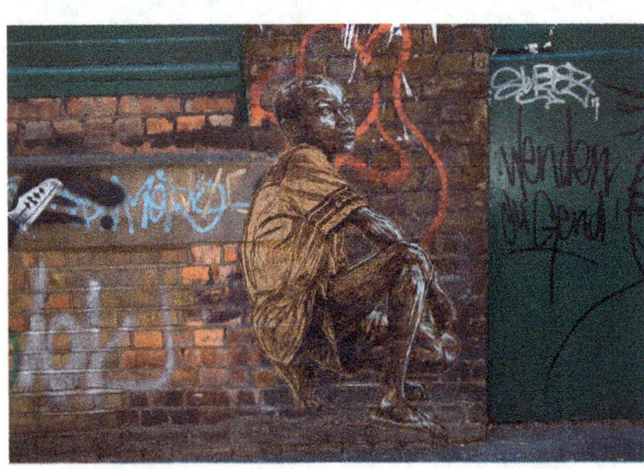

2.85 Example of street art by Swoon, 2016, Shoreditch, London. The street artist blends her work into urban settings, often adding them to the walls of disused buildings.

Materials and techniques: **Linocut**

The linocut is a form of relief printmaking closely related to the woodcut. The artist cuts their design into a sheet of **linoleum** using a sharp knife. Once the design is complete, the artist inks the sheet using a roller and then presses the sheet onto a sheet of paper or textile to produce the image. As with the woodcut, this requires some skill – it is the uncut, raised areas that show the printed image (and in mirror form). However, unlike the woodcut, the linocut is more readily achievable in a school environment.

Activity A: **Experiment with linocut mark-making**

Practise the linocut process by experimenting with lines and different kinds of marks. Try the following in order on a piece of linoleum and create your print:

- straight lines
- lines of different weights (thickness)
- lines that get thicker or thinner
- cross-hatch
- curved lines
- shapes or masses.

Activity B: **Create an Expressionist linocut**

1. Choose an object with personal significance to you.
2. Make a simple linocut in which you convey your personal feeling towards the subject matter.
3. Make some black and white sketches and design an image for a relief print.
4. Express your feelings through the way that you make your cuts into the printing block.

Critical thinking:

With a partner, consider and discuss each other's prints from **Activity B**. What is the emotional effect of your partner's print on you? Is it the same as the emotion that your partner wanted to convey in their work? Discuss what other factors came into the artistic process, apart from the emotion. Did these hinder or intensify the emotional impact of the work?

Further research

Explore more about the German Expressionists at the Brücke museum website.

To gain a feel for Expressionism as a wider cultural movement, watch the film *Metropolis* (1927, dir. Fritz Lang).

Search the internet for help and advice on how to make a linocut.

lino; linoleum Flexible, durable material made from linseed oil, originally made for flooring.
mortar Weapon that fires bombs out of a large barrel, used in World War I.
relief printmaking A printmaking process where the design is cut into a material, creating raised areas (relief).

Mixed media

Learning objectives:

- To understand how history has influenced artists
- To explore ways of combining media to express intentions

History has always provided artists with a source of inspiration. The term 'history painting' refers to a genre of painting first categorised in 17th-century Europe, where the subject matter was taken from classical history and mythology. In the 18th century, the term began to refer to work inspired by more recent historical subjects and events. There are works by more modern and contemporary artists that we can describe as history paintings and some artists as history painters. More broadly, many artists use their art to comment on and criticise society.

CONFRONTING HISTORY

The German artist Anselm Kiefer (born 1945) is an artist who uses his work to reflect on events from history and culture. Kiefer grew up in Germany just after the end of World War II in the wake of the Nazi period and the **Holocaust** – a traumatic period that many Germans wanted to forget. Kiefer, however, uses his art to confront difficult and controversial issues from the past. By using mixed media, such as ash, clay and straw combined with oil paint, he is able to create powerful, disturbing imagery.

Search online to view *Your Golden Hair, Margarete*, a response to a line from a poem by the Jewish poet and Holocaust 'survivor' Paul Celan (1920–70) entitled *Todesfuge* ('Death Fugue'). The poem evokes the horror of the Nazi concentration camps, in which millions of European Jews were murdered.

The heavy use of black paint gives the work an oppressive and threatening feel, while the burnt straw refers to the 'ashen hair' of a murdered Jewish woman. Kiefer also often includes lines of text, names or places within his work.

Materials and techniques: Using found objects in collage

Contemporary artists often combine unusual collage materials in their work. Anselm Kiefer frequently uses straw, sand, clay, lead and objects such as shoes and books, and these materials are usually linked to the concept of his work. They have significance to the overall meaning, as well as introducing interesting textural qualities.

When using found objects such as collage materials, there are no boundaries as to what you can incorporate. However, you will need to ensure that the support that you use is strong enough to hold the work and that the adhesive that you use is also strong enough. For example, PVA is good for sticking papers, card and light materials, whereas wood glues and hot glue guns can be used to hold heavier materials such as plastics, wood and stone.

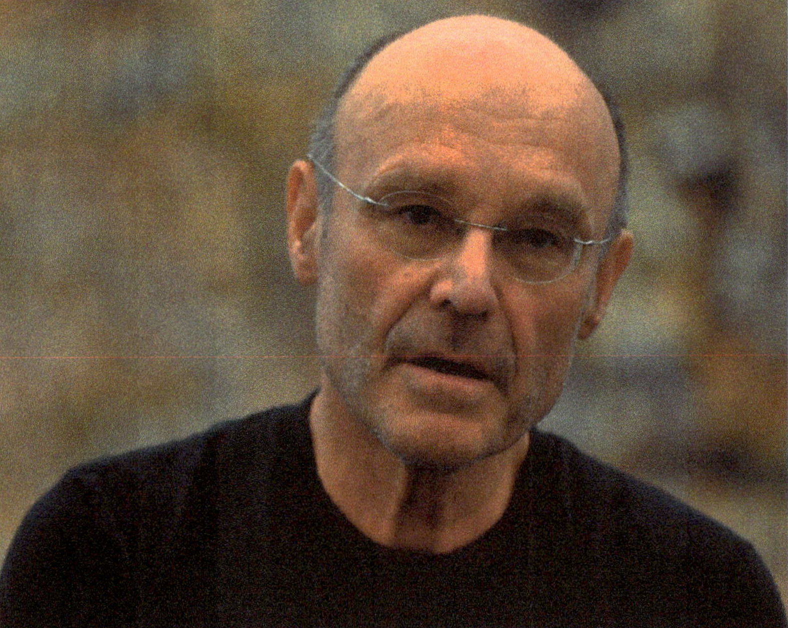

2.86 Anselm Kiefer in 2011.

ART AS SOCIAL COMMENT

Jean-Michel Basquiat (1960–88) was an African-American artist who referenced Black history and made social comments in his work.

Black history, also termed African-American history, refers to the history of black American ethnic groups, most of whom are descended from Africans taken by force from their homeland, transported to America, and sold into slavery between 1555 and 1865. Despite the abolition of slavery, and African-Americans being given their freedom, this did not lead to equal rights. **Segregation** between the racial groups existed in the southern states of the USA until well into the 20th century. The Civil Rights Act of 1964 banned discrimination in public, but civil unrest continued and racism is still an issue in society even today. In the mid-1960s to the mid-1970s, the Black Power Movement urged African-Americans to look to Africa for inspiration and emphasised living together in solidarity rather than **integration**.

Basquiat used his work to explore themes such as poverty and debates such as integration versus segregation. He used pre-existing drawings, paintings and poetry, bringing images and texts together to form semi-abstract collages. His style involved the use of bold colours, manic brush marks and skeleton-like faces and bodies. He worked with a range of contrasting materials, such as paper, acrylic paint and oil bar, and scratched into the layers of paint using a **sgraffito** technique.

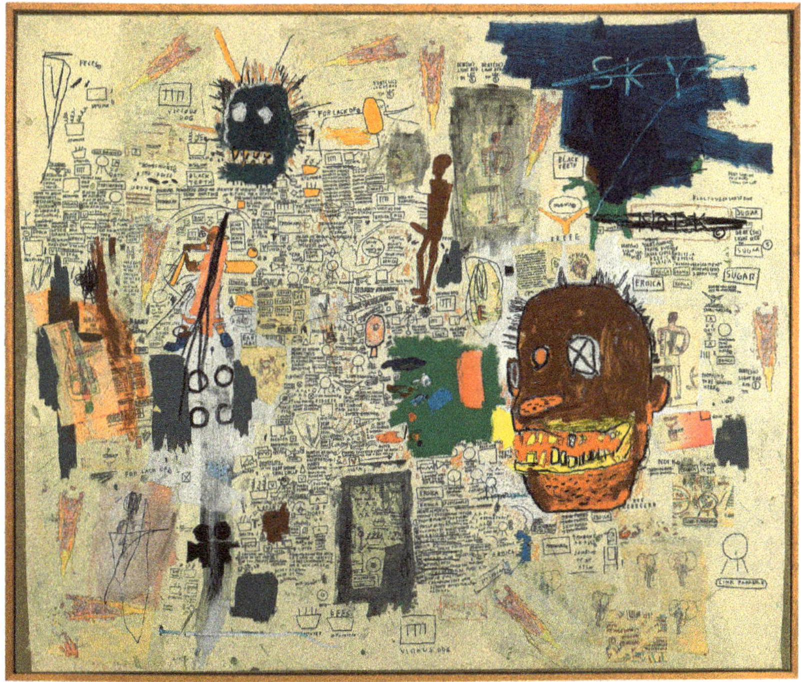

2.87 Jean-Michel Basquiat, *Untitled*, 1987, acrylic, oil stick, graphite, paper collage, and crayon on canvas, private collection. This mixed-media work shows the expressive approach to challenging society and our place within it.

Further research

Go online for more about the work of Anselm Kiefer and Jean-Michel Basquiat.

Read Paul Celan's poem 'Death Fugue' on the internet.

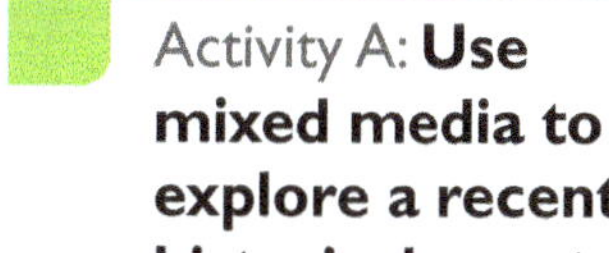

Activity A: Use mixed media to explore a recent historical event

Reflect on a national or world historical event and make a mixed-media collage in response to it.

Choose contrasting materials to help express your ideas as well as to create interesting textures.

Critical thinking:

Looking back at the work of Kiefer and Basquiat, think about how the choice of mixed-media materials can link to the concept. Now look at the work that you produced in **Activity A** above. Does your choice of materials reflect the concept of the work? Make notes to explain how you have done this.

Holocaust The mass murder of Jews and members of many other ethnic, social and political groups in continental Europe between 1940 and 1945 by the Nazi regime.

integration Where one set of people mix in with mainstream society, adopting its values and culture.

segregation The separation of people on grounds of their race or other characteristics – applied to the place where they live, the schools they go to and other facilities they use.

sgraffito A technique of scratching lines in a surface of colour to reveal the original surface or another layer of colour below.

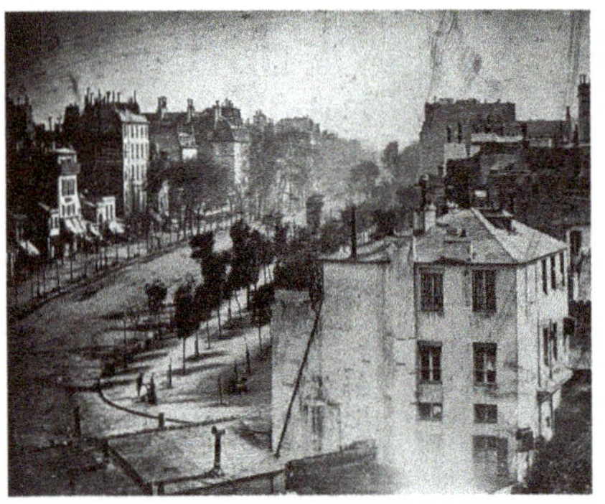

2.88 Louis Daguerre, *Boulevard du Temple*, 1838. Louis Daguerre (1787–1851) was a pioneer of photography. His image of a busy street in Paris is shaped by the technology he used – the exposure time was so long that the camera did not record the carriages and other vehicles in the street.

Photography

Learning objective:

- To understand how technology influences photographers

Photography is a discipline where the context of technology plays a very clear role. Developments in technology since the invention of photography in the early 19th century (see Figure 2.88) have shaped the nature of the artworks produced – for example, the development of practical colour photography (1900s) and instant photography (from 1948).

The rise of digital photography (c.1990) has meant that photographers face new challenges as well as opportunities. The growth of high-performing, affordable cameras within smart phones has meant that professional-looking photography is now within the reach of many people. This means that practitioners can explore different ways of developing photographic ideas. We look at some of these in this unit.

PANORAMA

The photograph in Figure 2.89 uses a panoramic composition. Some smart phones have a panorama setting. You can also create something similar by taking a sequence of images, each of which joins onto the next. If you are using a DSLR camera, you can experiment with the 'Joiner' facility. You can also explore vertical compositions that use this technique.

When creating sequential panoramic images like this, you will find that some of the images cannot be completely lined up in a neat manner – they overlap. The result is a **photocollage** or 'joiner' that look like a Cubist painting (see page 166).

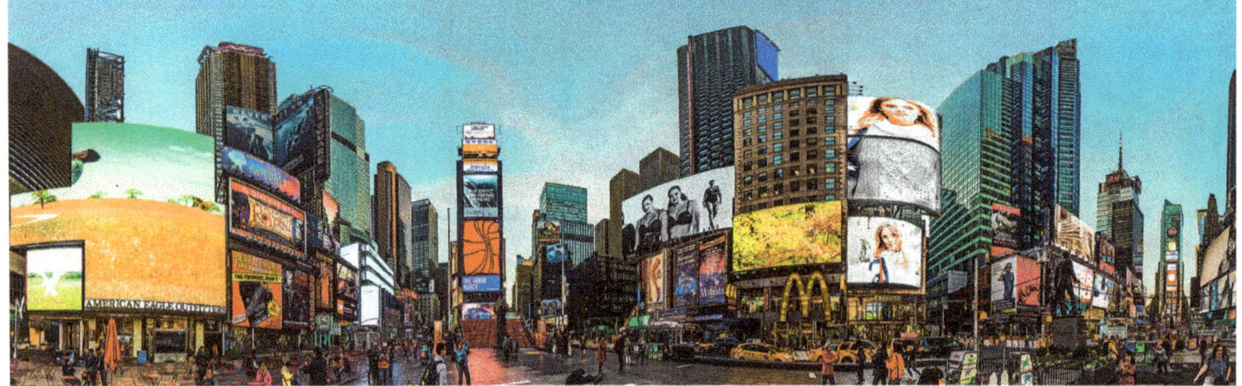

2.89 Panoramic photograph: Times Square, New York City.

Activity A: **Create a photocollage**

1. Explore photocollages created by the British artist David Hockney (born 1937) at his website.
2. Using the theme 'Street', take a sequence of photographs – at least eight.
3. Create a photocollage, allowing some images to overlap and others to 'jump' (miss out a slice of the subject).

CLOSE-UP

Many photographers have been inspired to look for inspiration in close-ups and details. Advances in sensor size have allowed cameras to record details both close and far away in minute detail. Files with higher resolution can be stored on removable memory cards, allowing practitioners to use digital editing software to explore close-up details of objects and textures. They may work with macro lenses at the same time (Figures 2.90 and 2.91).

In looking at surfaces close-up, photographs take on a different meaning. They stop being simple photographs of stone walls or wooden fences, and become studies of the colours, surfaces and forms in textures.

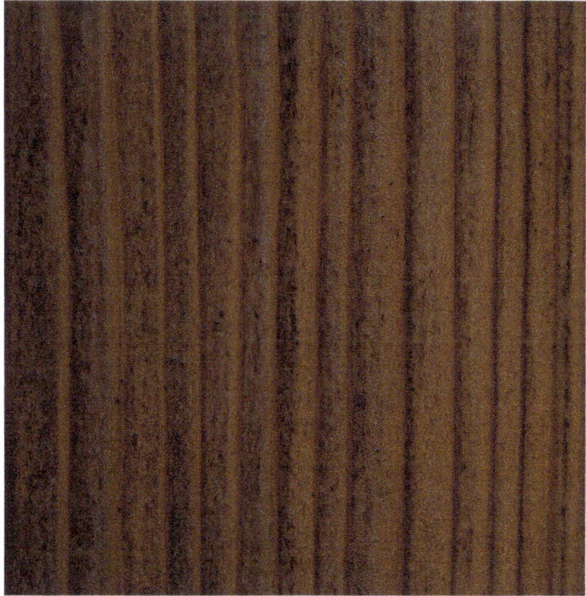

2.90 Alan Parsons, *Texture 2*, 2012. This close-up of a grain of cedar wood provides a striking image made up of horizontal bands.

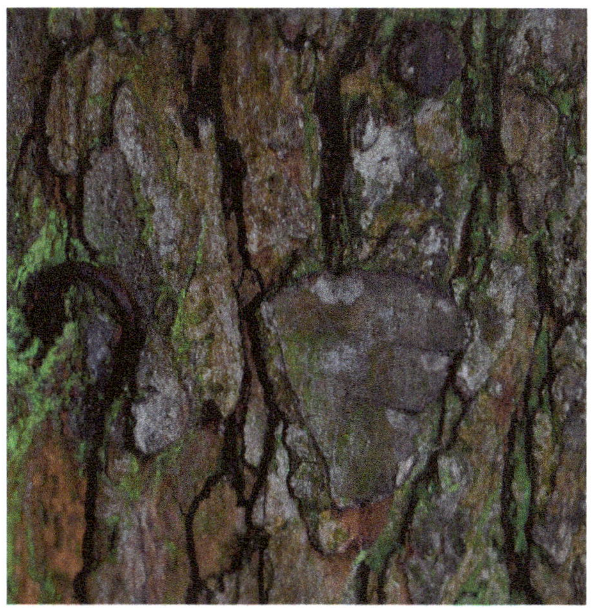

2.91 Alan Parsons, *Texture 3*, 2012. You can use a camera to record what is around you.

Activity B: **Create a close-up**

1. Return to the theme 'Street' that you explored in **Activity A**.
2. This time, take *five* close-ups of the same subject matter.
3. Consider composition, texture and other formal qualities.

Materials and techniques: **Composition**

When you are shooting close-ups, think about composition. You will see one version through the viewfinder, but you are not limited to using just this format. These images use the square format to emphasise that they are part of a set of images – there are 64 small squares in the complete piece, arranged in a grid of 8 x 8 squares.

Further research

Go online for more about the development of photography, the early pioneers of photography and advice on creating 'joiners'.

photocollage Collage made up of photographs.

Experimental/assemblage and construction

Learning objectives:

- To understand how context influences experimental fine art
- To explore a concept for an experimental fine art piece

In conceptual art, the concept or idea is the most important thing about an artwork. It relies less on technical skills, such as drawing or painting, and aesthetic concerns associated with traditional fine art. It asks the viewer to consider an abstract idea through the way it combines materials, or isolates objects and gives them new meaning.

MARCEL DUCHAMP AND READYMADES

Art historians often consider the French-American artist Marcel Duchamp (1887–1968) as the pioneer of conceptual art. At the beginning of the 20th century, he challenged – and enraged – the art world by raising the status of everyday things to art objects. He achieved this not by changing such objects in any particular way, or by using them as a basis for a sculpture. He believed that the object became a sculpture or art object simply because he had the idea or concept that it could be. He called this kind of object a 'readymade'.

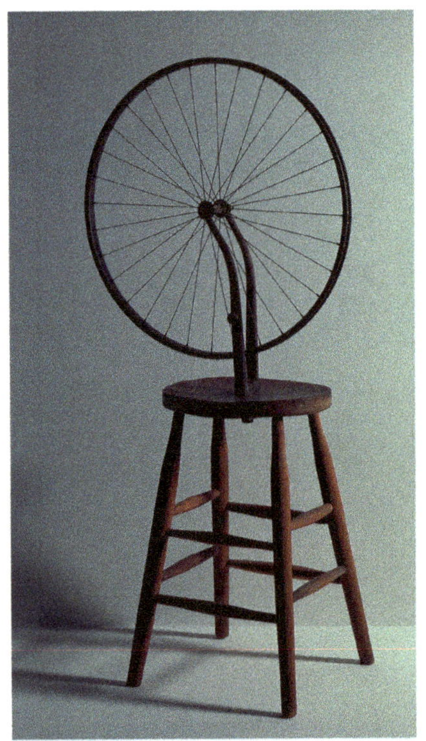

2.92 Marcel Duchamp, *Bicycle Wheel*, 1963, mixed media, private collection. An everyday object raised to the status of a sculpture. Is the artist asking us to revisit bicycle wheels and consider their formal qualities as objects, or questioning what can be thought of as an art sculpture, or both?

THE CONCEPTUAL ART MOVEMENT

Conceptual art developed into an art movement in the 1960s. At this time, many artists began to question the dominance of formalism in contemporary art – that is, art in which the formal qualities, such as colour, line and material, are the most important thing. They also argued that if art became mainly about ideas rather than finished art objects, they could free art from the constraints of the museum and the marketplace (Figure 2.92). A few artists got rid of the art object altogether by simply providing the instructions to make one!

Critical thinking:

Some art critics and 'ordinary' viewers have criticised conceptual art for what they argue is the lack of artistic skill. The conceptual artists may well have used drawing, photography and other art practices as they developed their ideas; these, though, are not visible in the exhibited work.

Hold a class discussion in which both sides of the argument are debated.

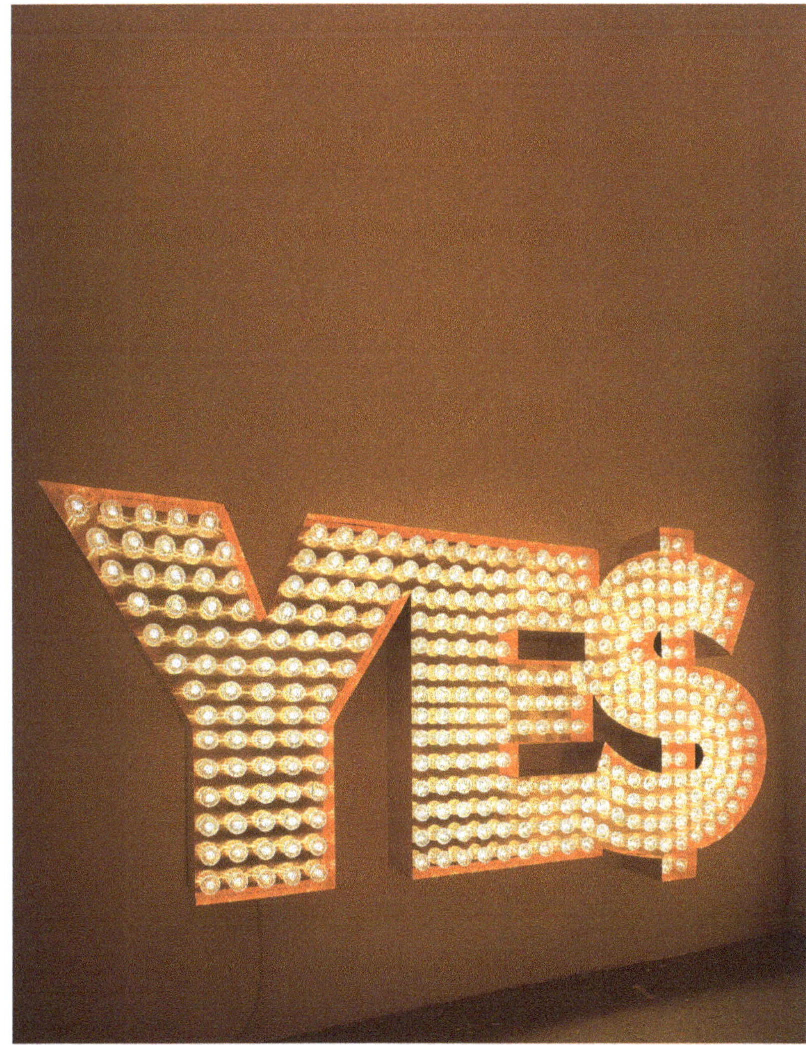

2.93 Tim Noble and Sue Webster, *YE$*, 2001, 335 ice white turbo reflector caps, lamps, holders and daisy washers, lacquered brass, enamelled paint and electronic light sequencer, private collection. Do you think the artists are celebrating or criticising the role of money in the art world – or both?

Activity A: **Plan a conceptual fine art piece**

Starting from the theme 'Environment', make a series of drawings and photographs that explore your ideas for a conceptual fine art piece. You can plan the piece using any materials, provided you have good access to them. For instance, if you were concerned about sustainability, you could source items that you feel have a particular impact – for example, throwaway non-disposable items that end up in landfill. If you are concerned about marine pollution, imagine making a tangled web of different wire and lines, with representations of animals trapped in this, as in a web. These are just suggestions – you can develop your own idea or concept.

Tip:

Much conceptual art poses an idea or question, rather than presenting a solution. Audiences leave an exhibition with a set of questions and thoughts inspired by the work. In this sense, there is no fixed answer; the audience interprets the signals and symbols within the work, and reacts to them. Sometimes the work is asking us to rethink an accepted idea. At other times it is just holding a mirror back to us and showing an aspect of our lives we may not consider or think about that much.

Critical thinking:

Display the work you have produced for **Activity A**, and ask your classmates to review it with you:

- Do you feel it has a strong concept behind it?
- What does it communicate to your classmates?
- Could it be interpreted in different ways or on several levels?

Further research

Read more about Marcel Duchamp in *Marcel Duchamp* by Dawn Ades, Neil Cox and David Hopkins (Thames & Hudson, 1999).

Explore more conceptual artworks at the Guggenheim museum website.

Module 3 Development and refinement

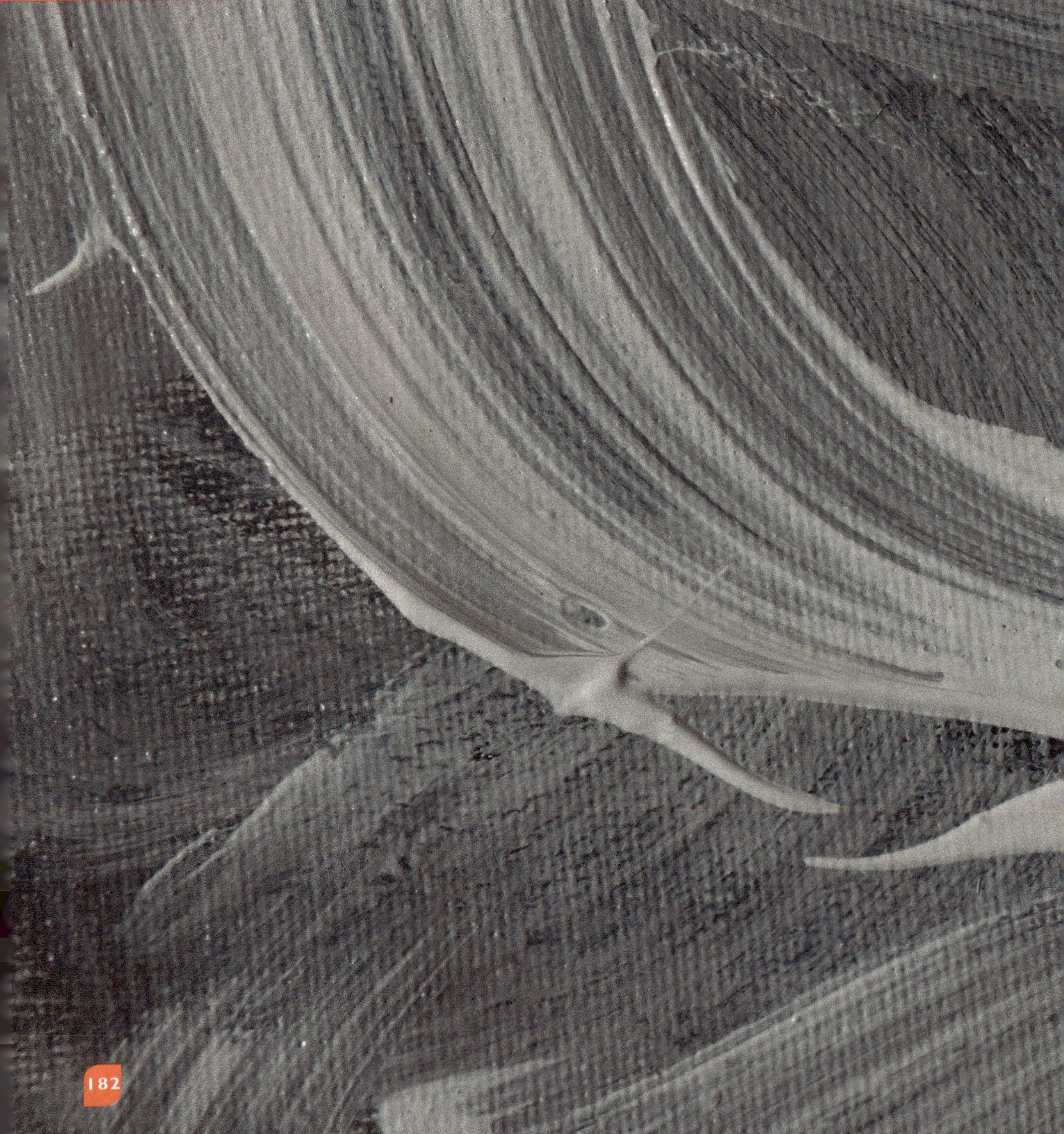

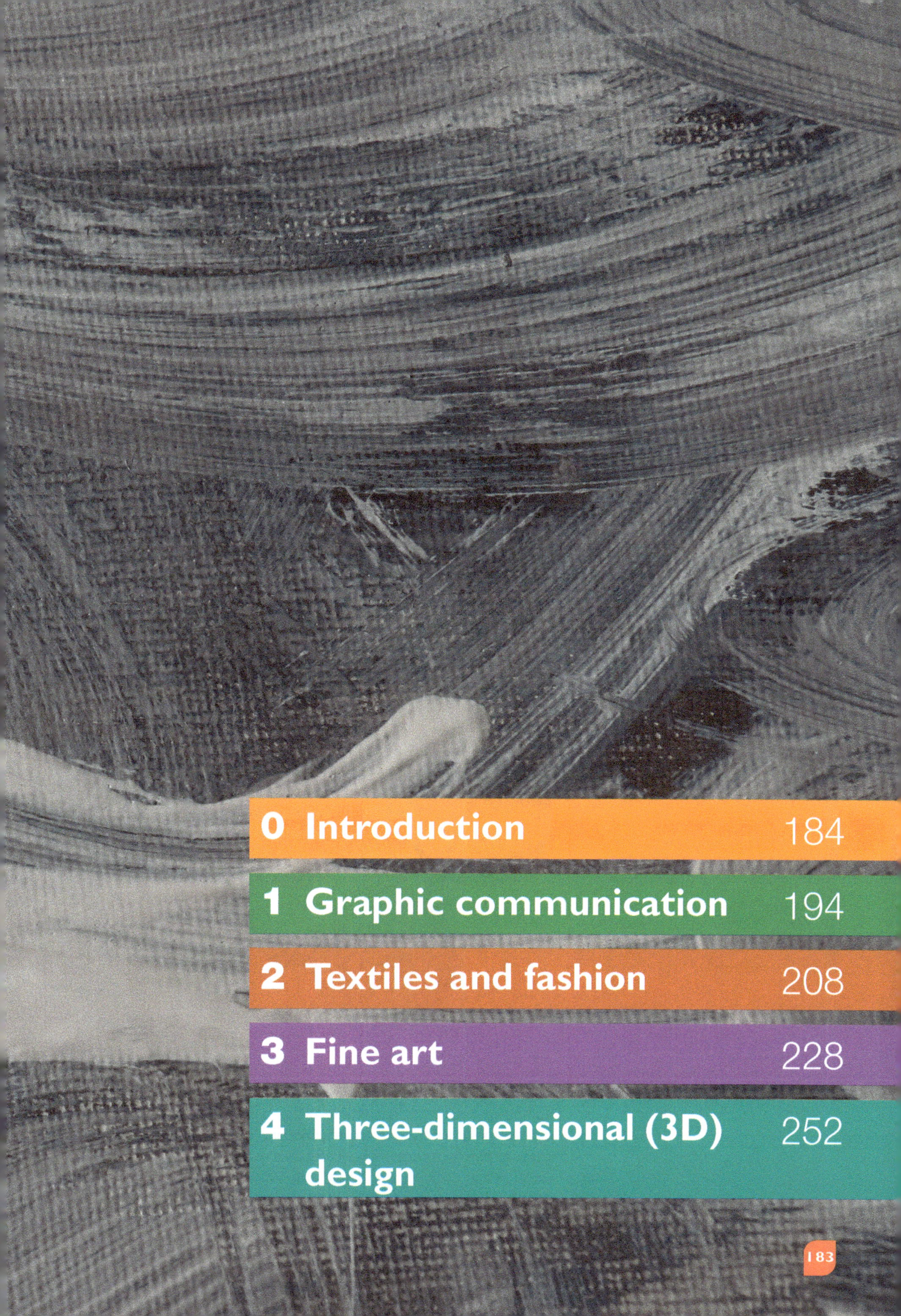

3.0 Introduction

This module introduces you to the idea of continual development as you respond to the visual information that you collect, through recording from first- and second-hand sources, and as you respond to the work of different artists and designers. Your ideas will develop as you gain a deeper understanding of the context in which you work. Through visual experimentation and annotation, you will begin to demonstrate critical understanding of what you do and how you do it. By being able to demonstrate critical understanding, you will be able to refine your ideas.

The module also introduces you to the ways that artists and designers use materials, processes and techniques to develop and refine ideas.

DEVELOPMENT AND REFINEMENT AS PART OF THE DESIGN PROCESS

Artists, craftspeople and designers often work through a set of stages from a brief or starting point to the final outcome. This creative journey is often referred to as the design process. The stages can be seen in Figure 3.1. You will study the design process in more detail later in this module (pages 261–262).

Tip:

Keep a record of everything that you do when developing and refining your work. You can work directly in sketchbooks or create worksheets, but don't forget to include printouts or screenshots of any development work that you do using a computer, and photograph any models, maquettes and samples that you make to try out your ideas. You will need to refer to these when you are producing your final artwork and as evidence for assessment purposes.

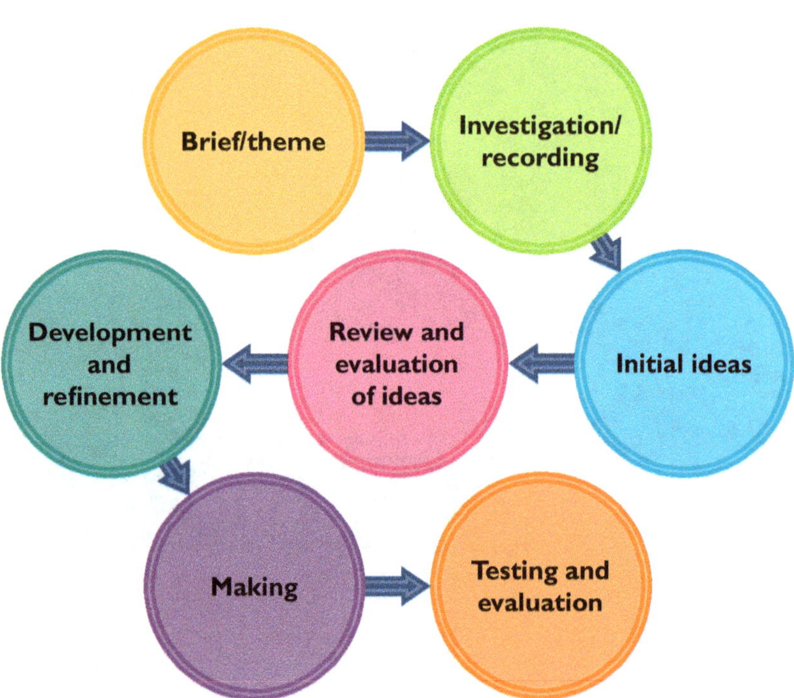

3.1 The design process.

Development is defined as the process of growing or progressing something, such as an idea or a technique. Refinement is about making small changes or additions to improve something, or add polish. Together they form a key step in the process where ideas are shaped and tested, often from small sketches and drawings to a bigger scale, or from two to three dimensions, and the choice and application of media and techniques can be explored. For example, architects and product designers make models from plans, and sculptors make three-dimensional (3D) maquettes from sketches. Graphic designers will experiment with font styles, layout and proof prints, and painters will experiment with composition.

USING SKETCHES TO DEVELOP A FINAL COMPOSITION

Traditionally, artists explored their subject matter through making sketches from observation. They then combined all the individual elements that they wanted to include, to develop a final composition. This can be seen in the work of the English landscape painter John Constable (1776–1837). Constable made many quick studies of the scenes that he painted, recording details such as cloud formations, and using a range of drawing and painting materials. He then made much larger finished paintings based on the sketches. Note how his brushwork is more refined in the finished version of the painting (see Figure 3.4), compared to the brushwork that you can see in the study of the clouds (Figure 3.3).

3.2 John Constable, *Sketch for Dedham Vale*, c.1827, oil, ink and graphite on canvas, Sterling and Francine Clark Art Institute, Williamstown, Massachusetts.

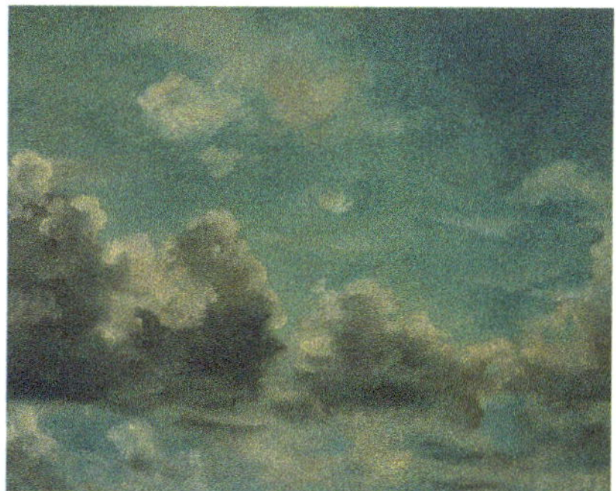

3.3 John Constable, *Study of Cumulus Clouds*, undated, oil on canvas, Touchstones Rochdale Museum.

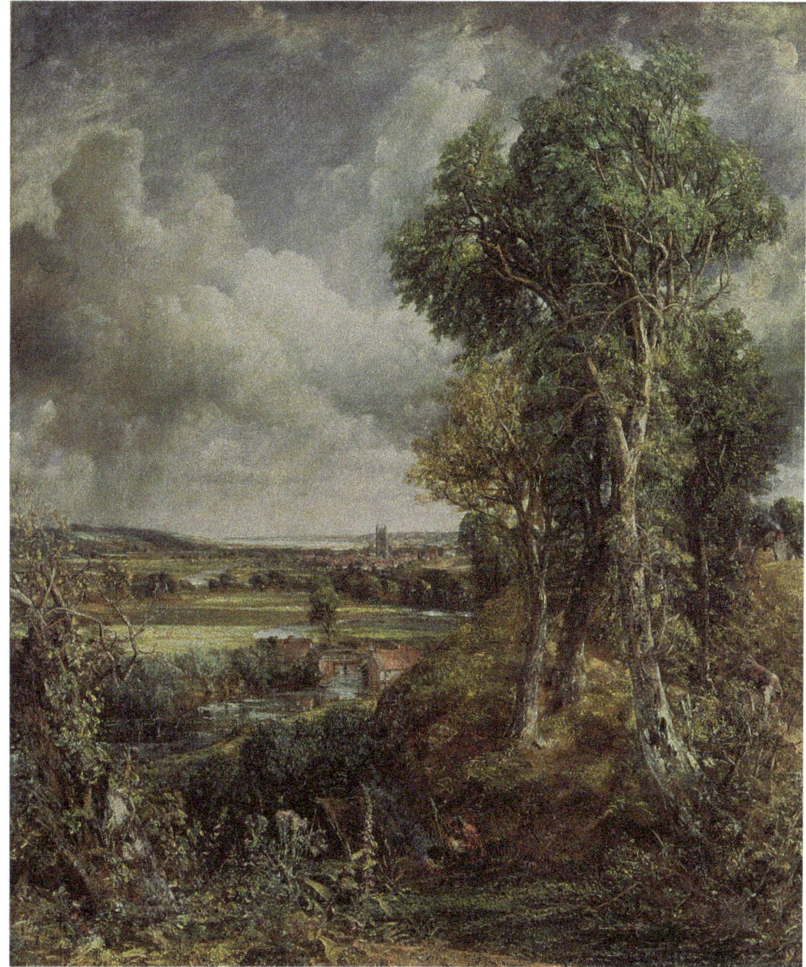

3.4 John Constable, *The Vale of Dedham*, 1828, oil on canvas, Scottish National Gallery, Edinburgh. The final painting is approximately two and a half times bigger than the preparatory sketch and the brush marks are much more refined than those seen in the studies.

Activity A: **Spot the difference**

1. Look carefully at Figure 3.2 *Sketch for Dedham Vale* and Figure 3.4 *The Vale of Dedham*. Make a note of the differences that you can see between the sketch and the final painting. What has been added to, or taken out of, the composition?
2. Why do you think that Constable has made these changes?

DEVELOPING ABSTRACT COMPOSITIONS

The art movement known as **Op art** is a good example of art that is technically very accomplished, requiring careful planning. 'Op art' is a term given to works that give the viewer a sense of movement by using patterns that seem to vibrate or swell when you stare at them. It developed as a movement in the 1960s and one of the main exponents was British artist Bridget Riley (born 1931). Riley developed ideas for her optical patterns by first using small-scale, hand-drawn grids, as can be seen in Figure 3.5. Using a grid system meant that she could easily recreate her designs on a larger scale when she was happy with the arrangement of the shapes and gradations in tone. Although at the start of the movement Op artists worked using a monochromatic palette, work quickly developed by introducing the use of colour, as can be seen in the work of Israeli artist Yaacov Agam (born 1928), whose work can be found online.

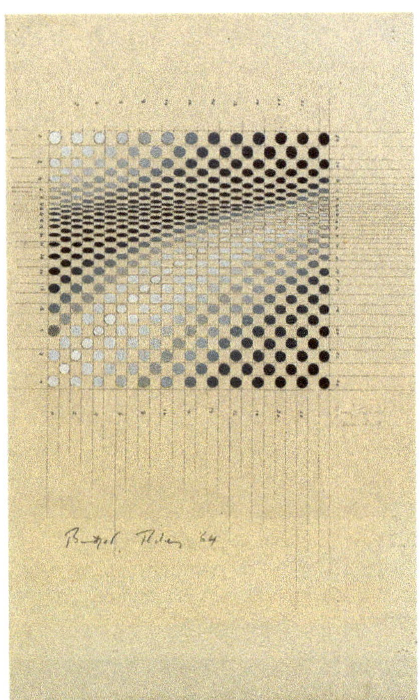

3.5 Bridget Riley, *Untitled*, 1964, gouache and pencil on paper, private collection.

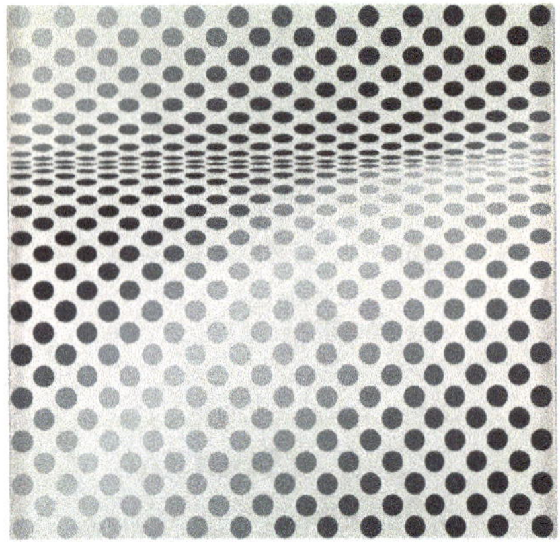

3.6 Bridget Riley, *Hesitate*, 1964, emulsion on board, Tate, London. *Untitled* shows Riley's use of a grid system to work out the composition for her later painting *Hesitate*, carefully working out the position of each circle and ellipse.

Activity B: **Using a grid to transfer, enlarge and distort an image**

Using grid systems to enlarge images was a technique also used by American Photorealists, such as Richard Estes (born 1932), who worked from photographs, recreating them using a very detailed and precise painting style on a much larger scale. The grid that Estes used to enlarge the image for *The Canadian Club, New York* (Figure 3.7) would have been a regular square or rectangular grid, whereas Riley used a carefully distorted grid to create the ellipses for her painting *Hesitate* (Figure 3.6).

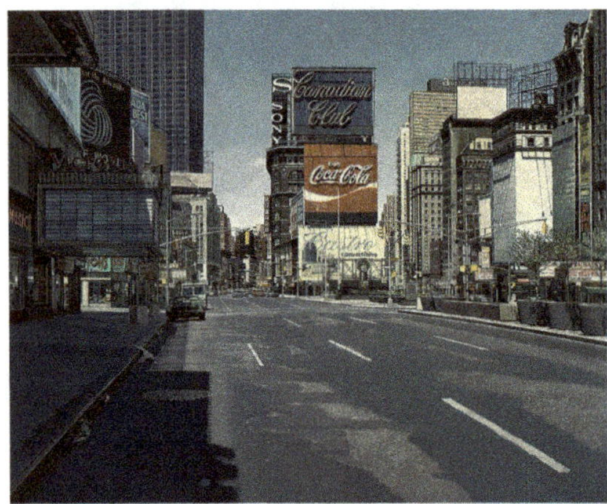

3.7 Richard Estes, *The Canadian Club, New York*, 1974, oil on canvas, private collection.

1. Working from a photograph that you have taken, print it out to an A5 size and draw a 2 × 2 cm, or 1 × 1 inch, grid over it.
2. Then draw a larger-scaled version of the grid on A3 paper and transfer the image by drawing a cell at a time.
3. You can experiment with creating distorted images by drawing a different-shaped grid on the paper. Create longer and thinner or shorter and fatter versions of an image by changing the cell shape to rectangles instead of squares. Just ensure that there are the same number of cells as in the grid covering the photograph and that you draw the image seen in the original grid cells to fit the shape of the cell in the drawing.

Using compositional techniques to refine artwork

There are a number of ways to achieve a sense of unity within an artwork, depending on the intention of the artist. A work of art is regarded as being aesthetically pleasing to the eye if the elements within the work are arranged in a balanced way. You can experiment with the way in which the elements of an image are organised to change the impact that your work has. You can alter the composition of an image simply by changing the format from portrait to landscape or by changing the **focal point**. Look at the two photographs of lotus flowers below. They are both the same image, but by changing the focal point and maintaining a shallow depth of field when taking the photograph, the resulting versions are quite different. In Figure 3.8 our eye is drawn to the top half of the picture, and in Figure 3.9 the reverse is true: we automatically look towards the flower in sharp focus. You can decide for yourself which composition you prefer.

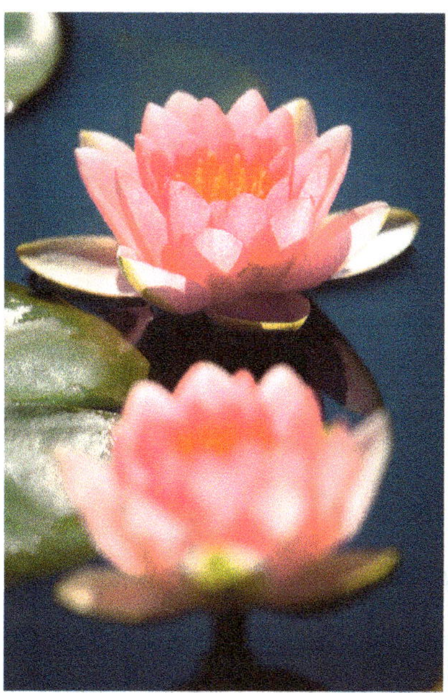

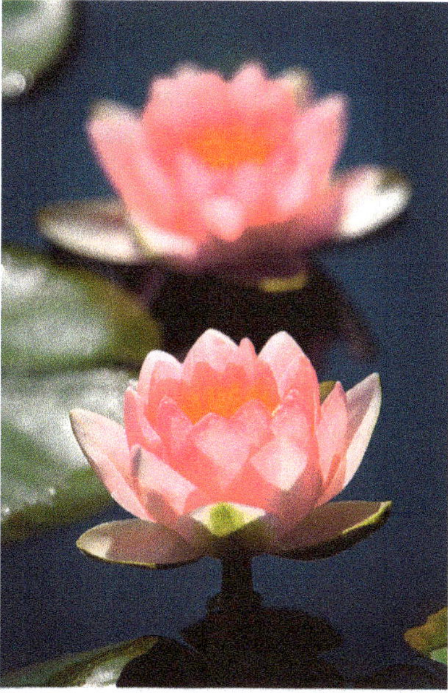

3.8 and **3.9** Charles Knox. Two lotus flowers in water with shallow depth of field. The composition of an image can be altered by changing the focal point, as seen in these two versions of a photograph.

Critical thinking:

Think about other ways in which the photographer could compose the image of the lotus flowers – for example, zooming in further on one of the flowers. Make sketches to illustrate your ideas.

The way in which the individual shapes are arranged within the image in relation to each other can make a big difference. You can use a formal or informal layout. The shapes might be arranged symmetrically or asymmetrically, but to create a more interesting composition artists usually avoid having a focal point that is directly in the centre of the page.

Materials and techniques: The golden section

A very traditional way of composing two-dimensional (2D) work relies on a mathematical concept known as the golden ratio, or golden section. In mathematics, two quantities are in the golden ratio if their ratio is the same as the ratio of their sum to the larger of the two quantities. This is believed to be the most aesthetically pleasing arrangement and is a device used by many artists across many centuries when composing their images. The concept is presented visually in Figure 3.10, where the focal point corresponds to the central point of the spiral. If you look back at Figure 3.4, you will see that John Constable placed the trees, which are the focal point of the landscape, using this technique.

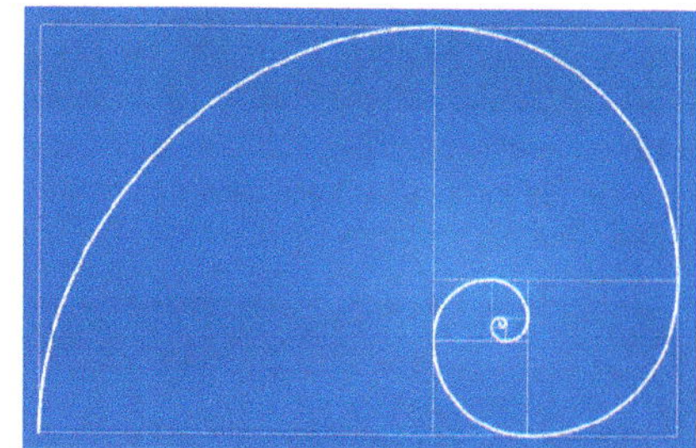

3.10 The golden section. The most aesthetically pleasing compositions are believed to have a focal point that corresponds to the centre of the spiral, a ratio of approximately 8:13.

focal point The part of the photograph to which the photographer directs the viewer's attention, generally where the image is sharpest.

Op art A style of abstract art chiefly concerned with the exploitation of optical effects such as the illusion of movement.

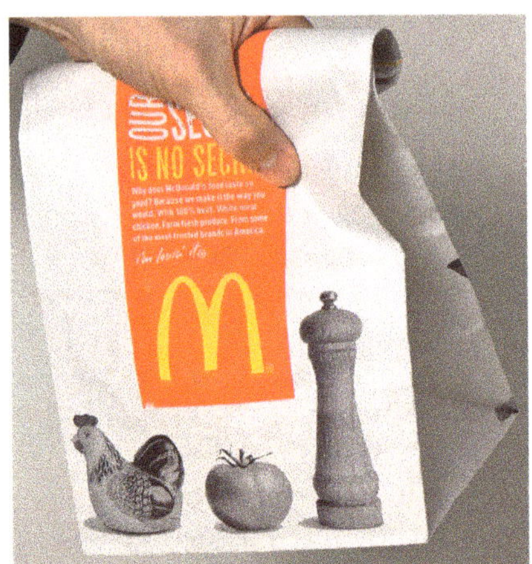

3.11 McDonald's paper bag, 2010.

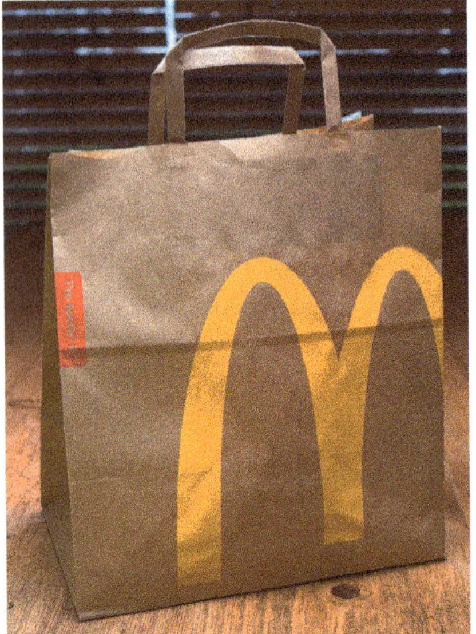

3.12 McDonald's paper bag, 2017. The scale and placement of the logo has been altered to refresh the visual impact.

> **Critical thinking:**
>
> Look at the way that O'Keeffe has applied the paint in her paintings of poppies in Figures 3.13 and 3.14. Think about the style of her mark-making technique and what impact this has on the finished work.

DEVELOPING AND REFINING WORK OVER TIME

Development and refinement can happen in the production of a single piece of work, but it can also be seen happening over time. Some artists, craftspeople and designers develop and refine work they undertake over many months or even years. For example, the design of the McDonald's logo is universally recognised and has remained unchanged for many years, but the way that it has been used on the packaging has changed over time. As well as the example from 2010 (Figure 3.11) having additional images included in the design, the placement and scale of the 'golden arches' logo is different on each of the two paper carrier bags seen here, so the look of the packaging has been refreshed.

REFINING ARTISTIC STYLE OVER TIME

Artists, craftspeople and designers experiment with their use of materials and develop a personal style over time. The examples in Figures 3.13 and 3.14 both show paintings of poppies by American artist Georgia O'Keeffe (1887–1986), *Poppies*, painted in 1926 and *Red Poppy No. VI* in 1928. Although the composition is very similar, the way in which the paint has been applied is different. In the 1926 painting, O'Keeffe shows less refinement than in the later version, which demonstrates a more mature style where the brush strokes are clean and sharp, with the result that the painting looks slick and more stylised. Practical experimentation and experience will help you develop your technical skills and understand the possibilities of the media that you are working with. This could be within one project, or seen across the work that you produce throughout your course.

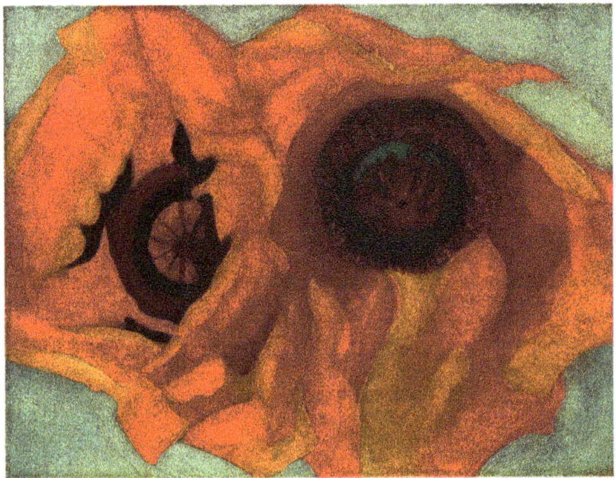

3.13 Georgia O'Keeffe, *Poppies*, 1926, oil on canvas, private collection.

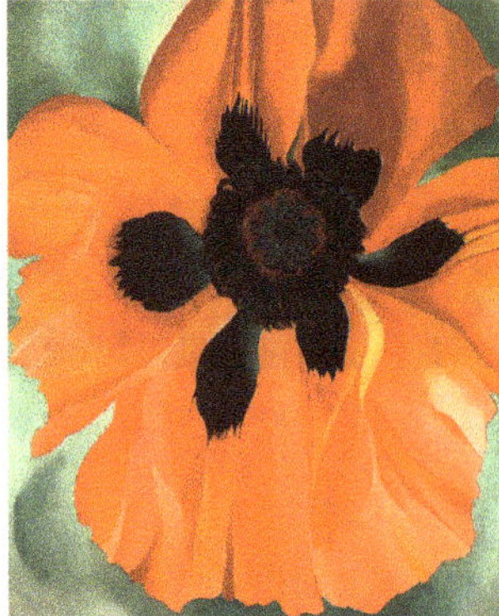

3.14 Georgia O'Keeffe, *Red Poppy No. VI*, 1928, oil on canvas, private collection.

DEVELOPING DESIGN IDEAS USING DIFFERENT MEDIA

For designers working in three dimensions, it is necessary to work with very different materials than the ones they use to record observations and ideas. The materials and processes that they use to develop their ideas can also be very different than those they eventually use to execute their final designs. A good example of this is the design development stages undertaken by German car designer Ferdinand Alexander Porsche (1935–2012). In the manufacture of cars, highly detailed scaled ceramic models are made as part of the design process. In Figure 3.15. you can see Porsche working on a model of the Porsche 911 from his very sketchy drawings on the wall behind him.

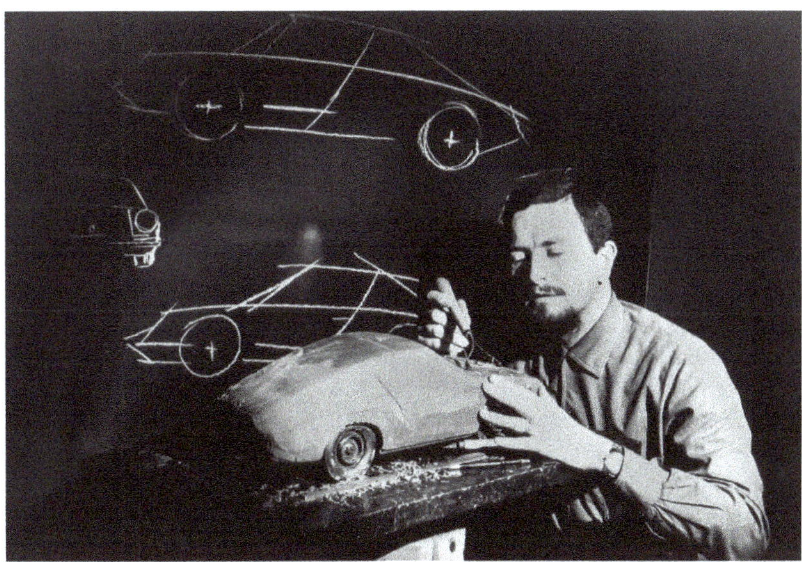

3.15 Ferdinand Alexander Porsche, grandson of the founder of Porsche, was a German-Austrian designer, whose best-known product was the first Porsche 911. In this studio photograph, he is working on a clay model of the Porsche 911 with his sketched drawing behind.

Many designers use computer-aided design (CAD) as part of the development process. Graphic designers will use CAD to explore the layout of their designs, which can then be sent digitally to be printed, because CAD enables designers to visualise accurate designs in 2D and 3D as well as to explore different colourways and font styles.

From using CAD, fashion designers will then develop their ideas in 3D, making mock-up garments, known as **toiles**, using cheap fabrics, so that alterations and experiments with the design, pattern and fit of the garment can be made.

Architects use 2D plans to visualise their ideas in 3D form by creating scaled models. They work with a range of sheet materials, such as card, foam board, balsa wood and plastics. The purpose of such models can be for the benefit of the designer, who can test out the feasibility of the design and help the client to see what the building will look like. Whatever your area of study, make sure that you explore your ideas using a range of media and techniques as your work develops.

toile An early version of a garment made up using inexpensive cloth so that alterations and experiments can be made.

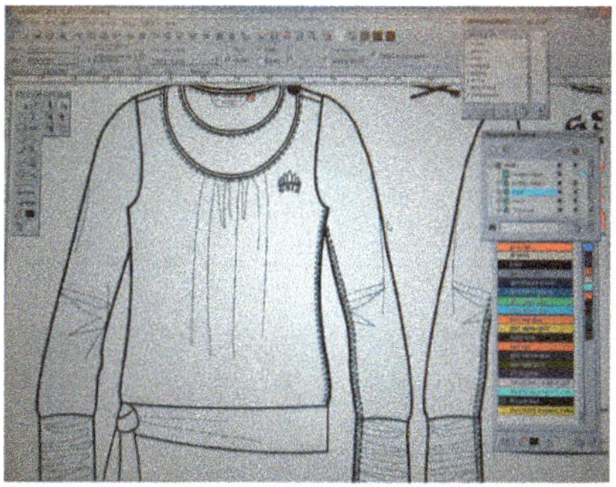

3.16 CAD being used by a fashion designer.

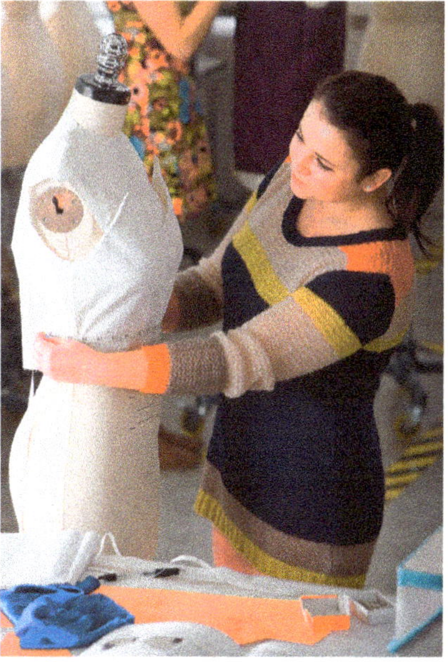

3.17 Fashion Design student working on a toile, developing the fit of the garment on the mannequin.

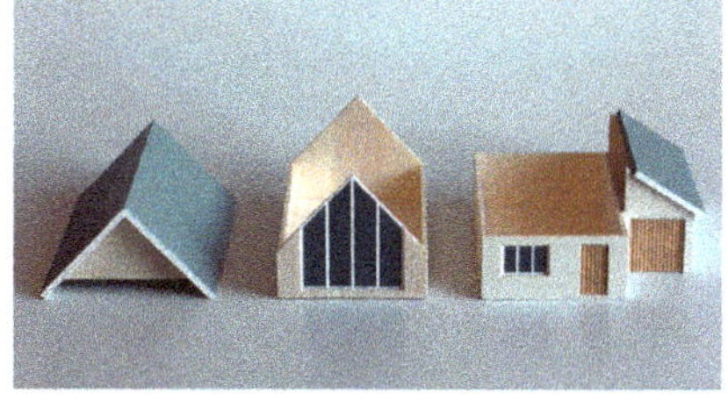

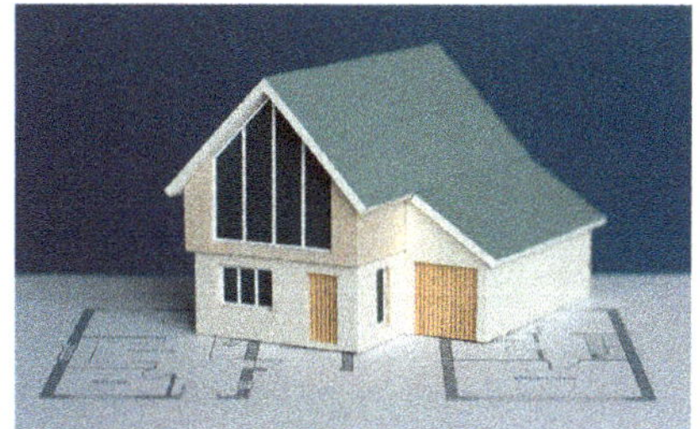

3.18 and **3.19** These images show how the building has been modelled in separate sections, so that the interior space and exterior can both be visualised . The model has been developed from the 2D plan.

Activity C: **From 2D to 3D**

1. Take a design drawing that you have created and use any appropriate media to create a 3D model of it. Make notes about any aspects of the design that you change as you develop your idea in 3D, and explain why you are making changes.
2. Once you have made your model, evaluate the outcome and suggest further **modifications** to improve the design further.

SUMMARY

Refinement and development is an important aspect of the creative process for all artists, designers and craftspeople. You can develop your ideas by reworking them using different media, materials or techniques, including the use of CAD. Every study that you make can provide you with evidence of the refining of your ideas, but when you are exploring the use of different media and techniques make sure that you are also developing other aspects of the work, such as composition and scale at the same time.

The media that you work with can help to determine the final form of your work. For example, when you work with 3D materials, such as clay, you begin to think through your ideas, taking account of real space.

The visual impact and form of any artwork will be affected by the characteristics of the medium that you work with. For example, a small-scale watercolour study will look very different if it is reworked as a large-scale oil or acrylic painting, where the brush marks may have a very different quality and colours may appear different because they have been applied in thicker layers instead of thin washes.

Critical thinking:

Think about the range of media and processes available for you to use for your area of study and make a list of those that you intend to work with. Reflect on your level of confidence and skill as you work with different media and processes, and make critical judgements about the impact that using different media and processes has on your work. Don't forget to continue making links to the work of other artists.

Tip:

Your work should reflect a 'journey' through the creative process. When developing and refining your ideas, make sure that you:

- produce a series of studies that use a range of media, processes and techniques, in 2D and 3D, as appropriate to your area of study
- experiment with the scale of your work, including the scale of the marks that you make
- explore composition and layout
- avoid simply reproducing the same image many times, just using different media
- annotate your work, critically evaluating what you do.

UNDERTAKING SECOND-HAND RESEARCH

Once you have undertaken first-hand research, which is required as part of the Personal Investigation, you should start to read around your subject to put your study into context and find out more about your theme, key artists or designers and other artworks. It is unlikely that you will be able to see all relevant artworks first-hand and you will need to do some analysis of work from second-hand sources. The main sources of second-hand research include books, the internet and film and video footage. It is important to remember that, unless the second-hand resource that you are using has been written or narrated by the artist or designer themselves, the views presented will be the author's viewpoint about the work or the theme that you are studying. Remember that the work that you produce for this component should focus on your personal response.

Using books

Books are a great source of information and will provide you with research on a wide variety of themes relating to all aspects of art and design. Popular themes, subjects and individual artists and designers will feature in work by a range of authors, so reading around a subject can help you to develop a balanced view of your subject matter and help you to form your own opinions. It is perfectly acceptable to agree with someone else's point of view, if you acknowledge that you are doing so. You can do this using quotation. For example:

I agree with Author A's point of view that artist X's representation of fire symbolises 'the spiritual and celestial realm, but also the presence of man', because …

You must then state where the quote has come from, usually as a footnote, and connect it to your line of thinking.

Tip:

Books do have limitations. If you are looking at images of works of art in books, you should be aware that when reproducing photographs in print, the colours that you see may be quite different to those you would see if looking at the work first-hand; they can seem very muted and dull in comparison. It is also very difficult to see textures in a photograph and you do not always have a sense of the size and scale of the work. If you are going to analyse works of art and design from photographs in books, take these limitations into consideration.

It is worth checking with your teachers to see what books the art department has. You will also need to check the art and design section of the school library and/or your local town library, if you have one. If you live in or near a town with a university, you may also be able to access the university library, which will have academic journals as well as books. If you use a local or university library, they might be able to source specific books or articles from other libraries for you to see or borrow, but they might charge a small fee for this service.

modifications Small changes or adjustments.

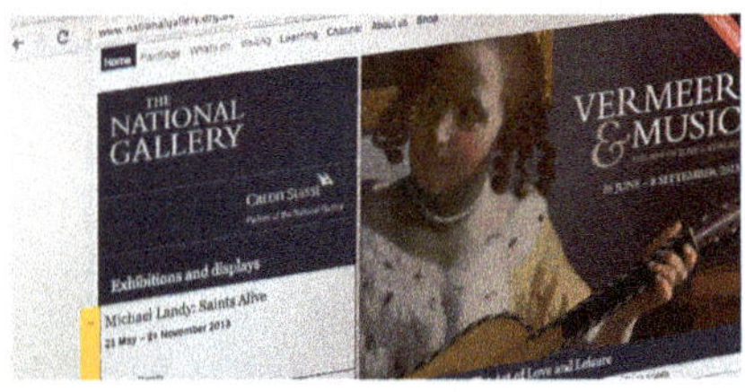

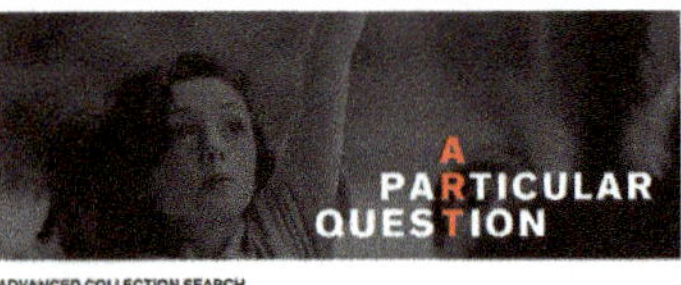

ADVANCED COLLECTION SEARCH

3.20 and **3.21** Gallery website search engines offer the opportunity to find specific artists or art works from the collection.

USING THE INTERNET

The internet is a good source of second-hand research, as you can easily search for information on global artists and designers. It is easy to find very contemporary work and research less well-known artists, often through their own websites. You can see artworks on museum and gallery websites from all the world's major collections, and many of these websites have the capacity to allow you to search for specific pieces of work.

Images in an online gallery collection have been photographed to be viewed on-screen and are often good quality. On-screen, the colours are more likely to be true to those in the original work, when compared to looking at a printout. Seeing a piece of work by taking a virtual gallery tour, or people interacting with art and design work, helps to give you a sense of size and scale.

However, be aware that not all information found on the internet is correct, and you should try and find more than one source to verify facts.

Activity A: **Internet searches**

1. Compile a list of useful internet sites that will potentially help you to research your Personal Investigation theme by searching the internet using key words, names and terms.
2. Save the web addresses of the most informative sites, using the 'Favourites' tab in your browser so that you can easily return to them later.

Critical thinking:

You must read around your subject matter or theme to help you to understand the context of your own work, but be prepared to question the validity of what you read. Be selective with what you research, ensuring that your written analysis, or annotation of your practical work, is relevant to your study. You need to synthesise, evaluate and interpret it as you go.

Remember: your opinion is as valid as that of someone else.

Activity B: **Selecting relevant information**

1. Either use an internet search, or look in books, and print or photocopy a section of information about an artist or designer that you are familiar with.
2. Now either underline or highlight key facts and information about them. Use the information that you have selected to write a paragraph about them in your own words, as concisely as possible.

USING FILM AND VIDEO FOOTAGE

Another source of second-hand research is film, DVD and video footage, which can also include television programmes about art and design. Some satellite services have dedicated arts channels that you might be able to access, or there are programmes available through on-demand or internet streaming services. Your school, college or community library might have a library of art and design-related programmes or films. If you use a visual source of research, you will need to take notes as you watch it.

You might need to watch the work of an artist who uses the medium of film, but in this instance the resource would be classified as a first-hand resource.

HOW TO USE THE INFORMATION THAT YOU FIND

It is very easy to gather a wealth of written information, but you will also be expected to use it selectively, in a way that supports the aims of your Personal Investigation. It is not acceptable to include long pages of general or biographical information, as it is your response to the theme that you are studying that is important. If you print out, photocopy or transcribe information, make sure that you read through it and highlight or underline key words and facts that you need to incorporate into what you write. Only use information that sets the context that is relevant to your work, supports your views or helps you to make judgements and form conclusions.

ACKNOWLEDGING YOUR SOURCES AND REFERENCES

It is a requirement of the Personal Investigation that you acknowledge and record your information sources. This should be done in the form of a **bibliography**. It should include any resources that you have used, including books, websites, articles in journals or film and video footage. You can also record the source of first-hand information by noting visits that you have made to galleries, museums or artist studios. It is also a place to acknowledge and thank artists you have interviewed or spoken to during the project.

There are slightly differing conventions when compiling an academic bibliography, but for your Personal Investigation it is acceptable to use a simple format. List the different sources of written information in alphabetical order, by surname of the author, followed by the book title, followed by the name of the publisher and date of publication. Add the page numbers if the source is an article. If the source is online, add when you last accessed it.

- For a book:
  Author, Anne, *Writing about Design*, Printed Books, 2008.
- For an article in a journal:
  Painter, Peter, 'What About Art?', in *The Gallery*, Volume 4, Issue 2 (2016), pp. 22–28.
- For an online source:
  Writer, William Wallace, 'How Do I Analyse Art?', <www.website.com>, accessed 20 January 2018.

Note that the book title and journal titles are italicised. Article titles and online sources have quotation marks. Commas are used between the author's surname and initial or first names; after the first name, or initial and full stop; after the title; and after the publisher name. If you are referencing an online journal or article, the date on which it was accessed should be included.

It is usual to expect a bibliography to list different sources of information in different sections. For example:

- books, articles and journals (including exhibition catalogues, online articles)
- websites (gallery or museum websites) – for example:
  www.moma.org Museum of Modern Art, New York
- other sources (a film, TV programme or video footage, artist interviews and so on) – for example:
  Local Artist Jane Doe, Environmental Sculptor, interviewed 24 May 2018.

It is usual practice to use double spacing when writing the list and only have one source on each line.

Tip:

- Make a note of books, articles and websites and so on that you use as you work through your project. It is much easier to compile your bibliography at the end if you have all the information to hand. If you do not use something that you have found in your research, then you do not have to acknowledge it, but it is easier to delete it later than have to add something in.
- Remember that it is fine to use secondary sources to gather information, but you must write up what you find in your own words and not just cut and paste chunks of text.
- Do not list the search engines that you used to find information online; just list the websites that your referred to.

Activity C: **Set up a bibliography record sheet**

1. Make yourself a record sheet where you can start to collate all the references that you use throughout your Personal Investigation in one place.
2. Create a table with columns for: the date when you accessed your source, the title, the author, publisher name and date of publication and/ or website addresses. You can also include a column for recording visits to galleries, museums of artist studios and a column for the artwork that you specifically went to look at there.

bibliography A list of books or other material on a subject.

3.1 Graphic communication

Printmaking and illustration

Learning objectives:

- To understand how printmaking and illustration can be developed and refined
- To explore printmaking and illustration techniques

Illustrators and printmakers develop work through using materials, techniques and processes. In this unit, we look at some of the techniques you can use to develop print-based illustration work. You will be exploring different techniques to create illustration work. One of these illustrations will use a printmaking technique called a **collagraph**.

USING TECHNIQUES TO DEVELOP WORK

Illustrators work using techniques suited to their intentions. They find the right technique by trying out different ways of working. These might be drawing-based illustration, using print techniques, painting or software. They can combine these if need be. They then reflect on the results of these experiments. Some illustrators use image and text to create work that communicates through both. In Figure 3.22, the Indian illustrator Sameer Kulavoor (born 1983) is using a photocopier-based technique to create an image which is itself based on local photocopier facilities.

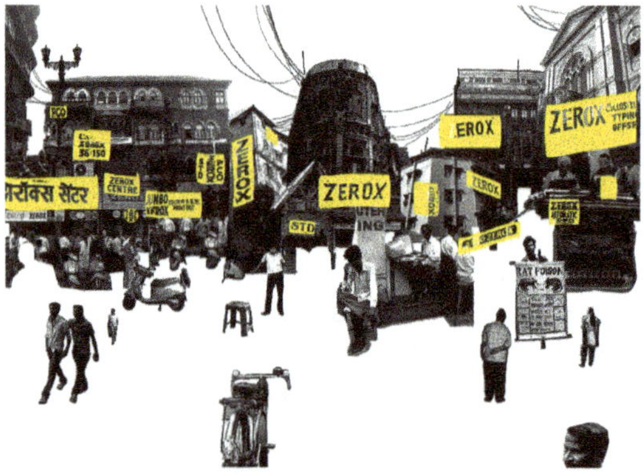

3.22 Sameer Kulavoor, *Zeroxwallah Zine*, 2011, Black screenprint on yellow card. This image uses the techniques of the Zerox shop, which is a photocopy shop, to make works that combine image and text. The use of yellow and black together with small sections of images from Mumbai gives it a distinctive cultural reference.

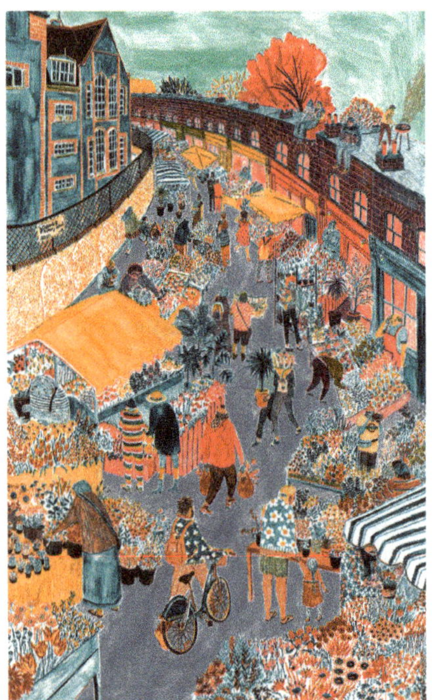

3.23 Mouni Feddag, *Columbia Road Flower Market, London*, 2015, ink and pencil and coloured digitally. An illustration recording an environment using layered pigments. The image captures the visual character of a busy market street.

DEVELOPING WORK – CAPTURING THE MOOD

Illustration is used to capture the mood of a subject, or to show its personality. It achieves this through exaggerating its **visual characteristics**. Many illustrators emphasise characteristics through the way they use formal elements. For instance, they might be illustrating a busy street scene with lots of noise, colour and movement, such as the market scene in Figure 3.23. In this example, the British illustrator Mouni Feddag has used bright colour and a higher viewpoint to illustrate the movement and busy nature of the scene. This uses recording skills and ideas about the subject to develop work.

TECHNIQUES FOR ILLUSTRATING AN IDEA

There are different techniques you can use to communicate an idea. Some of the main ways artists do this are by using:

- Drawing – many illustrators use drawing as they develop work, using different types of drawing media; these can be pencils, pastels, chalks, markers and so on.
- Paint media – these can be water-based or oil-based. There are examples of different paint media shown on page 232.
- Collage – this can be pieces of imagery pasted together, or digital collage using software where layers are used, each with different image – both of these make a **composite image**.
- Print – traditionally, illustrators have explored intaglio and relief printing. Screen and digital printing have further developed the possibilities in this area.

Illustrators use drawing to record their environment. One way is to make preparatory drawings and studies. This is a way of building up a personal library of drawn imagery. This is like having your own bank of images you can go to when you need ideas or information. You can make preparatory drawings and studies using illustration techniques.

Activity A: **Produce a set of studies**

This skills activity builds into the others in this unit. It also relates to skills activities in Module 1, where you were developing your recording skills, and understanding of how to use source materials. In this activity, you are going to capture the mood of a scene through the types of marks and media you use; these will be your illustration techniques. You will also use photography.

You should work on this activity in groups of three or four.

1. Find a local market, shopping centre, line of stalls or avenue of shops in your local area.
2. Arrange with your teacher to make a visit there in your group, including travel arrangements to get there, and make sure that there is no risk to your health and safety – if you prefer, you can use a playground or area at your school or centre.
3. Once there, set yourselves up close to each other.
4. Use drawing and painting illustration techniques to record the scenes in front of you. You will need to:
   - Work quickly.
   - Try drawing in a loose style – if people are moving around, you will have limited time to record them.
   - Explore different ways of recording them – you might find that you can use some lines, such as squiggles and small gestural marks, to record people.
   - Set them against the backdrop of the buildings/stalls.
   - Try using water-based colour if you feel confident.
   - Make sure that at least one drawing records the whole scene – make this A3 size.
5. Take photographs of the scene.
6. Bring the work back to the classroom, display it and discuss in your group.

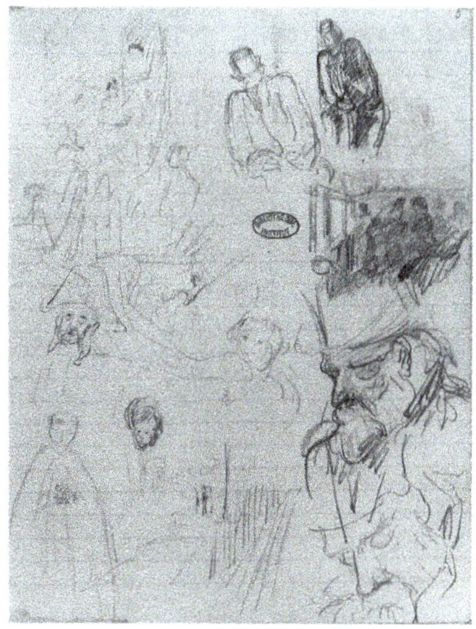

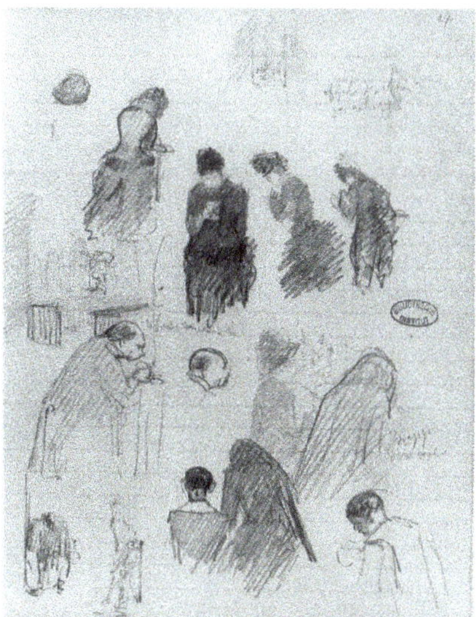

3.24 and **3.25** Édouard Vuillard, *Two pages of a sketchbook*, 1890–1940, pencil on lined paper, Bibliothèque de l'Institut de France, Paris. In these images, the French Impressionist artist Édouard Vuillard (1868–1940) has worked quickly, using line and basic shading techniques.

collagraph Printing block made by collaging and gluing surfaces together onto a card board.
composite image An image made up of different pieces, as in a physical or digital collage.
visual characteristics When formal elements are exaggerated to show the personality of a subject.

Tip:

Practise drawing from memory with simple objects with regular shapes to start with, such as flower pots and cups and saucers. You can move on to more complex subjects once you have practised on these.

Materials and techniques: Developing drawing from memory

This is a great way to extend your drawing and illustration practice, but it does take some getting used to. You have to look at a simple object for between one to two minutes without drawing it. Really study the shapes and forms of the object, and memorise them. When you feel you have a good mental picture of the object, turn away from it and draw it without looking at it.

This technique can help you actually become better at looking – an important stage to master when developing skills. Many artists and illustrators worked up details in their work from memory, such as the French artist Pierre Bonnard and the British artist J.M.W. Turner. They used their memories to develop and refine work by adding to or incorporating additional colours or textures in scenes they were painting. They did this to make the paintings communicate more directly to the viewer; they left out unnecessary details and focused on using colour and light.

LINKS BETWEEN ILLUSTRATION AND PRINTMAKING

Illustrators can take techniques from the printmaking process and apply these to their own work. There is a long history of book illustration using engraved or relief printing. Relief printing of imagery was developed as a result of editions; this is the number of prints of books that were required. Illustrators also explore printmaking techniques developed in other areas such as fine art or commercial graphic design, such as photo-based silkscreen printmaking.

The Japanese illustrator Mayuko Fujino has developed and refined a technique that explores the potential of paper cut-outs. She takes her inspiration from traditional Japanese craft technique katagami, the making of stencils for dyeing textiles. This led her to use cut-out paper shapes as key elements in the visual design. Her work explores rich pattern, form and the negative space between shapes. It has been featured in music packaging, editorial and advertising, as well as carpet design and print on fabric. This shows how illustration has a broad range of applications.

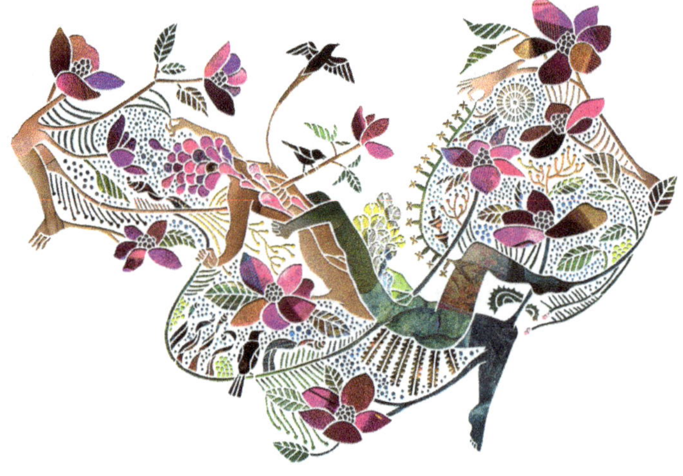

3.26 Mayuko Fujino, *Psychological Acrobatics*, illustration, undated, collage and paper. An example of Fujino's rich detailed work that can be produced using cut paper stencils.

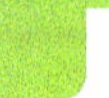

Activity B: **Developing a composition**

This activity develops from the work you did in **Activity A**.

In Figure 3.22, you saw how photocopies can be used to make a composition of a street scene. Some of these used different scales.

1. Take the A3 drawing you made of the scene, and photocopy it at least twice full size.
2. Print out your photographs of the scene.
3. Cut out figures and details in the photographs, and place them onto the larger A3 copy of the drawing.
4. When you have an interesting composition, glue them down – this is the first version.
5. Now go back to the copier and use the reduce/enlarge controls to change the scale of some of the other figures you still have.
6. Place these on the second copy of the scene, and explore different compositions.
7. Refine the placement of the figures until you feel that it works, then glue them down.
8. Discuss the two layouts with your classmates – which one works best?
9. How could you use this technique further to develop ideas for work?

> **Tip:**
>
> Introduce other formal elements by using coloured papers as backgrounds, by photocopying or printing onto acetate film, or by using handmade textures – for instance, you could wash paint onto paper, let it dry and then paste the cut-outs onto this.

Activity C: **Developing illustration using stencils**

1. Make another A3 copy of the drawing that you made on the scene in **Activity A**.
2. Take some of the smaller drawings you made for **Activity A** and photocopy them or scan and print these out.
3. Cut out the figures and put these to one side. You will need these later. Take the sheet they were cut out from, and position it on the larger sheet. This can be next to a drawing of a figure, or anywhere you like. It doesn't have to match exactly.
4. Experiment with different paint media to develop the illustration by careful dabbing of thin layers of paint through the stencils and seeing what effect they make.
5. Again, discuss the image with your classmates, and consider how could you develop this technique further.

Materials and techniques: **Cutting paper stencils**

To do this safely, you need a sharp craft knife. Blunt knives mean that you have to push harder to cut, and you should avoid this. You must use a suitable cutting surface. There are specialist **cutting mats** available from suppliers. You can also use strong, dense card if no mat is available. Draw your shape onto the paper, and use the knife to carefully cut out the shape – where possible, keep your other hand away from the cut, and make the direction of the blade go away from the body.

cutting mat Strong plastic mat specifically for cutting paper on.

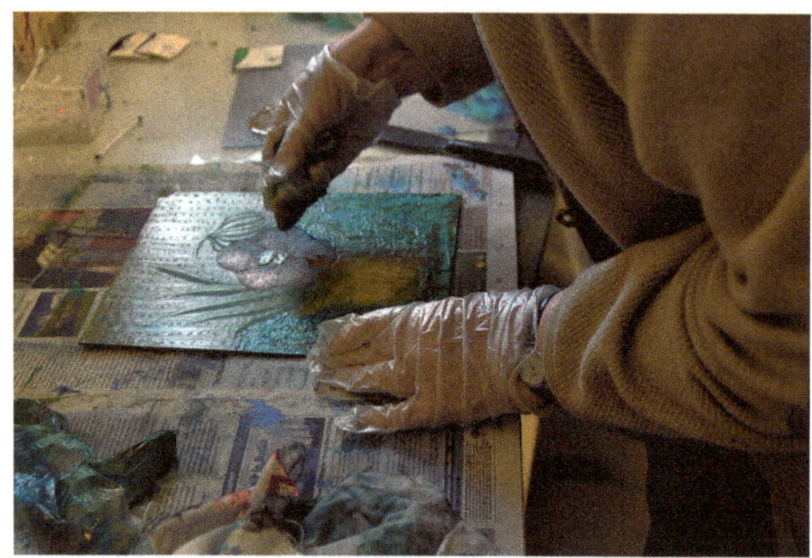

3.27 Inking up a plate in a printmaking workshop. Making a plate is a simple way to develop printmaking, as in collagraph or lino printing.

COLLAGRAPH PRINTMAKING

A collagraph is a simple printmaking block. Shapes, cut surfaces and materials are collaged together and glued to a background block material. Strong card can be used for this. The block is built up so it has raised surfaces. The surfaces of the collaged materials will pick up ink, so need to be made to fit the shapes of the subjects. Once theses surfaces are completed, they are varnished and allowed to dry. This is then inked up as a block, and printed using a press, or by sandwiching between sheets of paper and two boards and applying pressure. It can create richly textured imagery. It cannot be repeated limitlessly, as the board may start to break down with repeated use.

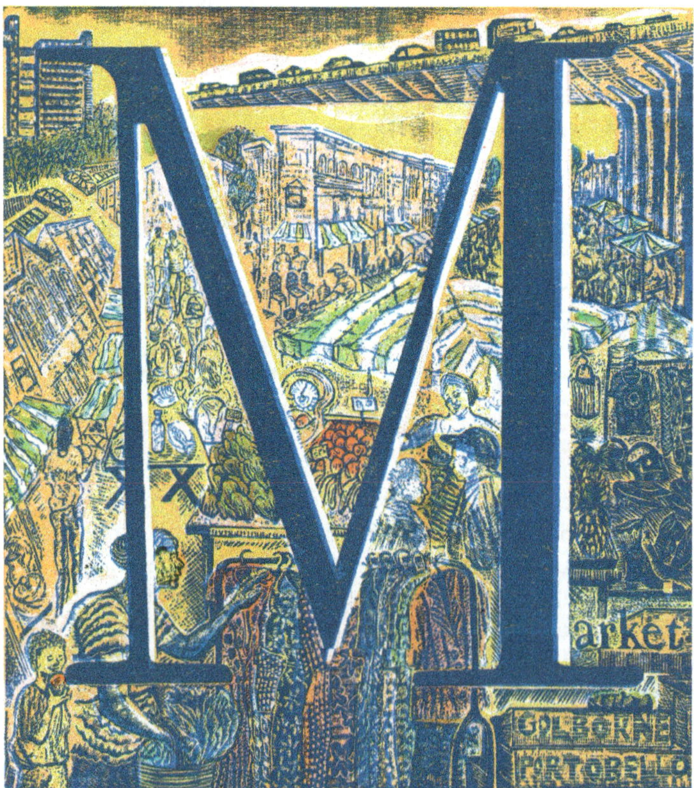

3.28 Mary Kuper, *Market: Portobello and Golborne Road*, 2015, vinyl engraving and collagraph print, private collection. In this image, collagraph printing has been used as part of the image-making process to produce a richly textured street scene.

DEVELOPING THE PRINT

Developing an idea from original starting point to finished print requires working through the stages in the creative process shown on page 184. Think about the different parts of your work being like bricks or blocks in a wall. They all need to go together to make the final piece work successfully. You are going to explore this idea further by taking your work in the skills activities so far, and use it as the basis for the next stage, where you will be using printmaking.

Activity D: **Collagraph printing**

This activity combines illustration and printmaking. To do this, you will need your A3 street scene and the paper figures you cut out and put to one side in **Activity C**. You are going to use these to develop your image using printmaking.

1. Take the A3 image and reverse it on the photocopier – most copies have an invert image facility. If you do not have this in your school, use a light box, turn your image upside down and trace the main parts onto another sheet of A3 paper.
2. Stick the A3 sheet onto a piece of good-quality strong card the same size – this is your block.
3. Collect materials with interesting textures, including string and cardboard to tear to see the internal structure. Use some of these to create background details on your A3 image. You can match these shapes to outlines on your drawing, such as buildings.
4. Glue these down.
5. Take your figure cut-outs and enlarge some of them. Glue a set of different-sized figures onto card and cut round them carefully. Repeat this at least one more time, making the figures much thicker.
6. Stick these figures down onto the A3 block.
7. Paint varnish over the block and allow it to dry. You want the surfaces to become one fixed surface. Repeat with another coat of varnish if you need to.
8. Now think about colours. You can hand-paint background colours onto sheets of paper before you print on them. Make up an ink to use (see mixing inks on page 53).
9. Print your block using a press. If you do not have access to this, place between paper and boards and apply pressure.
10. Display your prints – think about composition, positive and negative shapes and the overall visual effect.
11. Discuss with your classmates – is there anything you would want to change? Make notes.

Further research

For more on Mayuko Fujino, go to her website.

Search online for more on collagraph printmaking.

For more on printmaking techniques, read *Printmaking: A Complete Guide to Materials and Process* by B. Fick and B. Grabowski (Laurence King Publishing, 2015).

Critical thinking: **Evaluate your illustration and printmaking**

Display all of your work for all four activities in this double unit and critically review the work. Ask your classmates to help you, by commenting on your work with their own views. Write up a summary considering:

1. Can you see the stages in the development of the work from **Activity A** to **D**?
2. How well did you use formal elements, such as composition, or colour – what have you learned about these through doing these tasks?
3. What stages are the strongest – the ones where you really understood the tasks?
4. Which areas require improvement?
5. Make a note of your answers to step 4 and focus more on them the next time you are developing work.
6. What techniques and processes worked well?
7. Can you see any ways that you could use these techniques and processes in future work, to develop and refine ideas, preliminary work and final pieces?

Packaging and branding

Learning objectives:

- To understand how branding can be developed in packaging
- To develop and refine packaging design for a luxury brand

In this unit, you are going to look at the different stages in packaging design. You will research an example for a luxury brand, and produce a design idea for packaging.

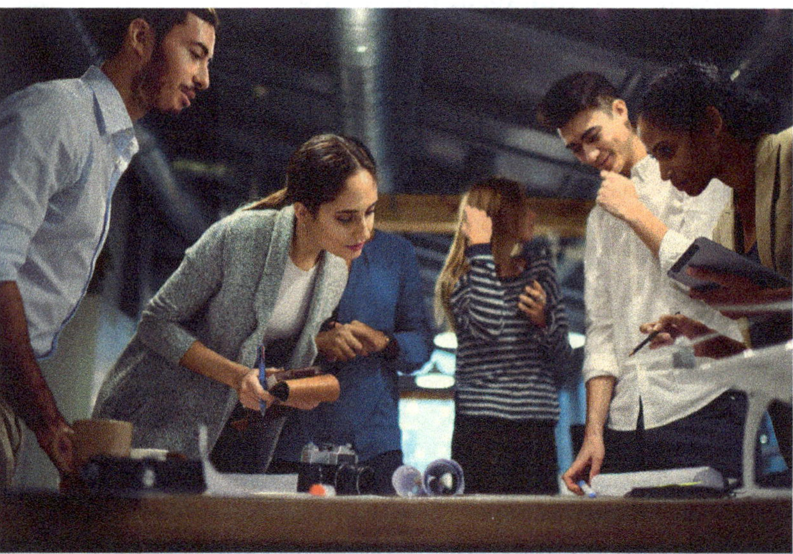

3.29 A design team considering ideas. Working through the different stages in a design is an important part of developing each stage, which needs to be covered properly in order to inform the next one.

DESIGN STAGES

The stages in developing packaging design are:

1. Drawing – rough sketching out of ideas.
2. Editing – selecting the best ideas.
3. Showing rough **die-lines** – these are the points for cutting, scoring and folding that will make the structure – these can be made with pencil at this stage.
4. Prototyping – this can be in paper and is sometimes called rapid prototyping – allows the idea to move from a 2D surface to a 3D object. It uses the die-lines made in previous stage.
5. Measurements – these are for shelves, cartons and anything that affect the production. They can be made by scanning paper mock-ups, using CAD software, to produce vector diagrams.
6. Working models – these are made in final production materials and used to test the design of the packaging.
7. Photographing the models – allows them to be tested in different conditions (for example, on shelves) and the results shared around the team as part of the testing phase.
8. Refining the designs by using the results of the models tested in different conditions to adapt the design, and go to production.

PACKAGING DEVELOPS THE BRAND

Images, text and materials are used to communicate the product's personality. Most packaging uses the logos and design elements from the brand, and states them simply on the box or outer surface. For some brands, this is the most direct way of reinforcing the personality of the product.

PACKAGING FOR A LUXURY BRAND

As a designer, you have to be aware of how this works. For example, if you were designing for a luxury brand, the packaging needs to promote the exclusivity of the brand. You might use design to produce refined packaging, using elegant fonts, and rich surfaces and textures. You are developing these designs to make the consumer feel that the product is special.

USING SURFACES AND COLOUR TO PROMOTE BRAND IN PACKAGING

The physical materials used in packaging are important. Examples of low-cost products will typically use stock, normally card that may have been recycled or cheaply sourced. Alternatively, a brand may want to create a specific packaging feel – and target this at a specific audience, who will react positively to this packaging. The Chanel example in Figure 3.30 shows packaging using heavier stock card, with reflective surface and a simple, elegant colour range, including gold – all reinforcing the brand, identifying the concept with luxury.

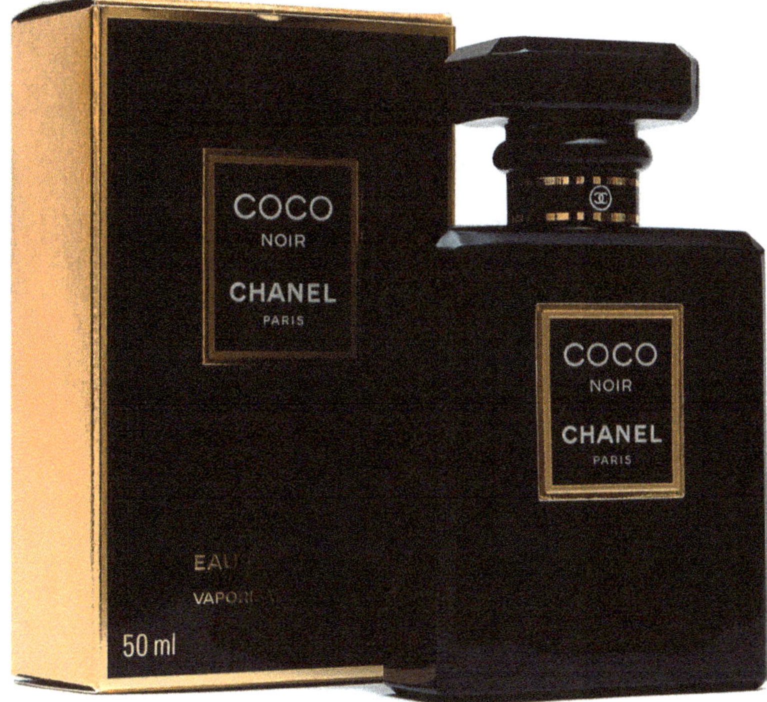

3.30 Packaging design, Chanel perfume. The original Chanel logo was designed by Coco Chanel herself in 1925. In this example, the designer has used a classic serif typeface and in a small, discreet type size. What do you think the designer is trying to express about this brand?

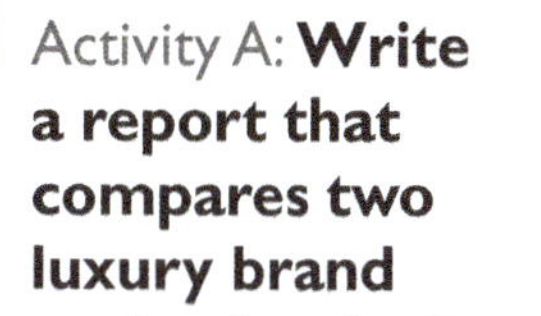

Activity A: **Write a report that compares two luxury brand packaging designs**

Work in pairs to produce packaging design for a luxury product.

1. Research examples of luxury brands.
2. Discuss and decide on two brands that you want to research further.
3. These can be similar, that is, both perfume or trainer brands, for example.
4. Use your visual analysis skillset to compare the two types of packaging and write a report for presentation to your classmates. You should include visuals of the packaging in your reports.
5. Your report should discuss:
   - brand identity
   - how this is achieved
   - use of formal elements
   - unique or special aspects of the packaging, such as the shape used, surfaces, layout and so on.

die-line Flat shape of package laid out on a single 2D sheet of material, showing lines to be cut and scored, to make a 3D package.

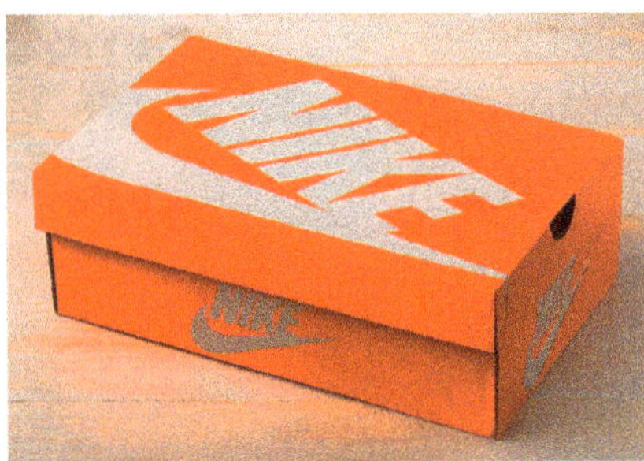

3.31 Nike, shoe packaging. This brand has become instantly recognisable through its use of colour, font and logo. These elements are all reinforced in this packaging example.

Activity B: **Develop a design for packaging for a specific brand**

Work in pairs to produce packaging design for a luxury product.

1. Research a brand and decide on a product you will design the packaging for.
2. Discuss your ideas, and produce some rough drawings for your packaging.
3. Display these drawings and edit them down to one final idea.
4. Take this idea and draw a rough die-line of the packaging.
5. Make a paper prototype of this, using the die-line as a guide for folding and cutting. You can refer to Figure 3.32 to give you an idea of how this can work.
6. Put your packaging on display and get feedback from your classmates.
7. Use this feedback to refine your design idea and make the package in good-quality card. Include logo details as part of this.
8. Photograph the final piece.
9. Present this to your classmates in a **pitch** for feedback, and make a note of the points raised – you will need these later in the unit.

Tip:

Practice makes perfect. You need to learn and practise the skills required for receiving and providing feedback. You can make notes about others' work as you listen to them, before you give feedback.

Materials and techniques: **Giving and providing feedback**

Presentation skills
To get feedback to help you refine work, you need to present it professionally. Avoid having bits of paper curling up, or dirty drawings – scan them and use a digital printout system, or make sure that the physical copies are well mounted on card.

Using persuasive language
This is important, because if you are justifying your work in a critique you may want to convince someone that your idea meets the brief, without sounding argumentative. If you are giving feedback to others, you need to do this in a way that is seen as positive, by offering options in a supportive manner.

Reaching conclusions
Make sure that you summarise the points in any feedback you either receive or provide. You have to go away from any team discussion knowing exactly what the action points are – otherwise, you will not know how to refine the work further.

pitch Presentation back to clients or audience, showing responses to a design brief, and potential creative solutions for consideration and feedback.

REFINING WORK – REVISITING THE DESIGN PROCESS

The process for developing packaging shown on page 200 at the start of this unit was laid out in a sequence. Sometimes you may not be able to go through each stage neatly. You may find that you need to go back to certain points in the process – for instance, if the results of your tests on how the packaging looks show any weaknesses, or the client is unhappy with some aspect. Whatever the reason, your ability to refine the idea by working through the processes will help you to resolve the design.

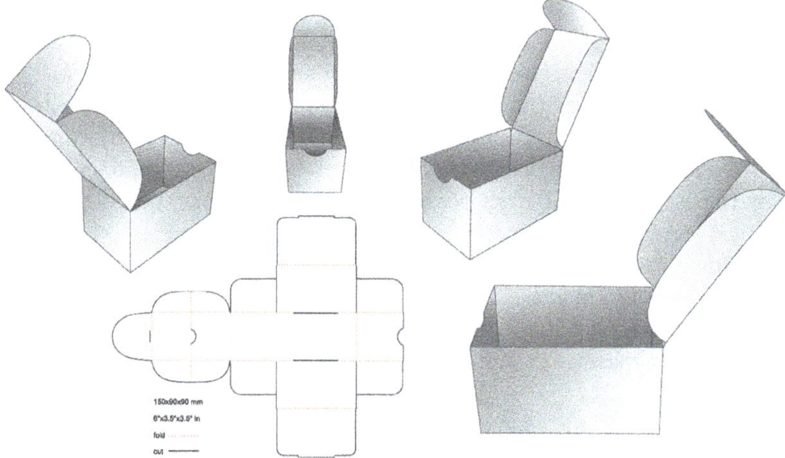

3.32 A die-line for a simple card box. This shows the basic shape that would need to be cut out of flat material to make the package, in this case a simple box, with lines for folding to make the structure work.

Activity C: **Refine your design ideas**

1. In your team, discuss how you would resolve the points raised in the pitch you did at the end of **Activity B**.
2. Think about how you could use these points to refine the design you produced.
3. List the points, and show how this would be incorporated to refine the visual design.
4. Write up your summary, and present it back to the team. Do they agree with your design responses?

Further research

For more on the packaging industry or brand identity and visuals such as logos, search online.

Tip:

The ability to refine a design idea is another key skill used by designers. This can be informed by feedback from different sources, such as other members of the design team, or the client themselves. Some designers will try to strike a balance between their intention for the brief, and the responses and feedback offered.

Critical thinking:

1. Consider what you learned about packaging design work on all three skills activities.
2. Can you describe the design development process that you used to develop your work in **Activity B**?
3. Was it informed by anything you learned in **Activity A**?
4. How did the use of visuals and materials reinforce and communicate the values of the product or brand?
5. How did you use formal elements to communicate these brand values?
6. What have you learned about the process for developing packaging design work and refining it through these activities?

Advertising

Learning objective:

- To understand how image and text are used together to develop and refine advertising

DEVELOPING ADVERTISING – IMAGE AND TEXT

Designers use techniques to develop and refine advertising ideas. Some of this depends on contextual factors, as we have seen in Module 2. Advertisers may produce topical campaigns that reference socially relevant ideas at that time. This affects the techniques that designers use and how they develop work, such as how they combine image and text. Here's an example:

Look at early car manufacturers' advertisements. These used performance statistics to highlight the desirability of their vehicle. This might be the time it took to get from 0 to 60 miles per hour. Are there that many advertisements that you know of that still mention this kind of information today?

If you compare the examples seen in Figures 3.33 and 3.34, you can see how much the use of image and text has been developed and refined.

This can be seen in the layout, the font and the illustration. However, has the underlying message changed?

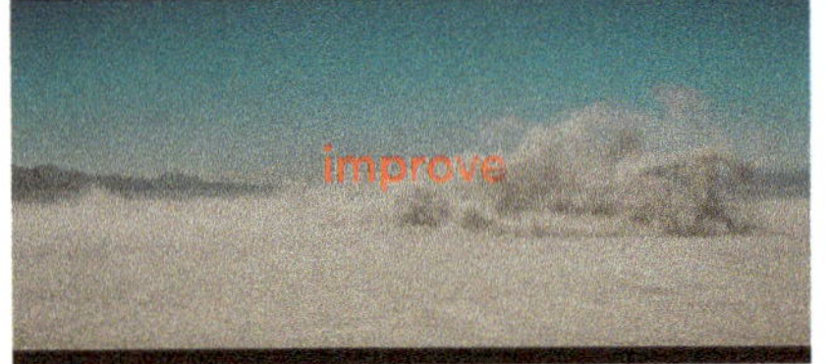

3.34 Still from Honda TV advertisement, 'Keep Up', 2015, Wieden and Kennedy, London. This advertisement uses the idea of speed but not in an image showing a car moving quickly. In this advertising campaign, it is the font itself that moves at speed. Watch the advert online.

Activity A: Image and text

1. Work in pairs.
2. Choose an existing advertisement that you feel has an interesting and eye-catching use of image and text.
3. Find visual examples of this advertisement.
4. Discuss how you could develop this.
5. Draw up a series of roughs and thumbnail sketches showing your ideas.
6. Now meet again and develop these sketches by selecting one and refining it in more detail.
7. Draw the design out, showing the font or typeface, or hand-drawn letterform, and the image in more detail.
8. Discuss this again and write a short statement explaining:
   - the inspiration behind the design you developed
   - how you used image and typography.

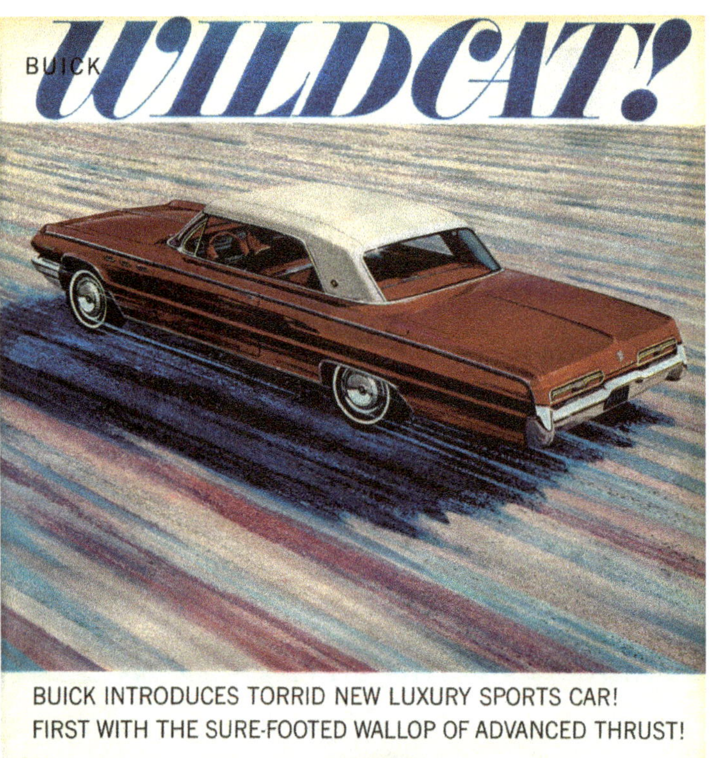

3.33 Magazine advert *Buick Wildcat!*, USA, 1960s. Note the use of the word 'Wildcat!' in this image. What are its associations? Are these emphasised by any of the details in the advertisement, or by the way the image of the car is presented?

HAS IT CHANGED?

The still from the advertisement in Figure 3.34 shows a development from the 1960s poster shown in Figure 3.33, but is it just a different way of saying the same thing? The advertisement featured a car in the desert, with fast-moving text **superimposed** one word on top of the other. This happened very quickly, almost too quickly to read. It was based on the concept that if you can read the words while they move fast, you are capable of more than you thought you were.

The advertisement was banned by the Advertising Standards Authority (ASA), as they said that its use of speed and specific phrases such as 'You can surprise yourself. Suddenly you find you can go faster than you thought' and 'keep pushing and get to better faster' encouraged speeding.

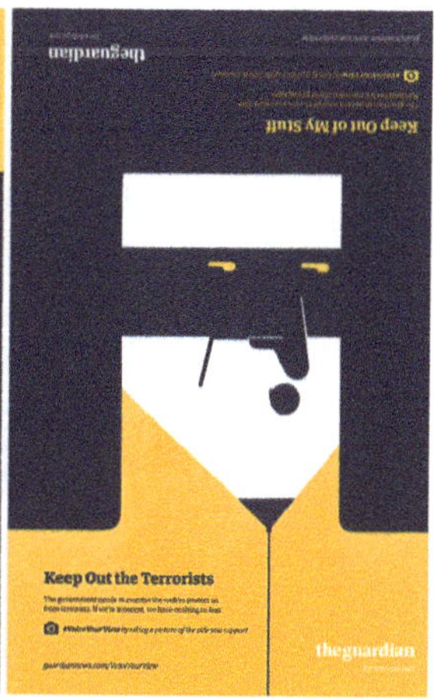

3.35 Print advertisement, *Guardian US*, Illustrations by Noma Bar, 2011. This figure shows an interesting use of images and words to communicate the idea of two sides to an argument.

DEVELOPING ADVERTISING – CONCEPTS

Image and text can be used to create images that communicate a message effectively. In Figure 3.35, the image on the left shows a person at a desk under a light, with a laptop. If the image is flipped, these elements become parts of a face. There are two separate sections of text, each stating a different message. These two images represent different views and arguments about controlling and viewing internet habits. The images were used as posters and mobile billboards. They were designed to promote the message that this publication would report on all sides of a current issue. Figure 3.36 shows an older, less integrated approach to using text with image in promoting the idea of books as presents.

Activity B: **Refining your work from Activity A**

In the same pairs, come up with an alternative design solution to the one you finished with in **Activity A**. Think about how your design used image and text, and refer to the examples in Figures 3.35 and 3.36. What could you do to refine your work?

1. How could you develop the visuals?
2. How would this affect the way you develop and refine the text?
3. Can you make the visuals and text have a message that is communicated more clearly after your revisions?

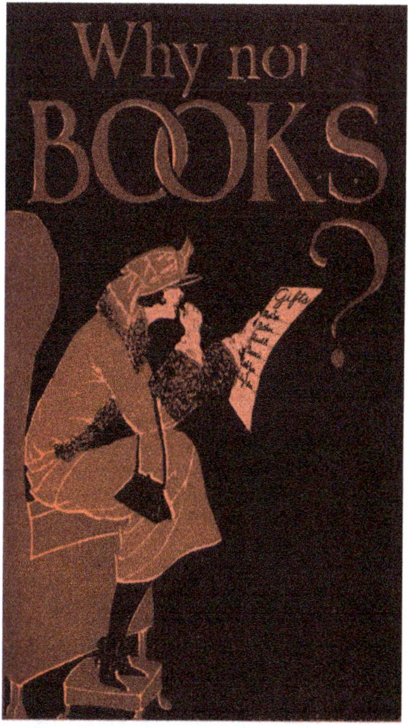

3.36 An American advert to encourage people to read books. American Bookselling Circular, c. 1922.

Critical thinking:

Present your design development on **Activities A** and **B** to your classmates.

Ask them to feed back to you on how;

- you used imagery and text generally
- you refined this use in **Activity B**
- the visuals work to create interest
- you could develop the design further.

superimpose To lay one thing over another.

Further research

Go online to find more on print advertising campaigns.

For more on examples of advertising, read *Advertising: Concept and Copy*, 3rd edition by G. Felton, (W.W. Norton & Company, 2013).

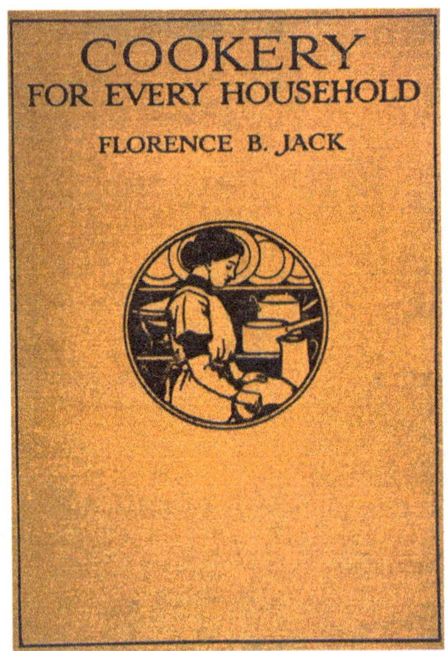

3.37 T.C.E.C Jack Ltd, *Cookery for Every Household*, Book Cover, 1924. A design that uses minimal imagery and a symmetrical layout to achieve a simple cover that communicates its meaning effectively, without any attempt to add mood or emotion through visuals and typography.

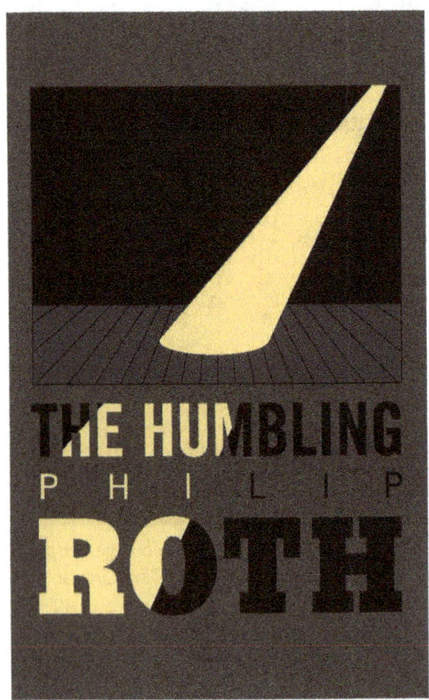

3.38 Milton Glaser, *Book cover for The Humbling by Philip Roth*. In this figure, the American graphic designer Milton Glaser (born 1929) has used typography and simple imagery to communicate the idea behind the story. This is the tale of an actor who becomes old and lonely and loses the ability to act.

Typography

Learning objective:

- To develop and refine practical typography skills in book cover design

TYPOGRAPHY AND INFORMATION

We have looked at how different typefaces can be developed to communicate certain types of information on signs and notices. Typography can also be used to communicate ideas and moods, as in magazine and book covers. The same techniques are also used in screen-based typography. Designers who explore this aspect of typography use formal elements to make it communicate an idea or meaning, beyond the words it spells out. This might be in the way they use scale, colour, shape, layout and so on. In this unit, you will develop a design for a new guide book on your country using typography.

LAYOUT

Typography is arranged as part of the composition of a book design. The example in Figure 3.37 shows a symmetrical layout, where the typography is centrally positioned. The type is in a single colour, and all upper case. The image is also placed centrally. This creates a balanced and ordered feel to the design.

COLOUR AND TYPOGRAPHY

In the design by the American designer Milton Glaser in Figure 3.38, the colours in the cover are monochrome and add to the sense of unhappiness that is contained in the story. This is an example of a book cover communicating an idea about the contents using colour, typography and layout in an effective combination. The typography is linked to the image by the way in which it continues the shaft of light coming from the off-stage spotlight.

Tip:

You can explore layout and typography in word-processing software by changing the position of text. This can be left-aligned, centred, justified and so on. It can show you how text can look in these positions. Desk-top publishing (DTP) software is designed for layout and will include ways of setting custom **margins**, gutters and so on.

DEVELOPING TYPOGRAPHIC DESIGN

You can use techniques to develop your typographic design. One way would be to:

- Work on paper to explore ideas about layout and font.
- Work up rough sketches into more defined ideas.
- Use digital software to work up designs into digital versions.
- Refine and output work using digital software.

ALTERNATIVE APPROACHES

You can explore other ways of developing typography. In the example in Figure 3.39, the typography is made up of drawn elements. It can still communicate meaning to us, as we recognise the letterforms and words. It can also go on to communicate another level of meaning to us. This happens when we realise the importance of the way the letterforms are made. In this novel by Lauren Beukes, people who have committed crimes are attached to an animal familiar. This links with the way the type is made from drawn elements that incorporate some animal parts. To develop handmade work, you may want to:

- explore handmade design solutions
- collage elements of imagery together to make letterforms
- scan and edit your handmade typography in digital software if necessary.

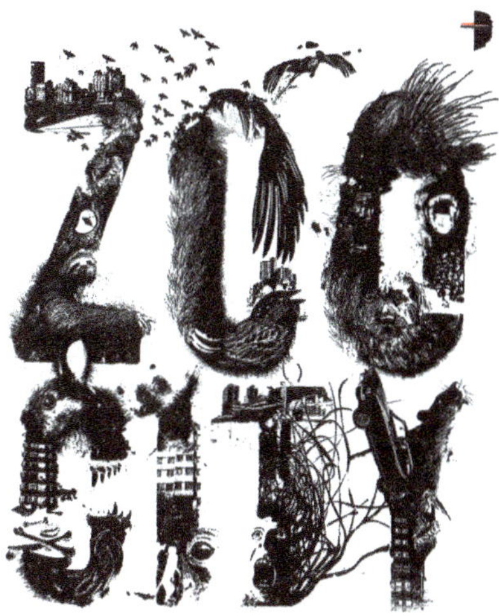

3.39 Joey Hi-Fi, book cover for *Zoo City* by Lauren Beukes, 2010. The typography here is made up of imagery that again relates directly to the idea behind the science fiction story. People who have committed crimes are linked to an animal familiar. This is represented by the way the type is made from drawn elements.

Activity A: **Design a travel guide book cover**

Create two versions of a book cover for a new guide book for travellers to your country. It should include 'Visit "name of your country"' on the cover – for example, 'Visit Japan'. It should *not* contain images, unless they are part of the letterforms themselves. One version is to be digital-based, so will use DTP. The other will be handmade.

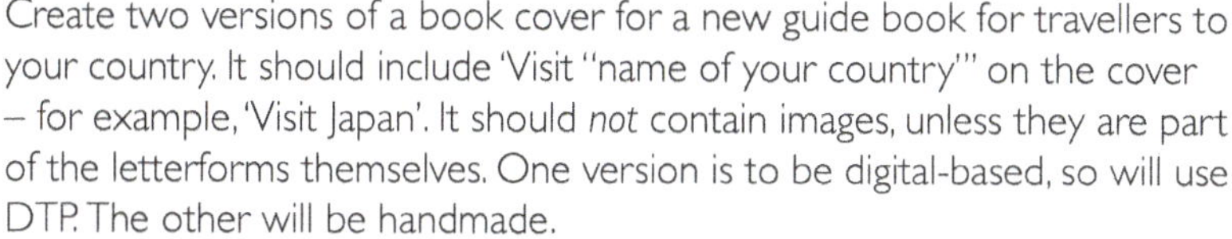

Work in groups of four on this activity.

1. Research information on the phrase 'reasons to visit your country'.
2. Write down any good reasons you can think of why people might want to visit your country.
3. As this activity is not about recording, you can use imagery from tourist information sources to get background visuals.
4. Develop a response in each of the two options.
5. Start by using handmade rough versions, and move on to the art-worked versions, where you mock up the actual pieces. Mock up one digitally, and the other by hand – these will show what the designs will look like.
6. Meet as a team and discuss the two pieces.
7. Select one and refine it further. You can develop and refine it by:
   - using formal elements in different ways
   - developing designs using alternative fonts or letterforms or layouts.
8. If working digitally, make sure that you save your version each time – that way you will not be overwriting existing work and losing it.
9. Print out and/or present the final piece to your classmates.

Critical thinking:

In your team, display your work for **Activity A**.

Discuss your work with your classmates, reviewing and evaluating:

- How effectively have you used typographic elements in the design?
- Clarity – is it easy to read? (Use feedback of others here.)
- Have you used formal elements in the design?
- Have you managed to communicate any ideas about your country in the way you have used typography?
- How could you improve the design?

Further research

For more on typography read *The Typography Idea Book: Inspiration from 50 Masters* by G. Anderson and S. Heller (Laurence King Publishing, 2016).

Go online to find out more on classic book covers.

For more on Milton Glaser, go to his website.

margin The edge or border of something.

3.2 Textiles and fashion

Printed and constructed textiles

Learning objectives:

- To explore different types of subject matter when developing pattern design ideas
- To be able to consider types of repeat for final outcomes
- To use critical thinking to support idea development

As a textile designer you need to be imaginative when choosing your subject matter for a pattern idea. First-hand observation is important if you want your designs to be unique. This information can be found all around us from everyday objects to human gestures and expressions. Once a *motif style* – for example, a floral, animals, ethnic, abstract, geometric or **conversational motif** – has been chosen, then you can decide how to compose and place the artwork onto cloth or paper.

This can be done in a few ways depending on the designer's intention for the overall effect. A couple of the important principles that a designer needs to consider when composing the design onto cloth or paper are scale and placement. If the print is for a child's garment, does the design need to be small? Or does the print need to be achieved by screen printing onto individually cut garment pattern pieces?

Activity A: Make repeat-pattern designs

Using the examples in Figure 3.40 as a guide, source five repeat-pattern designs and identify how they are repeated. What do you think a mirrored design would look like? Draw a grid like this one and make examples of your own:

1. straight repeat
2. random repeat
3. half-drop repeat
4. brick repeat.

USING FIRST-HAND RESEARCH TO DEVELOP A FINAL OUTCOME – 'REPEAT' SECTION

When designing a repeat pattern, decide whether you want a simple or complex design. The pattern needs to come together seamlessly and repeat across the length and width of the fabric. There are excellent examples of repeat pattern in the form of **tessellation** found in Islamic art and the art work of M.C. Escher. In textiles, however, it is the **block prints** of William Morris (1834–96) that present us with multi-coloured repeat complex patterns. In some of his designs, Morris used up to 80 colours, making his designs very labour-intensive. Go online to see how a William Morris design repeats. Try it yourself and see how intricate his designs are.

In this unit, we explore some examples of repeat images.

We will begin with a few simple repeat types seen here in Figure 3.40 and then look at how a student has developed her ideas for an all-over screen print

The examples here are typical basic repeat-image configurations. You will find these in most designs.

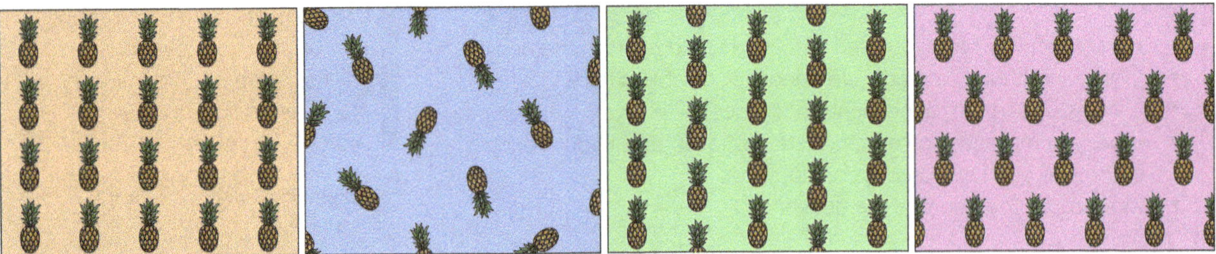

3.40 From left to right: straight repeat, random repeat, half-drop repeat, brick repeat.

The work featured here is by art student Jesse Howarth. In Figures 3.41 and 3.42, Jesse presents us with sketchbook pages of her ideas leading up to an all-over repeat design for a screen print. The drawings are a self-portrait drawn in pencil. She has drawn herself at different angles, as she wanted to convey different emotions and expressions for her print idea. Her final idea was to produce a piece of printed fabric expressing a person's varying emotions. She explored the quality of line in both pencil and paint to express contorted features (see Figure 3.43). The result is a multiple repeat on cloth in black textile ink that conveys a busy and lively design (see Figure 3.44).

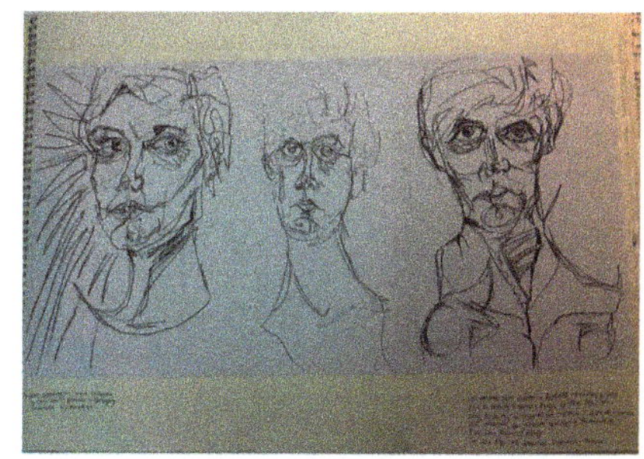

3.41 Jesse Howarth, sketchbook pages development work, self-portrait capturing emotion.

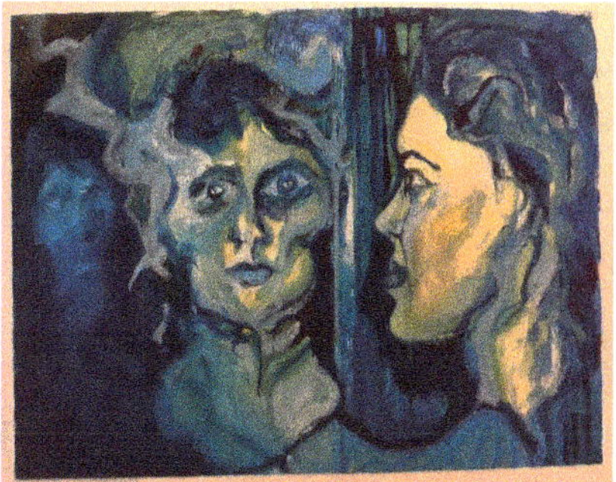

3.42 Jesse Howarth, sketchbook pages development work, self-portrait, acrylic. Jesse has captured a reflected image and used acrylic paint to explore mood and expression. She went on to experiment with distorting faces, playing with scale and overlapping her ideas until she decided on an image to repeat.

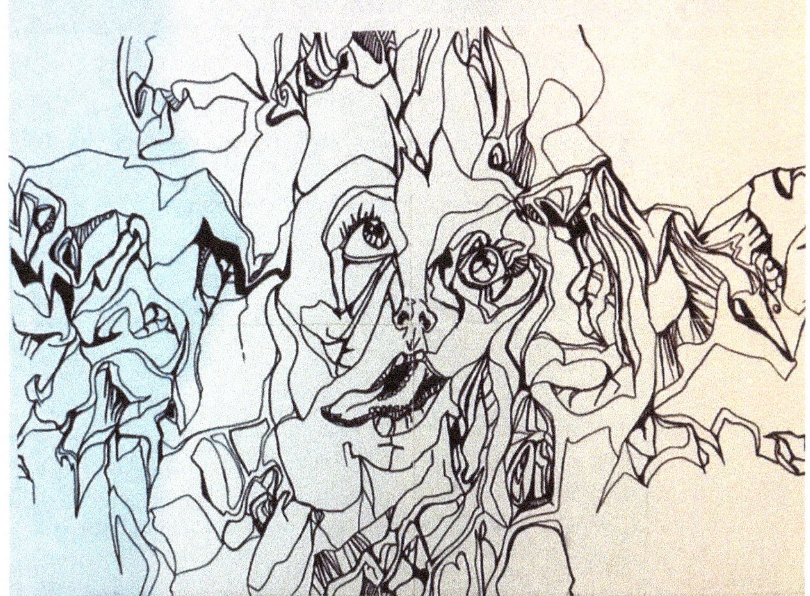

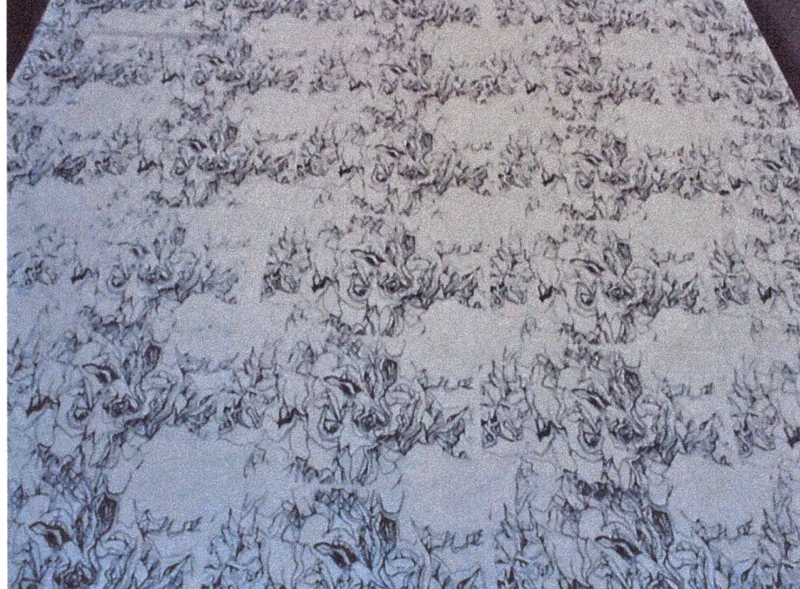

3.43 and **3.44** The image on the top followed the activity featured in this unit to achieve an all-over repeat. If you photocopy this image six times, you can see the design in repeat. The image on the bottom shows how this has been screen printed multiple times.

block printing A form of printing using an image carved into a material, usually wood, and covered in ink.
conversational motif One that has recognisable objects in the motif, from pencils, chairs, to embroidery threads and scenes from daily life.
tessellation An arrangement of shapes closely fitted together, without gaps or overlapping.

DEVELOPING PATTERN IDEAS

There are four main ways of creating repeating patterns (see page 208). Once you have chosen a theme for your fabric design or pattern, it is a good idea to explore it using different images and arrangements before making any final decisions. Sometimes an image may work well as a straight repeat, whilst another image may only look good as a random repeat.

Activity B: **Make a paper cut all-over repeat pattern**

This activity gives instructions for making an all-over repeat pattern for screen printing, block printing or any another textile application that requires an all-over repeat image. It may look a bit confusing but it does work!

1. Begin with a blank piece of paper. In the middle of your sheet, draw your design. Stay away from the edges of the sheet.
2. Turn your paper over and draw a four-part grid. Write the numbers:
   1 2
   3 4
3. Turn your drawing back over to the design side and cut the paper in half vertically. The number on the grid at the back of your paper will now read:
   2 1
   4 3
   Tape the pieces back together.
4. The middle of your drawing is now blank. Fill in the space, but stay away from the top and bottom edges.
5. Untape the drawing and rearrange back to its original configuration:
   1 2
   3 4
   Then tape it back together again.
6. Now cut your sheet in half horizontally and tape your pieces together. The numbers will read:
   3 4
   1 2
7. The middle of your drawing is now blank again. Fill in the space but stay away from the edges to the left and right.
8. Turn your drawing over and untape it. Rearrange the paper to the new configuration:
   1 2
   3 4

Your repeat is now complete. You can now photocopy the complete repeat image six times and to see whether it works. The photocopied image will reduce by a small percentage and will have white borders around it. Cut these off accurately with a sharp knife.

Tip:

To help you decide what the motif will look like as a repeat, superimpose the image onto your product.

Tip:

Working quickly at this stage in developing your pattern allows you to explore and choose from a range of ideas before spending more time realising a design. Computer art programs can be used to do this. Use a photograph or scan of your image in an art program. By flipping and mirroring copies of your image, you can make alternative patterns from your design without having to trace and redraw your work.

USING SKETCHBOOKS TO DEVELOP EMBROIDERY IDEAS

Embroidery designer Shannen McCusker develops her embroidery collection 'Aoife'. Her inspiration for her collection is an eclectic mix of plants from the botanical gardens in Belfast to Victorian patchwork embroidery. She pushes the boundaries of embroidery by using both hand and machine embroidery to produce elaborate and skilful textile surface designs for a series of deconstructed garment pattern pieces.

She begins her development with sketchbook pages displaying first-hand research of plants found in the botanical gardens. She focuses on the patterns and colours provided by the foliage and explores these surfaces using watercolour paint and paper collage. If you look closely at her annotation on her sketchbook pages, you can see that she has asked herself some questions on how she could use these new discoveries as part of her embroidery techniques.

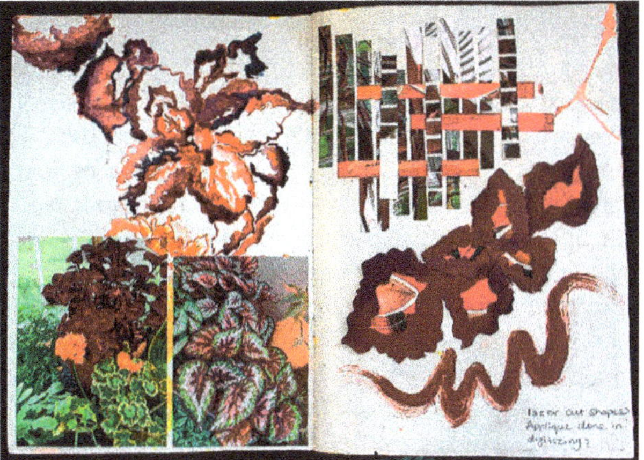

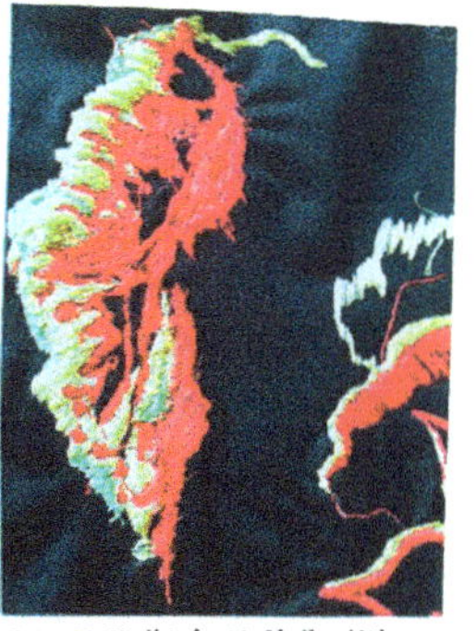

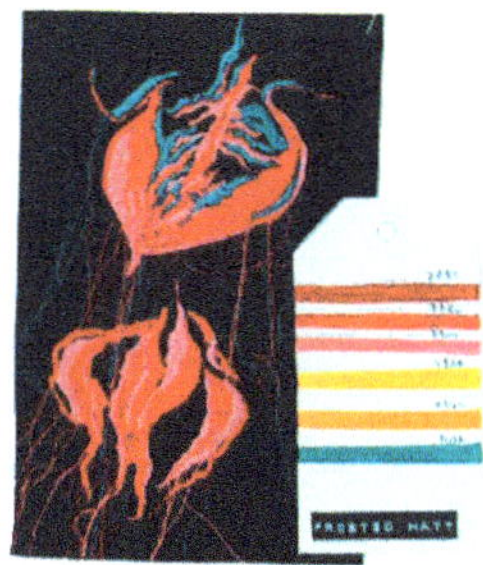

3.45 Shannen McCusker, sketchbook development pages with annotation, machine embroidery.

An example of her questions is: should she use a **laser-cut** technique for the outlining of the purple shapes of the leaves or use the appliqué technique? She makes a comment on the discovery of the irregularity of her stitches, which she now prefers and will take forward into her development ideas. Such discoveries can sometimes happen through accidents – for example, if a sewing machine has been threaded up with a looser bottom or top tension but the result is just what you're looking for! Remember to write down how you have discovered such things, as they can be easily forgotten.

Continually ask yourself questions to develop your ideas. This will encourage you to focus and move forward.

laser-cut A precise cutting tool that uses laser technology.

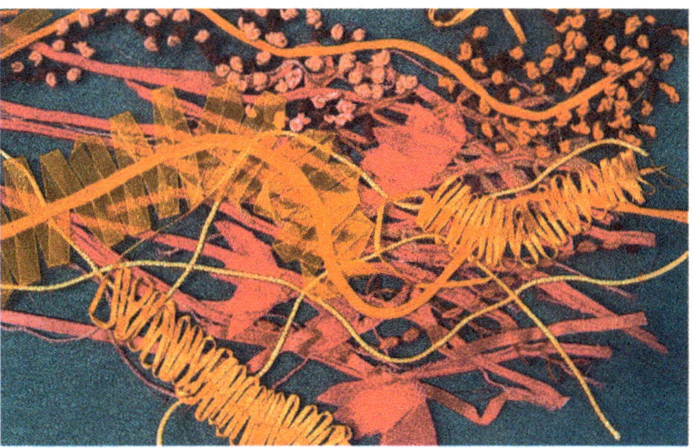

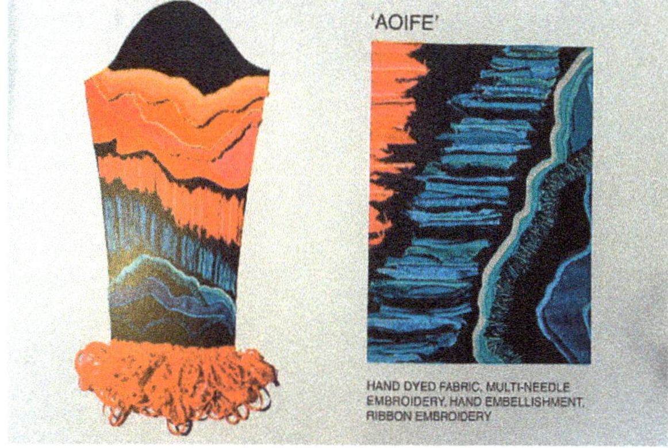

3.46 Shannen McCusker, hand ribbon embroidery sample.

Tip:

The three F's remind you of what you need to include when you are making a critical analysis of your work:

- **Facts:** What have I done? Explain what techniques and processes you have used.
- **Feelings:** Why have I done it? Explain how you feel about your discoveries. How successful are they?
- **Futures:** How can I improve it? What changes are needed for the next stage of your development?

Activity C: Draw from a natural still life

Set up a still life of found natural objects. These can be flowers or other natural materials, such as fruit or vegetables. Draw the unusual shapes and textures found on both the outside and inside of the objects.

Try cutting the fruit and vegetables up and use materials that allow you to explore the colours and textures you see. Use your viewfinder if it helps.

As you respond, be aware of what embroidery stitches you could use that relate well to the textures and colours in your still life. In translating your drawings into thread and fabric, you can make creative leaps. Your work can be more abstract or emphasise decorative patterns. Make five responses and, when you have completed the activity, make sample thread wraps using a piece of white card. Compare these colours with the original natural forms. They are probably quite different from nature. This exercise has helped you to develop your own colour scheme inspired by nature.

Tip:

When you have completed a piece of embroidery, turn the fabric over and view it from the wrong side. You might find some interesting results, as it can sometimes look irregular and have a softer texture.

Materials and techniques: Embroidery resources

You will discover a variety of embroidery threads and embellishment of varying qualities in textile supplies. Be mindful to choose the correct type of threads for your project. Fine shiny machine embroidery threads can slip around and fall off the **thread spool**, so you will need to secure these with a **thread sock**. Make sure that you have adjusted your sewing machine thread tension to suit the thread weight and thickness.

Critical thinking:

1. Consider the work that you produced for **Activity A**. How successful do you feel your repeat has worked? Did the pattern flow well across the page? Jesse's repeat is rather structured with a grid-like effect. Can you describe the effect of your design? Will it suit a dress fabric or an interior fabric? Can you now consider adding colour to your design?
2. Consider the work that you have produced for **Activity B**. Were you successful in identifying interesting patterns and colours? Did you have enough information to help you choose embroidery threads and embroidery stitches?

Further research

There are excellent collections of repeat patterns on the Victoria and Albert Museum website.

Explore the following books:

- *The Complete Guide to Designing and Printing Fabric* by Laurie Wisbrun (Bloomsbury, 2011)
- *Repeat Patterns* by Peter Phillips and Gillian Bunce (Thames and Hudson, 1992)
- *1000 Patterns* by Drusilla Cole (A&C Black Publishers Ltd, 2003)
- *How to Read Pattern: A Crash Course in Textile Design* by Clive Edwards (Herbert Press, 2009)
- *Dyeing and Screen-Printing on Textiles* by Joanna Kinnersly-Taylor, (A&C Black Publishers Ltd, 2012).

Go online to find out more on print, and pattern-focused articles on William Morris designs.

Explore the following books and websites for hand and machine embroidery:

- *The Left-Handed Embroiderer's Companion* by Yvette Stanton (Vetty Creations, 2010)
- *Textiles Now* by Drusilla Cole (Laurence King Publishing, 2008)
- *Stitch Draw: Design and Technique for Figurative Stitching* by Rosie James (Batsford, 2014).

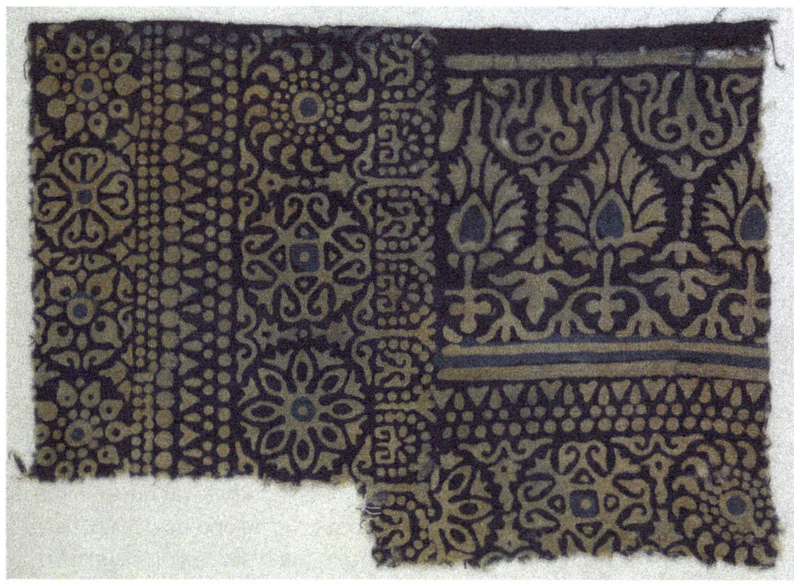

3.47 Block-printed textile fragment, Indian (cotton).

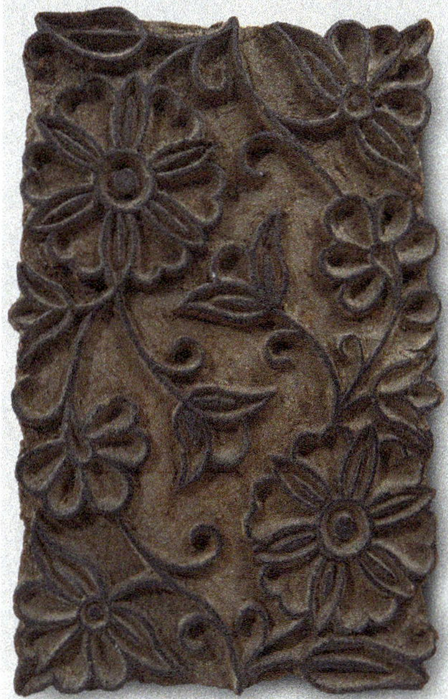

3.48 Traditional Indian wooden printing block used for fabric decorations.

thread sock A fine mesh that fits over the embroidery thread spool to prevent the thread from slipping off.
thread spool A small plastic tube that sewing-machine threads are wound onto.

Fashion design

Learning objective:

- To explore draping on the stand

Draping is a process of cutting, pinning, slashing and marking fabric in developing a pattern design on a mannequin or live model. It is an alternative method to **flat-pattern** development. This process is an excellent way for you to explore how a fabric behaves when on the body. How does it fall? How will you position a piece of fabric with a surface pattern on the body? To begin with, a toile is made on the mannequin using inexpensive fabric, such as **calico**, **jersey** or **muslin**. Toiles can be repeated many times to make small alterations until the final design is achieved.

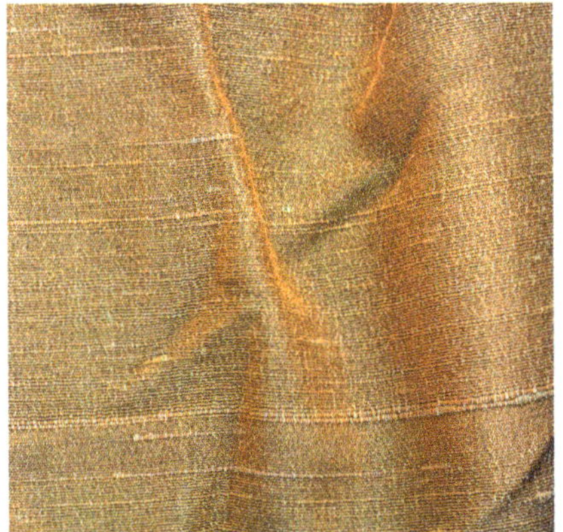

3.49 Grain lines visible in raw silk fabric.

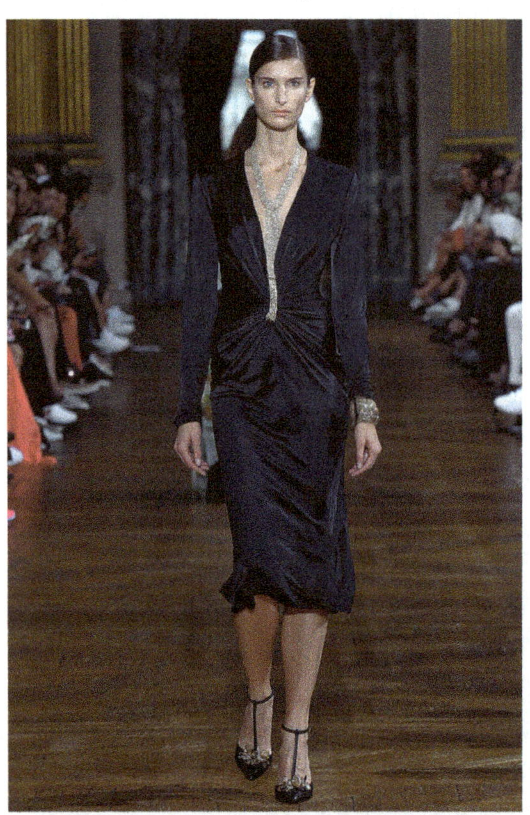

3.50 An example of a dress cut on the **bias grain**, Lanvin collection, silk jersey dress, S/S 2017.

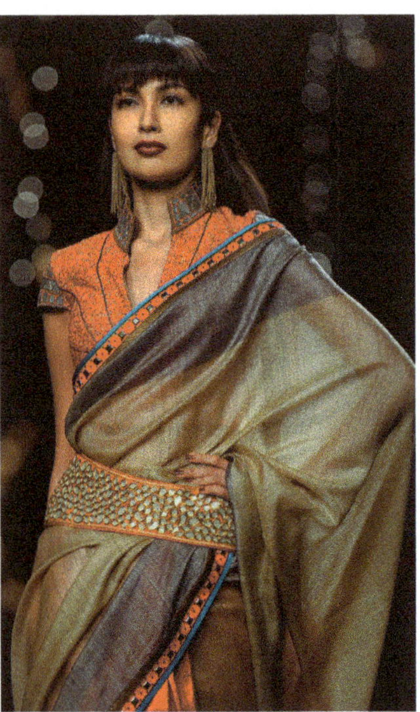

3.51 In this 2014 design, the Indian designer Tarun Tahiliani explores draping fabric over the body.

Before you use the draping method, it is important that you understand the basic principles of how woven fabric is constructed and how it will hang on the body. The example in Figure 3.49 shows the direction of the **grain lines of the fabric**. The straight grain or lengthwise grain (**warp**) runs parallel to the **selvedge** and is draped in a vertical direction on the body. If you want a close-fitting garment, this is the direction you place the fabric on the mannequin. If you want a little more stretch, then position the fabric with the cross grain (**weft**) horizontally so that the selvedge runs parallel to the bust and hip line. For a softer drape, like the garment in Figure 3.50, use a bias grain. This can be achieved by folding one corner of the fabric in a diagonal to the selvedge, now in a 45-degree fold line. Explore these grain lines yourself using a variety of fabrics, such as woven and jersey and discover the different draping effects.

Tip:

Take a piece of woven fabric, pull it in different directions and explore the three grains. Write on it where the grains are and place it in your sketchbook.

Materials and techniques: **Draping on the stand**

Draping on the stand by manipulating fabric or paper is a useful way to develop your ideas and understand how your garment will look. It is a technique that can help you to understand the relationship between a design sketch and a 3D form. It will also give you an insight into the volume and shape of the body you are designing for. Recording the work on the stand is very important. You can do this by photographing and drawing the shapes as your ideas develop. This is an essential part of your sketchbook development and must include annotation.

Tip:

Before taking the final design from the mannequin, sketch it on an A1 sheet of paper using a range of experimental techniques including collage and mix media.

This sketch could make an exciting fashion illustration. Use your imagination and add limbs and head by drawing or collaging them on from a magazine or the internet.

Activity A: **Working with paper or fabric on a mannequin**

You will need:

- a garment design sketch
- a mannequin – make sure that it's one you can push pins into
- a calico medium-weight fabric
- a pair of medium sharp scissors
- brown paper (alternative to fabric)
- pins (or masking tape if you are using paper).

Study your sketch. Remember at this stage that you are not making a complete fitted pattern, just exploring how the design will translate onto the body. Then start to manipulate your fabric onto the stand by folding, twisting, draping, pinning and cutting. Be brave and remember to keep recording with a camera or sketches. Let your choices be informed by the shapes you are creating. Try to contrast hard edges with soft folds, gathered cloth with soft hanging forms. Your ideas will change as you try out each idea. At this stage you do not need to worry about a final design, try to come up with several completely different arrangements.

If you have a favourite design, make sure that you have marked all the relevant information on the garment, such as centre front and back, seams, waistlines and so on before you take a final photograph.

bias grain A 45-degree angle to a fabric's warp and wefts.
calico Inexpensive cotton fabric.
flat-pattern Developed from a design sketch using a 2D template (a block) for a basic garment form.
grain lines of the fabric The direction of a fabric's yarns in a woven fabric.
jersey (fabric) Lightweight knitted fabric with good draping qualities.
muslin Inexpensive lightweight cotton woven fabric.
selvedge The edge of a piece of fabric.
warp The vertical direction of threads in a fabric.
weft The horizontal threads in a fabric.

Further research

Basics Fashion Design 03: Construction by Annette Fischer (AVA Publishing, 2009)

Draping: The Complete Course by Karolyn Kiisel (Laurence King Publishing, 2013)

Pattern Magic by Tomoko Nakamichi (Laurence King Publishing, 2010)

Draping for Apparel Design by Helen Joseph-Armstrong (Fairchild Books, 3rd revised edition, 2013).

Fashion illustration

Learning objectives:

- To be able to use fashion templates
- To be able to explore photo montage on a two-dimensional figure via CAD

In Module 1 we looked at the importance of communicating your ideas through fashion illustration. We looked at exercises in how to study the human figure, exploring gestures and poses to create a particular style and mood. It is important that you know the difference between fashion sketches and fashion illustration, as both have different roles. Fashion illustration, as we mentioned in Module 1, is about how the garment is perceived and what mood the designer is trying to put across to the audience. The work is more expressive and involves using a range of brush strokes and mixed media that does not fully show the garment in detail. A sketch, however, shows how a garment is put together and includes the details of the clothes – for example, the fabric, embellishments, colour and print. This is something you will need to do in order to construct your garments. These then become working drawings and include further details such as fastenings, seams and so on. All of this helps the **pattern cutter** to make the garment.

You will now discover ways to develop and refine your fashion design ideas using by-hand and digital drawing techniques.

FASHION ILLUSTRATION TEMPLATES

Fashion templates are pre-drawn figures found in illustration books or figures you have drawn yourself. They can be used by tracing them using a **layout paper** or tracing paper and then drawing your designs over the top. Layout paper, a semi-translucent paper, enables you to redraw your designs multiple times to change details of the garment until a more successful design appears.

You can use the drawings made in the activity below or find a template from a magazine.

Activity A: **Easy fashion sketching method using a template**

1. Find a fashion pose in a magazine, making sure that it is full length and that the clothes are close-fitting.
2. Using tracing paper, trace around the outline of the figure, working approximately 1–2 mm smaller than actual size.
3. Add in collarbone and bust definition.
4. Make shoes and legs slightly longer to add the illusion of length.
5. Exaggerate hair.
6. Mark the mouth and eyes.
7. Decide on the garment shape – for example, short-sleeved dress, full waist and flared skirt and ruffled collar.
8. Use flesh tone on the side of the body where the light falls.

layout paper Slightly transparent lightweight paper used to trace figures.
paint tool An illustration computer software tool for using colour digitally.
pattern cutter Someone who creates pattern templates based on drawings from a fashion designer.

Artists and designers: **Emma Benson and using CAD for fashion illustration**

CAD is a quick way of producing digital design ideas. We will be looking at the work of Emma Benson, a young designer who used CAD to illustrate her designs. The idea behind her collection 'Jaded Sugar' (Figure 3.52) was to reinvent the 1990s classic oversized sweater, and the result is a fun, brightly coloured hand-embroidered women's collection.

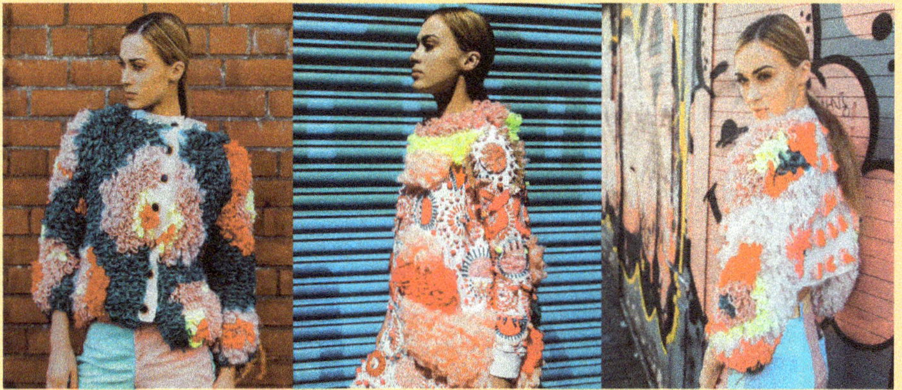

3.52 Emma Benson's line up for her final designs for 'Jaded Sugar'. Jersey white jumper customised with hand embroidery, 2017.

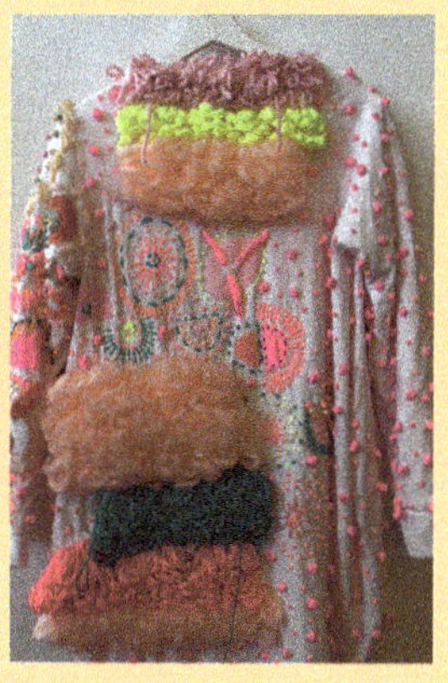

3.53 Close-up of garment. Mix of embellished techniques, 2017.

In Figure 3.54, Benson uses the **paint tool** to digitally render her embroidered surfaces. The results are a stylised version suggesting what the pattern and textures look like. Compare these to her original constructed fabrics in Figure 3.52. Do you think she has captured the essence of her designs?

The example in Figure 3.56 shows her original three figures imported into Adobe Photoshop and her CAD designs redrawn. She has used a more stylised approach to her CAD drawings. Compare these with her sketches in coloured pencil. Can you still appreciate and recognise her designs?

If you have access to a computer with basic Adobe Photoshop software, there are many websites and books to help you do this. The activity will give you a step-by-step guide to help you achieve this.

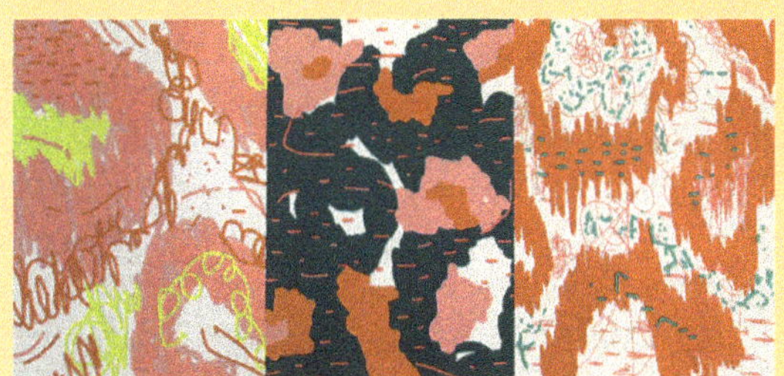

3.54 CAD-developed drawings describing Emma Benson's colourful embroidered fabric.

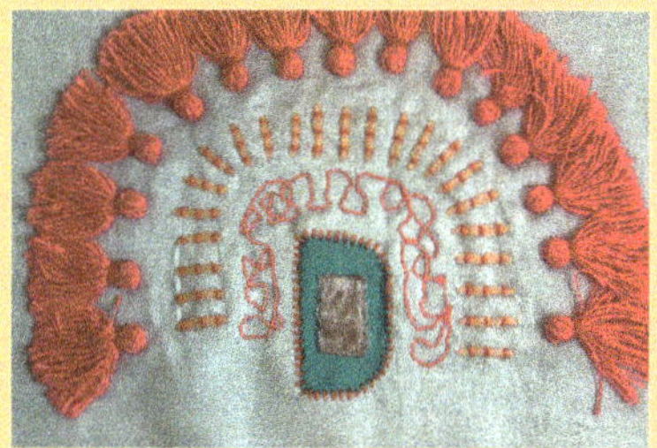

3.55 Original constructed hand-embroidery designs. Cotton embroidery theads, 2017.

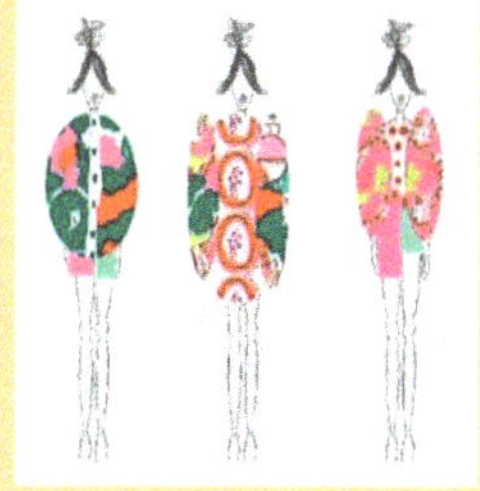

3.56 Three figures scanned into Adobe Photoshop with redrawn designs using Benson's digitally developed drawings.

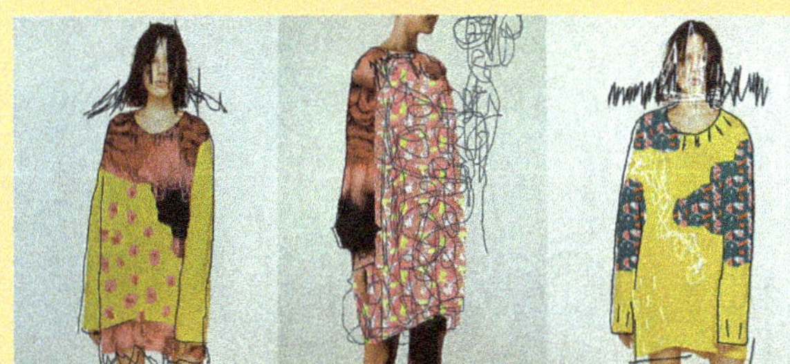

3.57 Emma Benson, final line up, CAD digital photomontage and drawing.

These CAD development illustrations are a combination of photomontages and digital drawings. This is a quick way to develop your ideas. You do not have to use CAD for this technique. Photograph your fabrics, print them out, cut them up and, as for the collage activity in Module 1, explore placement on a model from a magazine or the internet. Add in a personal touch by mark-making using a range of media, or simply a felt-tipped pen, as Benson has done in Figure 3.57 to personalise the illustration.

Tip:

Always use a technical notebook when using CAD to make notes on the digital design process you follow, to remind yourself how you did something.

Activity B: **Create a working drawing using Adobe Photoshop**

Draw your own model template, scan and send it to yourself.

1. Open a new file in Photoshop in A3 or A4.
2. File – select your scanned drawing.
3. Copy and paste two more drawings, spread evenly. Save your image as both a JPEG in Adobe Photoshop. Now you have a template to create quick fashion images.
4. With the Shape tool, create simple fashion drawings with circles, squares and triangles. Use the same methods to fill your image with patterns, colour and drawing with paint.

Activity C: **Creative use of your fashion templates**

Using Adobe Photoshop gives you the opportunity to explore a wide range of different development ideas with these templates. Name your file 'experiment01' and create a new layer. In this layer, paste images or patterns related to your theme. Erase areas, transform areas (Control+T) and alter the opacity of your layer to create new ideas for your designs. Sometimes random accidents and unplanned combinations can move you forward in your creative journey.

Further research

- *Fashion Computing – Design Techniques and CAD*, fashion design series by Sandra Burke (Burke Publishing, 2006)
- *Fashion Designers Handbook for Adobe Illustrator* by Marianne Centner (John Wiley & Sons, 2nd revised edition, 2011).

For figure and working drawings:

- Search online for a video lesson in fashion sketching.
- *The Fashion Designer's Directory of Shape and Form* by Simon Travers-Spencer and Zarida Zaman (A&C Black Publishers Ltd, 2008)
- *Figure Drawing for Fashion Design* by Elisabetta Drudi and Tiziana Paci (The Pepin Press, 2001).

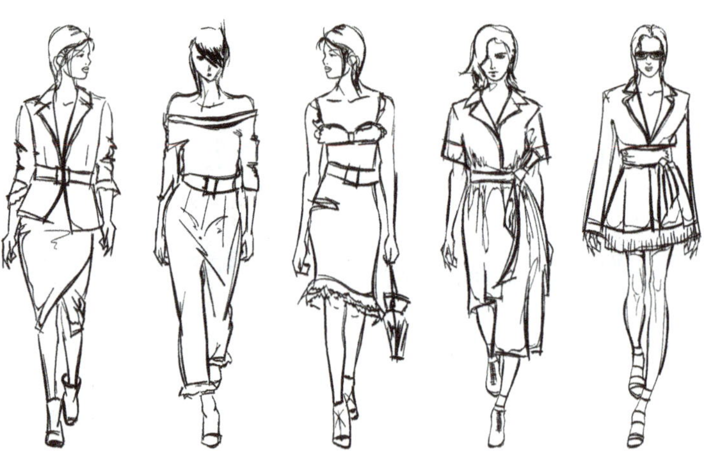

3.58 Sketches for a fashion collection.

Costume design

Learning objectives:

- To be able to consider authenticity when designing period costumes
- To develop and refine technical processes

When designing for a period production, some costumiers will be asked to design an exact replica of a specific historic garment or be given a looser, more generic brief. Either way, they will still need to be skilled and have a great understanding of historical garment processes, including dye techniques, pattern construction and fabric manipulation.

In this unit, we will look at how student costume designer Vicky Rodriquez uses her sketchbook to develop her different costume ideas, including those for the character Eva from the play *An Inspector Calls* by English playwright J.B. Priestley. Although this is a play set in England in the early 1900s, Vicky has chosen to set the design for her costumes in a 1300s medieval cathedral. This was partly inspired by the book *Pillars of the Earth* (Ken Follett), about a Gothic architectural building. By cross-referencing two literary works, Vicky has managed to combine elements from each source – she refers to Priestley's play for the colour palettes and to medieval symbols in Eva's costume.

Vicky Rodriquez uses her sketchbook for technical instructions as well as design development and includes important annotation on decisions she has made for future development stages.

Her designs are also an eclectic mix of Elizabethan costume and fantasy. She was inspired by many costume designs for film, including Gabriella Pescucci's Titania's costume in *A Midsummer Night's Dream* by director Michael Hoffman (see Figure 3.59). For her Eva costumes, Vicky has also looked to medieval architecture for structure and detail (see Figure 3.60).

Tip:

Cross-referencing is an essential part of thorough research. It is a research technique that makes sure that you look for related and or complementary visual references from a wide range of sources. These can be images of sculpture, architecture or natural objects. Look for similar qualities in texture, colour, shape and surface pattern. Try to make creative leaps in what sources you look at. In other subjects you are studying, there may be fascinating or relevant images to use – for example, in Biology or Geography. Once you have collected these, group them together. You will discover that you have formed new directions to base your designs on.

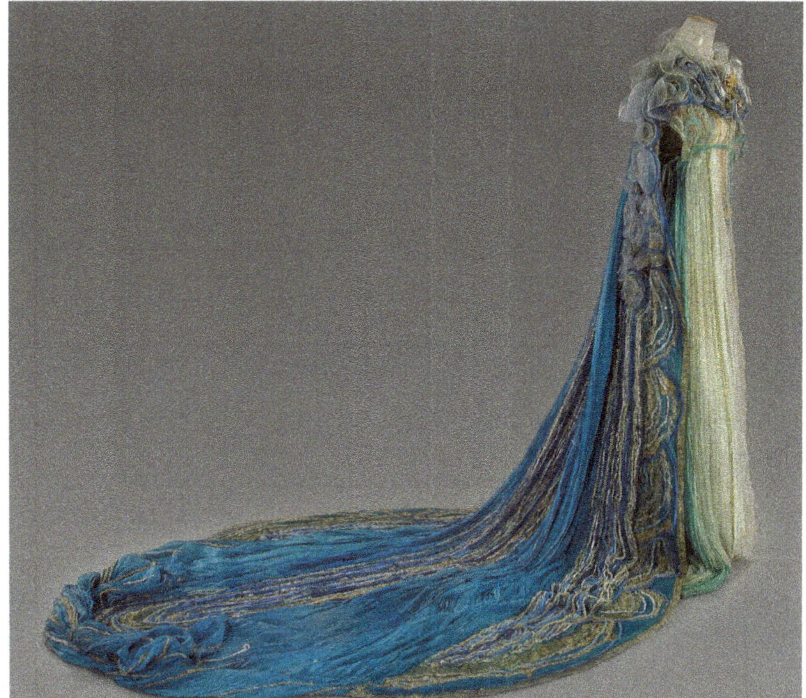

3.59 Costume designed by Gabriella Pescucci and made by Tirelli Costumi, Rome, for Michelle Pfeiffer in *A Midsummer Night's Dream* (1999).

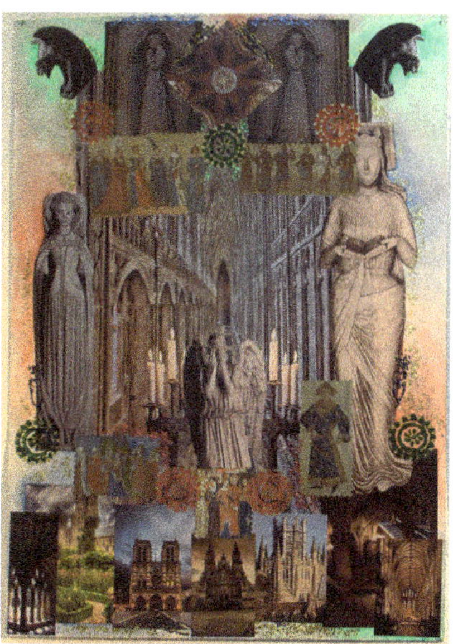

3.60 Medieval architecture mood board inspiration for Eva's costume.

Activity A
Authentic colour using natural dyes on fabric

Costume designers sometimes use authentic dyeing methods when making a costume. This is generally considered when a close-up shot of the costume will be used, such as in a film production. Below is a recipe for natural dyeing an animal or plant-based fabric, such as wool, cotton or silk. The colour will be yellow – use turmeric, a root spice used in traditional Indian cooking and an excellent beginner's dye recipe.

1. Soak fabric in water.
2. Put nine litres of cold water in a bowl. If you use hot water, the result will be a deeper colour.
3. Add one to two cups of turmeric powder into the bowl. (Use rubber gloves, as the turmeric will stain your hands.) Then add the fabric.
4. Leave soaking for an hour, depending on your preferred shade.
5. Rinse, and hang out to dry.

Looking again at Rodriquez's Eva costume, we can see in her sketchbook pages how she planned to construct the garment (see Figure 3.61). Notice how she records her development processes by photographing them and reflecting on each stage.

Rodriguez and other cosutme designers often need to create the authenticity of, for example, an expensive fabric such as **shot silk**. For this, the weft thread is dyed differently from the warp thread, allowing the fabric to look as though it is changing colour as it moves. The designer can create these illusions by simply dyeing the fabric. For her Eva costume, Rodriguez has again looked to *A Midsummer Night's Dream*, choosing the basis of her colour palette from the enchanted wood that the Fairy Queen, Titania, inhabits: earthy tones of browns, gold and soft grey-blues. She has used synthetic fabric dyes to do this, but she could have also experimented with natural dyes. See **Activity A**.

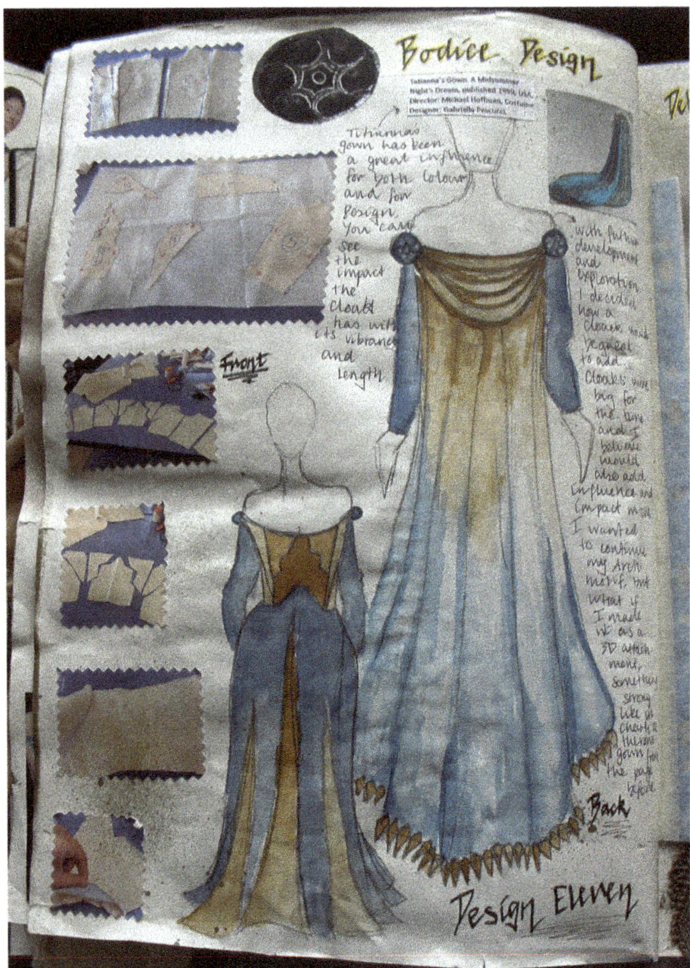

3.61 Vicky Rodriquez's sketchbook development pages for garment construction, with annotation.

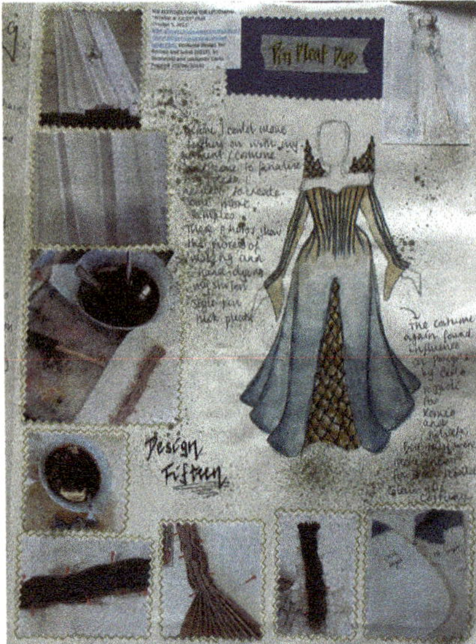

3.62 Rodriquez's sketchbook page exploring the **pin-tuck** method and dyeing textiles processes.

> **Tip:**
>
> When using natural dyes, it is possible to vary the shades using different types of **mordants**. You will find recipes for mordants in the book featured in the 'Further information' section of this unit.

Activity B: **Experiment with natural dyes**

Working in pairs, choose a colour and research how you could create a dye using plants, berries, bark and so on. Remember you will need to use a mordant (fixative). Ask your teacher to check your recipe.

Next, dye a textile using the colour. Remember to use rubber gloves.

Assess the result: has the colour turned out as you expected? How well has the textile held the colour? Is it even or blotchy? What would you do differently next time.

FINAL SELECTION

Figure 3.63 is a page where Rodriquez has decided on her final selection. This is an important procedure, realising her outcome for the first time. She selected the most successful designs so far from her sketchbook, using her reflections and experiments to help her make a decision. She was looking for a balanced view of back and front, keeping the manipulated fabrics to the sleeves and bodice.

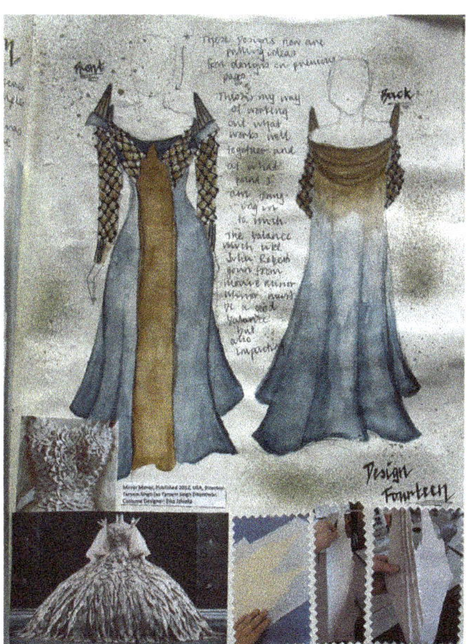

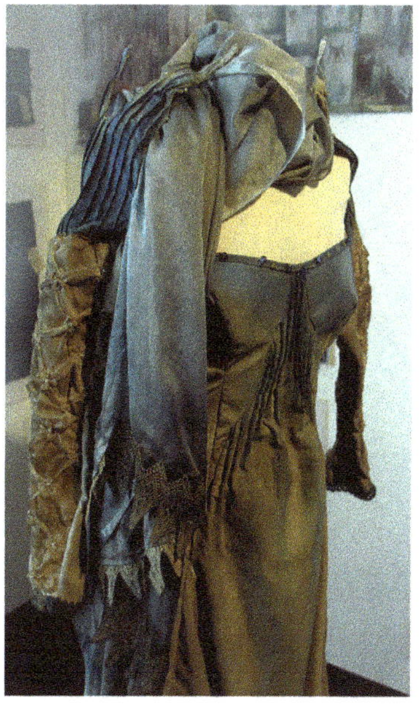

3.63 Vicky Rodriquez, development and refining ideas for a final outcome.

Further research

Search online to explore the technique of pin tucks and other manipulated fabric techniques.

Exploring dyeing techniques:

Shibori: Designs and Techniques by Mandy Southan (Search Press, 2008)

Wild Color: The Complete Guide to Making and Using Natural Dyes by Jenny Dean (Watson-Guptill Potter Craft, revised updated edition, 2010).

Critical thinking:

Rodriguez experimented with different techniques and materials, and when she reflected on her work she would ask herself questions such as: Was there anything that didn't work? What ways could I manipulate and alter my ideas to expose myself to new possibilities and routes for experimentation and sampling?

mordant This fixes dyes to fabric, depending on the type of mordant, such as alum. The shade will vary.

pin tucks A textile method of pleating fabric.

shot silk A woven fabric where the warp is one colour and the weft in another. The best examples are made in silk.

Accessories

Learning objectives:

- To understand wax-resist dyeing
- To explore colour mixing

Batik is a fun way to explore resisting dyeing with wax. There are other resist methods, such as **tie-dye** using clamps, elastic bands and string. In this unit, however, we will look at the tools and applications used for making batik. Your knowledge and understanding of the colour wheel is necessary when applying it to the batik method.

The example in Figure 3.64 shows a piece of cloth made using the traditional batik method using wax and natural dyes. The example in Figure 3.65 shows a commercial screen-printed batik version using synthetic dyes. Compare and identify the different design qualities. Does the quality and look of each design determine how they would be used? How would you use them?

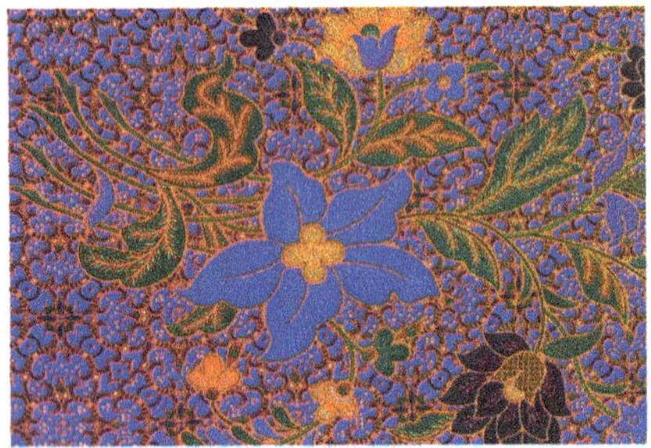

3.65 A screen-printed commercial batik version.

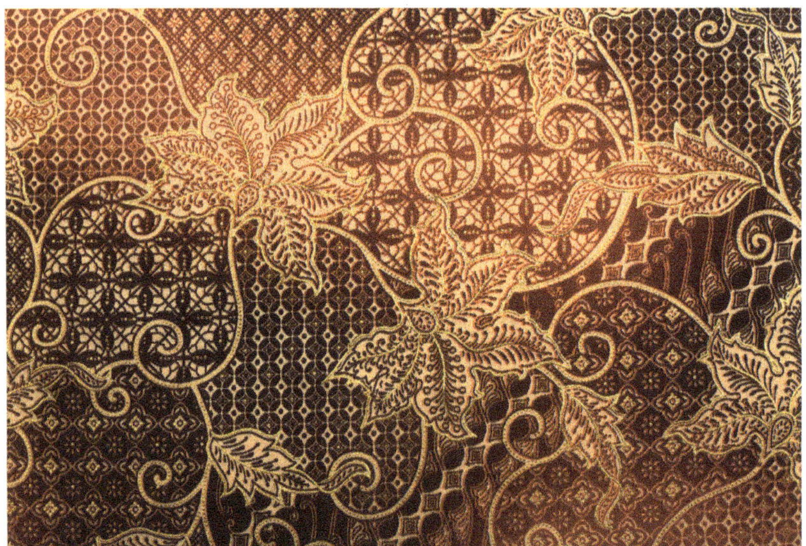

3.64 The beautiful art of Indonesian batik patterns using natural dyes.

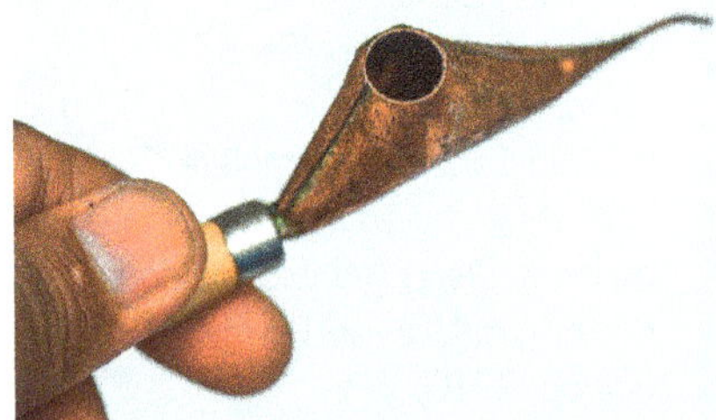

3.66 The tjanting tool, showing the well for the hot wax and the fine funnel where the wax pours out.

Figure 3.66 shows a tjanting tool filled with hot wax. The tjanting tool is used to draw/outline a design. The wax dries and the cloth is submerged into a dye bath or painted on using a brush or sponge. For multi-coloured designs, as shown in the example, the wax is applied to each colour so it protects the colour from additional layers of dye. The cloth is then boiled to melt the wax and, where the wax has resisted the dye, the colour of the cloth is exposed.

Tip:

Try to be creative in exploring the use of the tjanting tool and in drawing with wax. Apart from cloth, you can experiment with different papers, old prints you have made or even decorative fabrics. Not all these experiments will be successful. Decide what works for your ideas and plan how to use the techniques in more considered development work.

When dyeing the cloth, you need to use the lightest colours first, followed by the darker ones. For example, turquoise over yellow makes green, and so on. Use your colour wheel as a guide! See Figure 3.71.

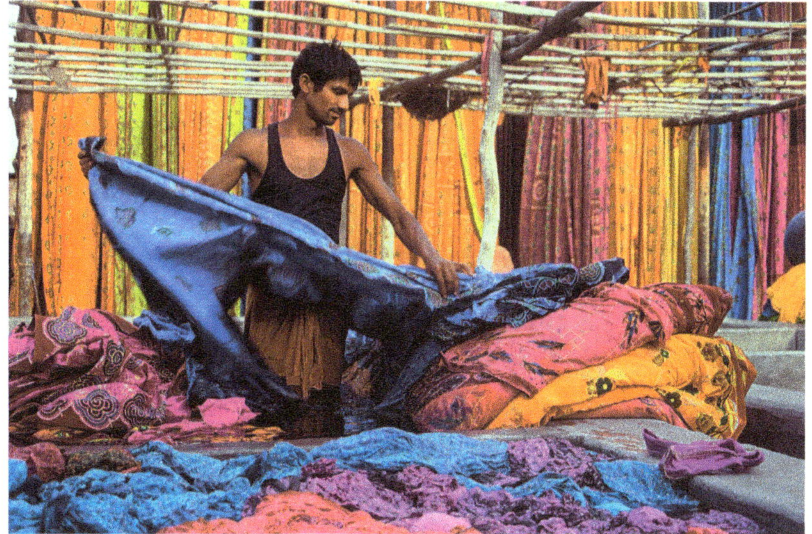

3.67 Fabric being pulled out of a dye bath.

3.68 Example of yellow fabric resisted with hot wax using a tjanting tool.

A cap or block can also be used instead of a tjanting tool. These wooden blocks or stamps are dipped into wax and printed onto the surface of the cloth. This method is suitable for repeating a design. They can also be used for **fabric block printing** using a fabric dye. You can make them or buy them in a craft shop. Block printing is also a traditional way of printing.

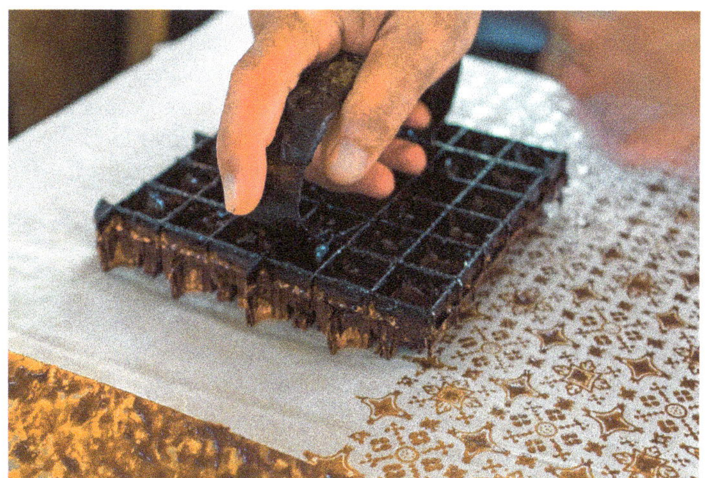

3.69 Using a wooden carved block for applying wax.

Activity A: **Try out block printing**

Do some research into this method and try out your own block printing samples using lino as a substitute for wooden blocks. Start with a small lino block and experiment with different types of repeat pattern. Make a mirrored block to extend the pattern. Try blending several colours on your roller. Choose the experiments that excite you for further development in your project.

fabric block printing Printing of designs, drawings and so on from engraved blocks.

tie-dye A resist dyeing method. It can be achieved by tying or clamping fabric in before dyeing. The coloured dye will only appear where the fabric has not been tied or clamped.

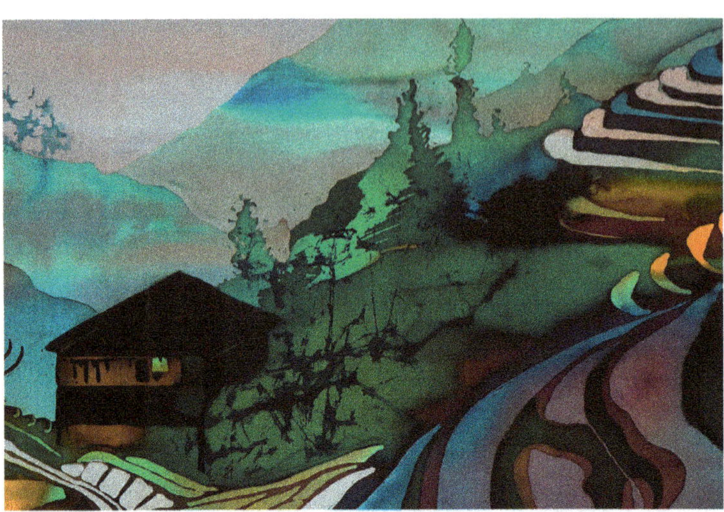

3.70 Handmade batik print on silk.

Figure 3.70 shows the use of a range of colours on a batik. The strength of dyes has been diluted to form graduated tones and **bokashi** brushwork has created blends between different colours.

Materials and techniques: **Becoming a collector**

Equipment for the batik process includes hot wax, tjanting tools of varying tip sizes, brushes, white cloth and **vegetable** or **synthetic dyes**. Originally the designs consisted of dots, lines and brush strokes, and depicted animals, flowers and geometric patterns such as **ogees** to create regular repeat patterns. Suitable wax pots are available from textile suppliers and are recommended, as they are safer and regulate heat temperature. Recommended dyes for batik are Procion MX Fibre-reactive dyes. These come in powdered form and are mixed with water and urea. Brushes, cloth and wooden sticks can all be used as tools for applying wax to cloth. Each will give a different texture and mark. Experiment to see how many unusual tools you can use.

Activity B: **Explore mixing colour with a colour wheel**

If you have already made a colour wheel using paints, you will understand how the colour wheel works. For this activity, you use the same procedure, but instead of paint you use **Procion MX Fibre-reactive dyes**. This is a great way to understand how batik dyes mix with one another before actually dyeing the fabric. Share this activity with a partner, or as a group, to save equipment, as dyes are expensive. You will have to approximate equal measures of dye when mixing. Remember: if they are not equal, you will get a different intensity of colour mix, which you might prefer, so experiment and discover!

You will need: three jars of dyes mixed with water (each jar must contain one of the primary colours – red, blue and yellow). You also need one pipette and twelve small plastic cups.

Fill each pipette with the primary colours and follow the colour wheel mixing system.

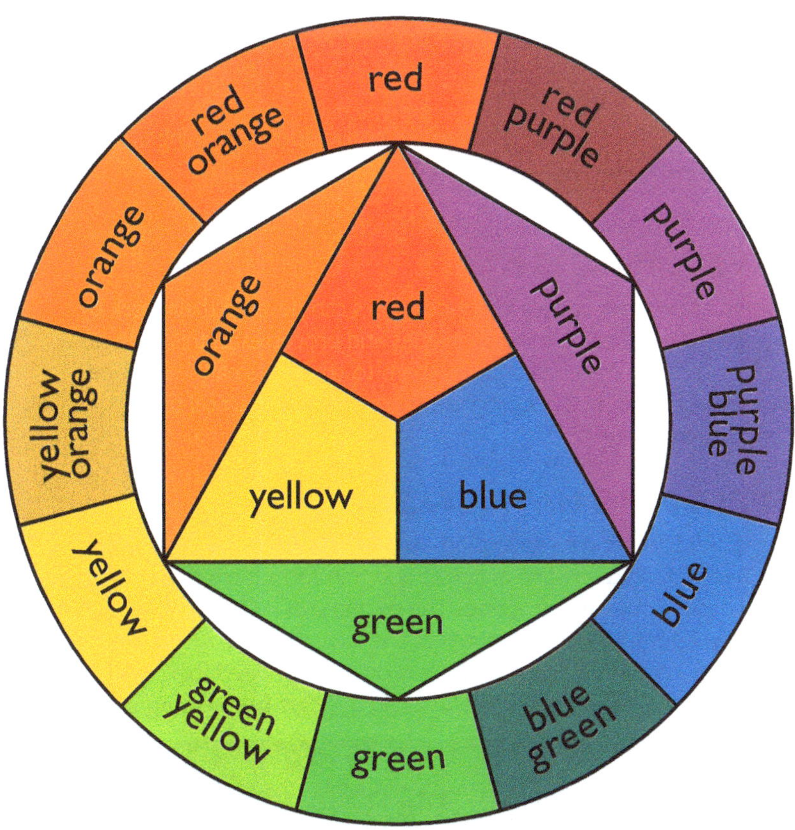

3.71 Colour wheel template for **Activity B**.

The hand-knitted design in Figure 3.72 makes careful use of the right-hand side of the colour wheel. The cool, harmonious colours provide a range of contrasts without using any warm green, yellow or orange.

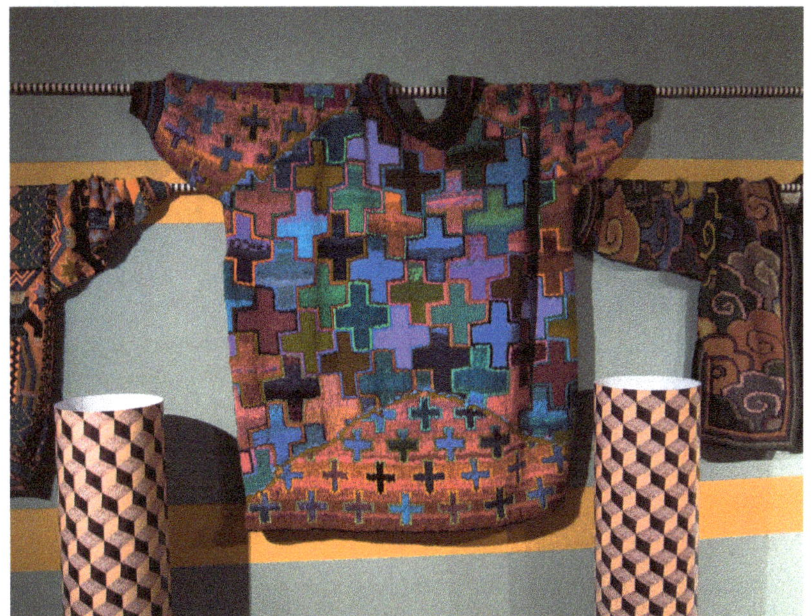

3.72 Hand-knitted designs by Kaffe Fassett, London, UK.

Critical thinking:

What discoveries did you make mixing dyes? If you followed the colour wheel using equal dye measurements, try exploring using unequal measures of dye and discover a variety of tones. Record your findings in a technical notebook, as you will need to remember your dye recipes when you come to make your actual dye pots ready for dyeing batik.

Further research

Search online for a guide to batik:

'Outer Doors and Inner Worlds' by Tunizia Abdur-Raheem, *Silkworm* (Autumn 2016)

Creative Batik by Rosi Robinson (Search Press, 2002).

Look at the website of Kaffe Fassett, an American-born artist known for his colourful designs.

bokashi The controlled dye shading that produces such luminous results on silk.

ogee An image based on an 'S' shape made by two unbroken opposing concave and convex curves.

Procion MX Fibre-reactive dyes Recommended synthetic dyes for fabric. They are used for screen printing and batik and general cloth dyeing. You can buy them from most textiles suppliers.

synthetic dyes Chemical dyes.

vegetable dyes Natural dyes made from vegetables.

Jewellery

Learning objective:

- To develop a piece of jewellery or body adornment using recycled materials

DEVELOPING JEWELLERY WORK

Fashion accessories and jewellery designers can develop their work by exploring different materials, techniques and processes. In this unit you will explore recycled materials and use them to create a small-scale piece of jewellery, or larger body adornment piece. This is a practical task, so you will start by using materials.

EXPLORING MATERIALS

There are different ways to explore using materials in jewellery. One approach is to take existing materials and transform them through applying specific techniques and processes. The example of Pre-Columbian jewellery shown in Figure 3.73 uses seashells as the basic materials. These are then worked to create the final piece. This is one way of developing work through using specific techniques with materials, in this case **burnishing** and polishing.

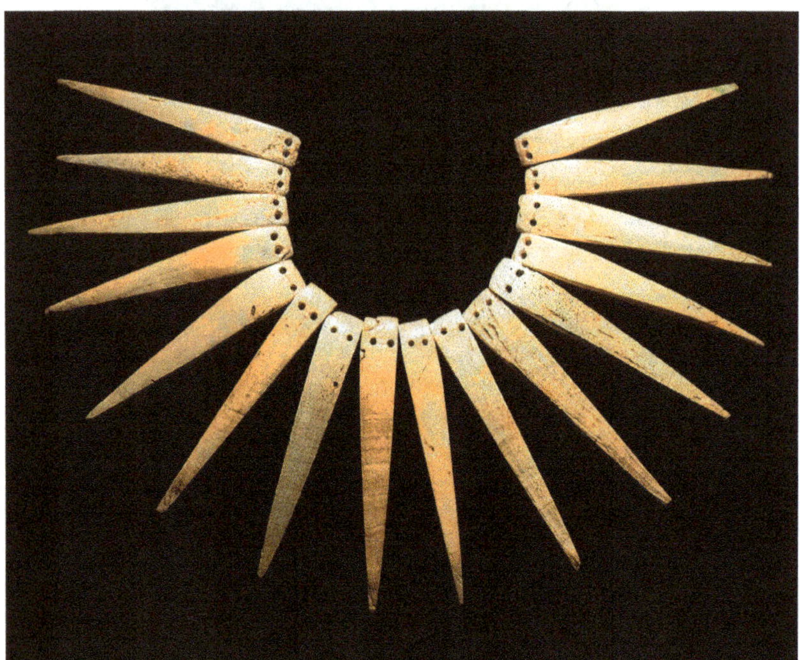

3.73 *Breast plate*, polished and burnished seashell, Mochica Period, 1–800 CE, Pre-Columbian Peru. Jewellery can take objects from everyday life and transform them into objects of beauty, as in this example, which uses seashells as the basic material.

EXPLORING RECYCLABLE MATERIALS

We should be aware of how important resources are, and of the need to use them considerately. Many of these resources are around us every day. These are paper, glass, metal and so on. The designer makes us think about resources by using basic materials for jewellery.

The example shown in Figure 3.74 uses shredded paper, creating a design that references traditional stoles or scarves. There is also a visual pun or joke, as this material is not normally associated with these items. The viewer sees the juxtaposition between the item and the material it is made from.

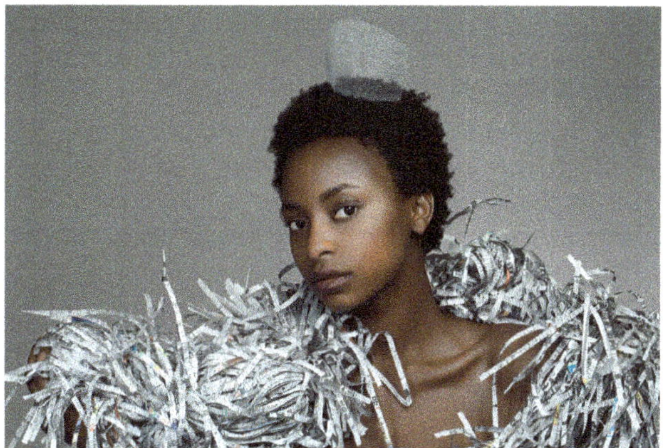

3.74 Accessory, recycled materials. Accessories can communicate ideas about recycling. The use of material is obvious and makes a very straightforward statement about recycling.

SELECTING AND USING MATERIALS

You can select materials from their physical characteristics. This could be how they look, or how they can be used – for example, materials that might provide interesting surfaces are glass, metals and wood. These materials have **inherent qualities** that you can explore, such as texture, colour and so on.

These kind of materials may require you to use more techniques with them than other materials, such as paper and card. Paper and card are easier to work with, so can be glued, joined, laminated, cut and coloured.

Activity A: **Designing a small-scale piece of jewellery or a larger-scale body adornment using recycled materials**

1. Select one recyclable material to use in your work.
2. Explore the potential in this material to make your piece.
3. Develop and refine your work as you go.
4. You can do some drawing and design to help you.
5. Make notes about the techniques you use.
6. Record your work in progress using a camera or your phone.

Critical thinking:

Evaluate your work on **Activity A**, considering and reflecting on:

- your selection of recyclable materials
- your use of specific techniques when working with this material
- how well you developed and refined the work in progress
- whether you used the characteristics and inherent qualities in the materials
- how well you used formal elements in the making of the piece.

Tip:

You can also use materials from other sources. For instance, you may be able to recycle materials by taking apart other garments or accessories, and reusing them in your own work. This is shown in Figure 3.75.

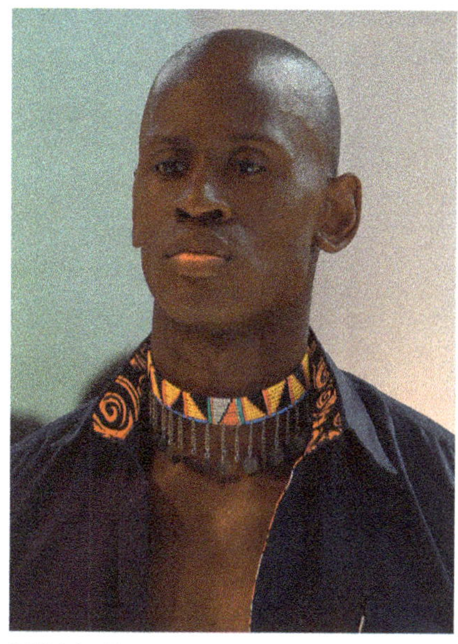

3.75 John Kaveke, *Body Adornment*, mixed media. The Kenyan designer John Kaveke uses mixed media and combinations of recycled fabrics – as well as leather, suede, knitwear, tie-dye cotton and denim – in his work. He has been involved in different projects, including M-Net's face of Africa and Catwalk Kenya.

Further research

For more about international jewellery, go to JMA International Jewellery Design website.

For more on contemporary jewellery design, go to The Jewellery Editor website.

burnishing A process of repeated hard polishing and working of a surface, flattening and hardening it to produce a patina or shine.
inherent qualities The natural characteristics of materials, such as the shininess of metal, the textures in wood, the transparency of glass.

3.3 Fine art

Painting

Learning objectives:

- To understand how painters develop and refine themes and ideas in fine art
- To explore techniques to develop and refine paintings
- To understand how experimentation can inform development in painting
- To select subject matter and develop a painting response to a theme

DEVELOPING PAINTINGS

Looking at paintings can provide insights into how painters have developed their work. This can be in different ways, such as:

- Developing an idea or theme in a series of pieces:
    - working from specific subject matter
    - simplifying the formal elements in successive paintings
    - recording your work's development to direct it.
- Refining an individual piece or response through applying specific painting techniques:
    - using different primers
    - exploring painting techniques used by other artists
    - experimenting with different painting materials, techniques and processes.

Both ways of working use critical reflection as a way of measuring progress against intention, and making a judgement on how an individual piece or series can be improved. In this unit, we look at how painters develop an idea or theme, so that you can apply this in your own painting. We also look at materials, techniques and processes that you can use to refine and improve your own work.

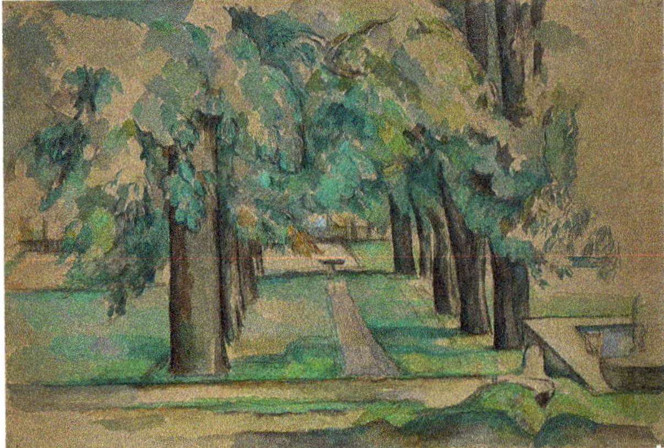

3.76 Paul Cézanne, *Avenue of Chestnut Trees at the Jas de Bouffan*, 1880s, watercolour and pencil on ribbed hand-made paper, Städel Museum, Frankfurt am Main. Painters sometimes use a different medium to explore a painting idea before developing it. To see the oil painting based on the same subject, go to the Tate Gallery website.

DEVELOPING PAINTINGS – SUBJECTS

Many painters work with the same or very similar subjects throughout their working lives. They find that they can develop their understanding of the subject through repeatedly observing it. To achieve this, they need to concentrate on the subject, and identify the unique parts of it that really interest them. This is especially true with figurative painters, who will often observe the same subject over time.

Other painters work with an idea or concept, such as the abstract colour field painting shown in work by the American artist Mark Rothko (1903–70). Rothko explored the potential in this approach to painting by repeatedly trying out different versions of it.

You can apply the same process to your own work, by selecting a subject that interests you and using it as a starting point again and again. You need to feel an **affinity** with the subject. It must be something that appeals to you, and has enough interest for you to return to repeatedly.

We can try out this process on the first type of subject – one that you observe directly.

Activity A: **Find a subject with which you have an affinity**

This activity involves some of the critical reflection discussed in the Introduction to this module. You are going to be exploring different potential starting points through direct observation, and making a judgement on which one/s you prefer. These starting points might be scale, viewpoint, location, light source and so on. You can work on this in pairs, using a combination of photography and drawing.

1. The human face/form:
   a. Using each other as models, make a set of studies of the head and figure in different settings.
   b. Some of these should be portraits, and some half- or full-figure, to get an idea of different ways of representing the figure.
2. Architecture:
   a. Explore a range of different architectural subjects in your neighbourhood.
3. Nature:
   a. Explore natural forms in a garden or parkland in your local area.
   b. You can record spaces in the subject, such as fields and trees, or work with close-up details of organic forms.
4. Machinery:
   a. Record examples of machinery/mechanical form.
   b. These can be engineered and/or digital-based types of machinery/equipment.
5. Print out your photographs and display them, together with your drawings.
6. Select the subject matter that you feel most attracted to, and offers you the most potential to work with.
7. Explain this to your partner, using critical reflection to justify your view.
8. Add additional subjects to the list if you want to.

DEVELOPING PAINTINGS – TECHNIQUES USED BY OTHERS

We looked at contextual influences in Module 2, and many artists have developed their painting as a result of these influences. For example, they might take ideas from other painters, or actually copy the way that others work to learn about their techniques. As you develop and refine your own work, be prepared to clearly acknowledge your influences. This is an important and valid way for you to find out about painting in general, and painters' approaches to using materials, techniques and painting processes. The Dutch artist Piet Mondrian (1872–1944) used techniques that he borrowed from other artists. There is more on this on page 113. He used these painting techniques through a series of stages where he continually strove to refine his work. We will look at the progression in some of Mondrian's work in more detail.

Materials and techniques: **Keeping a record**

What is important is that you have a record of the development of your work, and you can use this to see how you refine the painting as you continue. You may find that earlier stages have more energy in the way you paint, and that your final version is overworked, or that you want to change the colours that you use. This is difficult to predict, but sometimes paintings can be worked on too much, and they lose the freshness or energy of the early stages. Alternatively, you may see mistakes that you make with drawing proportions that you can learn to correct earlier.

These records are also really useful in presentations. They can help tell the story of your work's development. You can also see whether you lose something from an earlier version of the painting that you prefer, and re-introduce it.

affinity Having a natural feeling of liking a thing, subject, location, person or idea.

Artists and designers: **PIET MONDRIAN**

Developing work – progression

Piet Mondrian was inspired by scenes in his native country, the Netherlands, and by movements in art at the time, such as Impressionism, Post-Impressionism, Fauvism, Cubism and Abstraction. He was influenced by elements of all these movements while experimenting with different techniques. He developed painting where he tried to record his sensations, at the same time working out how to represent the subjects using different painting techniques. In this way, he developed his work through experimentation and refined it through different stages. We can use the three examples here to look at how he achieved this.

The painting in Figure 3.77 shows a strong sense of the tree's structure; Mondrian is recording an object faithfully. He is using heightened colour, so although the structure is very tree-like the colour is not naturalistic. He was absorbing the techniques shown in examples from the art movements he knew, such as Fauvism, and using these to work out his own personal approach to painting.

In the painting in Figure 3.78, Mondrian has begun to refine the shapes of the tree branches into a slightly more deliberate and simplified series of shapes and lines. He has also dropped the heightened colour in the previous image, and reduced the colour range. He is developing his approach to the subject and how he will apply the influences of others.

In Figure 3.79, Mondrian has further developed his approach to the subject by leaving out a lot of the branch shapes. He has refined the image by applying a systematic approach to the subject. He is now showing us just the basic, main shapes of the tree and the geometry of its structure. This process of simplification has been achieved through his experimentation and refinement of his techniques. He has also further refined and reduced the colour range, and the image is now on the edge of becoming a fully abstract painting.

Mondrian continued his experimentation towards full abstraction. Can you find an example of a painting of his from his **neo-plasticism** phase? Describe how it is painted. What subjects are shown, if any?

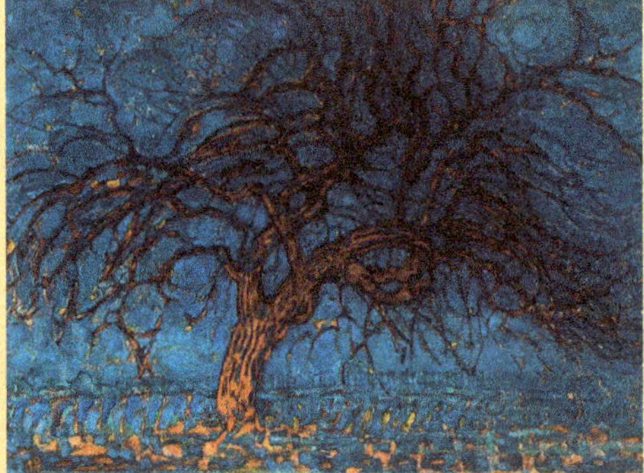

3.77 Piet Mondrian, *Evening: The Red Tree*, 1908–1910, oil on canvas, Haags Gemeentemuseum, The Hague. In this painting Mondrian is studying the tree, and referencing time of day; the colours are bright, like those of Vincent van Gogh.

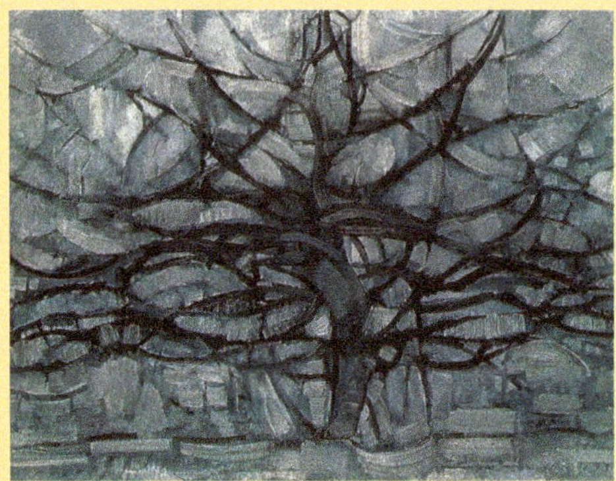

3.78 Piet Mondrian, *The Gray Tree*, 1911, oil on canvas, Haags Gemeentemuseum, The Hague. In this painting, Mondrian has developed and refined the image of the tree by limiting the colour range and using techniques he has adopted from Cubism to simplify the space and perspective.

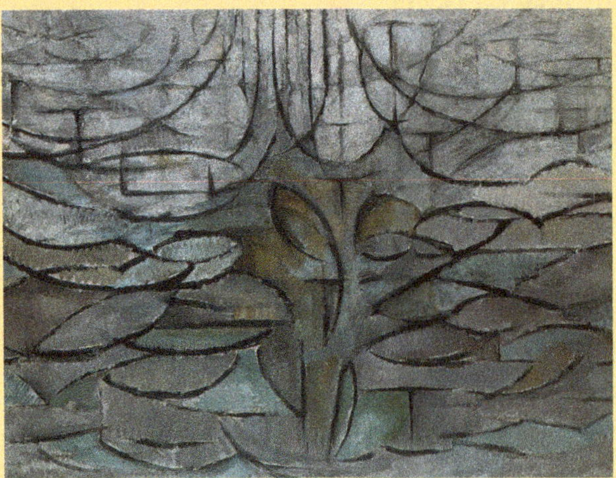

3.79 Piet Mondrian, *Flowering Apple Tree*, 1912, oil on canvas, Haags Gemeentemuseum, The Hague. Mondrian has now further simplified and refined his technique to create an image that is a balance between the delicate structure of an apple tree and an abstract painting.

DEVELOPING WORK – THEMES

Many painters develop themes in their work. One way they do this is by selecting and combining subject matter and techniques to develop imagery. This might give their paintings a clear intention or message. Another approach is more intuitive: painters might work with same subject repeatedly and see what comes out of this process. They then review this work, applying critical reflection as you have been doing at the end of each of your activities.

Painters can use this to help them select imagery, techniques or approaches to develop and refine their work. It is possible to see how they have refined work by comparing and contrasting an earlier and later image, if they are working with the same theme continuously.

Activity B: **Developing a themed response**

This activity builds on from **Activity A**, where you were asked to select a subject that you felt an affinity for. Use that subject as a starting point.

1. Working in the same pairs, display the studies you made from your chosen subject.
2. Take some time to develop a discussion with your partner, to see whether you can identify any potential themes in the work. These could be:
   - compositional
   - colour, contrast, tonal
   - mood, emotion, sense of drama
   - structural, complexity
   - using specific techniques.
3. Make notes on your findings as you go along, identifying a theme you would like to explore further.
4. You can also identify any artists' painting techniques that you might want to experiment with.
5. Working individually, take the subject matter and the notes and make painting studies from that subject, which incorporates this theme and any techniques you have selected to use. This might be through:
   - using paint combinations, specific colour(s) such as bright colours, or muted colours
   - simplifying the subject into flat colours and shapes
   - creating atmosphere and mood through a controlled use of light/dark
   - using energetic, expressive marks to convey an emotion
   - developing complex compositional ideas in paint to refine the subject and theme.
6. Make at least three studies that explore and develop your treatment of the subject and theme.
7. Remember to photograph/record your progress in individual studies.
8. Display your studies and discuss these with your classmates.
9. Summarise how effectively you have developed your theme and paintings of the subject.

Tip:

You can use preparatory studies of a subject to make smaller paintings in preparation for larger or studio versions. These allow you to experiment with materials, techniques and approaches, and formal elements, and can help you make a plan for the larger work.

Materials and techniques: **Recording your work's development**

You will learn how to recognise and direct your development in your work if you can record it happening. One way of doing this is to take regular photographs of a piece of work as you develop it. You can decide to do this at regular points – say, on the hour every hour, or more spontaneously.

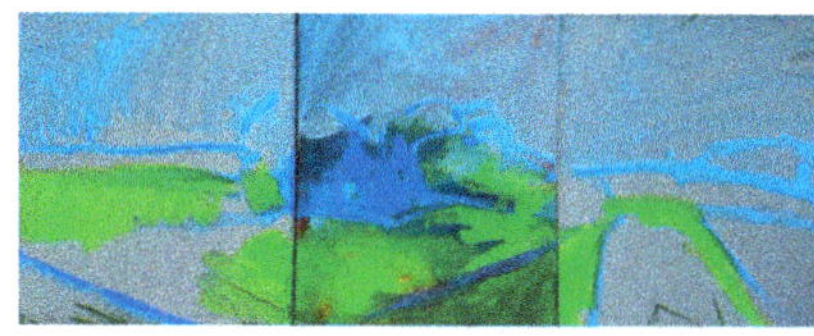

3.80 Alan Parsons, *Study, Chellington Hill*, 2017, acrylic on canvas. The first stage of a **triptych** painting, worked in plein air, showing the early composition and laying out of the subject. Note how the drawing is made using a brush.

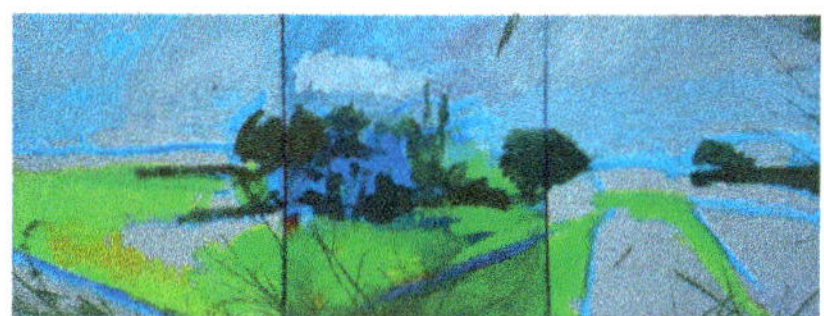

3.81 Alan Parsons, *Study, Chellington Hill*, 2017, acrylic on canvas. The second recorded stage of the triptych painting. The painting is developing through the use of additional colours and a wider range of lights and darks.

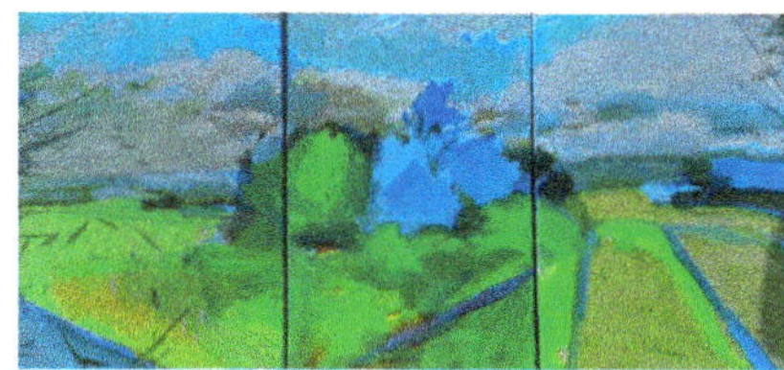

3.82 Alan Parsons, *Study, Chellington Hill*, 2017, acrylic on canvas. The third recorded stage of the triptych painting. The painting now covers the entire canvas surface. There is a wider range of colours used, and a more defined sense of perspective in the sky.

neo-plasticism Term adopted by Piet Mondrian for his paintings that used only vertical and horizontal lines and shapes, and primary colours.

triptych A painting made up of three separate panels or canvases, showing separated or related imagery, or imagery spreading across all three panels.

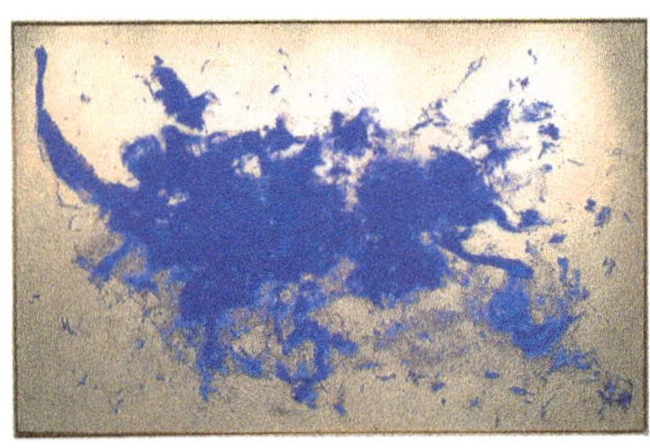

3.83 Yves Klein, *Anthropométrie, 'Le Buffle', (Ant 93)*, 1960–61, pigment and resin on paper laid down on canvas, private collection. In this series of images, the French artist Yves Klein (1928–62) reinterpreted the idea of the 'painter's model' by using models as tools when making paintings. The model became the brush by being covered in paint and transferred this to paper by laying on it as part of a performance.

Tip:

Try out painting on paper or card primed with white, and with other colours: use the Venetian idea of Mars red, for instance (painters in the 18th and 19th century would use this; think of John Constable, whose work is shown page 185). You will find that your use of white will be very different when working on a Mars red-coloured primed surface.

DEVELOPING WORK – EXPERIMENTATION

You can develop work through experimenting with materials, techniques and processes. All these are linked, but it is useful to identify them separately and how they can work.

Materials

You can experiment with different types of painting materials and media. Before we look at paint, we need to think about what it will be applied onto. Experimentation can begin at this point, by thinking about the type of surfaces to be used as the base for the painting.

- Supports – this is a term for the surface or material you are painting onto, so could be canvas, paper, wooden board, canvas-board, cardboard, Perspex, metal, found surfaces. Look at the section on priming and sizing below to see how supports can be used as part of the development process.

Each type of paint media has its own different set of characteristics. Keep a technical log of the painting media and techniques you are using, so you can remember details about how they behave.

- Water-based paints – these are acrylic, gouache and watercolour. Each has a different quality:
    - Acrylic – dries quickly, good for overpainting quickly/in layers; good for strong colours on large scale, versatile, can be painted on different supports.
    - Gouache – a designers' paint in small tubes, strong colours designed for art working and taking to print; cannot be overpainted without disturbing layer beneath, used in small-scale work.
    - Watercolour – generally used in small works, though can sometimes be larger; uses white of paper in optical mixing of colour, transparent washes, becomes body colour when mixed with white.
- Artists' oil-based paints – slow-drying, allows for painting wet into wet, strong colours.
- Mixed-media paints – these are any combination of paints that are not normally seen as artists' paints, such as emulsion, oil-based household paints, varnishes, stains.
- Tools – these can be any combination of brushes: household and artists, scrapers, palette knives, rags, fingers.
- Customised tools – you can make or collect your own set of tools, like card scrapers, cloths and so on.

Sizing and priming

Sizing means protecting the surface of the support from the oils in oil-based paint. This can be applied to papers and cards as well. Traditionally, hot animal-skin glue size was painted on the support. This has been replaced in some areas by thinned acrylic medium or primer. Size acts as a barrier to oil, which will otherwise rot the surface.

Priming means preparing the surface of the support for paint. Many pre-primed canvases and boards use white acrylic primer. Venetian painters used variations on primers, such as greens, and Mars red to provide a different type of surface to work on. Primer can be applied to any surface, such as canvas, paper, card, metal and so on.

Processes

The processes used often depend on the selection of materials and techniques. Like a lot of things in painting, these are all interchangeable.

- Working from observation – often used by painters at the start of the development process, to source information on the spot. Some artists react to the scene or subject in front of them so have to work outside or from observation. This is sometimes called 'working from life'.
- Working up from studies – artists take a group of studies and develop their subject, often into a larger piece. This has been used extensively in history to produce work that was made in the studio, but whose subject was external, such as historical events at sea, or outdoor scenes.
- Working with abstraction, working from intuition/imagination – used by painters throughout history, often to create striking scenes. Think of the fantastical paintings by the Dutch/Netherlandish artist Hieronymus Bosch (1450–1516). Abstract painting was used by painters in the 20th century in areas such as Constructivism, Colour Field Painting and Action Painting. In these works, the painter will respond to colours and shapes on a surface, rather than considering their resemblance to the exterior world. These images tend to have their own logic in how they use visual elements and language.

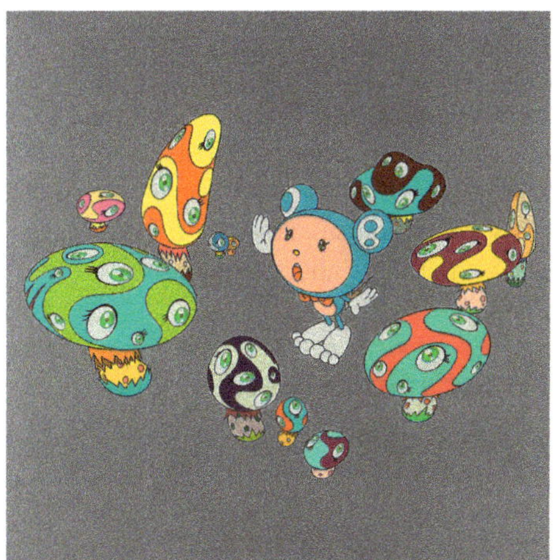

3.84 Takashi Murakami, *!IN CHA!*, 2001, acrylic on canvas, private collection. In the painting, the characters are floating in an open grey space, appearing as separate objects. This work has imaginative qualities. It presents a space and objects that has its own logic. It is not a representation of an observed scene.

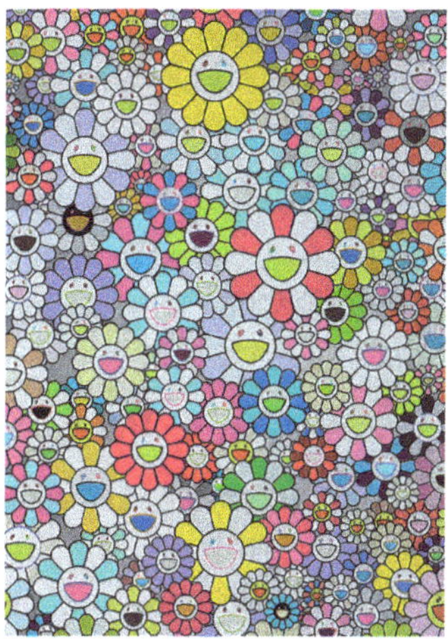

3.85 Takashi Murakami, *Multicolour Flowers*, 2012, acrylic and platinum leaf on canvas, private collection. The painting shows the development of a different style in Murakami's work. In this painting he treats the surface of the canvas entirely, creating a rich network of shapes in a complex, cellular-like matrix.

Refining work

Painters reflect on the strengths and areas for development in their work. They use different methods to reflect on their progress, depending on the context they are working in. For example, work being produced to self-generated themes may be reviewed and refined quite slowly and privately in the artist's studio. Work that is going straight into an exhibition needs to be reviewed quickly and any refinements worked on at that point. As you develop your painting, you can get used to trying out different ways of applying critical reflection and using this to inform the refining of your work.

Materials and techniques: Painting techniques

Try out the following to experiment with paint:

- Painting wet to wet – this way of working allows painters to blend colours together, and create smoother surfaces. This was used historically when the intention was to hide the texture of the paint.
- Overpainting – this means painting over the top of other sections of painting. It can be used in oil or water-based work. It normally means the whole surface of the support is covered, then dried, and then smaller parts of the image are worked on. These are then then allowed to dry, and smaller sections painted over, and so on, until completed.
- Glazing – used to create depth and mystery in work, and to represent the effects of light and shadow with great detail. Colours are thinned with a glazing agent, such as oil and turpentine, or a specialist medium if using oil-based paint, or acrylic if water-based paint is being used. The colour washes are painted in successive layers, each being allowed to dry before the next is applied.
- Scumbling, dragging – these involve working thinner washes of darker colour over lighter-coloured textures, and allowing the texture of the paints to show.

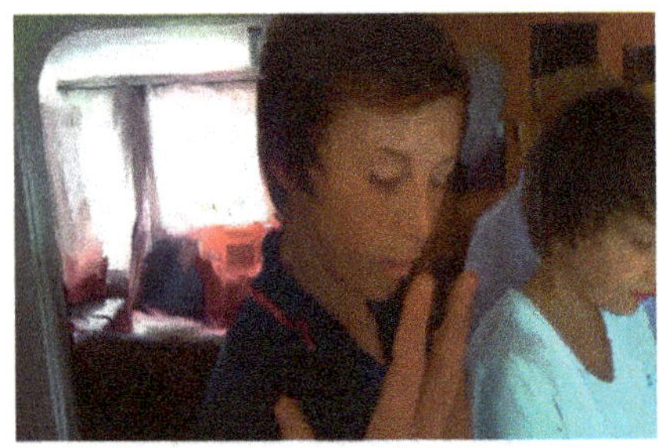

3.86 Alan Parsons, *Alex and Ed, Version 1*, 2012, photography, acrylic and oil paint on canvas, laid on board. 40 cm x 98 cm. This image shows the first stage in developing this painting. Note the composition in this version is cutting off the figure on the right, and the way the perspective of the opening on the left is angled.

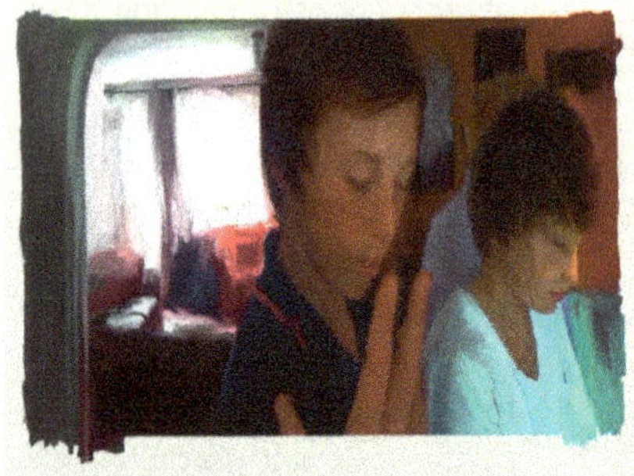

3.87 Alan Parsons, *Alex and Ed, Version 2*, 2012, photography, acrylic and oil paint on canvas, laid on board. 40 cm x 118 cm. This shows how the painting was refined after critical reflection. The painting was repositioned onto a larger board, with more canvas added, and additional areas painted in to refine the composition. The figure on the right is now shown in full, and the perspective in the composition in the background has been straightened to be vertical.

Reflecting on progress

This is important, as it will help you understand what you need to do to improve your work, through developing and refining it.

- Peer review – many artists have used each other as critics and advisers in the past. Think about Picasso and Braque working slowly and carefully through early Cubism paintings (it had no name then, and it's easier to see the movement as a whole with hindsight). They would meet up and discuss each other's paintings, looking at how they were treating the subject, using colour, developing their ideas, and would use the discussions to help them refine their work. This is exactly the same process that you use when you work with a classmate (peer) in **Activities A** and **B**.
- Group review – this tends to provide more information, and works best when the group are all working to the same theme or ideas.
- Exhibitions – this will bring in comments and feedback from the public. Painters can find out whether their intention is actually being communicated by their work. It is also fascinating to see how others view a piece of work, and how widely interpretations can differ.
- Artist's Statement – many exhibitions and events require an artist's statement. Think about some online competitions, for example. The process of planning and writing a statement forces artists to think about their work and what it means, and this can help define their ideas and processes.
- Critiques and presentations – these are used to provide a forum for painters to discuss their work and to receive feedback, and for others to put across their views. Lively discussions can happen in critiques.
- Online – painter's websites and blogs have become areas where work is discussed and evaluated, and artists can again use information from these to help them consider how they communicate, and to refine their work.

Activity C: **Write an Artist's Statement**

Based on your work in **Activity B**, write an Artist's Statement in two paragraphs:

- Paragraph 1 should introduce the subject and theme, and why you chose these.
- Paragraph 2 should contain information about your approaches to using materials, techniques and processes, use of formal elements and any contextual influences.
- Present your Artist's Statement to your classmates for feedback.

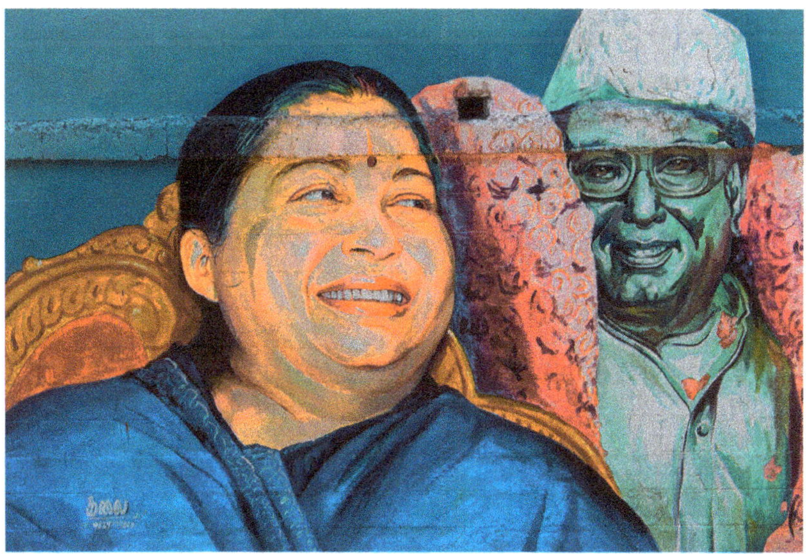

3.88 Wall painting, Madurai, Tamil Nadu, India. This shows a wall painting depicting the Tamil actress and politician Jayalalithaa Jayaram. Think about scale when developing your theme. For instance, portraits do not necessarily need to be small; you can explore larger versions, as in this image.

Activity D: **Develop a painting to a theme**

Produce a painting that shows development of one or more of your studies from **Activity B**, and your intention in your Artist's Statement from **Activity C**. You should:

1. Aim to make your subject and theme clear to the viewer, through controlling your use of formal elements and visual language.
2. Show experimentation in your painting and/or associated tests or studies.
3. Refine your choice of painting techniques, materials and processes in order to improve your work.
4. Record the developmental stages of the piece.

Critical thinking:

Display your work on the activities in this unit. Evaluate your work, considering how you:

- developed your use of materials, techniques and processes
- used experimentation to inform your development
- refined your work as you developed it
- used feedback from others to refine your work
- used visual language and formal elements to communicate the theme
- could further develop and refine your painting work on this subject.

Further research

For more on examples of contemporary painting, see *Vitamin P3: New Perspectives in Painting* (Phaidon Press, 2016).

For more on examples of paintings and resources, go to the Museum of Modern Art (MOMA), New York, website.

For more on examples of historical and contemporary paintings, go to the National Gallery, UK, website, showing examples of historical and contemporary painting, with resources.

If possible, visit your local and national museums and galleries for more examples of painting.

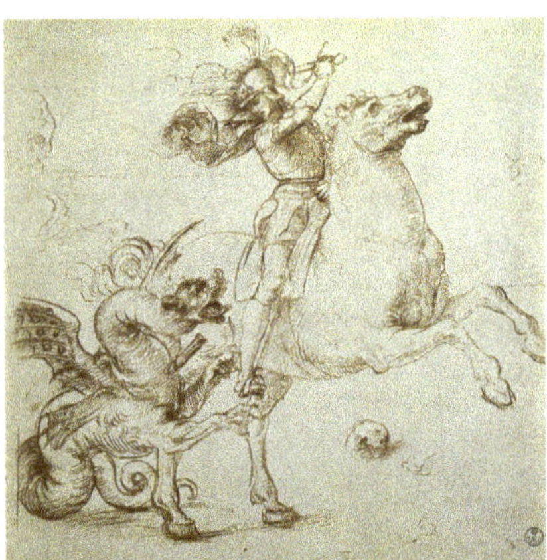

3.89 Raphael (Raffaello Sanzio of Urbino), *St George and the Dragon*, undated, pen and ink on paper, Galleria degli Uffizi, Florence.

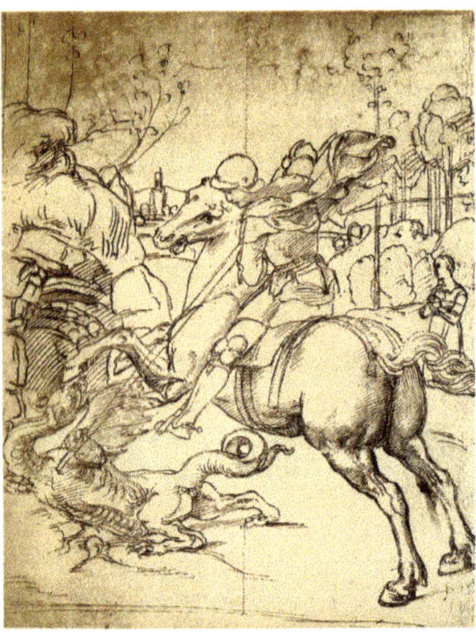

3.90 Raphael (Raffaello Sanzio of Urbino), *St George Killing the Dragon*, undated, pen and ink on paper, Albertina, Vienna. The placement of the components within each version alters the dramatic impact of the scene.

Drawing

Learning objectives:

- To understand how artists use sketches to develop compositions
- To understand that artists can develop ideas and themes across several pieces of work
- To understand how artists compose images with consideration for space, balance and dramatic impact

In this unit, we will look at how artists develop and refine ideas by producing many studies. They consider the placement of objects within their drawing and the impact that the composition has on the viewer.

DEVELOPING AND REFINING COMPOSITION

Artists often use themes and subjects more than once in their work. They create many sketches – quick responses to observation and studies – which are drawings that develop and refine the composition, to inform more than one outcome. This can be seen in the work of Italian artist Raphael (1483–1520), who used drawing to develop and refine his compositions.

He made pen and ink preparatory studies that were inspired by the legend of St George killing a dragon, by drawing the figure of St George on horseback from different angles. In each study the focal point is the dragon in the bottom left-hand corner, but the placement of St George on his horse creates a very different drama in the work and experience for the viewer.

In the first composition, seen in Figure 3.89, where the horse and St George are facing us, we are involved in the action. It feels as though we occupy the space in the foreground, with the horse rearing above us and the dragon to our left-hand side. In Figure 3.90, we are behind the horse and we are behind the action, looking in on it, almost as a **voyeur**. In this drawing Raphael has suggested a landscape background, creating a greater **pictorial** depth in the picture. However, it is the first composition that seems more dramatic, because of the placement of the individual components.

Raphael went on to paint two versions of *St George and the Dragon*. The first version, painted around 1504, hangs in the Louvre, Paris, France. Its composition is based on Figure 3.89. The second version, painted around 1506, can be seen at the National Gallery of Art, Washington DC, USA and can be viewed online at the National Gallery of Art website. You will see that the composition of the second version of the painting is very similar to Figure 3.90.

Activity A: **Develop a composition for dramatic effect**

1. Look at Figures 3.89 and 3.90 by Raphael.
2. Now develop ideas for a composition based on a theme that you are working on. Use the same components but arrange them in different ways. Think about using different viewpoints and imagine where the viewer would be within the composition.
3. Consider the dramatic impact that each composition idea has and make notes about each arrangement.

COMPOSING IMAGES WITH CONSIDERATION FOR SPACE AND BALANCE

Creating balanced images that are interesting to look at and lead the viewer's eye across the whole drawing is a skill that artists develop through preparatory work. They make studies to explore the scale and arrangement of objects and consider the negative space between the objects.

The Czech artist Alphonse Mucha (1860–1939) produced studies for book illustrations where he explored visually interesting and engaging composition. He was associated with the decorative Art Nouveau movement that spread across America and Europe in the 1890s.

In his pencil studies of crockery and cutlery, Figures 3.91a and 3.91b, Mucha has composed all the elements within his drawings so that they are balanced. Each drawing is a collection of still-life objects that are placed in close proximity on the same sheet of paper, seen from different viewpoints. Some are seen from the side, some from above. Whilst the objects are highly detailed and closely observed, their overlapping positions and layout creates a decorative feel. His use of multiple viewpoints makes his drawings interesting to look at and helps to lead our eyes to all corners of the studies. The empty space surrounding the objects helps to create balance within the composition. Note how Mucha has used white to highlight the drawings, which helps to suggest the surface textures of metal, glass and glazed porcelain effectively.

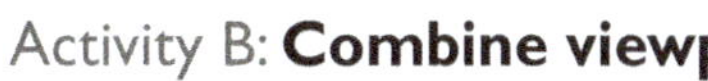

Activity B: **Combine viewpoints**

1. Look carefully at Figures 3.91a and 3.91b.
2. Using still-life objects such as items of crockery and cutlery as your starting point, compose drawings that combine different viewpoints of the objects. Do this in the style of Mucha.
3. Consider working in a range of different scales. Draw part of some objects close-up and some as complete objects.
4. Think about the balance between the spaces and the objects within your compositions, and work in detail to capture the surface texture of your chosen objects.

Further research

For more information on Raphael and Alphonse Mucha, go to their websites.

Alternatively, read:

Creative Drawing by Howard J. Smagula (Laurence King Publishing, 2002).

Tip:

Think about the impact that you want your work to have, and demonstrate that you have developed and refined your ideas by exploring different compositions.

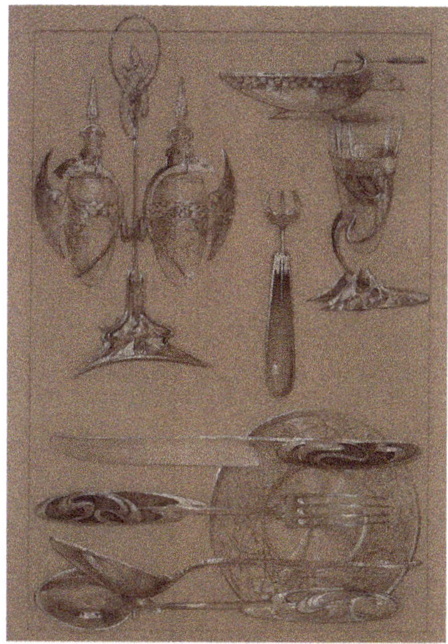

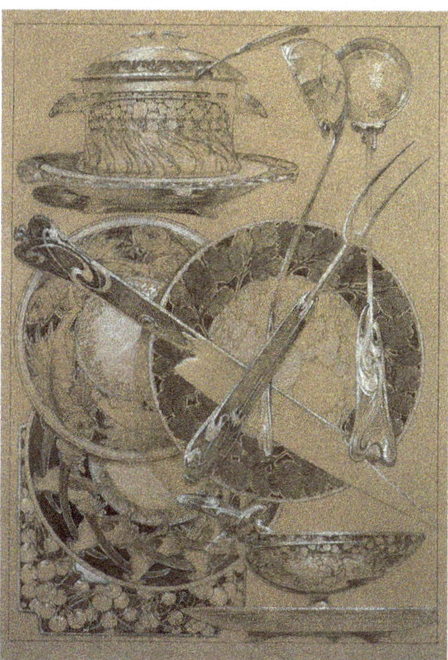

3.91a Alphonse Marie Mucha, *Study for plate 69 of 'Documents Décoratifs'*, 1902, pencil, watercolour and white on paper, Mucha Trust, Prague, and **3.91b** *Study for plate 59 of 'Documents Décoratifs'*, 1902, pencil, watercolour and white on paper, Mucha Trust, Prague. In these works, Mucha combined different viewpoints within his composition to create a sense of balance. His compositions are highly decorative.

pictorial Of, containing or expressed in pictures.
voyeur A person who obsessively watches others.

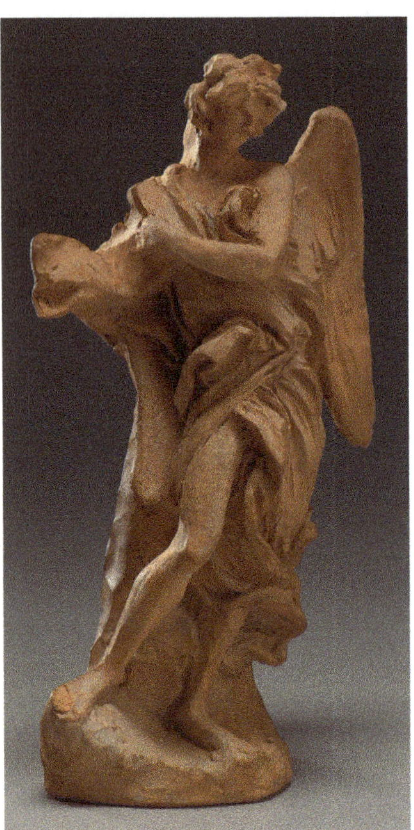

3.92 Gian Lorenzo Bernini, *Angel with the Superscription*, 1668, terracotta, Kimbell Art Museum, Fort Worth, Texas. Maquette for a carving on the Ponte Sant' Angelo bridge, Rome.

Sculpture

Learning objectives:

- To understand why artists use maquettes to develop and refine ideas
- To know which materials sculptors use to make maquettes
- To understand the purpose of using an armature when making a sculpture

As sculptors develop and refine their ideas, they often use maquettes to translate two-dimensional (2D) sketches into three-dimensional (3D) forms. These models are usually worked on a much smaller scale than the finished sculpture. This unit looks at how artists use different media and materials to create their working models as part of the creative process.

Media and processes used in making maquettes

Different sculptors develop their own working methods as part of the process of creating their work. The Italian artist Gian Lorenzo Bernini (1598–1680) developed his finished sculptures having first created maquettes using terracotta clay or wax. *Angel with the Superscription* (1668) is one of a series of 10 models made by Bernini using clay. (Clay and wax are both soft and malleable materials, so easy to work with, as you can add more material or take it away, as needed.) Commissioned by Pope Clement IX in 1667, this is a model of one of the decorative sculptures used as part of the renovation of the Ponte Sant' Angelo bridge, the ancient bridge linking the city of Rome to the Vatican. The sculptures were designed to stand on the bridge's **balustrades** and guide the pilgrims' approach, physically and spiritually, toward St Peter's Cathedral. From using clay or wax models, Bernini went on to carve his full-sized sculptures from marble and stone. Sculpting with clay or wax is a very different technique to carving marble, but clay and wax are cheap materials. By using cheap materials, Bernini could practise and perfect his design before starting to carve the marble. This reduced the risk of making mistakes and wasting a very expensive material.

Search online to see pictures of the final carvings.

In contrast to Bernini, American artist Alexander Calder (1898–1976) made maquettes from materials that were like those that he used to produce his final sculptures. His sculpture *L'Araignée Rouge* is made from cut pieces of thick sheet metal that have been joined together. The maquette *Araignée* has been created using thinner sheets of metal that have been riveted together to create his abstract form.

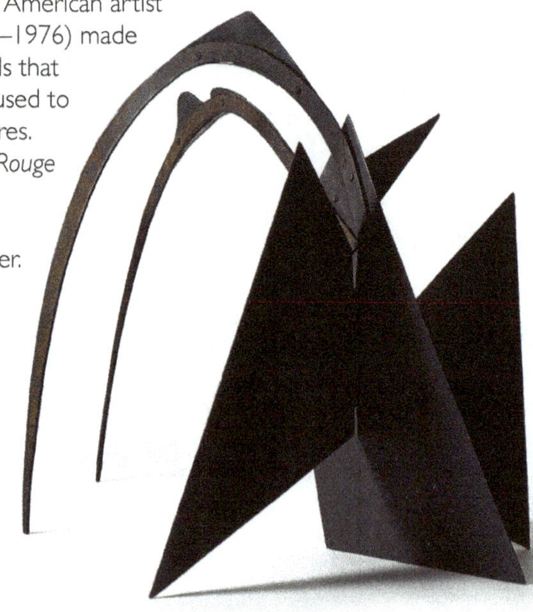

3.93 Alexander Calder, ***Araignée*** (Maquette), c.1958, sheet metal and paint, private collection.

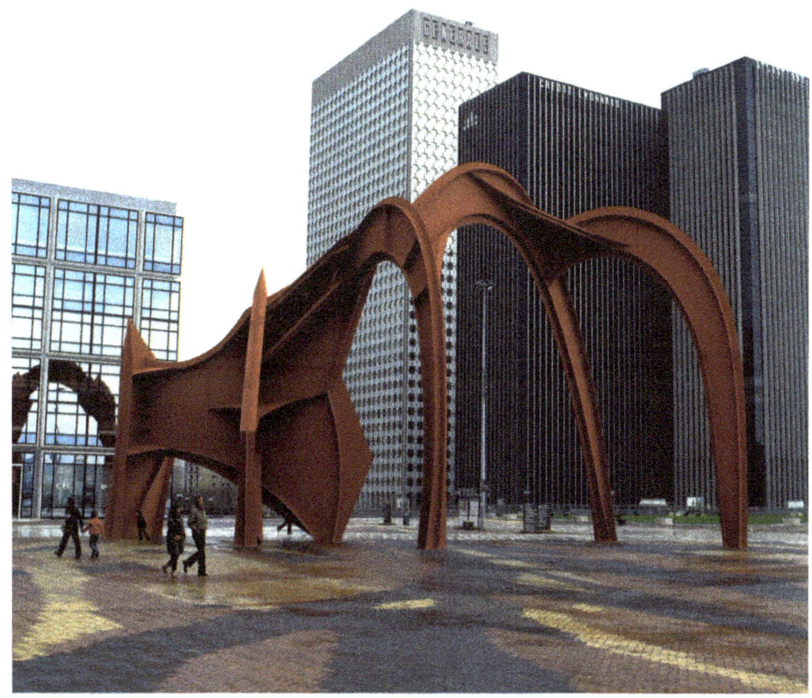

3.94 Alexander Calder, *L'Araignée Rouge*, 1976, sheet metal, bolts, and paint, La Défense, Paris. Alexander Calder uses sheet metal to create both his maquettes and monumental sculpture, as can be seen in the two different works shown here. While not the actual model for *L'Araignée Rouge*, how does the maquette compare to the full-sized sculpture?

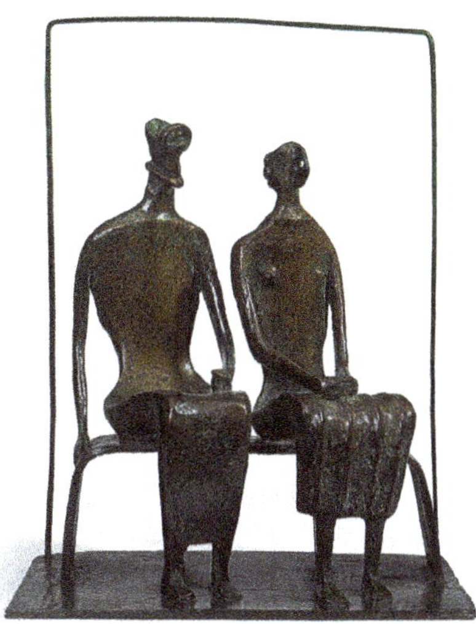

3.95 Henry Moore, *Maquette for King and Queen*, 1952, bronze with brown and green patina, private collection. Moore used small-scale casts of his work as part of the development and refinement process, using the maquettes to trial surface finish.

British sculptor Henry Moore (1898–1986) also used the same process when making maquettes that he used for his full-sized work. He made small casts of his large-scale sculptures. First, he made a model in clay or wax, as Bernini would have done, and then from the model made a plaster mould and then poured in liquid metal. As part of the process of refining his work, Moore also used his maquettes to try out the surface textures and effects that he wanted to create. This can be seen in *Maquette for King and Queen* (1952), where he has used a **patina** of oxidised bronze that is also seen in the full-scale version of the sculpture.

Look back at Figure 1.43 on page 68 – Henry Moore's *Reclining Woman* (1982), created using charcoal, gouache and chalk on paper – to remind yourself of how Moore draws to inform his sculptures.

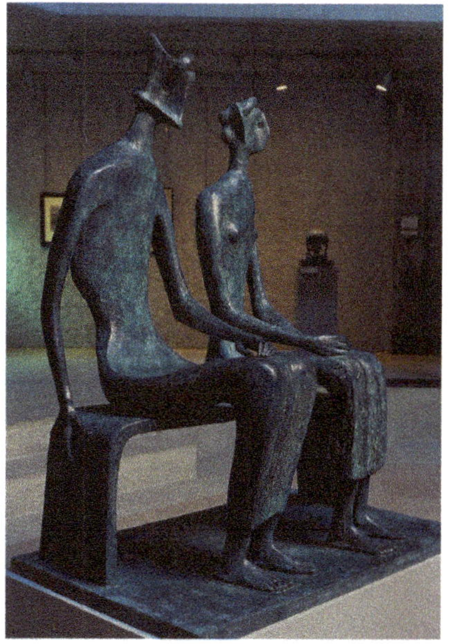

3.96 Henry Moore, *King and Queen*, 1952–53, bronze, Henry Moore Foundation, Perry Green, Much Hadham, Hertfordshire.

Materials and techniques: **Using an armature**

An armature is a framework, or a 'skeleton', around which materials, such as clay, wax or plaster can be built up. The armature provides structure and stability to the sculpture. It is usually made from stiff wire that can be twisted into the required shape and fixed to a base, usually wood, so that it can be free-standing.

araignée The French word for 'spider'.
balustrade An ornamental rail or wall on a balcony, bridge or staircase, with its supporting set of balusters.
patina A film of oxide formed on the surface of a metal, especially the green oxidation of bronze or copper.

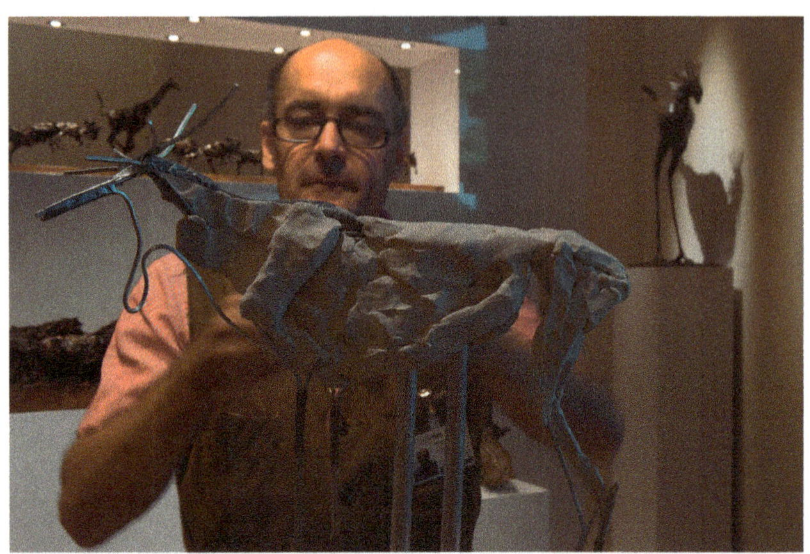

3.97 An example of a sculptor using an armature as he builds a clay maquette.

Activity A: **Make maquettes**

Using your own sketches and drawings of the human figure as a starting point, make a series of small maquettes for a sculpture.

1. First, begin by making an armature from wire and then work with clay to build up the figure.
2. Next look back at the work of Alexander Calder in Figures 3.93 and 3.94 and use sheet material, such as cardboard, to create a maquette inspired by your figure drawings.
3. Photograph the outcomes and make notes about your work, comparing the techniques that you have used.
4. Think about which materials and processes you would choose to use if making final versions of your work.

Critical thinking:

What are the advantages of using the same materials for a maquette as the finished sculpture? Think about the work that you have produced for the activity above. How does using a different material or process help you to develop your ideas?

Further research

For more information about Bernini's maquettes, go to the website of the Museo dei Bozzetti, Pietrasanta, Italy, a museum specialising in collections of maquettes.

Printmaking

Learning objectives:

- To understand how proof printing enables printmakers to develop and refine imagery
- To understand how artists develop the use of colour within relief print techniques
- To understand how artists develop themes through their work

This unit will look at how printmakers develop and refine their visual imagery when using intaglio and relief processes, and consider different approaches to developing coloured relief prints.

PROOF PRINTS

The only way in which a printmaker can see what is happening to a printing plate when they apply the initial design is to take a trial print. (To remind yourself what a printing plate is, read the section about printmaking in the 'Introduction to the disciplines' section on pages 72–73.) This process is known as **proof printing**. It is an important part of the development and refinement process when using relief and intaglio techniques, such as lino and woodcuts, etching and drypoint. Once printmakers have a printed version of the image, they can look closely at it, perhaps drawing over it, to decide how to develop the image further by making more marks, or cuts, on the plate. They will then repeat the proofing process until they are happy with the image and have reached the point at which they will print the final version.

Proof printing also allows the printmaker to experiment with the amount of ink that is applied to the plate, which will also impact on the quality and appearance of the print.

Activity A: **Taking a proof print**

1. Working from drawings that relate to a project that you are working on in class, make an intaglio or relief print plate.
2. Now take a proof print.
3. Next, look at the print compared to your original drawing and decide what you need to do to refine the plate further.
4. Now develop the marks that you make on the plate, taking more proof prints as you go. Keep all the proof prints that you make and annotate them to explain how you have developed and refined your work.

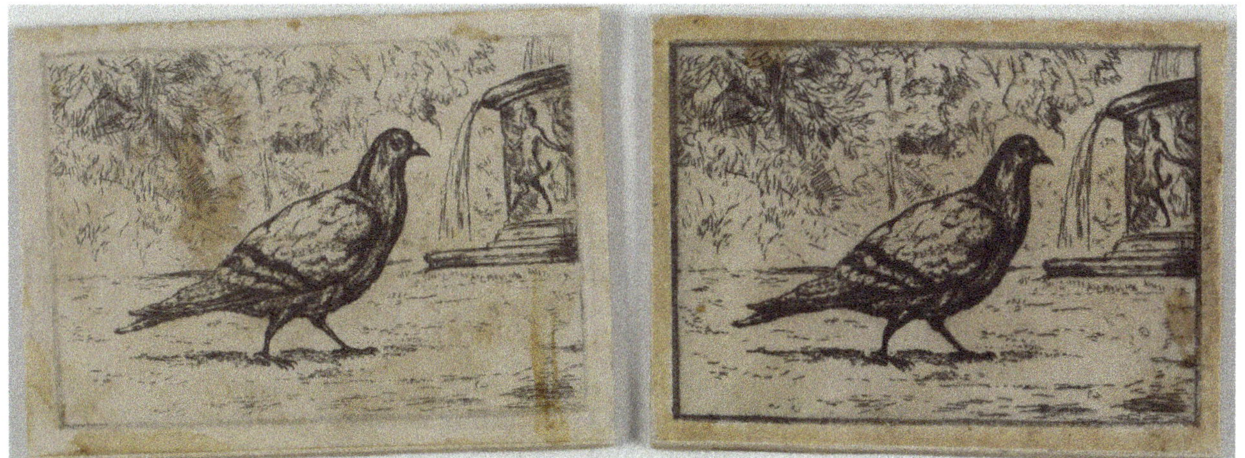

3.98 Chester Leich, *Print Processes*, undated, copper plate, Dallas Museum of Art, Texas. This intaglio print plate has been proof printed. The image of the left-hand side is quite pale and the marks are much lighter than on the second proof print. On the right-hand print, the lines drawn on the plate have been strengthened and hold more ink, thereby printing as a stronger image.

proof printing Taking a trial print to assess what's happening with the printing plate when the initial design is applied.

Tip:

When using proof prints to develop your design, you can draw directly onto the prints to visualise the refinement of the image before making changes to the plate.

DEVELOPING PRINT IMAGERY THROUGH USE OF COLOUR

Some artists develop their prints by using different colour combinations to create a series. Andy Warhol (1928–87) often screen printed many versions of the same image, changing the colours he used. For example, his 1964–5 print *Flowers* looks very different when seen in its different states. When you compare the black and white print (Figure 3.99) with the coloured version (Figure 3.100), the first thing that you notice is that the black and white version has not printed cleanly; there is an area on the left-hand side where the ink has not fully pulled through the screen mesh.

The use of different colours and different number of colours to recreate the same image means that we read the image differently. (Refer to the section 'Colour', pages 12–13.) Colour creates a very different visual impact and evokes a very different mood. Compare Figure 3.101 with the version in the collection at the Museum of Modern Art in New York, which you can see online.

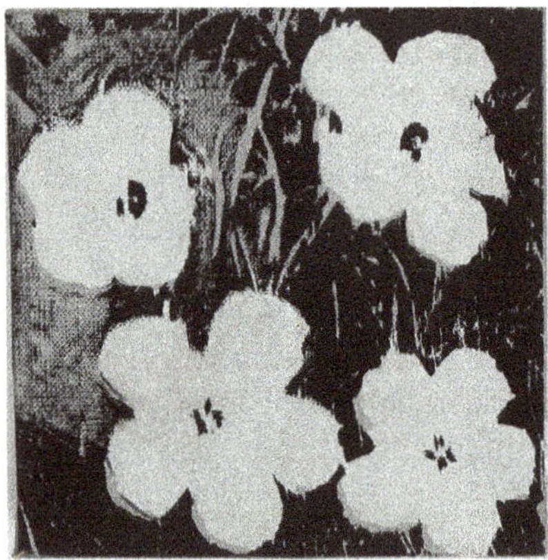

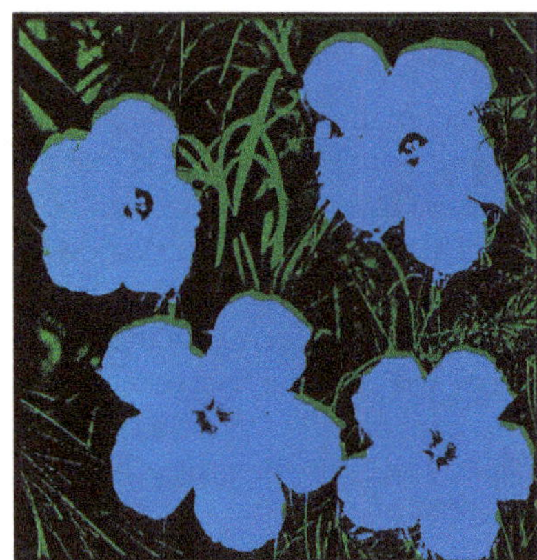

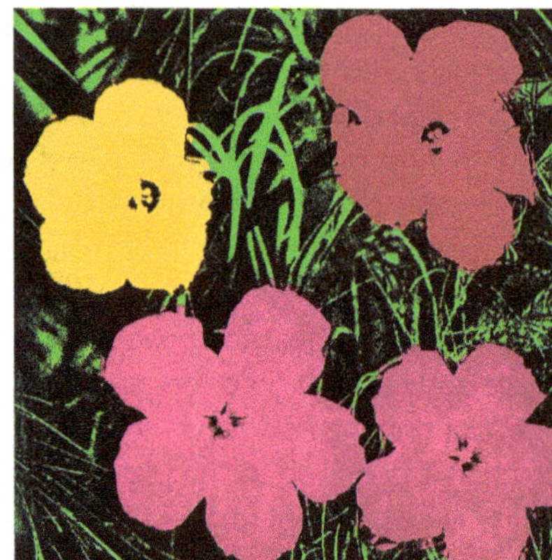

3.99, **3.100** and **3.101** Andy Warhol, *Flowers*, 1964–65, synthetic polymer silkscreened on canvas, private collection. Three versions of the same print. How does the use of colour create a different mood to the black and white version?

Critical thinking:

Compare the different versions of Warhol's print *Flowers*. Think about the impact that using different colourways has on the image. Use your knowledge of colour theory to consider why certain colourways have particular effects. Why do you think that Warhol has used different colourways? Which version do you prefer, and why?

Activity B: **Use colour to vary the impact of the image**

1. Working with an image that you have already created, draw the design onto to a piece of lino and cut it.
2. Proof print the image in black, and continue making marks and taking proof prints until you are happy with the image that you have created.
3. Next, experiment with printing the block using different colours.
4. What impact does changing the colour have on the image that you have created? Record your thoughts.

Artists and designers: **Katsushika Hokusai**

The Japanese printmaker Katsushika Hokusai (1760–1849) was a master artist and printmaker of the *ukiyo-e*, 'pictures of the floating world', school, which flourished in Japan from the 17th to 19th century. Hokusai used the image of Mount Fuji many times in his work. Between 1826 and 1833, he produced a series of prints entitled *Thirty-Six Views of Mount Fuji*, which is regarded as being a high point in the history of the Japanese landscape print.

In this series Hokusai sometimes used the same woodcut block, but inked it differently. He used different colours to create effects to represent different weather and lighting conditions.

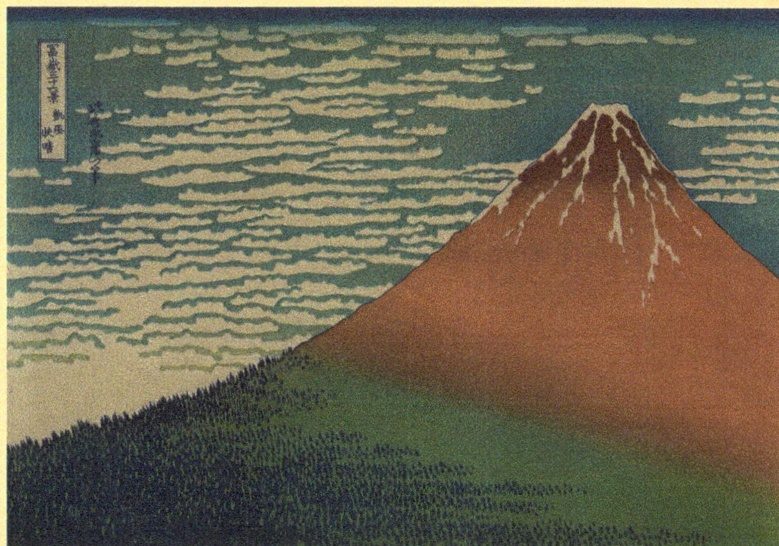

3.102 Katsushika Hokusai, *Clear Day with a Southern Breeze ('Red Fuji')*, from the series *Thirty-Six Views of Mount Fuji*, 1831, hand-coloured woodblock print, Library of Congress, Washington, DC.

Hokusai made other prints in the same series where the composition of the image is varied. In Figure 3.103, *Fuji above the Lightning*, the size and position of Fuji remain unchanged, the background hills are also visible and the angular lines in the right-hand corner represent the lightning, as viewed from above. Figure 3.104, *Mount Fuji Reflected in Lake Misaica*, presents us with the same view of Fuji, but from much further away, looking down on, and across, the lake.

Hokusai used a very similar composition in his two views of Mount Fuji. The development and refinement of the image here is seen through the addition of the lightning bolt. What other differences can you see between the prints?

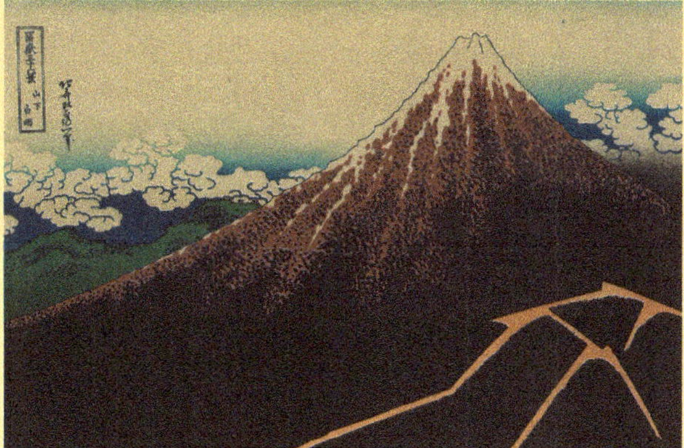

3.103 Katsushika Hokusai, *Fuji above the Lightning*, from the series *Thirty-Six Views of Mount Fuji*, 1831, coloured woodblock print, Library of Congress, Washington, DC.

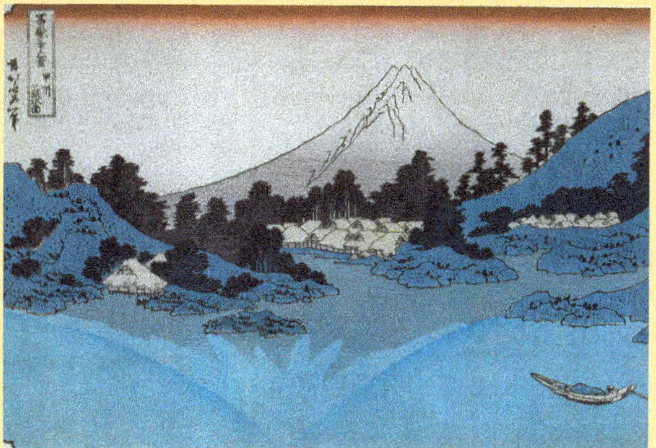

3.104 Katsushika Hokusai, *Mount Fuji Reflected in Lake Misaica*, from the series *Thirty-Six Views of Mount. Fuji*, 1831, coloured woodblock print, Leeds Art Gallery. Slight variations in the composition of the imagery enable Hokusai to develop a theme across a series of prints.

Materials and techniques: **Developing multi-colour prints**

There are two different approaches to developing multi-colour relief prints. In one method, you can make a separate block for each colour that you want to print and print them on top of each other. In the second method, you can use one block, print one colour at a time and cut away the areas that you want to remain that colour. In the latter method, you print the colours from lightest to darkest. Either method of developing colour prints will require the correct alignment of the printing block so that the print is in exactly the right place on the paper. This is known as **registration**.

The process of building a print by using separate blocks can be seen in the example from American printmaker Gustave Baumann (1881–1971) in his print entitled *Palo Verde and Ocotea* (see Figures 3.105 and 3.106). Each colour is proofed separately and then the image is built up and developed by printing successive layers on top of each other.

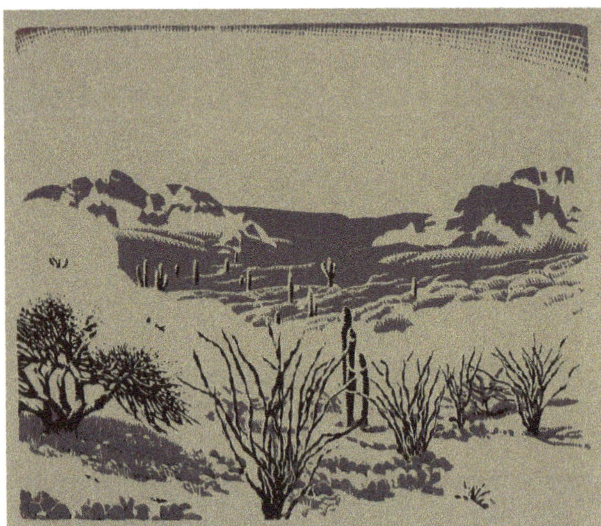

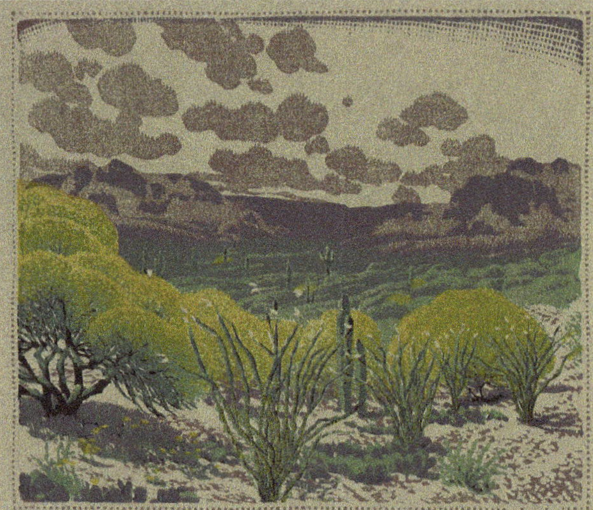

3.105 and **3.106** Gustave Baumann, *Palo Verde And Ocotea*, 1926, progressive proofs black and purple (3.105) and then black, purple, green, rose and yellow (3.106), colour woodblock print, Indianapolis Museum of Art at Newfields. The example shows how the colours are proofed and printed separately to build the image in layers.

Further research

Search online for more information about the work of Hokusai and Gustave Baumann. For information about printmaking techniques, read *Printmaking: A Complete Guide to Materials and Processes*, 2nd edition, by Bill Fick and Beth Grabowski (Laurence King Publishing, 2015).

Critical thinking:

Discuss with your classmates the advantages and disadvantages of the different approaches to making multi-colour relief prints. Why do you print the lightest colours first when using the single block reductive method?

registration The alignment of the printing block on the paper.

Mixed media

Learning objectives:

- To understand how artists compose images with consideration for space, balance and colour
- To understand how artists use a mixed-media approach to develop and refine ideas
- To understand how artists develop themes through their work

Artists develop their ideas and refine their work in many ways, using a wide range of mixed media to help them achieve their intentions. This unit considers a range of approaches: how artists develop their compositions, and the way that they combine formal elements to develop a theme, over time and across different pieces of work.

EXPLORING SPACE, BALANCE AND COLOUR TO DEVELOP IMAGERY

Scottish artist Elizabeth Blackadder (born 1931) provides a good example of an artist who considers space very carefully in her compositions. Her work is influenced by the principles of **Zen**, which place great importance on the idea of empty space. She has painted and drawn many still-life compositions where the objects are placed across the whole page, without overlapping or touching each other. The objects themselves are represented as being strongly three-dimensional, but there is no pictorial depth behind the objects. She has developed this approach to her work throughout her long career, and it can be seen in her mixed-media composition *Japanese Still Life with Origami Swan*, 2008 (see Figure 3.107).

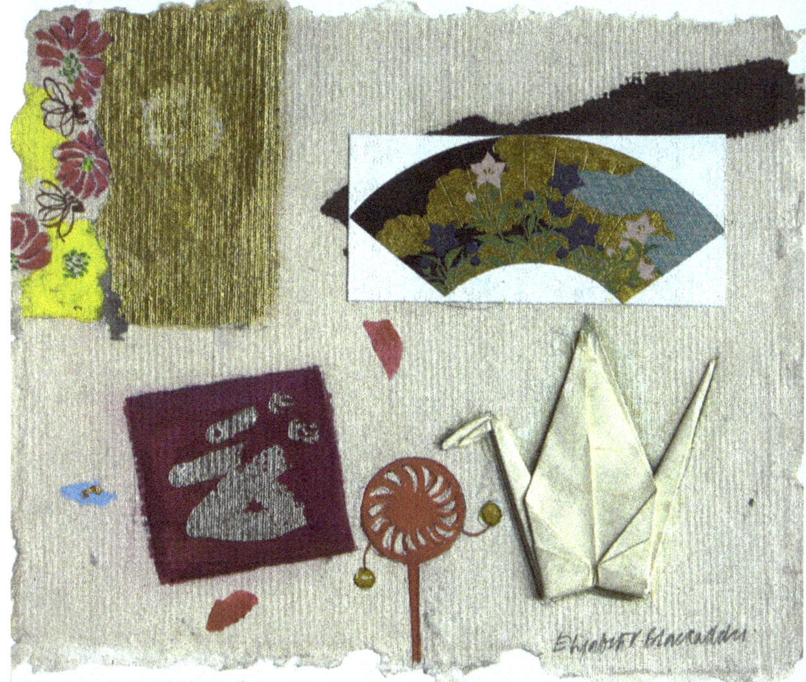

3.107 Elizabeth Blackadder, *Japanese Still Life with Origami Swan*, 2008, watercolour and collage on paper, private collection. Here you can see the careful placement of the objects, where the space becomes as important as the objects themselves.

Activity A: **Still-life arrangement**

1. Look carefully at Figure 3.107, the collage *Japanese Still Life with Origami Swan* by Elizabeth Blackadder.
2. Now create your own still life, using any appropriate mixed-media and collage materials. Place the objects so they do not overlap on your page. Consider the space in between the objects, known as negative space, as carefully as the objects themselves.
3. Try arranging the composition in different ways, making a sketch or taking a photograph of each variation, before deciding on the final version.
4. Make notes and justify your choice of final composition.

Zen Japanese school, of 12th-century Chinese origin, teaching that contemplation of one's essential nature to the exclusion of all else is the only way of achieving pure enlightenment.

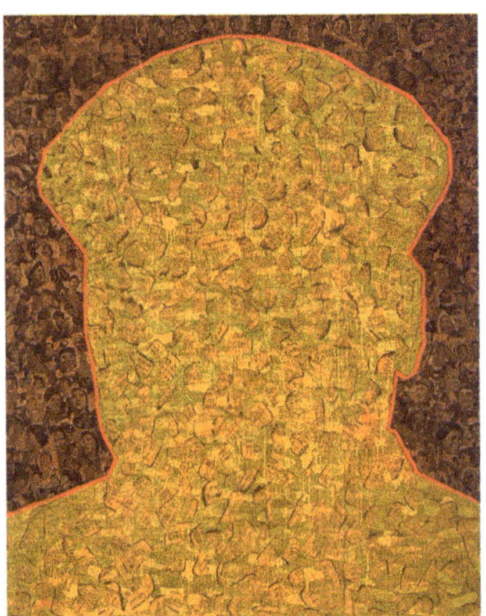

3.108 Xue Song, *Mao*, 2005, acrylic and burnt paper collage on canvas, private collection. One of a series of works on the same theme, *Mao* balances shape, colour and line in a flat, decorative way. See other works from the series at the chinesecontemporary.com website. How do different colour combinations affect the impact of the work?

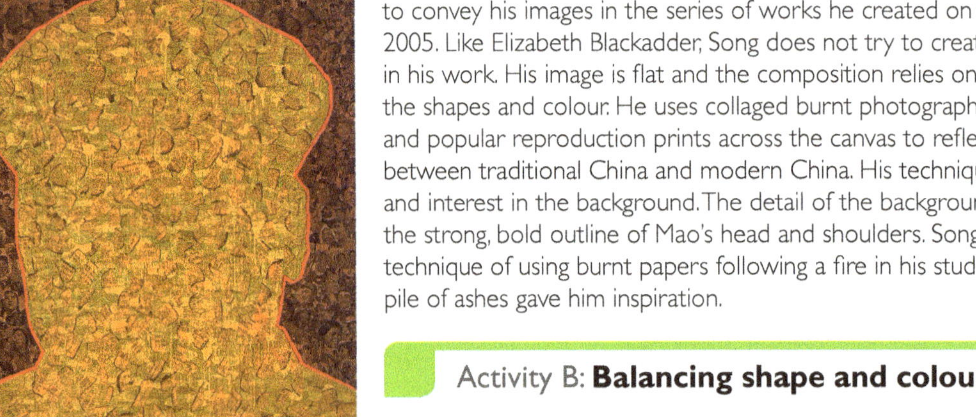

Chinese artist Xue Song (born 1965) uses strong line, shape and colour to convey his images in the series of works he created on the theme of *Mao*, 2005. Like Elizabeth Blackadder, Song does not try to create pictorial depth in his work. His image is flat and the composition relies on the balance of the shapes and colour. He uses collaged burnt photographs, flyers, magazines and popular reproduction prints across the canvas to reflect the contrasts between traditional China and modern China. His technique creates texture and interest in the background. The detail of the background contrasts with the strong, bold outline of Mao's head and shoulders. Song developed his technique of using burnt papers following a fire in his studio, where seeing the pile of ashes gave him inspiration.

Activity B: **Balancing shape and colour**

1. Begin by looking at the way that Xue Song has painted *Mao* in Figure 3.108. Also go to the website chinesecontemporary.com to see more examples of his work and look carefully at his style.
2. Using a photographic portrait, make several photocopies of the image.
3. Outline the head and shoulders using acrylic paint to split the image into two main shapes – the background and the figure.
4. Now paint the shapes using colour to balance them visually. Experiment with using different colours and reflect on the impact that this has on the image.

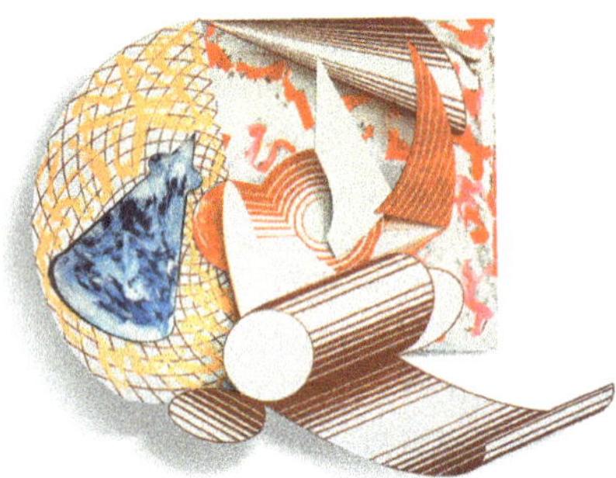

3.109 Frank Stella, *Giufà e La Statua de Gesso*, 1984, oil, enamel, fluorescent alkyd, acrylic and ink on canvas and metal panels, Cincinnati Art Museum, Ohio.

DEVELOPING AND REFINING IDEAS THROUGH THE USE OF MEDIA

Artists can spend many years developing themes and ideas within their work, sometimes using different media as a way to develop their creative thinking. In his abstract compositions, American artist Frank Stella (born 1936) developed and refined his use of media across two and three dimensions, over time. He used 2D collages, which he referred to as maquettes, to inform larger mixed-media pieces. From these 2D works in the mid-1980s, he went on to work in three dimensions, working with sheet metals to create relief sculptures, as can be seen in Figures 3.109 and 3.110.

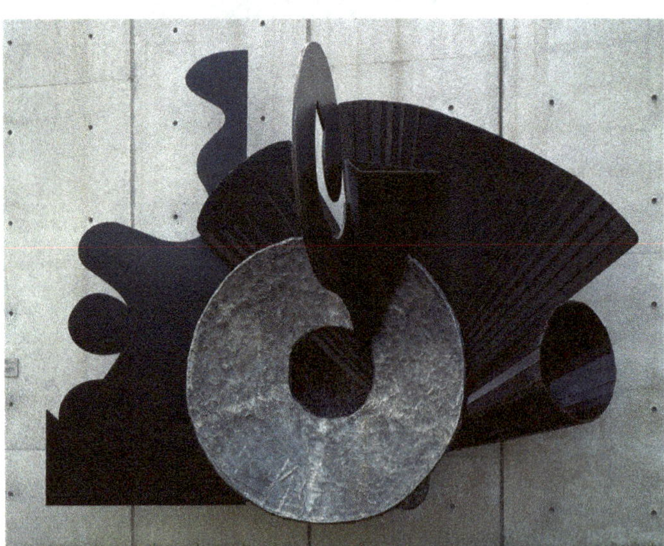

3.110 Frank Stella, *Decanter*, 1987, steel and bronze, Museum of Fine Arts, Houston, Texas. You can see how Stella has used abstract shapes using mixed media in 2D form in *Giufà e La Statua de Gesso* (Figure 3.109), to later develop 3D outcomes. The geometric shapes have been transformed by shaping sheet metal in his 1987 sculpture *Decanter*.

RECURRING IMAGERY

The American artist Joseph Cornell (1903–72) is an excellent example of a mixed-media artist who has developed a theme across successive pieces of work. In 1948, he used a photograph of the portrait painting *Bia de Medici* by the Italian artist Agnolo Bronzino (1503–72) as the central image in his mixed-media box collage, entitled *Medici Princess.* The work also contains other printed materials and **recurring** smaller-scale photographs of the same portrait. Over the next six years, Cornell used the same photographic image repeatedly in similar mixed-media collages, combining the photographs with different found objects. He experimented with repetition, arrangement and scale of the photograph of the *Medici Princess* and limited his use of colour to blue on the parts of the work that are paper.

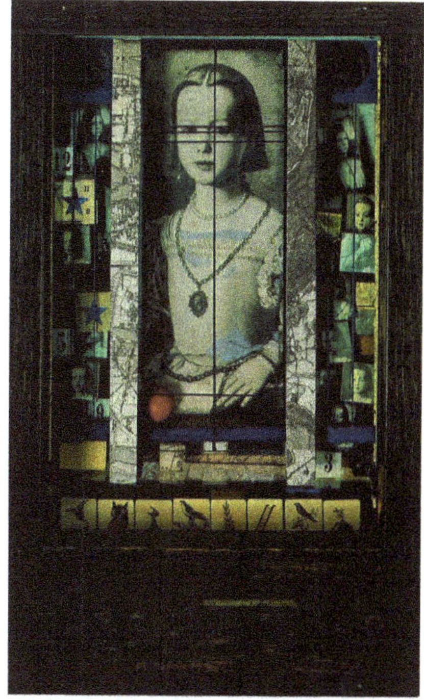

3.111 Joseph Cornell, *A Medici Princess*, c.1948, three-dimensional object, private collection.

Activity C: **Repeated images**

1. Look at the examples of Joseph Cornell's work in Figures 3.111 and 3.112.
2. Using a photograph of a person or object as a starting point, print or photocopy the image several times at different scales.
3. Arrange the copies in different ways, combining them with other collage materials or found objects to create different, yet similar, compositions. Use found objects that have some meaning or connection to the original image.
4. Make notes about the creative process that you are using and evaluate your outcomes.

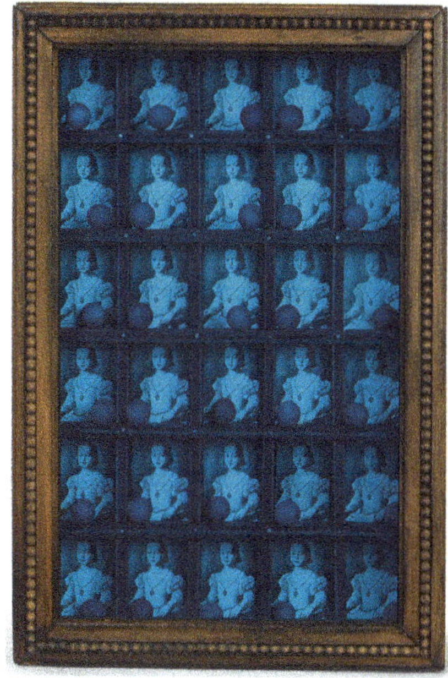

3.112 Joseph Cornell, *Untitled (Compartmented Medici Princess [Bronzino])*, c.1952–54, tinted glass, wood, printed paper collage, wooden balls, paint and nails, private collection. Cornell explores his theme of the *Medici Princess* across several pieces of work, experimenting with size, placement and scale of the main photographs.

Tip:

- To ensure that you have plenty of evidence for assessment, experiment with using and combining a wide range of media and approaches when developing your own work.
- Remember that you can explore your theme by combining the same components in many different ways.

Further research

Search online for more information about the work of Elizabeth Blackadder, Xue Song and Frank Stella.

recurring Happening again at regular intervals.

Photography

Learning objectives:

- To understand how to develop photographic work
- To explore techniques to refine photographic work

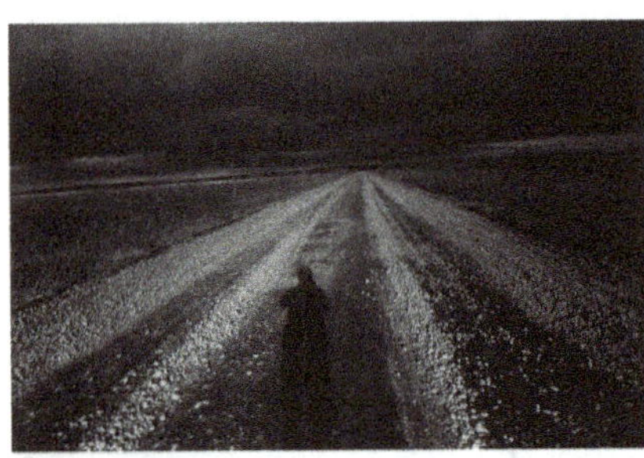

3.113 Daido Moriyama, *Hokkaido*, 1972–8, silver gelatin print. Japanese photographer Daido Moriyama (born 1938) is using perspective and the shadow cast by his own body as key elements in the image.

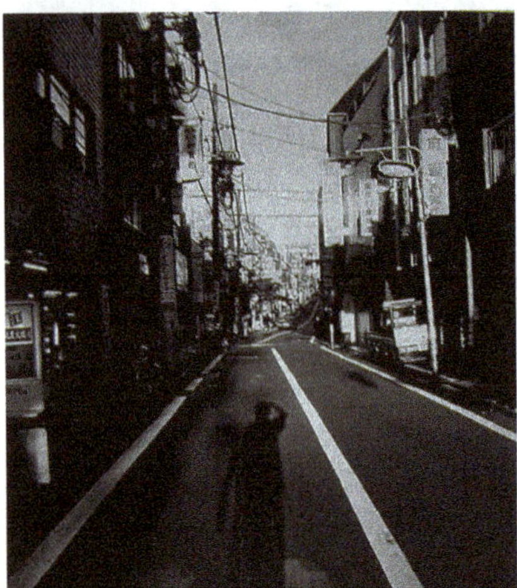

3.114 Daido Moriyama, *Untitled (Shadow/Street Scene)*, 2002, silver gelatin print. Photographers will often return to the same theme and subject and refine their work by shooting in a different way.

Photography can be used in its own right or as part of the creative process to develop ideas. Photographers can explore combinations of techniques in camera and on-screen to refine work. Some photographers in fine art have maintained an interest and practice in chemical-based photographic work. Others have developed work in digital formats. You can develop exciting and interesting photographic work through understanding how to refine your ideas and photographic techniques.

In this unit we are using the word 'develop' in the sense of progressing an artwork creatively rather than making a photograph out of film using chemicals.

DEVELOPING PHOTOGRAPHIC WORK

Like most areas within art and design, photography involves a balance between creative and technical skills. Understanding how these two areas work together is an important part of developing and refining photographic work. The photographers or artists, who are working with a creative approach, still need to apply the right techniques to make their ideas become a reality. They also need to reflect on their work, to understand how they need to develop it.

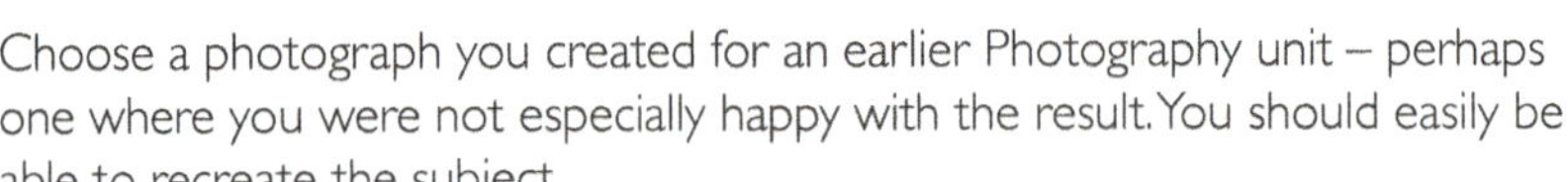

Activity A: **Reshoot one of your photographs**

Choose a photograph you created for an earlier Photography unit – perhaps one where you were not especially happy with the result. You should easily be able to recreate the subject.

1. Consider your photograph in terms of its formal elements and visual language. Make notes about each of the following (if relevant):
   - composition
   - tonal values and contrast
   - colour
   - line
   - texture
   - scale
   - shape
   - perspective
   - any other aspect.
2. Select three elements you would like to improve, or use to explore creative approaches.
3. Return to the subject and reshoot, this time paying attention to how you are recording the subject and the elements you want to improve.
4. Output or print your imagery and display it.
5. Reflect on your work – have you been able to develop your work creatively?
6. Discuss your work with your classmates, making notes on their responses.

liquid light A wet, light-sensitive medium that can be painted onto surfaces, then exposed to light, brushed with developer, wash and the fix to make photographic images on non-paper surfaces.
transfer medium Solution painted into photographic images, allowing the image to be transferred onto other surfaces.

DEVELOPING WORK – SHOOTING TECHNIQUES

There are different ways of generating and developing creative photography. Some photographers work with a subject and theme and build this slowly, taking time to set up shots, and editing carefully. Other photographers work very quickly, and record what their eye sees, in a very intuitive manner. This approach can be used in street photography, and in some documentary photography. The way in which a photographer works dictates the techniques they use, and has to be matched to the kind of work intended. Creative approaches can use either long set-ups or fast shots.

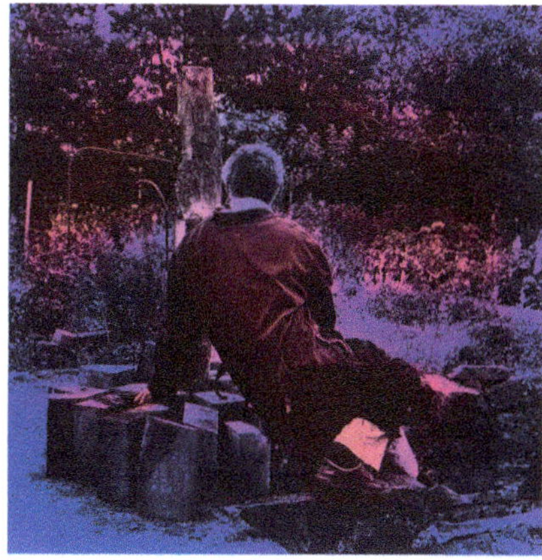

3.115 Li Yuan-chia, *Untitled*, 1993, hand-coloured black and white print, LYC Foundation. Some photographers explore the potential to combine materials, such as hand-colouring prints, as seen in this example.

Materials and techniques: **Creative approaches**

Photographers can develop work by exploring different materials and processes, as seen in Figures 3.115 and 3.116. Examples of these approaches include:

- using montage and collage
- printing onto other surfaces with a **liquid light**-type medium
- combining photography with other media, such as paint, when making imagery
- printing onto canvas and then painting, or painting onto photographic prints
- using **transfer medium** to transfer photographic images onto other surfaces
- using techniques from other areas, such as stitch.

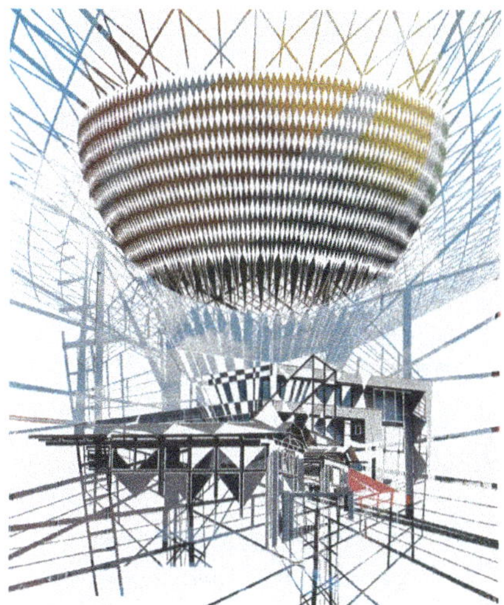

3.116 Richard Galpin, *Noosphere*, 2006, excised photograph, The Lodeveans Collection. This photograph has been made using an experimental technique. The photographic emulsion of the print is peeled away from the paper backing.

IDENTITY

Identity is one of the underlying concepts explored by contemporary fine artists today. Artists use photography to question some of the roles and systems that society is built on. Cindy Sherman develops work in series that explore roles and gender stereotyping; she will often be the model in the image. These photographs are portraits; they act as self-portraits, and also portraits of all women in roles in society. She has continued to explore these themes throughout her career, developing and refining her approach to the subject, and her photographic techniques.

The image in Figure 3.117 is part of a set of large printed images. This photograph is 246.7 cm high and 162.4 cm wide. This gives the image the proportion and importance of an historical portrait. Within the image, the subject is wearing what appear to be expensive clothes, which add to the impression of importance. However, look closely and you can see the shoes look like a cheap pair of pink slippers. By doing this, Sherman is saying to us, 'What you think you see is maybe not what is actually there.' So we think we see a wealthy figure in splendid clothing, but it is really an image she has created. She is presenting herself through a made-up, constructed identity.

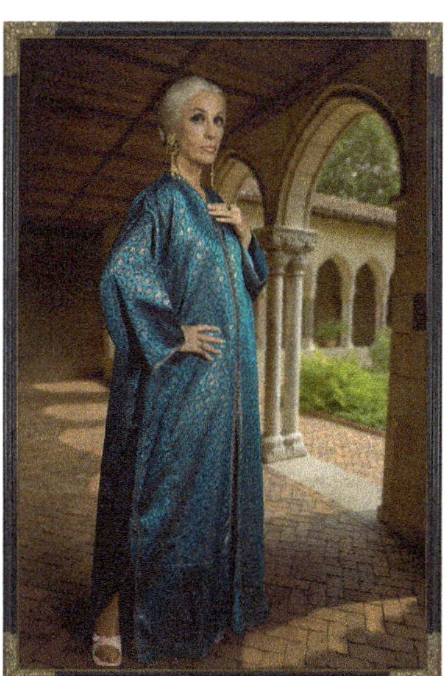

3.117 Cindy Sherman, *Untitled #466*, 2008, chromogenic colour print. In this image, the American artist Cindy Sherman (born 1954) is exploring ideas about identity, how people see themselves and wish to be seen. These large-scale photographic portraits have a similar visual effect as historical paintings of important or wealthy patrons.

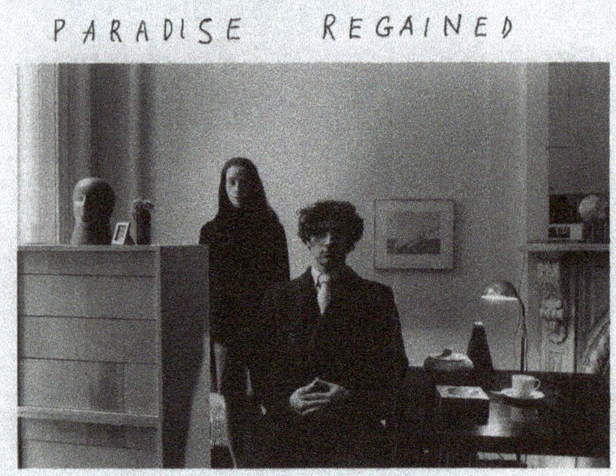

3.118 Duane Michals, *Paradise Regained*, 1968, gelatin-silver photograph (detail from a sequence of six gelatin-silver photographs), The Israel Museum, Jerusalem. Some photographers use imagery to create stories through using series of images, or by including written text as part of the work.

NARRATIVE

Photography can be used for storytelling. The American photographer Duane Michals develops imagery in a sequence to tell or suggest a story. Sometimes these images use Surrealistic juxtapositions of objects, setting and people. The story is not always obvious. As in other types of contemporary fine art, we may have to interpret it. You can find examples of photography in advertising that uses Surrealistic devices. This is achieved by juxtaposing two or more objects that do not normally fit together, which makes the viewer look harder at the images to try and work out the story or puzzle. Digital technology has enabled photographers to develop rich imagery that can narrate stories in more detail, using higher resolution and image editing software.

Critical thinking:

Evaluate your photography. Reflect on the work you produced for **Activities A** and **B**. Write or present a short response, showing:

- how well your work showed or communicated your idea about identity
- how you developed your photographic techniques to improve your work
- specific areas where you refined your ideas and techniques
- how you could refine and improve your work further.

Activity B: **Developing and refining photographing techniques**

Shoot a series of four photographs based on the theme 'Identity'. Work in pairs for this activity.

1. In your pairs, discuss the theme 'Identity'. Think about what people do to control and present their identity.
2. Now think about each of your own identities. How do you want people to see you? What do you want to present to them?
3. Define this by writing a short project proposal.
4. Shoot two photographs each, where you are the model. Use any combination of clothing, make-up and props to present your identity.
5. Print out the images and discuss as a pair. Ask yourselves how the images could be developed. Could this be through: refining techniques, such as lighting, or camera techniques? Consider:
   - using a different composition
   - moving the subject
   - creating a background effect or using props.
6. Make notes about the refinements you want to make.
7. Reshoot the two images, making the refinements as you go along. You will have two original and two refined photographs each.
8. Compare and discuss the second batch of images, and consider how you achieved the refinements.
9. If you have time, extend this task by creating a fantasy version of your identity. You can research artists such as Andy Warhol, Cindy Sherman and Marc Quinn to see how they create images that present a different identity or fantasy story.

Further research

For more on Cindy Sherman, go to the New York Museum of Modern Art's website website.

For more on identity in photography, go to the Victoria and Albert Museum (V&A) Study Room website.

For more on Cindy Sherman's *Untitled #466*, search on You Tube.

Experimental assemblage and construction

Learning objective:

- To develop and refine an experimental piece of constructed fine art

Developing work and refining ideas is a key part of experimental art and design practice. Artists select themes and use subject matter alongside specific techniques and approaches to communicate their ideas. The ability to continually evaluate work and propose solutions and improvements is part of professional practice.

DEVELOPING WORK TO A THEME

Artists working experimentally may explore a theme through working and reworking the same idea. There may be subtle refinements each time. Conceptual artists are always working with ideas that they refine to improve or take their work in new directions.

Activity A: **Develop and refine a constructed figure made from found objects**

In this activity, you will be developing and refining fine art work.

1. Start collecting found objects that interest you – there is no limit to what these objects are, as long as they are not harmful in any way, and you obtain them safely.
2. Use some drawings that you have of the figure, or make some new drawings, again of the figure (the pose is up to you).
3. Take the drawings and see whether you can interpret them in 3D by using some of the objects and joining them to make a constructed fine art piece (again, do this safely – you can use strong gaffer tape and or masking tape just to try out the constructions).
4. Make drawings and take photographs of your construction.
5. Make notes on how you could refine the model – to improve its resemblance to the figure in the drawing.
6. Refine the piece and photograph it when complete.

Critical thinking:

Evaluate your developmental work and constructed fine art piece.

Further research

Go online to find out more on Lawrie Simonson or found objects in art.

For additional images and information on found objects, go to the Tate Gallery website.

Materials and techniques: **Found objects**

Artists may look for the potential in materials around us, such as found objects. This makes the audience consider their relationship with resources. There can be playfulness in the way materials can be combined to make imagery.

Tip:

It can help to really focus on a single idea rather than dipping into a whole range of them. For instance, if you are interested in reusing materials and exploring our relationship with them, make this a focus, and research artists that work in this way to help you get an understanding.

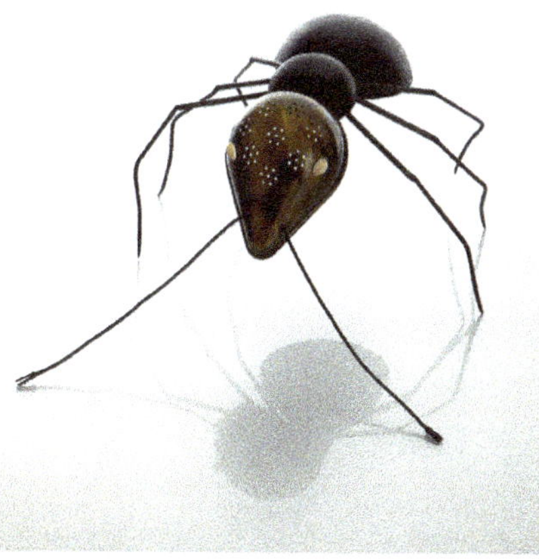

3.119 Lawrie Simonson, *Ant*, 2013, metal spanners, tools and found objects, private collection. The British artist Lawrie Simonson (born 1950) has joined metal kitchen utensils to create an interpretation of an ant. This is an example of everyday found objects being used to create an interesting figure.

Architecture

Learning objectives:

- To understand how architects develop and refine design work
- To develop and design an environment within an architectural space
- To develop a piece of sculpture to be sited in the development

Architects create environments for people to use as part of their daily lives by developing and refining design work. There is a complex relationship between the design and the way that users interact with it. You have looked at recording and contextual influences in Modules 1 and 2. In this section, you will bring some of these ideas together and combine them in a group activity. This activity will also include environmental design and sculpture.

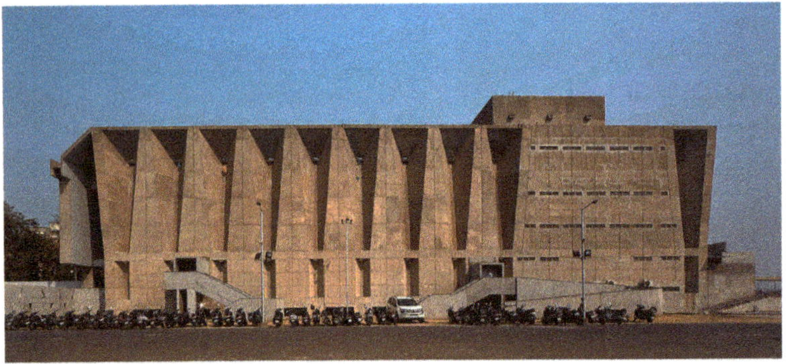

3.120 Balkrishna Doshi, Tagore Memorial Hall, completed in 1966, Ahmedabad, India. As a student of Le Corbusier, Doshi was inspired in his early career to develop work in the Brutalist style, as shown in this image.

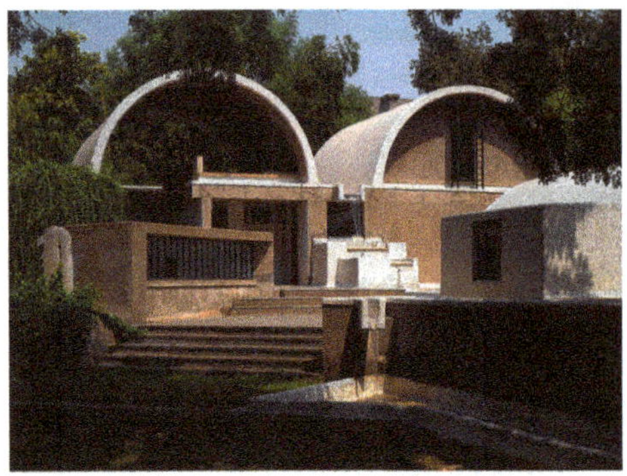

3.121 Balkrishna Doshi, Sangath, 1981, Ahmedabad, India. Doshi refined his ideas by developing his style towards Postmodernism. He designed buildings that were individual, rather than conforming to any particular style.

DEVELOPING STYLE

The Indian architect Balkrishna Doshi (born 1927) studied under Le Corbusier (see Module 2, page 126), and continued his ideas connected to Modernist principles. You have covered Modernism in Module 2, so you should be aware of the characteristics of this style of architecture. Modernist buildings were often huge, and made from materials that were modern in their day, such as poured concrete, hung glass walling and steel structures. As Doshi developed and refined his style, he began to soften this approach. His studio space, Sangath, shown in Figure 3.121, is designed to be in harmony with its local environment, rather than dominating it in a **Brutalist** style. The building and plot acts as a lecture area, with vaults sunken into the ground to create different levels, and outdoor spaces for slide shows and events. It acts as a focal point for community activities and as a research centre. This architecture shows how Doshi has developed his own style. He is not just repeating the ideas of Le Corbusier. His ideas for Sangath represent the **individualistic** approach seen in Postmodernism (Module 2, pages 125–127). Buildings in this style can be shaped to individual needs and purpose.

Brutalist Architectural style that developed from Modernism, based on the term 'Beton Brut' or 'raw concrete'; surfaces are often cast in concrete and allowed to show this construction method.
individualistic (or expressive) architecture A style that allowed individual designs to develop, rather than following a prescribed style.

THE JOURNEY OF A BUILDING – USING DRAWING

Architects' drawings are the accurate to-scale visual diagrams or blueprints for a building. They develop the ideas from the concept stage in more detail. They show the sizes and proportions of the building, and how it fits in to the planned location. In community or commercial-based projects, they can also show communal, shared spaces.

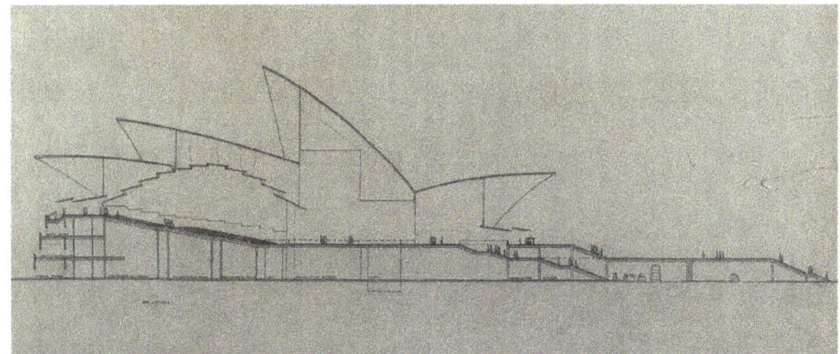

3.122 Jørn Utzon, *Sydney Opera House*, 1957, architectural drawing. This shows one of a set of competition drawings submitted by Jorn Utzon to the Sydney Opera House Committee.

ELEVATIONS

Drawing is an important part of the planning process. This can be in the form of concept drawings, elevations and plans. Elevation drawings are views of the planned building, seen from the sides, front and rear. Examples of elevation drawings are shown in Figures 3.122 and 3.123.

The Danish architect Jørn Utzon (1918–2008) responded to an international competition for a 'National Opera House at Bennelong Point'. He presented his ideas in drawing format. One of these drawings is shown in Figure 3.122. Utzon was then commissioned by the New South Wales Government to produce final drawings for the Opera House, and to supervise its construction.

Some architects use drawing to refine their ideas and sketch out visualisations of buildings with their clients. This means that they can amend details, and show their clients how this would look. This also allows ideas to be shared around the design team and discussed before being developed further.

3.123 Balkrishna Doshi, *Elevation drawings for Sangath*, Ahmedabad, India. Doshi is showing how the South face of the building will look, and some of the details that link different areas, such as steps.

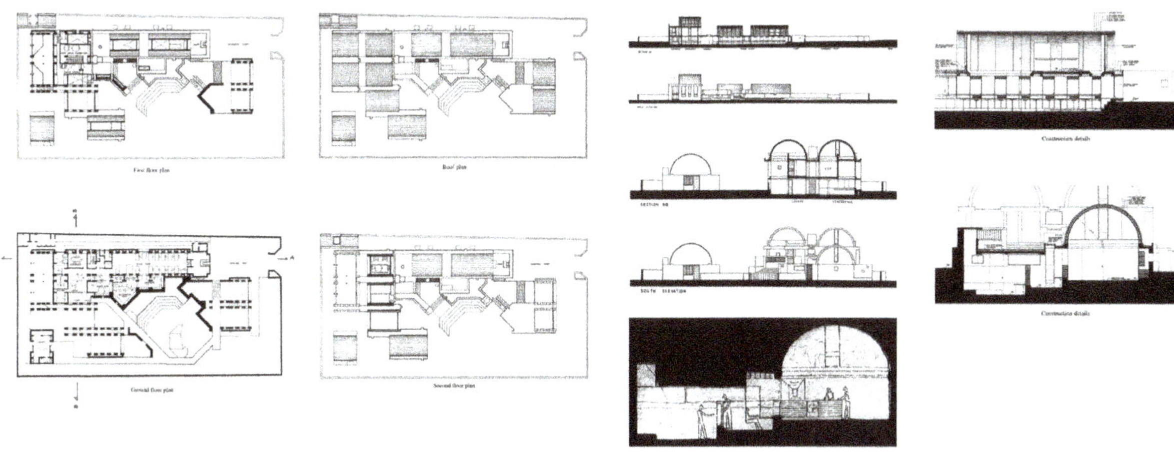

PLANS

Plan drawings are used to show the building and its surrounding spaces seen from above. These can be used to show how communal spaces are **integrated** within the overall design for the building and its location. An example of a plan drawing is shown in Figure 3.124. These drawings would then be produced in CAD software.

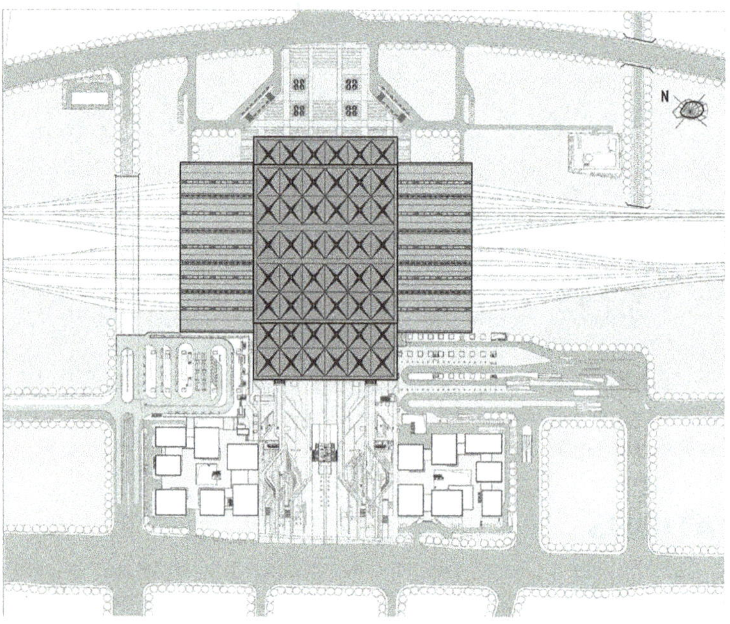

3.124 CSADI Architects, Taiyuan South Railway Station, China, Plan drawing, 2014. A plan drawing showing the layout of spaces around the main building.

Activity A: **Design a communal space**

You are asked to produce technical drawings for a shared space in a municipal setting. Your design should show an awareness of the need to care for the environment, and feature one sculpture.

The theme is 'Relaxation and nature – a break from work'.

- Your design must include features that show an awareness of environmental issues.
- This could be in the materials proposed for construction, or in visual themes such as plants.
- The scheme is to be located in the quadrangle between office buildings, so is meant to be an area of rest and relaxation – an oasis of calm.

Get into teams of three.

1. Research examples of architectural design for communal spaces in areas such as concourses and terminus design.
2. If you know of any similar local areas, visit them and make drawings and take photographs.
3. Use your research to produce:
   - 1 × elevation drawing, from a side of your choice, on an A3 page
   - 1 × plan drawing, on an A3 page.
4. Discuss your work in your team as you are producing it, making notes about your progress and how you are meeting the brief.
5. Extension task: If you have time, make a technical drawing of your work. This can be in isometric or orthographic projection.

integrated Made whole or completed by adding or bringing together parts.

DEVELOPING WORK – MODEL-MAKING

Model-making is another important stage in developing work. This is the stage where architects and designers produce scaled versions of their planned buildings in three dimensions (3D). Models are often used in pitches and presentations to clients, and where urban schemes are presented to the public or clients for consideration. Model-making allows for further development and refinements, as the design for the building can be seen as a real structure.

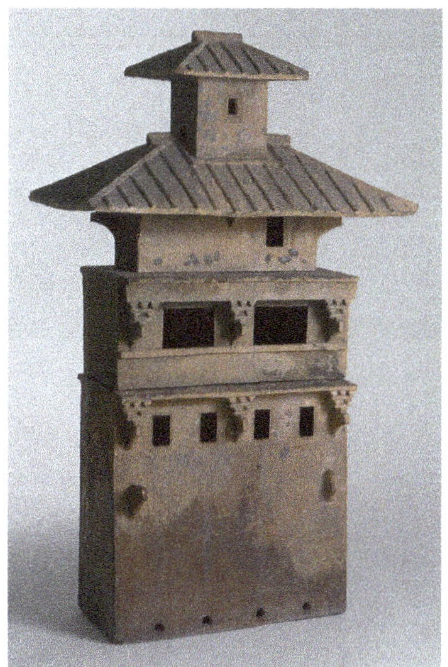

3.125 Model of building, Zhandge, Henan Province, 100–300 CE, earthenware, Philadelphia Museum of Art. Models have been used throughout history as a way of visualising structures.

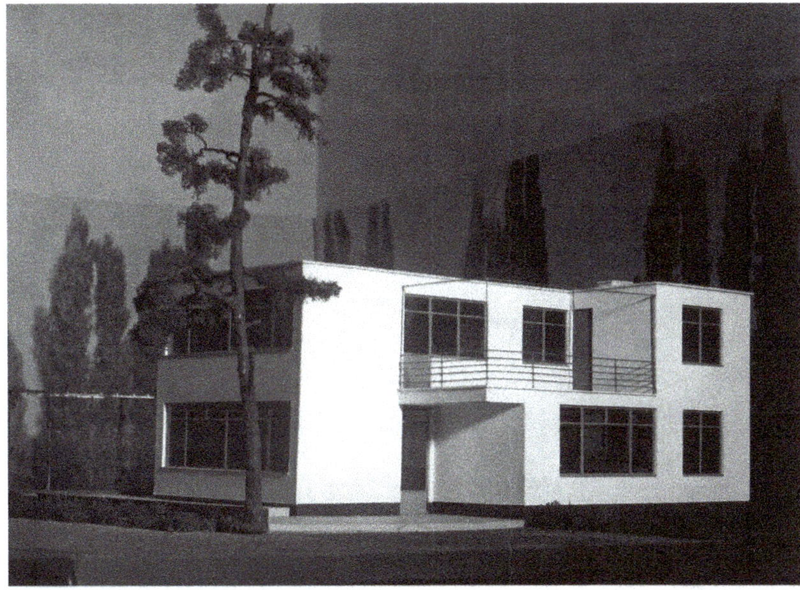

3.126 Walter Gropius, Model of single-story building, 1930–39. Architects and designers such as those in the Bauhaus movement have used models to inform the development and refinements in their work.

Activity B: **Model-making**

1. In your team of three, gather your elevation and plan drawings, and any detailed drawings you have made and use them to make a scale model of your building. You should research examples of architectural models to find out what sort of scale to work with. The model should fit on top of a standard 1250 mm-long table.
2. Use simple white card for the model.
3. You can add trees and other details. These can be ordered on the internet, to scale.
4. Consider how you will represent the theme.
5. It is important that you use good craft skills:
   a. cutting the shapes out carefully
   b. using gluing and joining techniques without smearing glue over the white surfaces.
6. If your school or centre has a laser cutter, you may use this for some of the finer details; these techniques are used in industry.
7. If your school or centre does not have one, cut out the shapes carefully.

ADDRESSING THE THEME

Your team needs to include the environmental awareness theme in their design work. It should be a space where people, mainly office workers can relax. If the space is in an open area it might also be used by other people, such as visitors to the site, and it must have a 'Relaxation and nature – a break from work' theme. How can you do this?

You could achieve this in a number of ways. For instance:

- What sort of environment do people find relaxing?
- Can your designs use materials that are renewable, or from a sustainable source, such as in seating or benching?

Many architectural developments include natural materials in communal areas to break up the harshness and uniformity of the office building environment. Designers can use planting to make a space interesting by using plants that react throughout the seasons, such as blossoming or flowering cherry trees.

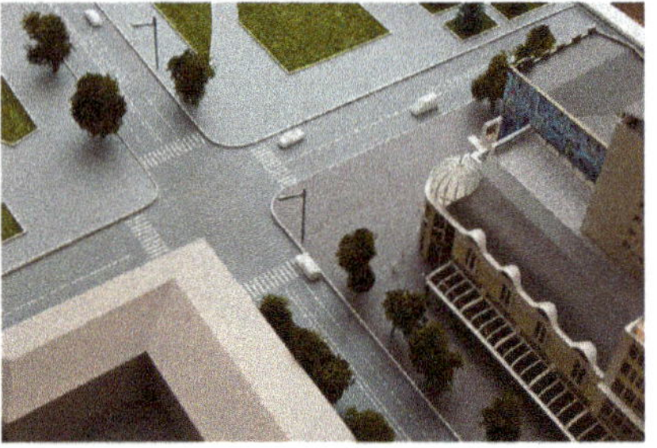

3.127 Model-making can be used to bring architectural detail to life. You can use your model-making to provide detail on your layout and arrangement of spaces.

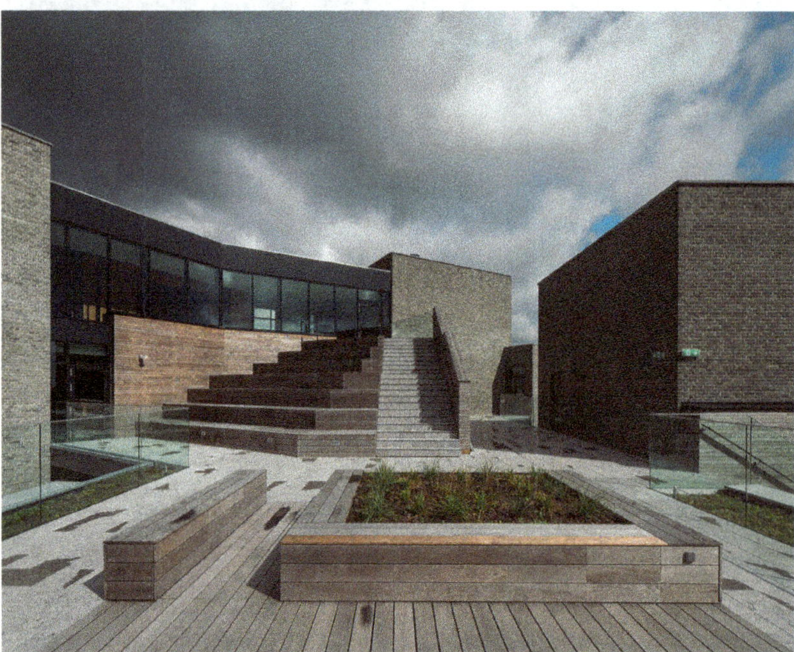

3.128 C.F. Møller, Campus Hall, University of Southern Denmark, 2016. An example of a communal space – your design work could include ideas for raised areas, steps and communal seating.

Activity C: **Design the sculpture**

This could be made jointly in your teams of three or passed to one of the team if preferred.

1. Develop drawings that show the sculpture in situ.
2. List the materials the sculpture will be made from (you can refer back to pages 238–239).
3. Annotate your drawings to explain how this reflects the theme.
4. Make a small maquette.

Developing the design for the sculpture

As you develop your model, you need to include the sculpture. Research examples of public sculpture in your local area. Sculptors can address themes through their use of materials. They will also use specific formal elements to communicate their ideas and intention for the sculpture. Is it meant to be a part of its location, in harmony with it? Or is it meant to dramatically stand out from its background? You should make notes, drawings and take photographs of examples you see.

Refining design work

Creative teams rely on their ability to be open and honest about their design work. They need to be able to articulate their criticism and evaluate how designs can be improved. To refine work, they need to compare it against the original aims and objectives in the brief. They will also consider their own creative ideas and intentions. As a student, you need to refine and change your ideas as you develop project work in assignments. It is important that you understand why you are changing your ideas. You should aim to improve your work by refining it as it develops. You should record these changes and refinements, as they are a reminder of your design thinking.

Activity D: **Team meeting**

This team-based activity brings the units in this module to a close. To complete it, you will need:

- your work on all three activities so far, including:
- all sketchbook research and rough drawings/notes
- records of discussions
- A3 technical drawings, including how your theme is being addressed
- designs and maquettes for sculpture
- models of design
- photographs of models – there is more on this in Module 4, on pages 278–283 'Presentation methods'.

In your team, present your work back to your group, describing:

- how you developed your ideas – your research sources and how you addressed the theme
- how you refined your ideas
- how well you worked as a team
- the importance of your drawings in the design process
- the effectiveness of your model-making
- how your building could be improved.

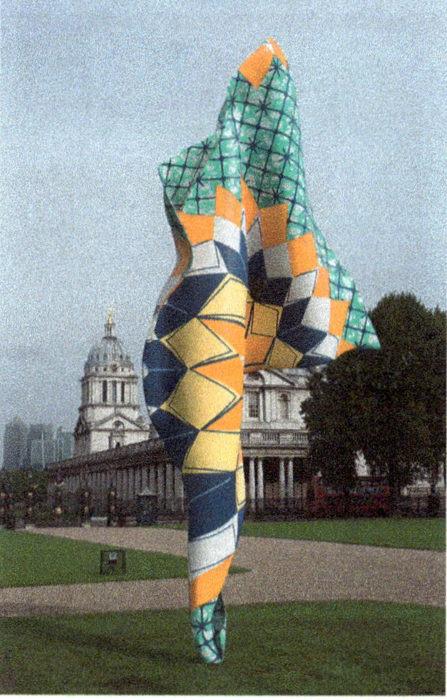

3.129 Yinka Shonibare, *Wind Sculpture II*, 2013, steel armature, hand-painted fibreglass resin cast, Royal Museums Greenwich, London. Sculpture can reference the natural elements by being animated by them. This sculpture reacts to the wind. Its textile areas move as the wind blows.

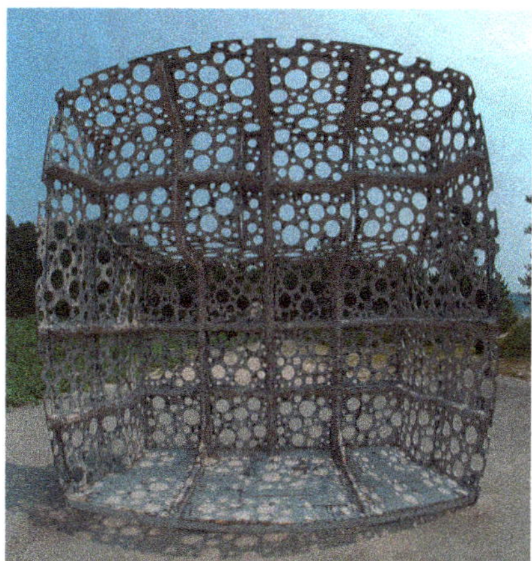

3.130 Shinro Ohtake, *Shipyard Works – Stern with Hole*, 1990, Benesse Museum, Outdoor installation on Naoshima Island, Japan. Sculpture can represent a theme by recycling objects that relate to its location. In this piece, the Japanese sculptor Ohtake (born 1955) is using parts from fishing vessels to reference the location's reliance on fishing.

Critical thinking:

Using your displays for **Activity D**, reflect on your work as a whole on these units, evaluating how:

- you worked as a team
- you used communication skills to discuss, develop and refine work
- you feel your designs refined the theme
- effectively your designs worked visually
- you could improve work further.

Further research

For more on architectural design that incorporates nature and the environment, go to the Benesse House Museum website.

For more on architecture, interiors, design and technology, go to the Dezeen website.

For more on examples of public sculpture, visit the Public Monuments and Sculpture Association website.

For more on examples of projects in drawing and model form, look at the Studio Libeskind website.

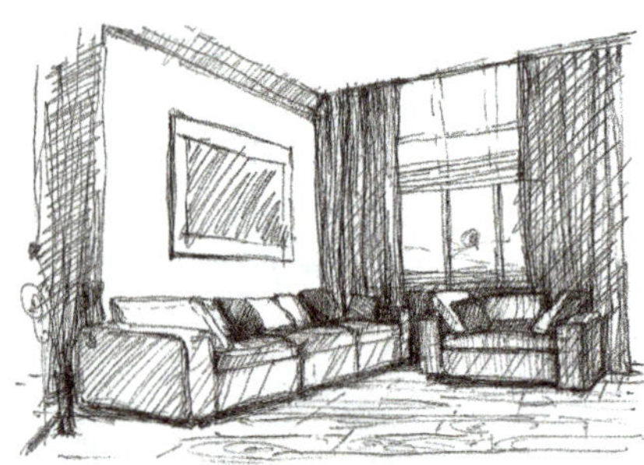

3.131 Freehand drawing of an interior. Drawings can be made in simple linear formats to show physical space.

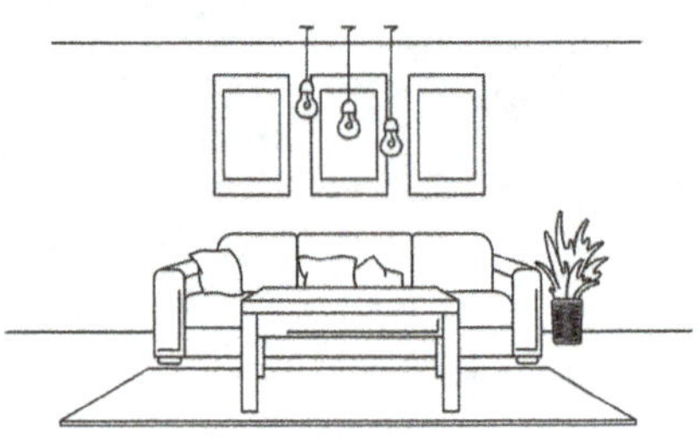

3.132 Vector drawing of interior. CAD can be used to simplify and clarify the design work, making the details clear.

3.133 CAD **render** of living room. CAD software can add more definition to the details. It can show an accurate version of the room and props, and be used to decide whether the design needs to be further developed and refined.

Set design

Learning objective:

- To develop working drawings and a model in response to a set design brief

Set designers work with ideas and concepts and express these through drawings, models and final pieces. They work as part of a team to organise the materials that they produce and, with the director or production company, to ensure their work meets the client's needs. In this unit, you will work in a production team to develop designs for a television set. You will develop two different set designs for this room, using computer-aided design (CAD) or traditional freehand drawing and colour work. You will then select one example and make a model of it.

DEVELOPING WORK WITH DRAWINGS

You can use drawing to help your communication skills. Imagine that you are a designer in a meeting with a director. They are asking you to refine your initial designs. You can take your pencil and paper and make some sketches showing them how this could be done, and get their approval.

WORKING WITH AVAILABLE TECHNOLOGY

Some designers use CAD to develop and refine their ideas once they have researched and visualised their concepts. CAD can be used as a basis for manufacturing sets and props, as information can be provided to different people working in the production team. It can also be used to send information digitally to production workshop equipment.

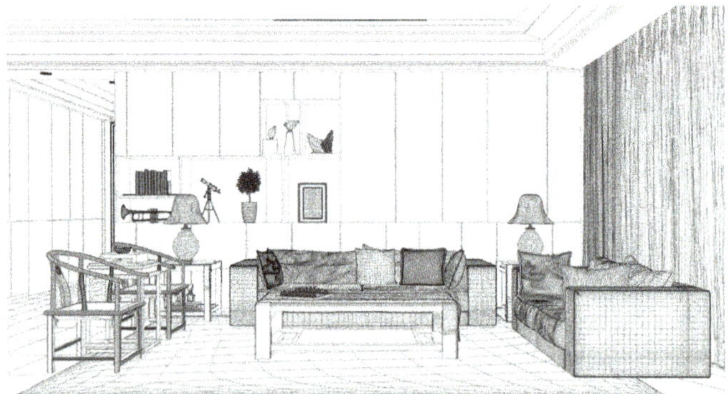

Activity A: **Developing drawings for two set designs for television**

This is based on the theme 'Family life', and features one living room where all family members meet.

This is a team-based project – you need to work in teams of three.

1. Find examples of living spaces you think could be used as starting points for drawings. These can be from magazines, your own drawings and photographs, or downloaded from the internet.

   You will refine these once you have decided on the characteristics of the family in the programme. This could be in the type of furniture, the layout, decoration, spaces between people and chairs and so on.
2. In your team, discuss the set design to come up with a direction for it.
3. Define the physical characteristics of the set.
4. Make CAD or freehand drawings that visualise your ideas – if you have the facilities and time, you could make both.

REFINING THE RESPONSE

Set designers have to interpret and refine themes in productions, plays, film and events in their design work. They develop this interpretation while thinking about technical aspects of a production. These might be the physical space, lighting and performance within the set. There is an element of teamwork involved in developing set design work, as it has to work for all the different people involved.

Activity B: **Refining the set design**

Meet as a team and discuss the drawings you did for **Activity A**.

1. How well do they show the characteristics?
2. How could you refine them?
3. How could they make the theme in the set stand out more?
4. Make a list of actions that you as a team believe will improve the designs.
5. Choose one of the designs to take forward into model-making.

INCORPORATING INFLUENCES

In Figure 3.134, the French artist Robert Delaunay (1885–1941) has reinvented an original set design by the Russian artist Léon Bakst (1886–1924). He has produced a simpler interpretation based on colour combinations, while retaining the themes of the piece. He was a founder member of the Orphism art movement, which made work that used bright colour combinations and geometric shapes. In your team, you may want to show the influences of artists and designers you admire in your model-making. This might be in the use of colours, shapes and so on.

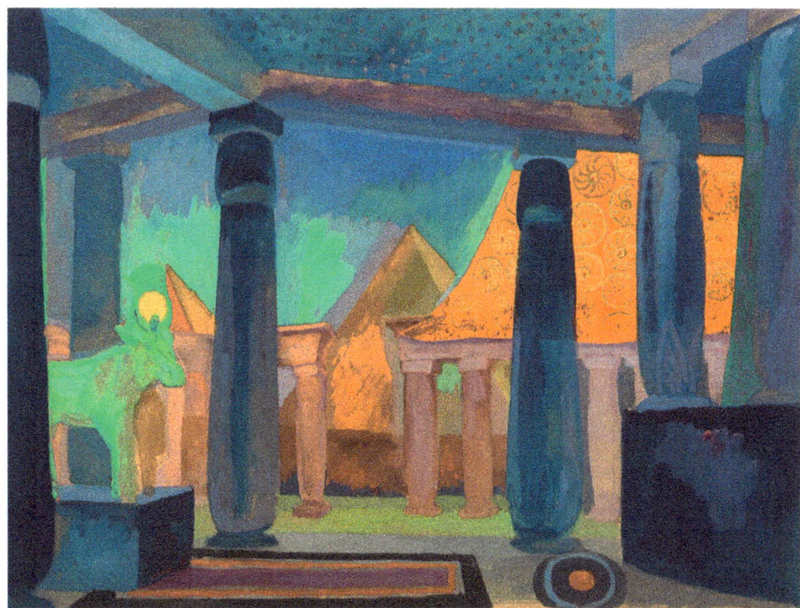

3.134 Robert Delaunay, *Stage design for 'Cleopatra'*, c.1918, watercolour, gouache, metallic paint and graphite on paper, Metropolitan Museum of Art, New York. A reinterpretation of themes in a production, influenced by the designer's interest and own work in painting.

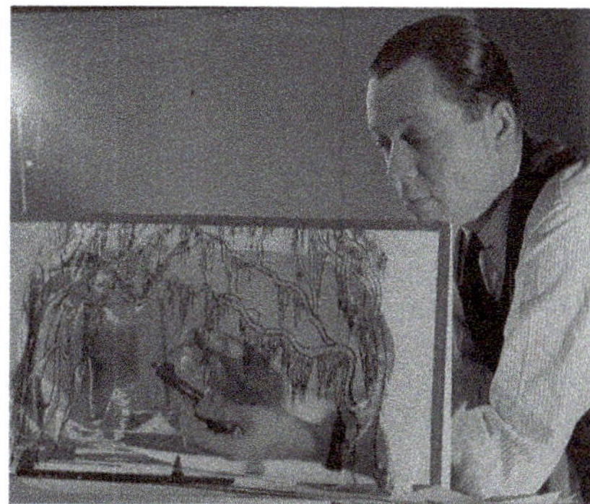

3.135 Jo Mielziner, set design, figurine and design on glass, 1945. The American theatre and lighting designer Jo Mielziner (1901–76) is making changes and refining the set design as he is making it. You can do this as you make your own set designs.

render A Photorealistic image developed from either a 2D drawing or a 3D model.

Tip:

As a set designer, you are working as part of a team, so you need to have good communication skills. As you work through the task in the unit, practise your teamworking skills. Can you listen effectively so you know what to do, or what is going on? Can you communicate your own ideas and views clearly to others?

Activity C: **Make a model of one of your set designs**

1. Use one of your drawings as a basis to make a model of your design for the television set, using suitable materials.
2. Think about formal elements as you do this, and any influences that you want to include.
3. Photograph your model under lighting.

Critical thinking:

Present your work on **Activities A** and **B** back to your team. As a team, describe how you developed and refined your ideas. Evaluate your work, reflecting on:

- Your teamworking skills – how well did each of you communicate in the team?
- Developing and refining your drawing – what drawing techniques did you use?
- Refining the work – what factors emerged from your midpoint discussion, and how did these affect the refinement of the set design?
- How effectively did the model work?
- Theme – do you feel that your design would make an interesting set for the television programme?

Write up a brief summary of your conclusions.

Further research

For more on resources and information on set design, go to the American Association of Community Theatre website.

Go online to find out more on CAD software, including some student free trial packs.

Find out more on different approaches to theatre design, including sculpture. Try Ralph Koltai's website.

Product design

Learning objective:

- To understand how developing models can assist designers in exploring form and surface details when developing and refining their ideas

Design is an **iterative** process. This means that ideas are modelled as prototypes, the models are tested and evaluated against the original brief and specification, and the design can be developed and refined further as a result. The next stage of the design process is to take 2D ideas and drawings and develop them into 3D models or prototypes.

MAKING MODELS

Models can be very simple, made to help you test out shapes or the use of colour and surface decoration. An example of a very simple 3D model can be seen in Figure 3.137. Models can also be more complex working prototypes, as can be seen in Figure 3.138.

You will be expected to explore and develop the forms that you design by making hand-built model prototypes. You should use scale drawings such as orthographic projections to work from when making models. You can use the drawings that you have made to create **templates** for cutting your modelling materials, so that you can accurately cut pieces the same size. You should experiment working with and combining a wide range of modelling materials (for example, card and styrofoam block, which can be cut and sanded easily into shapes), acrylic, wood, composite materials such as medium-density fibreboard (**MDF**) and metals.

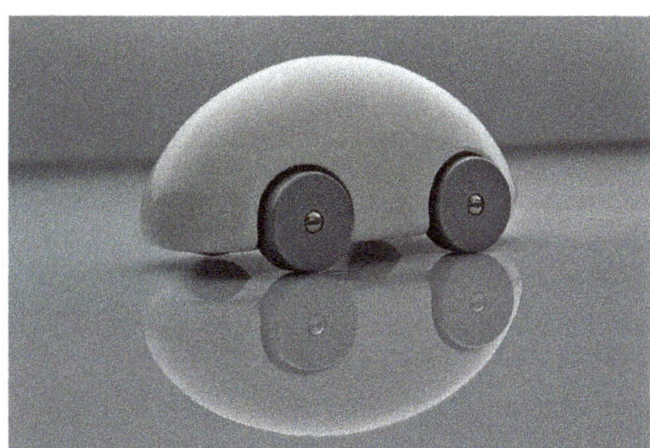

3.137 and **3.138** White Model Car on grey background. The model in Figure 3.137 (left) is a very simple design that focuses on the shape of the vehicle. Compare the simplistic model design to Figure 3.138 (below), which is the prototype design of Google's self-driving car.

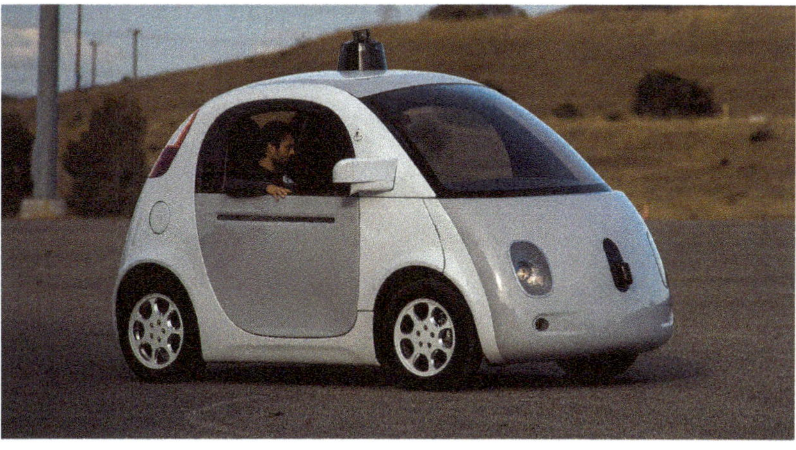

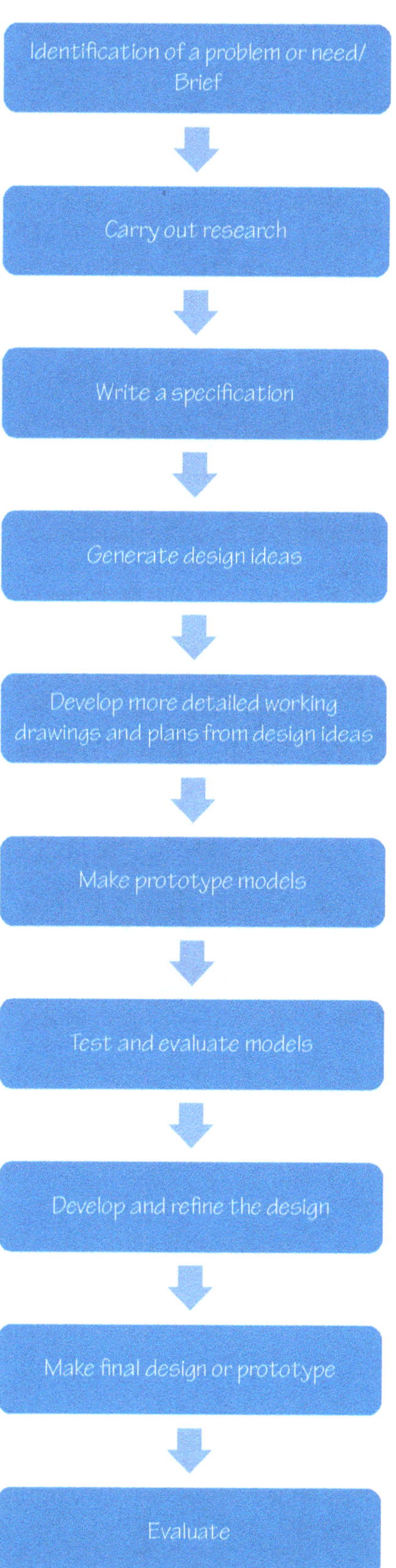

3.136 The design process.

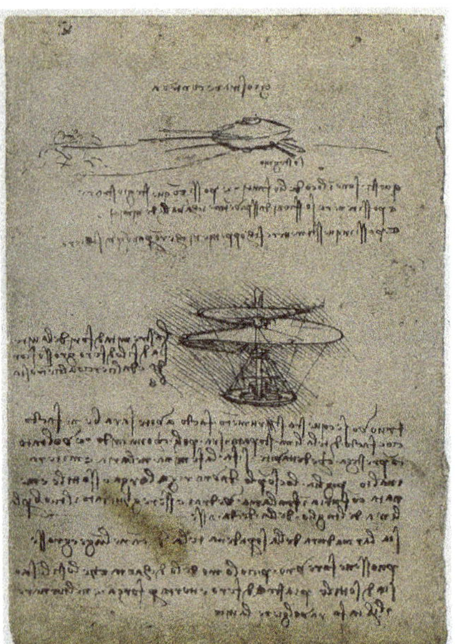

3.139 Leonardo da Vinci, *Studies of an air screw*, 1488–90, pen and ink on paper, Bibliothèque de l'Institut de France, Paris.

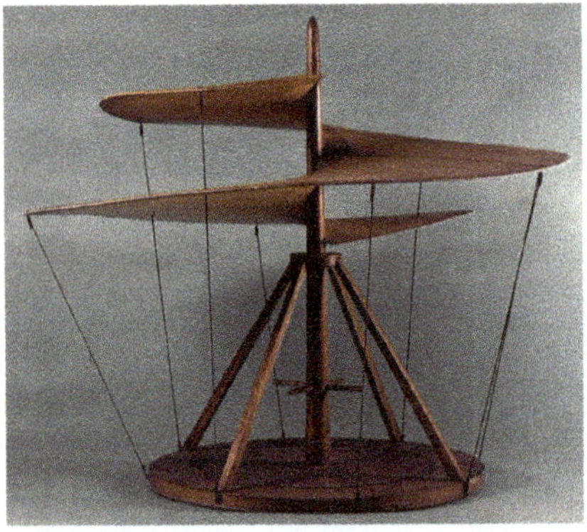

3.140 This helicopter flying machine illustrates how CAD has been used to make computer-generated 3D models from the original drawings by Leonardo da Vinci, enabling the design to be seen from all angles.

Activity A: **Develop your ideas in three dimensions**

Make a 3D model of a hand-held device, such as a remote control or games console.

1. Begin by making scaled drawings of your design. Use the drawings to form templates.
2. Work with any suitable materials that you have available and use the templates to cut any identical shapes.
3. Build up the surface details and consider use of colour and texture as part of the design development.
4. Evaluate your outcome and ask others to give you feedback about the size and feel of the model, your use of colour and surface textures. Use the feedback to help identify possible modifications so that you can refine and improve the design further.

Materials and techniques: **Making models using computer-aided design (CAD) and computer-aided manufacture (CAM)**

Today, models can be made easily using the computer-aided manufacture process of 3D printing. Another term for this is 'additive manufacturing'. The process involves a 3D object being formed from a CAD model by adding layers of material, commonly plastic, in a printer that is linked to the computer. Virtually any shape can be produced, but size is limited by the size of the printer. Different colours and surface textures can be created through the 3D printing process. You may have access to a 3D printer in your school or centre, which you can use as part of the designing process.

Modern-day CAD and CAM techniques have been used to develop the design ideas of Leonardo da Vinci (1452–1519), who between 1488 and 1500 made drawings of an 'air screw', one of the first designs resembling a modern-day helicopter. In the 21st century, it has been possible, using CAD, to create virtual 3D models of the original drawings, showing their form from all viewpoints. From this information, it has also been possible to build real prototypes of the designs and test them, so providing an example of the design process, working from drawings to develop a 3D prototype.

iterative Repetitious or frequent.
MDF Medium-density fibreboard (MDF) is an engineered wood product.
template A thin piece of sheet material such as card or plastic that is shaped and used to reproduce the same shape many times.

Ceramics

Learning objective:

- To understand how to develop surface decoration in ceramic work

Studio potters may find that they become fascinated with a single type of ware, and spend considerable time in developing their ideas around this type of ceramics. These ideas will address both form and surface decoration.

MAKING FORM AND DECORATION WORK – GLAZES

As we have seen in Module 2 (pages 130–131), ceramicists use glazes as surface decoration in their work. These glazes are available in a range of colours, depending on the type of pottery being made. You will develop your understanding of glazes through experimentation and refining your working methods. There are other types of glazes you can use to develop your work: these are shown in the 'Materials and techniques' box.

Materials and techniques: **Types of glazes**

- Underglazes – can be bright colours; behave as watercolours.
- Slips – are coloured liquid clays, used to create texture and surface detail, as well as colour, sometimes called englobes (Figure 3.141).
- Oxides – chemical compounds mixed in water.
- **Earthenware** or stoneware – specific glazes designed to be fired to certain temperatures:
    - earthenware fires up to around 1100 degrees centigrade
    - stoneware fires up to around 1260 degrees centigrade.
- Enamels – can be used as an overglaze, added over the top of an existing glaze, then fired again.

Pablo Picasso produced many of his pieces alongside potters, who would make the form. He would then decorate the work with glazes. Picasso had an understanding of how colour, line and other formal elements would work together. He had explored this in painting, drawing, print and 3D work. Ceramicists work out how to use glazes as surface decoration to enhance the form of their pieces. This means making sure the form of the piece works with the way it is decorated (Figure 3.142).

Tip:

A general way of working is as follows. If you make a simple form, you can explore complex decoration; if you make a complex form, it might work better with a simple decoration. However, this is only a general tip, and you could explore different combinations of the two.

earthenware Clay body and glaze, slightly porous, used in garden pots, fired to around 1100 °C.

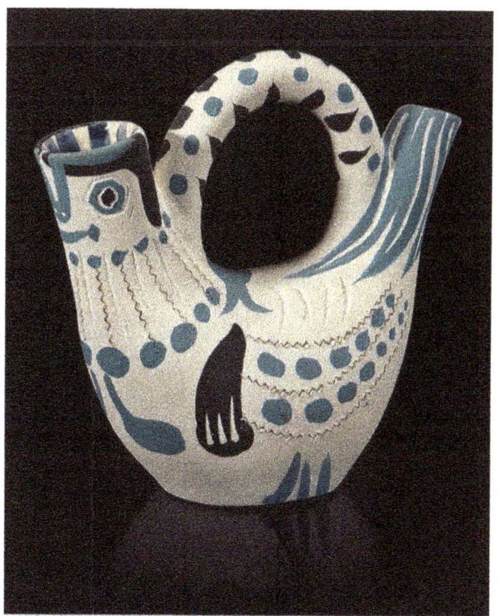

3.141 Pablo Picasso, *Pichet Espagnol*, 1954, partially glazed ceramic, private collection. Picasso decorated this using englobes, using surface decoration and form together.

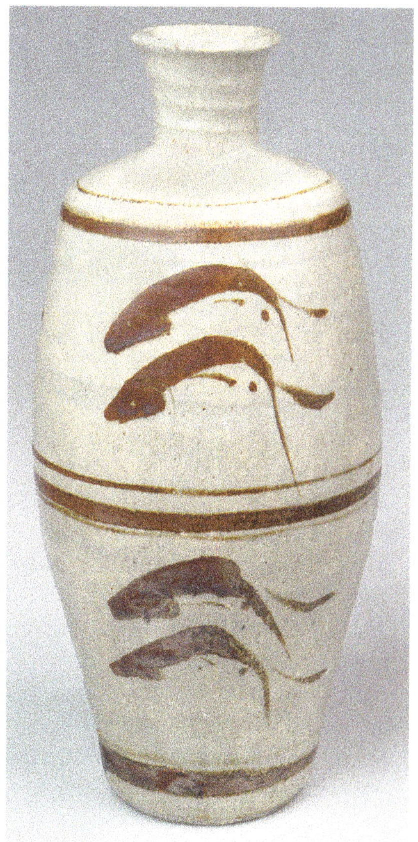

3.142 Bernard Leach, *Tall bottle with leaping fish*, 1970s, stoneware, matt cream glaze with brushed iron, Crafts Study Centre, University of the Creative Arts. In this vase, the British potter Bernard Leach (1887–1979) developed his ideas on surface decoration and form through working with the Japanese potter Shōji Hamada (1894–1978) and the influence of Japanese pottery.

Artists and designers: **Ladi Kwali**

Hajiya (Dr) Hadiza Ladi Kwali was known as Ladi Kwali. She was born in Nigeria in 1925, in the village of Kwali, and died in 1983. She is known for developing ceramics that embodied an African sensibility in the way they were made and decorated. She was exposed to Western ideas through her work with the British potter Michael Cardew, and combined this with her knowledge of traditional Nigerian ceramics to create her own personal style of ceramics.

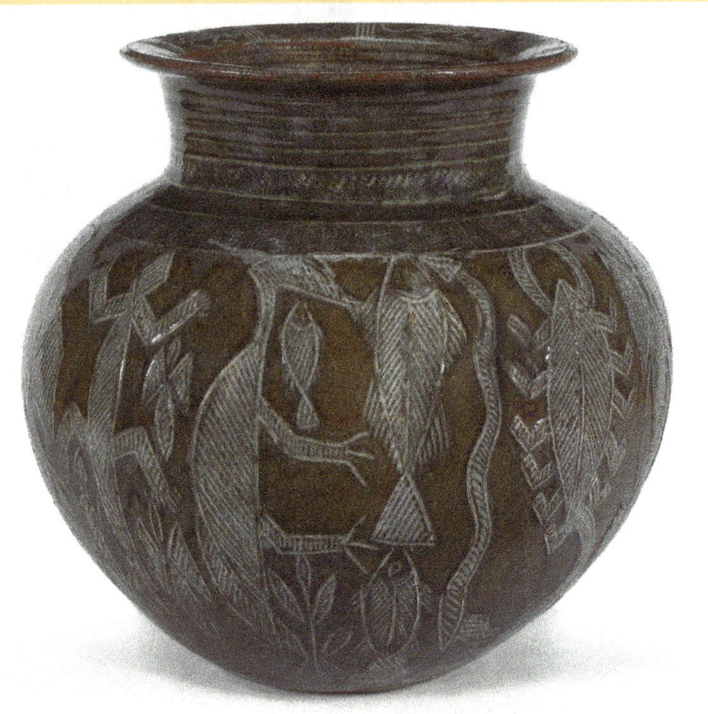

3.143 Ladi Kwali, Pot, 1969, glazed stoneware. An example of Ladi Kwali's decorative work, applying sgraffito on a traditional form. The mixture of horizontal bands and upright shapes emphasises the form of the piece.

Kwali used a blend of coiling and pinching techniques learned in childhood, and traditionally passed from mother to daughter. Pottery was seen as a female occupation in Africa at this time. She developed and refined skills in using building techniques, alongside detailed decoration, with an instinctive sense of shape and its relationship to the surface decoration. Her work was seen by Cardew as having exceptional qualities, being both beautifully thought out and made, as well as extremely strong and functional. Her vessels were made in the traditions of African pottery for the home.

Kwali's functional ceramics corresponded to ideas in Europe about the craft of the potter and interest in localised potteries and makers. Kwali's use of **celadon glaze** also inspired Cardew and others to pursue similar ways of working in their own ceramics. Kwali had fired her work in traditional grass and wood firings in the open. Her firing techniques developed with her understanding of glazes and firing kilns. She referenced her heritage in using sgraffito, inlay and mark-making ideas from African culture. Her work influenced the idea that ceramics could represent a maker's cultural heritage and interests.

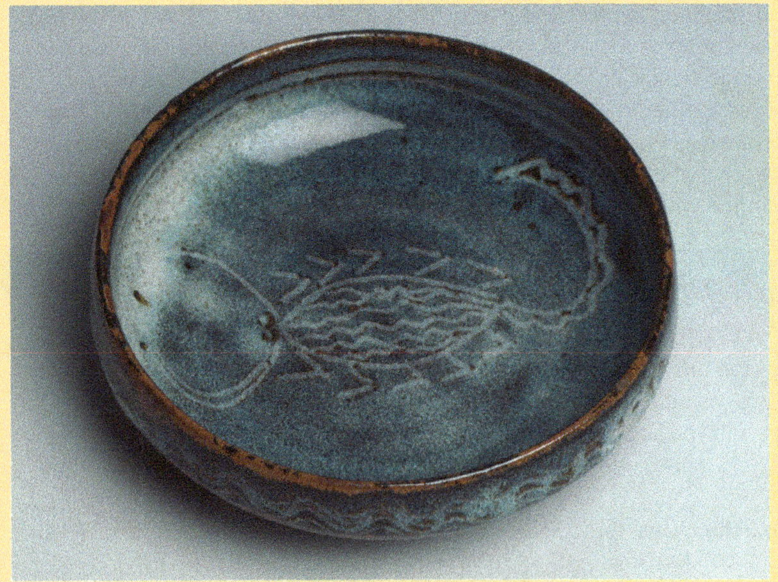

3.144 Ladi Kwali, Stoneware dish with an incised scorpion design, from about 1960. Kwali developed work that used a blend of African and Western forms and surface decoration.

REFINING WORK – USING DRAWINGS

Ceramicists will often make drawings that show different ideas for forms and decoration. These are likely to be linear with minimal shading, as they will develop their ideas further as they begin to work in three dimensions with maquettes. Drawings may often be annotated with ideas and references to possible surface decoration.

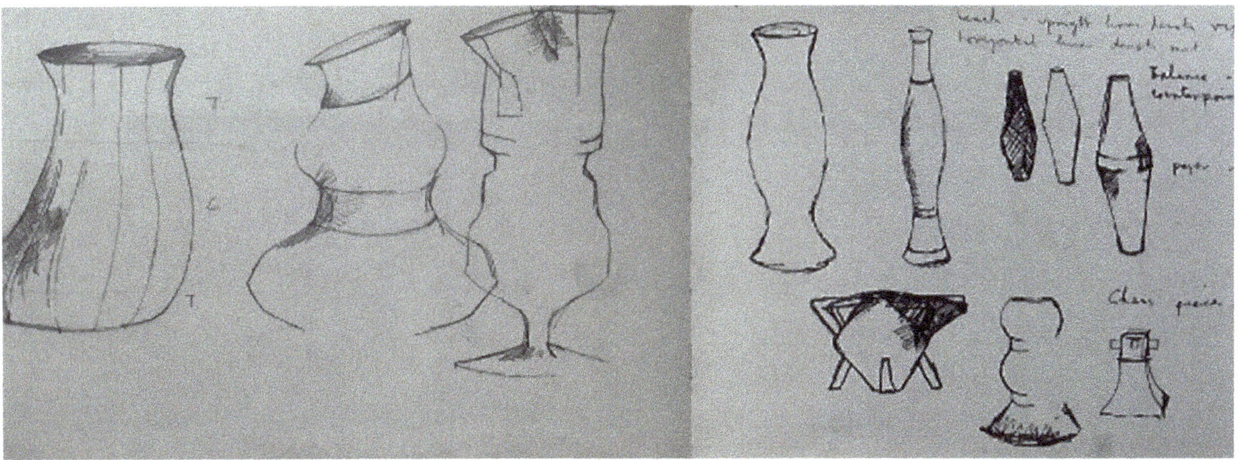

3.145 Alan Parsons, sketchbook page, drawings for ceramic forms, 1999. A quickly drawn double spread of visualisations of potential shapes and forms.

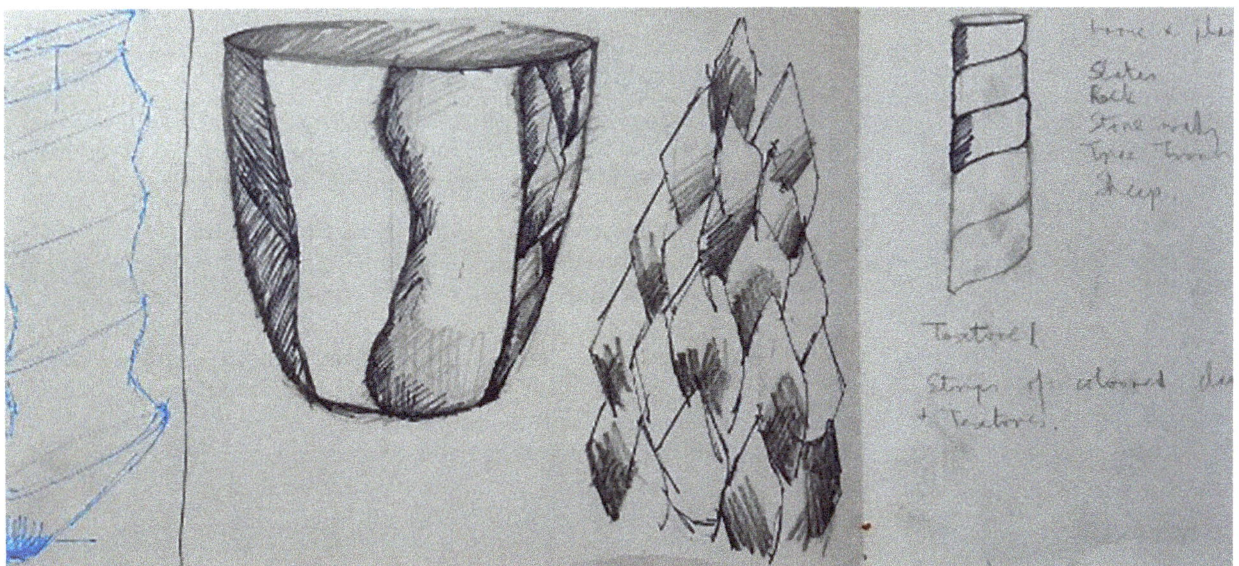

3.146 Alan Parsons, sketchbook page, drawings for ceramic forms, 1999. A quickly drawn double spread of visualisations of potential shapes and forms.

celadon glaze Pottery glazed with jade green celadon colour, also transparent glaze, often with small cracks.

DEVELOPING AND REFINING – MAQUETTES

Ceramicists will use maquettes to develop their ideas about glaze surface decoration, textures and glazes. This way of working can help them understand how their work is progressing by providing visual examples of glaze testing and sampling. They can also use this process to test out firing temperatures and how these affect their choice of glazes.

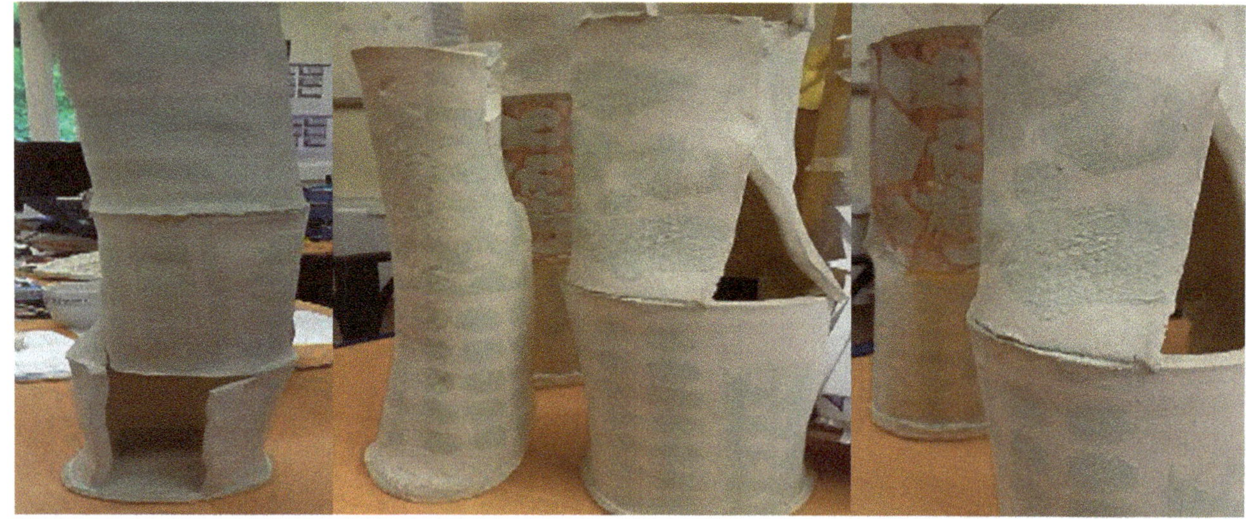

3.147 Alan Parsons, *Towers*, clay maquettes, once fired, with screen-printed slip decoration, 2007. These maquettes were used as test pieces for once firing, and to see how the screen-printed slip decoration would react to matt transparent glazes.

TECHNIQUES FOR GLAZING

You can develop your work with glazes by trying out different techniques for applying them on maquettes. You can then use the results to select techniques to achieve the surface decoration you require. Some techniques are:

- painting, dabbing or sponging underglazes, added pre-biscuit firing, onto wet to leather-hard clay
- using a **slip trailer**, printmaking or hand painting to apply slips
- brushing or sponging oxides in water onto surface of leather-hard and/or biscuit-fired pottery and wiping away; suited to picking up texture details
- hand painting or printing enamels to bring colour and detail to a background glaze surface
- pouring, dipping or spraying glazes onto biscuit-fired work.

Materials and techniques: **Make a ceramic form with glazes**

Design and make a ceramic form that uses a specific set or combinations of glazes in its surface decoration; you can get ideas for this from ceramic traditions in your local area, or from international ceramics if you prefer.

- To get you going on this, research and decide whether you will use ceramics in your local area or country, or international ceramics, as your source.
- Make drawings of the kind of forms and decoration that inspire you.
- Develop a design for a single ceramic form.
- Design a surface decoration for the form that explores different glazes and techniques.
- Make a maquette based on your form that you can use to test ideas for kiln-fired glazes.
- Test glazes on the maquette – be sure to note the full details about the glaze (you can get information on the glaze composition from the manufacturer's website, or your centre or school technician).
- Develop and refine your ideas and the results of the glaze samples, and produce a final piece.

Critical thinking:

Display your work on ceramic form and glazes. Evaluate the work, thinking specifically about:

- your use of drawings
- the balance between surface decoration and form/shape
- how well you used maquettes, and what these told you
- your use of building and glazing techniques
- how you could develop and refine your glaze techniques further.

Further research

You can find out more about contemporary and historical international ceramics, including resources and case studies, by visiting the *Ceramic Review* website.

For more about Picasso's ceramics, go to the Masterworks Fine Art website.

Find out more about the history of Nigerian ceramics and Ladi Kwali online.

slip trailer Tool used for dripping, drawing with/or running a line of slip across pottery surface.

Module 4

Audience and setting

4.0 Introduction

This module aims to develop your understanding of how and where art and design is presented and communicated to audiences. It will introduce you to:

- the methods used to present art and design work, and show how these are adapted according to the specific needs of the audience or users
- the relationship between audience and **setting**, through considering the different examples
- recognising audience needs and requirements when planning your practical work
- presentation methods, providing you with a basis to make your own decisions about the best way to present your work.

AUDIENCES

We have looked at how artists and designers are influenced by contextual factors in Module 2. Audiences are also influenced by the contextual factors of their time. Much contemporary fine art involves the audience in reading or interpreting signs and symbols in fine art work. Most galleries have information available to support this process. This might be in

- printed information and introductions in each gallery room
- video-based statements
- audio aids
- catalogues.

Work made in design areas of study is a mixture of the designer's own creative ideas and a solution to the target audience or users' needs. To solve these creative problems, the designer needs to be aware of their target audience's demographic and aspirations. We are all generally familiar with technology in our daily lives, from computers, tablets and phones that we use to share information and follow events in the world. Designers understand this and use technology as a way of connecting with their audience, through using:

- websites
- interactive design using technology
- apps.

Let us look at how art and design was traditionally presented.

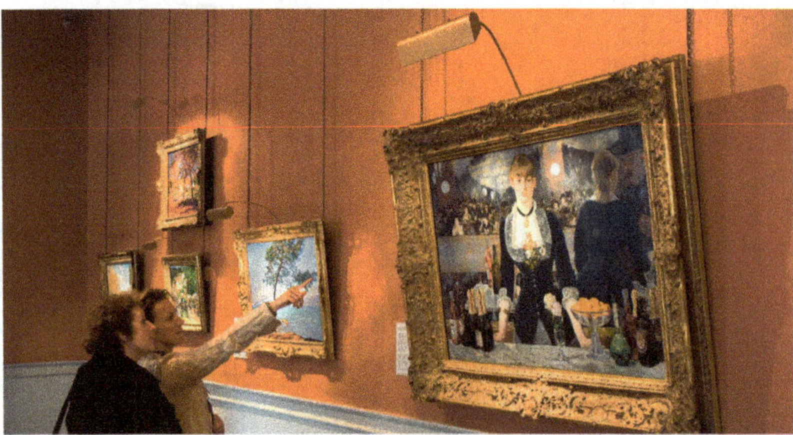

4.1 Courtauld Gallery, Impressionist and Post-Impressionist paintings, London. Traditionally, major art exhibitions were arranged formally. This painting by Édouard Manet, *A Bar at the Folies-Bergère*, 1882, has a picture light included in its ornate gilded frame.

Exhibition design

Exhibition design is another branch of design, and these designers have to be extremely aware of the evolving needs and requirements of audiences. They aim to develop displays and presentations that fully engage the audience in the exhibitions, through interesting uses of space, information and technology. Figure 4.2 shows a different way that audiences can become involved with a painting. Post-Impressionist paintings by Paul Cézanne have been transformed by technology into a multi-faceted exhibition piece. Cézanne's portraits were made much smaller than these projections. Technology has been used to enlarge sections of paintings, and create an **immersive** environment. This is very different from people crowding around a single painting, taking it in turns before they move onto the next one, as if in a procession. What benefits do you think the example in Figure 4.2 offers to the audience? Can you list these?

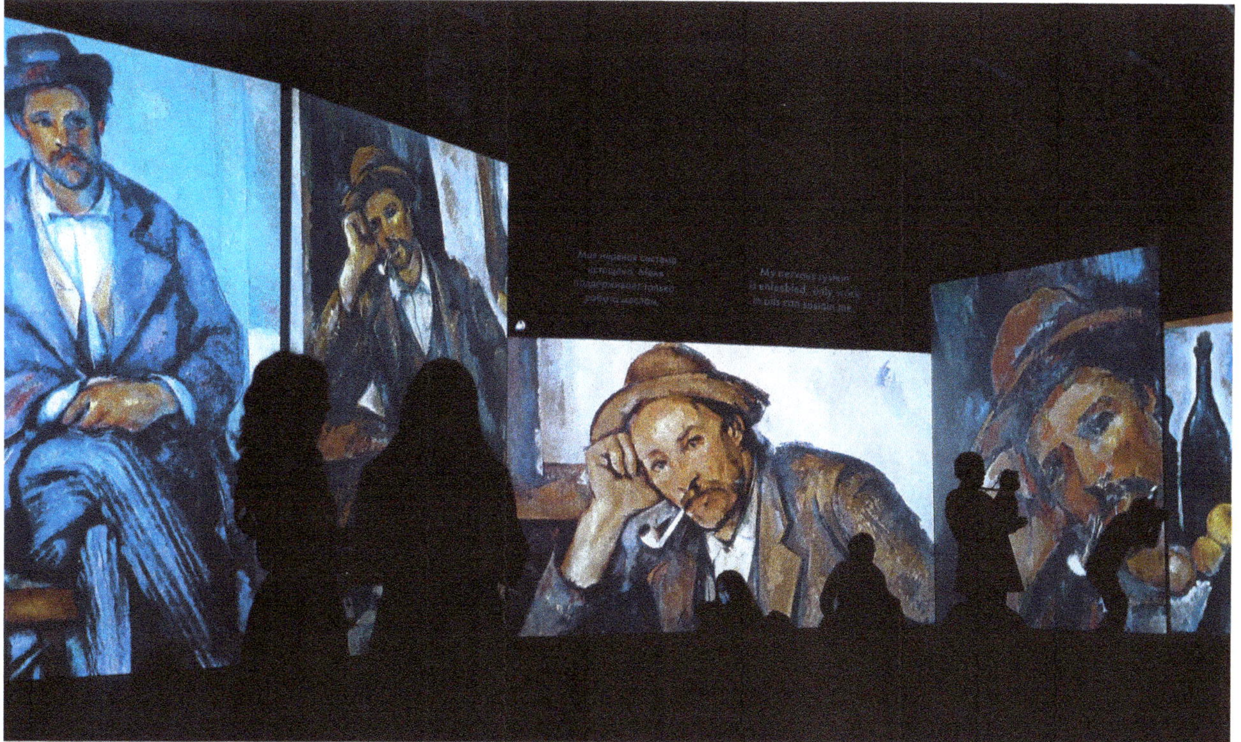

4.2 Exhibition, 'The French Impressionists - From Monet to Cézanne', Artplay Design Centre, Moscow, Russia, 2015. Post-Impressionist paintings seen in a new way: viewers interact with larger-scale projected images of paintings, showing details of the works, such as brush marks, close-up.

Activity A: **Comparing exhibitions**

Find at least two exhibitions in your local area, town, city or location. Visit the exhibitions and make notes on how they function. Ask the following questions:

1. How is the exhibition arranged and set out – traditional, non-traditional?
2. How is information about the exhibits displayed?
3. Is technology used to support or deliver parts of the exhibition?
4. If so, for what specific purpose is it used?
5. If not, could they have used it to improve the exhibition?
6. In your opinion, which exhibition works the best? Why?

immersive Providing an experience for all the senses.
setting In this module, setting can mean the physical setting, as in a gallery, or the context, such as a design brief.

Developing audience involvement

Audiences can become involved in the way that museums and galleries present their work, influencing the way this happens. To do this, museums and galleries have to collect the views of the audience. In 2015, the Museum of Modern Art (MoMA) in New York asked visitors to complete a sentence on a piece of paper 'I went to MoMA and …' These were posted into a collection box and the results were automatically scanned, and recorded by the museum.

Curators have realised they have to engage with their public and use their views to inform the way their exhibition involves audiences. This kind of **feedback loop** helps plan for future exhibitions, and where to allocate resources. For example, they may find that their audience does not use printed materials in guide forms, preferring audio aids. They can use this information to redirect resources, and improve the audience experience in their exhibitions.

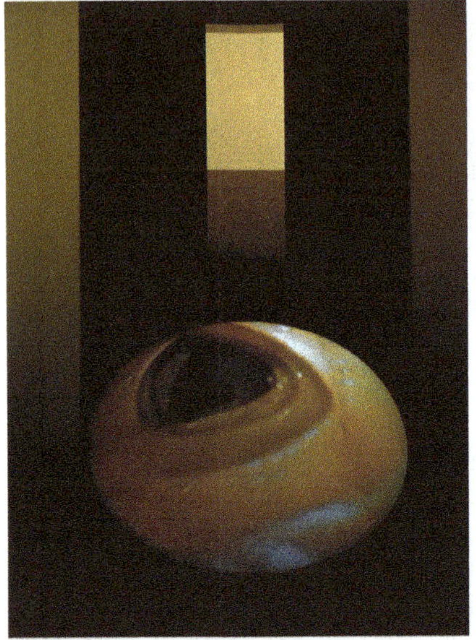

4.3 Mona Hatoum, *Corps étranger*, 1994, Video installation with cylindrical wooden structure, video projector and player, amplifier and four speakers, 350 × 300 × 300 cm, Installation view at Centre Pompidou, Paris. Viewers are forced to interact with the space used as part of the creative process. This is a very deliberate part of the way this work was made.

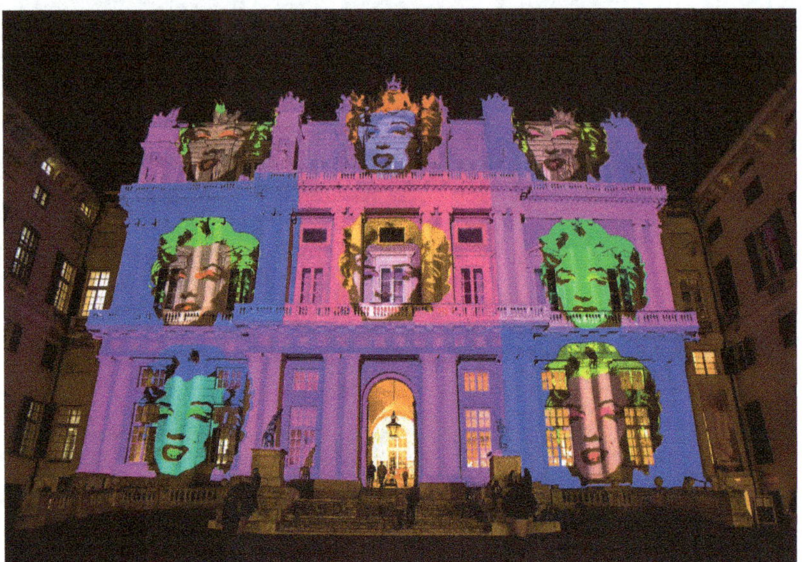

4.4 Projection can take imagery into a new format and present it in a new way, as in the iconic Marilyn imagery projected onto the façade of the Palazzo Ducale, Genoa, Italy, in 2016. Projection technology offers exhibition designers the chance to explore ways of showing work that takes art and design out of normal gallery spaces.

Activity B: **Create a mind map of audience or user needs**

In groups of three, discuss audience or user needs for an exhibition of contemporary work in your area of study.

1. What sort of exhibits would you imagine there to be in the exhibition?
2. What would visitors to the exhibition need to see?
3. How would these be displayed or presented?
4. Would you need to plan to use any technology to assist your presentation?
5. Write this up on a sheet of A1 paper, and present back to your classmates.

THE SETTING

Exploring the setting in art-based work – physical space

Different artists explore settings for their artwork. They do this through using a specific space as part of the creative piece, as in installations where the viewer's experience is controlled to some degree by their proximity to the piece, or involvement in it by being forced to stand or sit in certain place.

Installation art specifically uses the involvement of the audience in where they are placed. In the video *The Viewer*, 1996, by the American artist Gary Hill (born 1951), a line of projected figures confronts the gallery audience in a set space. See Figure 4.5. How does the audience react to this image?

- The natural tendency for the audience visiting this space is to line up opposite the projected images.
- These figures are from a cross-section of society, and wear a variety of different types of clothing.
- This creates a mirror-imaging-type situation.
- The audience viewer stares across at the opposite projected figure, which is mostly still, and then suddenly moves or shuffles their feet.

This artwork seems to be asking the audience who exactly is viewing whom here, exploring aspects such as eye contact and the action of **mirroring**. This is when the person opposite you unconsciously mimics your pose or stance.

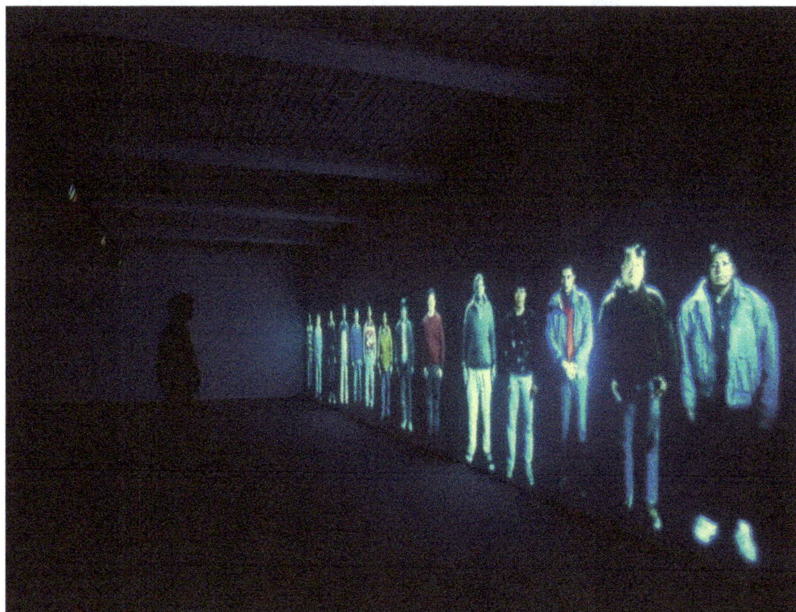

4.5 Gary Hill, *The Viewer*, 1996, five-channel video installation, silent. A video installation that explores mirroring, and the role of the subject and audience. As a viewer standing in front of this, you could ask 'Who exactly is looking at whom?'

feedback loop Process of sourcing feedback from users, collating information and using it to inform and modify the way the audience experience is delivered; its impact can be tested by running the feedback exercise again.

mirroring Term used in psychology, where one human mirrors or reflects back the speech, posture or gestures of another. Mirroring is sometimes seen as a form of empathy between people.

Exploring the setting in art-based work – environment

Other artists explore the relationship of a space by using it as a backdrop for an event involving the audience. In Figure 4.6, Japanese artist Fujiko Nakaya's (born 1933) *London Fog*, installation is created with water vapour. This is an example of an immersive sculpture, where the audience is immersed into a sensory experience involving sight, soundscapes, temperature and water vapour. All of this happens against a backdrop of city buildings. What sort of message do you think Nakaya wants to communicate to her audience in this work? Discuss this with a friend and summarise what you think she is trying to get her work to say.

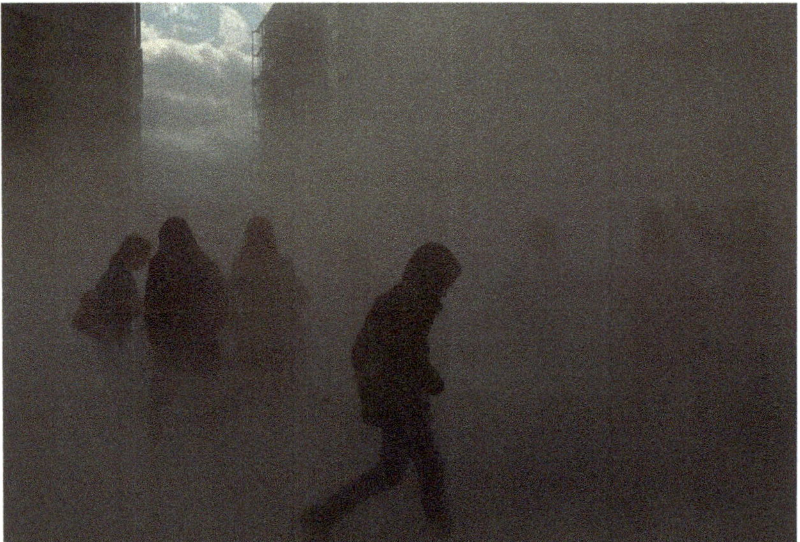

4.6 Fujiko Nakaya, *London Fog*, 2017, on the South Terrace of Tate Modern's Switch House, London. This is presenting artwork that pushes the boundaries for viewer experience of art installations. This work involves steam in an exterior location.

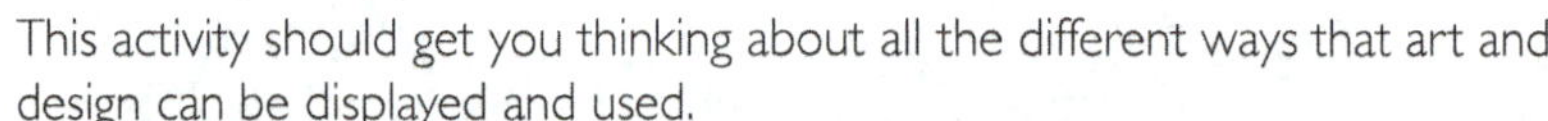

Activity C: **List as many settings and contexts as you can**

This activity should get you thinking about all the different ways that art and design can be displayed and used.

1. Work in pairs and make headings for all the different art and design areas within your chosen area of study. For example, if you are working in fine art, you should list drawing, painting, photography and so on.
2. Then list as many examples as possible of how each of these areas is communicated, such as:
   - galleries
   - museums
   - magazines (and so on).
3. If you are working in a design area of study, for example, graphic communication, list all the areas (typography, illustration and so on) and then list examples of the contexts these are used in, such as:
   - printed materials
   - web-based work
   - signs and so on.

Exploring the setting in design-based work – technology and interactivity

Designers have to consider how their audience will use technology when thinking about the setting or context for a brief. This is particularly important when it is part of the brief, as in games design or design for the web, because:

- These applications rely on how well the user can interact with the technology used in the design.
- Developments in smart phones and virtual reality technology are allowing more users to engage with this type of experience, in virtual platforms from education to entertainment.
- These have the potential to become part of the audience experience in exhibitions.

A design idea in this field has to take into account the audience and the users' requirements to be truly fit for purpose. Have you ever tried to use an app or website that was difficult to navigate? If so, you will know how much of a negative effect this has on a user's perception. In fact, they may avoid using it in the future if it is too difficult to manage.

Artists and designers are making use of the potential in technology to assist in the interactive experience and provide information as they create specific exhibitions.

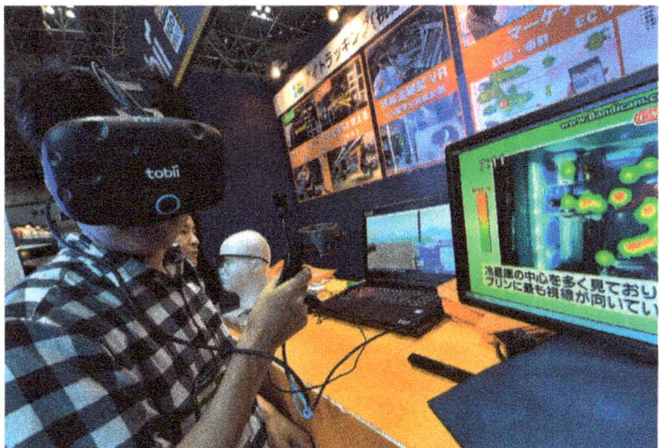

4.7 'Advanced Content Technology Expo', exhibition featuring innovations in gaming and interactive technology, Japan, 2017. This shows technology at the heart of gaming development, used to present work to the audience and also shows users how they will engage with the product.

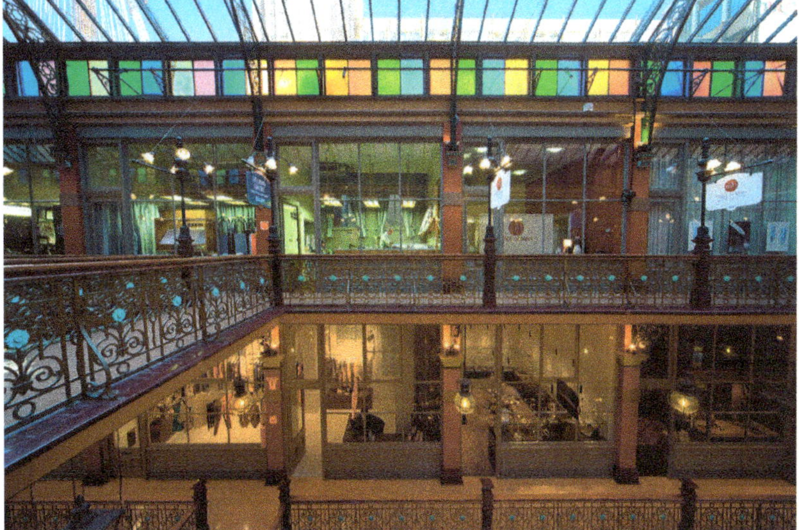

4.8 Traditional shirt-maker and designer fashion shops, The Strand Arcade, Sydney, New South Wales, Australia. Designers will be planning to engage with their audience through retail outlets such as the designer shops shown here.

Activity D: **Collecting information on users' needs**

Designers use information on demographics and target audiences to inform their design process. You are going to conduct a user focus group. The aim of this group is to collect information on what users think the next generation of smart phones should be able to do.

1. Work in a small group of five or six people.
2. Ask each member of the focus group to explain how they use their phone, specifically how much time for communicating by spoken voice, how much by text, how much watching videos and so on.
3. Ask them to try to guess these roughly as a percentage of the total time they use their phone.
4. Collate the results and see whether there are any patterns emerging. You can also average out the results to get a rough usage figure.
5. Now ask them what would they want a future model smart phone to be able to do. This should be a discussion, and you can make notes as you go along. It may be that the conclusion is 'nothing else', in which case what would be the message back to the designers and product developers?

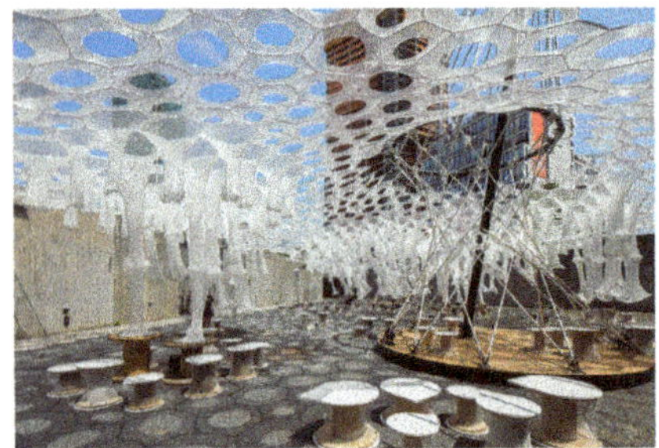

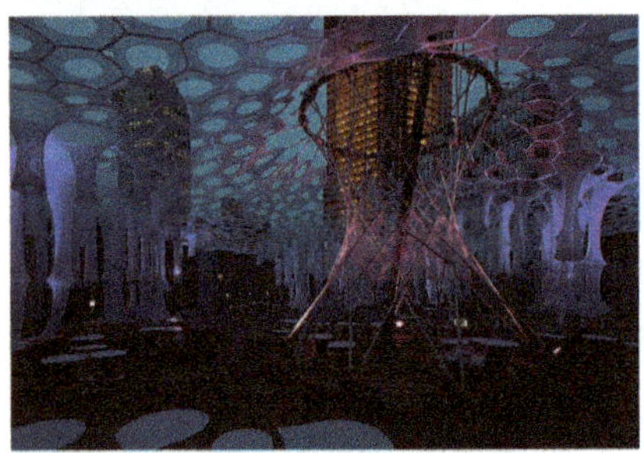

4.10 Jenny Sabin Studio, *Lumen*, 2017, digital knitted and woven fibres, Responsive textiles installation, MoMA, PS1, Long Island City, New York. Textiles-based installation that evolves and changes according to light conditions. Some contemporary work explores an idea or theme with an audience as it changes.

PLANNING PRACTICAL PROJECT WORK: REACHING OUT TO THE AUDIENCE

We have looked at how exhibition and setting can be designed as an integral part of the audience experience when experiencing art and design work. Artists and designers also have to consider the audience when they plan and make their work.

You need to consider your audience when you are planning your work. It can be exciting to begin working quickly; however, it is worth spending some time thinking about how you are working, and whether this is the right method to connect to your audience. You may not be able to communicate your intention clearly if you have not thought this part through. There are different ways that you should consider your audience when planning, for example:

- *Intention or purpose of the work:* This is your own intention, and that of any client.
- *Format:* Are you working to a format that suits the intention and audience needs?
- *Audience:* Who are they, and what are their needs?
- *Communication:* Is there any specific message that you or the client want to communicate?
- *Materials, techniques and processes:* Which ones will you use, and how does this choice suit the audience?

Format

When you choose a format to work with, you should consider how it fits your intentions, the setting you will show the work on, and your audience's needs. Artists and designers who want to explore narrative in their work should understand which format works best for this. Sometimes this can be achieved through the use of single images.

However, much art and design work explores the potential that a series of images can have, for example, documentary photographic recording of an event. A series of images can also help to create a narrative that is more connected to storytelling than to social or documentary purposes.

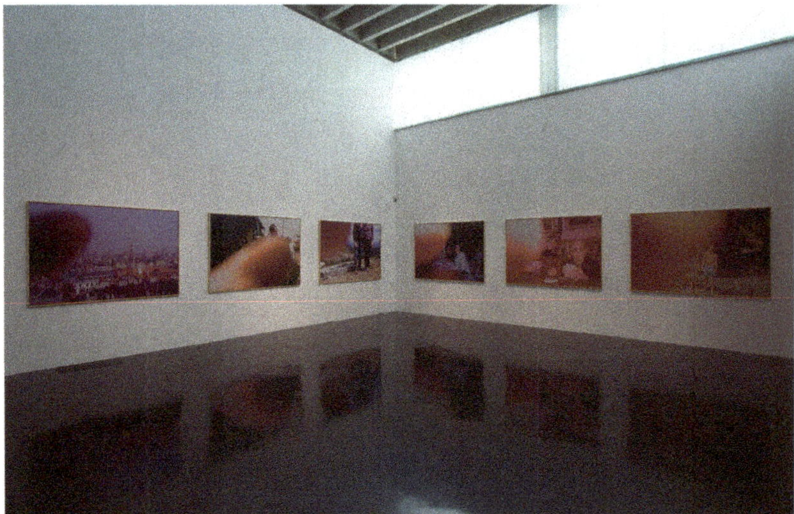

4.9 Erik Kessels, *In almost every picture #13*, at the FOUND exhibition, 2015, The New Art Gallery, Walsall, UK. Some practitioners present imagery as part of a series. This allows the audience to see a larger set of related work that explores a theme, such as documentary.

Activity E: A commissioned contemporary work

Work individually on this task. You have been asked to produce a piece of commissioned contemporary work in your area of study. As it is commissioned, it will involve a client (this is the audience or intended user). Plan your response, considering the following:

- How will you find out the needs or requirements of your users or audience?
- Can you define the setting and/or context?
- How would you use this information in the creative process?
- How could you tell whether you have successfully met their needs or requirements?

Scale

It is important to work to a scale that will help you communicate your idea to your audience. For instance:

- If you were planning a set of detailed portraits made from life, you would have to make sure the size of the paper, canvas or board was suitable for this type of work. This would enable you to complete your work to its full potential, and communicate this detailed work to your audience.
- However, you might want to create bigger portraits with large-scale texture and mark-making, to communicate an idea about how paint can be expressive. In this case, a small scale would not work; it would be the wrong size for your intention, and would not communicate to your audience.
- If you were developing an idea in product design or 3D ceramics, you would need to make sure that the scale was suited to the building or construction methods you intend to use.

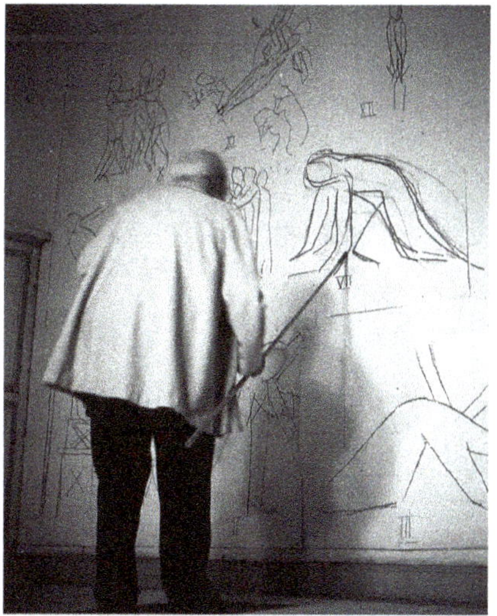

4.11 Henri Matisse, designs for decoration of Chapelle du Rosaire de Vence, 1947–51. You can see here how Matisse is developing ideas by working on preliminary work that explores the scale of the final pieces.

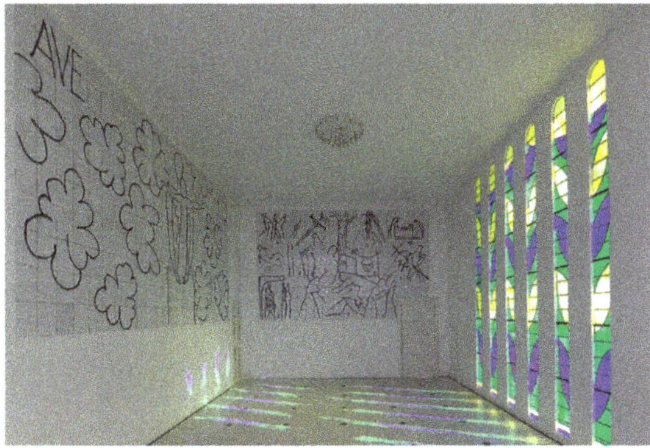

4.12 Henri Matisse, Decoration, Chapelle du Rosaire de Vence, 1951, stained glass windows and wall decoration. This image shows designs developed from preliminary work in Figure 4.11, realised in the finished building.

Clarifying your intention

This should be an integral part of your planning phase for your assignments and projects. It should state what it is you want to achieve. It might not say exactly what your work will look like, or how you will achieve it. That is the bit you are going to be working on. Having a clear intention makes you focus on what it is you are trying to communicate to your audience. These can be seen in Artists' Statements, which are covered on pages 234 and 235.

Choosing materials, techniques and processes

Your choice of these will also need to be linked to your intention, the proposed setting or context for the brief, and what it is you want to communicate to your audience. If we look at the portrait example we used above:

- You want to produce intricate, small-scale portraits.
- You would choose techniques and materials suited to working this scale, such as:
  - small brushes
  - acrylic or oils in glazes and so on.
- Alternatively, if you wished to explore mark-making in larger portraits, you would use materials such as:
  - larger brushes and scraper tools
  - acrylic or other water-based paints, such as emulsion.

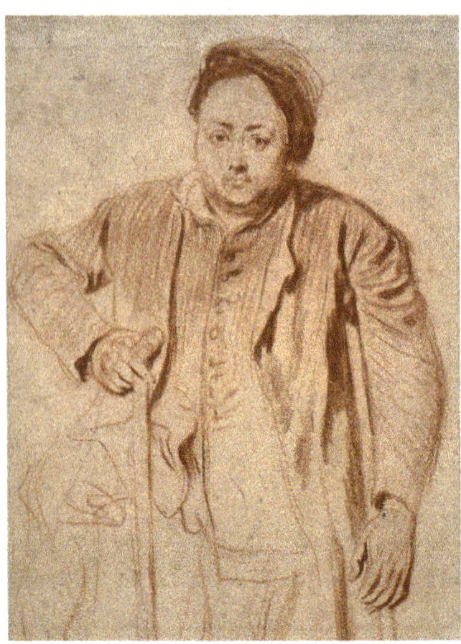

4.13 Jean Antoine Watteau, *Portrait of Antoine de la Roque*, undated, red chalk on paper, Fitzwilliam Museum, Cambridge. Artists and designers can present visual recording in drawings and studies as part of their working practice.

PRESENTATION METHODS

In this section, we will look at the methods and techniques you can use to present your work. Firstly, we need to clarify the different types of work that you can present.

- *Research:* this may be folder-based or annotated sketchbook work, downloads, screenshots.
- *Ideas generation:* this may be mind maps, rough sketches, thumbnail drawings, text.
- *Visual recording:* this may be any mixture of drawing, painting, photography, frottage and so on.
- *Exploration and experimental work:* this may be studies, samples, mock-ups, tests, digital files, test shoots.
- *Refinement:* examples showing how you have refined the idea, techniques and so on.
- *Outcome:* your final piece or pieces in response to an assignment.
- *Information:* this may be statements, screenshots, annotation, conclusions.

Selecting work

The first stage in presenting work is to select the examples that you want to show. This will depend on the setting and context you are presenting in. For example:

- If this is a critique in mid-assignment, you may want to show a whole selection of developmental work, such as:
  - research
  - visual recording
  - ideas generation.
- Alternatively, it may be at the end of an assignment, when you will need to make a selection of work across a wider range of stages and examples in your creative process.
- To do this, you need to understand how you can use work to explain how you have worked through the project.

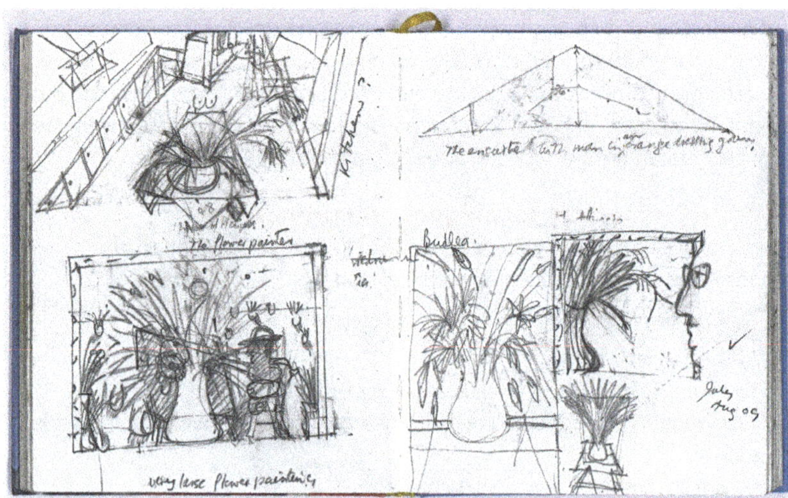

4.14 Anthony Green, *Page from a sketchbook*, 2009, pencil on paper, private collection. You may find it useful to present sketchbook pages as part of your preparatory work, if in a mid-assignment critique, or as part of a **portfolio** of images at the end of a project.

Activity F: **Making a selection**

Work individually on this task. Use an assignment you have already worked on.

1. Take all the work you provided for the developmental or preparatory stage and make a selection to support a verbal presentation where you will be explaining:
   - how you worked on the research
   - your ideas generation
   - your visual recording stages.
2. Pin these up and present back to your classmates. Ask them to give you feedback on how well your selection of images supported your explanation.

Creating a presentation board

When you are mounting work, you may find you need to present a sheet that is a collage of smaller images. This might be to make up one of your sheets showing your supporting studies of the externally set assignment, or it could also be a process for your coursework portfolio submission. You may have a set of smaller images that would work better as one sheet. It helps to be aware of the following points:

- It is a composition – you need to arrange the smaller images to achieve a balanced overall image. This is a bit like arranging sections of a design or painting – the same rules apply.
- Keep the work clean, and cut any edges cleanly.
- Add text if you need to – this might be a title for the page. This can be used to explain the purpose of the sheet to your audience.

You might also use this technique to show studies of a single subject, made with different materials. Alternatively, you may have explored different illustration ideas that work best mounted on one A2 sheet. It is also an effective way to mount samples and test pieces, such as fabric or printed imagery from textiles or fashion.

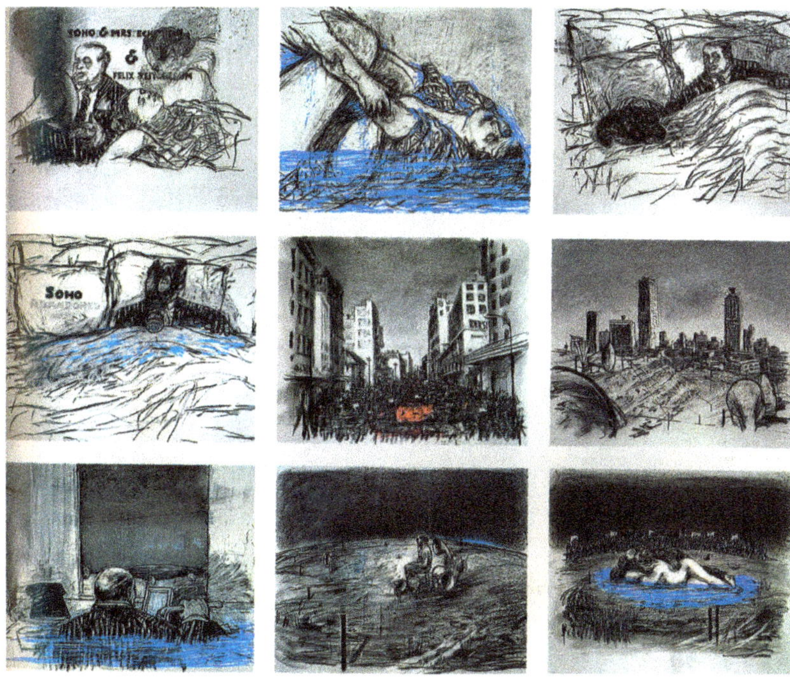

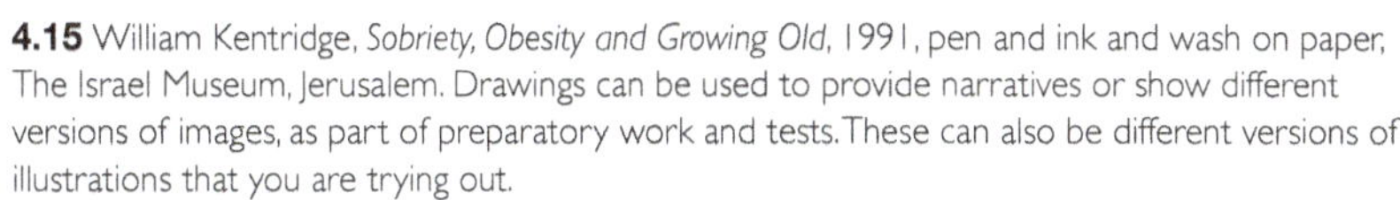

4.15 William Kentridge, *Sobriety, Obesity and Growing Old*, 1991, pen and ink and wash on paper, The Israel Museum, Jerusalem. Drawings can be used to provide narratives or show different versions of images, as part of preparatory work and tests. These can also be different versions of illustrations that you are trying out.

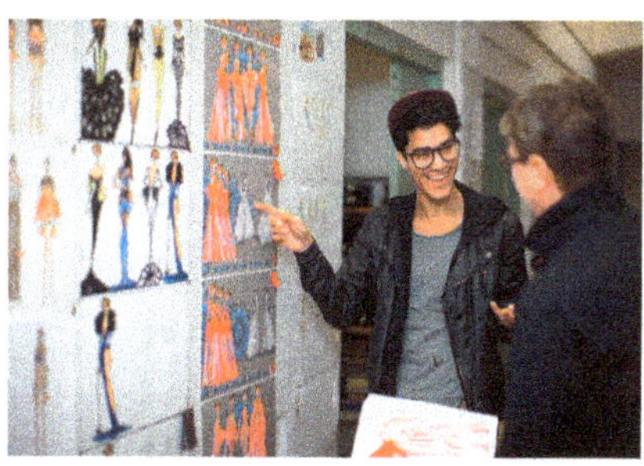

4.16 Fashion work and presentation. Ideas and responses to users' needs and contexts can be presented and discussed at critiques.

Critiques

Critiques are one way to engage directly with your audience. In critiques, you present your work back to an audience in an informal setting. This is a different kind of presentation to that used in a formal lecture. You will be asked to explain your work, including your preparatory stages. You may decide to hold up sketchbook pages to support your explanation. Once you have finished, your audience is invited to contribute by commenting on the work. This can develop into a question and answer session.

Materials and techniques: **Digital techniques**

You can use digital techniques to make a presentation sheet. These can be set up in software in a grid format to allow you to reposition images until you have a balanced sheet. Remember that you can only output this to the size of printing in your school or centre, unless you want to send it to print externally.

portfolio A selection of final pieces of work for an examiner or tutor to see.

Mounting work

The purpose of mounting work is to make it look more finished and professional. Mounting also makes it stand out from its surroundings, as with framing. Mounting can also protect work to some degree. You can use different-coloured mounts and frames to make your work stand out.

Remember, your final work must be bound and packaged securely, as it will be sent to Cambridge, in the UK, for final assessment. It may not be possible to mount and present work in certain ways due to this requirement. However, it is good to know how you can mount and present work as long as you bear this final packaging in mind.

So how should you mount work?

> **Tip:**
>
> When you measure for the position of your mount, make sure that you measure accurately. A useful maxim is 'measure twice, cut once'. This means that you should check your measurements twice before cutting the mount.
>
> You can also experiment with leaving a larger gap at the bottom of the mount compared to the top. This makes the image sit nicely on the mount.

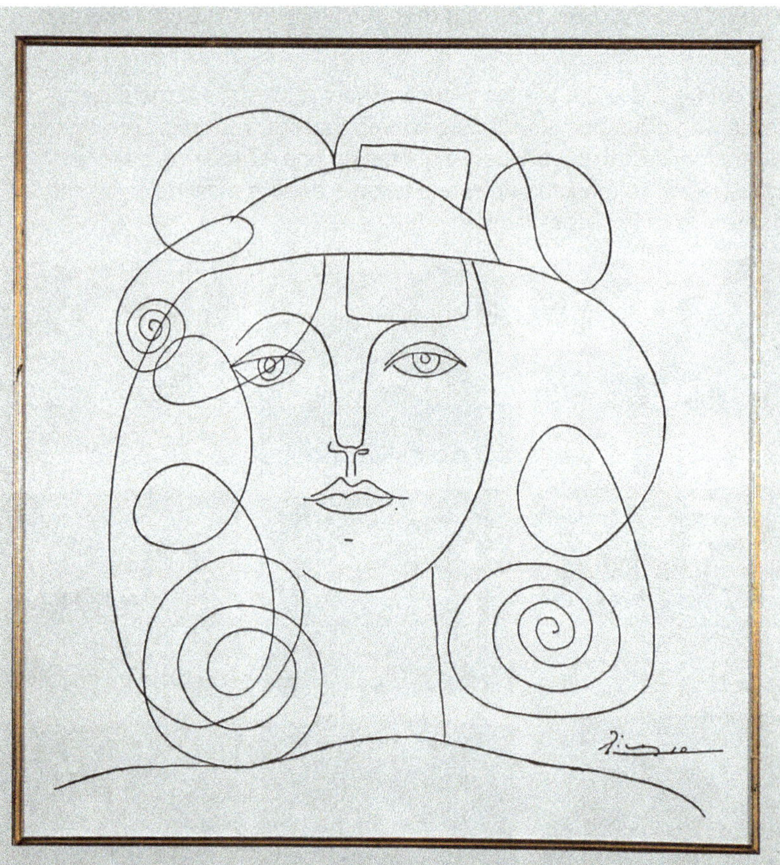

4.17 Pablo Picasso, *Head of Girl*, c.1950, lithographic print, private collection. Simple framing techniques can enhance images. Here, the drawing by Picasso is simply framed by a gold border. This can be a frame or a mount.

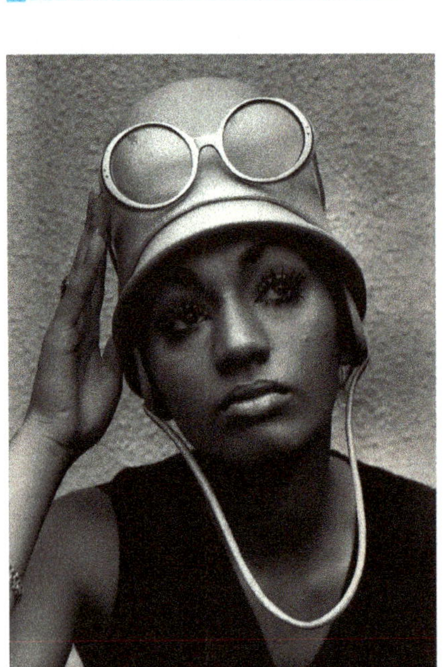

4.18 Japanese millinery, model wearing straw motoring hat, Tokyo, 2012. You can present examples of work such as fashion accessories by photographing the object as it would be worn, as in this instance. This is particularly useful in fashion- and accessories-related work.

The example in Figure 4.17 shows an example of a simple frame around an image. We can analyse how the surrounding frame has worked in making the image stronger:

- The image itself is made in line, so might get overpowered by a more colourful piece if put next to it in a display.
- It might a not stand out enough from its background, and be overlooked if left unframed.
- The contrasting surround works to show the image effectively.

Framing work

You can frame 2D work for exhibitions in galleries. This is matter of practicality and choice. For example:

- Some exhibitions require work to be framed, so the organisers know that it will be protected, as in drawing competitions.
- Some artists prefer not to frame paintings; they neatly paint the edges of their canvases a neutral colour like a pale grey or white, as in Figure 4.20.

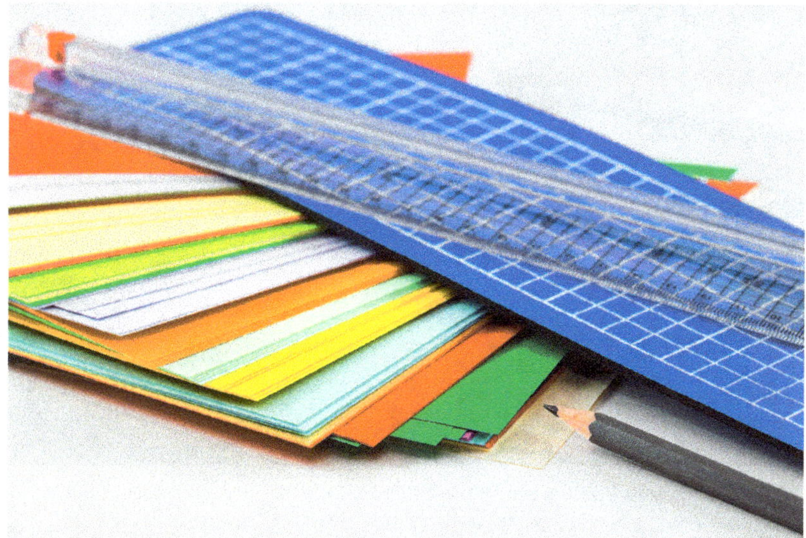

4.19 Use the right tools, as in cutting mats and guides, when mounting with card.

4.20 You can frame art and design work or, in the case of stretchers, just paint the edge of the stretcher a neutral colour when you have finished the painting.

Using peers as the audience

As you plan your selection and framing of work, think about what it is you want to communicate. You may find it easier to use your classmates to help you decide what to put up to communicate an idea, especially in projects you work on earlier in your course. For instance, if you are presenting midpoint about your progress, you may be unsure of which pieces of work you should show. The process of selecting and framing images for a mid-project critique can help you understand what has gone well, and what needs further development. You can ask your classmates for their views about the work you select. Is it showing your development off well?

Tip:

Always make sure that you have the right tools with you when mounting and getting your work ready for presentations – it will save you a lot of time in the long run to be prepared.

> **Tip:**
>
> Practice makes perfect. Using software is a skill, and like any skill you can improve with practice. Work on using image editing software to help you produce presentation-ready images of your work. Key tools and settings to control are exposure, contrast and curves or levels.

Photographing work

You can use photography to record examples of 3D work for your portfolio or presentation to an audience. You can see a simple lighting diagram in Figure 4.21.

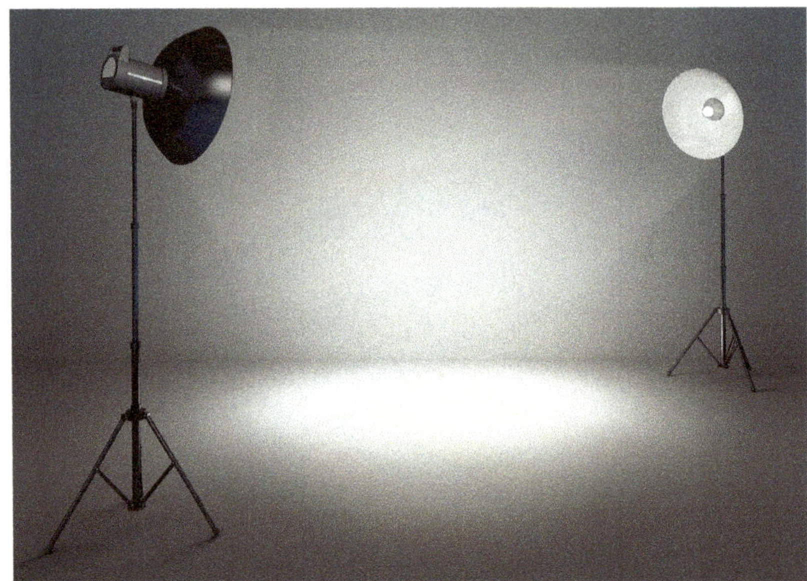

4.21 Basic photographic set-up, two lights in a studio. You can use a very simple set-up in a studio if you can access this. Alternatively, you can use a room well-lit with daylight.

Backgrounds

If you are photographing 3D work, remember that you need to plan the background to the photographs. You may need to spend some time setting this up by finding the right venue. It is worth doing this; the reaction you receive from the audience will be based on the kind of images you show them. The image in Figure 4.22 shows an example of 3D work that is well photographed.

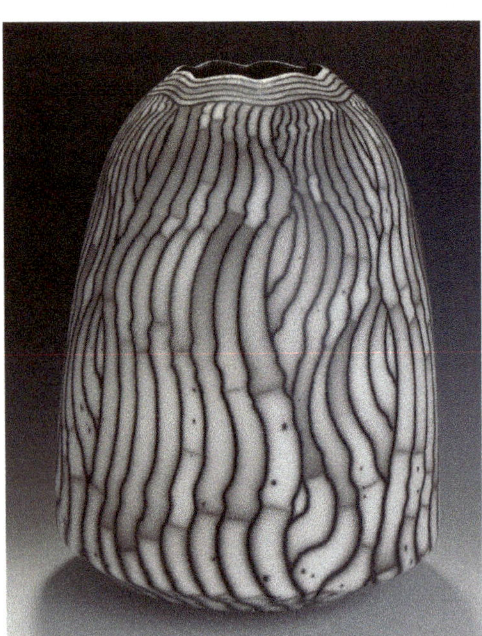

4.22 David Roberts, *Weeping Landscape*, 2011, coil built and raku fired ceramic. You should aim to take photographs that pick out the details of your 3D work, such as colour and form. This photograph effectively records shape and surface detail in a ceramic work.

Activity G: **Editing images**

Work individually on this task. Use a photograph you have already of a piece of your work. Note: only printed photographs can be submitted for assessment – no digital files.

1. Take the image and use it to explore tools in the image editing software in your school or centre, exploring the following:
   a. cropping
   b. exposure
   c. contrast.
2. Save the final edited file, print it and present it to your classmates. Ask them to give you feedback on how well you used the software editing tools to improve the image. Is it ready to be used in a presentation?

Critical thinking:

Think about the activities in this introduction. Write a short report on what you have learned about understanding the audience, settings for displays and presentation techniques.

Further research

Research online to find out more about presentation techniques and critiques.

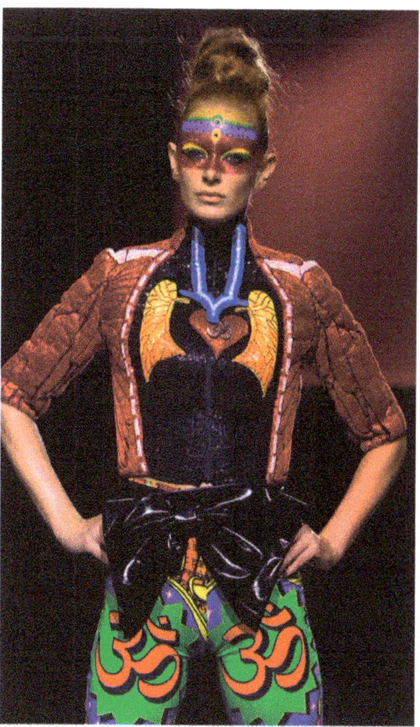

4.23 Manish Arora, Fashion Show retrospective, Victoria and Albert Museum, London, 2007. Some design work can use textual cultural elements in its visual design. This can reference influences behind the work, to communicate to an audience, as in this fashion example. You can plan how your work will communicate cultural ideas.

You are reminded that there are two elements to the Personal Investigation:

- the written analysis, which must be in **continuous prose** and contain detailed research
- the practical work.

The written analysis *must* support and link to the practical work.

WRITING UP YOUR RESEARCH

Having completed the research for your Personal Investigation, you must finalise and present the written analysis. The written analysis should be planned carefully. There should be three main sections:

1. It must start with a *short introduction*, where you:
   - set the context
   - make links to the wider practical project
   - explore a personal response through to an informed conclusion.
2. The *main section of the study* is where you discuss, analyse and compare the artworks that you have researched.
3. You need to end the written analysis with a *short conclusion*, where you:
   - summarise what you have covered
   - draw out your main ideas
   - realise intentions to a personal response.

In addition, you must include a bibliography, covering all your main sources of information – books, articles, websites and so on.

There is a word count of between 1000 and 1500 words for the written analysis. If you exceed this word count slightly, it will not be a problem. However, if you are significantly over the 1500-word limit, go back and revise what you have written. Try taking out any unnecessary information from second-hand sources and any lengthy biographical information about artists or designers. Remember to be concise in what you say.

Your bibliography does not count towards the word limit.

Tip:

Ask a teacher, a friend or a family member to proofread your work, checking for clarity, spelling and grammatical errors. Include time for you to respond to any critical feedback.

PRESENTING THE WRITTEN ANALYSIS

The written analysis can be either handwritten or word-processed. Word processing has the advantage in that you can easily make edits, corrections and changes as you go without having to make lengthy rewrites if you make a mistake.

However you choose to present the written component, it must be legible and in English, with correct use of spelling and grammar. You must make use of specialist subject vocabulary that is relevant to the theme of the study.

If you word-process your work, it is good practice to use double spacing, as this makes it easier for the examiner to read and mark your work. Print your work on one side of the paper, as eventually you will have to submit the whole project for assessment mounted on A2 sheets. Your teacher will give you guidance about submitting work for assessment.

You should plan the visual appearance of your work carefully. Think about the style of fonts that you use and select a style that is clear and easy to read and that is appropriate to your theme. For example, look at the images of **Art Deco** design and note the style of fonts used at the time. If your Personal Investigation centres around the theme of Art Deco, it would be appropriate to use a similar style of font within your work to reflect the style of the era (Figure 4.24).

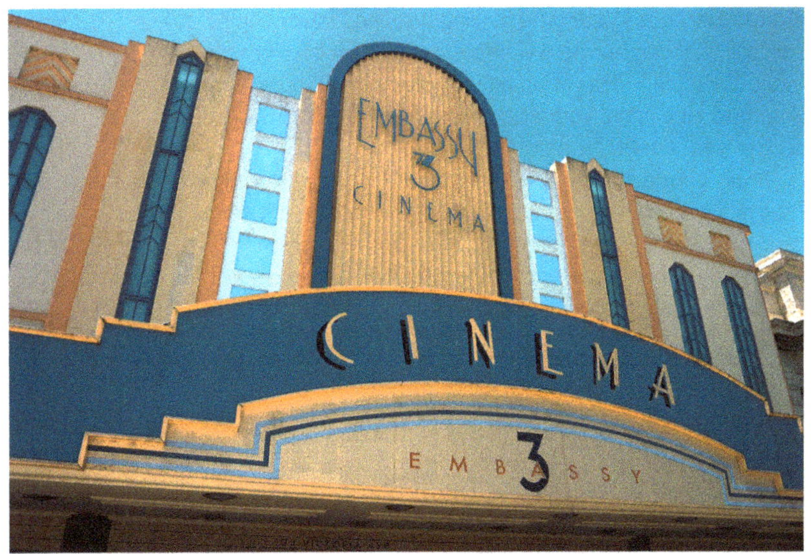

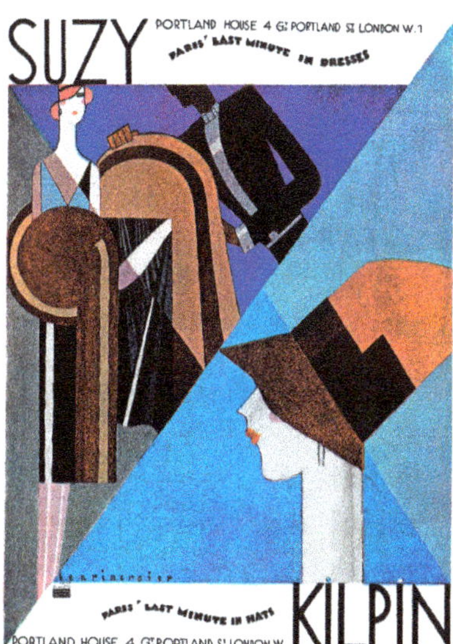

4.24 Examples of Art Deco architecture and advertising that typify the style of the era.

Font styles such as **Broadway** or ***Harlow Solid***, might be appropriate to use, as they link to the visual theme of the study. However, if you are using a very decorative font it might make the text harder to read and you should consider using it for the titles and headings only and combine it with a simpler style of font for the main body of the text. A style such as Ariel or Tahoma, which are clear and modern-looking, would work well in this instance.

Art Deco A style of interior decoration, jewellery, architecture and so on, at its height in the 1930s and characterised by geometrical shapes, stylised natural forms and symmetrical functional designs adapted to mass production.

continuous prose Writing set out in full sentences and well-structured paragraphs.

Activity A: **Experiment with font styles**

Experiment with presenting the title of your Personal Investigation using different font styles.

1. Look at the range of fonts that you have available to you in your word-processing program. Think about which font styles reflect or link visually to the theme of your study.
2. Type out the title and a few lines of text from your study. Try out several different fonts to compare.
3. Experiment with varying the font size for main titles, headings and subheadings. If it is visually appropriate to do so, consider creating interest by changing the colour of your font.
4. Ask your classmates to give you feedback as to which look best and which are clearest to read.

You can illustrate the written text with photographs that you took and drawings that you made as part of your first-hand research. You can also use images that you have sourced from the internet and books as part of the second-hand research. Ensure that the images you use are good quality and clear, but do not waste time making detailed, drawn copies of work that you are talking about, as you will be demonstrating your practical skills elsewhere in the Personal Investigation and it will not help you to achieve more marks. You must label all of your illustrations and place them close to the relevant section of the text.

Finally, consider the paper that you are writing or printing onto as an integral part of the presentation. You can use different-textured papers, thin card or colours to create interest. It might be interesting to experiment with including pages of architect's tracing paper, which is semi-transparent, or a handmade paper, if these are appropriate to your work.

Tip:

You can research fonts online if you cannot find a suitable font included in programs such as Word. Some font styles can be downloaded free of charge, but always check that you are downloading information from a safe website and that your computer has up-to-date virus protection.

Also, check what paper thickness and type can be used in your printer if you are experimenting with different surfaces to work on.

INTEGRATING THE WRITTEN ANALYSIS AND PRACTICAL WORK

The two aspects of the Personal Investigation, the practical project and written analysis, must be presented together in a cohesive and integrated way that is appropriate for the subject of the study. The written analysis could be presented as part of an illustrated study that combines your practical work throughout. Another way could be to present an outcome, such as a sculpture or product, photographed and displayed alongside the related written analysis. Alternatively, the Personal Investigation could start with the focused written analysis. For example, you could compare the style or technique of two artists, which you then use in practical work influenced by the style of one or both artists.

Examples of students' practical work can be seen on pages 356–374 in the 'Practical guidance' section.

Personal Investigation checklist

Before you are ready to hand in your work, make sure that you have:

- written legibly, in English
- used subject-specific vocabulary
- checked the accuracy of your spelling and grammar
- kept to the word count
- labelled your images and placed them at appropriate places within the text of the written analysis
- included a bibliography
- answered the question that you set yourself at the start
- linked the written analysis to your practical work and presented the two sections in an integrated way.

4.1 Textiles and fashion

Activity A: **Write a statement of intent**

When you begin your research and development, you need to have some idea what your intentions are for the final piece. One way to do this is to research something topical or relevant in your local area or internationally that holds your interest, and present it in a creative way.

It could be a social or environmental issue, such as:

- global warming
- endangered animals
- freedom of speech.

Or it could be an issue more personal to you.

1. Find out as much as you can about the topic and research how other artists have presented their work addressing the same or similar issues.
2. Make a list of the technical processes – including materials, colour palettes and so on – remembering that this is a guideline.
3. Write up your list in more detail for a 'Statement of Intent'. This is approximately 500 words on what your project is about and where it will lead.

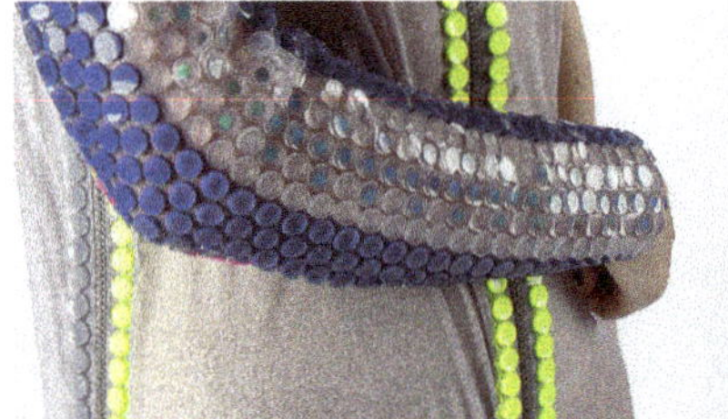

4.25 Zeba Safdar, 'Ath-Opulance', 2017, moulded silicone. This is a collection about tactile textured surfaces with highly decorative elements for future premium sports products.

Constructed textiles

Learning objectives:

- To be able to demonstrate the importance of cultural and social factors when making and exhibiting work
- To define the function and purpose of final outcome
- To be able to identify an audience for a final outcome
- To explore how textiles and fashion design can be used to communicate an idea

It is important designers are very clear from the outset how they want their audience to respond to and understand their work. It may be the outcome has a specific function or a message that the designer wants to communicate with the audience. Design isn't just about aesthetics – for example, British fashion designer Stella McCartney promotes animal welfare with her recent 'skin-free' collections in Paris, March 2017. She has considered and satisfied a client base that shares her own concerns about animal cruelty. A designer will often work to a given or self-directed brief and with this in mind the final outcome must always be the focus when the project is being developed.

Designers who construct fabric from raw materials should have the skill and understanding of how the fabrics they create will behave when used. Japanese fashion designer Issey Miyake works very closely with his own fabric technicians to create fabrics that are both functional and aesthetic. In 1993, he designed a clothing range called 'Pleats Please' that had a unique aesthetic that combined comfortable, modern and functional design with advanced pleating techniques. He wanted to design clothes to fit different size and body shapes and so constructed them to stretch across these varying shapes. This is one example of how a designer carefully considers the functionality of his work. Can you identify another designer who uses specialist fabrics for a specific function?

As we have become more and more concerned about our environment and healthy lifestyles, we see designers reacting to these needs with new and exciting work. Earlier we mentioned Stella McCartney and how she designs clothes considering animal welfare. The examples below are students who have investigated and promoted human well-being in their garment collections – in particular, physical and mental health.

Zeba Safdar is a textile designer who creates **interactive textiles**. Her clothing range 'Ath-Opulance' includes highly decorative and tactile textural surfaces that offer remedial body healing for the sports clothing industry. She chose to use the material silicone because of its healing properties and experimented with heat-treating and moulding patterns to suggest muscle anatomy (see Figure 4.25). Her aesthetic and functional approach using a sporty colour palette of primary colours and unusual surface pattern interests both a fashion and specific sports market.

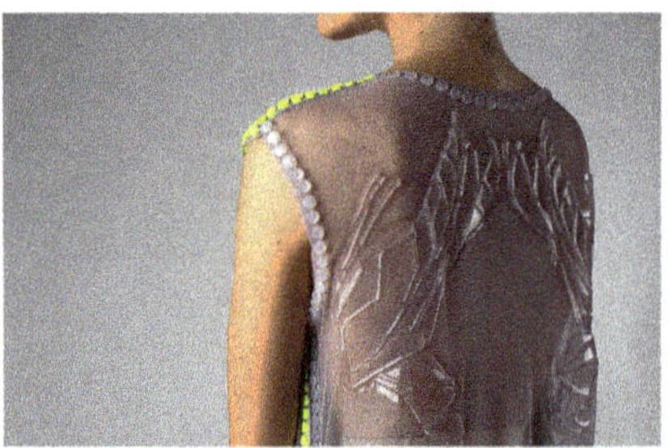

Anna-Maie Southern has based her clothing collection entitled 'Mind's Eye' on concerns she has for mental health and well-being among young men aged particularly between 18 and 30. The collection of well-being fabrics is inspired by art therapy and Surrealism, a movement that visually translates the subconscious or hidden meaning.

She uses natural dyes, such as turmeric, for their healing properties and weaves them into colourful, symbolic imagery and text that highlight what the men are thinking and feeling. Her choice of soft cashmere yarns evokes the comfort and sense of security they should feel when safe in their surroundings. As a young designer, her brand targets are for the skateboarding, hip-hop and youth culture market, such as the American clothing label Supreme.

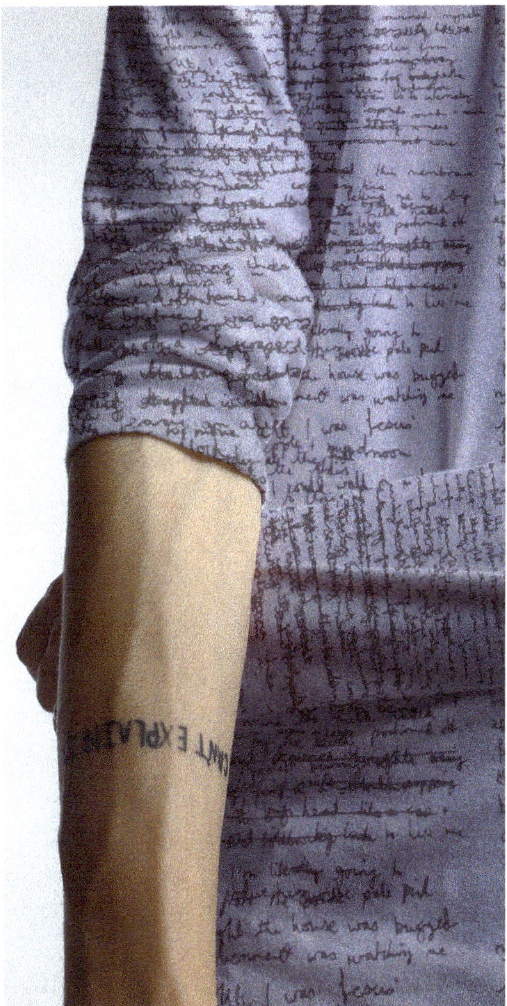

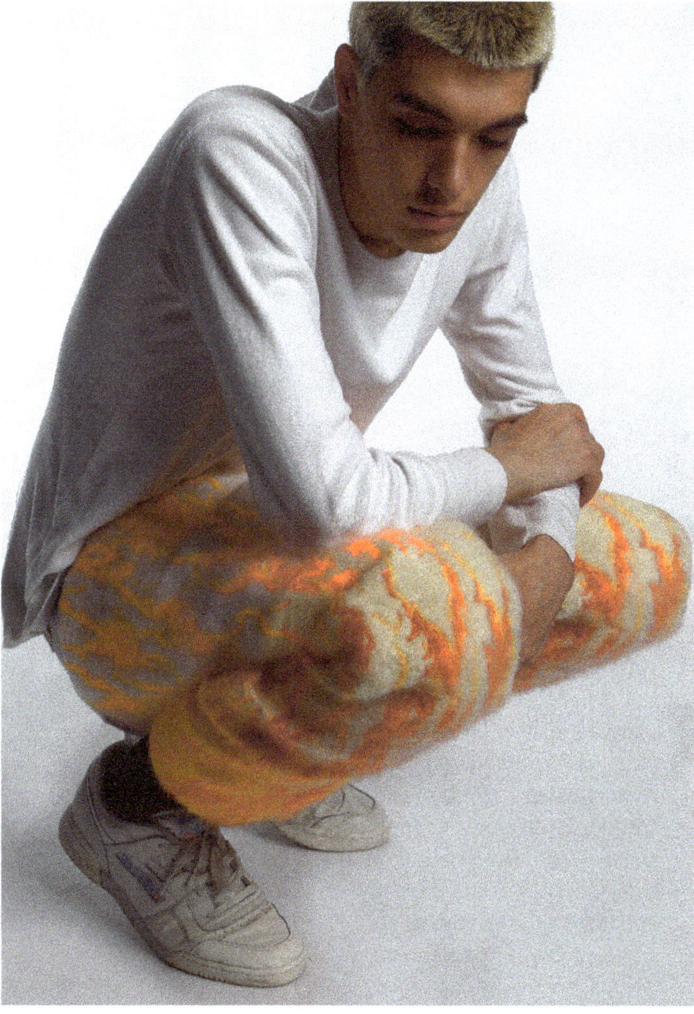

4.26 Anna-Maie Southern, 'Mind's Eye' collection, jacquard weave, cashmere. Digital printed, cotton jersey.

The collection allows the wearer to actively wear their 'mind' on their sleeve, thereby reducing social isolation and shame surrounding mental health difficulties. The image on the left uses the power of text to make a clear statement. The designer has used a model with an appropriate tattoo that helps explain the meaning behind her collection. When finding models to present your work, keep in mind the 'look' or 'style' of the model that will suit your collection and communicate it best.

interactive textiles Textiles that are able to work closely with the environment and react or adapt to it in a programmed way.

Tip:

One quick way of seeing what your design will look like on a garment or interior product is to superimpose it onto a photograph or image from the internet. This is how Anna-Maie Southern could visualise her idea before taking the time to make it. This will give you an idea of scale and placement.

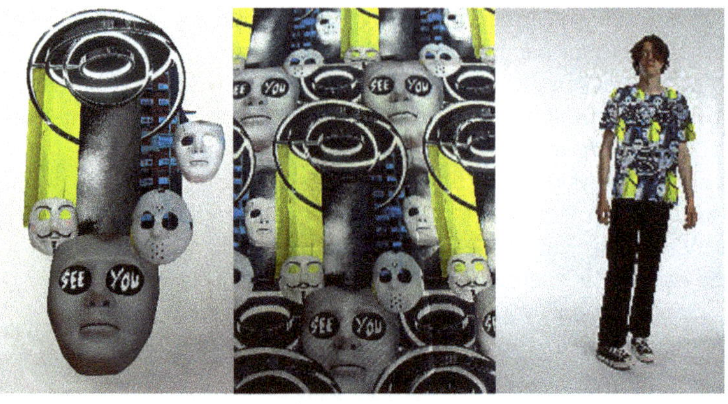

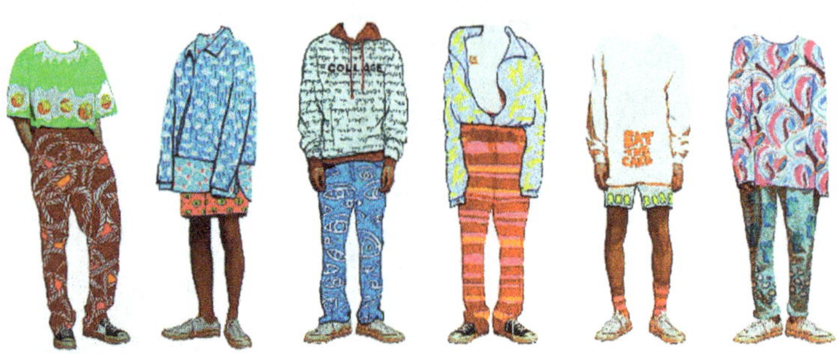

4.27 Development board sequence for 'Mind's Eye' collection, original collage mood board for T-shirt design. Illustrations superimposed onto model's bodies.

Critical thinking:

Whatever the framework you have set yourself, make sure that you stick to it! There will be plenty of room for experimentation and exploration, within the development period but never lose sight of the ultimate goal you have set yourself. Each time you make a new discovery, ask yourself 'Does this demonstrate what I'm trying to say or do? Am I keeping to the guidelines of the brief?' By keeping to this mantra or set of rules, you will become more disciplined in your approach and make quicker and more effective decisions.

Activity B: **Explore superimposing your work onto secondary images**

- Find a selection of images of potential products that your fabrics could be made for. For example, if you intend to use your fabrics for interior design, take photographs of chairs, curtains or wall space (you can easily find these on the internet or cut them out of magazines).
- Photocopy or scan your designed fabric so you have printouts. Remember to reduce or enlarge the size so it matches the scale of the photograph of the product or human figure.
- Use tracing paper to trace the outline of the photographed image. Transfer this to your designed fabric printout.
- With scissors or a craft knife, carefully cut around the traced outline of the fabric printout and collage your design images onto the models or products. You may have to add in more detail, such as shadows, hem lines and so on, to make it as realistic as possible.

Further research

Search the internet for more on presentation formats.

You might also like to explore the following books:

- *Advanced Textiles for Health and Wellbeing* by Professor Marie O'Mahoney (Thames & Hudson, 2011)
- *Smart Textiles for Designers: Inventing the Future of Fabric* by Rebeccah Pailes-Friedman (Laurence King Publishing, 2016).

Surface design

Learning objective:

- To be able to explore ways of displaying and presenting work to different audiences

When the creative process is complete, it is time to consider how you will present your work to your tutors, in an interview and most importantly to yourself! If you are considering a career in fashion and textiles, you will need to prepare portfolios for interviews. When selecting work, you must be very careful to select your best work. When you have done this, you then need to consider how best to display or present it. You can do this by presenting work on a mount board or reorganising your original sketchbook so you only show your best experiments and ideas. A good presentation can make a significant difference to your grades and success when continuing your further education.

The example given below in Figure 4.28 shows how a design student has presented her work.

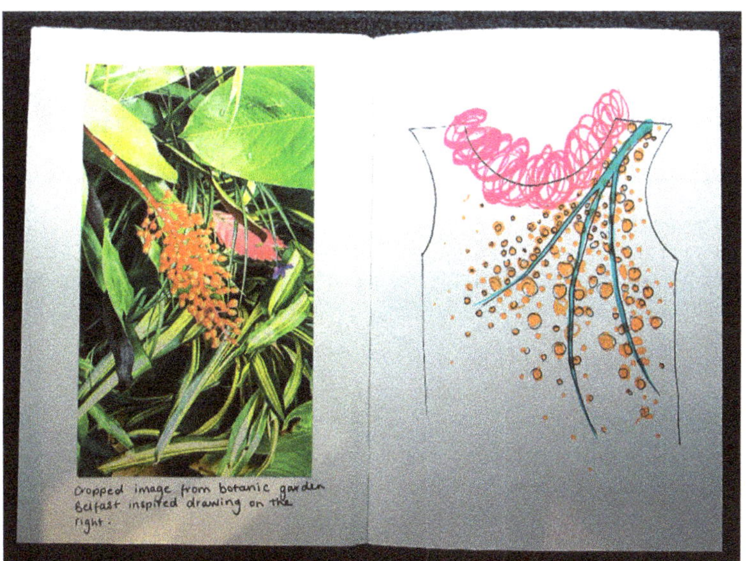

4.28 Shannen McCusker, sketchbook pages, artist's own photograph and annotation with developed design, 2017. This example shows how the student has carefully selected two images that best represent her work. She has decided to crop to the plant structure and focus on the area she is interested in to support her ideas. The illustration is simple but it does well to translate her first-hand research onto a garment.

The example in Figure 4.29 presents us with lively embroidery and paper collage ideas. This student has chosen to use a black background to make her colourful patterns stand out. These work well as support pieces for her presentation portfolio.

Natalie Percival hand-paints her fabrics with fabric dyes and overlays her designs with screen printing. Her inspiration is from the surrounding countryside in Norway. She presents her work by displaying her wall hanging as a piece of art but also shows how her fabric can be functional as cushion covers (see Figure 4.30). Sometimes, when presenting work, you need to remember that an audience needs to feel secure with understanding its meaning and purpose. This is a helpful way to show the audience alternative outcomes.

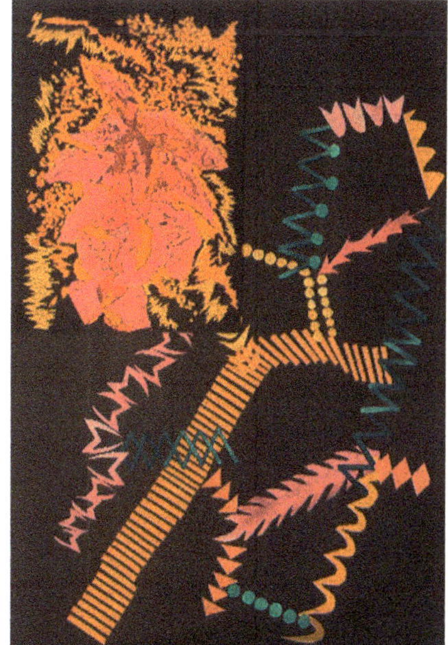

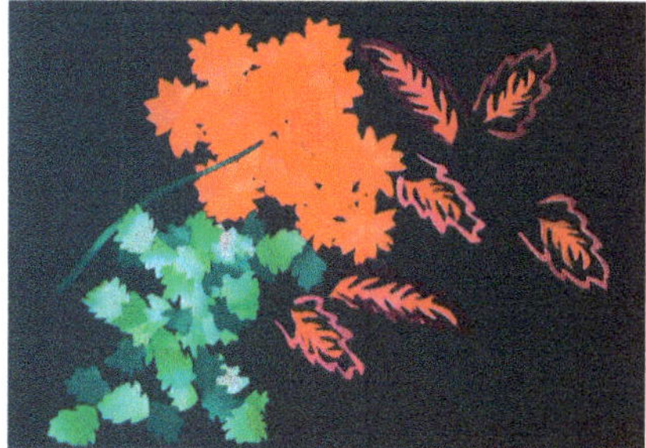

4.29 Shannen McCusker, hand embroidery and paper collage on card, 2017.

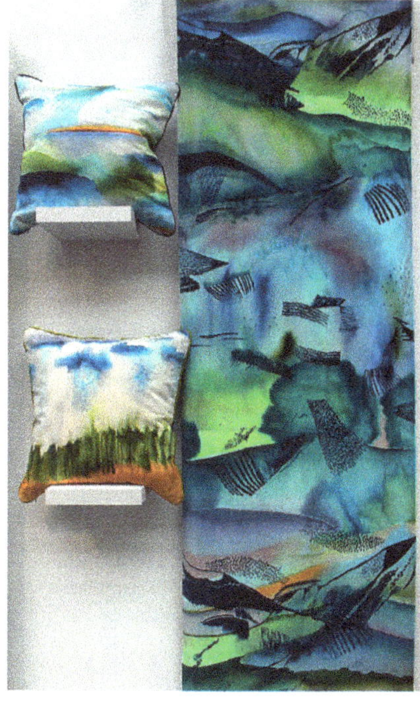

4.30 Natalie Percival, hand mono-painted overlaid with screen print on cotton velvet, 2017.

Activity A: **Explore how to mount work**

- Use the example in Figure 4.31 as a guide and explore mounting your work.
- Use white mount paper or card throughout the portfolio, as this will be **consistent** and uniform.
- Do not use heavy board, as this will be difficult to carry around.
- If you have large pieces of work – for example, A1 or 3D sculptures – you need to reduce the scale by photographing them and mounting them onto paper.
- Be very selective, and remember less is more! A less busy board can communicate your idea more clearly to an audience.
- The order of work is important. The first and last pages should be your best pieces of work and describe you as an artist or designer. Then, your audience will remember you!

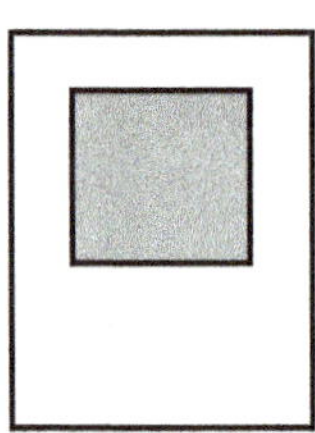
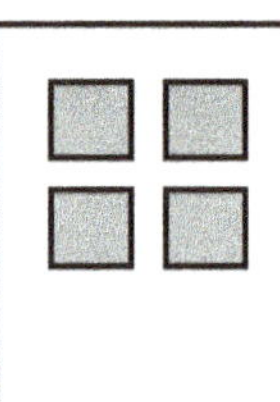
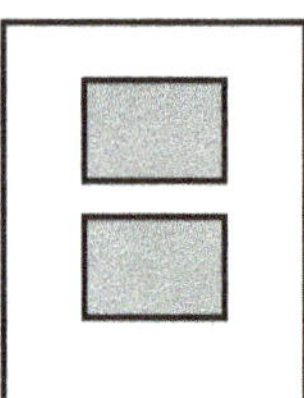
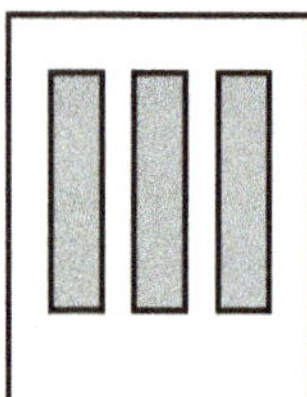

4.31 Different positions to mount up work.

4.32 A simple fabric header. You can display your fabric samples and write the title of the project and other notes on them. By placing the samples together, you can create the overall mood and look of the collection at a glance.

Tip:

A good portfolio of work needs to:

- visually record and archive all past work, accurately and professionally
- be well-ordered, coherent and communicate all aspects of your work in your absence for tutors to read.

Materials and techniques: **Equipment you will need for mounting up work**

Make sure that you use good-quality materials to display your work on. Quality mount card such as a 1400-micron weight is suitable to hold work. Preferably, use white, as it is often requested by art colleges because it shows the work clearly without any distractions. Use adhesive spray mount so you can reposition work on the paper. Use a metal ruler when cutting down work, for accuracy, and always cut on a cutting mat with a sharp knife!

Fabric samples can sometimes be heavy, so either limit what you put on or attach card headers to them (see Figure 4.32) and write clearly what project they relate to.

Remember: any marked or untidy boards with images or samples that have been put on unevenly can be disappointing and will not show your work at its best. So, take your time when preparing.

PLACES TO PROMOTE AND DISPLAY FASHION AND TEXTILES DESIGNS

The next stage you need to be prepared for, once you are satisfied with your designs, is presenting them to a wider audience. There are a few ways to do this depending on how you would like your designs to be received and by whom.

First, you need to decide on how you want to document your ideas. This can be done in a studio or on location. Using lighting and backdrops well is essential for quality photographs. Finding a good accessible location can be lots of fun and can be a great way to present unique images. The following examples offer different ways to display and present work.

New Designers exhibition in London is a trade fair where young designers present their work to the fashion and textiles industry. Places like this are very useful to visit when you are looking for inspiration for your own projects and a good opportunity to talk to the exhibitors for advice. Local colleges and universities also have their own open days or final year shows and these are another excellent opportunity to help you decide on where you might go for further education. If possible, try to visit places like this in your local area.

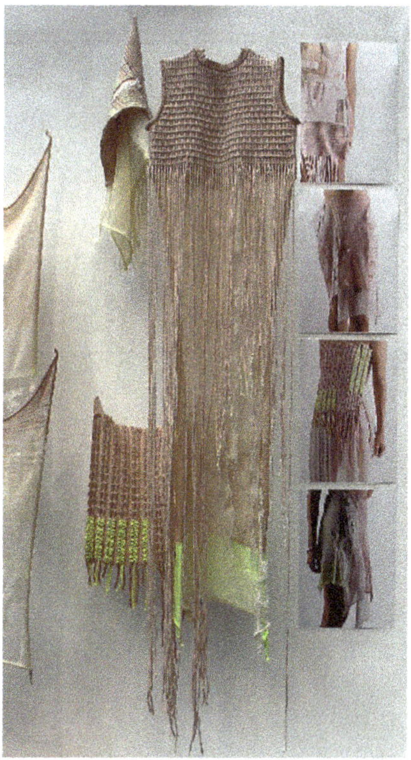

4.33 Azra Iqbal, knitwear display at New Designers, London, 2017.

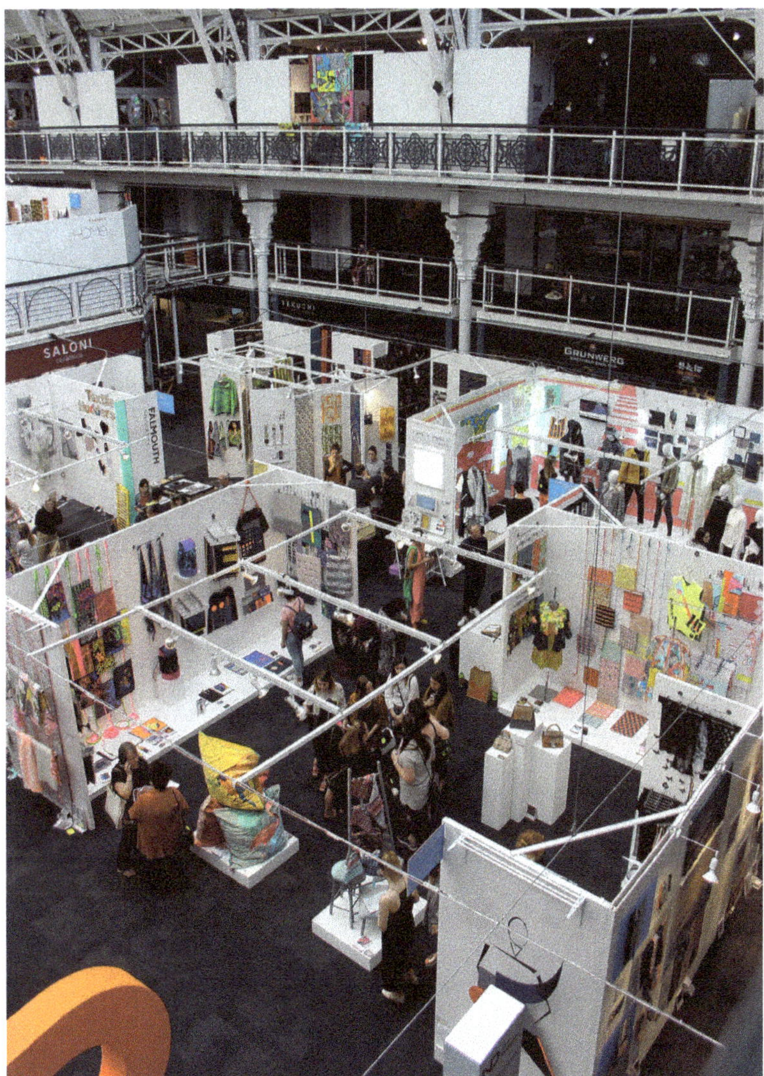

4.34 New Designers trade fair exhibition, London, 2017.

Tip:

It is always a good idea to present your final piece with photographs of a model wearing the garment, displaying the functional possibilities.

consistent Steady, even.

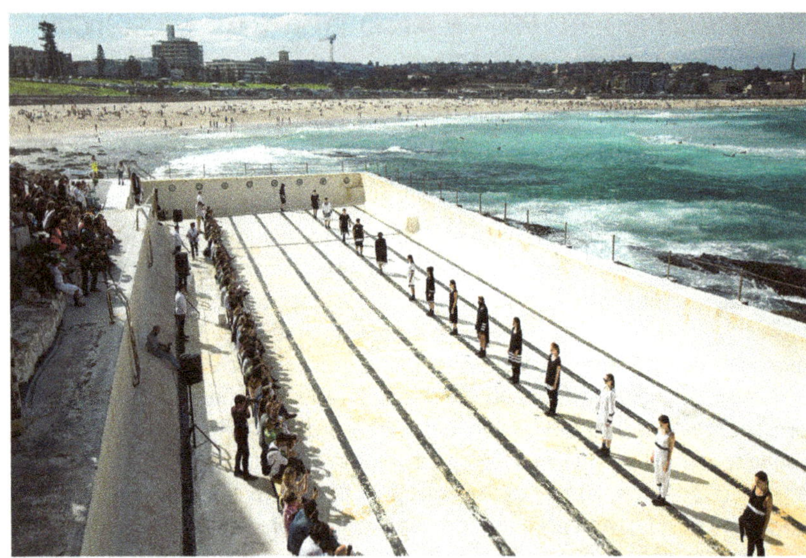

4.35 Australian fashion label TEN PIECES on location in Sydney's Icebergs pool, 2017.

Figures 4.35 and 4.36 show two examples of unusual locations for catwalk shows. Figure 4.35 is in Sydney, Australia, where an iconic outdoor swimming pool has been drained and acts as a runway for models to walk through. The backdrop is stunning and adds to the mood of the 2017 collection by Australian fashion label TEN PIECES.

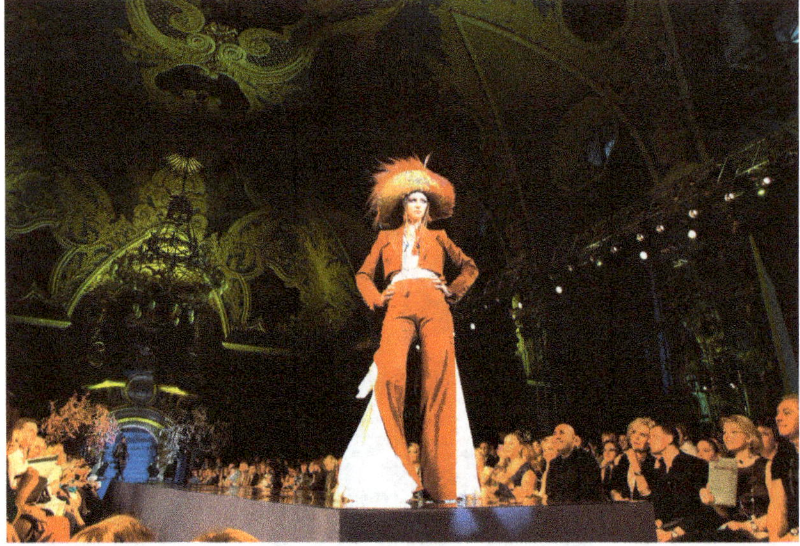

4.36 Russian designer Alexander Terekhov holds a fashion show inside a Moscow metro station.

Figure 4.36 is an image from Alexander Terekhov's collection, shown in an underground metro station. Try to find an urban or rural location in your area that is easily accessible. You will have to make sure that you can get permission to use out-of-the-way places. Find places that will complement your designs. For example, if you have a garment that has geometric design lines, perhaps try to find an urban setting with architectural qualities; or, for a more organic sensibility, perhaps a wooded landscape.

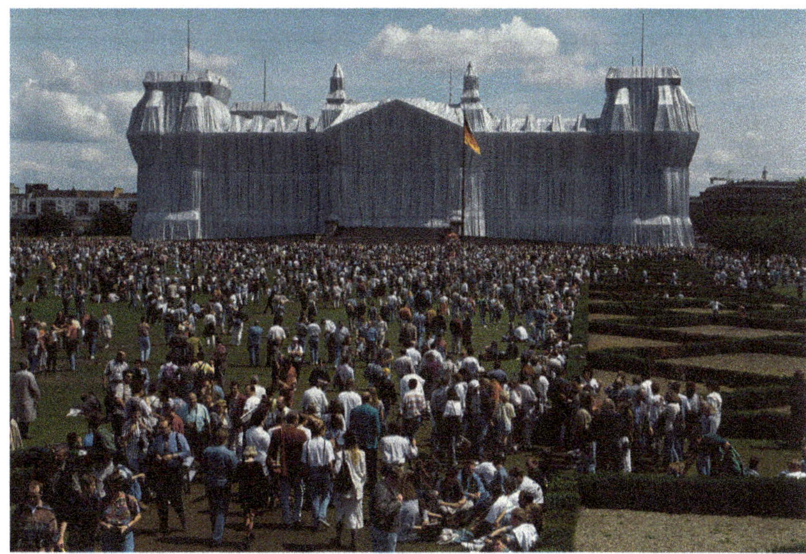

4.37 Christo and Jeanne-Claude, *Wrapped Reichstag*, 1995.

We have mentioned alternative locations for garment presentation, such as catwalk shows. But if you have textile art to display, how can you creatively present these? The example in Figure 4.37 shows how two designers, Christo and Jeanne-Claude, used 100,000 square metres of thick woven polypropylene fabric with an aluminium surface for the wrapping of the Reichstag in Berlin. The façades, the towers and the roof were covered by 70 tailor-made fabric panels, twice as much fabric as the surface of the building! Although a massive accomplishment, can you find simpler ways to present your fabrics that interact with the environment for added effect? American artist Eva Hesse used the disused interiors of a factory, where she found materials for making her textile sculptures.

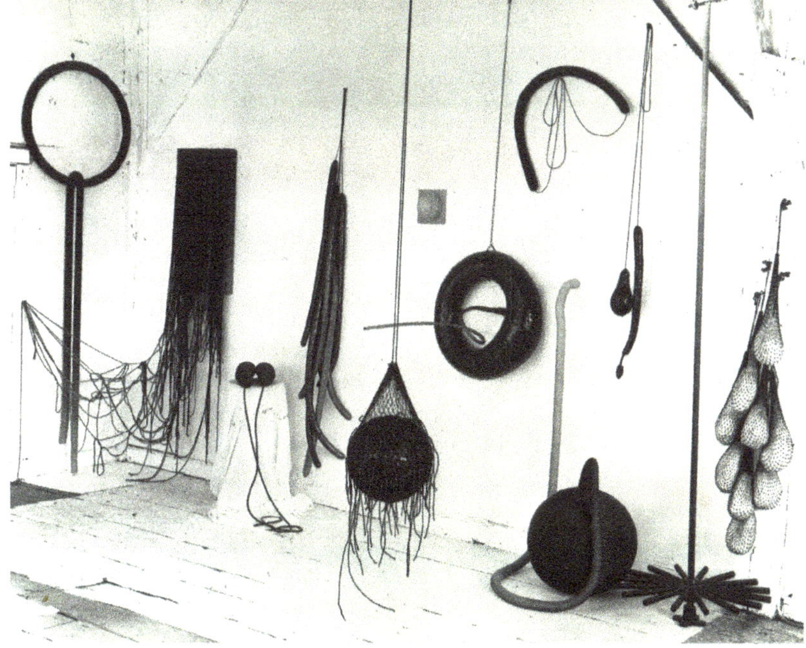

4.38 Works from 1965–66 in Eva Hesse's studio, photo by Gretchen Lambert.

Activity B: **Planning and presenting work for a critique**

A **critique** is where you present your work or ideas to your tutors, and sometimes your fellow students, for general feedback or formal assessment. The purpose of the critique is to help you to appreciate your progress and resolve potential problems in your work. It is a time when ideas can be exchanged. As a student designer, this is a very important stage of your development and one that you must take seriously. You need to be well prepared and on time, as you will only have a certain number of minutes to present to your audience.

To help you plan and present a critique, you need to:

- Select work that clearly shows the intentions of your brief. You may have limited space, so you need to present only a few images showing the initial ideas and developments, including problem solving and finished products. Therefore, the work needs to be specific and relevant.
- Decide on how to present your work – on mount boards, PowerPoint slide presentation, on a life model or mannequin and so on.
- Use photographs or designs of your work that describe how it might be used – for example, fashion illustrations or working sketches or location images.
- Practise your presentation to a classmate, or video yourself. This can be daunting but it will help with your presentation skills.
- Choose work that you can confidently talk about. If you know what you are talking about, so will your audience!
- Make sure that your work is mounted accurately, and is clean and tidy with no fingerprints or glue marks.
- Begin your presentation with sentences such as 'My intention for this brief was to…' or 'For this brief I wanted to explore the idea behind…'
- Finally, be prepared for questions at the end of your presentation. Don't forget to ask your audience questions as well, so you have feedback to help you improve on your work.

Critical thinking:

After your critique, reflect on **Activity B** and ask yourself if your presentation was a success. How could you have improved on it? Did your audience fully understand what your brief was about? Were you able to keep to the presentation timeframe? Were you able to extract the useful information during the feedback session to help you improve your ideas? Lastly, stay positive! Designs cannot be forced on people – they must be accepted. If you have a negative response from your audience, don't let it affect you too much. It is important to bounce back from disappointing experiences.

Further research

For a book that features presentation skills:

Fashion Design (Portfolio) by Sue Jenkyn Jones (Laurence King Publishing, 2011).

atelier An artist's or designer's workshop or studio.
choreographer A person who invents steps and dance.
critique This is the occasion when tutors evaluate your response to a project.
public relations or **PR** A person who is responsible for managing and communicating another person's business to a wider audience.
stylist A person who puts together objects or clothes to improve their appearance.

Artists and designers: **How a designer puts together and organises a catwalk show**

Once a fashion designer has finalised a collection, they need to promote and publicise their work to a wider audience. More recently, designers are finding new ways to showcase their designs through social media, such as videos and live Instagram feeds or informal presentations that bring models and journalists together. However, the live prestigious catwalk shows are still the most popular method of introducing fashion design work to a wider audience, and are presented to the world twice a year in Europe, New York and Asia. In the late 19th century, British-born fashion designer Charles Frederick Worth became the first designer to present seasonal collections on live models in his **atelier** in Paris. Catwalk shows are still the most preferred presentation method for designers to showcase their work.

Organising a fashion show takes weeks of preparation and can be very expensive, so it is important to have a professional team to help with the arrangements. The team is made up of **stylists**, models, make-up artists, **choreographers**, lighting engineers and the designer's **public relations** or **PR** department.

To begin with, designers must find a suitable location or venue for their catwalk that can accommodate important guests such as buyers, magazine editors, press photographers and sometimes celebrities. Designers often look for unusual settings or stage performances to ensure that their audience remembers the occasion.

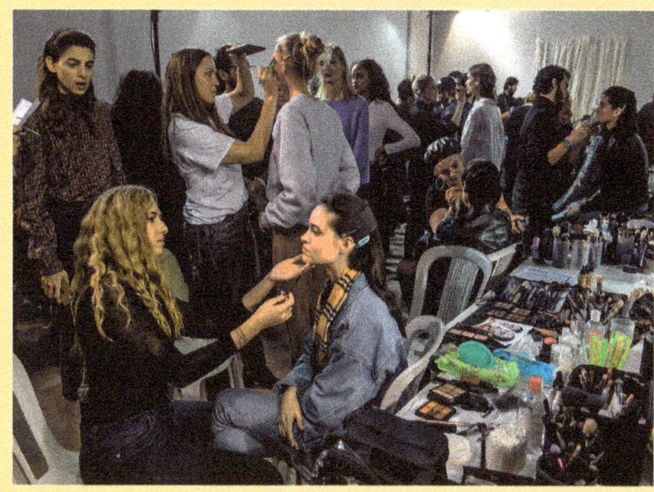

4.39 Backstage preparations at a fashion show.

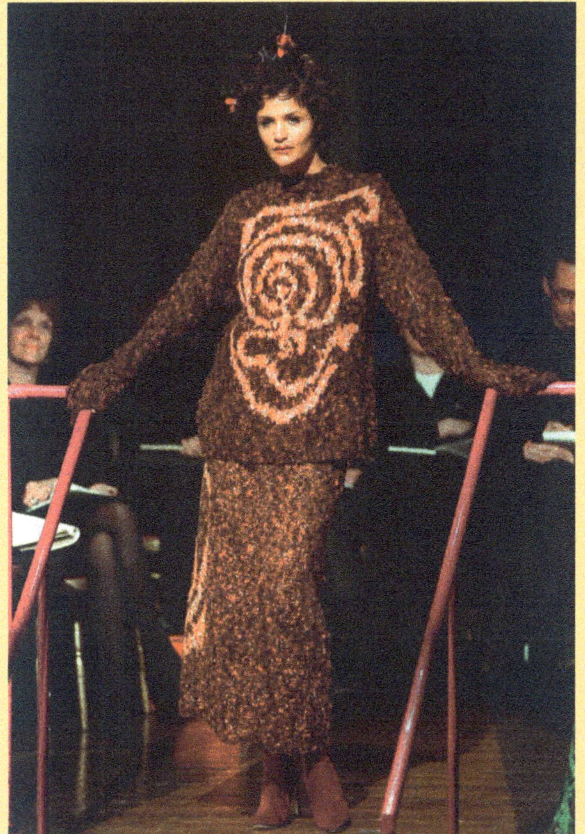

Below is a brief account of an up-and-coming designer in the mid-1990s who successfully showcased her first catwalk show in London. The success of the show was not only due to her ground-breaking knitwear designs but also the skilled and famous team of people that worked alongside her. Lainey Keogh's vision was always for quality and fashionable knitwear to be accessible to all her audience.

In 1997, she presented her work at the Cobden Club, a small venue in London. Her design team was made up of avant-garde British *Vogue* stylist Isabella Blow, who at the time had famously introduced British fashion designer Alexander McQueen to the world fashion stage. Isabella had the ground-breaking idea to invite an unknown plus-size model, Sophie Dahl, which challenged the trending size 0 models of the time. This radical decision was swept up by the press and as a result sensationalised Lainey's catwalk show, making her designs an overnight success.

4.40 Lainey Keogh, knitwear, model Helena Christensen, catwalk show, London, 1997.

Surface pattern

Learning objective:

- To be able to consider cultural contexts for a setting and audience

CULTURALLY INSPIRED

Often fashion and textile designers, and artists, want to inform people how rich and culturally diverse their work can be by exploring their own cultural identity. The focus can be just on the aesthetics of the designs, such as surface pattern and colour, combining traditional and contemporary techniques, or the outcomes can have a more profound meaning behind the ideas. Either way, these artists attempt to bring cultural awareness to a wider global audience.

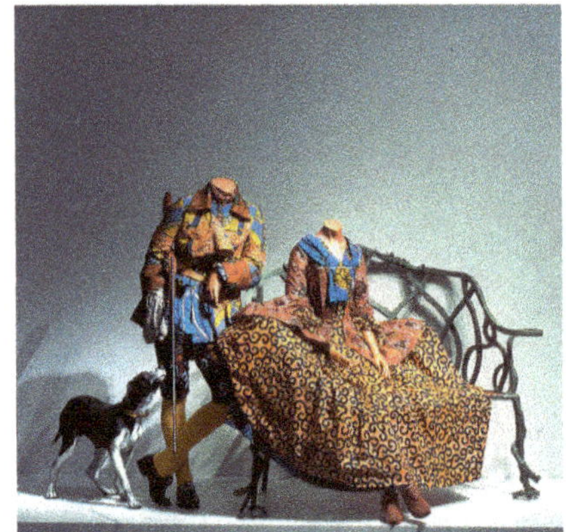

4.41 Yinka Shonibare MBE, *Mr. and Mrs. Andrews Without Their Heads*, 1998, two life-size mannequins, bench, gun, dog, Dutch wax printed cotton, National Gallery of Canada, Ottawa.

Yinka Shonibare MBE (RA) (born 1962) is a British-Nigerian artist. His life and experiences living in the UK have allowed him to explore his own cultural identity. He is particularly interested in the effects of globalisation and how this has impacted on people's authentic identity in an ever-changing, global, modern world.

The example in Figure 4.41 presents us with two black, headless mannequins in European 18th-century costume made with cloth from traditional African batik designs. These sculptures are a direct representation of a famous painting by British artist Thomas Gainsborough in 1750, depicting a wealthy British couple who owned trading ships during the colonisation of Africa (Figure 4.42). Shonibare is particularly interested in race relations and the role of power and class during this time.

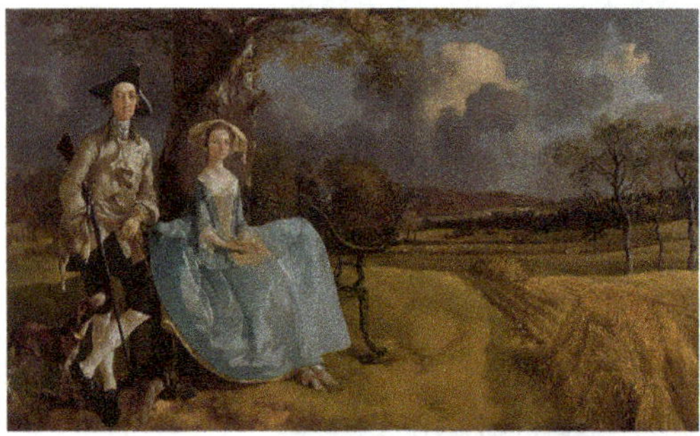

4.42 Thomas Gainsborough, *Mr and Mrs Andrews*, 1750, oil on canvas, National Gallery, London.

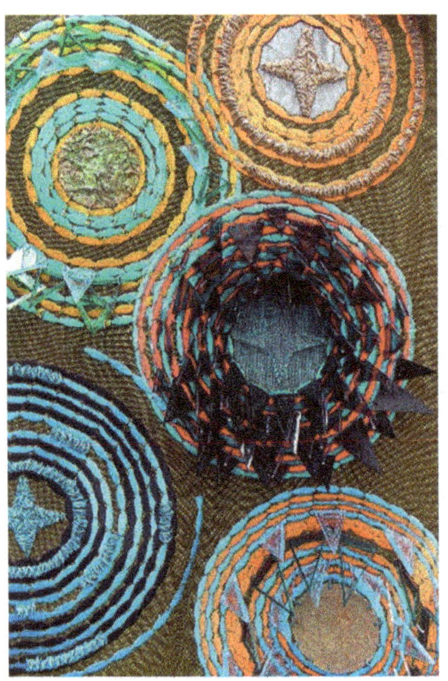

4.43 Sunna Yasin, *Manus x Machina*, 2017, machine and hand embroidery, Perspex, leather and metal.

The fabric used to dress the mannequins was, in fact, manufactured in Indonesia and bought in London and did not even reach the shores of Africa. Yinka wanted to suggest to his audience, how, like the African fabric, a person's cultural identity can become a hybrid of cultures as a result of globalisation. Therefore, if a person has no true identity, any negative race relations can become resolved. His fabrics are bright and colourful, inviting his audience to truly engage in his work. He believes that the more engaged an audience is, the more sympathetic they will be to understanding and accepting his work.

Fashion and clothing is a powerful commodity and has the potential to reach the corners of the globe and bring people together. In contrast to Shonibare's work, surface pattern designer Sunna Yasin shares the beauty and positivity of her Islamic culture with other faiths. Her collection *Manus x Machina* is about the exploration between the handmade and mechanisation in fashion, and combines hand and machine embroidery with Perspex, leather and metal embellishment (see Figure 4.43).

She finds inspiration in all things Islamic, including the mosaic tiles found on the façade of buildings and geometric patterns. The symbolism in shapes are an important aspect to her work: squares symbolise foundation, circles symbolise unity and triangles symbolise wisdom.

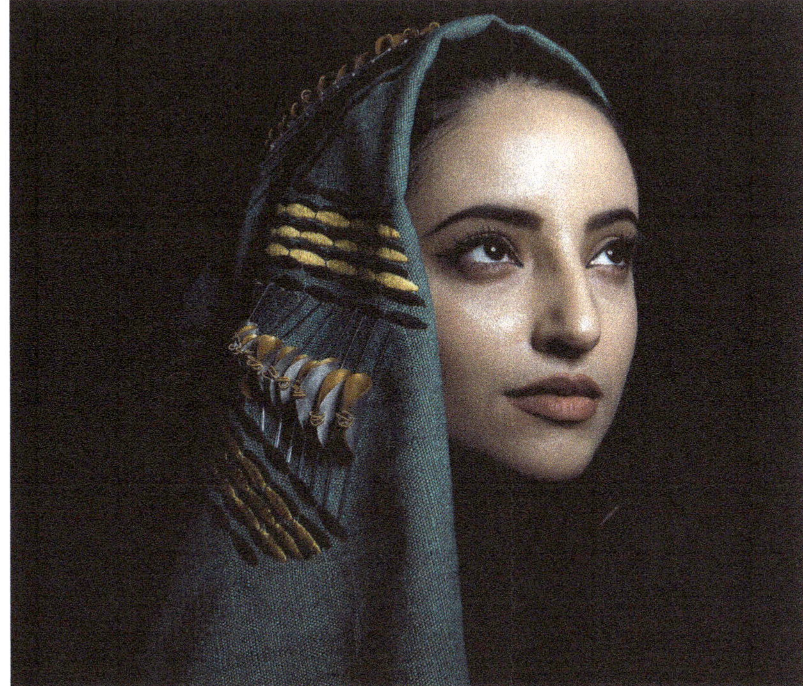

4.44 Sunna Yasin, Shayla headscarf showing her application of embroidery in modest fashion, 2017, embellished with leather and machine embroidery on cloth.

Activity A: **Define and present your own cultural identity to an audience**

Research:

1. Begin by exploring your history, culture, politics and social behaviour. Gather research by interviewing older members of your family and friends. Visit museum archives. Read journals. Collect images.
2. You may find that your generation has moved away from traditional values. Find out why and how this has happened.

Define a target audience:

3. Do you want to create work with an aim to simply celebrate your culture and create work that is aesthetically pleasing? Or do you have a message you want to share with other cultures or faiths that reignites issues and challenges concepts?

Present work:

4. Think about how you might like to present the work to others; computer social networking is an obvious form of connecting your ideas to a wider audience, such as online pinboards like Pinterest and Instagram. Alternatively, consider staging and recording your work in a public domain in front of a heritage site/building. If you have made garments, then maybe a performance piece might be appropriate.

Further research

For more on surface patterns and the rich cultural influences that shape them, read: *The Pattern Sourcebook: A Century of Surface Design* by Drusilla Cole (Laurence King Publishing, 2009).

4.2 Fine art

Drawing

Learning objectives:

- To understand the meaning of iconography and that the iconography in an artwork can work on different levels
- To understand how to help an audience engage with drawings when they are displayed

Someone can look at a work of art and like what they see, but do they always understand what the artist is trying to say through the work? In this unit, we look at how an artist can convey their meaning to an audience using iconography, or give an insight into their work through the way it is displayed in a gallery.

As you will recall from Module 1, iconography is the use of visual symbols and images to convey an idea or subject. Knowing what the symbols mean can help us to **decode** artworks and understand them, but this is not always an easy thing to do. Iconography can be universal, cultural or personal.

4.45 Pablo Picasso, *Dove with Flowers*, 1957, coloured pencil on paper, private collection. Both the subject and the use of colour have symbolic meaning in this Picasso drawing of the dove.

CULTURAL AND UNIVERSAL ICONOGRAPHY

The symbol of a dove is a good example of iconography used in works of art from different cultures and religions, where it can represent **fidelity**, a messenger, the human soul and the Holy Spirit. It is also a universally recognised symbol of peace. In 1949, the World Peace Congress, held in the wake of World War II (1939–45), used an image of a dove, created by the Spanish artist Pablo Picasso, as its symbol.

Picasso used the dove in his work as a recurring theme during his career, moving away from realistic drawings to simplified, stylised versions. The simple, yet elegant line drawing still carries the powerful message as a symbol of peace. In the version illustrated in Figure 4.45, the use of the colour blue also has symbolic significance – blue is widely accepted as representing peace, harmony, tranquillity, calm, trust and faith.

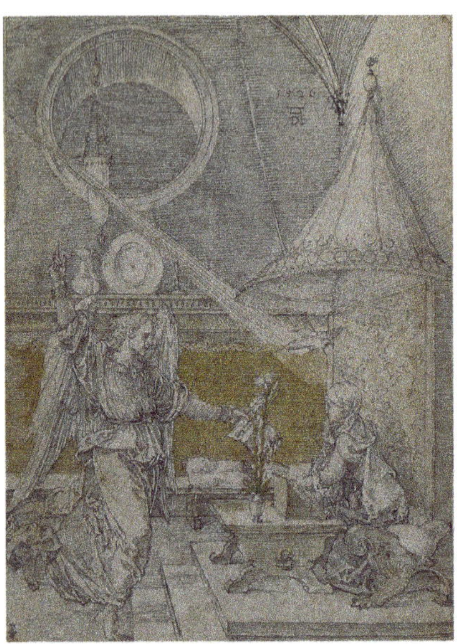

4.46 Albrecht Dürer, *The Annunciation*, 1526, pen and ink wash on paper, Musée Condé, Chantilly.

Activity A: **Decode a drawing**

The **Annunciation** is a subject within Christianity that many artists have depicted, but can you decode all of the symbols?

1. Look carefully at the drawing of *The Annunciation* by the German artist Albrecht Dürer (1471–1528) (Figure 4.46).
2. Try to decode what the figures and the objects in the drawing represent, and write a short description (150 words) of its iconography.
3. Go to the website of the Fitzwilliam Museum in Cambridge, UK, where the drawing is kept. The webpage explains the symbols used by artists portraying this theme. How well did you do in decoding the iconography?

Annunciation In Christianity, the Annunciation was the announcement by the Archangel Gabriel to the Virgin Mary that she was going to give birth to the son of God (Jesus).
decode If you decode a work of art, you manage to understand its meaning.
fidelity Faith or loyalty to a belief.

PERSONAL ICONOGRAPHY

As is seen in Figure 4.45, sometimes artists use well-known and understood symbols in their work. Sometimes, however, they create their own personal **metaphors** that are not immediately obvious without some explanation. The Japanese avant-garde artist Yayoi Kusama (born 1929) has developed a personal iconography through her use of dots (Figure 4.47).

The dots, or abstract 'cells', are a recurring theme throughout her career. According to Kusama, they represent cosmic infinity and the personal obsession that she has developed with pattern, repetition and brilliant colour. Kusama began to develop her personal iconography as a child, when she began drawing dots in response to **hallucinations** that she suffered.

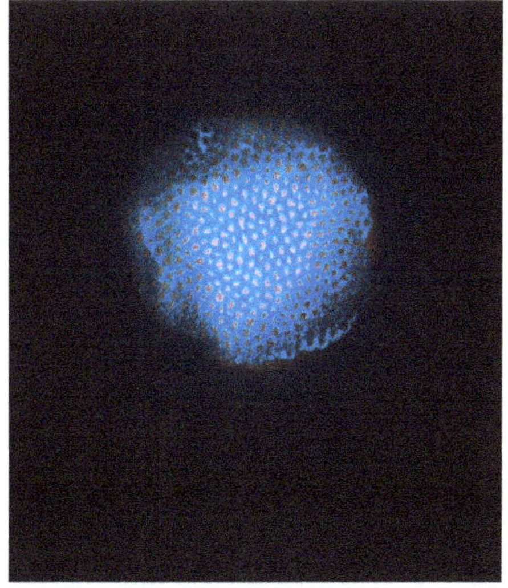

4.47 Yayoi Kusama, *Untitled*, 1954, pastel and watercolour on paper, Butler Institute of American Art, Youngstown, Ohio. Consider how you respond to this artwork – to what extent would you be able to decode it without knowing anything about the artist and her work?

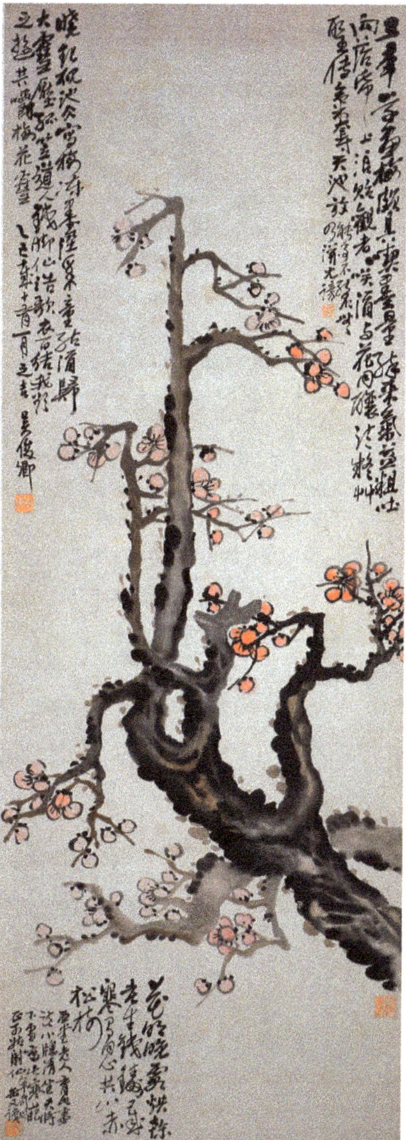

4.48 Wu Changshuo, *Red Plum Blossoms*, 1905, hanging scroll, pen and ink and colour on paper, private collection. The artist, who was famous for his skill as a calligrapher, has enhanced his image by adding a poem.

INFORMING AND ENGAGING AUDIENCES THROUGH DISPLAY

Does it matter if you do not understand the artist's intention? If you have to be told what it means, does that mean that the work is unsuccessful? When exhibited in a gallery setting, drawings and paintings are often explained through curators' words, or, in the case of contemporary work, through an Artist's Statement. In the traditional art of East Asia, drawings and paintings often include written words in the form of poems, to explain or enhance the meaning of the image or to explain how the work came about.

In the East Asian art of China, Japan and Korea, hanging scrolls are a traditional way of displaying work. Figure 4.48 shows a typical example by the Japanese artist Wu Changshuo (1844–1927). Drawings and paintings that are presented as hanging scrolls are usually intended to be displayed for only a short period of time. The custom is to rotate them according to the season and the occasion. The support onto which the picture is worked can be paper or silk, and the work is then mounted with decorative brocade silk or satin borders. Usually, the size and format of drawings and paintings presented in this way means that only a small number of people can view the work at one time, offering a closer, more intimate experience.

hallucination Someone has a hallucination if they experience sights and sounds that are not actually present; hallucination may occur in certain mental disorders.
metaphor If one thing is a metaphor for another, it is intended or regarded as a symbol of it.

Activity B: **Hold a class debate**

Using Figures 4.47 and 4.48 as your starting point, hold a class debate on the following questions:

- Do you think it is necessary to be able to decode an artwork?
- Should an artwork be meaningful to an audience without their having to know about the artist's intention?

Critical thinking:

Look back at the work that you have produced as part of your course:

- Does the way in which your work is displayed help engage your audience?
- What kind of iconography have you used?
- Is it personal, cultural or universal?
- Do you think that your audience, including the examiner, will be able to understand your work?
- To what extent do your annotations help to explain it?

Activity C: **Write an Artist's Statement**

Refer back to the section on Artists' Statements in Module 3 (pages 234–235), then write an Artist's Statement about one of your drawings. Explain your intention and the iconography of your work. Your statement should enhance the meaning behind your work and help the viewer understand how it came about.

TECHNOLOGY AND DISPLAY

When we view artworks in a gallery, we are usually only able to see the final outcome. Occasionally – especially in displays of work by **Old Masters** – a gallery exhibits one or two studies that led up to the production of a final piece of work. Sometimes, too, documentary video footage of an artist working is shown alongside their work.

New technology is enabling artists to communicate with the viewer in different ways. For example, British artist David Hockney (born 1937) often experiments with digital art and has produced a large series of iPad drawings, which he displays on large screens when he exhibits his work. Through displaying his work in this way, he can give his audience a unique insight into his creative process, because as he draws he records the sequence of his mark-making and plays this back as an animation. We can watch his drawing progress from start to finish and this helps us to engage with his work more deeply (Figure 4.49).

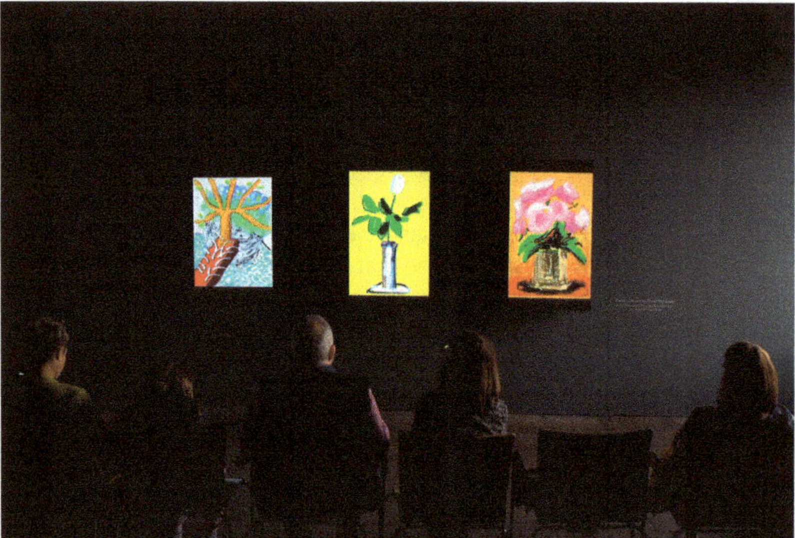

4.49 David Hockney, iPhone drawings on display screens, Salts Mill, Saltaire, West Yorkshire, UK, 2017.

Old Masters Term sometimes used to describe outstanding European artists working before the 19th century.

Further research

Discover more about iconography and symbols by visiting the British Museum and the National Gallery (UK) websites.

Find out more about Yayoi Kusama at the Tate Gallery website.

Sculpture

Learning objectives:

- To understand how audiences engage with sculpture
- To understand how the siting of sculpture can impact on the audience, both in terms of space and setting
- To understand that an artwork can have more than one interpretation

Sculpture is usually made to be viewed from all angles. It can invite the viewer to physically interact with it in some way, sometimes through touch or by moving around or even through it. In this unit, we look at how the space in which a sculpture is displayed can affect the way that the audience interacts with it. We also look at how the siting of sculptures can influence how we respond to and interpret the work.

SCULPTURE AND SPACE

The space in which a sculpture stands can add to the experience that the viewer has when interacting with the work. A good example of this can be seen in the piece *20:50* by the British artist Richard Wilson (born 1953) (Figure 4.50).

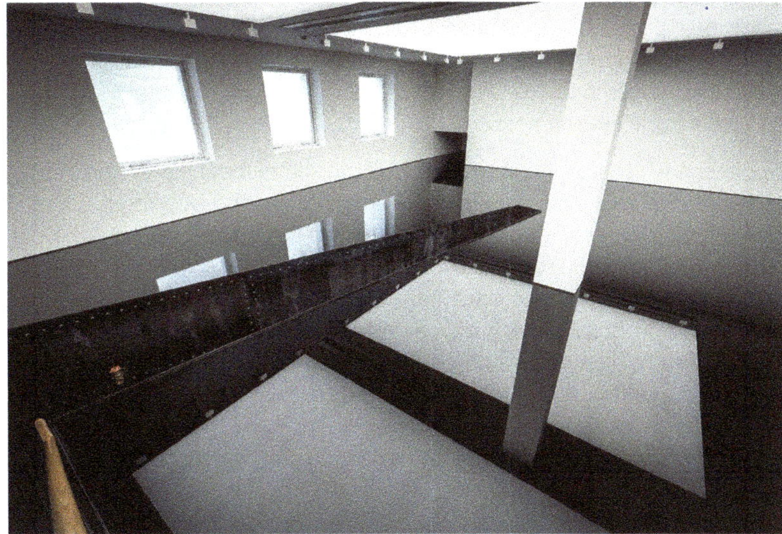

4.50 Richard Wilson, *20:50*, 1987, used sump oil, steel, and wood, Saatchi Gallery, London. The audience engages with this sculpture by walking into the heart of it. The space in which it is exhibited impacts on its visual appearance, becoming part of the work.

Wilson invites the viewer to engage with his work by walking into the middle of it, along a narrow gangway. The large-scale sculpture appears to turn the gallery space into a container, into which used sump oil (used engine oil) has been poured. The oil looks deep, and as the viewer walks to the centre of the structure they are meant to feel as though are wading, waist-deep, through it. In fact, the oil is in a shallow tray, attached to a raised, steel-clad wooden block.

The highly mirrored surface of the oil reflects the architecture of the gallery space. Therefore, the visual appearance of the sculpture changes when the location in which it is **sited** changes. The architectural features of the gallery space make a dramatic difference to the way that the work looks.

Activity A: **Create a space for a sculpture**

Using a sculpture that you have been working on, plan the space in which you could exhibit it.

1. Make sketches and notes about the space that you want to use. It could be an indoor or outdoor space.
2. Think about how you want your audience to interact with it. Do you want them to see it from above or below or from the side? Should they be able to walk all around it? Can they touch it?
3. Photograph your sculpture and, using an image manipulation programme such as Adobe Photoshop, combine the image of your work with an image of a gallery or outdoor space to show it in that location.
4. Add annotations to explain how you would like your audience to interact with your work.

Tip:

You could create your own ideal space in which you could site your sculpture, by drawing or painting an imaginary gallery or other location.

sited If something is sited in a particular place or location, it is placed or built there.

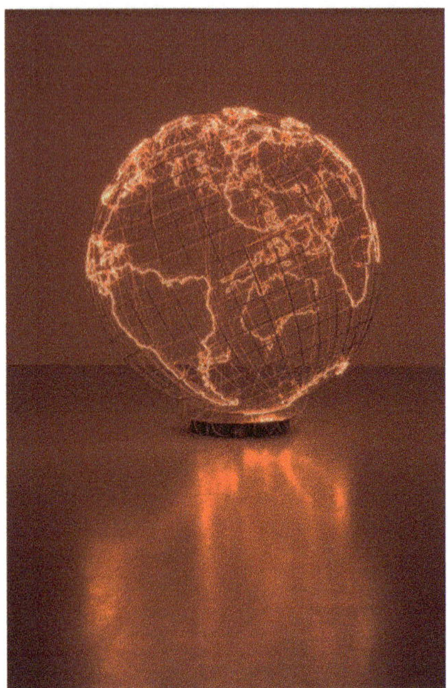

4.51 Mona Hatoum, *Hot Spot III*, 2009, stainless steel and neon tube, 234 × 223 × 223 cm, on display at MdBK Leipzig, 2016. Hatoum uses space, neon lighting and sound to engage audiences with her work. What is your interpretation of this work? Justify your interpretation and discuss with your classmates.

ENGAGING THE AUDIENCE

Space is not the only way in which an artist can invite an audience to engage with their work. The Palestinian artist Mona Hatoum (born 1952) is a sculptor who wants her audience to walk around her work to engage with it, but she also uses light and sound to draw the viewer in and help communicate her intention. This can be seen in her piece *Hot Spot III* (Figure 4.51), which challenges the notion of boundaries and borders. The sculpture takes the form of a globe tilting on its axis, just as the Earth does, where the neon outlines of the map glow and buzz.

Two interpretations of this piece are possible:

1. We can read it as referring to political hot spots, with the glowing lines representing contested borders.
2. We can see it as symbolising global warming, with the neon and buzzing noises reflecting the wasteful amount of heat generated by human activity.

Hatoum has stated that, above all, she wants to provoke an emotional and psychological response in her audience, unique to each person.

SCULPTURE AND SETTING

Sculptures can be seen in a variety of settings – for example:

- indoor galleries
- sculpture parks
- religious spaces, such as churches or temples
- on the façades of buildings
- in public spaces in towns
- in the natural environment.

The place in which a sculpture is exhibited can sometimes help us to understand the artist's intention or have an impact on the work itself. Sometimes, if it is possible to interpret a work in more than one way, where it is sited will influence our understanding.

For example, the Brazilian artist Ana Maria Pacheco (born 1943) is a sculptor who produces work with meanings linked to the Roman Catholic faith, the main religion of her homeland, Pacheco also refers to the history of Brazil in her work, exploring the brutality and violence used against ordinary people when Portugal ruled Brazil as a colony (1500–1815). Pacheco's work has been exhibited in galleries, but also in church and cathedral settings (Figure 4.52), thereby making a direct link to the Roman Catholic references.

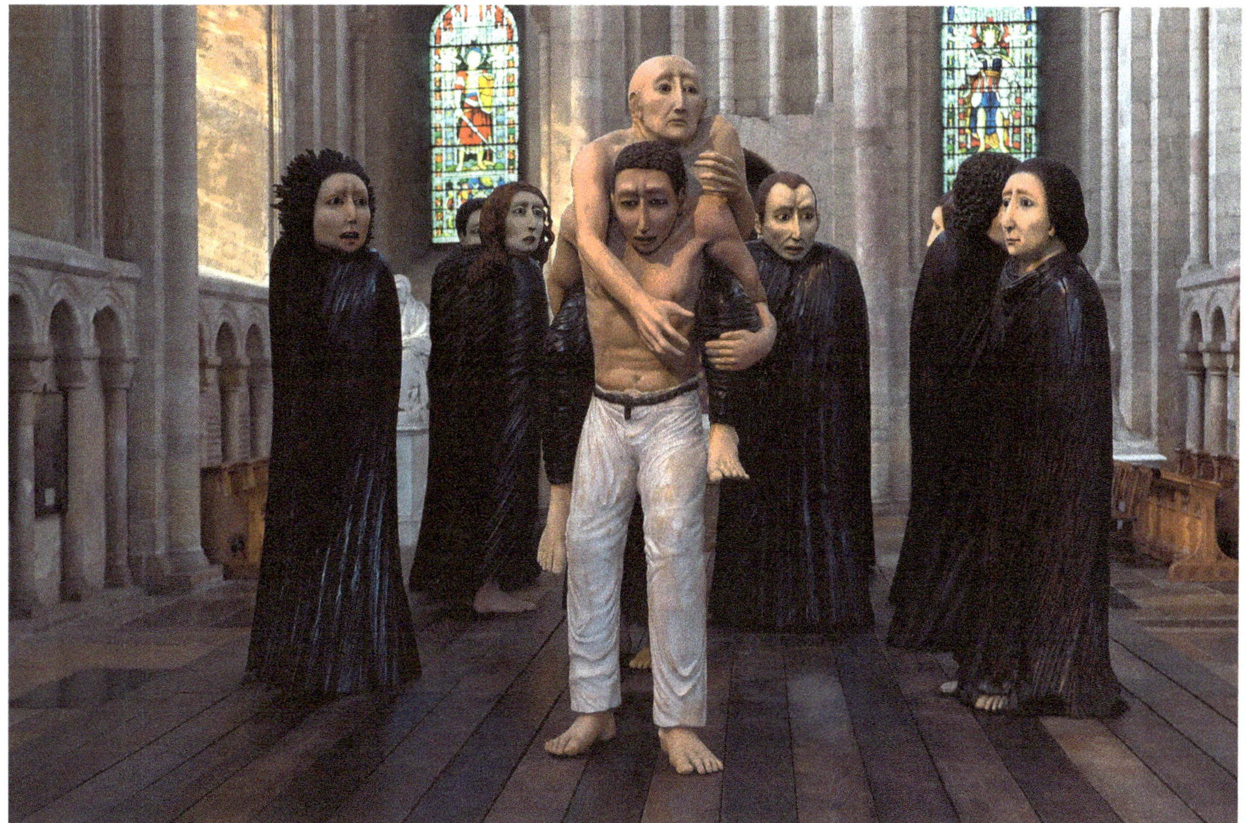

4.52 Ana Maria Pacheco, *Shadows of the Wanderer*, 2008, polychrome wood, on display at Salisbury Cathedral, Wiltshire. How does the setting influence the way in which we interpret the sculpture? Does the setting turn the work into a 'religious' work of art? Now imagine it in a different setting – for example, a park. Do you think your response to the sculpture would be different?

Activity B: **Change the setting of a sculpture**

1. Choose one of the following well-known sculptures: a) *Winged Victory of Samothrace* b) Michelangelo, *Moses*, c) Auguste Rodin, *The Thinker*, d) Alberto Giacometti, *Walking Man II*, e) Arturo Di Modica, *Charging Bull*.
2. Discuss the sculpture with your classmates and try to interpret the artist's intention.
3. Next, using an image manipulation program such as Photoshop, take the image of the sculpture that you have chosen and put it into different types of setting. For example, place it in an outdoor location, or in spaces with very different architectural features, or in a place with special meaning attached to it.
4. Make notes about how each different setting changes the way that you see the sculpture. Does a different setting affect the way that you interpret the work?

Further research

To find out more about the work of Mona Hatoum, Ana Maria Pacheco and Richard Wilson, go to the Tate Gallery, National Gallery (UK) and Saatchi Gallery websites.

Printmaking

Learning objectives:

- To understand what is meant by the term 'edition' in printmaking
- To understand how contemporary printmakers experiment with the presentation of their work

In this unit we look at how fine art printmakers present their work, both in traditional and more experimental ways. We look at how artists print editions, consider the use of shaped plates within the design of the print, and the way that contemporary printmakers are using mixed-media techniques within their practice.

EDITIONS AND NON-STANDARD EDITIONS

Artists can decide to present their prints to the audience either as editions or non-standard editions.

- An edition is where the artist creates a fixed number of copies of the final print. For example, an edition of 25 refers to 25 identical prints being taken from the same print plate or screen print. Editions are numbered, usually in the bottom left-hand corner, directly below the image. A print numbered '2/25' represents the second print taken from a run of 25 in total.
- A non-standard edition is where the artist takes prints from the same print plate or screen stencils, but individually colours them or otherwise makes them different. Non-standard editions are not usually numbered, as each is a unique variation.

Activity A: **Print an edition**

1. Using a printing plate that you have created, make an edition of five identical prints. Remember that you will have to proof your print first, prior to creating your edition, so refer back to Module 3, pages 241–242 if necessary.
2. The quality of printed image should be consistent across all your prints.
3. Number the edition in the order that you made the prints.

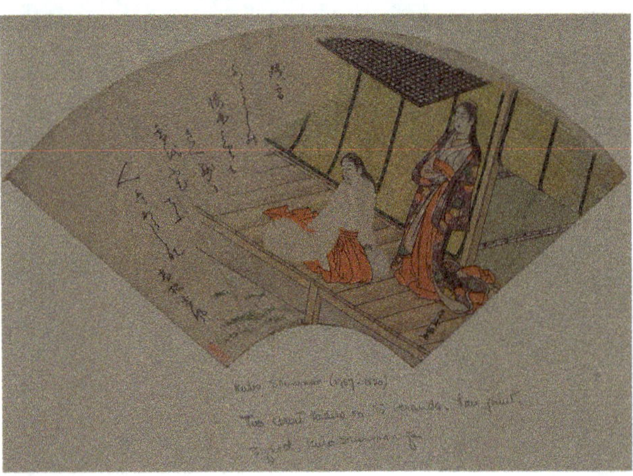

4.53 Anonymous, *Snow on Mount Koro*, c.1795–1805, woodblock print, private collection. The fan-shaped woodblock used here adds interest to the overall composition of the design, as well as having cultural significance.

DIFFERENT-SHAPED PLATES

Printmakers usually choose to work using a square or rectangular format. However, the shape of an intaglio or relief plate does not have to be like this. The shape of the printing plate can be designed to contribute to the overall composition of the image, providing interest for the viewer.

Japanese printmakers in the 18th century sometimes experimented with different-shaped blocks, as can be seen in *Snow on Mount Koro* (Figure 4.53). Here the artist has presented an image of two women of the Japanese court on a veranda in the shape of a fan. In Japanese culture, the fan has a long history in religion, folklore and poetry and was an important part of formal dress for both men and women.

Activity B: **Make a different-shaped print**

Make and present a relief print where the shape of the printing block either reflects the imagery of the subject matter or has cultural significance related to your work.

Materials and techniques: **Chine-collé**

The surface on to which artists choose to print can impact on the final presentation of the work. The process known as chine-collé can be used to add a background colour as well as delicate detail to a monochrome print plate.

1. The printmaker cuts a shaped piece of fine tissue paper to size and places it on the inked plate.
2. They then spread a small amount of glue on the topside of the tissue paper.
3. The print is then taken. The tissue paper sticks to the paper, onto which the print is transferred when the plate passes through the press.

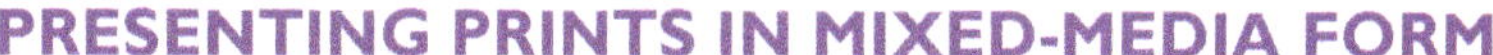

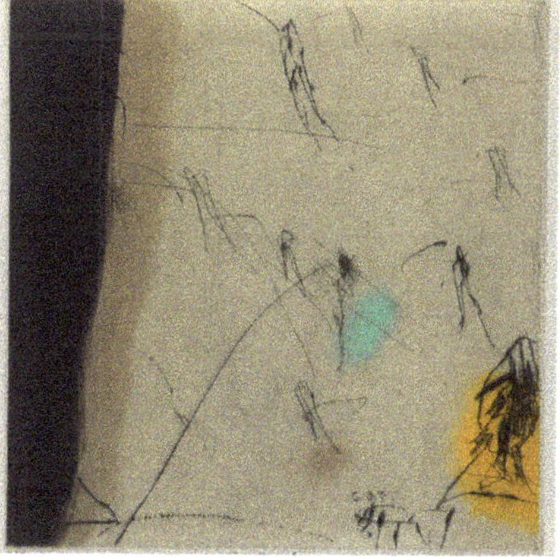

4.54 Takashi Itoh, *Square*, before 1978, intaglio with chine-collé, Brooklyn Museum of Art, New York. The coloured areas have been created using the chine-collé process.

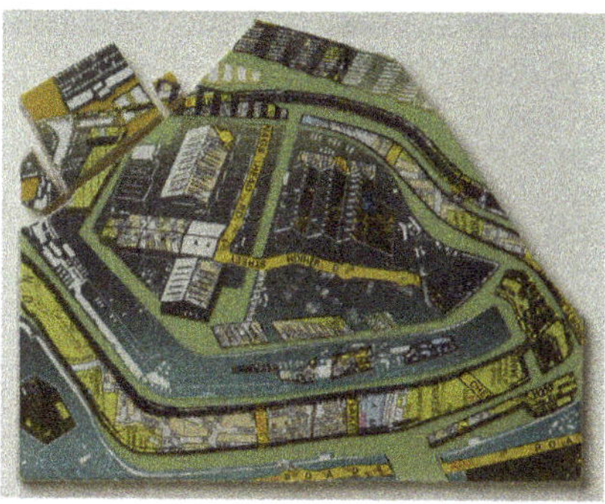

4.55 Anne Desmet, *Pieces of History*, 2010, private collection. Here the artist has printed wood engravings on to pages from a London A–Z street atlas, and then collaged them onto four pieces of ceramic tile.

PRESENTING PRINTS IN MIXED-MEDIA FORM

Printmaking has gradually become more experimental in nature, with some contemporary artists presenting prints in very different ways – for example, using prints to create collages or installations, or printing on surfaces other than plain papers. Go to the website of American artist Yashua Klos (born 1977) to see how he creates large-scale heads from woodblock prints of different textures that are collaged together. Now look at the introduction page of German artist Thomas Kilpper's (born 1956) website to see a large-scale print installation.

The work of British printmaker Anne Desmet (born 1964) provides a good example of an artist printing onto different surfaces when she makes her non-standard editions. She prints her images of urban buildings directly onto pre-printed surfaces such as maps so that the original printed surface becomes integrated with her own imagery. She also uses her prints as collage materials (Figure 4.55). This complex process of producing prints reflects Desmet's interest in how cities and buildings undergo change, both destruction and **regeneration**.

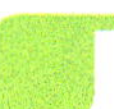

Activity C: **Print onto pre-printed papers**

1. Collect different commercially printed papers, such as pages from newspapers, magazines, maps or gift wrap.
2. Now print an existing relief plate onto the different surfaces.
3. Print the plate onto plain white paper to compare the outcomes.

Critical thinking:

Look at your outcomes from **Activity C**, and think about the impact that printing onto pre-printed paper has on your own visual imagery. Record your thoughts in your annotations.

Further research

To find out more about the work of Anne Desmet, go to her website.

For more information about printing editions, see *Printmaking: A Complete Guide to Materials and Processes*, 2nd edition, by Bill Fick and Beth Grabowski (Laurence King Publishing, 2015).

regeneration To renew and revive a run-down or economically depressed area of a town or city.

Mixed media

Learning objectives:

- To understand how artists convey intention and meaning to audiences
- To understand how artists can plan to exhibit their work as an integral part of the piece

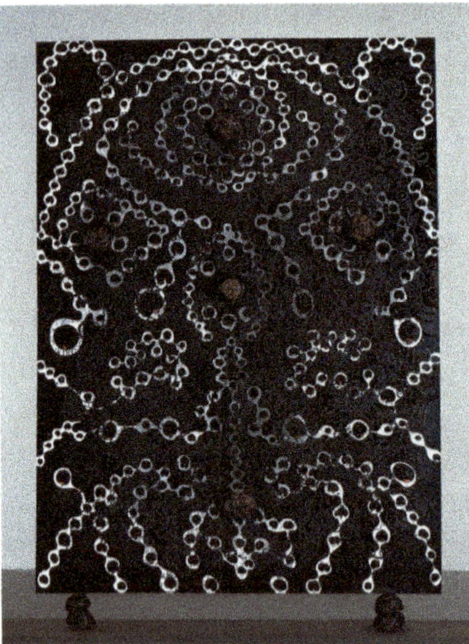

4.56 Chris Ofili, *Afrobluff*, 1997, acrylic paint, oil paint, paper collage, polyester resin, glitter, map pins, elephant dung on linen. Ofili plans how he wants his work to be presented in a gallery in order to give his work a relaxed feeling.

In this unit, we look at how the way artists present their work to the public is an integral part of their creative journey. This builds on ideas from pages 300–301 in this module, about the use of iconography and how artists engage with their audience. We also look at how they communicate their intentions to their audience.

Today artists can easily communicate their intentions and explain the meaning of their work across a wide range of media platforms, such as blogs on Tumblr or WordPress, personal websites and through newspaper or magazine interviews. This can influence how we view and understand their work more easily than ever before.

The usual way to exhibit a work on canvas is to frame it and hang it on a gallery wall, but some artists want us to see their work in a different way. For some artists, planning how their work will be presented to the audience is an important part of the process of creating it. This is because the presentation can add something to the way in which the audience experiences the work or can enhance the meaning of the work.

An example of this can be seen in the work of the British artist Chris Ofili (born 1968), who, by drawing on his African heritage and visits to Zimbabwe, uses the highly unusual medium of elephant dung in some of his mixed-media paintings. Ofili designed canvases such as *Afrobluff* (Figure 4.56) to be displayed in a gallery space leaning against the wall and propped in position by dried elephant dung supports. This move away from the convention of hanging art on a wall allows the viewer to see his artwork from a different viewpoint, providing a fresh perspective. Ofili does this to make the painting feel more relaxed and 'friendly'.

Critical thinking:

How do you want an audience to view your work? Has it been made to be hung on a wall, or would seeing it from a different viewpoint engage the audience in a different way? Discuss your thoughts with a partner.

Activity A: **Interview the artist**

Work with a partner and interview each other about the work that you have produced as part of your course.

1. Begin by preparing some questions to ask. Refer back to the 'Personal Investigation' section in Module 3, pages 191–193, to get some ideas for questions to ask when interviewing an artist.
2. Using your questions, interview your partner about their work and record their answers.
3. Write a short (400-word) report, as if writing a newspaper article or an online blog.

Further research

To find out more about the work of Chris Ofili, go to the Tate Gallery website.

impetus Force or motivation.
Sufism Spiritual aspect of Islam in which believers seek direct inner experience of God.

Artists and designers: **Faiza Shaikh**

Faiza Shaikh is a contemporary Pakistani artist who exhibits internationally and who uses a range of media sources to explain her work to her audience. Using everything from blogs to newspaper and magazine interviews, she is able to ensure that her audiences are able to understand the meaning of her work.

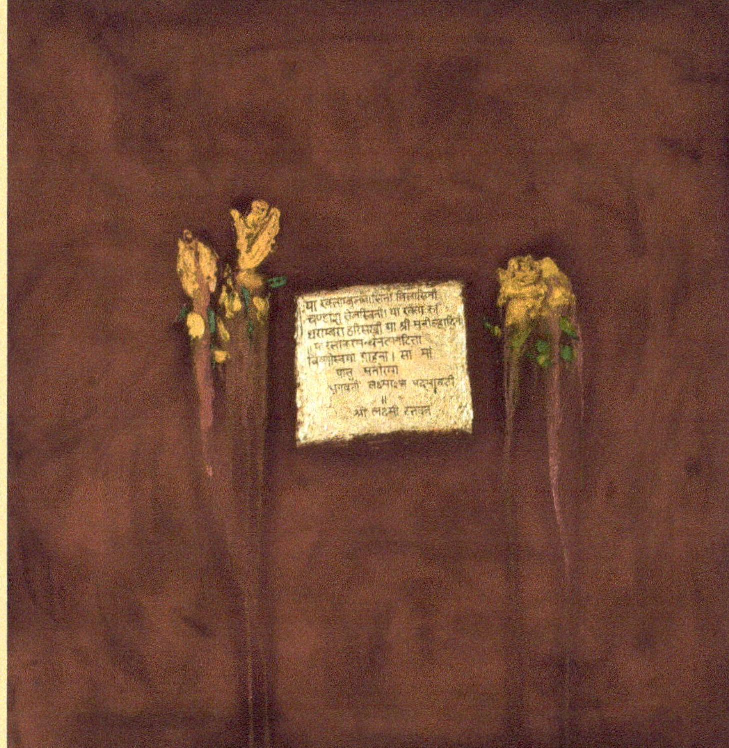

4.57 Faiza Shaikh, *Laxmi*, mixed media, 2007, private collection. This work includes direct references to philosophical texts that inspire the artist.

Faiza Shaikh's work is based around her personal responses to Islamic philosophy. In her artworks she often includes delicate Arabic calligraphy, collaged against bold colours on carefully treated canvases that look as though they are made from luxury fabrics such as velvet (Figure 4.57). Shaikh takes inspiration from the work of the Persian poet Rumi (1207–73) and from **Sufism**.

According to Shaikh, her work 'presents the quest for perfection, taking **impetus** from this world, but without depicting its content'. Although her paintings use direct quotations from philosophical or poetic texts, Shaikh intends her work to be open to countless interpretations, dependent on the response of each person who views them (Figure 4.58).

To find out more about the work of Faiza Shaikh, go to her website.

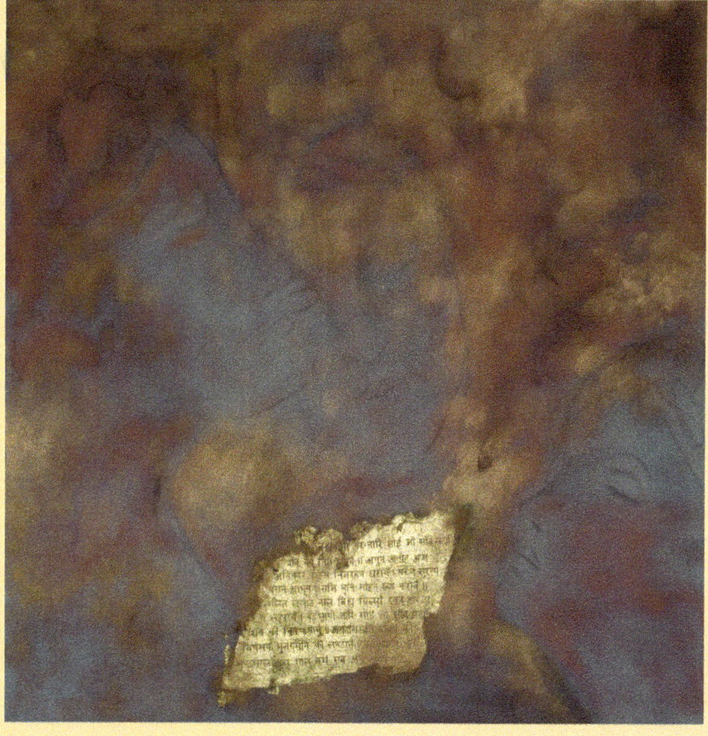

4.58 Faiza Shaikh, *Satyam Shivam Sundaram [The Truth, the Good and the Beauty]*, 2007, mixed media, private collection. Here, Shaikh includes the delicate outline of female faces in the painting. How do you respond to and interpret this painting? To help you, research Faiza Shaikh's own words in blogs and interviews.

Painting

Learning objectives:

- To understand how painters present their work to an audience
- To explore techniques used to present painting work to an audience

Painters use different ways to present their work to their audience. They show work through specific outlets, such as in solo or group exhibitions at galleries or trade fairs. They can also show work online through a website. They use different techniques when they present their work, such as mounting and framing, photographing and so on. Some of these formats have been covered in earlier units in this section. In this unit, you will look at different ways that painting can be presented, focusing on presenting work using different formats, mounts and other surfaces; exhibiting work in galleries; and presenting work digitally.

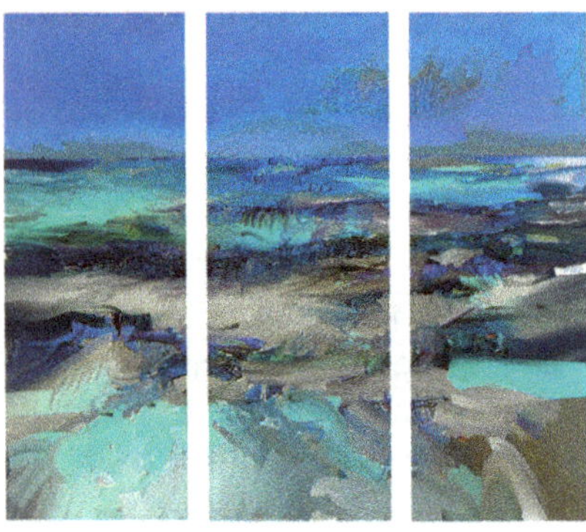

4.59 Alan Parsons, *The Sea*, Cyprus, 2014, digital print, oil, acrylic, collage. The original painting has been photographed and reworked to create a triptych. What effect do you think this presentation has on the image?

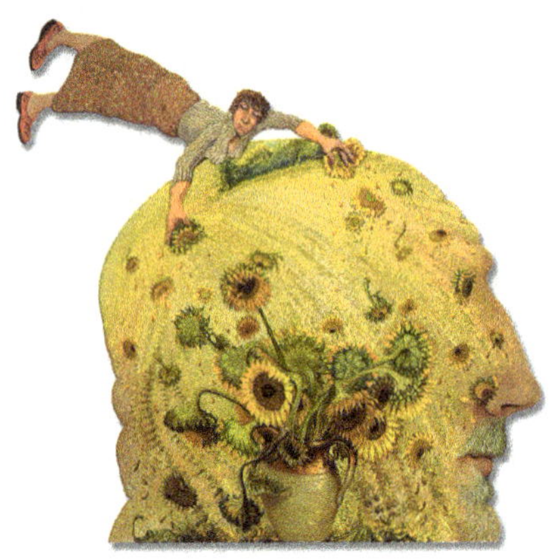

4.60 Anthony Green, *Vase of Sunflowers*, 2009, oil on MDF board, private collection. Again, what effect do you think this presentation has on the image?

PRESENTING WORK

Exploring formats

Painters explore different formats for their work. This is normally linked directly to the kind of image that they want to create. This in turn relates to their intention, and what they want to communicate to the audience. Formats can take many shapes and sizes:

- Very large paintings, such as those by **Abstract Expressionists**, are designed to draw the viewer into a powerful, almost physical experience. The work is often physically larger than the viewer and completely fills their **field of vision**.
- Small-scale work often creates a more intimate experience for the viewer and draws them into a private, inner world that will remain unseen unless the viewer looks really closely.

Formats such as the **diptych** and triptych were traditionally used in Western art for paintings with a religious purpose (for example, for display in a church to encourage prayer and meditation). However, these formats can be also used to reformat and enrich an image, as in the paintings in Figure 4.59:

- This was originally a single painting.
- It was photographed and made into a triptych, by digitally separating the image into three sections.
- These were printed out onto three different strips of wide-format canvas.
- Each one was worked on further with paint.
- The strips were then stapled to a stretcher.

Painters sometimes explore unusually shaped canvases or boards, as in the oil painting of sunflowers by the British artist Anthony Green (born 1939) (Figure 4.60).

Activity A: **Create a diptych or triptych**

1. Using one of your own existing paintings, consider how you could re-present it as a diptych or triptych.
2. Use the method outlined above to create a new work out of the painting.
3. In discussion with a classmate, consider whether the new format has brought something new to the artwork.

Exploring mounts

You can use mounts or mount board to control the size and shape of your work when you present it. Mounts are typically made from card or foam board. They can be used to show flat work produced on paper or similar supports. They provide a clear edge around the piece. They can be:

- *window mounts* – these show the artwork through a 'window' cut into the middle of the card, with the margins carefully calculated.
- *surface mount* – these have the artwork literally spray-mounted to the surface. The work being surface mounted needs to be clean and neatly cut, with straight or sharp lines. You have already learned about cutting mounts on page 292.

Exploring murals or wall paintings

Some of the earliest images made by humans are found on cave walls. Since ancient times, artists have also created paintings known as murals on the walls of important buildings. Sometimes this type of painting has been used to narrate a religious story or event, as in the fresco cycles found inside many Italian medieval and Renaissance churches, which told the story of key events in the Bible or in the lives of saints (Figure 4.61).

At other times, wall paintings can commemorate political ideas or historical events. They are a very public way to show work. There is no entrance fee or charge to look at murals in public buildings. Painters such as the Mexican artists Diego Rivera (1886–1957) and José Clemente Orozco (1883–1949) believed that murals were essential so that everyone had access to important art-based images. You can see a contemporary example of a 'political' mural in Figure 4.62.

Today street artists use the outside walls of houses and other buildings as their 'canvas'. In this way, they can communicate directly with their target audience – often people who would rarely go into a museum or gallery to view art. A well-known artist of this kind is Banksy. This British artist keeps his identity a secret so that his art and his message are always the most important thing rather than his personality or celebrity.

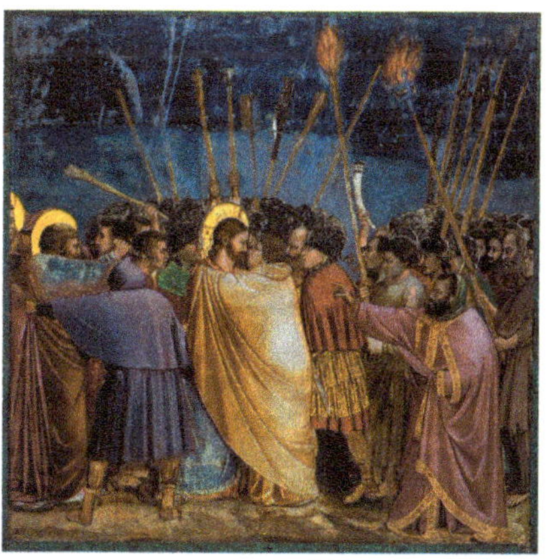

4.61 Giotto, *The Kiss of Judas*, about 1305, fresco, Scrovegni Chapel, Padua. This scene is part of a fresco cycle showing the life of Christ painted by the Italian artist Giotto di Bondone (about 1270–1337).

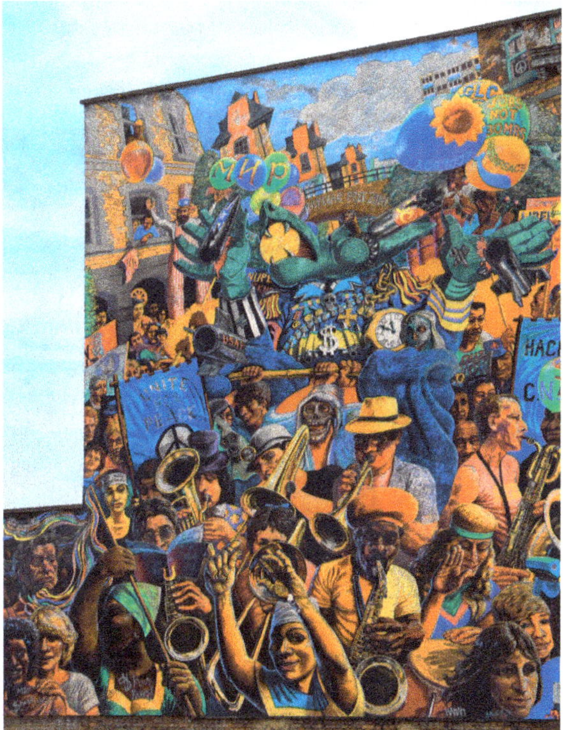

4.62 *Hackney Peace Carnival Mural*, Dalston, London, England. Images can become monumental when produced on a larger scale, communicating ideas to a mass audience. What message do you think this artist wanted to convey?

Abstract Expressionists Art movement based in the United States in the 1940s and 1950s in which artists made large-scale painting often using energetic mark-making and/or intense, vibrant colour. Key artists include Jackson Pollock (1912–56) and Mark Rothko (1903–70).

diptych A painting made up of two separate panels or canvases, showing separate but related imagery, or imagery spreading across both panels.

field of vision The area you can see without turning your head.

PRESENTING WORK IN GALLERIES

Galleries are managed in different ways, depending on who owns or runs them:

- Some galleries have been set up to house a private collection of paintings given to the state – many of the larger or national galleries in countries have been set up in this way. Such galleries often show paintings from historical periods.
- Some galleries are publicly run by arts groups or locally funded organisations.
- Other types of galleries are run on a commercial basis (Figure 4.63). They show well-known (established) as well as up-and-coming artists and sell their work to customers. These types of galleries charge a **commission**. This covers their cost of running the gallery as well as generating profit.

Activity B: **Hold a class discussion**

The kind of gallery an artwork is shown in can influence the way we look at the artwork. Hold a class discussion to consider in what ways and why this might happen.

The gallery space

Presenting work in a gallery is called hanging a show. Artists and technicians spend a lot of time planning out exhibitions in galleries. Some artists make scale models of the spaces, rooms and exhibits to be able to see how the exhibition will look. These are used to work out the running order of paintings and the way they are spaced, and to preview the experience of a visitor to the exhibition. Some exhibitions are dense, with lots of paintings hung together. Other exhibitions are more formal, with large amounts of space around each picture to focus the viewer's attention on the work (Figure 4.64).

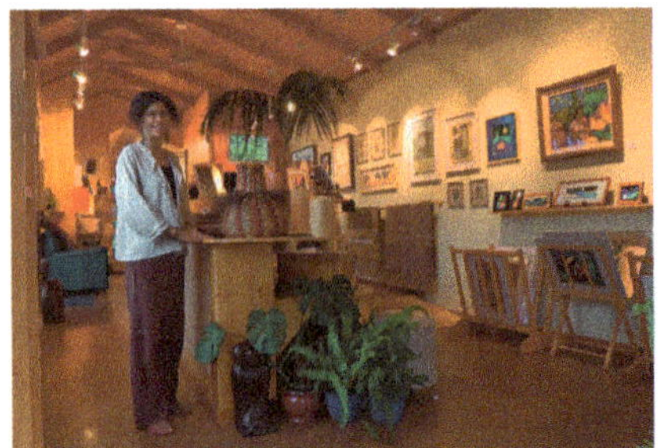

4.63 Kirsten Bunney Gallery, Makawao, Maui, Hawaii. This figure shows a commercial fine art gallery. There are artworks both on the walls and in print racks. A commercial galley will run short exhibitions, so that there is always lots of new work for people to buy.

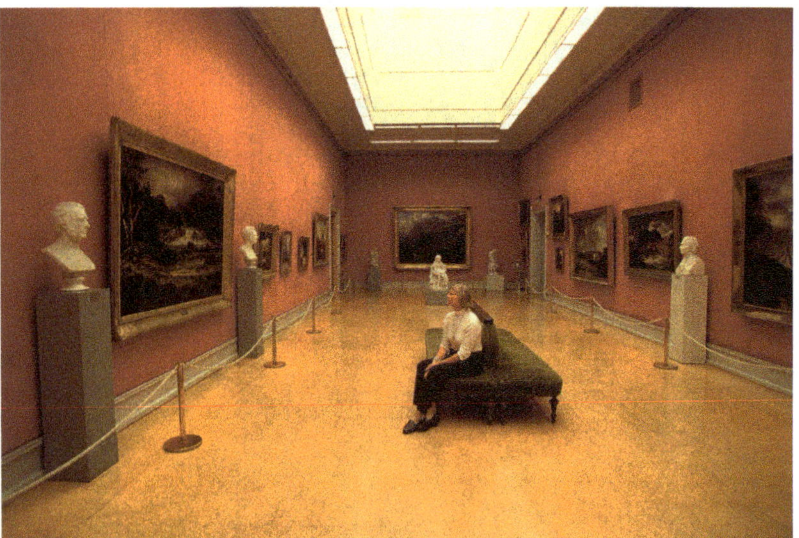

4.64 Display of paintings at the National Gallery of Norway, Oslo. In this prestigious state-run gallery, the paintings have been hung with lots of space around each work. What do you think that this way of hanging suggests to the viewer?

Ways of hanging pictures change, not only according to the types of venue but also over time. In past centuries in Europe, for example, pictures were hung very close to one another, not only side by side, but stacked one on top of the other (Figure 4.65).

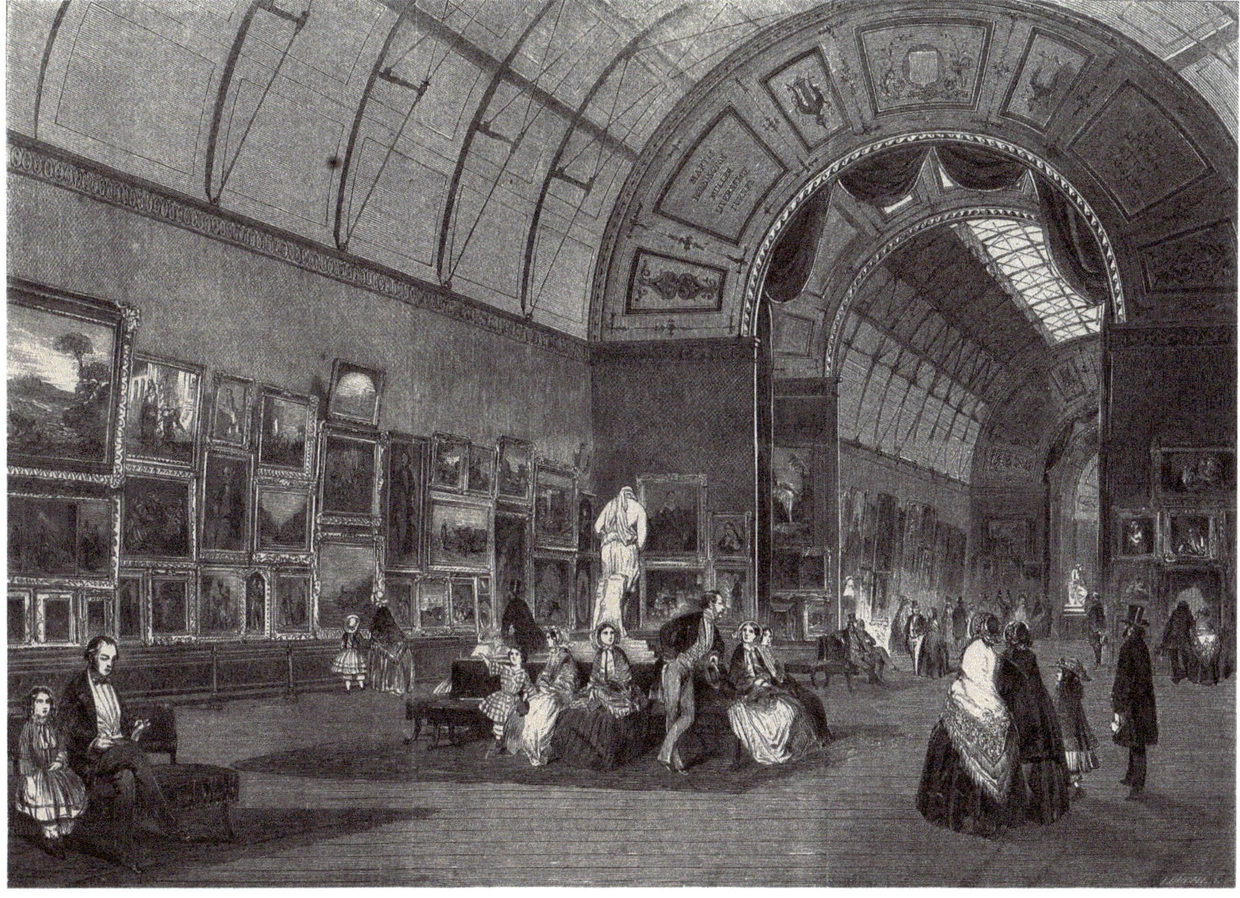

4.65 A typical display of paintings in a gallery in the 19th century. Some images would have been so high that they would have been hard to see. What effect do you think viewing paintings in this way would have had on the audience?

Activity C: **Research local galleries**

1. Working in threes, get tourist maps of the nearest large town or city to your location.
2. Make arrangements to travel safely to this town or city and use the maps or points of interest (POIs) on Google to find the location of galleries – large and small, public and commercial.
3. In your groups, visit the galleries, and make notes on the following:
   - Is the gallery commercial or public?
   - Who is the intended audience?
   - How is the work displayed?
   - What type of work is being shown?
4. Back at your school or centre, discuss your research as a group.
5. Create a digital presentation of no more than six slides and present your findings back to your classmates.

Tip:

Artists have to understand the context of the venue or location where their work will be shown. Part of this includes developing an understanding of the kind of audience that will be seeing the work, and what their expectations will be. This is used to inform the layout and the sequencing of exhibits.

commission A percentage of the sale price of an artwork taken by the gallery at point of sale. It will vary according to gallery and location.

DIGITAL PRESENTATIONS

Artists also increasingly use digital formats for presenting their work. There are various ways of doing this:

- Artists develop websites that show their work across their career, providing background information, artist's statements and a list of exhibitions they have taken part in (Figure 4.66).
- Some artists use digital formats to present the work itself. For example, the British artist David Hockney includes the development of his iPad drawings (see page 302) in the gallery setting.
- Students also use digital presentation methods as part of the submission and application process to study in further or higher education.

A gallery or agent will also use websites as a platform for showing artists' work (Figure 4.67).

4.66 Exchange + Draw, 2016. Example of a webpage showing arrangement of work and icons. Each icon opens up a series of further images, allowing the user the chance to see a large amount of digital-based work.

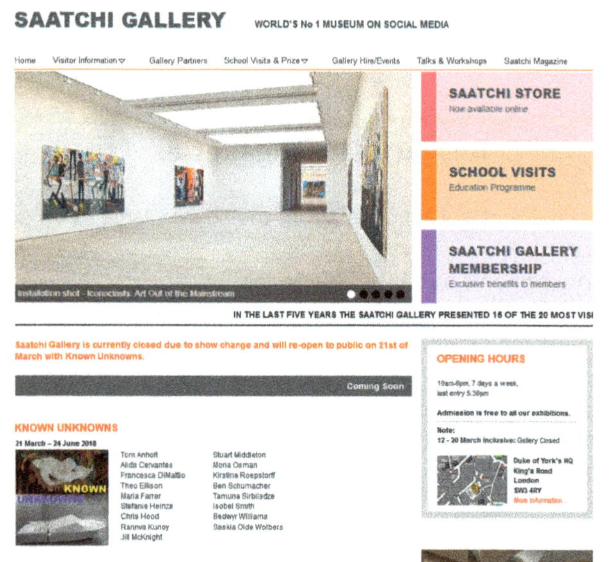

4.67 Saatchi Gallery, internet homepage. Artists are promoted by galleries and art organisations through the internet.

Critical thinking:

1. Evaluate your approach to presenting your work.
2. Reflect on the materials, techniques and processes you used for the presentation activities.
3. Write a short response, identifying:
    - strengths in the way you presented work
    - areas for development
    - how you addressed the audience requirements or needs.

Activity D: **Display your painting work**

To carry out this activity, you will need a complete body of painting work that you have produced for a project. Display your work in a physical setting:

- Mount or frame the final piece(s).
- Use appropriate techniques safely to hang the painting work.
- Write an Artist's Statement to support the work, and display this alongside the work.

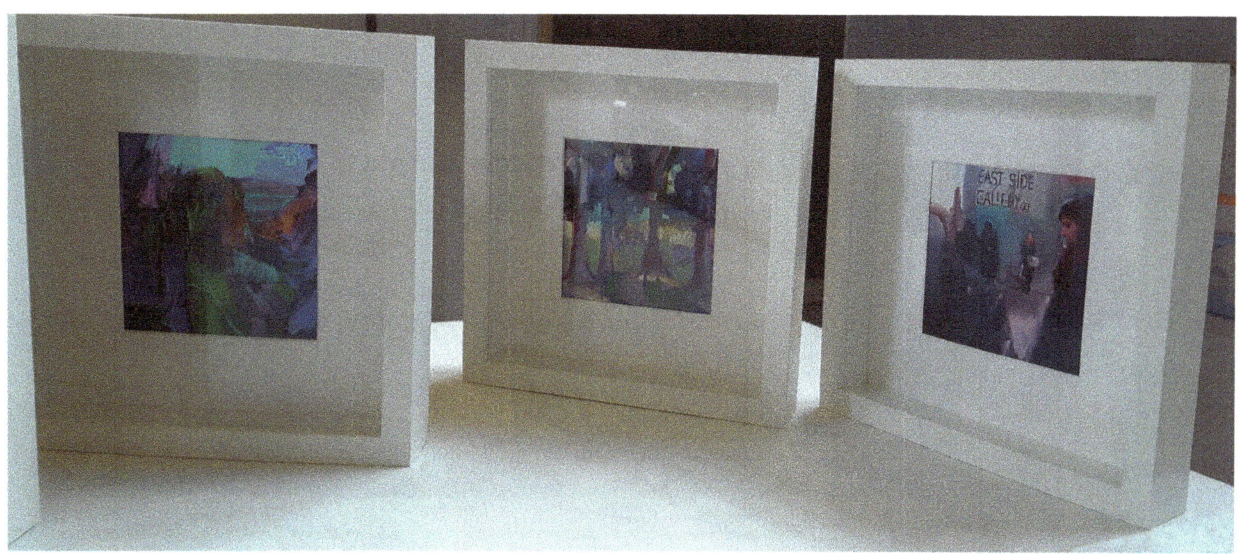

4.68 Alan Parsons, Set of three painting studies, 2016, box frames. Here the artist has used frames that are coordinated and neutral.

Further research

Go online to find out more on mounting artwork and painting, and digital presentations.

For more on framing and displaying work, read *The Complete Photo Guide to Framing and Displaying Artwork* by V.C. Kistler (Creative Publishing, 2009).

Photography

Learning objective:

- To explore techniques to present photographic work

There are similarities in displaying and presenting photographic work to that of painting. This unit will look at some of the approaches to presenting photographic images, and how photographers appreciate and understand how presentation techniques affect or involve the audience.

NARRATIVE PHOTOGRAPHY – PHOTOBOOKS

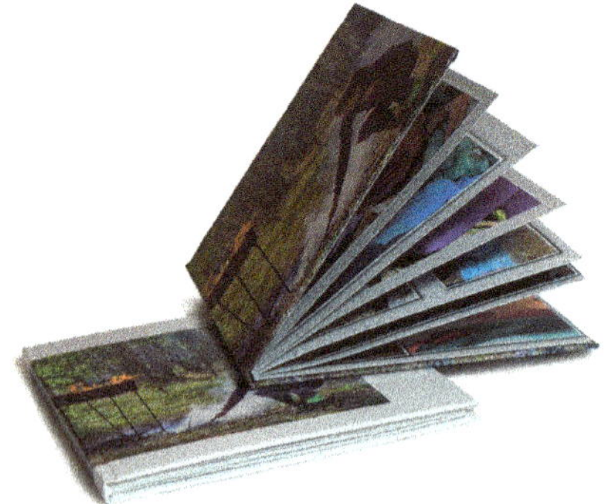

4.69 Example of a photobook. Photobooks are often used to present narrative imagery, or simply for collections of photographs. Sequence and layout are important things to consider when designing photobooks.

Some photographers who specialise in narrative image making use photobooks – published sets of images – to present their work (Figure 4.69). Photobooks allow photographers to reach a very wide audience and to take advantage of the book format to tell a story, as the 'reader' (viewer) flicks through.

For example, for one project commissioned by the Fondation Cartier pour l'Art Contemporain in Paris, the Japanese photographer Nobuyoshi Araki (born 1940) took a single photograph each day over one year. Initially, the artist published the images online as a weekly slide show. At the end of the project, however, he gathered the images together in a single book, *Hi-Nikki (Non-Diary Diary)*, published in 2016.

Photobooks are also often used by journalistic and documentary photographers.

Activity A: **Create a simple photobook**

Note: only printed photographs can be submitted for assessment – no digital files.

1. Using your own existing photographic work or by creating a fresh series of images, present your work in the form of a short hand-crafted photobook.
2. Consider the sequence of images and the layout, so that you tell a strong story as the reader/viewer turns the pages.
3. Consider including captions to enhance your audience's experience of your work.

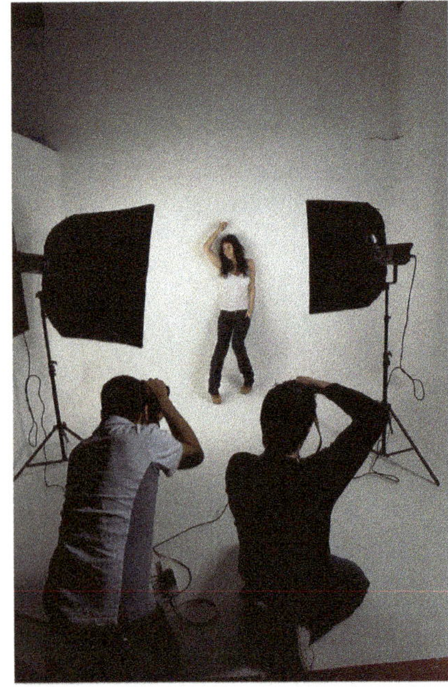

4.70 A model on a fashion shoot. Sets and lighting are used to create an effect that makes the model stand out.

FASHION PHOTOGRAPHY – MAGAZINES AND WEBSITES

Fashion photography is aimed at a specific audience. It uses techniques and considerable effort to make images that meet the needs of its audience, be they readers of magazines or websites. Whole teams of assistants, make-up artists, set designers and photographers work on shoots, coordinated by an art director. They will have considered and targeted their audience using data and information provided by the client. This may also link to the target audience of any brand or fashion product.

PROJECTING PHOTOGRAPHIC IMAGES

Some photographers use projection to present their work, often as part of an installation. They may choose to show photographic or lens-based imagery on its own or combine with sound within a defined space (Figure 4.71). The viewer may be directed to sit or stand at a particular spot and see a projected display of images that are much larger than still or printed imagery. This work can often have a powerful emotional impact.

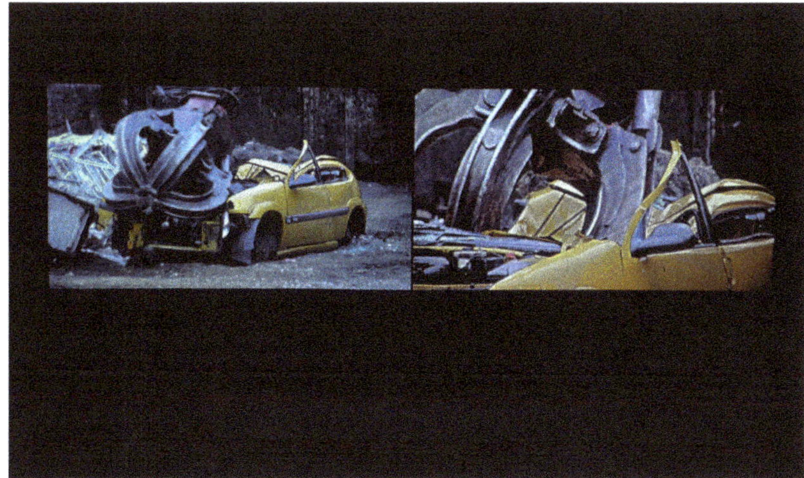

4.71 Zineb Sedira, *The End of the Road*, 2010, Double video projection (color, sound), super 16mm, 13 min 44 s, 16:9 format, soundtrack by Mikhail Karikis, Commissioned by and collection of Mathaf – Arab Museum of Modern Art, Doha.

Activity B: **Compare two presentation techniques for photography**

Take a set of images that you used for a project. You will need at least eight images. Try out two different presentation techniques – the first is printing, mounting and hanging; the second is projection:

Technique 1:

- Print your images onto good-quality paper.
- Mount them using the techniques shown on page 292.
- Hang or stick these images to the wall of your 'gallery' space.
- Ask your classmates to view your work and give you feedback.

Technique 2:

- Now take the same images and use them to create a digital presentation that you can project. You will need to use a data projector for this. If you do not have access to a projector, use the largest TV screen you can.
- Use a digital software package to edit your images into a projected/ television screen presentation that lasts two minutes.
- You may choose to control the way your viewers interact with the imagery – for example, by arranging the seating in the space.
- Ask your classmates to view the display and give you feedback.

Finally, ask your classmates which presentation technique they liked the most, and why. Make notes on their responses.

Note: only printed photographs can be submitted for assessment, not digital files.

Critical thinking:

Evaluate the responses to your presentations and write or present a short response. Consider the following questions:

- Which presentation technique did your audience prefer, and why?
- Which technique did you prefer, and again why?
- Were your audience's preferences and reasons the same as yours?
- How will this process of evaluation influence the presentation of your photographic work in future?

Further research

Find out more about making photobooks in *Create Your Own Photo Book* by Petra Vogt (Rocky Nook, 2012).

Go online to find advice on creating photo slideshows.

Explore the use of photography in installations at the MoMA website.

4.3 Three-dimensional (3D) design

Architecture

Learning objectives:

- To understand how architecture meets audience needs
- To understand the links between audience and architect and how this influences designs
- To develop and present an architecture response considering audience needs

Architects design buildings with people and spaces in mind from the very beginning. Architects and designers need to consider the needs of the users as they develop their designs and structures, as these will be environments that people will use. In this unit, we focus on public architecture – buildings such as town halls, libraries, concert halls and hospitals that are created for (at least potentially) everyone.

UNDERSTANDING AUDIENCE NEEDS

Understanding audience needs is a vital part of the design process used to develop a public building. In order to do so, they will quite often consult the local community, sometimes through focus groups. To consider audience needs, they ask questions such as: What is the purpose of the building? How is it going to be used? How will it engage with the existing fabric of the town and, crucially, with the people who live there?

Public building can be designed to:

- provide local **amenities**, such as public libraries
- raise awareness of and reflect pride in a local culture, as in the Harlem Hospital Pavilion (Figure 4.74)
- create a landmark as a key part in a program of urban regeneration, as in the Guggenheim Museum, Bilbao (Figure 4.75).
- host, celebrate or commemorate a national event, such as when a country hosts the Olympic Games (Figures 4.76 and 4.77).

We will look at all each of these aims in more depth below. More than one of these factors may come into play when creating any particular public building. The Guggenheim Museum, for example, is not only a landmark in the city's fabric but, with its ship-like shape and 'fish-scale' reflective panels, reflects the culture of the ancient port city of Bilbao. The general public also wants to see that public money has been well spent.

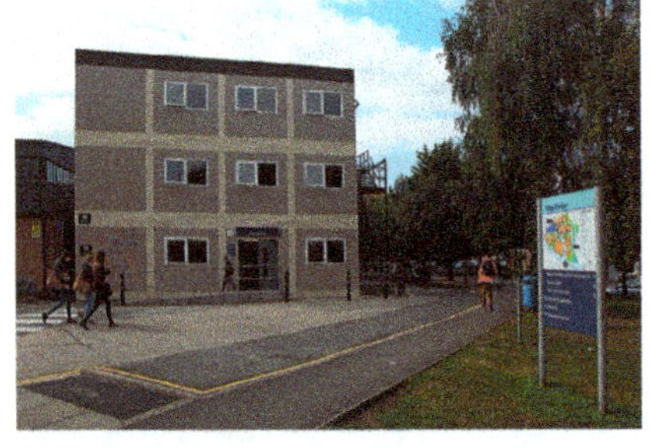

4.72 This contemporary building provides seminar rooms for a university and was built quickly to meet a shortage of space. However, do you think this would be a good place to learn? Would the building contribute to a positive 'learning environment' that encourages thinking and communication?

amenities Useful buildings or facilities that serve the local community.

PROVIDING LOCAL AMENITIES

Buildings built to provide services and amenities for local communities can sometimes have a poor reputation. Tight budgets and deadlines as well as a limited approach to the functionality of the buildings can result in designs that are unimaginative and unappealing (Figure 4.72). This can have negative results: for example, people may be unwilling to visit a library or sports centre that fails to make an impression in the cityscape or is simply just ugly and patients are less likely to get better in a hospital that feels gloomy and oppressive.

In many cases, such buildings show that the architect has failed to take a broad enough view of functionality. For example, a home for older people living with dementia needs to take into account their need for open, light-filled environments that stimulate all the residents' senses.

However, there are, of course, plenty of examples of well-designed local buildings, even on the smallest scale. Figure 4.73 shows a ferry passenger shelter on a remote island in Scotland. This small but dramatic building serves a very simple function: to protect passengers from the wind and rain. At the same time, however, its design allows the passengers inside to experience the beauty of the rugged landscape, while the radical, Modernist design seems to offer a visual link between this lonely island and the outside world.

Many of the sections below will show how architects can design buildings as 'meaningful' places.

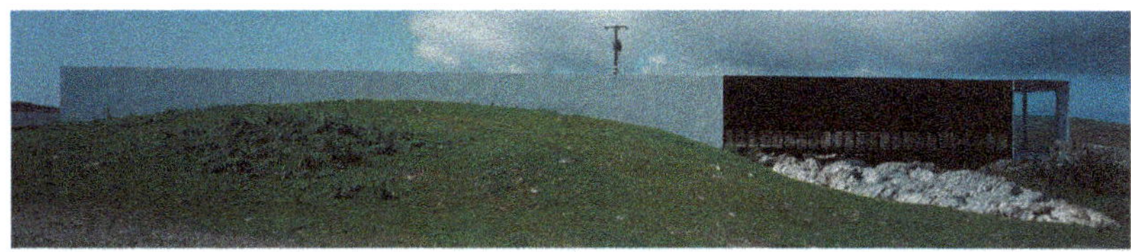

4.73 Sutherland Hussey Architects, 'An Turas' (The Journey) Ferry Shelter, Tiree, Scotland.

Activity A: **Develop a concept for a public building**

For this activity, work in pairs. You are asked to produce concept drawings for an extension to a public building in your local area – it can be either a hospital library or a new part of a railway station, such as a café.

- Visit the site and use drawings/photographs to record the existing building.
- Include some ideas or imagery linked to the local area or population.
- Discuss your ideas and develop an A2 presentation sheet showing your concepts.
- Ask your classmates to be the audience and present your ideas to get feedback.

Tip:

The architect always needs to design with an imaginative feeling for the lives of the people who are going to use a building.

REFLECTING A LOCAL CULTURE

Architects may design buildings that reflect their immediate surroundings or the people that live there. These might be in terms of the materials used to make it (for example, by using a local stone or brick), or in the surface treatment, as in using visual representations of local culture. This creates a relationship between audience and building, and gives it a sense of being part of the neighbourhood.

The Harlem Hospital was founded in 1887 and is a municipal hospital in Harlem, an area in New York City that has long been home to African Americans and a vibrant black culture. In 2012, the hospital was expanded and upgraded through the addition of a new building designed by Helmuth, Obata and Kassabaum (HOK) (Figure 4.74). The main façade reproduces on a grand scale three panels from a series of murals originally painted for the hospital by the American artist Vertis Hayes (1911–2000). The murals, commissioned by the US government in 1935, celebrated black and African cultural achievements.

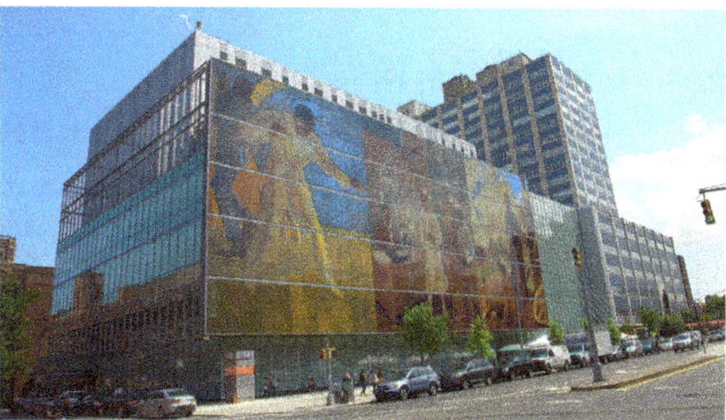

4.74 Helmuth, Obata and Kassabaum (HOK), Harlem Hospital Pavilion, Harlem, New York, USA, 2012. The murals ensure that the hospital continues to reflect the black heritage of the neighbourhood.

CREATING LANDMARKS

Towns and cities have always needed landmark buildings. These can:

- symbolise the main centres of power, whether political, religious, cultural or judicial – a parliament building, a mosque, a museum or palace of justice
- provide visual focus points that help give the town or city its structure and geography
- be emotional 'anchors' for the people who live in the town or city – these buildings can symbolise home.

Today architects often design landmark buildings as part of a program of urban regeneration, to give a run-down area or district a new lease of life. For example, the government of the Basque region of Spain worked alongside the private US Solomon R. Guggenheim Foundation to commission a new museum for Bilbao, which was economically depressed. They hired a 'celebrity' architect, the Canadian-born American Frank Gehry (born 1929), to design the building.

The resulting building (Figure 4.75) was a spectacular success, both as a piece of architecture and as an economic boost for Bilbao. Millions of tourists went to Bilbao to see this landmark building, injecting millions of dollars into the local economy. The city has given its name to the way that architectural landmarks can rejuvenate a city – the 'Bilbao effect'.

There are many examples of areas within towns and cities that are known for their relationship to a landmark building. What landmark buildings can you think of that are recognisable symbols in your own town, city or country?

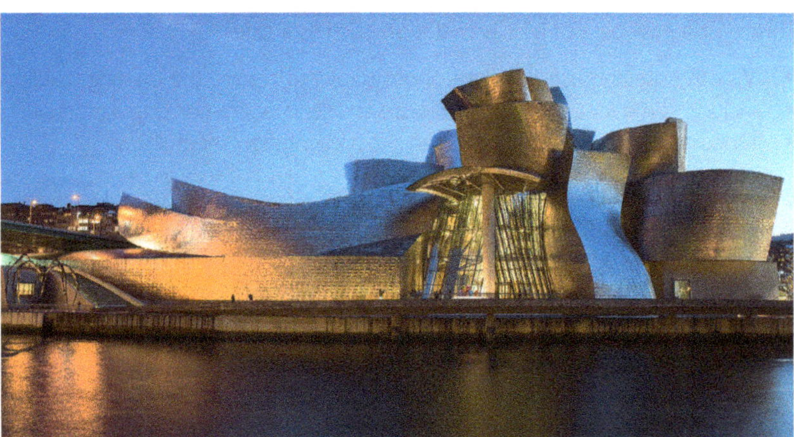

4.75 Frank Gehry, Guggenheim Museum, Bilbao, Spain, 1997. This public building became a landmark piece of architecture and was part of an urban regeneration plan for a run-down harbour area of Bilbao.

Activity B: **Research an Olympic stadium**

1. Choose an Olympic stadium to research. Search the web for a complete list. Avoid the Beijing National Stadium, which is discussed opposite.
2. Try to find out as much as you can about:
   - what made the design distinctive as a building
   - its success in meeting the needs of the spectators and athletes
   - its appeal as an architectural showpiece both for a national and international audience.
3. Create a short presentation to give to your classmates.

CELEBRATING NATIONAL EVENTS

Architects are also commissioned to design landmark buildings to celebrate regional, national or international events, especially relating to sport. This often takes the form of an arena or a stadium, and can act as focal point for local national pride.

When a country is awarded the right to hold the Olympic Games, its government will often invest a lot of money in building a spectacular range of buildings for the sporting events. The centrepiece is always a landmark stadium (see 'Artists and designers' box, opposite), which not only provides a focus point for the Games but a way for the country to make its mark internationally.

Artists and designers: **Herzog and de Meuron and the 'Bird's Nest' Stadium**

The Beijing National Stadium in China was designed and constructed for the 2008 Summer Olympic and Paralympic Games. As in other examples of national buildings (see the Sydney Opera House example on page 253), the government invited bids from architecture companies to design the building. Bids are concepts and outline plans showing ideas for a building project.

In this case, the design had to include ideas for the purpose of the building after it had hosted the Games – how the public would continue to use it. The commission was awarded to the Swiss architecture firm Herzog and de Meuron (named for its founding partners Jacques Herzog and Pierre de Meuron, both born 1950). The project also included the Chinese artist Ai Weiwei (born 1957) as consultant.

As a concept, the design was inspired by Chinese ceramics: it would contain the public just like a ceramic pot can contain materials. It was originally designed to include a retractable roof, and clusters of steel supports were included to hide the mechanism. In the end, the roof idea was dropped from the project, but the steel supports remained, giving the building its unique appearance and its nickname, the 'Bird's Nest'.

The National Stadium incorporates design principles to make the setting more comfortable for a large audience. For example, the two stands at the east and west of the building are higher, to improve spectators' views. Pipes under the stadium surface collect heat in winter and circulate warmth. These are cool in the summer and are used to provide ventilation.

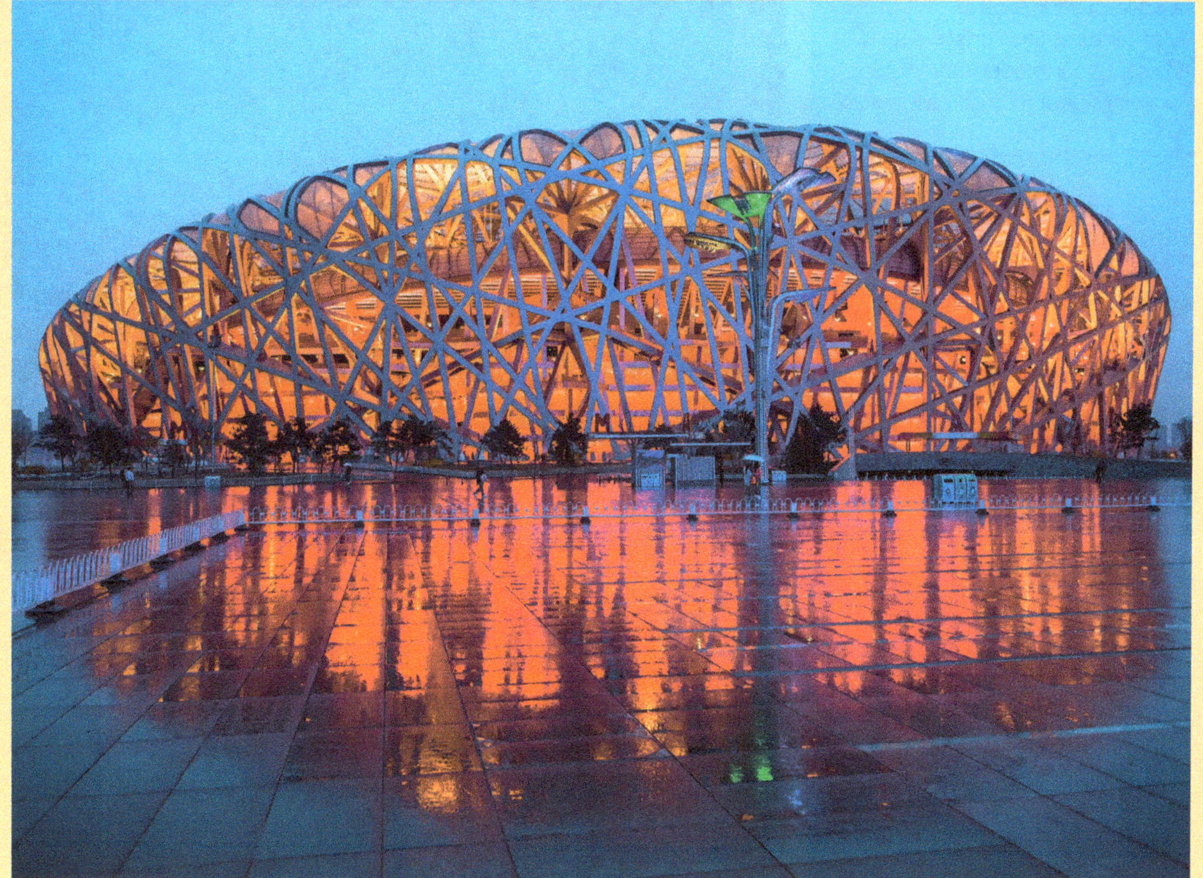

4.76 Jacques Herzog and Pierre de Meuron, Stefan Marbach, Ai Weiwei and CADG, The National Stadium, Beijing, China, 2008. The Beijing National Stadium is a collaborative venture to design and construct a public space for large-scale audiences. The design and construction consider the audience's needs through specially designed seating arrangements and temperature control.

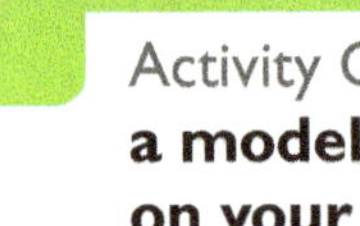

Activity C: **Make a model based on your concept drawings**

For this activity, continue to work in the pairs you worked in for **Activity A**.

- Using your presentation sheet, make a technical drawing of your design. This can be in the form of a plan and details in isometric or orthographic projection.
- Select materials for a model, based on your drawings – think carefully about your choices (for example, if you want to show clear surfaces in your model, use Perspex or acrylic).
- Make a model of your extension, to a scale of your choice.
- Use textures and surface details.
- Present your model and concept drawings back to your classmates.

ETFE (ethylene tetrafluoroethylene) A strong weatherproof plastic that is resistant to chemicals, corrosion, and very high and low temperatures.

Materials and techniques: **New materials**

Architects can appeal to their audience by using materials in their buildings in new and exciting ways. The Beijing National Aquatic Centre (Figure 4.77) is the largest **ETFE**-clad building in the world. The Aquatic Centre was used in the 2008 Chinese Olympics and afterwards turned into a water park. The water theme was developed in the ETFE exterior panelling, using the Weaire-Phelan structure, based on the natural patterns that develop in soap lather. This gives the building its visually strong appearance when lit from within, making the building stand out from its surroundings and so become a landmark.

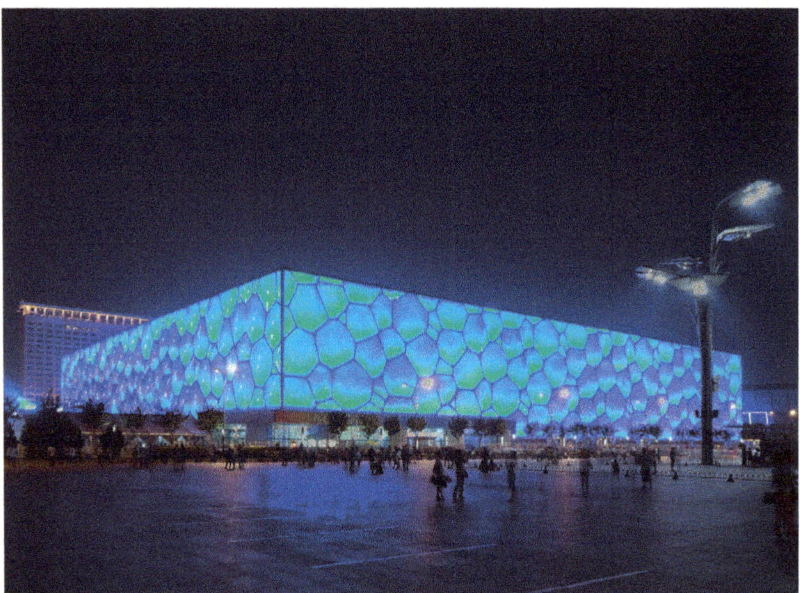

4.77 PTW Architects, Arup engineering, China State Construction Engineering Company (CSCEC), and China Construction Design International (CCDEI), The Beijing National Aquatic Centre, 2008.

Critical thinking:

Reflect on your work in **Activities A**, **B** and **C**, considering:

- how you addressed the needs of the users/audience in your design work
- how your concept and design reflected the intended purpose of the extension
- how your choice of materials was related to the users and audience.

Further research

Go online to find out more about Vertis Hayes, the WPA Harlem Hospital and the Beijing National Stadium.

To discover more about stadium design, read *Construction and Design Manual: Stadium Buildings* by M. Wimmer (DOM, 2016).

Set design

Learning objective:

- To understand the relationship between set design and audience

Set designers produce work that acts as the backdrop for the audience's view of a play, film or event. Addressing the interaction between the stage and the audience is a critical part of set design. The focus of this unit is the concept of theatrical space and the audience.

CONCEPTS OF THEATRICAL SPACE

The concept of theatrical space has been developed in different ways. In each new development, the relationship between audience and set is different and the set designer faces a different challenge:

- *Open-air theatre* – this uses the natural environment as its setting and backdrop. The theatres of ancient Greece were of this kind and used the landscape in terms of its shape, setting and acoustics (Figure 4.78).
- *Renaissance theatre* – in the UK, for example, public theatres flourished in the period 1562–1642. Theatres like The Globe in London (1599; reconstructed nearby 1997; Figure 4.79) featured a central stage area and set, with stalls built three storeys high around the edge. Earlier theatres such as The Globe were open-air. The audience would become involved in the play, exchanging comments with the actors.
- *Proscenium theatre* – this is sometimes called box-set stage design and became the standard theatre type from the 18th century onwards. The proscenium is the invisible 'fourth wall' that fronts the box-like stage. Many theatres of this type surround the proscenium with an elaborately decorated frame, turning the stage into a kind of picture or view seen through a window. The audience are typically removed from the action of the play.
- *Theatre in the round* – the stage is located centrally, with the audience placed around this. Productions using this form of theatrical space usually have little set scenery or props.
- *Ambulatory theatre* – this involves the audience following the performers from place to place. The theatrical space becomes fluid, extending into the real world.

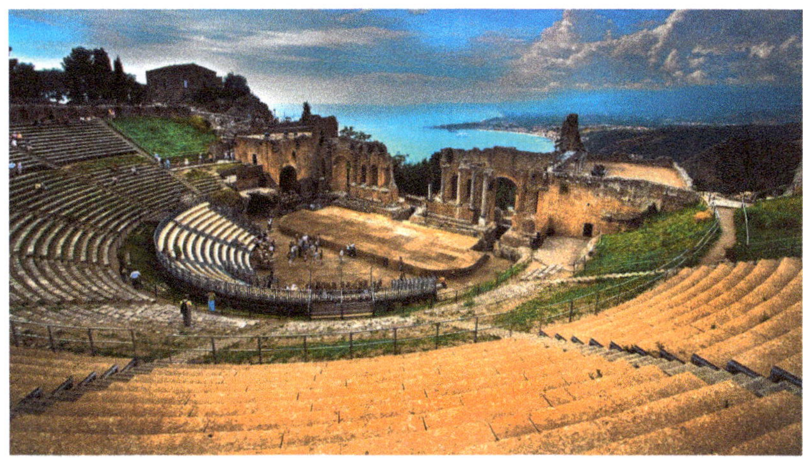

4.78 Ancient Greek theatre in Taormina, Sicily, 3rd century BCE.

Tip:

Use photography when you are recording information about your potential site for an open-air theatre. Take photographs from lots of different viewpoints, and combine these with drawings to understand the space as much as possible. You can also use measurements made on site to help you draw up plans showing details such as the position of the stage.

Activity A: **Find a venue for an open-air theatre production**

For this activity, work in groups of three. You might like to work in collaboration with your school's drama students or drama group, with a view to putting on a production.

- Find a suitable venue for an outdoor production of a play of your choice, to be produced in an open-air theatre.
- The venue must be within the boundary of your school or centre.
- Think about how you could use available space and natural features. For instance, are there any raised areas that exist already?
- Take photographs of the site.
- Make drawings showing your ideas for how the stage and seating would be placed.
- Make sure that you are aware of health and safety rules – you will need to show exit walkways.

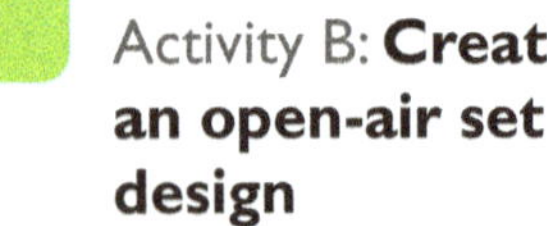

Activity B: **Create an open-air set design**

Based on your initial drawing ideas in **Activity A**, design and make a model showing how your set would work for the open-air theatre within the venue you have chosen.

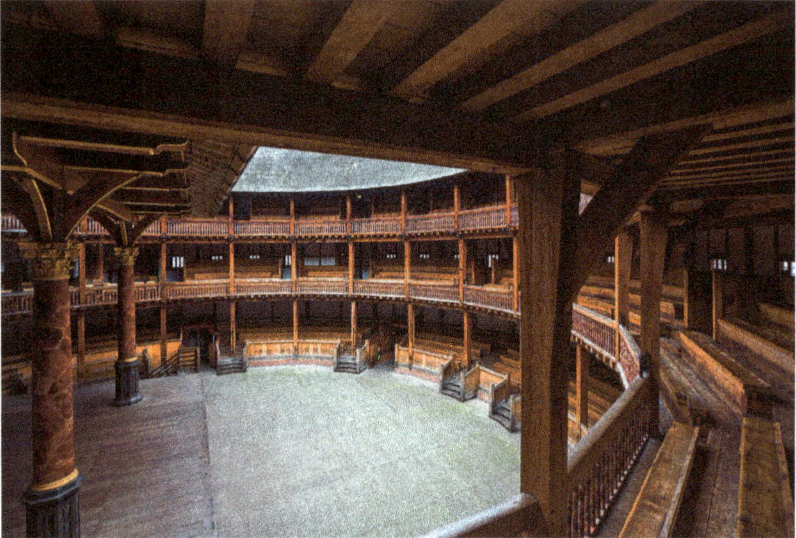

4.79 The Globe Theatre, Bankside, London, UK. This modern building recreates a Renaissance theatre that stood on the same site. The English playwright William Shakespeare (1564–1616) staged many of his plays in the original building.

Further research

Go online to find out more on open-air theatres or modern amphitheatre design.

Find out more about Shakespeare's Globe theatre at their website.

Critical thinking:

Display your work on **Activities A** and **B**, and evaluate it:

- How well did you understand the audience's needs in your planning?
- Could you improve your design work further?

If your set design has been used for a school production, you will be able to assess how well it works during rehearsals.

Product design

Learning objectives:

- To understand that products should be finished to a high standard, then tested and evaluated by the target market against the original brief to inform future design developments
- To understand how products need to be packaged and advertised for sale

A designer can say that a product design is finished when the needs of the original brief are met and the product functions as intended. However, as we have seen across the previous modules, the process of design is driven by the changing needs of users and consumers, and advancements in technology and materials, and so products continue to evolve. Continual testing and evaluation by the target market can help inform designers about the success of their designs as they are, and provide key information to use in subsequent modifications.

Product designers also need to consider the placement of their product in the marketplace and the role of packaging design and marketing in how successful the product is, especially in comparison with other similar products on the market.

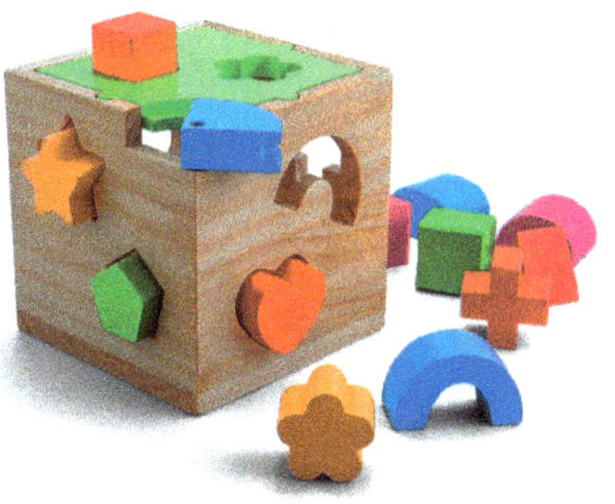

4.80 The product is a wooden educational toy, aimed at very young children.

TESTING THE SUCCESS OF YOUR DESIGN

Your final design should be made including any modifications that you identified during the development and refinement process. It should function as intended and have a good quality of finish to give it visual appeal.

Once the product is completed, you will need to test how successful it is. You can do this by:

- creating a questionnaire and asking your target market their opinion – this is a form of **qualitative research**
- running a product testing session, where you observe and photograph people using the product
- checking the product against the original brief and specification.

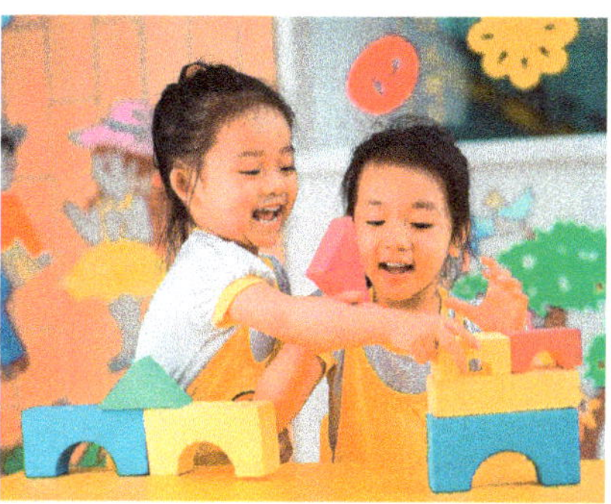

4.81 By including an image of children interacting with the product, it is possible to comment on more aspects of the design – for example, the scale of the parts of the toy in relation to the size of the children.

Activity A: **Evaluate the success of a product**

1. Start by looking at Figure 4.80, which shows a wooden educational toy, and think about the target market.
2. Write down the questions that you would need to ask to evaluate the success of this design, with regard to (a) its educational value; (b) visual appeal; and (c) safety.
3. Now look at Figure 4.81, an educational toy being played with by children. What additional aspects of the design can you evaluate when you can see the product in use?

qualitative research Research that explores people's opinions and responses. Compare quantitative research, which focuses on the collection of numerical data.

PRODUCT PROMOTION

As a product designer, you should also think about how you want your product to be packaged and/or advertised, to help complete the concept of your design. Aim to include design ideas to show your intentions. Packaging design and advertising are both disciplines within graphic communication and you will find information and ideas about them in the Graphic Communication sections of each module in this book. Other design activities related to the concept of your final product design might include the design of a user manual or a set of visual instructions for assembling the product.

Activity B: **Create a packaging design**

1. Look at Figure 4.82 and think about the how the product relates to the design of the packaging.
2. Next, sketch some design ideas for the packaging for a product that you have made.
3. Annotate your design ideas and indicate how your packaging will help protect and advertise the product.

Remember: you will find it helpful to refer to the Graphic Communication units to help you undertake this task.

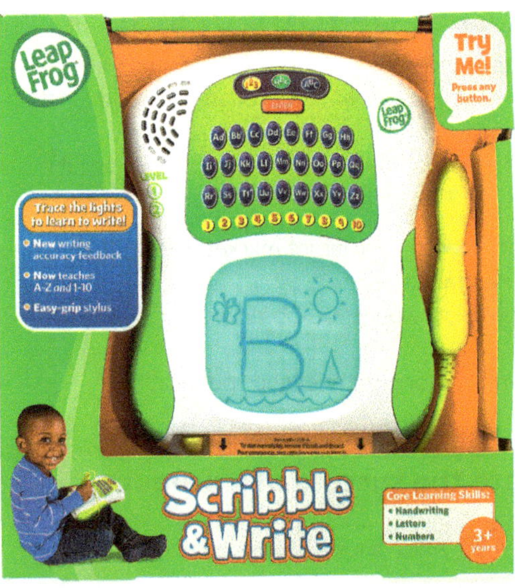

4.82 In this example of packaging for the 'Scribble & Write' educational toy made by LeapFrog, the toy is visible and there is an image of a child playing with it, as well as information about the product for the parents.

Activity C: **Evaluate your design**

Thinking about a product that you have made and ideas for packaging that you have designed in **Activity B**, how successful is your design against your original intention? How appropriate are your packaging ideas?

1. Using a maximum of *ten* questions, design a questionnaire to test the product against your original brief.
2. Ask a minimum of *five* people from the intended target audience to evaluate the product for you.
3. Think about what the questionnaire results tell you and how the feedback can help inform you about future design developments or opportunities.

Tip:

- There should be a focus on the *quality of finish* of your three-dimensional work. If your outcome is largely made using computer-aided manufacture (CAM), ensure that your making skills are evident in hand-built models that you made during the development and refinement process.
- Photograph your product from different angles and include shots of your target audience interacting with your completed product in your project.

Further research

For ideas about what questions to ask when evaluating product designs, go online.

Ceramics

Learning objectives:

- To understand how ceramicists market their work to audiences
- To develop your own marketing plan

Ceramicists need to engage with their audience to promote and sell their work, through developing a marketing strategy to reach out to commercial markets. They develop a marketing plan that uses specific formats and media, such as websites and social media, to make sure that the audience is aware of their work.

In this unit, we will look at some of the ways ceramicists market their work to audiences. Of course, practitioners of all kinds – from painters to jewellery makers – will need to develop marketing plans for their work.

MARKETING DESIGN WORK

Ceramicists, jewellers and designers use different formats and media to show examples of their work to a wide audience and make customers aware of what they make. These include:

- *Solo websites* – these are used by designers to show their portfolio and can include visual records and examples of commissions. They often include an ordering and shopping facility.
- *Group websites* – these bring together practitioners linked by geography or by their discipline. They may be linked because they all exhibit at a gallery (Figure 4.83).
- *Commercial websites* – e-commerce websites such as Etsy act as a kind of online craft fair for makers and buyers.
- *Trade fairs* – these are used by buyers as well as designers (Figure 4.84). They are an ideal place for designers to show work that is available for purchase on the spot. Orders for work can also be placed at fairs by buyers for an outlet or a shop. Galleries also use these events to look for up-and-coming talented designers to represent.
- *Agents* – this involves a practitioner using a person who has a business background and links with lots of organisations to promote and sell designers' work. They will have a network of contacts they use for connecting designers with buyers, and will charge a commission (fee) for doing this.
- *Social media* – many designers use social media as a way of marketing their work. They maintain their online presence by delivering and updating a constant stream of information for people who follow them, such as photographs of new works. They also use it to promote events like workshops or summer schools they are involved in or hosting.

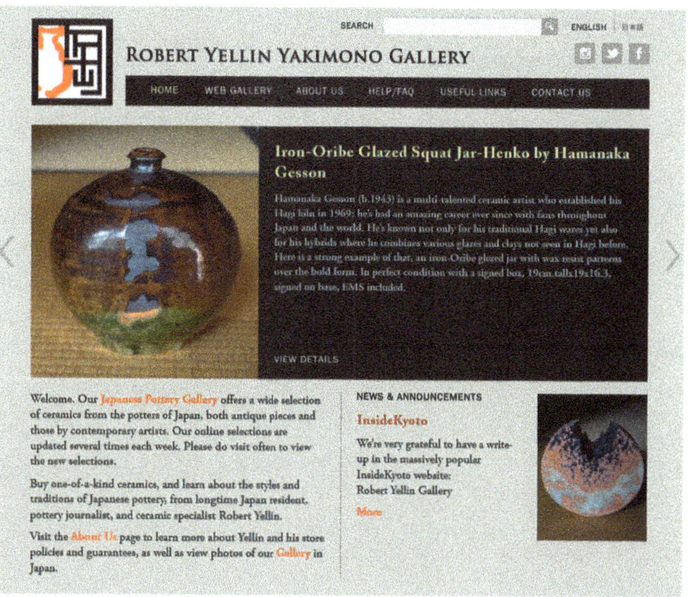

4.83 Website homepage, Robert Yellin Yakimono Gallery, 2017. An example of a ceramics-based web page. This page has a mixture of images and information. Some creative websites have less information on their homepage, or even none at all, focusing instead on an eye-catching image.

ATTENDING TRADE FAIRS

Ceramicists showcase their work at these types of professional events. Attendees can include buyers for retail outlets, gallery owners, makers, private customers, and other people associated with their design discipline, such as writers for craft magazines. Trade fairs give designers the chance to:

- present a body of work that shows their particular skills, or how their work is developing, such as recent work using a new technique
- evaluate work made by others in their field and 'size up' their competitors, in terms of what they are making, how they marketing it and the prices they are asking.
- engage with customers directly – they may be able to use face-to-face discussion to personalise orders, discuss prices and so on
- network – make contact with key people in the industry.

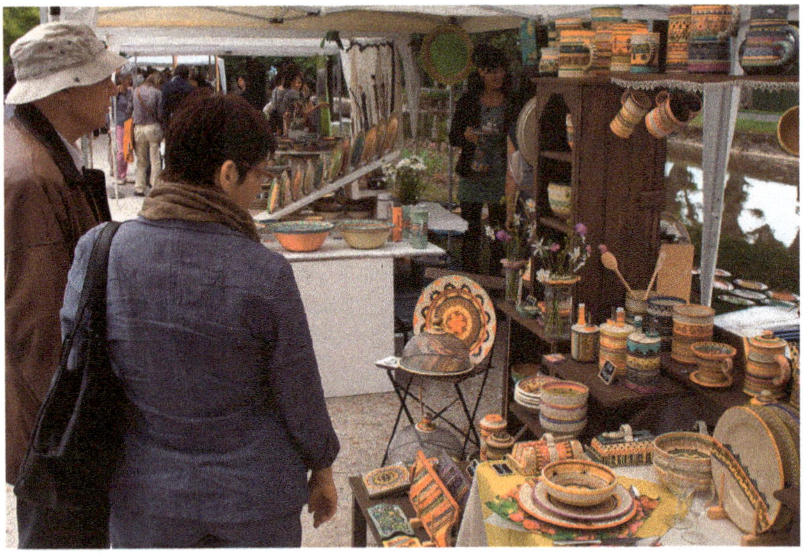

4.84 A pottery fair in Morges, Switzerland.

CREATING A SOLO WEBSITE

Websites provide a showcase for your work and so need to be designed with care.

- You must put thought into the design, as potential customers will see your website as reflecting the design values you express in your craft.
- The website must be simple to use and navigate.
- You must keep the website up to date. Keep refreshing the site with your latest work and 'news' such as events that you are taking part in.
- Invite users to sign up to your customer base, perhaps by offering the chance to win one of your works.
- Link your website to your other social media accounts.

Activity A: **Create a homepage for a design or craft-related website**

You will need to include:

- images of your work
- some form of introductory text – this could take the form of an Artist's Statement (see pages 234–235)
- links to other areas of the site – these do not need to be functional, but should show where the link would take you, such as:
  - techniques and technical data
  - commissions
  - workshops
  - endorsements
  - shopping area.

GETTING COMMISSIONED WORK

Most designers make commissioned work as part of their creative practice. These commissions may be one-off, bespoke pieces made to order for a single client, or the production of a limited number of pieces for a retail outlet. To undertake commissions effectively, designers need to understand the audience they are making for. They need to consider how their work will meet the needs or requirements of the clients who are commissioning it.

Activity B: **Develop a marketing plan for your designs**

Create a one-page document outlining how you would promote and market your work. You need to include or discuss the following factors:

- Will you attend trade fairs or local events to market your work? Research local opportunities.
- Websites – will you set up a solo website or try to join a group one?
- Galleries – how will you find the right places to exhibit your work?
- Social media – how will you use platforms such as Twitter and Facebook to market your work?
- Commissions – will you seek out private commissions and, if so, how will you do this?
- Pricing – how will you make the price of your work competitive?

Critical thinking:

In pairs, evaluate your partner's marketing plan written for **Activity B**. Offer constructive criticism and advice on how their plan could be improved, and share your own ideas.

Further research

Go online to find out more on ceramics trade fairs.

For more on marketing across the art and design disciplines, read *Craft a Creative Business: Making & Marketing a Successful Creative Business* by Fiona Pullen (Search Press, 2014).

4.4 Graphic communication

Advertising

Learning objectives:

- To understand how graphic designers use digital technologies in advertising, both offline and online
- To develop ideas for a public safety viral advertisement

Technology has revolutionised how graphic designers think about advertising and communication, in terms of both:

- increasingly sophisticated software that enables them to manipulate imagery and typography quickly and efficiently, and
- digital platforms such as social media that enable them to reach and target new audiences in new ways.

Some digital forms of advertising can be seen as evolutions of conventional, non-digital forms, such as the billboard, the printed ad in a newspaper/magazine or on TV. Some, however, are entirely new and have developed in response to the internet and mobile technologies, and their ability to target individuals on a global scale.

This technological revolution is setting graphic designers new challenges. They need to:

- develop and expand their skills constantly
- keep themselves up to date with the latest digital and online technologies and software
- be able to cope with the pressures imposed by the demand for speed and ease of communication – users want to see and consume images and messages much more quickly than in previous times
- face up to the challenge of an increasingly digitally **literate** audience, who are increasingly able to develop and publish their own graphic communications.

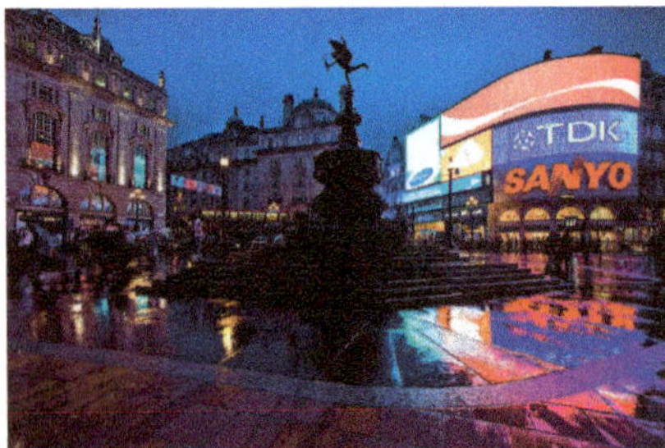

4.85 Digital billboards in Piccadilly Circus, London, UK. The billboards in this world-famous traffic intersection are now confined to a single building. Bold colour and a minimum of text create an eye-catching display.

DIGITAL BILLBOARDS

Billboards (or hoardings) first appeared on city streets towards the end of the 19th century. Displays of advertising could often be spectacular, as in London's Piccadilly Circus (Figure 4.85), a landmark traffic intersection which was once surrounded by illuminated billboards, or the hoardings alongside the Dōtonbori Canal in Osaka, Japan. Billboards need to be graphically very simple and very bright, to catch the attention of passers-by, who are often moving at speed. Typically, text/typography is kept to a minimum, often including no more than the brand name, if that.

Digital billboards follow the same principles, but the images are produced by computer software. Images can be changed at short intervals, enabling several companies to share a billboard, to advertise more than one product and to target different audiences at different times of day. For example, a single digital billboard could show a different stream of advertising for daytime office workers and night-time clubbers.

Digital technology has also enabled advertisers to use iconic buildings as temporary backdrops and canvases for advertising imagery.

Activity A: **Assess a local digital billboard**

If safely and easily accessible, assess the impact of a digital billboard in your neighbourhood. Consider:

- the siting and shape of the billboard
- the number of advertisements shown and the length of time each is shown
- the graphic qualities of each advertisement, in terms of colour, imagery, logos and text.

Take photographs, print them and present a short report to your classmates. Together, discuss the qualities that you think make an effective digital billboard from the design point of view.

ONLINE ADVERTISING

Since the first banner ad appeared online in 1994, online advertising has developed rapidly. Today, online advertising is widely used across all industries and generates income that often matches or surpasses that of traditional advertising platforms, such as TV. The internet is increasingly saturated with advertising imagery, making it hard for designers to make their mark. Audiences become blind to imagery, and/or find it intrusive and manipulative. They may be willing to pay for ad blocking.

Graphic forms of online advertising (rather than other marketing techniques such as search engine marketing (SEM) and optimisation) are often collectively known as display advertising. Some of the main types of display advertising are:

- *banner ads (or web banners)* – these are **embedded advertisements** on a web page. This form of digital advertising is closest to the traditional printed ads found in newspapers and magazines. The ad serves to inform the reader about a company and its products/services and why they should buy these. It will certainly also include a link to the company's website but also other media content such as audio or video.
- *pay-per-click (PPC) ads* – this is an internet-based form of advertising where the viewer clicks on an online ad on one website and is directed to the website of the advertiser. The publisher of the first website earns income based on the number of times the advert is clicked or opened.
- *pop-up ads* – these use a user's internet habits and marketing data to generate targeted adverts that 'pop up' in a new browser window as the user surfs the internet.
- *video advertising* – here companies use an online video stream to advertise their products or services. The video adverts may use a platform such as YouTube or be incorporated into another form of online advertising such as a banner ad.

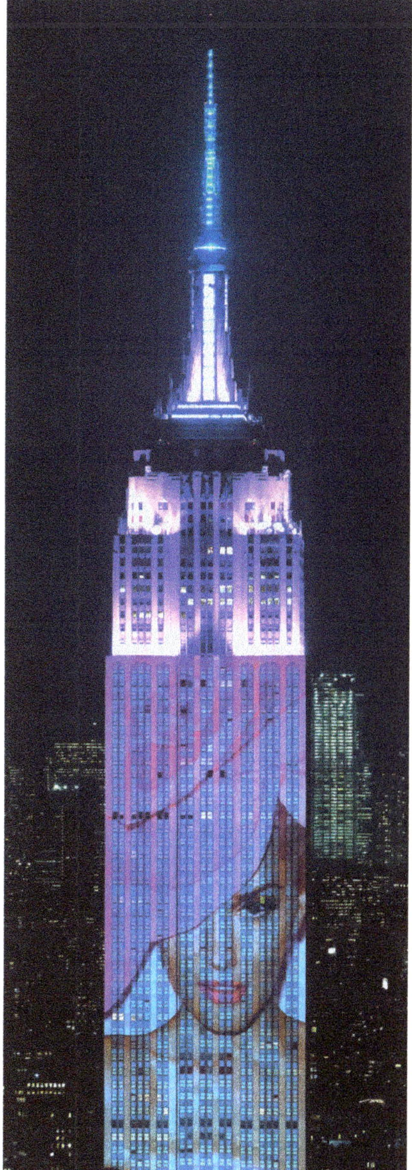

4.86 Advertising, *Harper's Bazaar*, Projection, 2017, Empire State Building, Manhattan, New York, USA. What kind of message do you think this image communicates to viewers? Does it make the product seem more important or somehow powerful?

embedded advertisement A link on a page that takes a user to the product or service's website once clicked.
literate Skilled.

Activity B: **Design a banner ad**

Working in pairs, design a banner ad layout for a company of your choice. You need to include:

- the company name and logo
- some form of imagery – drawn, photographed or digitally made
- some advertising copy, including text for a button link, such as 'Available Now'.

Put the design onto a digital slide and present to your audience – in this case, your classmates. Ask for feedback.

In all of these cases, technology has allowed designers to reach a target audience immediately, and present them with a high-quality advertising product. Advantages include the following:

- costs are reduced
- there is no need to run a design through an expensive design and print process
- the design can be developed on a mobile device and uploaded later that same day.

Because the user is likely to look at a display ad for one or two seconds at most, the design must create images with instant impact if it is to draw the user in.

VIRAL MARKETING

This type of online marketing often uses surreal imagery (see page 113) that may have little or no obvious connection to the product. Its aim is not necessarily to physically reflect the product, but to get people talking about the advert and asking what it is about. This gathers momentum and spreads from person to person through the internet or social media, like a biological virus. Can you think of a current or recent viral advert that got your attention?

There are examples of YouTube video-based advertisements that have recorded millions of views. These will often be supported by Tumblr or Facebook campaigns and spread through people sharing and discussing their content, or the way they use imagery and visuals. Sometimes they may just tell a story.

Viral marketing can be used in positive ways, as in the **public information film** *Dumb Ways to Die* (2012), shown in Figure 4.87. The city train operator Metro Trains Melbourne developed this campaign as a result of dangerous behaviour around train tracks and stations in Melbourne, Australia. The campaign also included billboards (Figure 4.88), a children's book, and a website where people could interact with the message by making a pledge to behave safely around train stations. The advert also crossed into phone apps, where different interactive games were developed. Metro Trains reported a 21 per cent drop in dangerous behaviour by 2013.

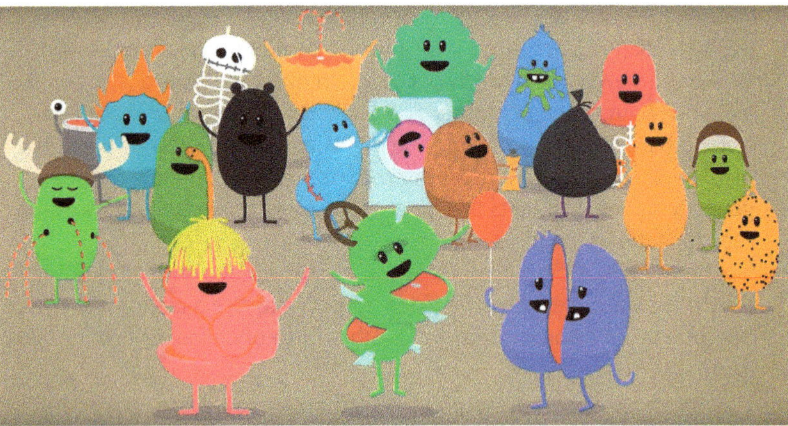

4.87 *Dumb Ways to Die*, Public Safety Film, Metro Trains Melbourne, 2012. An example of viral marketing used for public safety that grew in popularity and developed into a series of other digital platforms, such as an app and game.

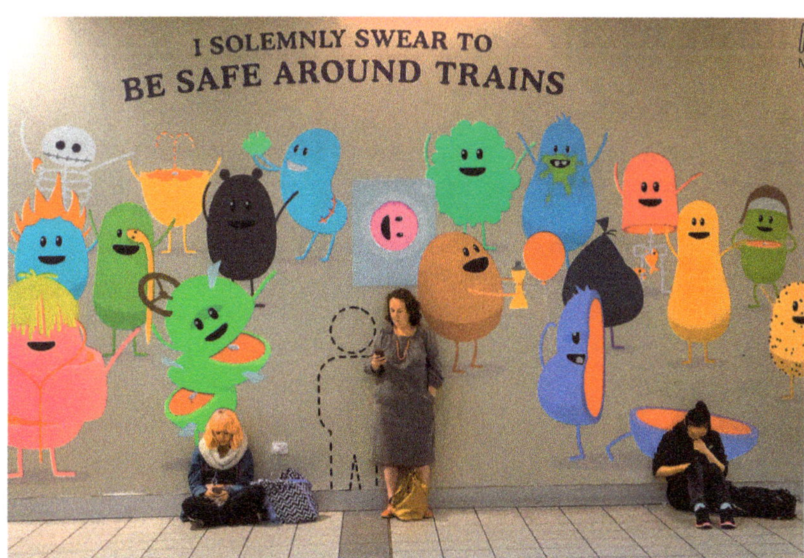

4.88 *Dumb Ways to Die*, Shelter advertising, Metro Trains Melbourne, 2012. The strength of the idea behind the advertising campaign meant that it could also be developed to include traditional posters and billboards.

Activity C: **Plan a viral marketing campaign**

Working in terms of three, develop a set of visuals showing your ideas for a viral marketing campaign based on safety in schools. Use these to create a 60-second presentation.

1. Identify at least three hazards or dangers in your school or centre.
2. Make drawings and take photographs illustrating these, applying what you have learned about the way that designers use formal elements.
3. As a team, work out how you would advise fellow students to avoid these dangers and make a series of drawings and photographs illustrating these points.
4. Put both sets of images together and produce a narration describing both the hazards and the ways of avoiding them. Use images and basic transitions/animation techniques or more advanced methods to link the images if you want. You could also add a backing track or music.
5. Present your viral advert to your group, explaining how you think it would become a viral advertisement and its potential to be used in other media, such as in apps and posters.

Critical thinking:

Review your work produced for **Activity C**:

- How well did your viral advertising work?
- Did it communicate the dangers you listed effectively?
- How versatile was the imagery you created? Would it cross easily and effectively into other media?
- What would you improve in the future if you made this viral advertising again?

Tip:

Keep a visual log. It is useful practice to keep an ongoing log of examples of interesting viral marketing that you come across. Make notes about how they use image and text to communicate their message. Summarise this information in your sketchbook or journal, with screenshots. You can also keep a digital notebook of viral marketing campaigns, saved in a folder.

Further research

Go online to find out more on banner advertising, and search for 'Dumb Ways to Die' for more on this safety campaign.

public information film Sometimes known as a public service announcement. A (usually) short film created to educate the public about a key issue such as road safety, health, protecting the environment, or how to vote.

Illustration

Learning objective:

- To understand how illustration is used to present infographics to an audience

Infographics (information graphics) is the graphical representation of information or data or a set of instructions. It is used to present complex information in a way that an audience can understand easily and quickly. Types of infographics include:

- pie charts
- graphs
- exploded diagrams
- flowcharts
- subway/metro maps
- weather maps
- electronic circuit diagrams.

Infographics makes use of a full range of graphic imagery (including colours, shapes, lines and icons), as well as small amounts of text, to communicate information in infographics. These can be used to:

- show a wide variety of information in a unified way, such as research data
- show a sequence of actions as in instructions to make flat-pack furniture
- describe a process, such as the journey that raw materials might make on the journey to becoming an item of clothing
- reveal and communicate aspects of data that might remain hidden or be hard to take in when presented in tables of figures or large amounts of text.

Developing design work for infographics involves researching the target audience's needs (Figure 4.89). When designing infographics, always ask yourself:

- What is the information to be communicated?
- What will it be used for?
- Who is the audience?
- What sort of images and text are they likely to understand best?

For example, if a designer is creating a graph for a group of university scientists, it will look very different from one created for young schoolchildren.

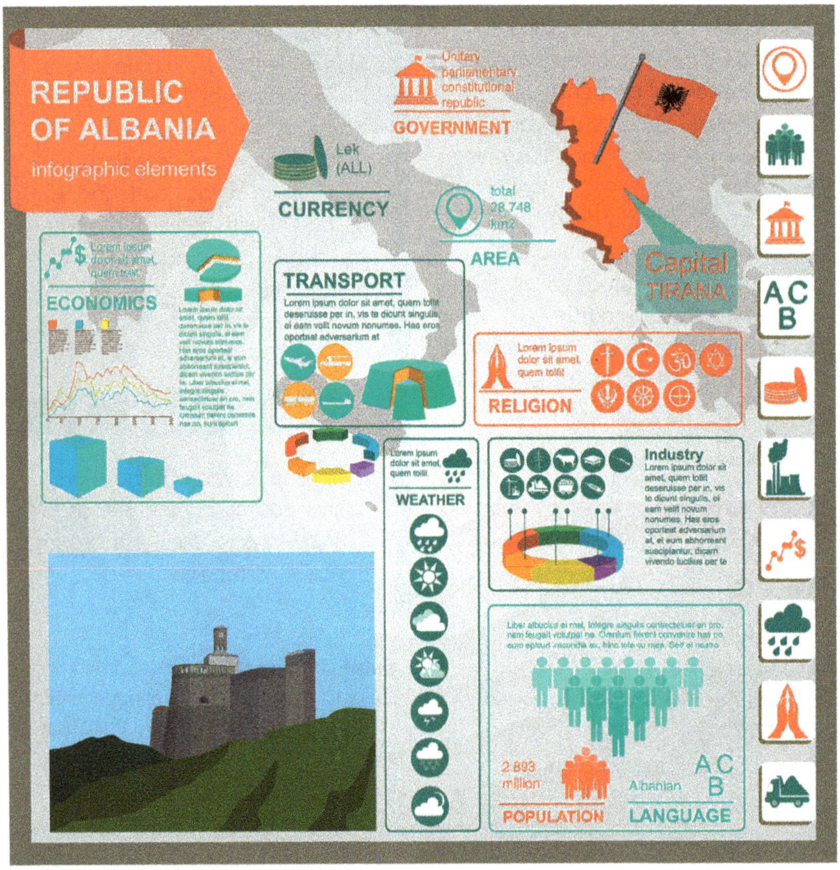

Materials and techniques: Infographic software

There is plenty of free software online to help you create infographics. Try the following:

- Canva Infographic Maker
- Easel.ly
- Google Charts.

However, as a designer you should be attempting to create your infographic ideas **from scratch** – whether that is by using drawing skills or a graphics program such as Adobe Illustrator.

4.89 Infographic summarising information about the country of Albania. Who do you think this infographic is targeting?

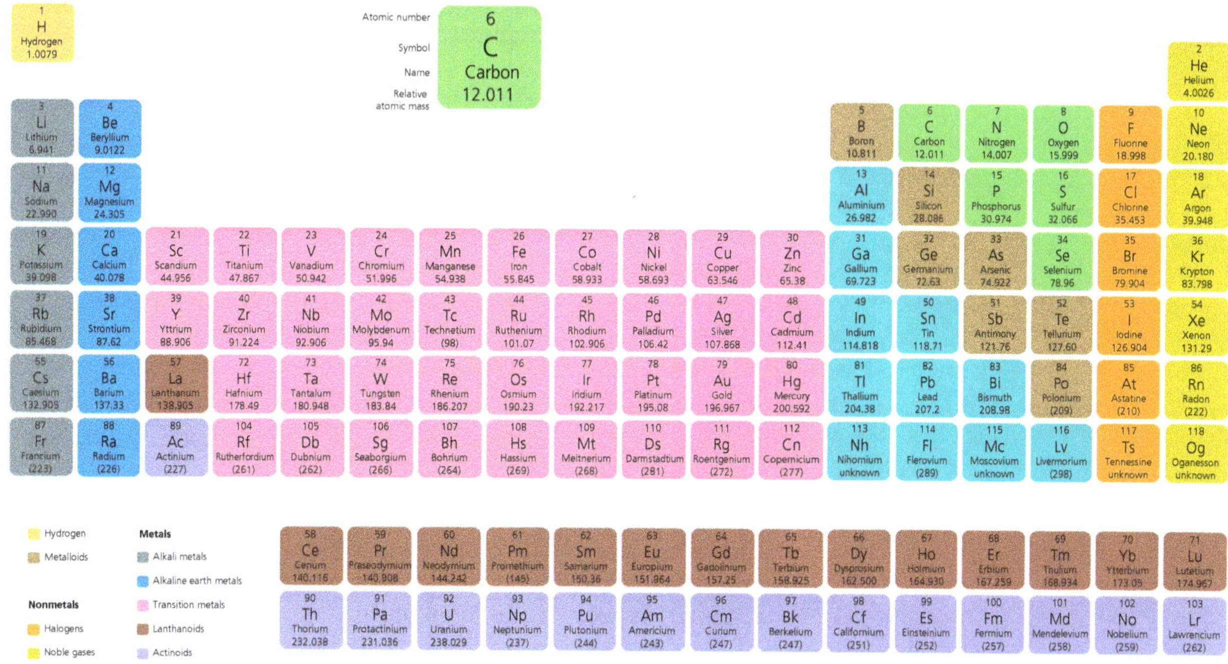

4.90 The periodic table, including a key. This very well-known diagram orders the chemical elements according to a whole range of features, including atomic number and chemical properties. However, scientists have come up with other ways to display the elements graphically, including a spiral version.

Activity A: **Create an infographic diagram**

For this activity, work in groups of three. You are asked to create an infographics diagram of part of your school or centre. This is more than just a map: your infographic needs to include icons that indicate the activity or subject that takes place in each room or set of rooms. For instance, think about how you could use an image to sum up the different rooms in the science block, so that anyone seeing it would recognise them. The intended audience will be new students and their parents. It could also be used by visitors to the school.

1. Working in your group, conduct research on the kind of information new students might expect to see on the diagram.
2. Using either drawing skills or software, create your infographic. Remember to include a key.
3. Ask permission to trial the infographic with the target audience, and ask for their feedback.

Tip:

Remember to include a key (or legend) within the infographic. A key helps the user decode the meaning of the icons, colours and so on (Figure 4.90). Sometimes the icons are so well known that a key is not needed – for example, on a weather map.

Critical thinking:

Consider the work you produced in **Activity A** and write a summary of the journey your design work went through. Think about:

- how you addressed the needs of the audience
- the balance of illustration and text you used to produce the diagram
- how you could improve the work further.

Further research

Go online to find more examples of infographics.

from scratch Without making use of anything that has been done before.

Packaging

Learning objective:

- To understand how technology is being used to develop packaging tailored to manufacturers' and users' needs

Packaging is using technology to develop new formats that take into account changes in demographics and audience needs. In this unit, we will look at examples of packaging where technology is driving new developments.

RETHINKING PACKAGING

In the past, packaging has been considered simply as a necessary part of the journey of product from manufacturer to customer. It has typically provided:

- protection for the item during transportation and delivery
- an idea of the nature of the item
- basic advertising for the company and brand
- a way of enhancing the consumer's experience of the product, by suggesting its 'luxury' status, for example.

Digital technology, however, has enabled the functions of packaging to be extended, for both producers and users/consumers. It can do this through using the information that can be sourced as the digital packaging moves along its journey from warehouse to user. This information can include:

- numbers of items sold, based on barcode scans – providing information on sales
- stock availability – providing consumers with information about whether the product is available
- reordering requirements – ensuring that supply meets demand
- sales and user profiles – which items are popular and who is buying them.

Printed packaging

Printed packaging is using technology to become personalised. There are online retail outlets that can personalise delivery labels that are printed out onto packaging. These can be updated with specific delivery details, such as where to leave a package. This information is personalised by being linked by technology to information the user types in on their keyboard as part of the ordering process. This connectivity builds a stronger link between the user and retailer, and encourages loyalty between the consumer and the brand or service.

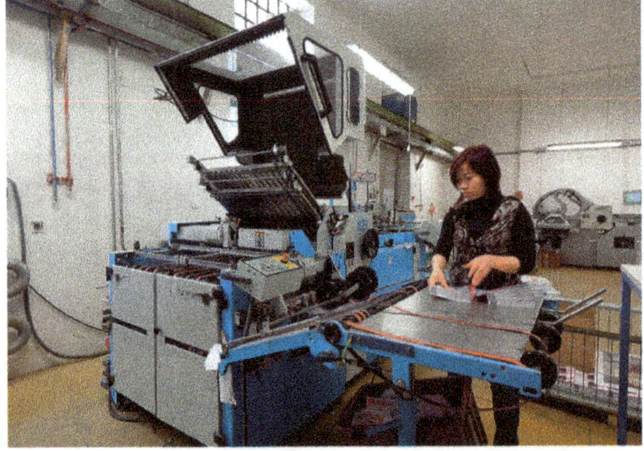

4.91 Production machinery for printed and digital packaging, GZ Digital Media A.S. Facility, 2010. Ongoing advances in digital-based technology are allowing companies to design and produce packaging in a wide variety of formats and materials.

SMART PACKAGING

Smart packaging takes the idea of personalised packaging to a new level. It uses digital technology to provide companies and users with information on, for example, stock availability, **ambient conditions** and location. It is sometimes known as active packaging.

It is possible to develop packaging that uses a 'smart-cap' technology. This could be used in the **pharmaceutical** industry to help users follow the correct **dosage**. This technology is built into the packaging, and will record and display the number of times the medication is taken, **monitoring** the dosage and frequency. This information can then be used by healthcare professionals to remotely check on a patient's medication regime. Smart packaging can also be used in food packaging to extend shelf life and monitor freshness.

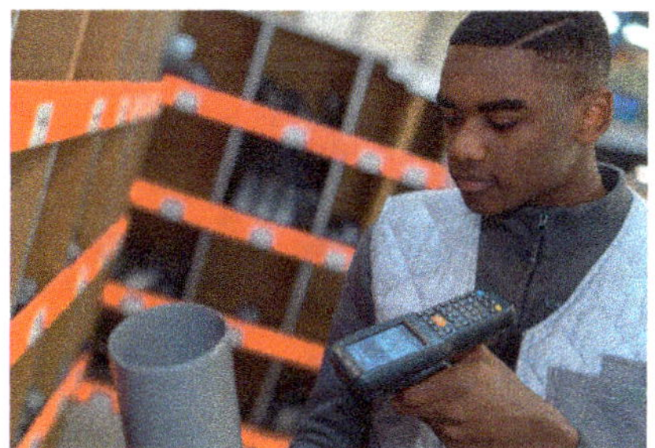

4.92 Here a barcode reader is being used to scan and identify packaging. Printed information can allow the fast distribution of items, as well as update stock levels immediately through the use of digital technology.

INVOLVING THE AUDIENCE

Technology has opened up interactivity in packaging. For example, food producers have used a printed label that the user can scan to gain access to a recipe linked to that product. Other producers have used packaging to interact with customers through social media. Other developments driven by technology may include computer chips and heat-responsive labels.

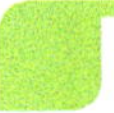

Activity A: **Create ideas for an item of digital packaging**

Find an example of fresh food packaging in a local supermarket, consider the type of packaging used and reinvent this using digital packaging technology. Based on your understanding of digital technology and packaging, how could your design improve the information available to users in terms of:

- shelf life
- ingredients and nutritional value
- safety (including allergies)
- recipes
- serving suggestions?

Write up your ideas and present them back to your classmates.

Critical thinking:

Consider your outcome for **Activity A**:

- How effectively do you feel that your ideas communicated the information to the user?
- How is it an improvement on the original packaging material?
- What could you do to improve the packaging?

Further research

Go online to find out more about printed packaging and smart packaging.

ambient conditions The temperature, moisture level, atmospheric pressure and so on in a particular place.
dosage The correct amount of a medicine.
monitor To observe and check the quality of something.
pharmaceuticals Medical drugs.

Practical guidance

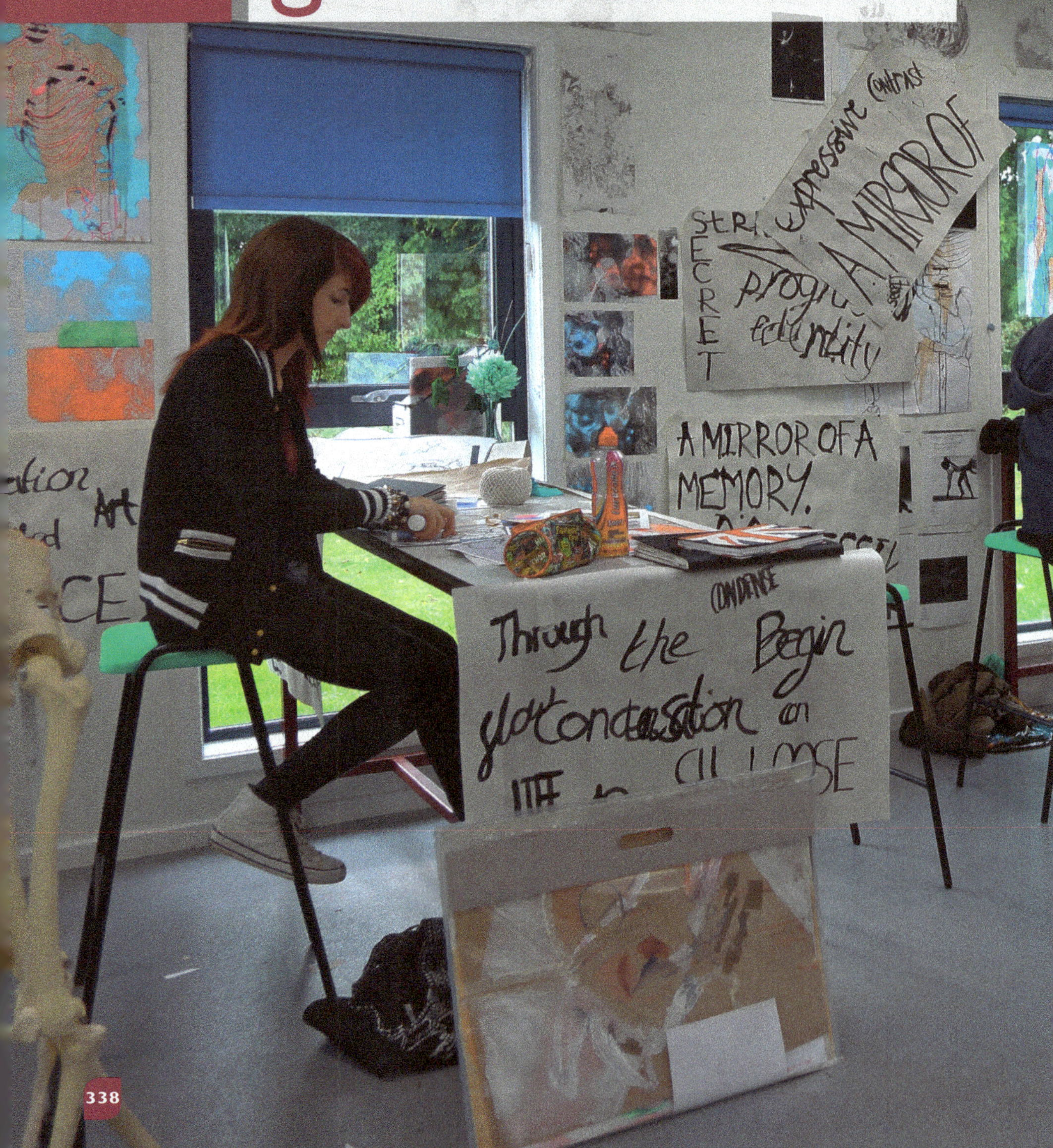

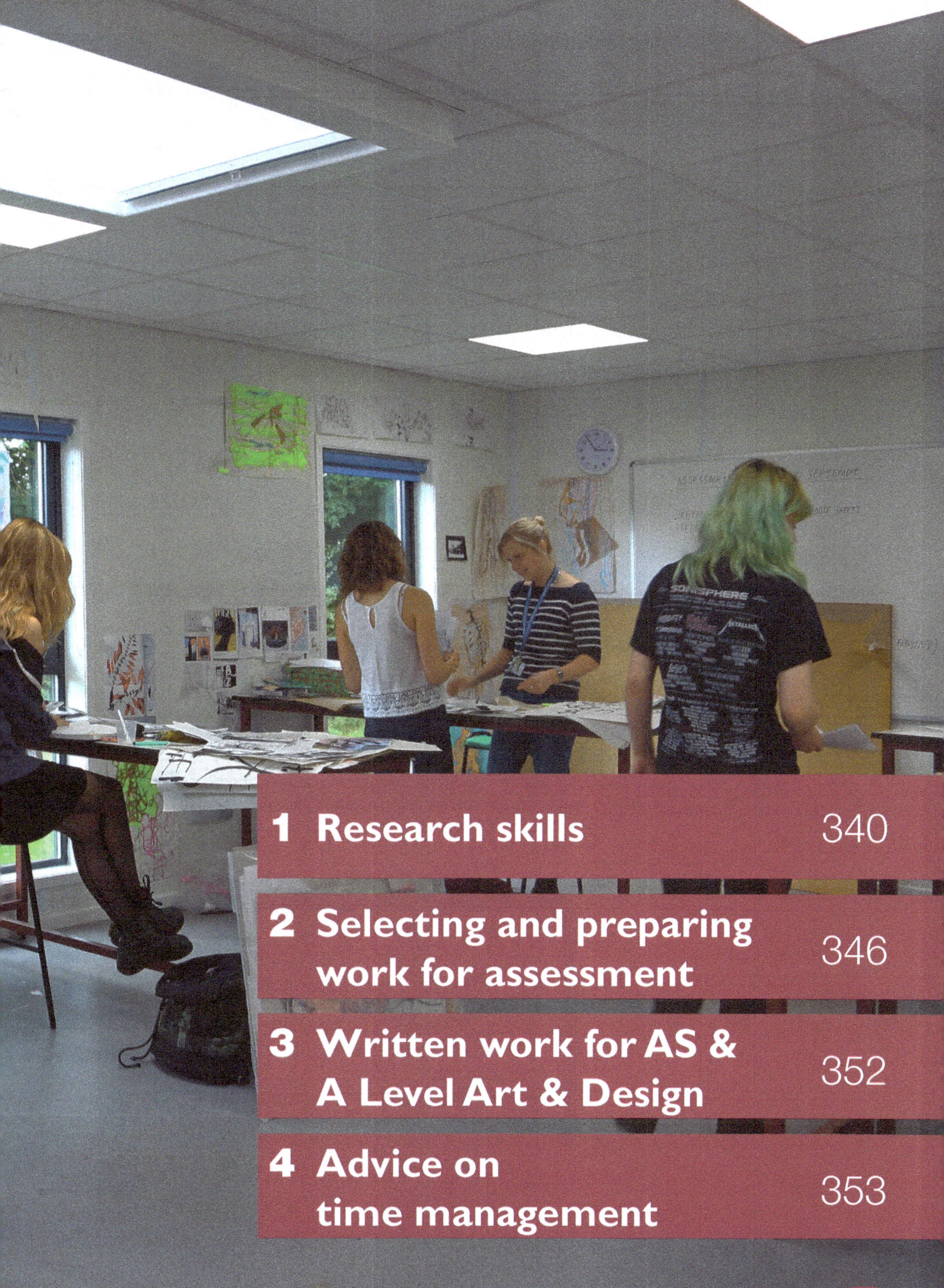

Research skills

Research is a key skill in studying art and design and in every component of the Cambridge Assessment International Education AS & A Level externally set assignment. You need to be able to demonstrate that you can undertake research at various levels, investigating not only the work of other artists but also by exploring a theme or idea through your own work.

There are three main research skills that you should aim to develop throughout your A Level/AS Level course:

1. looking at the work of other artists/designers – for example, in galleries, at art fairs, in books and online
2. investigating the work of other artists/designers – using second-hand sources such as books, exhibition catalogues, journal articles and so on
3. carrying out visual research into a theme in your own art and design work.

Not all of these skills will have equal weight in every component. In Components 1 and 2, for example, visual research in your own work will be at the forefront, while in Component 3 you will have to give roughly equal weight to all three of these areas of research.

In this section, we look at each of these areas in turn.

LOOKING AT THE WORK OF OTHER ARTISTS/ DESIGNERS

In general, throughout your course you should try to look at the works of as many other artists and designers as possible. Visit as many galleries, museums, exhibitions, fashion shows and art fairs as you can. Make yourself aware of any new buildings or pubic sculptures that may have been constructed/erected in your city, town or neighbourhood.

Don't just look at the disciplines that interest you most, but expose yourself to as many kinds of art and design as possible. Art and design is often at its richest where it takes inspiration from other fields. There are no real boundaries between the area of study and disciplines, as we hope this course will have shown you.

Tip:

Keep an eye on what is going on in your area by checking a listings magazine or website on a regular basis. These will let you know that there is an exhibition coming up or that a group of artists are opening up their studios for a day or two. Your teachers will also be a good source of information, so remember to ask!

When visiting galleries or studios, try to go with other students. This is not advised just as a matter of safety, but because you can gain a lot from discussing what you have seen. Other people will have insights and experiences that you may not have.

For much the same reason, also make sure that you look at the work of both historical and contemporary artists. You may initially find some historical art, for example, hard to understand or 'irrelevant' to your life and work. However, with patience you will almost always discover something useful or inspirational, such as the artist's use of colour and line.

Above all, keep your eyes and mind open!

Looking at art and design is not as easy or straightforward as it might sound. You need to look at works of art and design, not as a casual observer or passer-by might, but *as an artist and/or designer*, as a practitioner. This means that you must look at them critically – exploring and assessing the formal elements and components that we examined in the Introduction of this book and working out how the artist or designer is likely to have reached the outcome you are now looking at. Even if you take an instant dislike to an artwork, try to work out why you don't like it. This can sometimes be as fruitful as working out why you do like something!

If you are lucky enough to visit an artist's or designer's studio, ask them whether you can take a look at their preparatory studies and so on. They will probably be very happy to let you do so, and also to talk to you about their working practices.

Tip:

Give other people's artworks and designs time and respect. It is better to look at a handful of works closely and attentively than to rush around an exhibition or studio, just glancing at every piece. You will take a lot more away from the experience and your own work may be all the better for it.

This is also, however, about respecting other artists' and designers' work. Try to look and respond to other practitioners' work as you would hope others would look at and respond to yours!

Further research

You may find the following books on looking at art and design inspirational:

Ways of Seeing by John Berger (Penguin 2008)
About Looking by John Berger (Bloomsbury, 2009)
How to Look at Art by Susie Hodge (Tate Publishing, 2014)
On Photography by Susan Sontag (Penguin, 1979).

Tip:

While exhibition captions can provide insights into the work you are looking at, do not allow them to become the sole focus of your attention. Try to look at the artwork first, then briefly read the caption, and finally look at the artwork again. It is your response and interpretation that matters most, not the exhibition curator's!

For Component 3 – the Personal Investigation – you need to take your secondary research much further. It will also need to be much more focused: you need to have a clear idea of your goals – what you are trying to find out – before you start your research. Detailed guidance on undertaking research for the written analysis aspect of Component 3 is covered in the Personal Investigation section of Module 3 (pages 191–193).

INVESTIGATING THE WORK OF OTHER ARTISTS/DESIGNERS

Looking is the basic research skill of every artist and designer. However, you will almost certainly need to back this up with second-hand research as well if you are to gain a full appreciation and understanding of what the artist or designer has sought to do.

Get into the habit when planning a visit to a gallery, building and so on of finding out something about the artist/designer or movement *before* you go, by reading reviews or doing a basic search on the internet. This will equip you with some of the context to help you look at and understand the work when you get to the exhibition.

Similarly, while at the gallery, take some time to read the gallery leaflets, exhibition captions, artists' personal statements, exhibition catalogues and so on. Exhibition catalogues and other relevant books are often available for visitors to look at while in the exhibition, so you do not need to buy them!

Below is a summary of some of the ways that you can undertake second-hand research.

Books

Books are the traditional way to carry out second-hand research. Remember that, although your school or local library may not keep a book on a particular subject, it may be able to get hold of a book that you want through an 'inter-library lending scheme'. Ask the librarian to help you.

To find out what kinds of books may be available, look at the bibliography or 'Further reading' section of a book on the subject that you do have. Another way is to search on Amazon or a similar bookselling site. Sometimes you may be able to purchase books very cheaply.

Further research

There are a several art and design book series that can provide you with excellent introductions to artists, designers and art/design movements/periods. These can often be very useful places to start your research. Try the following:

- Art & Ideas (Phaidon) – excellent, well-illustrated surveys of key artists and movements
- Oxford History of Art (Oxford University Press) – useful introductions to major artists, themes and art movements aimed at students
- World of Art (Thames & Hudson) – this includes a large number of short introductions to artists and movements aimed at the general reader.

There are also useful dictionaries and encyclopaedias of art and design:

- *The Concise Dictionary of Art Terms* by Michael Clarke (Oxford University Press, 2010)
- *The Thames & Hudson Dictionary of Design since 1900* by Guy Julier (Thames & Hudson, 2004)
- *The Thames & Hudson Dictionary of Graphic Design and Designers* by Alan Livingston and Isabella Livingston (Thames & Hudson, 2012)
- *The Penguin Dictionary of Art and Artists* by Peter and Linda Murray (Penguin, 1997)

- *The Thames & Hudson Dictionary of Art and Artists* by Herbert Read and Nikos Stangos (Thames & Hudson, 1994)
- *The Grove Dictionary of Art* by Jane Turner (ed.), 34 volumes (Grove, 1996).

Journals and magazines

Journals and magazines can be another useful source of information about artists and designers. However, be aware that many articles are highly specialised and academic. It may be more useful at this level to look at the more 'popular' magazines and journals aimed at the general reader:

- *Aesthetica*
- *Apollo*
- *Creative Review*
- *Flash Art*
- *Frieze*
- *Studio International.*

Your school or local library may stock copies of these, and some are available online.

The internet

The internet can be a rich source of information. However, it is also one of the most difficult to use successfully for research. Books and magazines have their content checked by experts before being published. This is not often the case with websites, so you need to treat the information with caution.
In general, it is wisest to use only websites linked to major galleries and museums, which are a rich source of factual and opinion-based information. You can refer to these with confidence.

Using questionnaires

You can use questionnaires to find out information about artists and designers. Some practitioners prefer this way of being contacted as they can answer the questions when they get a spare moment. Test out your questions on your classmates. You should also write a covering letter or email, explaining that you are a student on this course and that you are researching examples of art and design work. You could add that you admire the work and would value their input.

How much research do you need to do?

While there are no hard-and-fast rules for this, your research into art and design practice, contextual factors and visual recording should be in depth and purposeful. This means studying your sources in detail, and developing your own response. Research is a highly effective tool in developing creative work if used and applied with commitment and purpose. There are two questions that summarise research in this context: What are you trying to find out? How can you use these findings to help you in your own practical work?

Tip:

When undertaking research, you need to strike a balance between using a good variety of second-hand sources and not 'spreading your net too wide'. Try to access a range of viewpoints and interpretations, but at the same time keep your research goal in focus. This can be tricky!

CARRYING OUT YOUR OWN VISUAL RESEARCH

Recording from life/direct observation is an essential part of the research and starting points you will need to undertake as part of both the components for the AS Level and all three components of the A Level. Module 1 covers approaches to recording visual research and you should reread the Introduction and sections relevant to your chosen area of study carefully. Through direct observation, you are able to experience objects and places with all five senses, as well as your wide field of view. This makes it possible for you to record a far wider range of sensations and experiences, including changes over time.

You can undertake visual research at school, by bringing in objects and images to work from, or you can use your environment at home, around where you live or go on a field trip to a specific location. If you are working at your centre (school or college) you will be able to use the full range of media and materials available to you in the art and design department and easily work at a range of scales. However, if you are working away from the classroom, you will need to take your appropriate media and materials out with you and this might limit how you work and the size of your work.

A basic range of media and materials that you should take out with you can include:

- drawing materials, such as pencils of different softness, charcoal and pastels
- an eraser – you can use this as a drawing tool as well as for rubbing out any mistakes
- a sketchbook, or paper and a board to lean on
- a camera or a smart phone camera.

If you want to work in paint, take pans or tubes of watercolours or gouache, brushes and a mixing palette. Remember to take a container or bottle of water to use with the paint and to clean the brushes!

Tip:

Keep asking yourself questions as you plan and work on your visual research to keep it focused:

- Have I chosen the best format for the research?
- Could I extend my research by working on other formats, or combinations such as paper-based and digital?

Tip:

There are other approaches you can take to recording. For example, if you are interested in recording texture to inform your work in ceramics or textiles, you could use frottage techniques, taking rubbings directly from different-textured surfaces. Alternatively, you could press objects into slabs of clay to record different-textured surfaces.

Format

Your research can be collated in different formats:

- Research folder – this can be an A4 binder.
- Sketchbook – some students prefer this, as it gives their research a personal touch, and becomes like a visual diary.
- Digital folder – some of your research can be scanned or screen-shot using digital techniques. This is useful if you are researching video, photography and other digital formats. You will have to print out your work as evidence for assessment.

Remember that you may want to use all these techniques combined in different ways to make your research work for you.

Tip:

Always carry a sketchbook with you. Use a small A6 sketchbook for this. You can use this alongside your smart phone camera any time you are inspired by something that you see.

Selecting and preparing work for assessment

All three components of the Cambridge Assessment International Education A Level and two components for the AS Level externally set assignment require you to submit your work and/or photographs of your work on A2 paper or card for external assessment. For Component 1, you can provide five sheets (ten sides) of A2 for the portfolio, and one sheet (two sides) of A2 for the final outcome. For Component 2, you should provide a maximum of three sheets (six sides) of A2 for the supporting studies, and up to one sheet (two sides) of A2 paper for your final outcome.

This means that you will have to select the work that you submit for assessment by Cambridge Assessment International Education carefully from the total amount of work that you produce during your course and when preparing for the externally set assignment. The work that you select must demonstrate that you have met each of the assessment criteria for each component. There is no limit to the number of A2 sheets that you can use to present your work for Component 3, the Personal Investigation, but you should still be selective. There is a word limit for the written portion of Component 3, of between 1000 and 1500 words.

Discuss with your teacher what work you will submit to the examiner, who will help you to select the best of what you have produced and make sure that it covers all four assessment objectives.

COMPONENT 1: COURSEWORK PORTFOLIO

Your coursework is presented in two parts: the portfolio and a final outcome. The portfolio comprises the work that you do in response to a project based on a theme. The theme for this component will normally be set by your teacher following guidance from Cambridge. You will work through the different stages of the coursework, producing art and design work as you go along. This work must evidence how you have:

1. Recorded ideas and observations
    - from first-hand sources
    - by using drawings and photography
    - from second-hand sources and imagery.
2. Explored and experimented
    - with different media, techniques and processes.
3. Researched artists, designers and cultural influences
    - to inform the development of your ideas.
4. Selected, reviewed and refined
    - your work throughout the creative process
    - to plan and present a personal and coherent outcome.

You can achieve the same number of marks for each of the four stages, so you need to treat them equally within the project. Avoid the temptation to rush into an outcome when you have spent limited time on research, recording and exploration of materials. Your portfolio is meant to show the selected highlights of your work through the creative process of your project. It will present your creative journey to the examiner and represent the best of what you can do.

The creative journey should:
- start with your exploration of the theme
- show the range of your research
- include observation and recording
- demonstrate how you have developed and refined ideas through exploration and experimentation with media and materials
- set a clear direction for the final outcome.

Selecting work for the coursework portfolio

You have up to five sheets (ten sides) of A2 to work with. As you can use both sides, that makes ten sides of A2 maximum. You should consider the space you use well, to present a cohesive and integrated presentation that can include the following:

1. Work that shows how you recorded ideas and observations showing drawing, painting, photography and other recording from first-hand and second-hand sources.
2. Work that shows how you explored and experimented, showing your exploration of different media, techniques and processes.
3. Work that shows how you researched artists, designers and cultural influences, showing how you used your research to inform the development of your ideas.
4. Work that shows how you selected, reviewed and refined your work throughout the creative process, showing how you reviewed and refined work to plan and present a personal and coherent outcome.

Some of the A2 sides are likely to feature mounted examples of work, possibly from different sources – for example, sketchbook pages, studies on different pieces of paper and so on. You need to make sure that the examples you select are described and explain your work in a strong manner. There are different ways you can achieve this, as shown below.

COMPONENT 1: FINAL OUTCOME

The final outcome is presented in addition to, and alongside, the coursework portfolio of up to five pieces of A2 paper or card. The portfolio should support the final outcome.

You must select and refine the work on the theme to produce a coherent final outcome. This means an outcome that has developed consistently and whose source can be traced back through the work in your portfolio. The final outcome should ideally bring together your ideas and exploration to produce a strong, creative piece. The final outcome can be more than one piece – for example, it can be a series of related prints or paintings, photographs, graphic designs, textiles, 3D work and so on.

Remember that all your work must be presented on A2 sheets, so you might have to photograph the final outcome, depending on its size and the materials that it is made from. For example, a large-scale painting or a fashion garment will need to be photographed and printed out at a reduced size.

Presenting work for assessment

The advice given here is also relevant to preparing work for assessment in Components 2 and 3.

The way that you present your work can impact on the overall quality of your portfolio. You must present your work in the best way possible that does not detract from (take away from) the work itself. To do this, you must consider the following points;

- Arranging the work – you have limited space on which to display your work, so you must use the space fully and effectively. Each side is basically a composition made up of the pieces you are going to mount onto it. You need to arrange the pieces in such a way that they look well balanced and neatly laid out. Think about the sizes of the pieces and how much space you leave around them.
- Cutting out neatly – you need to trim your work when using sketchbook pages or separate pieces of paper. You also need to use a scalpel or craft knife safely.
- Arranging in sequence – this means your drawings, photographs, studies, research, experimentation, samples and so on are arranged in a logical sequence. They will be telling the story of how you developed your project and how you used the creative process.
- Photographing work – try to make the photographs as clear and as well-lit as possible, without any background detail. Aim to achieve strong images through proper use of camera controls, rather than relying on post-capture editing. This is particularly the case when photographing larger-scale or three-dimensional (3D) final outcomes.

Tip:

An infinity cove is an all-white space with no corners, designed to create the impression that the background of a subject stretches to infinity. You can make a simple infinity cove by bending a piece of card into the intersection of a wall and floor, or table and wall. This will give you a flat white surface for shooting models, maquettes and smaller 3D items.

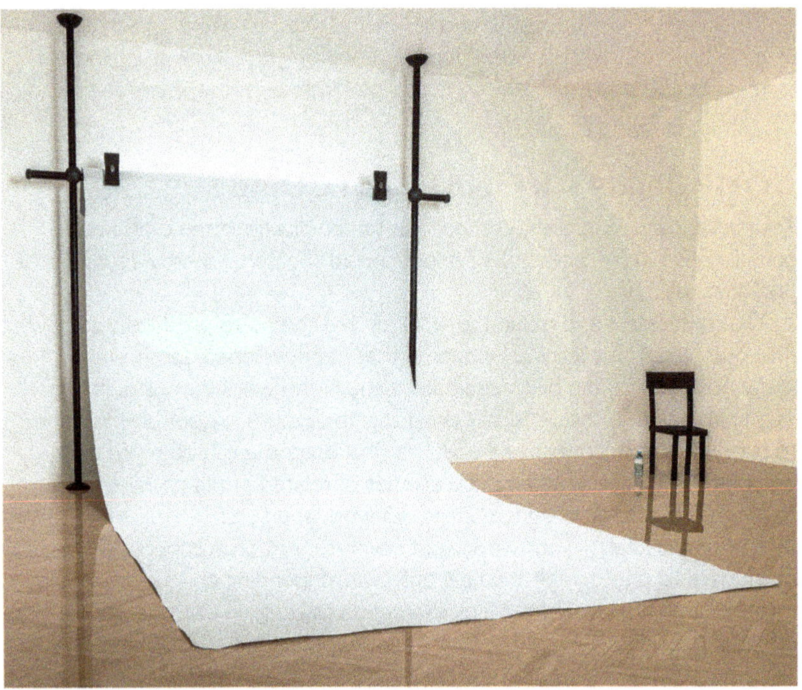

5.1 An infinity cove set up in a photography studio. Ask your teacher to show you how to set up a smaller version in your school studio.

COMPONENT 2: EXTERNALLY SET ASSIGNMENT

When you are given the question paper by your teacher, you have to select one starting point to work on. There is a preparation period before the date of the externally set assignment, when you produce your supporting studies based on your chosen starting point.

You have to explore and develop supporting studies in response to the starting point, producing a body of work leading to a final outcome. The final outcome is produced during the 15-hour supervised test over several days under examination conditions. You can use a broad range of stimuli to develop ideas, from visual arts to theatre, prose, music, textiles, literature or film. You must take your supporting studies into the test with you.

Interpreting the question paper

The question paper will contain instructions and general information. You need to read through these carefully. It will also feature a selection of possible starting points, presented as words or phrases, such as these examples taken from a fictional sample paper:

1. An interior space
2. Vessel
3. Enclosed
4. Spiral
5. Detail.

You will select one of the five and use it as a theme for your work in the test, following the same processes that you worked through in developing your coursework responses. You will use these to develop your supporting studies, take them with you into the test, and use them as the basis for your final outcome.

Generating ideas

It is a good idea to discuss the starting points with your teacher, and explore the potential of each before deciding which one to follow. You can start generating ideas by creating a mind map (refer to Module 1, page 38) or, taking the example of 'An interior space', you can list as many different examples of 'interior space' that you can think of – for example:

- small room
- courtyard
- sports hall or stadium
- concert hall
- the inside of a car
- aircraft cabin
- the circuitry of a computer...

You could also break the phrase down into less literal examples, such as:

- the inner or spiritual self
- the mind
- in the womb...

You also have the option of looking at sources from wider fields. For instance, are there any examples in literature or film that feature the same theme?

Supporting studies

The supporting studies part of Component 2 has the same function as the portfolio part of Component 1. This is where you must explore and develop ideas in response to the chosen starting point. You must take your supporting studies with you into the externally set assignment, as they inform the final outcome that you produce in the 15 hours. You should approach the work in the same way that you approached Component 1 coursework, although you will have to work to a tight time scale set by your school or college, and you only have three A2 sheets (up to six sides) on which to present your preparatory work.

Getting started

Start to research examples of work in your study area on your theme. Look at how other artists, craftspeople and designers have used materials, techniques and processes, and consider how they have used formal elements in their work.

As with your coursework, you must show that you have used recording from direct observation. You must not rely on second-hand sources, such as photographs by other people.

Exploring your theme or subject

In the early stages of the assignment, be prepared to explore different versions of the same starting point. It is important to make a start quickly, and refine your ideas by exploring them practically.

Changing your theme or subject

You can change your mind about which starting point to refer to once you have started, although the guidance in the question paper advises against it unless vital. You have a limited amount of time to produce your preparatory studies and you will not be given extra time if you start again!

Remember, the supporting studies for this assignment need to show that you have:

- recorded ideas and observations
    - from first-hand studies – for example, your own drawings and photography
    - from secondary imagery
- explored and experimented with different media, techniques and processes
- researched in depth into artists, designers and cultural influences, to inform the development of ideas
- selected, reviewed and refined your work throughout the whole creative process, to plan and produce a personal and coherent outcome.

The 15-hour externally set assignment

Your school or centre will set the timing of the externally set assignment and run it over several sessions. You must be prepared for the first session and bring all your supporting studies into the test to refer to throughout the 15 hours. At the end of the test, the supporting studies must be mounted onto a maximum of three sheets (six sides) of A2 paper or card. These will be sent to Cambridge Assessment International Education, along with your final outcome – or photographs of the final outcome if it is 3D, larger than A2 or fragile.

Before the externally set assignment, talk to your teachers about your work and plan what materials you will need. Try to be relaxed and confident when you go into the test. If you have prepared properly, you will already know what you have to do during the 15 hours and practised using the materials and techniques beforehand.

Use your time wisely during the externally set assignment. If something does not go as planned, don't panic. Try to reflect critically on what you are doing and be prepared to stop work on the final piece and try out more ideas if necessary to work through a problem. Use the time when you return to the test room after a break to stand back and look at your work with fresh eyes before continuing.

COMPONENT 3: THE PERSONAL INVESTIGATION (A LEVEL ONLY)

The specific sections within each module (pages 48–51, 118–123, 191–193 and 284–287) provide you with a detailed framework of support for the written analysis part of this component.

The second part for this component is practical work. The practical work for this component should be approached in the same way as you approach the coursework for Components 1 and 2.

All the work for this component must be presented on A2 sheets. However, there is no limit to the number of sides of A2 sheets you can use.

Written work for AS & A Level Art & Design

Although there is no specific requirement to produce any written work in Components 1 and 2, it is good practice to do so. Written notes (annotations) can help explain your ideas for your own benefit, as well as helping to make your intentions clear to your teacher and the examiner.

The written analysis is a key part of Component 3: Personal Investigation, and detailed guidance on this section is given throughout this book.

ANNOTATING YOUR WORK

There are two main types of annotation:

- The first is the annotation made by practitioners when recording in front of an object, scene, situation or event. This type of annotation might be details about the scene, and serves to remind them of what they have seen when back in the studio. It might say 'very bright light in clouds above buildings, almost white', or 'deep shadows on side of face, blues and greens', and so on. Some of your drawings might have this kind of annotation on them.
- The second type is the annotation that is meant to provide information after something has been produced. This is more of an explanation or description, and can serve as a kind of critical reflection. It might, for example, be technical information written underneath a set of samples using different print techniques. It could explain the processes used, or identify a preferred example, or show critical analysis of the work in progress through self-reflection and evaluation.

You can add annotation to examples of work on your A2 portfolio sheets, to help clarify specific details about what it is you were doing or working on at that particular time. You can also use it to highlight a selection you made, such as a technical refinement.

Tip:

Where you annotate your work, you must use the correct terms and subject-specific vocabulary. There are many points within this book where terminology and vocabulary are covered – refresh your memory about these before you begin annotating. Use the Glossary to help you.

Advice on time management

You need to manage your time as you work through the coursework and externally set assignments and on the Personal Investigation. The creative process is a complex one and, as mentioned previously, there is no real right or wrong answer to set assignments. While this is exciting and gives you a creative freedom to interpret and produce your own individual response, the process does require a degree of self-management. You should follow a plan that provides mini-deadlines for your activities. *Remember that any deadline set by Cambridge Assessment International Education is not negotiable and cannot be changed.*

A **Gantt chart** or a **spreadsheet** may be useful ways for you to plan the different stages of your research.

You can list the stage along one edge, and then include deadlines that provide each separate acitvity with a specific cut-off point. You can also add to these by including spaces for ordering of any specific materials you need, or organising any technical assistance. Use an example of an existing Gantt chart and adapt it for your own use.

Tip:

The creative process is not necessarily linear. This means that you will not always work through the different stages one after another, in a neat sequence.

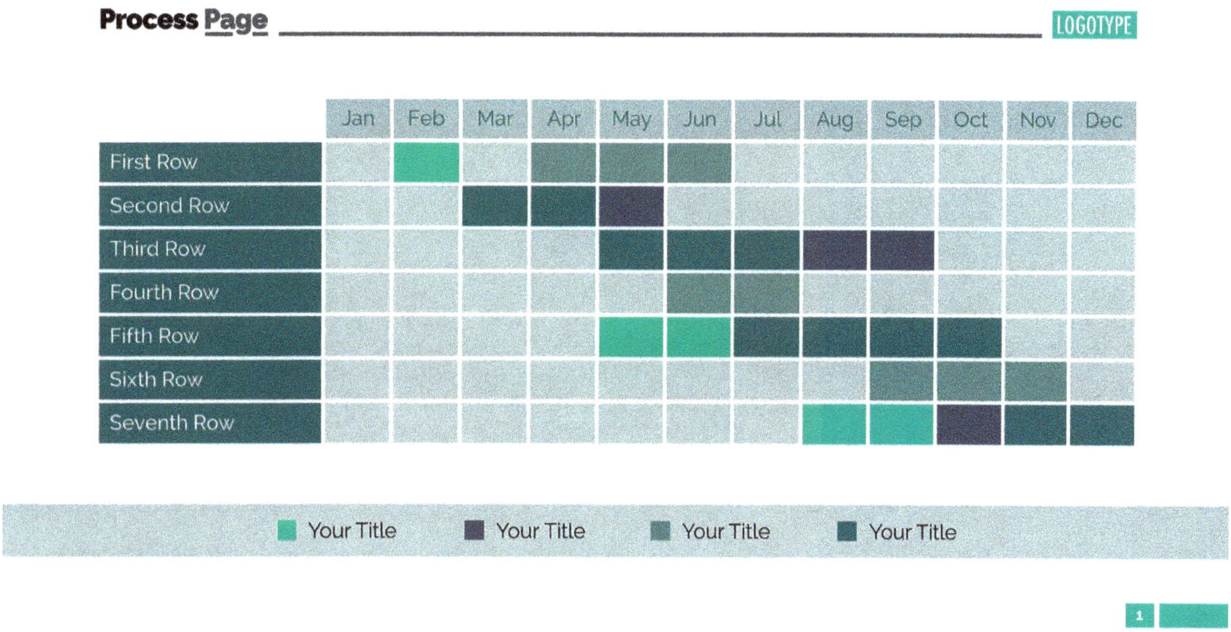

Process Page LOGOTYPE

	Jan	Feb	Mar	Apr	May	Jun	Jul	Aug	Sep	Oct	Nov	Dec
First Row												
Second Row												
Third Row												
Fourth Row												
Fifth Row												
Sixth Row												
Seventh Row												

Your Title Your Title Your Title Your Title

1

5.2 Example of a Gantt chart – you can use a Gantt chart to plan out the milestones or mini-deadlines in your project.

Tip:

Build in time for unexpected changes. Your project may not go completely to plan, and you may need to adapt your ideas. Build in time, too, for review and subsequent refinement.

Gantt chart A type of spreadsheet that displays actual work done over a certain period in relation to what was planned for that time period.

spreadsheet An electronic document with cells that contain data (usually numerical), which can be recorded and manipulated.

Gallery of student work

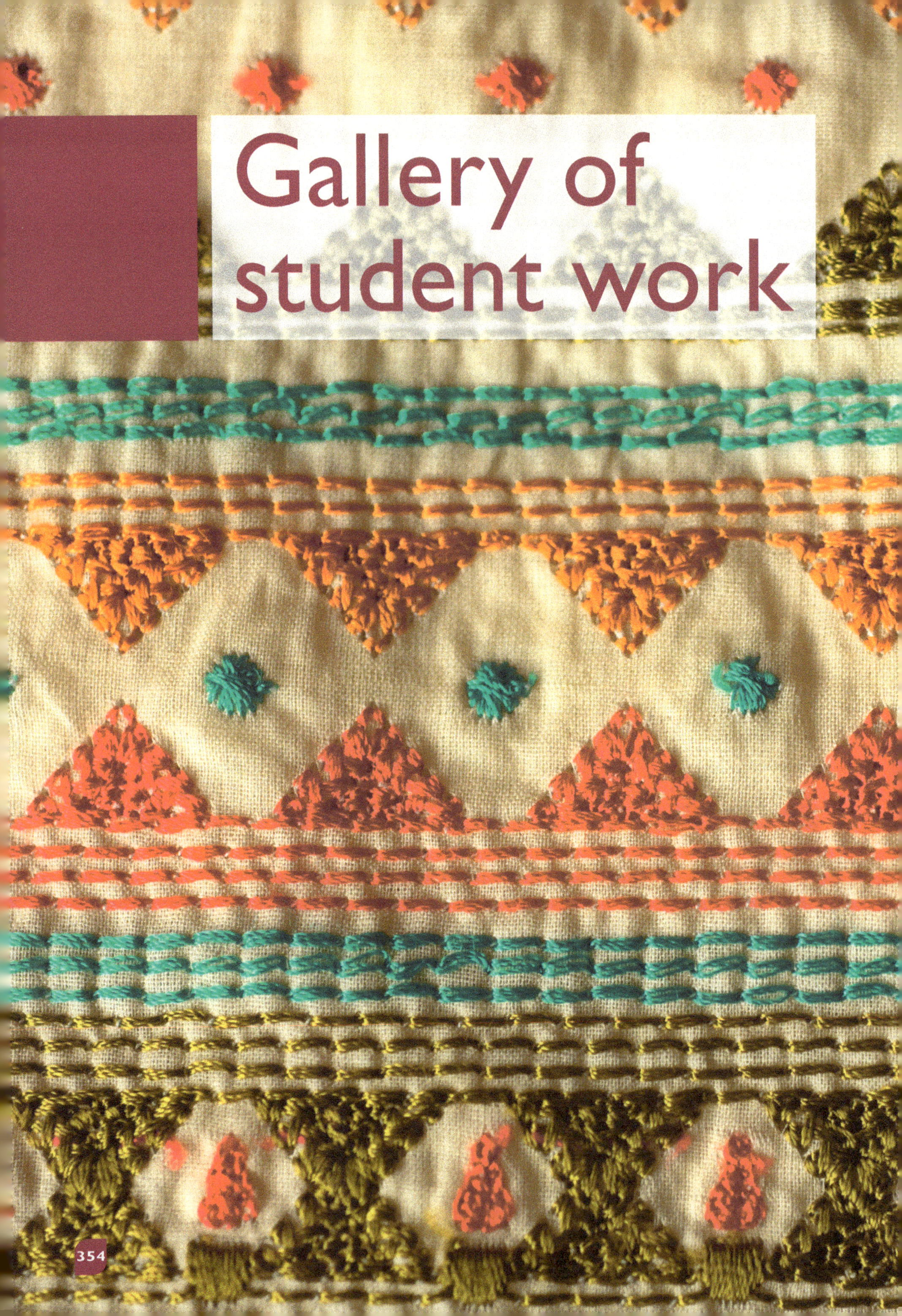

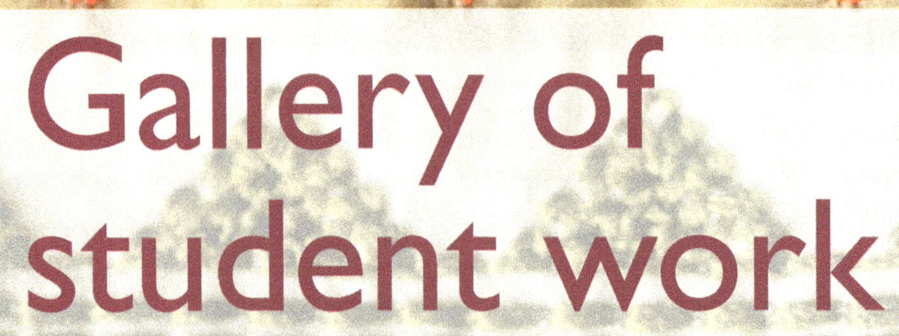

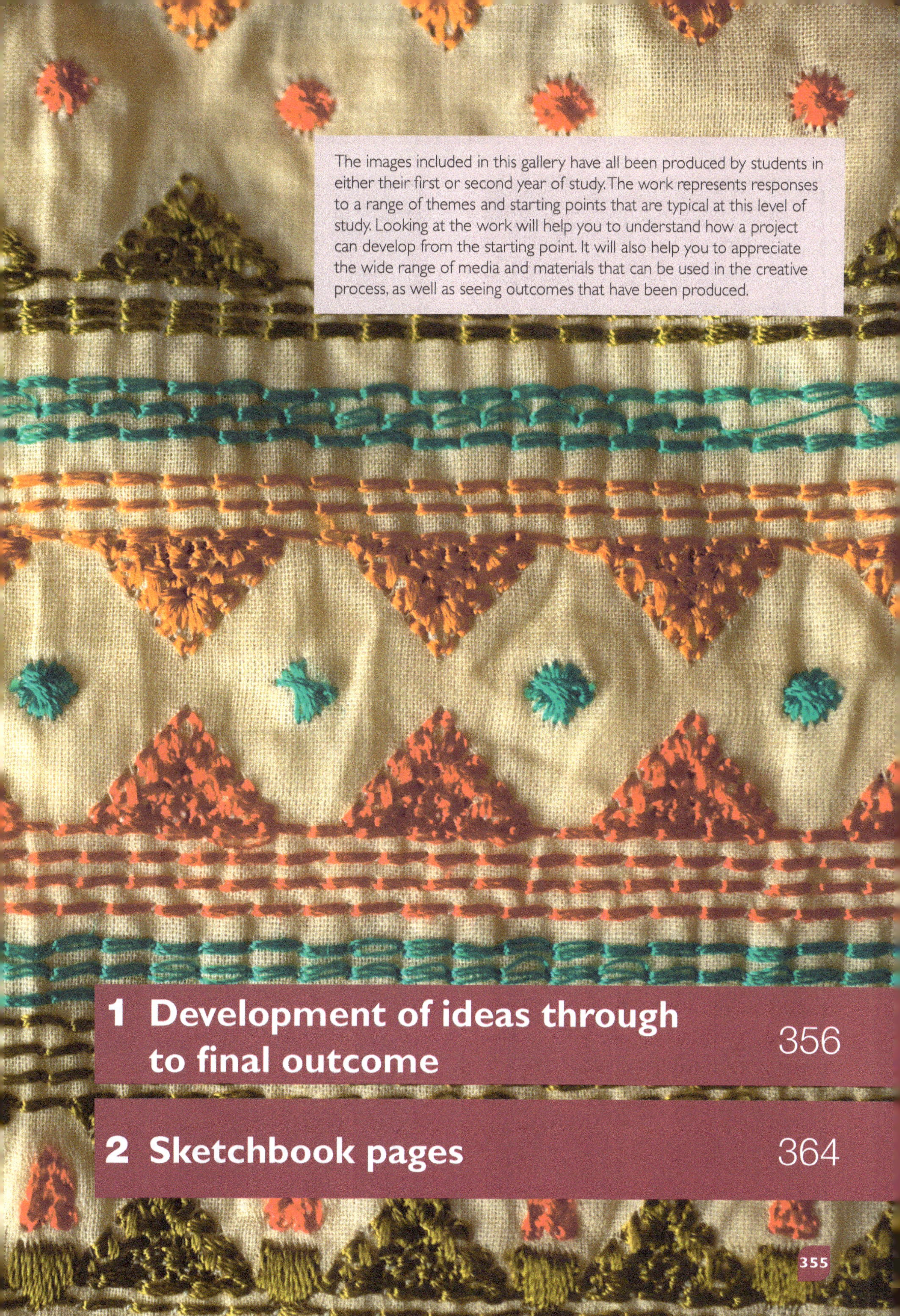

The images included in this gallery have all been produced by students in either their first or second year of study. The work represents responses to a range of themes and starting points that are typical at this level of study. Looking at the work will help you to understand how a project can develop from the starting point. It will also help you to appreciate the wide range of media and materials that can be used in the creative process, as well as seeing outcomes that have been produced.

Development of ideas through to final outcome

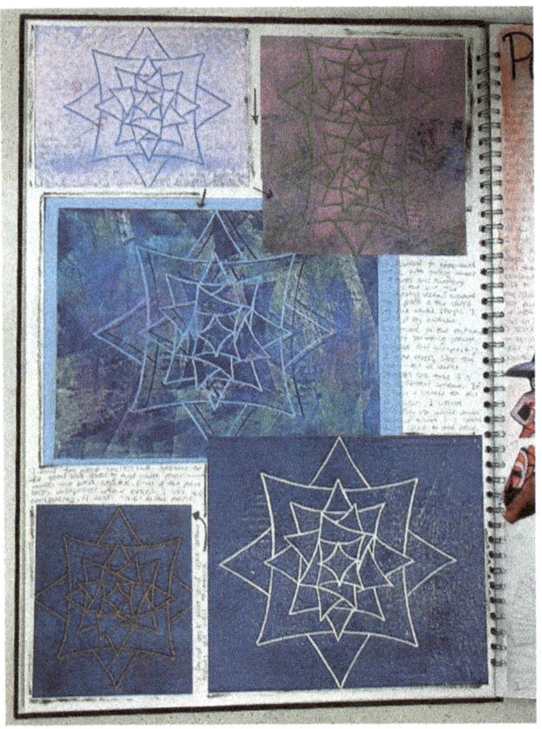

6.1 Anna Buriak: Anna's work shows how ideas can be developed from initial research to a final design by experimenting with media, materials and processes.

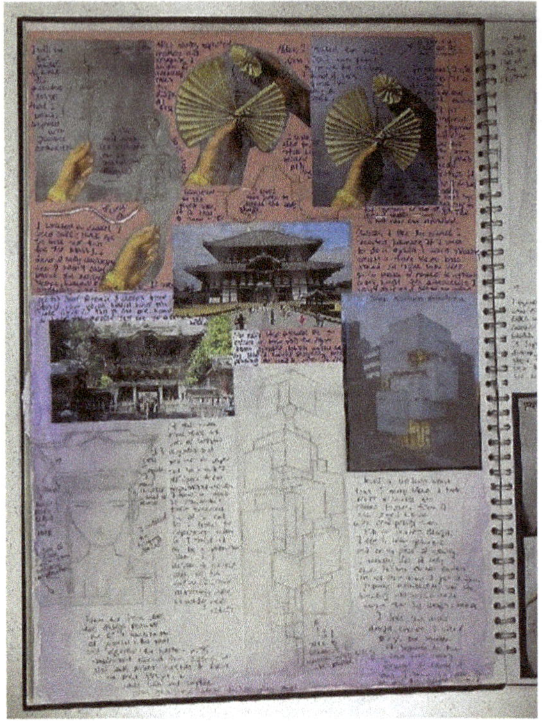

6.2 Anna Buriak.

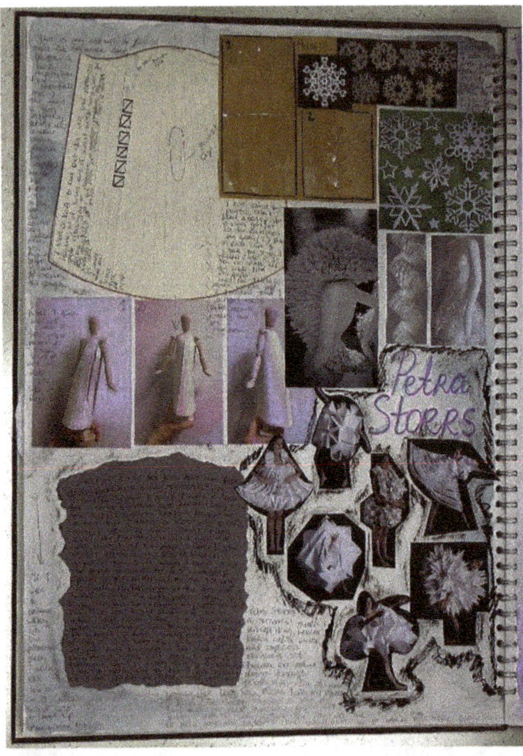

6.3 Anna Buriak.

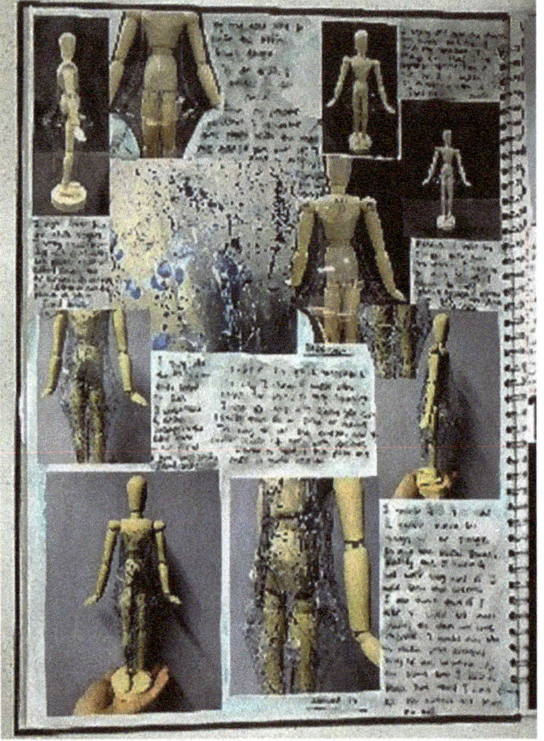

6.4 Anna Buriak.

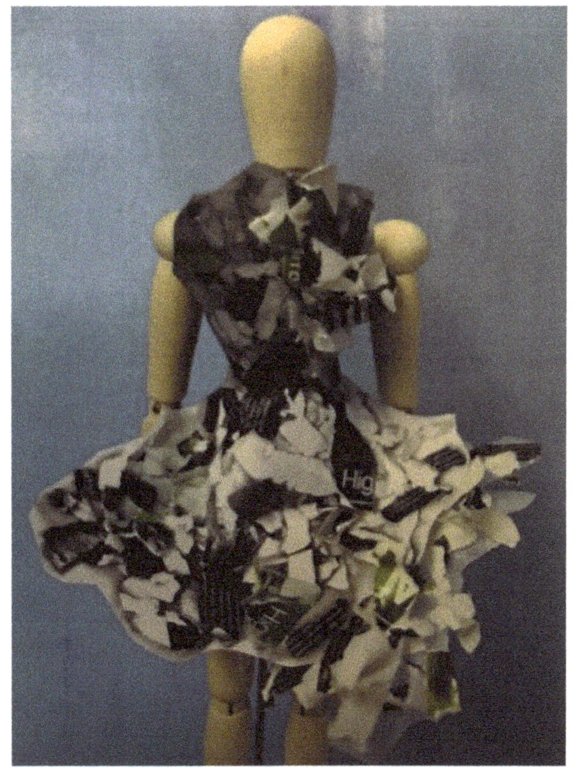

6.5 Anna Buriak: Trying out an idea as a maquette.

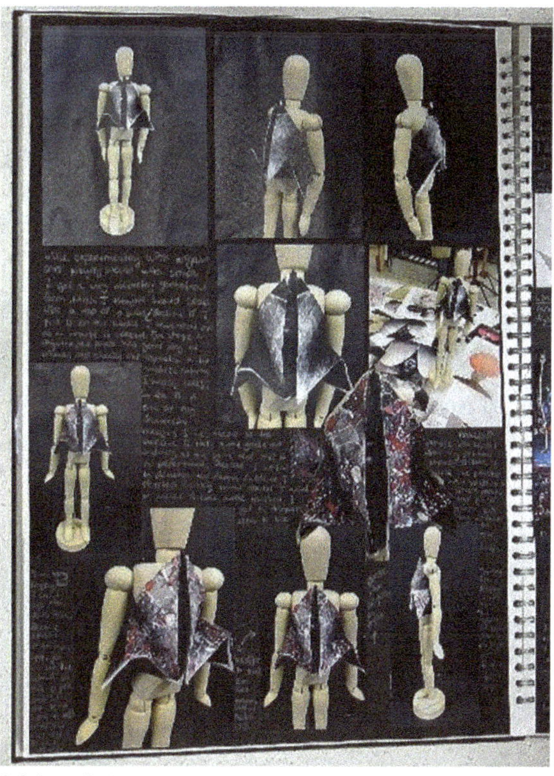

6.6 Anna Buriak.

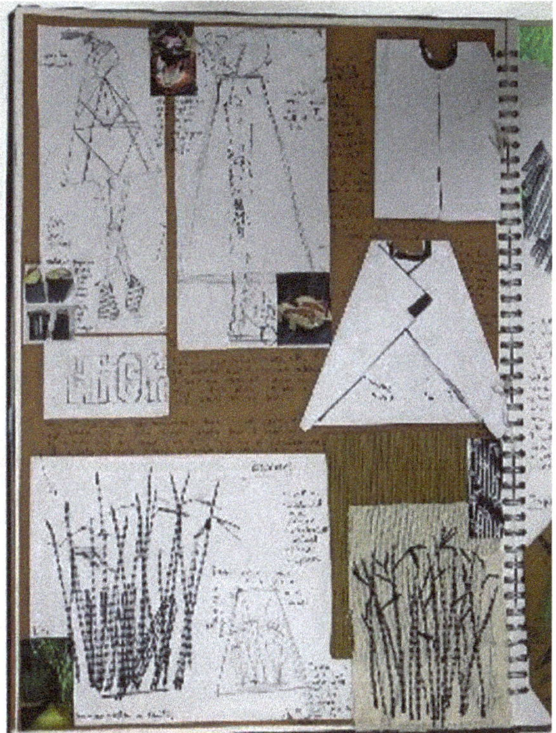

6.7 Anna Buriak: Consider the range of media and materials that Anna has worked with across her project.

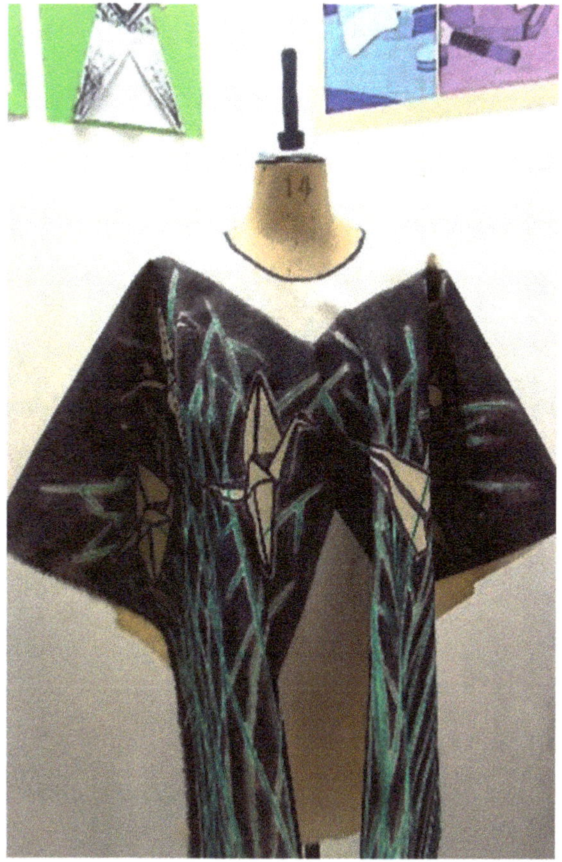

6.8 Anna Buriak: The final outcome. What do you think has influenced Anna most in this project?

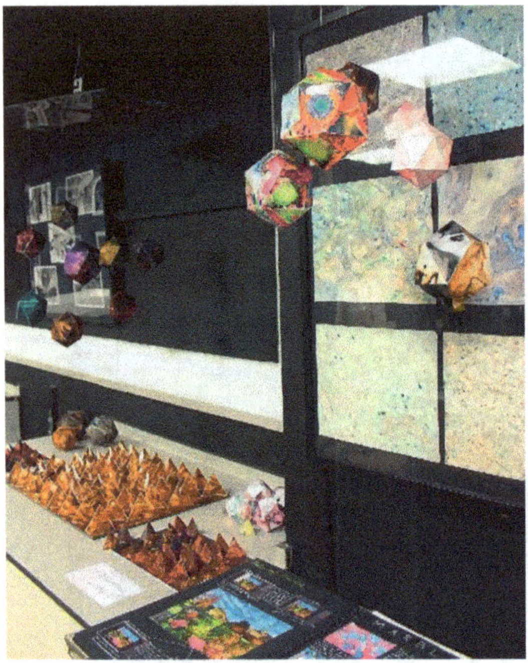

6.9 Suki Fong: Developing sculptural work from photographic images and abstract patterns.

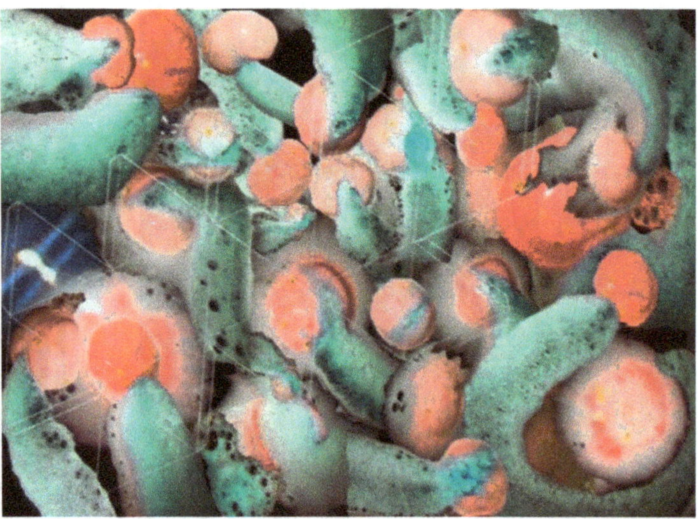

6.10 Suki Fong: The net of the geometric form has been overlaid onto a photographic image.

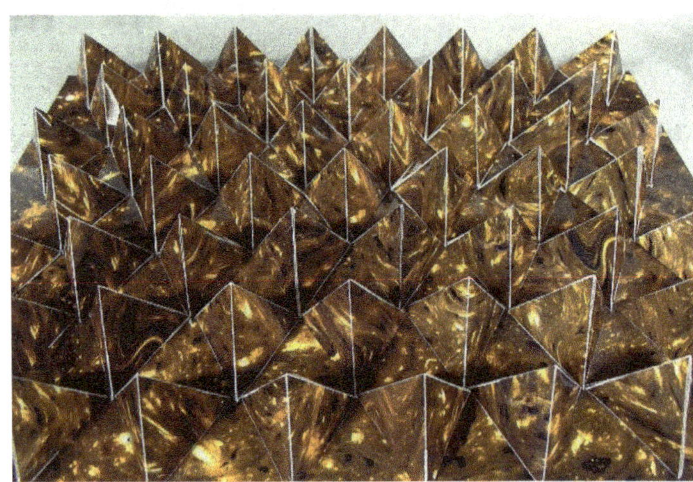

6.11 Suki Fong: Folded geometric sculptures.

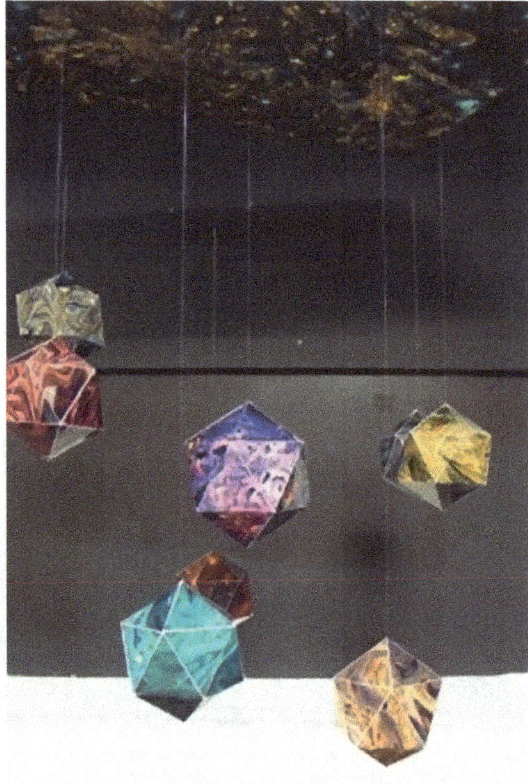

6.12 Suki Fong: Hanging folded geometric sculpture.

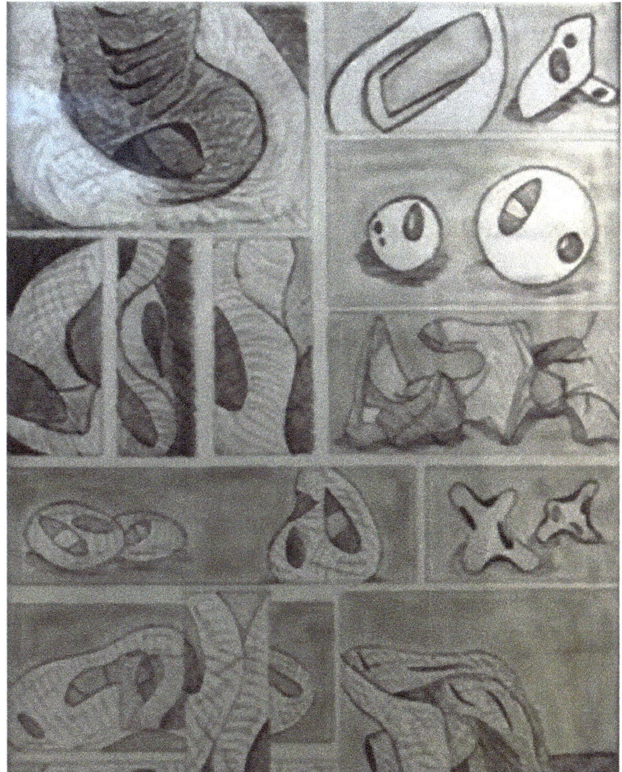

6.13 Thomas Bailey: Pen and ink studies.

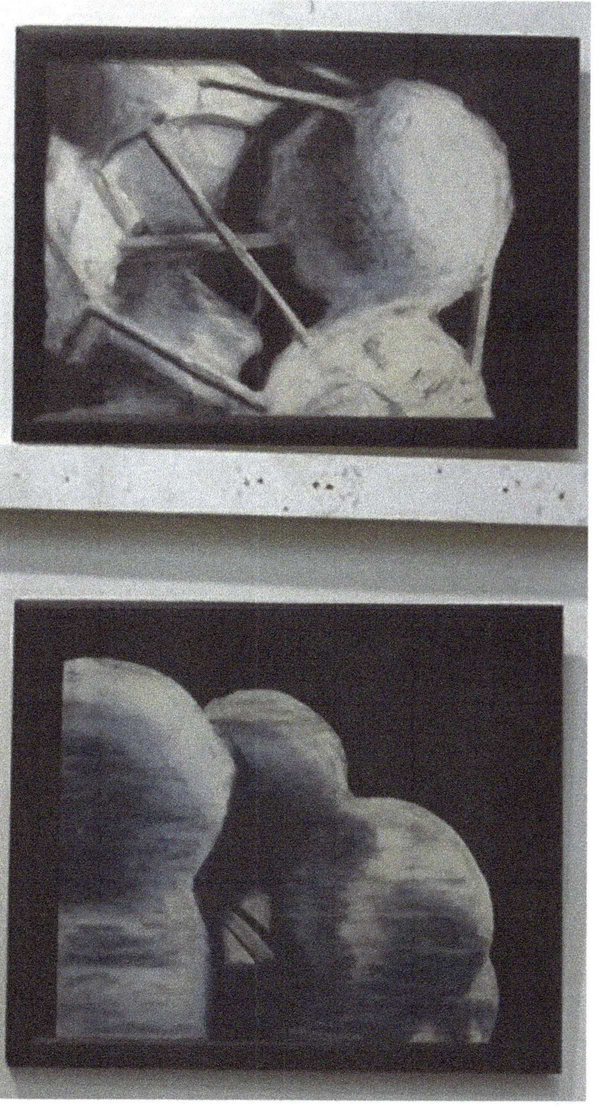

6.14 Thomas Bailey: Chalk drawings on black paper.

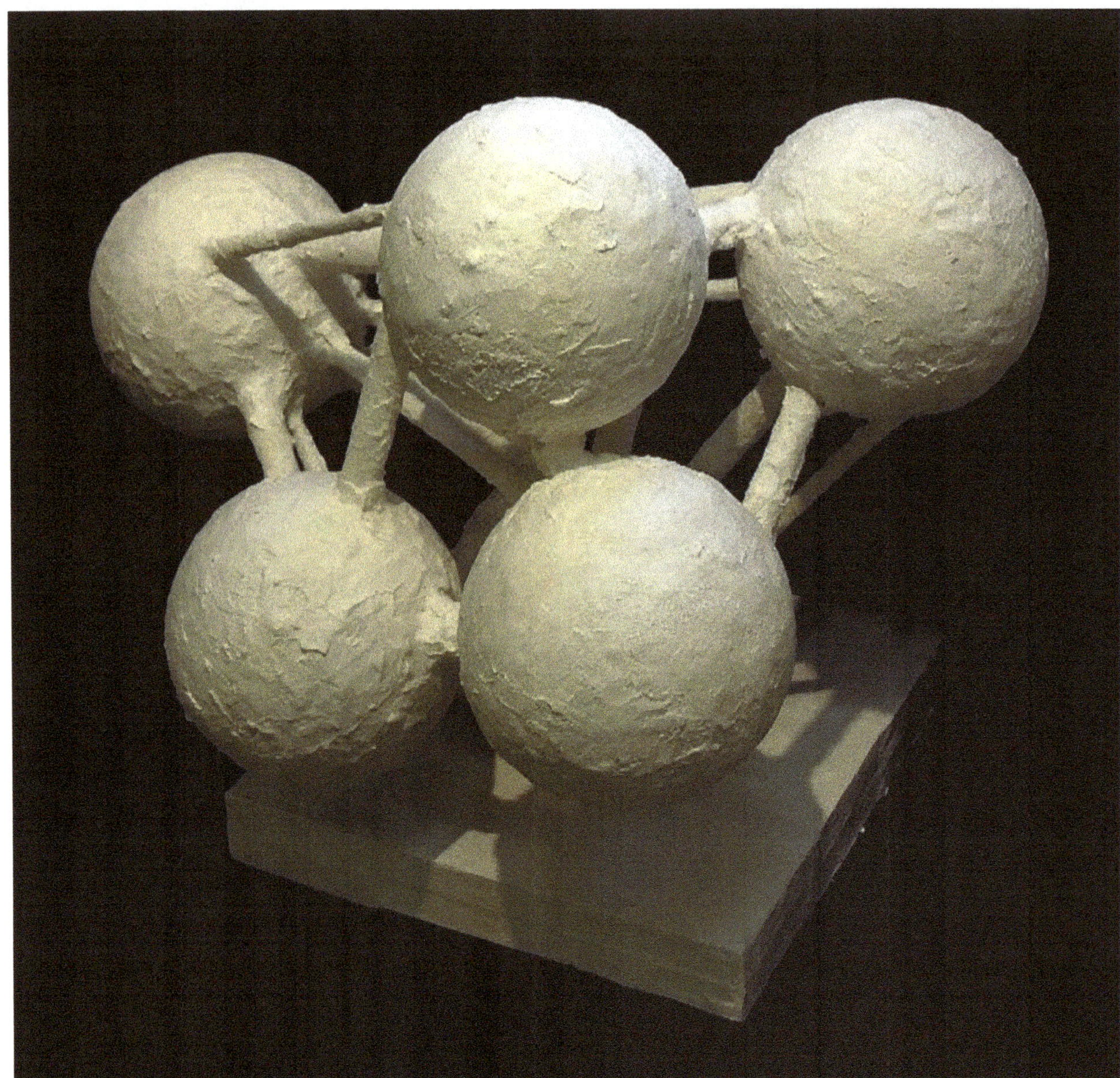

6.15 Thomas Bailey: As you can see across these three images (Figures 6.13, 6.14 and 6.15), Thomas has explored form through his use of monochromatic drawing, before developing a 3D outcome.

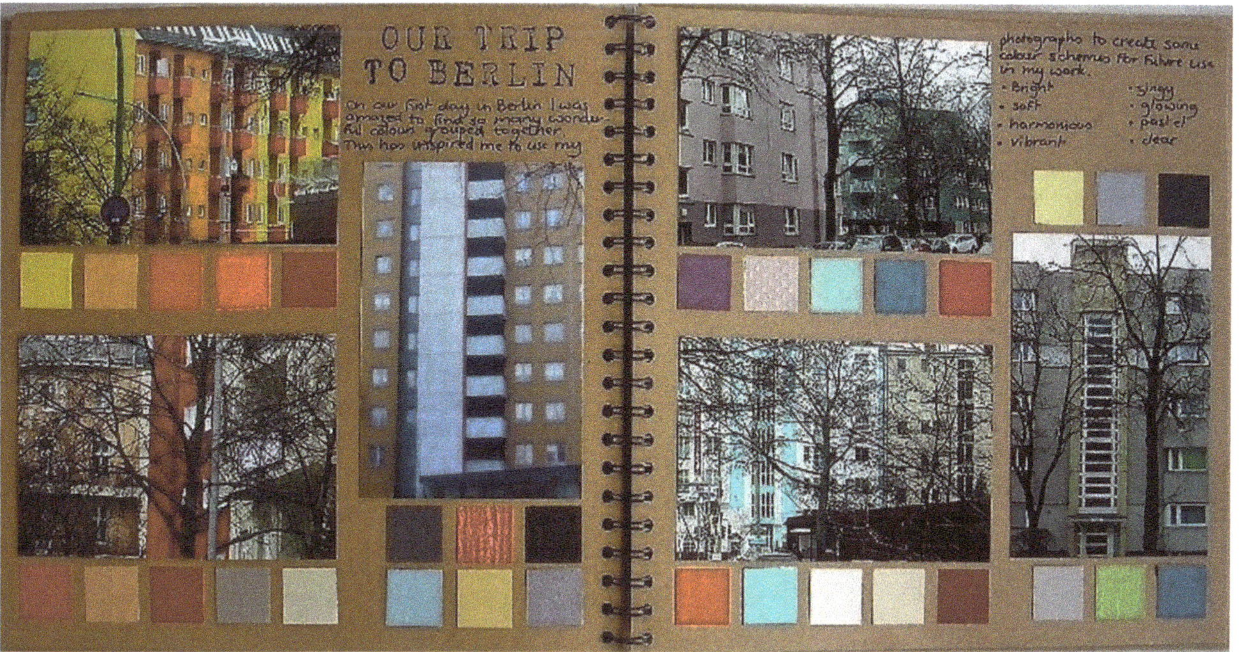

6.16 Alison Page: First-hand research of architecture is undertaken during a trip to Berlin, Germany.

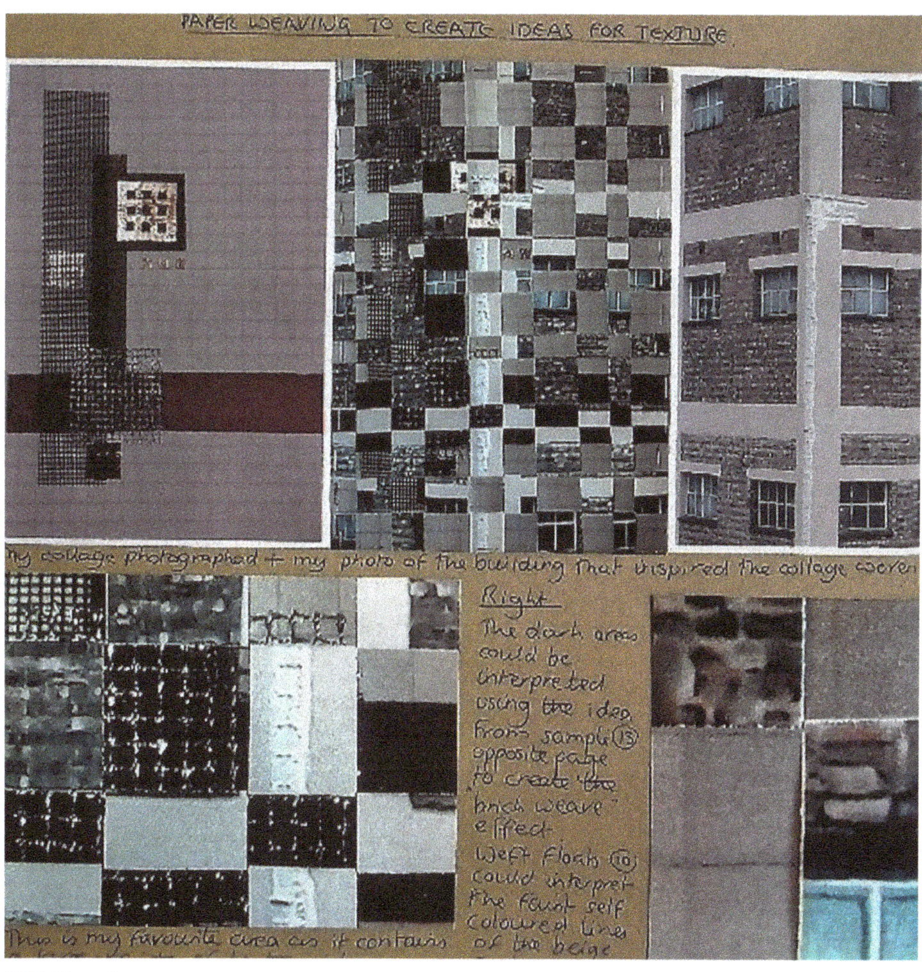

6.17 Alison Page.

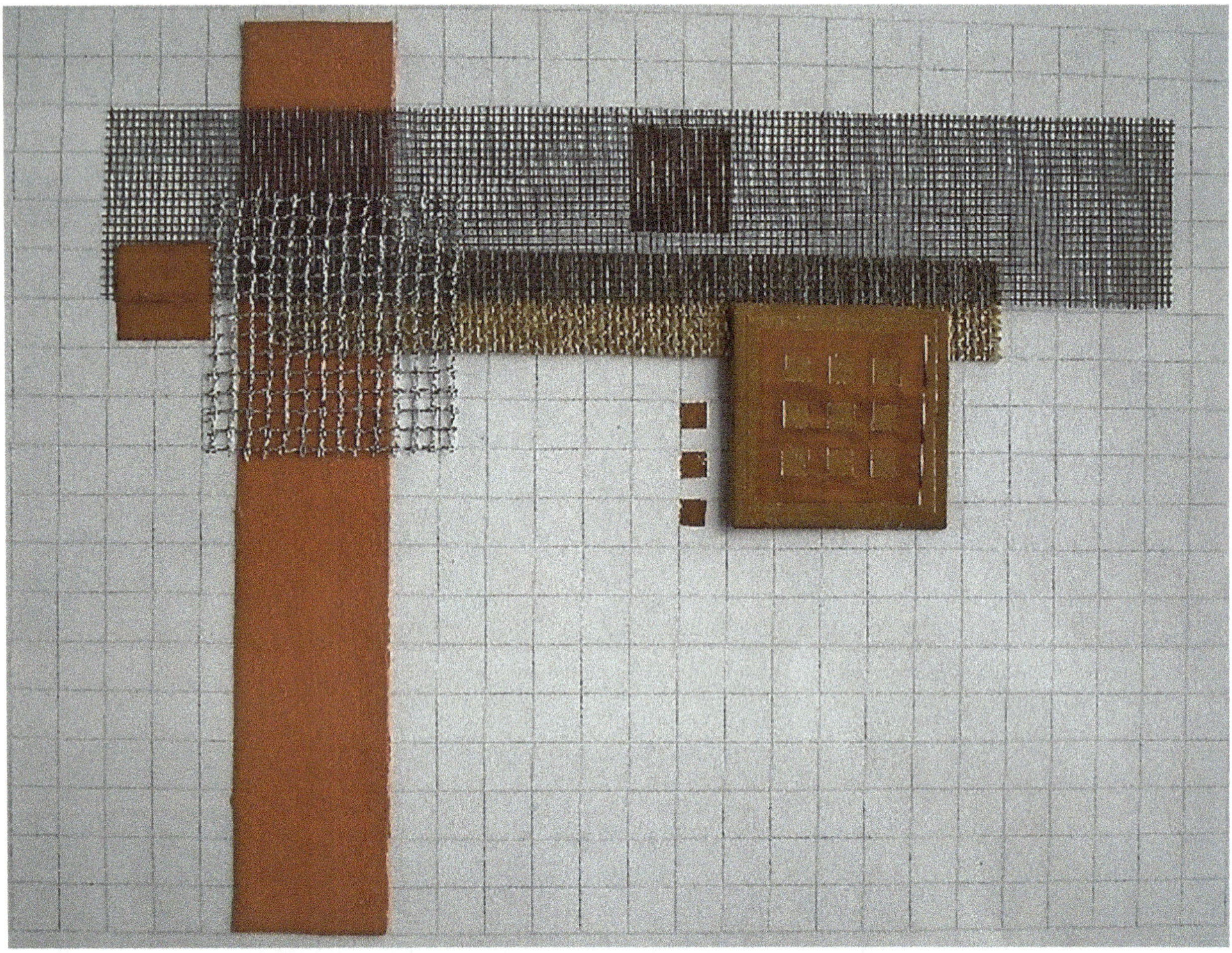

6.18 Alison Page: Alison explores her theme by experimenting with a wide range of media.

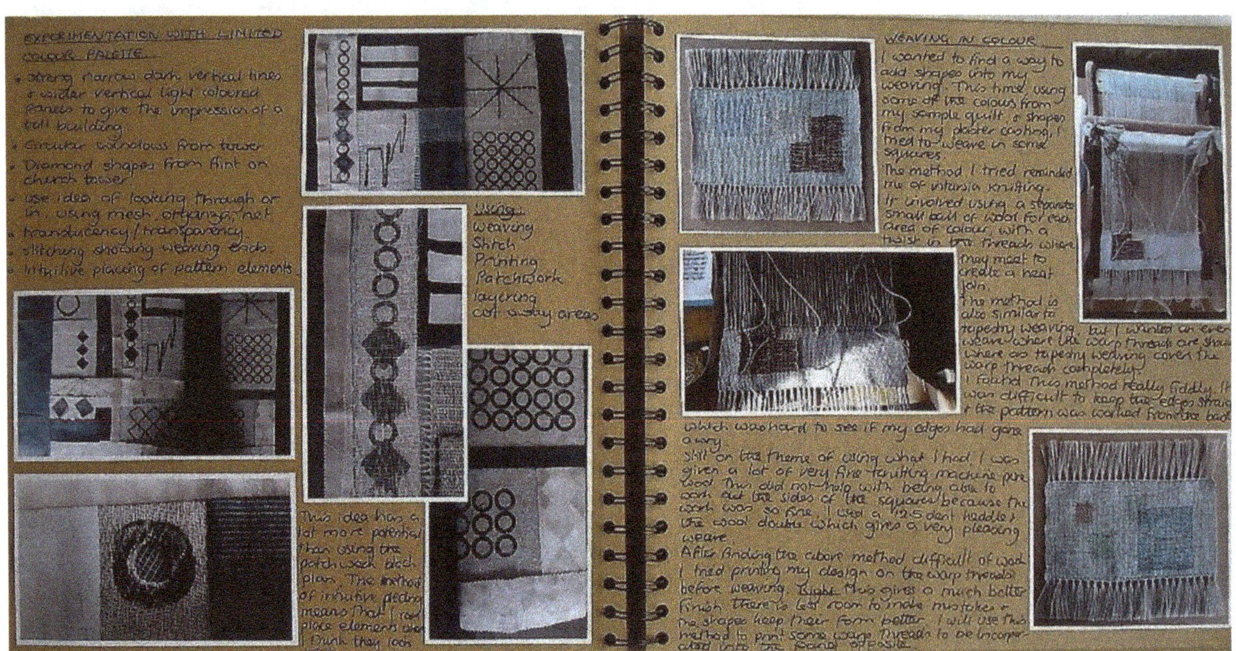

6.19 Alison Page.

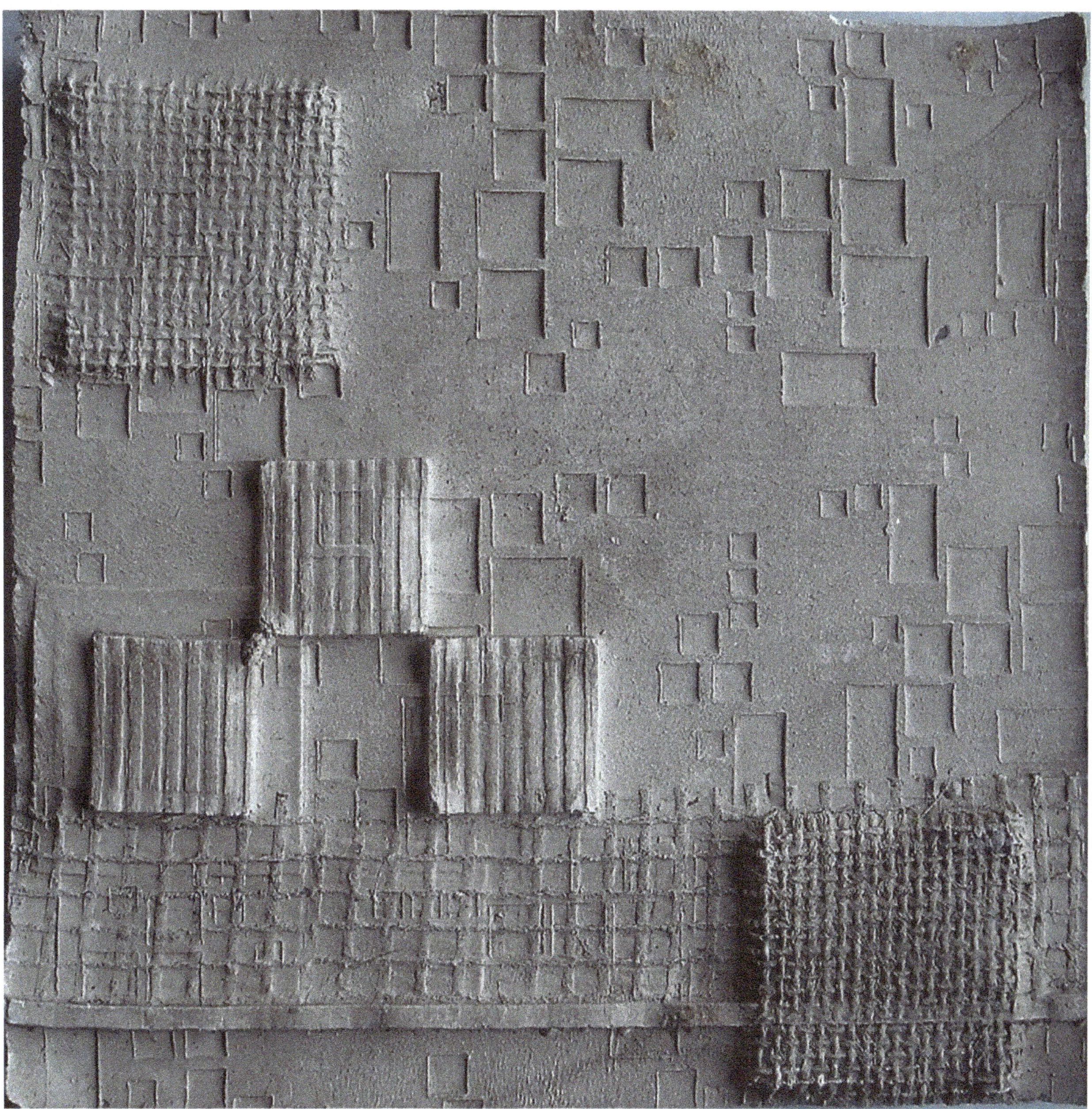

6.20 Alison Page: The resulting work is developed through the medium of woven textiles.

Sketchbook pages

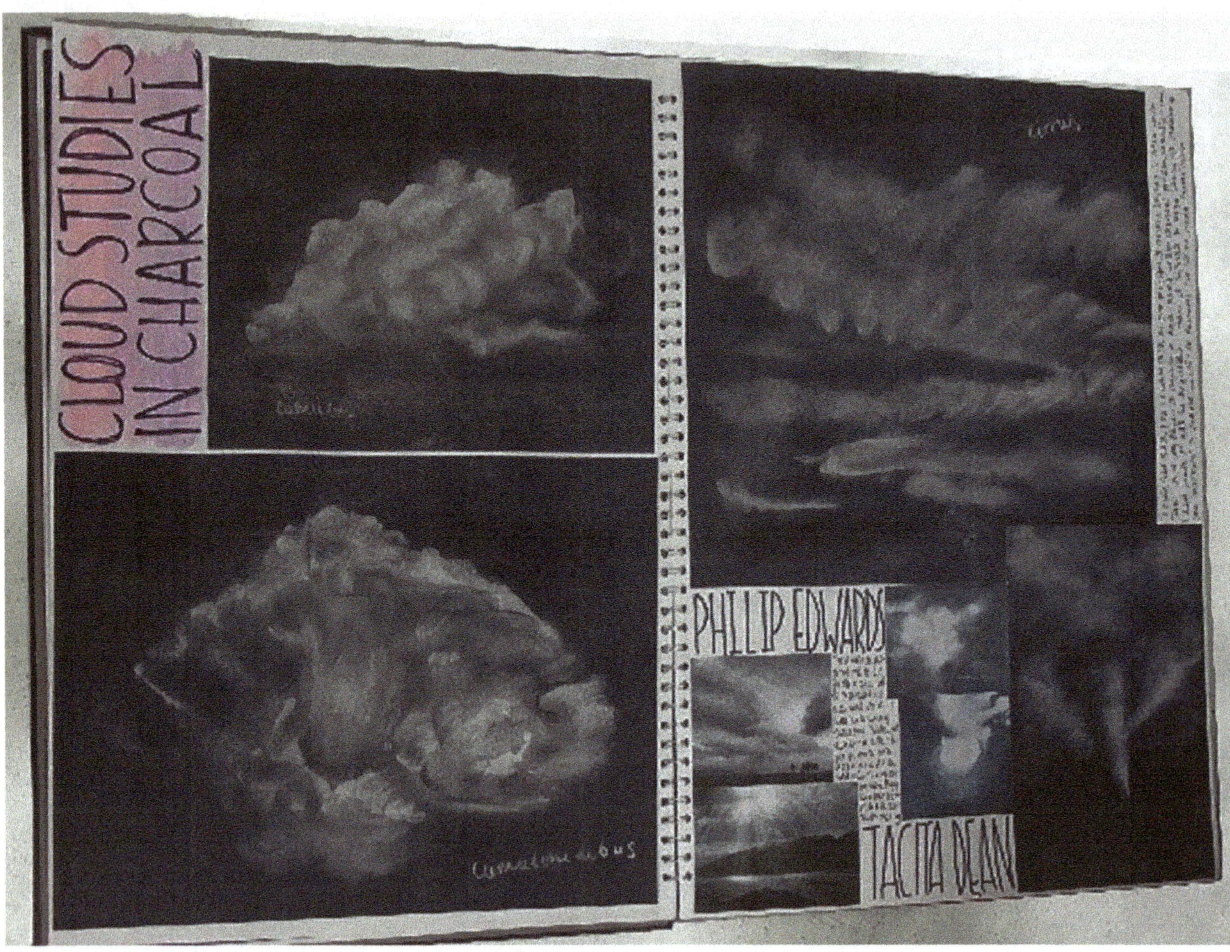

6.21 Eloise Groves: Charcoal sketches of clouds from observation and research into the work of artists.

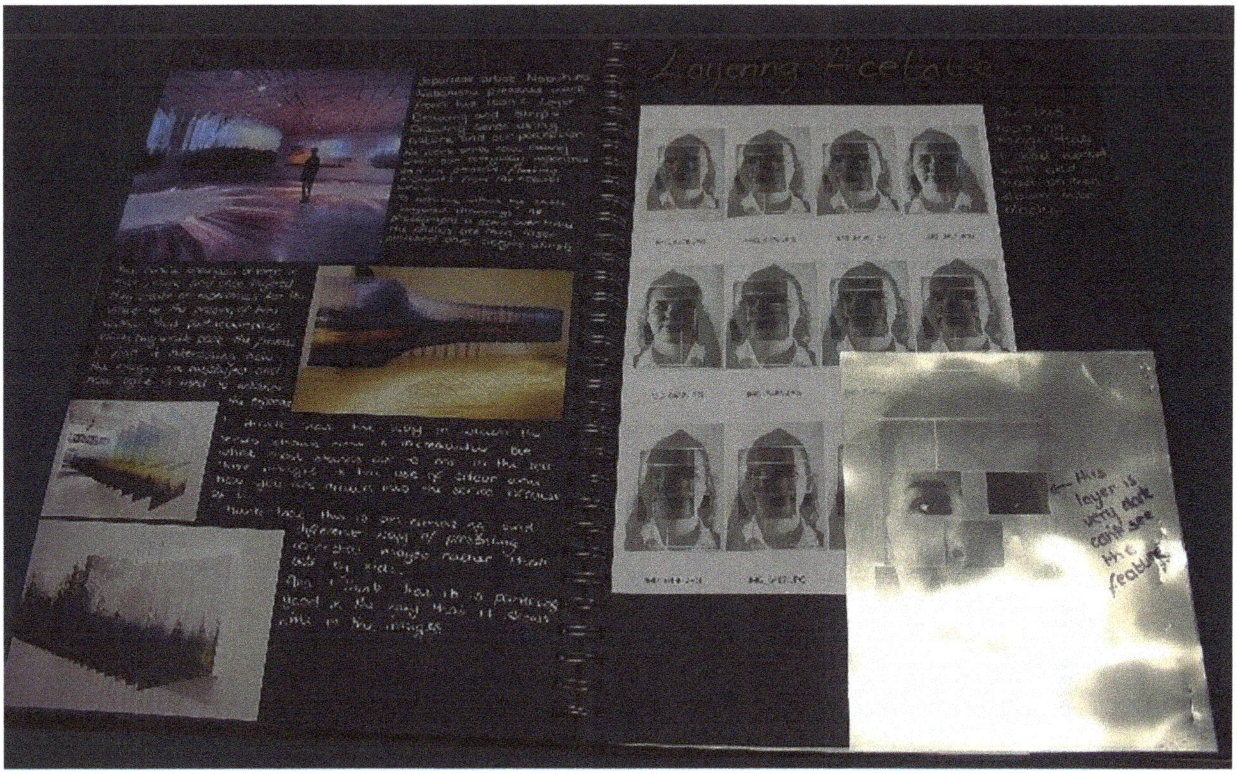

6.22 Jackie German: A record of a visit to an exhibition and subsequent development of practical work in response to the work seen.

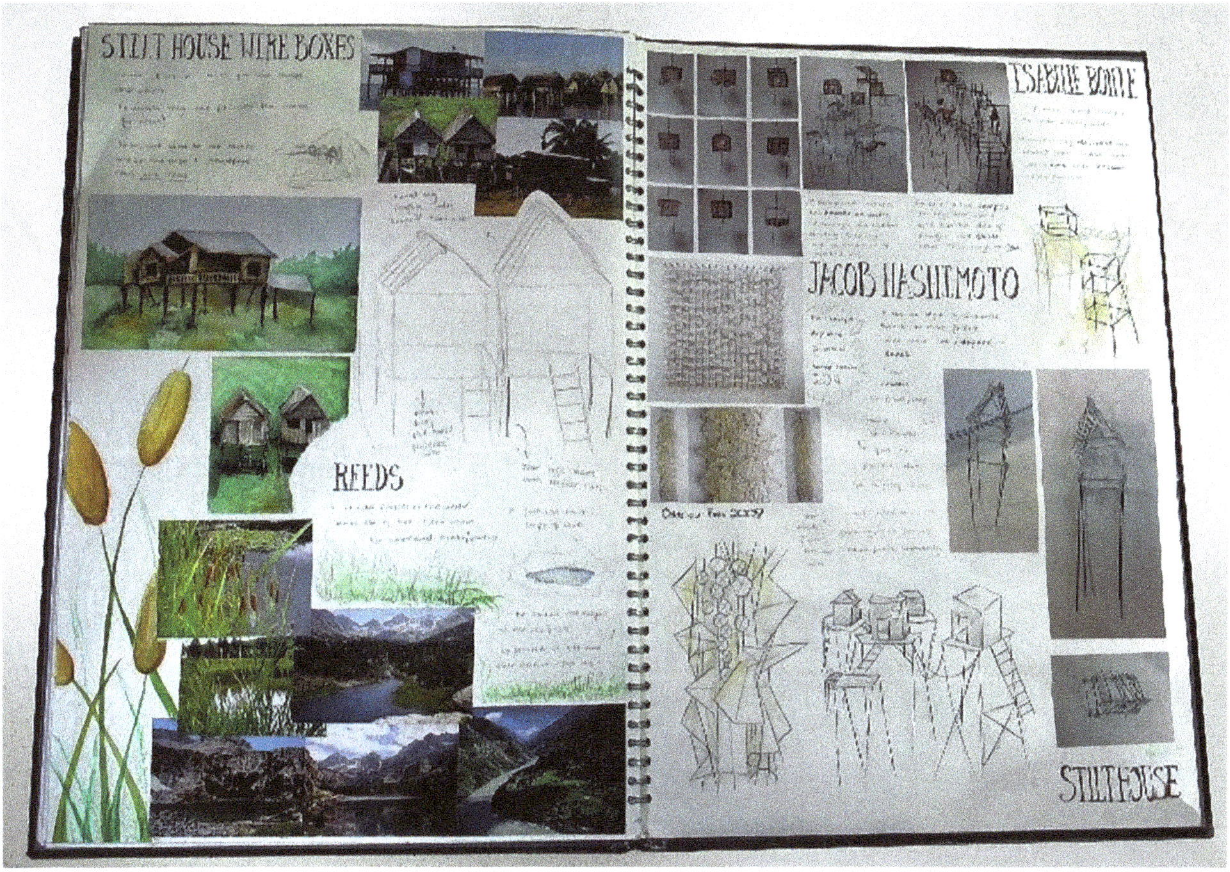

6.23 Ashlea Philips: Visual and artist research pages.

Recording from observation

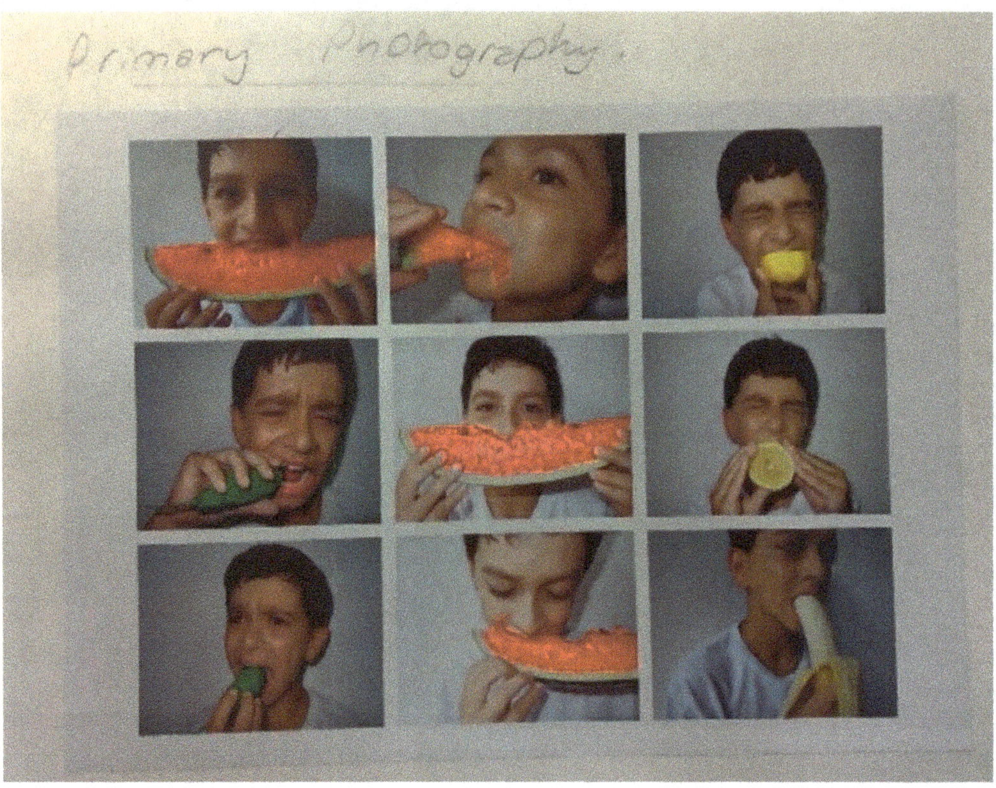

6.24 Mahnoor Abassi: Initial photographs. In this selection of images, you can see how Anna has taken her own photographs and made carefully observed coloured drawings and paintings from her images to explore her subject matter further.

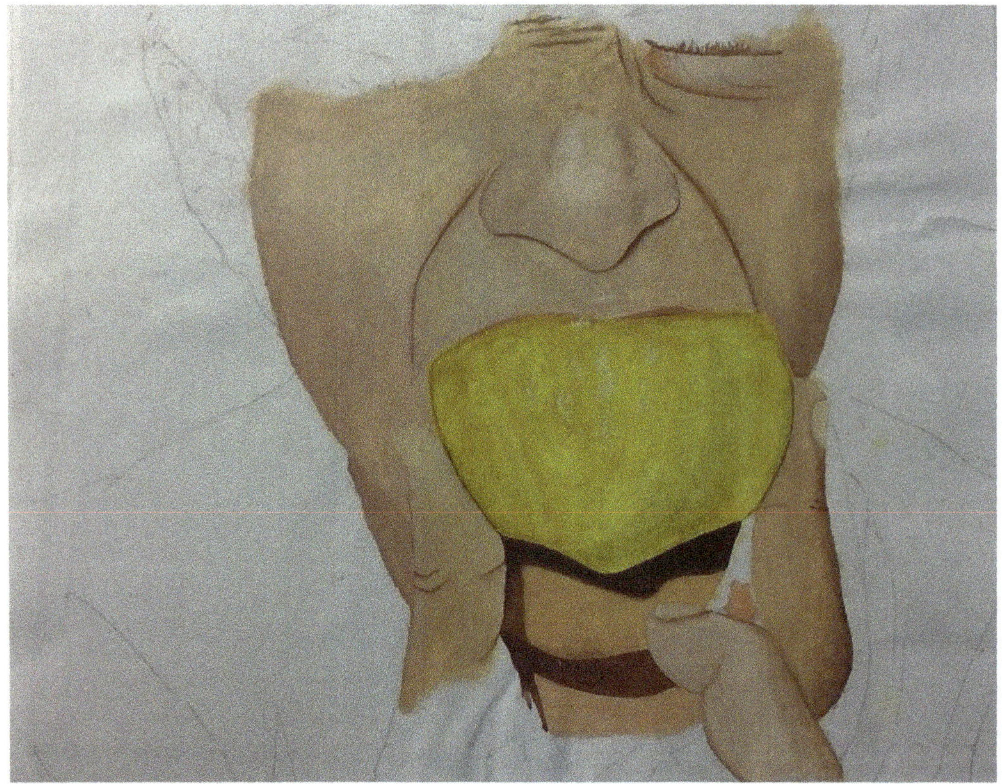

6.25 Mahnoor Abassi: Painted sketch.

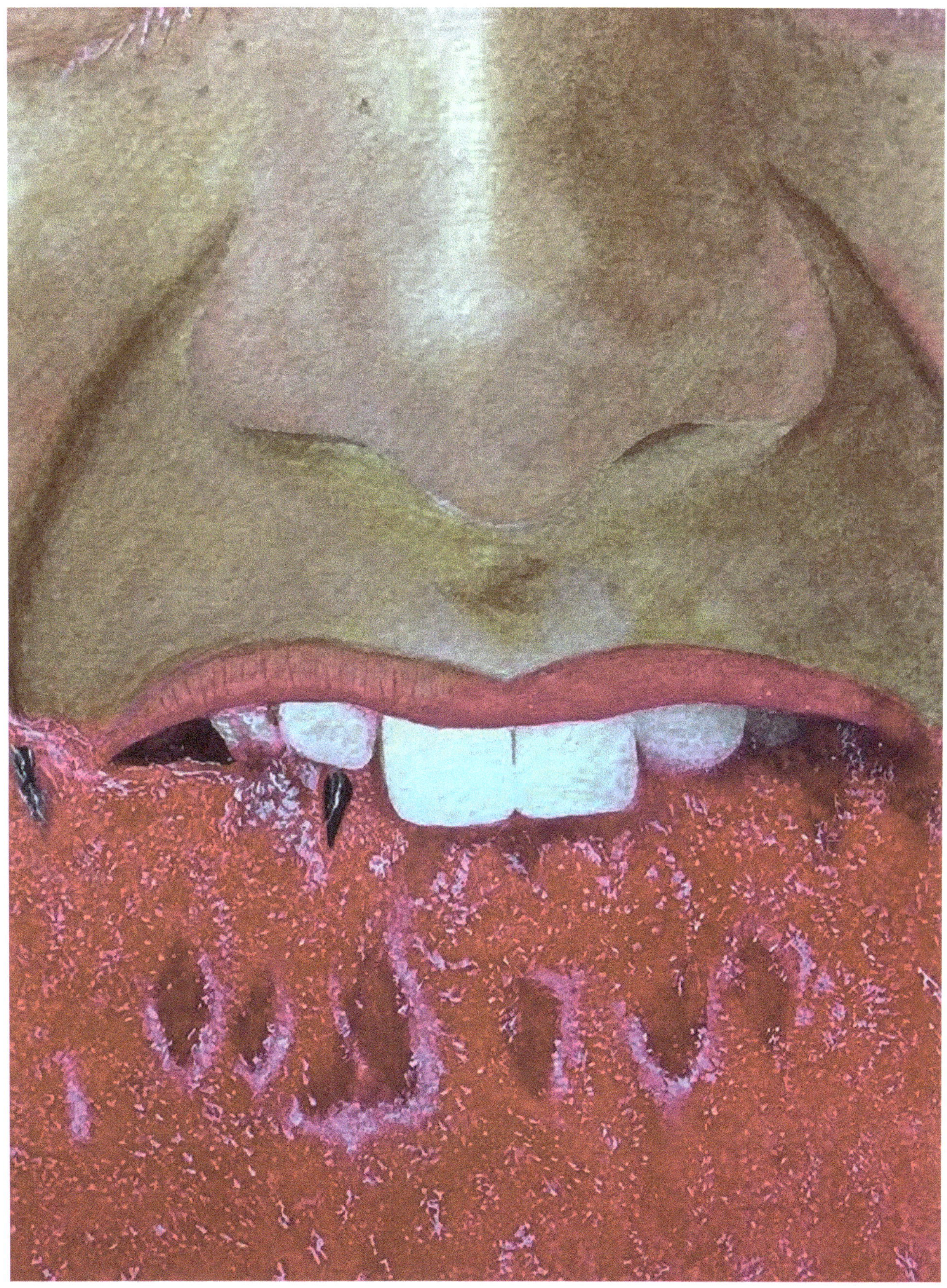

6.26 Mahnoor Abassi: Colour drawing.

Outcomes that show the use of a wide range of media and materials

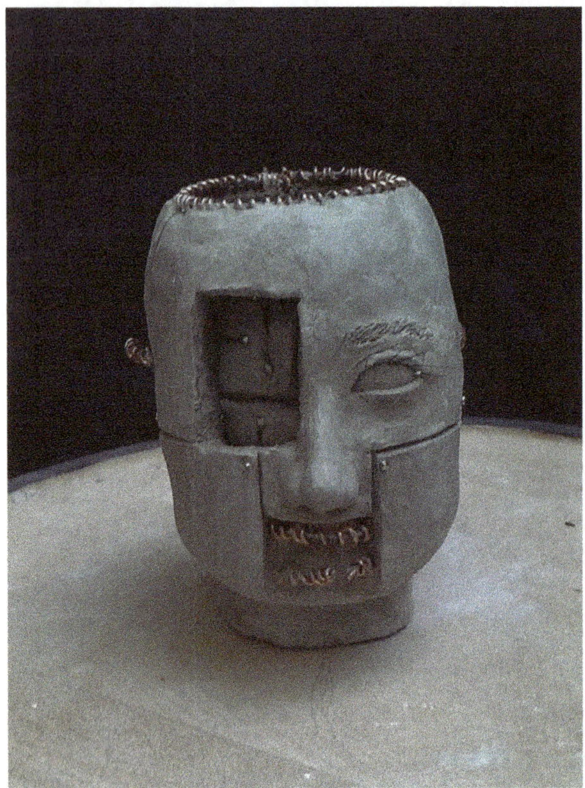

6.27 Isabella Vanackere Castellano: Ceramic head, front view.

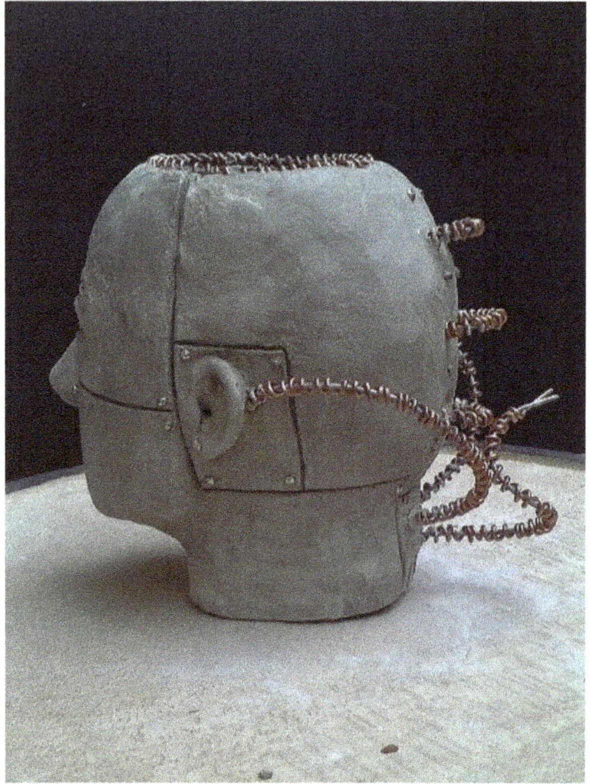

6.28 Isabella Vanackere Castellano: Ceramic head, rear view.

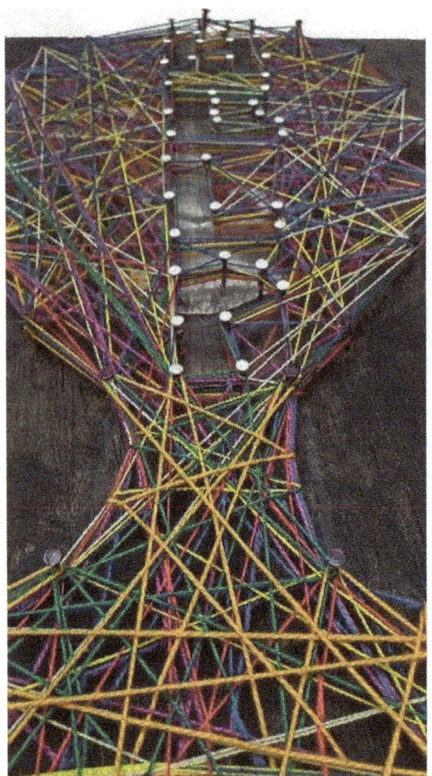

6.29 Blaze Chapman: String and nail portrait.

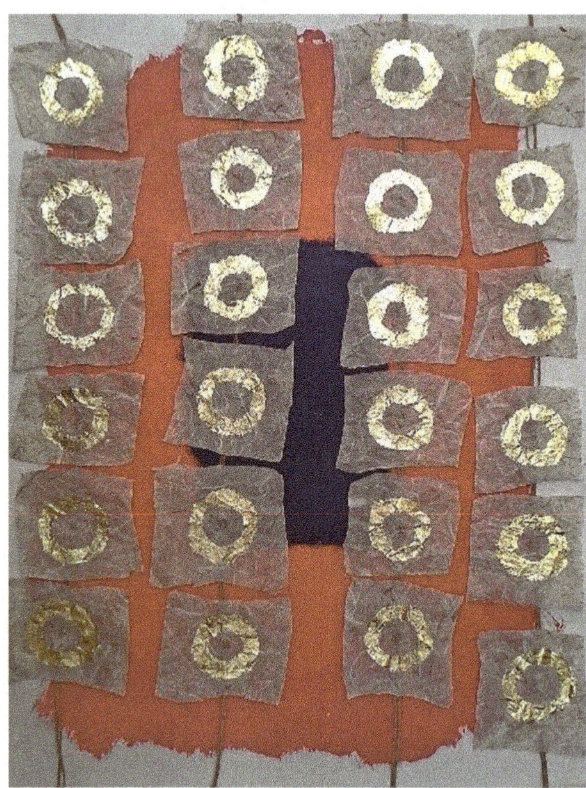

6.30 Julia Vila Rosell: Mixed media and gold leaf.

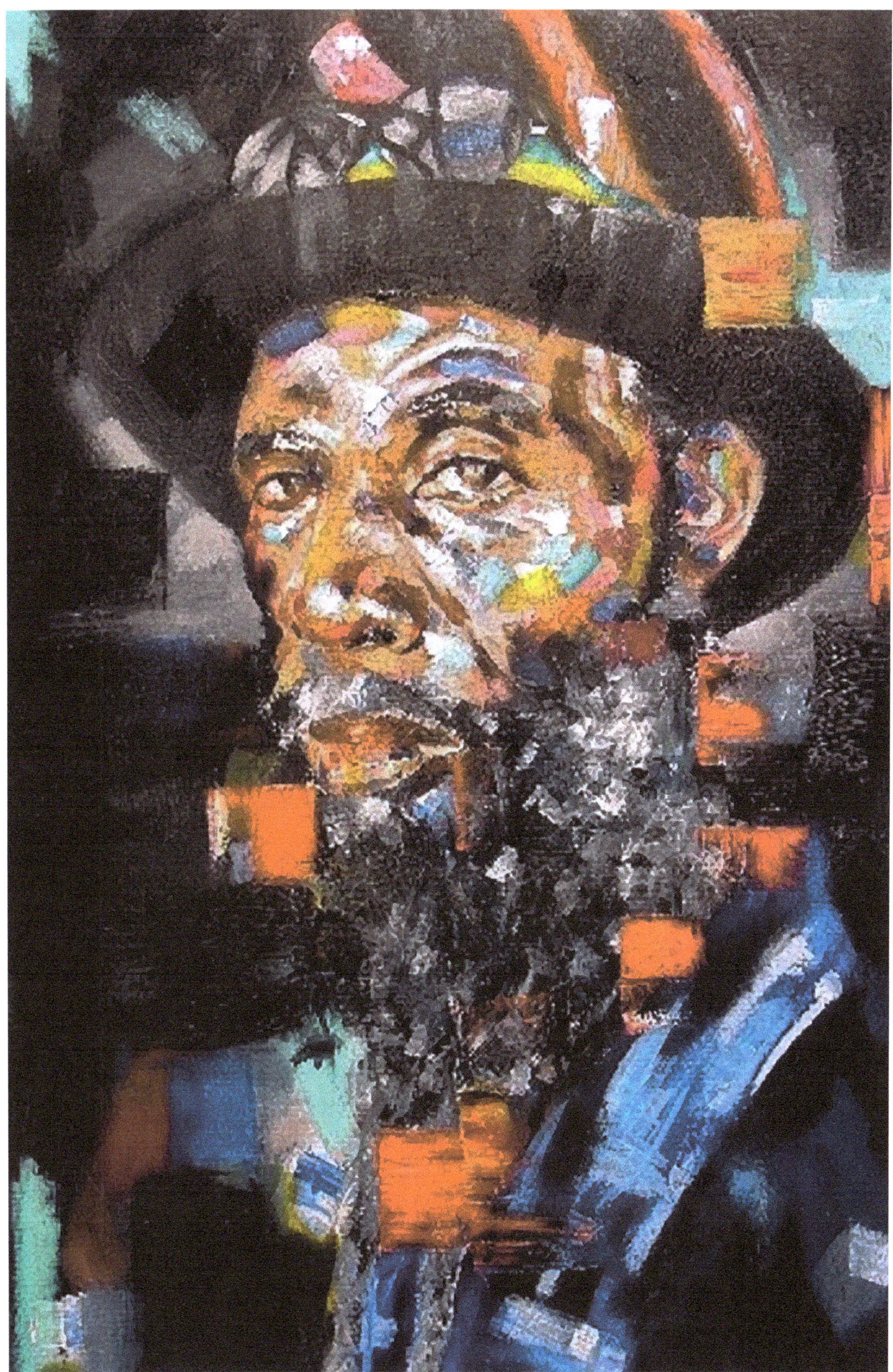

6.31 George Groves: Painted portrait.

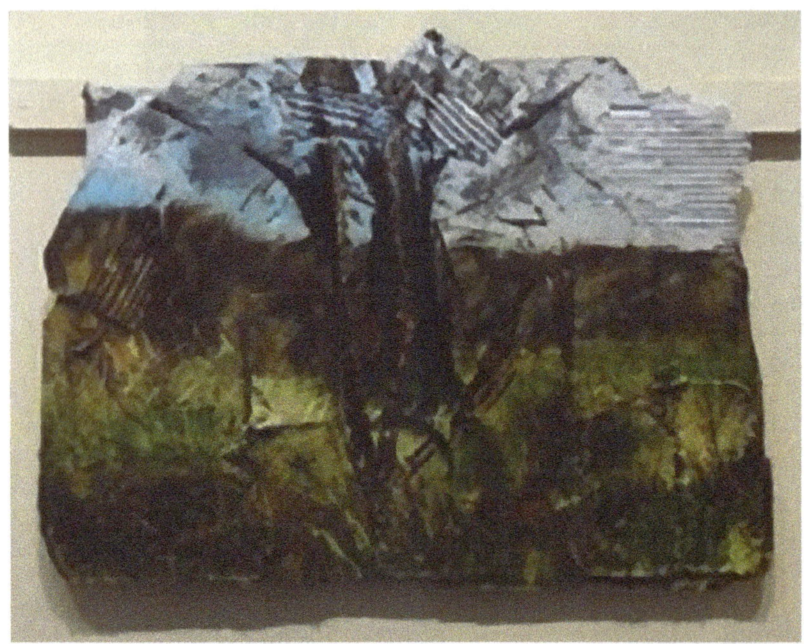

6.32 Stefan-Marc Seymour: Mixed-media landscape.

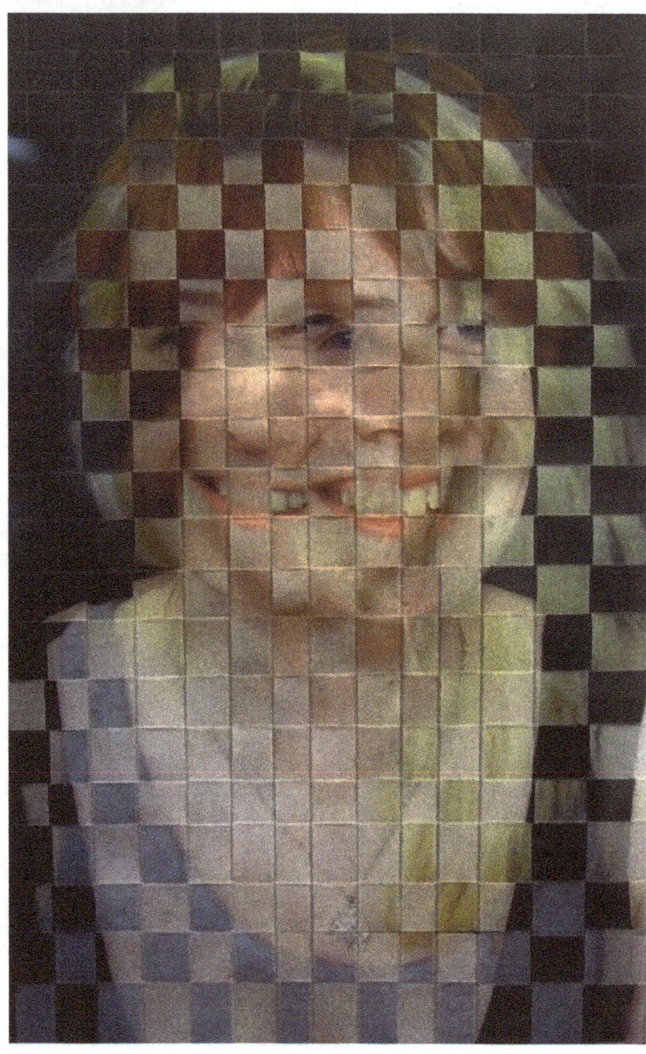

6.33 Jackie German: Interwoven portrait.

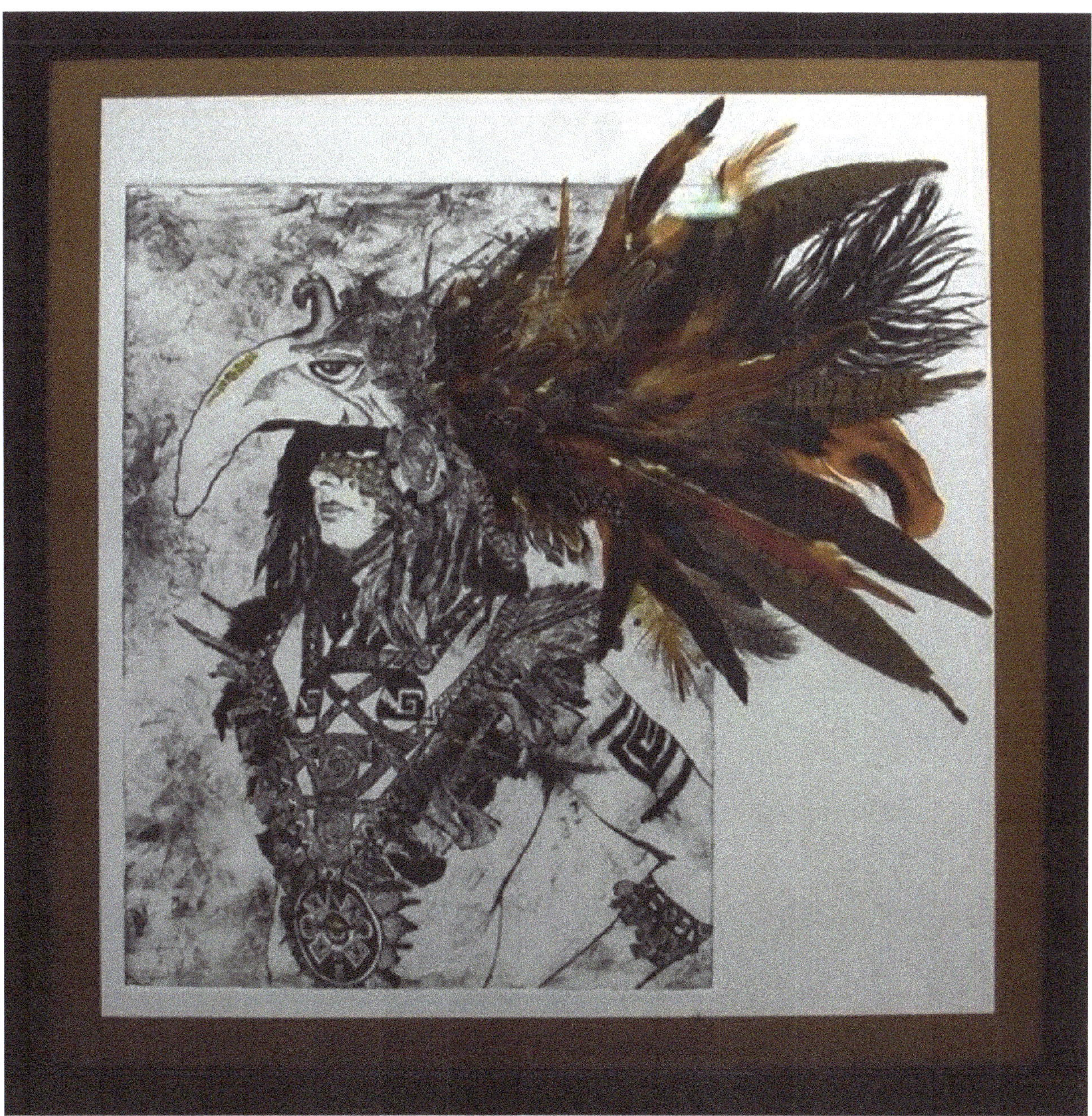

6.34 Christine Wiggil: Mixed-media drawing and collage.

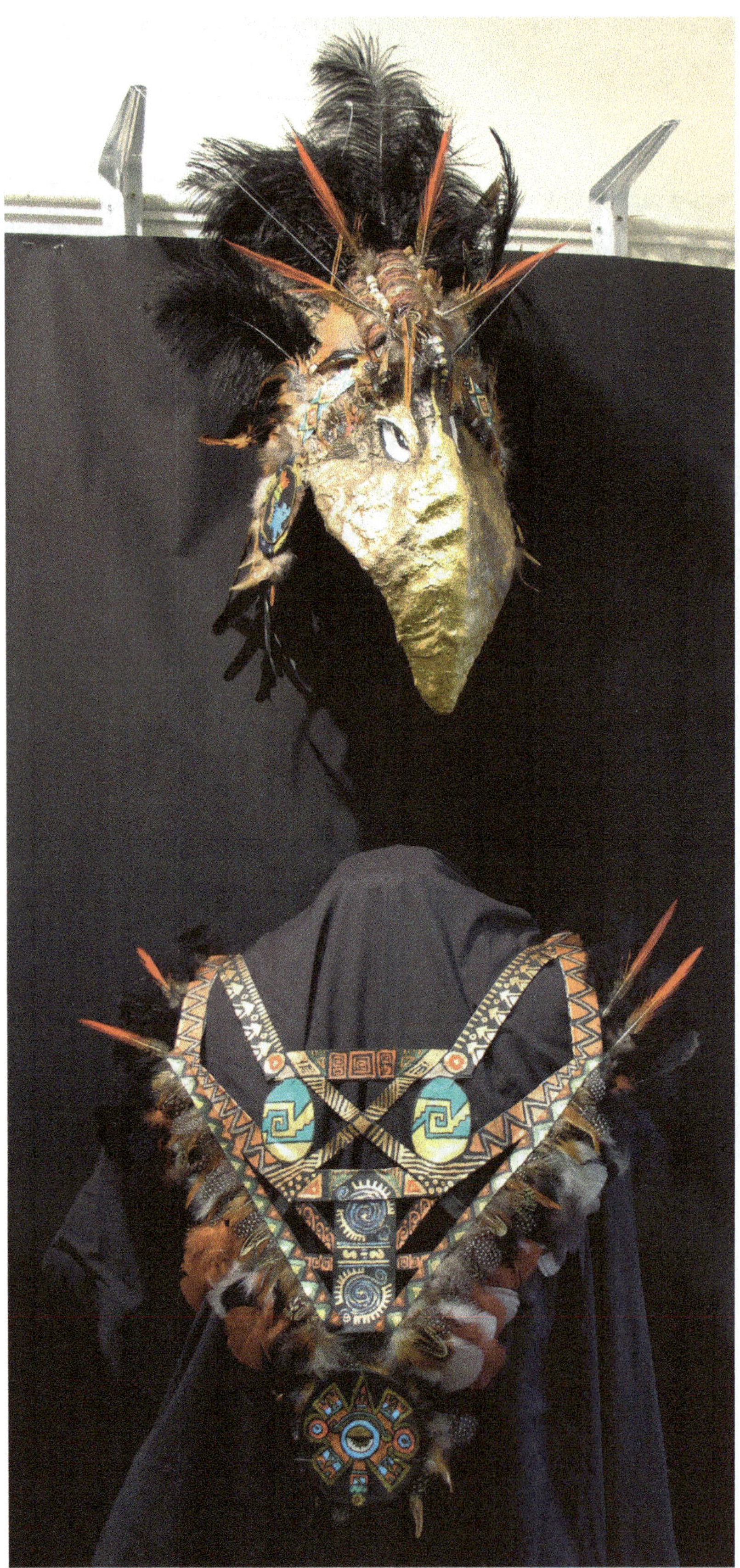

6.35 Christine Wiggil. Costume design.

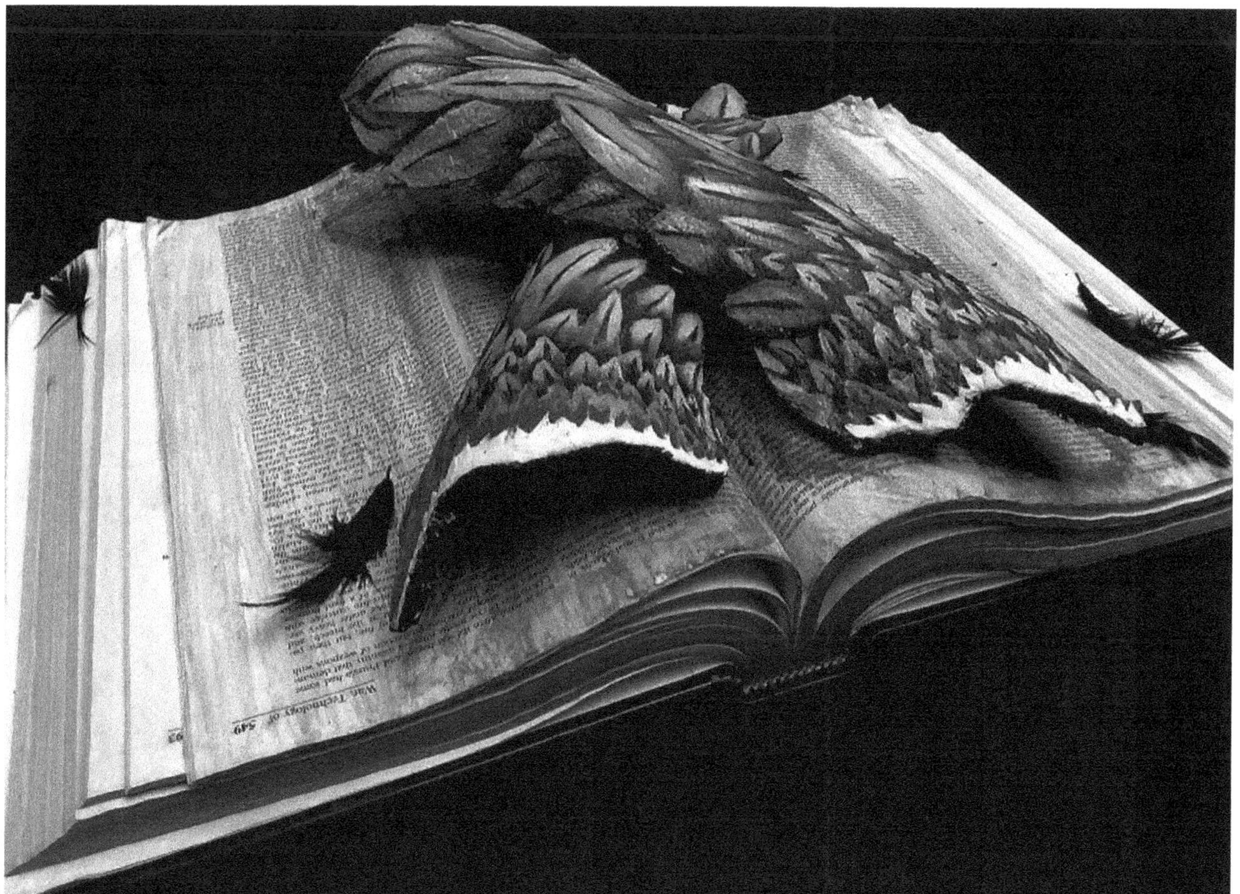

6.36 Naomi Flowers: Wing Book.

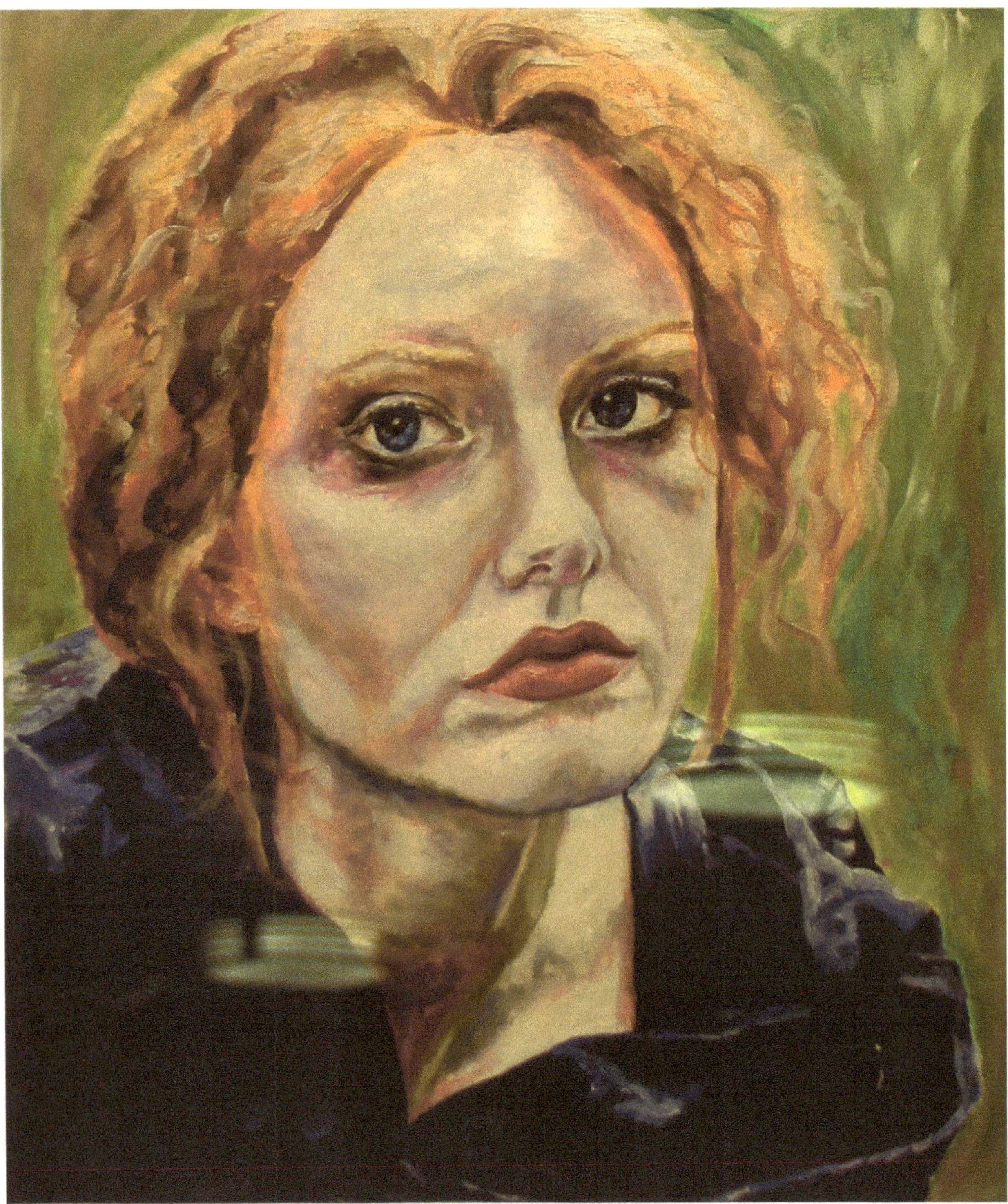

6.37 Jessica Bennett: Portrait.

Outline proposal form

Centre number		**Centre name**	
Candidate number		**Candidate name**	
Component			
Exam series		**If this is a resubmission, please check the box**	
Title of proposal			

Details of proposal (see guidance notes)

Teacher's initials   **Date**

Advisor's comments

Advisor's initials   **Date**

For Advisor's use only

Approved	Approved (with proviso)	Not approved	More information required	Approval not required (see comments)

Glossary

A

abstract Work that uses formal elements such as shape and colour in ways not limited by reproducing visible subject matter.
Abstract Expressionists Art movement based in the United States in the 1940s and 1950s in which artists made large-scale painting often using energetic mark-making and/or intense, vibrant colour. Key artists include Jackson Pollock (1912–56) and Mark Rothko (1903–70).
accent colour Small amounts of colour used to lift or to add impact to a colour scheme.
acetate A transparent sheet used in photocopying and printing.
additive Produced by adding material; compare reductive.
adhesive spray mount A spray glue that allows you to move and reposition your images.
adjacent Next to something.
aesthetic Relating to beauty rather than other considerations.
aesthetics The study of beauty and of the human responses to beauty.
affinity Having a natural feeling of liking a thing, subject, location, person or idea.
'after' Used in an artwork title, this tells us that the image is based on another's work (for example, 'after Millet').
alignment The setting of the text on the page or other background – common terms are 'flush left', 'flush right', 'centred' and 'justified'.
ambient conditions The temperature, moisture level, atmospheric pressure and so on in a particular place.
amenities Useful buildings or facilities that serve the local community.
Analytical Cubism The early phase of Cubism known for its geometric shapes and monochromatic use of colour.
anatomical Relating to the structure of the body or an organism.
Annunciation In Christianity, the Annunciation was the announcement by the Archangel Gabriel to the Virgin Mary that she was going to give birth to the son of God (Jesus).
aperture The hole through which light passes to reach the film or image sensor.
appliqué Textile technique where one material is added to another by means of stitch or adhesive for decorative effect.
araignée The French word for 'spider'.
archive A collection of historical documents or artefacts.
area of study This term refers to one of the broad areas of art and design: fine arts; three-dimensional (3D) design; graphic communication; textiles and fashion.
armature Framework to support the clay or other material used in modelling.
Art Deco A style of interior decoration, jewellery, architecture and so on, at its height in the 1930s and characterised by geometrical shapes, stylised natural forms and symmetrical functional designs adapted to mass production.
Art Nouveau ('new art') International style of art, architecture and decoration that flourished around 1890–1910 and took its inspiration from the natural world, especially plants.
aspirations The goals, values and lifestyle an individual or group of people aim to achieve.
assemblage Art technique involving the construction (assembling) of an artwork out of existing objects. It is like a 3D version of collage.
asymmetry Where the parts of an object are unequal and do not balance; the lack of symmetry.
atelier An artist's or designer's workshop or studio.
atmospheric A way of indicating distance in gradation of clarity, tone and colour, especially blue.
austerity Strict simplicity.
automatic drawing A drawing made without the drawer thinking about it. Another word for this is 'doodle'.
avant-garde People who work in a highly creative and experimental way.
Avignon City in south-east France.

B

balance Harmony in the parts of a whole.
balustrade An ornamental rail or wall on a balcony, bridge or staircase, with its supporting set of balusters.
Bassa A people of coastal West Africa.
batik A process for printing designs on cloth. Wax is put on those areas of the cloth that you do not want to be coloured by dye.
Bauhaus The architecture and design school founded by the German architect Walter Gropius (1883–1969) in Germany and which lasted from 1919 to 1933. The school's ethos, summed up in the statement 'Form follows function' (functionalism), was hugely influential on modern design.
beading Application of beads of varying sizes and weights to fabric, usually by stitching.
bias grain A 45-degree angle to a fabric's warp and wefts.
bibliography A list of books or other material on a subject.
block printing A form of printing using an image carved into a material, usually wood.
bokashi The controlled dye shading that produces such luminous results on silk.
Bollywood Name given to India's film industry.
boogie woogie A style of piano jazz.
brand image The 'personality' of a brand built up over time. It should be consistent so that customers develop a relationship with, and loyalty towards, the brand.
bric-a-brac Everyday household objects that people no longer need and have thrown away.
brief Outline of a task or project given to the artist or designer before they start work.
Broadway New York street famous for its theatres.
brocade Richly decorated woven fabric.
Brutalist Architectural style that developed from Modernism, based on the term 'Beton Brut' or 'raw concrete'; surfaces are often cast in concrete and allowed to show this construction method.
burnishing A process of repeated hard polishing and working of a surface, flattening and hardening it to produce a patina or shine.

C

CAD Computer-aided design – the use of computer technology in the creation of designs.
calico Inexpensive cotton fabric.
calligraphy Handwriting as an art, highly prized in many Eastern cultures.
camera obscura A darkened box with an aperture or lens that projects the image of an external object onto a screen inside the box.

campaign A project undertaken by an advertising company for a product or brand.
caricature Image of an individual that focuses on and exaggerates their most obvious features.
cartoon In this context, a detailed study for a mural or fresco showing the final arrangement of the composition, tonal ranges, figures and design.
celadon glaze Pottery glazed with jade green celadon colour, also transparent glaze, often with small cracks.
chisel Tool that has a long metal blade with a sharp edge at the end. It is used for cutting and shaping wood and stone.
choreographer A person who invents steps and dance.
cohesive Consisting of parts that fit together well and form a united whole.
collage Artwork technique where a range of materials, such as newspaper, textiles, photographs and so on, are fixed or glued onto a surface (paper, canvas and so on).
collagraph Printing block made by collaging and gluing surfaces together onto a card board.
colour theory Practical guidance on colour mixing and colour combinations.
commemorate To remember and honour an event or person.
commission A percentage of the sale price of an artwork taken by the gallery at point of sale. It will vary according to gallery and location.
complementary A colour is described as complementary when it contrasts with and reinforces another colour. Green and red, for example, are complementary colours.
component Part, quality or aspect.
composite image An image made up of different pieces, as in a physical or digital collage.
composition The way something is put together.
concept An idea or abstract principle.
concise Brief and to the point.
consistent Steady, even.
consumerism An economic system (such as capitalism) that encourages people to buy goods beyond what they need.
context The situation, background or environment in which an artwork is made.
continuous prose Writing set out in full sentences and well-structured paragraphs.
contours The shape or surface of a curving form.
conventions The use of shapes, colours and scale in signs to communicate – for example, using red as a colour in hazard signs.
converge To draw closer.
conversational motif One that has recognisable objects in the motif, from pencils, chairs, to embroidery threads and scenes from daily life.
copyright If someone has copyright on an image, piece of writing or music, it is illegal to reproduce or perform it without their permission.
counter The negative space within a fully closed letter, such as O, A, D. Some letterforms have non-enclosed negative space, such as G, U, C – these are also called counters.
counterculture Subculture that rebels against the conventions of the dominant culture.
crackle Pottery surface covered with fine cracks.
cradle to cradle From the 'birth' of a product to its 'rebirth' as a new one.
craft knife A knife with a fine blade for cutting paper.
critique This is the occasion when tutors evaluate your response to a project.
cross-fertilisation Where two or more cultures enrich one another with new ideas.
cross hatch Fine crossed lines used to suggest darker areas of tone.
Cubism An early 20th-century movement in modern art that represented the real world in an analytical way, often using multiple views of the same subject at the same time.
culture A particular society or civilisation, considered especially in relation to its beliefs, way of life or art.
cutting mat Strong plastic mat specifically for cutting paper on.

D

decode If you decode a work of art, you manage to understand its meaning.
deconstruct To take apart.
decorative Something that is intended to look pretty or attractive; ornamental.
demographics The study of a population based on factors such as age, race, sex and other characteristics.
design process The act of creating a plan for the construction of something.
die-line Flat shape of package laid out on a single 2D sheet of material, showing lines to be cut and scored, to make a 3D package.
diptych A painting made up of two separate panels or canvases, showing separate but related imagery, or imagery spreading across both panels.
discarded Thrown away, forgotten or set aside.
discipline This term refers to a specific type of work within each area of study: for example, drawing and painting are both disciplines within the field of fine arts.
dosage The correct amount of a medicine.
dramatic Filled with action, emotion or exciting qualities; vivid, striking and so on.
draughtsman/woman/person Someone who prepares detailed drawings.
drawn threads A technique involving the pulling out of threads in a fabric. The remaining threads are stitched into place with embroidery.
drypoint Technique of intaglio engraving using a hard steel needle, without acid, on a copper or acetate plate.
durable Lasting.

E

earthenware Clay body and glaze, slightly porous, used in garden pots, fired to around 1100°C.
eclectic Showing a wide range of influences.
elevation Technical drawing showing front, side or plan view of a structure.
ellipse Shape like the orbit of a planet around the Sun.
embedded advertisement A link on a page that takes a user to the product or service's website once clicked.
embellishment (in fashion) A decorative detail added to an item of clothing to make it more beautiful – for example, a ribbon, button or trim.
embroidery Technique to embellish fabric using a variety of threads and stitches, including French knots, chain stitch and cross stitch. This can be done by hand or by machine.
embroidery foot An attachment for a sewing machine that makes free-motion stitching.
embroidery frame A metal or wooden ring, designed to keep fabric stretched while an embroiderer works on it.
encapsulate To sum up.
end user The person who will ultimately use the product.
engrave To cut a design or image into a surface.

enhance To enrich; to add additional layers of meaning.
ensemble Outfit.
ephemeral Lasting only a short while.
equate with To be equivalent to; have the same effect as.
ergonomic Designed for comfort and efficiency.
essence The basic nature of something.
etching Technique of intaglio engraving in which the image or design is engraved into the plate using acid.
ETFE (ethylene tetrafluoroethylene) A strong weatherproof plastic that is resistant to chemicals, corrosion, and very high and low temperatures.
ethos Ideas and attitudes of a particular group or movement.

F

fabric block printing Printing of designs, drawings and so on from engraved blocks.
fabric manipulation Using different techniques to change the surface of a fabric.
façade The front or 'face' of a building.
faience Tin-glazed earthenware.
fashion plate An illustration of a new fashion in a magazine.
faux fur Synthetic fur-like material.
feedback loop Process of sourcing feedback from users, collating information and using it to inform and modify the way the audience experience is delivered; impact can be tested by running the feedback exercise again.
fidelity Faith or loyalty to a belief.
field of vision The area you can see without turning your head.
figurative Art that directly represents the visible world.
film noir From the French for 'black'. Genre of Hollywood crime films of the 1940s and 1950s featuring low-key lighting, gritty urban settings and dramatic use of shadow.
first-hand source An object – for example, a painting or sculpture – that was created during the time period being studied.
flat-pattern Developed from a design sketch using a 2D template (a block) for a basic garment form.
floral Made up of flowers.
flourish To do something with flowing, sweeping strokes.
focal point What the eye or interest is drawn to, the thing that people concentrate on or pay most attention to; the part of the photograph to which the photographer directs the viewer's attention, generally where the image is sharpest.
found objects Also known as *objets trouvés*, this means objects used for art that were not designed for an art purpose.
fresco Method of painting images onto freshly plastered walls. Fresco was often used to decorate the interiors of public buildings in medieval and Renaissance Italy and formed part of a decorative programme, or cycle, telling a story from the Bible or history.
from scratch Without making use of anything that has been done before.
functionality How well a building meets its function.

G

garment An item of clothing.
genre Category – in film, for example, horror, comedy, romance, drama and so on; a type of art distinguished by subject, theme or style.
geometric Patterns or shapes made up of regular lines.
gesso A mixture of glue, chalk and white paint.
glaze Thin washes of paint that allow areas of paint (underpainting) to show through – creating a sense of depth and effects of light and shade.
Gantt chart A type of spreadsheet that displays actual work done over a certain period in relation to what was planned for that time period.
grain lines of the fabric The direction of a fabric's yarns in a woven fabric.

H

hallucination Someone has a hallucination if they experience sights and sounds that are not actually present; hallucination may occur in certain mental disorders.
hatching Fine parallel or crossed lines to create shading, used in drawing and engraving.
heraldic shield A traditional shield-shaped badge used by countries, cities and families, incorporating symbolic images and colours.
Holocaust The mass murder of Jews and members of many other ethnic, social and political groups in continental Europe between 1940 and 1945 by the Nazi regime.
horizon In perspective, an imaginary line in a drawing or painting that would be level with the viewer's eyes if they were looking at a real scene.
hot wax Paraffin wax (or beeswax) used for sealing the parts of cloth to be protected from dye.
Huari (Wari) People and culture of Peru that flourished 500–1000 CE.
hybrid Blended.

I

idealise To make something look better than it is in reality.
ideology A system of ideas.
Igbo A people of Western Africa, in what is now south-east Nigeria.
imagery Visual images of a piece considered as a whole.
immediacy Spontaneity and freshness – brings an instant response.
immersive Providing an experience for all the senses.
impasto Where oil paint is applied very thickly to a surface (such as a canvas), often creating a dense, uneven texture.
impetus Force or motivation.
Impressionism A style of painting developed in France from the late 1860s. It concentrated on showing the effects of light and colour rather than clear and exact detail, and on ordinary everyday life rather than on grand scenes from history or religious images. Key Impressionist painters include Claude Monet, Berthe Morisot, Camille Pissarro, Pierre-Auguste Renoir and Alfred Sisley.
Impressonistic Something that is similar to the work of the Impressionist painters – not including every detail but suggesting the mood of a scene.
improvisation Something carried out without a plan.
in situ In the original position.
individualistic (or expressive) architecture A style that allowed individual designs to develop, rather than following a prescribed style.
inherent qualities The natural characteristics of materials, such as the shininess of metal, the textures in wood, the transparency of glass.
installation An artwork that is constructed in an interior space, such as a gallery; a work of art requiring construction or elaborate setting up at its exhibition site.
insulator A non-conductor of electricity or heat/cold.
intaglio A printing technique using a carved or engraved surface to create a design in relief.

integral A part of something that is necessary to it or that cannot be removed without affecting its 'wholeness'.
integrated Made whole or completed by adding or bringing together parts.
integration Where one set of people mix in with mainstream society, adopting its values and culture.
interactive textiles Textiles that are able to work closely with the environment and react or adapt to it in a programmed way.
interplay Where two or more features work together.
ISO This shows the level of light sensitivity a camera is set at – 'low ISO' means low sensitivity to light; 'high ISO' is high sensitivity to light. The acronym 'ISO' stands for 'International Organization for Standardization', which sets commercial and industrial standards worldwide.
isometric Technical drawing using 30° and 60° angles.
isometric projection Method for showing 3D objects in two dimensions, in which two of the three axes are drawn at 30° to the horizontal.
italic font A sloping typeface.
iterative Repetitious or frequent.

J

jersey (fabric) Lightweight knitted fabric with good draping qualities.
juxtapose To set two contrasting objects side by side.

K

kanji Characters used in the Japanese writing system that are borrowed from Chinese.
kerning The adjustment of space between the letters of words to improve the appearance of printed text, used especially in larger type.
key design elements Parts that make up a textile outcome.
kiln Oven or furnace used for firing pottery.
Kingdom of Benin Powerful kingdom of the Edo people of Western Africa that lasted from the 9th century to almost the end of the 19th century.

L

lamination Sheet materials glued or bonded together to form a strong construction material.
laser-cut A precise cutting tool that uses laser technology.
layout paper Slightly transparent lightweight paper used to trace figures.
legibility The clarity of a typeface, enabling the almost-instant communication of a message.
letterform The shape or design of an individual letter or character.
linear Consisting of straight lines.
lino; linoleum A strong, flexible material made from linseed oil used for floor covering but also for carving out designs on its surface.
linocut Technique of relief printing, similar to a woodcut, where the design is created using a sheet of linoleum.
liquid light A wet, light-sensitive medium that can be painted onto surfaces, then exposed to light, brushed with developer, wash and the fix to make photographic images on non-paper surfaces.
literate Skilled.
lithography Printing technique invented at the end of the 18th century, originally using an etched stone plate.

M

macro lens Setting used for photographing close-up detail.
malleability The ability of a material to be pressed into various shapes without breaking.
malleable A substance that is malleable is soft and can easily be made into different shapes.
mannequin A life-sized model of a person, usually used to display clothes.
maquette A sculptor's small trial or experimental model – a kind of '3D sketch'.
margin The edge or border of something.
matt A non-shiny surface.
MDF Medium-density fibreboard (MDF) is an engineered wood product.
metaphor If one thing is a metaphor for another, it is intended or regarded as a symbol of it.
mirroring Term used in psychology, where one human mirrors or reflects back the speech, posture or gestures of another. Mirroring is sometimes seen as a form of empathy between people.
modifications Small changes or adjustments.
monitor To observe and check the quality of something.
monochromatic Made up of one colour.
monochrome A design in one colour or values of one colour, usually black, grey or white.
monogram A motif made up of an individual's initials (a kind of logo).
monoprint Simple printmaking technique that produces a single print.
mood board An arrangement of images, materials and pieces of text on a board – used to explore and express a style or concept.
mordant This fixes dyes to fabric, depending on the type of mordant, such as alum. The shade will vary.
mortar Weapon that fires bombs out of a large barrel, used in World War I.
motif In the visual arts, a decorative image or design.
mould A hollow container that you pour liquid into. When the liquid becomes solid, it takes the same shape as the mould.
mount board Stiff paper card to mount work onto and display. Mount boards come in sizes A1, A2 or A3.
movement In art, a group of practitioners who work with similar artistic goals.
Mughal A period in the history of India from the 16th to 18th century when foreign Muslim emperors ruled much of South Asia, known for its flourishing arts.
municipal Run or owned by local government.
muslin Inexpensive, lightweight cotton woven fabric.
mutual Two-way.

N

Ndebele A native people of southern Africa.
negative space The space between objects in an image that have a value as a shape within the composition.
Neo-Impressionism A movement of mainly French artists who in the 1880s and 1890s took the experiments of the Impressionist painters further. They especially used the technique known as pointillism – dots of painted colour on a canvas that appear to blend when seen from a distance.
Neolithic 'New Stone Age' – period in the development of human cultures from about 10 000 bce to about 4000–2000 bce. During this time both farming and the making of pottery became widespread.
neo-plasticism Term adopted by Piet Mondrian for his paintings that used only vertical and horizontal lines and shapes, and primary colours.
niche A small target group with highly individual characteristics.

non-linear Used to describe marks that are not lines.

oblique projection A simple way of making three-dimensional drawings from a front view of an object.
ogee An image based on an 'S' shape made by two unbroken, opposing concave and convex curves.
Old Masters Term sometimes used to describe outstanding European artists working before the 19th century.
one-point perspective Method for creating perspective in a picture that uses a single vanishing point.
Op art A style of abstract art chiefly concerned with the exploitation of optical effects such as the illusion of movement.
organic Derived from nature.
Orientialism Term used to describe Western artworks, especially of the 19th and early 20th century, that took inspiration from many Asian cultures. Asian countries were loosely described at the time collectively as 'the Orient', meaning the East.
orthographic Technical drawing using 45° and 90° angles – the 90° plane is shown parallel to the picture plane.
orthographic projection Method for showing 3D objects as a flat view in two dimensions, in which the object is shown separately in two or more accurate, scaled-down views, as from the top, front, and side. The views are typically displayed with the top view above and the side view alongside the front view.

P

paint tool An illustration computer software tool for using colour digitally.
painterly Method of painting that exploits and draws attention to the quality of the paint itself, so that brush strokes are visible in the final artwork.
palette In this context, the thin board used by painters to lay out and mix colours.
panel Wooden board used as a surface for painting on; single image in a comic book.
parameters Limits.
patina A film of oxide formed on the surface of a metal, especially the green oxidation of bronze or copper.
pattern cutter Someone who creates pattern templates based on drawings from a fashion designer.
perspective The art of making some objects or figures in a picture look further away than others.
pharmaceuticals Medical drugs.
photocollage Collage made up of photographs.
Photorealism Extremely realistic style of painting that mimics the look of photographs.
photoscreen A screen print where the stencil has been made using a light-sensitive process.
pictogram A simple drawing, the earliest form of writing.
pictorial Of, containing or expressed in pictures.
pigment A material often in the form of a dry powder that, after being mixed with oil, water and so on, is used for adding colour in artworks.
pin tucks A textile method of pleating fabric.
pitch Presentation back to clients or audience, showing responses to a design brief, and potential creative solutions for consideration and feedback.
pixel The smallest area on a computer screen that can be given a separate colour by the computer.
placement Arrangement or position.
plane Flat and smooth.
plaque A tablet fixed to a wall as a way of remembering a person or event.
pleating A permanent fold that is made in the cloth by folding one part over the other and sewing across the top end of the fold.
plein air French term that means 'open air', used where an artist works outside directly from the subject.
plumage The feathers of a bird.
point Measurement used in printing and typography – in desktop publishing, 1 point equals 0.353 mm or 1/72 in.
polychromatic Made up of many colours, multi-coloured.
Pop art Art movement of the 1950s and 1960s that used popular culture for inspiration, from film stars to cartoons to household brands. Key figures include Andy Warhol and Roy Lichtenstein.
portfolio A selection of final pieces of work for an examiner or tutor to see.
positive space The main focus or subject of an image; negative space refers to the background.
Post-Impressionism Various styles of painting that took the experiments of the Impressionists further, often using bold colours, clear outlines and flat, decorative compositions. Key Post-Impressionist painters include Henri de Toulouse-Lautrec, Paul Gauguin, Édouard Vuillard and Pierre Bonnard.
practitioner Catch-all term used to describe an artist, craftsperson or designer.
Pre-Columbian Term used to describe the cultures of the Americas before the arrival of the explorer Christopher Columbus in 1492.
preliminary drawing Rough unfinished drawing to show initial ideas; used to describe an artwork carried out in preparation for a final artwork – for example, a sketch.
preparatory Term used to describe artworks that prepare for a final artwork. They represent an experimental phase in the artistic process.
prepared canvas A canvas made ready for painting with a layer of gesso.
prescriptive Laying down rules.
Procion MX Fibre-reactive dyes Recommended synthetic dyes for fabric. They are used for screen printing and batik and general cloth dyeing. You can buy them from most textiles suppliers.
proof printing Taking a trial print to assess what's happening with the printing plate when the initial design is applied.
propaganda Information used to promote a political cause, often in the form of posters and leaflets.
prototype The product design in its first trial form; model of a product which is tested so that the design can be changed, if necessary, before the product is manufactured commercially.
public information film Sometimes known as a public service announcement. A (usually) short film created to educate the public about a key issue such as road safety, health, protecting the environment, or how to vote.
public relations or **PR** A person who is responsible for managing and communicating another persons business to a wider audience.

Q

qualitative research Research that explores people's opinions and responses. Compare quantitative research, which focuses on the collection of numerical data.

R

readability How easy a typeface is to read over a period of time; how easily a

reader can read and understand a text as a whole.
realism Term used to describe art that captures very closely the look of real things. When used with a capital R (Realism), it refers to a specific art movement in 19th-century France.
receptacle Another word for container.
rectilinear With all lines at 90 degrees to one another.
recurring Happening again at regular intervals.
reductive Produced by taking away material; compare with additive.
regeneration To renew and revive a run-down or economically depressed area of a town or city.
registration The alignment of the printing block on the paper.
relief plate A printing plate where the parts to be printed are in relief (raised).
relief printmaking A printmaking process where the design is cut into a material, creating raised areas (relief).
Renaissance The 'rebirth' of culture and learning that took place in Europe during the 15th and 16th centuries. It took much of its inspiration from ancient ('Classical') Greece and Rome.
render A photorealistic image developed from either a 2D drawing or a 3D model; to add colour or shading to make an object look three-dimensional.
representational Art that seeks to represent (i.e. depict) real things. Also known as figurative.
roman font An upright typeface.
Rub el Hizb Islamic symbol made up of two overlapping squares and used as a marker to divide up parts of the Qur'an.

S

sancai Chinese type of pottery decoration using slip or glaze and in three colours – brown, green and cream.
scope The area covered by an activity, topic and so on.
screenshot Image of a screen-based operation, taken from the working screen and saved as a digital file.
screentone A dotted pattern applied as the backdrop of an illustration to create an overall shade or texture, using pre-printed sheets or computer graphics.
second-hand source A secondary source of information created by someone at a later date; for example, a book, the internet.
segregation The separation of people on grounds of their race or other characteristics – applied to the place where they live, the schools they go to and other facilities they use.
selvedge The edge of a piece of fabric.
semiotics The study of signs and how they communicate and work.
sepia Reddish-brown colour once used to add a warm tone to black and white photographs.
setting Setting can mean the physical setting, as in a gallery, or the context, such as a design brief.
sgraffito A technique of scratching lines in a surface of colour to reveal the original surface or another layer of colour below.
Shell A British–Dutch oil and gas company.
shooting mode A selection made to determine the way a camera functions, such as Aperture Priority shooting.
shot silk A woven fabric where the warp is one colour and the weft in another. The best examples are made in silk.
shutter A shield in a camera that, when tripped, allows light to pass onto the film or plate for a period of time, usually a fraction of a second.
silhouette (in fashion) The outline or the shape of a body when clothed.
silkscreen Traditionally, the mesh used in the screen-printing process was made of silk (not polyester, as it is usually is today), so you will sometimes still see the term 'silkscreen printing'.
sited If something is sited in a particular place or location, it is placed or built there.
site-specific Artwork created to exist only in one place.
sitting A painting session in the production of a portrait; the subject 'sits' for the artist even if they are not literally sitting down.
slip Mixture of clay and water used for decorating wares or joining parts.
slip trailer Tool used for dripping, drawing with/or running a line of slip across pottery surface.
spandex Stretchy fabric often used in sports clothing.
sparingly In a small quantity or economically.
speed lines Parallel lines used in comic books to suggest movement.
spontaneous Unplanned.
spreadsheet An electronic document with cells that contain data (usually numerical), which can be recorded and manipulated.
squeegee Tool with a rubber blade or roller used to remove and/or apply ink.
stage props Short for 'stage properties' – anything portable used on stage, including ordinary items such as food, and constructed items such as light balsawood furniture.
stencil Piece of paper, plastic or metal with a design cut out of it. You place the stencil on a surface and paint it so that paint goes through the holes and leaves a design on the surface.
stimulus Something that provides the inspiration or starting point for an artist's work. It could be, for example, something in nature, something glimpsed in a city street, another work of art, a piece of music, a poem or a personal experience. The plural is 'stimuli'.
stoneware Non-porous clay body and glaze, capable of being fired at higher temperatures than earthenware (to around 1260°C).
story The overall theme of a design.
stretcher Wooden frame or support for canvas, which is stretched tightly across and stapled/pinned into place along the rear or edge.
study A smaller or more quickly executed drawing or painting, made primarily as an aid in the production of a larger painting.
stylised Term used to describe an artwork that has a definite or non-realistic style.
stylist A person who puts together objects or clothes to improve their appearance.
subculture Alternative ideas and art different from the rest of society.
subjective Based on personal taste or opinion. The opposite is 'objective', meaning based on fact and unaffected by personal feelings and opinions.
Sufism Spiritual aspect of Islam in which believers seek direct inner experience of God.
superimpose To lay one thing over another.
support The surface that the artist uses to create artwork on, for example, wall, canvas, paper.
Surrealism Art and literary movement of the 1920s, 1930s and beyond that sought to explore the world of dreams and the unconscious mind through irrational, fantastic imagery. Surrealism took much of its inspiration from the ideas of the Austrian psychoanalyst Sigmund Freud (1856–1939). Key

Surrealist artists include Salvador Dalí, Max Ernst and Hans Arp.
sustainability Preserving natural resources to ensure the future of that industry as well as the planet.
sustainable Careful use of natural resources so as to minimise damage to the environment and preserve them for the future.
symbol An object that represents or stands in for an idea. The adjective is 'symbolic'.
synthetic dyes Chemical dyes.

T

taxidermy The craft of preserving an animal by stuffing and mounting it.
tea ceremony Tea making and drinking ritual practised in Japan and other countries in the Far East for religious or spiritual reasons.
technical Showing technique.
tempera Fast-drying paint made up of a pigment and (traditionally) egg yolk. It was the form of paint used for artworks in European art until the rise of oil painting in the 15th century, though it was used by some Chinese and Indian artists many hundreds of years before.
template A thin piece of sheet material, such as card or plastic, that is shaped and used to reproduce the same shape many times.
tessellation An arrangement of shapes closely fitted together, without gaps or overlapping.
tessha A Japanese rust-coloured glaze.
theme The underlying idea of a work of art.
thread sock A fine mesh that fits over the embroidery thread spool to prevent the thread from slipping off.
thread spool A small plastic tube that sewing-machine threads are wound onto.
tie-dye A resist dyeing method. It can be achieved by tying or clamping fabric in before dyeing. The coloured dye will only appear where the fabric has not been tied or clamped.
tint Another word for shade.
tjanting tool Pen-like tool used in batik for applying melted wax to fabric in order to draw pictures and patterns.
toile An early version of a garment made up using inexpensive cloth so that alterations and experiments can be made.
tonal value The lightness or darkness of a shade.
'total work of art' A translation of the German word *Gesamtkunstwerk*, used to describe creative projects that draw on a wide range of disciplines to create a unified aesthetic impression.
transcription In art, the reworking of the work of one artist by another. The verb is 'transcribe'.
transfer medium Solution painted into photographic images, allowing the image to be transferred onto other surfaces.
triptych A painting made up of three separate panels or canvases, showing separated or related imagery, or imagery spreading across all three panels.
tweed Rough woollen fabric made in Britain and Ireland, often with flecks of colour or a herringbone pattern. The material is associated with clothes designed for outdoor pastimes such as shooting and hunting.
typeface A designed 'family' or set of letters and numbers with a shared set of characteristics – for example, Bodoni, Futura, Caslon, Times New Roman.

U

unambiguous With one clear meaning.
unconscious Without realising something.
unconscious mind According to Sigmund Freud, the part of the human mind (psyche) that is full of the anxieties and desires that are repressed (buried) in daily life.
upcycle To recycle an object while adding value to it.
upper case The capital letters of a typeface – A, B, C and so on.
urn Vase-like container, often made out of ceramic and often designed to hold human ashes.
utilitarian Designed to be useful rather than attractive.

V

value The lightness or darkness of a colour.
vanishing point The point in the distance where parallel lines seem to meet.
vegetable dyes Natural dyes made from vegetables.
vessel A container, especially for holding liquids.
viewfinder Device on a camera showing the field of view of the lens.
viewfinder frame Open frame made from two L-shapes, used to view areas through – to decide on composition/selection of image for recording.
visual characteristics When formal elements are exaggerated to show the personality of a subject.
visual communication The communication of an idea, intention, message or theme to an audience using visual materials, techniques and processes.
visual device A playful or eye-catching image that sums up an aspect of a brand or product.
visual identity The look of a brand.
visual language How formal elements are used to convey a sign or symbol, such as colour, shape, line and composition.
visualisation A drawing, painting or other artwork that communicates a concept in a visual way.
voyeur A person who obsessively watches others.

W

wardrobe master/mistress In the theatre, the person charged with supervising the making of clothes for a production and then maintaining the costumes during the run.
ware Pottery type – for example, stoneware, Delftware.
warp The vertical direction of threads in a fabric.
wash A thin layer of paint; thinned paint applied in a layer over part of a canvas or support.
weft The horizontal threads in a fabric.
White Balance A feature many digital cameras and video cameras use to balance colour accurately.
work into To build on your first mark-making in an image, adding new media and ideas.
working drawings Detailed drawings of design work highlighting the construction components of the garment including seams, darts, pockets, fastenings and topstitching.

Y

yukata A casual summer kimono.

Z

Zapotec Ancient civilisation of central Mexico that lasted from around 700 BCE to 1521 CE.
Zen Japanese school, of 12th-century Chinese origin, teaching that contemplation of one's essential nature to the exclusion of all else is the only way of achieving pure enlightenment.
zigzag Like the shape of a 'Z'.

Index

Acknowledgements

The publishers gratefully acknowledge the permission granted to reproduce the copyright material in this book. Every effort has been made to trace copyright holders and to obtain their permission for the use of copyright material. The publishers will gladly receive any information enabling them to rectify any error or omission at the first opportunity. The publishers would like to thank the following for permission to reproduce copyright material:

Key: (l = left, r = right, t = top, b = bottom)

p8–9 The National Trust Photolibrary/Alamy Stock Photo; p10tl Photo © Christie's Images/Bridgeman Images, bl Archivision Inc./Bridgeman Images, r © Estate of Roy Lichtenstein/DACS 2018, photo: Eileen Tweedy/REX/Shutterstock; p11l Elena Zaripova/Shutterstock.com, r David Wall/Alamy Stock Photo; p12t Antun Hirsman/Shutterstock.com, b Peter Hermes Furian/Shutterstock.com; p13 Museum of Fine Arts, Boston, Massachusetts/The John Pickering Lyman Collection – Gift of Miss Theodora Lyman/Bridgeman Images; p14tl Indianapolis Museum of Art at Newfields, USA/Gift of Dr. K. S. Lo/Bridgeman Images, cl © Estate of George Rickey/DACS, London/VAGA, New York 2018, photo: B.O'Kane/Alamy Stock Photo, bl FashionStock.com/Shutterstock.com, r Dallas Museum of Art, Texas, USA/Foundation for the Arts Collection, gift of Mr. and Mrs. Alfred L. Bromberg Foundation for the Arts Collection, gift of Mr. and Mrs. Alfred L. Bromberg/Bridgeman Images; p15l Antony McAulay/Alamy Stock Photo, r Art Collection 3/Alamy Stock Photo; p16 The National Trust Photolibrary/Alamy Stock Photo; p17 Jeremy Richards/Alamy Stock Photo; p18l Indianapolis Museum of Art at Newfields, USA/Gift of Mr and Mrs Eli Lilly/Bridgeman Images, r robertharding/Alamy Stock Photo; p19t © ADAGP, Paris and DACS, London 2018, photo: Indianapolis Museum of Art at Newfields, USA/Gift of Robert and Lisa Kessler/Bridgeman Images, b Stefano Ravera/Alamy Stock Photo; p20t © 2018 Mondrian/Holtzman Trust, photo: Martin Shields/Alamy Stock Photo, b The Metropolitan Museum of Art, New York, H. O. Havemeyer Collection, Bequest of Mrs. H. O. Havemeyer, 1929; p21t Arco Images GmbH/Alamy Stock Photo, b Chris Hellier/Alamy Stock Photo; p23 © DACS 2018, photo: Universal Art Archive/Alamy Stock Photo; p24t Jean-Pierre Courau/Bridgeman Images, c Art Collection 3/Alamy Stock Photo, b © Anish Kapoor. All Rights Reserved, DACS/Artimage 2018, photo: Dave Morgan; p25 Library of Congress, Washington, D.C.; p26 Dinodia/Bridgeman Images; p27l Mark Andrews/Alamy Stock Photo, tr © Deborah Butterfield/DACS, London/VAGA, NY 2018, photo: Jim West/Alamy Stock Photo, cr Westend61 GmbH/Alamy Stock Photo, br Hero Images Inc./Alamy Stock Photo; p28t Aaron Coury/Alamy Stock Photo, c Royal College of Art, London/Bridgeman Images, b Leon Harris/Getty Images; p29 © Subodh Gupta, photo © Christie's Images/Bridgeman Images; p30t Michele Molinari/Alamy Stock Photo, b PjrStudio/Alamy Stock Photo; p31t RosalreneBetancourt 14/Alamy Stock Photo, b imageBROKER/Alamy Stock Photo; p32 View Pictures/UIG/Getty Images; p33 Pierluigi Praturlon/Reporters Associati & Archivi/Mondadori Portfolio/Getty Images; p34t © Katrina Kirk, c © Kat Tunwell, b © Emma Benson; p35 Werner Forman Archive/Bridgeman Images; p36–37 DeAgostini/Getty Images; p39 DEA PICTURE LIBRARY/De Agostini/Getty Images; p40 Cat_arch_angel/Shutterstock.com; p41 Bridgeman Images; p42tl © Anthony Butera/Bridgeman Images, photo: Bridgeman Images, bl © Banco de México Diego Rivera Frida Kahlo Museums Trust, Mexico, D.F./DACS 2018, photo: Detroit Institute of Arts, USA/Gift of the Artist/Bridgeman Images, r DeAgostini/Getty Images; p43 Bridgeman Images; p44 © Alan Parsons; p45 © Alan Parsons; p46 Andrew Ray/Alamy Stock Photo; p47 © Janet Cardiff; Courtesy of the artist and Luhring Augustine, New York. Sung by Salisbury Cathedral Choir, Recording and Postproduction by SoundMoves, Edited by George Bures Miller, 'The Forty Part Motet' by Janet Cardiff was originally produced by Field Art Projects with the Arts Council of England, Canada House, the Salisbury Festival and Salisbury Cathedral Choir, BALTIC Gateshead, The New Art Gallery Walsall, and the NOW Festival Nottingham, photo: Keith Morris/Alamy Stock Photo; p48 Fototeca Gilardi/Getty Images; p49l Oscar Cardenas/Alamy Stock Photo, r Realy Easy Star/Giuseppe Masci/Alamy Stock Photo; p50 Dinodia Photos/Alamy Stock Photo; p52 © Lucien Freud/Bridgeman Images, photo © The Lucian Freud Archive/Bridgeman Images; p53 Bridgeman Images; p54 © Chuck Close, courtesy Pace Gallery, Collection of the Akron Art Museum, Purchased with funds from an anonymous contribution, an anonymous contribution in honor of Ruth C. Roush, and the Museum Acquisition Fund; p55t © The British Sporting Art Trust/Bridgeman Images, b Bridgeman Images; p57l © The Estate of Jean-Michel Basquiat/ADAGP, Paris and DACS, London 2018, photo © Christie's Images/Bridgeman Images, r © 2005 Kehinde Wiley. Used by permission, photo: B Christopher/Alamy Stock Photo; p58 James Jackson/Alamy Stock Photo; p59l Armand-Photo-Travel / Alamy Stock Photo, r © The Andy Warhol Foundation for the Visual Arts, Inc./DACS/Artimage 2018; p60t © Stuart Franklin/Magnum Photos, b © Barbara Kruger, courtesy Mary Boone Gallery, New York; p61 © Alan Parsons; p62t © Salvador Dali, Fundació Gala-Salvador Dalí, DACS 2018, photo © Tate, London 2018, b © The Joseph and Robert Cornell Memorial Foundation/VAGA, NY/DACS, London, photo Peter Willi/Bridgeman Images; p63 © Estate of Eileen Agar/Bridgeman Images, photo: Bridgeman Images; p64t © British Library Board. All Rights Reserved/Bridgeman Images, b Noppy2016/Shutterstock.com; p65t © CSG CIC Glasgow Museums Collection/Bridgeman Images, b Bridgeman Images; p66t © Purix Verlag Volker Christen/Bridgeman Images, b Photo © Christie's Images/Bridgeman Images; p67t © Liz Macfarlane, b Photo © Christie's Images/Bridgeman Images; p68 Reproduced by permission of the Henry Moore Foundation; p69 Zeljkica/Shutterstock.com; p70 © ADAGP, Paris and DACS, London 2018, photo

Bridgeman Images; p71r © Liz Macfarlane; l © Robert Rauschenberg Foundation/DACS, London/VAGA, New York 2018, photo Bridgeman Images; p72t ZU_09/Getty Images; b © Heirs of Josephine N. Hopper, licensed by the Whitney Museum of American Art, photo San Diego Museum of Art, California/Museum purchase through the Edwin S. and Carol Dempster Larsen Memorial Fund/Bridgeman Images; p73 © Paul Riley/Bridgeman Images, photo: Bridgeman Images; p74tl Robert Morris/Alamy Stock Photo, bl © Denis Kelly/Dreamstime.com, r © Anish Kapoor. All Rights Reserved, DACS 2018, Boykov/Shutterstock.com; p75 Carolyn Eaton/Alamy Stock Photo; p76t robertharding/ Alamy Stock Photo, b Dinodia Photos/Alamy Stock Photo; p77 © Andy Goldsworthy, © Photograph Bernardo Palmeiro; p78t Pictures from History/David Henley/ Bridgeman Images, bl Elnur/Shutterstock.com, br Gerry Boughan/Shutterstock.com; p79t, c & b © Alan Parsons; p80t Vanzyst/Shutterstock.com, b Courtesy Zaha Hadid Foundation; p81 Courtesy Bblur architecture; p82 Ovidiu Hrubaru/Alamy Stock Photo; p83 AF archive/Alamy Stock Photo; p84 Butterfly stools from Vitra, photo Bequest of Ise Gropius/Bridgeman Images; p85t Valerijs Kostreckis/Alamy Stock Photo, ct Photographee.eu/Shutterstock.com, cb & b Barry Barnes/Shutterstock.com; p86t Bridgeman Images, b Photo © Chris Beetles Ltd, London/Bridgeman Images; p87t © Alessandra Manfredi/Bridgeman Images, photo: Bridgeman Images, b © Junichi Nakahara/Himawariya, photo Pictures from History/Bridgeman Images; p88 © 2018 The Andy Warhol Foundation for the Visual Arts, Inc./ Licensed by DACS, London, photo Bridgeman Images; p89l © Succession H. Matisse/DACS 2018, r Granger/ Bridgeman Images; p90l fontStocker/Shutterstock.com, r PRISMA ARCHIVO/Alamy Stock Photo; p91t Campillo Rafael/Alamy Stock Photo, b Pictures from History/ Bridgeman Images; p92 Mark Thomas/Design Pics/ Bridgeman Images; p93 Ira Berger/Alamy Stock Photo; p94t Chones/Shutterstock.com, b Denis Radovanovic/ Shutterstock.com; p95l Jevanto Productions/Shutterstock.com, r JuliusKielaitis/Shutterstock.com; p96 imageBROKER/Alamy Stock Photo; p97t Mis-Tery/ Shutterstock.com, b Natalya Levish/Shutterstock.com; p98 Muilee/Shutterstock.com; p99l © Ellamae Statham, r © Azra Iqbal; p100l & r © Louise Arnould; p101 Basso & Brooke; p102t AMPIRION/Shutterstock.com, c FRANCOIS GUILLOT/AFP/Getty Images, p102b © Louise Arnould; p103t & b courtesy Dionne Swift, www.dionneswift.co.uk; p104t & b © Louise Arnould; p105l akg-images/Gerd Hartung, r © Nina Shirokova/Bridgeman Images, photo: Gamborg Collection/Bridgeman Images; p106l Mode 1947/ Photo © Collection Gregoire/Bridgeman Images, r Roger-Viollet/TopFoto; p107 © Jackie Thomson; p108t University of Bristol/ArenaPAL/TopFoto, b © Gregg Barnes; p109l AF archive/Alamy Stock Photo, r Royal Collection Trust © Her Majesty Queen Elizabeth II, 2018/Bridgeman Images; p110–111 © Yuko Shimizo; p112l Rose Carson/ Shutterstock.com, r Eugenio Marongiu/Shutterstock.com; p113t © Banco de México Diego Rivera Frida Kahlo Museums Trust, Mexico, D.F./DACS 2018, photo © Christie's Images/Bridgeman Images, b © Estate of Hans Schleger, courtesy of the Shell Heritage Art Collection, photo © Christie's Images/Bridgeman Images; p114t Archivart/Alamy Stock Photo, bl National Gallery of Art, Washington, D.C., Chester Dale Collection, br Museum of Fine Arts, Boston, Massachusetts/Keith McLeod Fund/ Bridgeman Images; p115 Bridgeman Images; p116t photo © Rijkstudio, b Granger Historical Picture Archive/Alamy Stock Photo; p117 Universal History Archive/UIG/ Bridgeman Images; p119l Archives Charmet/Bridgeman Images, tr Minneapolis Institute of Arts, MN/The Mary Ingebrand-Pohlad Endowment for Twentieth Century Paintings, the Frank Meyers Steiner American Western Art Fund, and the William and Harriet Ludwick Endowment for Western Art/Bridgeman Images, br DaTo Images/Bridgeman Images; p120 © The Josef and Anni Albers Foundation/VG Bild-Kunst, Bonn and DACS, London 2018, photo: James Goodman Gallery, New York/Bridgeman Images; p121t Indianapolis Museum of Art at Newfields, USA/Carl H. Lieber Memorial Fund/Bridgeman Images, b Museum of Fine Arts, Boston, Massachusetts, USA/Museum purchase with funds donated from the Marshall H. Gould Fund, Joyce and Edward Linde, and an anonymous supporter/ Bridgeman Images; p122l JonathanCollins/Shutterstock.com, r past art/Alamy Stock Photo; p124 Iain Masterton/ Alamy Stock Photo; p125 saiko3p/Shutterstock.com; p126t © FLC/ ADAGP, Paris and DACS, London 2018, photo: Bildarchiv Monheim GmbH/Alamy Stock Photo, b © FLC/ ADAGP, Paris and DACS, London 2018, photo: Galit Seligmann/Alamy Stock Photo; p127 Marshall Ikonography/ Alamy Stock Photo; p128 Bridgeman Images; p129 Ariadne Van Zandbergen/Getty Images; p130l Bashir Osman's Photography/Getty Images, r © Estate of the Artist, photo: Byron Slater; p132 Bridgeman Images; p133 Courtesy Nardi Mobili in Cartone, Italy, photo Germano Poli/Alamy Stock Photo; p134l Moviestore collection Ltd/Alamy Stock Photo, r Chronicle/Alamy Stock Photo; p136t POM POM/ Shutterstock.com, b Thawornnurak/Shutterstock.com; p137t jocic/Shutterstock.com, b Leszek Kobusinski/ Shutterstock.com; p138 © Alvar Aalto Foundation, Helsinki; p139 Chronicle/Alamy Stock Photo; p140 SIHASAKPRACHUM/Shutterstock.com; p141l INTERFOTO/ Alamy Stock Photo, Philip Bigg/Alamy Stock Photo; p142t Courtesy Makita, b StockImages/Alamy Stock Photo; p144l Jeff Morgan 04/Alamy Stock Photo, r Felipe Trueba/Alamy Stock Photo; p145 Dinodia Photos/Alamy Stock Photo; p146tl © Yuko Shimizo, tr Bridgeman Images, b © Yuko Shimizo; p148 Robert Wallwork/Alamy Stock Photo; p149 Grimgram/Shutterstock.com; p150t INTERFOTO/Alamy Stock Photo, b Tallandier/Bridgeman Images; p152t © Erin Daniels, b ZUMA Press, Inc./Alamy Stock Photo; p153 Victor Boyko/Getty Images; p154t The Print Collector/Alamy Stock Photo, b Private Collection/Bridgeman Images; p155l Moviestore collection Ltd/Alamy Stock Photo, r Divyakant Solanki/Epa/REX/Shutterstock; p156l © 2018 The Metropolitan Museum of Art/Art Resource/Scala, Florence, r thislife pictures/Alamy Stock Photo; p157t © 2018 The Metropolitan Museum of Art/Art Resource/Scala, Florence, b Trinity Mirror/Mirrorpix/Alamy Stock Photo; p158 Paul Hartnett/PYMCA/UIG/Getty Images; p160 © Staatliche Kunstsammlungen Dresden/Bridgeman Images; p161 © Idelle Weber, courtesy Broadway 1602, New York, photo © Christie's Images/Bridgeman Images; p162 Bridgeman Images; p163 Bridgeman Images; p164l Bridgeman Images, r Museum of Fine Arts, Boston, MA/Gift of Quincy Adams Shaw/Bridgeman Images; p166 Photo © Lefevre Fine Art Ltd., London/Bridgeman Images; p167 © ADAGP, Paris and DACS, London 2018, photo San Diego Museum of Art, USA/Gift of Mrs. William T. Burch/Bridgeman Images; p168l © Frank Auerbach, courtesy Marlborough Fine Art, photo Bridgeman Images, r © Whitfield Lovell, Courtesy of DC Moore Gallery, New York, photo Bridgeman Images; p170l Photo © Brian Seed/Bridgeman Images, r Collection of the Lowe Art Museum, University of Miami/Gift of Mr. and Mrs. Raymond Bell/Bridgeman Images; p171l National Gallery of Art, Washington, D.C., r The Israel Museum, Jerusalem, Israel/The Arthur and Madeleine Chalette Lejwa Collection/ Bridgeman Images; p173t © Andy Goldsworthy, b South West Images Scotland/Alamy Stock Photo; p174t © DACS 2018, photo © Christie's Images/Bridgeman Images, b Andrea Heselton/Alamy Stock Photo; p176 © dpa picture alliance archive/Alamy Stock Photo; p177 © The Estate of Jean-Michel Basquiat/ADAGP, Paris and DACS, London 2018, photo © Christie's Images/Bridgeman Images; p178t Paul Fearn/Alamy Stock Photo, b Songquan Deng / Shutterstock.com; p179t & b © Alan Parsons; p180 © Association Marcel Duchamp/ADAGP, Paris and DACS, London 2018, photo Cameraphoto Arte Venezia/Bridgeman Images; p181 © Tim Noble and Sue Webster. All Rights Reserved, DACS 2018, photo © Christie's Images/ Bridgeman Images; p182–183 TyC26/Shutterstock.com; p185t Sterling and Francine Clark Art Institute, Williamstown, MA/Gift of the Manton Art Foundation in memory of Sir Edwin and Lady Manton/Bridgeman Images, 185bl & br Bridgeman Images; p186t © Bridget Riley 2018. All rights reserved. Dimensions: 48 x 29cm, photo © Christie's Images/Bridgeman Images, bl © Bridget Riley 2018. All rights reserved. Dimensions: 106.7 x 112.4cm, photo © Tate, London 2018, br © Richard Estes, courtesy Marlborough Gallery, New York, photo Bridgeman Images; p187l & c Charles Knox - Creative/Alamy Stock Photo, r YAY Media AS/Alamy Stock Photo; p188t Peanutroaster/ Dreamstime.com, bl Lenscap Photography/Shutterstock. com, bc & br © Georgia O'Keeffe Museum/DACS 2018, photo © Christie's Images/Bridgeman Images; p189l Uber Bilder/Alamy Stock Photo, tr ton koene/Alamy Stock Photo, ctr Juice Images/Alamy Stock Photo, cbr & br D Core/3D Models/Alamy Stock Photo; p192t Chris Ridley - Internet Stock/Alamy Stock Photo, b Courtesy of the Auckland Art Gallery Toi o Tāmaki; p194l © Mouni Feddag courtesy of Bright Art Licensing, r An excerpt from the 'Zeroxwallah Zine' by Sameer Kulavoor; p195t & b Bibliothèque de l'Institut de France, Paris/Archives Charmet/Bridgeman Images; p196 © Mayuko Fujino courtesy Illustration Web; p198t Valerie Armstrong/Alamy Stock Photo, b © Mary Kuper, photo Bridgeman Images; p200 GaudiLab/ Shutterstock.com; p201 Magi Bagi/Shutterstock.com; p202 aperturesound/Shutterstock.com; p203 elfishes/ Shutterstock.com; p204t Courtesy of Honda and Wieden+Kennedy, b Image Courtesy of The Advertising Archives; p205t © Guardian News & Media Ltd. 2018; b Lebrecht Music and Arts Photo Library / Alamy Stock Photo; p206t Classic Image/Alamy Stock Photo, b courtesy Houghton Mifflin Harcourt; p207 courtesy Joey Hi-Fi; p209 all © Jesse Howarth; p211 all © Shannen McCusker; p213l Ashmolean Museum, University of Oxford/ Bridgeman Images; r Dorling Kindersley/UIG/Bridgeman Images; p214tl Bunwit Unseree / Alamy Stock Photo, bl Xinhua/Alamy Stock Photo, r Victor VIRGILE/Gamma-Rapho/Getty Images; p217 all © Emma Benson; p218 DOCTOR BLACK/ Shutterstock.com; p219l Costume made by Tirelli Costumi, Rome - Photo by Claudia Primangeli, r © Vicky Rodriquez; p220l & r © Vicky Rodriquez; P221l & r © Vicky Rodriquez; p222tl & r bayualam/Shutterstock.com, bl Mejini Neskah/ Shutterstock.com; p223tl Franck METOIS / Alamy Stock Photo, tr pzAxe/Shutterstock.com, b Steve Photography/ Shutterstock.com; p224 Sergey Kozienko/Shutterstock. com; p225 Dudley Wood/Alamy Stock Photo; p226 Stefano Ravera/Alamy Stock Photo; p227l Image Source Plus/Alamy Stock Photo, r david mbiyu/Alamy Stock Photo; p228 Heritage Image Partnership Ltd/Alamy Stock Photo; p230t, c & b © 2018 Mondrian/Holtzman Trust, photo Artepics/ Alamy Stock Photo; p231t, c & b © Alan Parsons; p232 © The Estate of Yves Klein c/o DACS, London 2018, photo Nathan King/Alamy Stock Photo; p233l & r © Takashi Murakami/Kaikai Kiki Co. Ltd. All Rights Reserved, photo © Christie's Images/Bridgeman Images; p234t & b © Alan Parsons; p235 imageBROKER/Alamy Stock Photo; p236t Bridgeman Images, b © Purix Verlag Volker Christen/ Bridgeman Images; p237t & b Mucha Trust/Bridgeman Images; p238t Bridgeman Images, b © 2018 Calder Foundation, New York/DACS London, photo: Bonhams Auctioneers, London; p239l © 2018 Calder Foundation, New York/DACS London, photo © Louis Monier/Bridgeman Images; tr Reproduced by permission of the Henry Moore Foundation, photo © Christie's Images/Bridgeman Images; br Reproduced by permission of the Henry Moore Foundation, photo: De Agostini Picture Library/G. Dagli Orti/ Bridgeman Images; p240 Malcolm Park editorial/Alamy Stock Photo; p241 Bridgeman Images; p242l, c & r © 2018 The Andy Warhol Foundation for the Visual Arts, Inc./ Licensed by DACS, London, photo © Christie's Images/ Bridgeman Images; p243t & bl Library of Congress, Washington, D.C., br Leeds Museums and Galleries (Leeds Art Gallery) U.K./Bridgeman Images; p244l & r © the Ann Baumann Trust, photo: Indianapolis Museum of Art at Newfields, USA/Gift of Stephen and Elaine Ewing Fess/ Bridgeman Images; p245 © Elizabeth Blackadder/ Bridgeman Images, photo courtesy of The Scottish Gallery, Edinburgh/Bridgeman Images; p246t Reproduced courtesy of the artist, photo © Christie's Images/Bridgeman Images, c © Frank Stella. ARS, NY and DACS, London 2018, photo: Cincinnati Art Museum, Ohio/ Gift of the Douglas S. Cramer Foundation/Bridgeman Images, b © Frank Stella. ARS, NY and DACS, London 2018, photo: Museum of Fine Arts, Houston, Texas/Museum purchase funded by the Alice Pratt Brown Museum Fund/Bridgeman Images; p247t & b © The Joseph and Robert Cornell Memorial Foundation/VAGA, NY/DACS, London 2018, photo: Bridgeman Images; p248t © Daido Moriyama Photo Foundation, Tokyo, b © Daido Moriyama, courtesy of Tepper Takayama Fine Arts, Boston; p249t © Estate of Li Yuan-chia. All rights reserved, DACS/ Artimage 2018. Photo: Phil Gammon, c © Richard Galpin. All Rights Reserved, DACS/Artimage 2018, photo: Richard Galpin, b Courtesy of the artist and Metro Pictures, New York; p250 © Duane Michals, courtesy of DC Moore Gallery,

New York, photo: The Israel Museum, Jerusalem, Israel/Gift of Nohra Haime, New York/Bridgeman Images; p251 © Lawrie Simenson/Bridgeman Images, photo: Bridgeman Images; p252l & r VIEW Pictures Ltd/Alamy Stock Photo; p253t © NSW State Archives and Records, b courtesy Vastushilpa Foundation, Ahmedabad; p254 © Li Chunfang, courtesy CSADI Architects; p255l © SZ Photo/Scherl/ Bridgeman Images, r Philadelphia Museum of Art, Pennsylvania, PA/ Gift of Charles H. Ludington from the George Crofts Collection, 1925/Bridgeman Images; p256l Konstantin Rodchanin/Shutterstock.com, r VIEW Pictures Ltd/Alamy Stock Photo; p257t © Yinka Shonibare MBE. All Rights Reserved, DACS/Artimage 2018. Image courtesy Stephen Friedman Gallery, London and James Cohan Gallery, New York. Photo: Stephen White , b STEPHEN FLEMING/Alamy Stock Photo; p258t Alexey Kashin/ Shutterstock.com, c Arkadivna/Shutterstock.com, b Robert Kneschke/Shutterstock.com; p259l Bridgeman Images, r Ann Rosener/Pix Inc./The LIFE Images Collection/Getty Images; p261t Adrian Gale/Alamy Stock Photo, b SiliconValleyStock/Alamy Stock Photo; p262t Alinari/ Bridgeman Images, b Granger Historical Picture Archive/ Alamy Stock Photo; p263t © Succession Picasso/DACS, London 2018, Photo © Christie's Images / Bridgeman Images, b Crafts Study Centre, University for the Creative Arts; p264t Courtesy of Bonham's, London, b cm studio/ Alamy Stock Photo; p265t & b © Alan Parsons; p266 © Alan Parsons; p270 Alex Segre/Alamy Stock Photo; p271 ITAR-TASS News Agency/Alamy Stock Photo; p272l © Mona Hatoum. Courtesy Centre Pompidou, Mnam-CCI/Dist RMN-GP (Photo: Philippe Migeat), r faber1893/ Shutterstock.com; p273 © ARS, NY and DACS, London 2018, photo: Gary Hill; p274 claire doherty/Alamy Stock Photo; p275t Aflo Co. Ltd./Alamy Stock Photo, b Wiskerke/ Alamy Stock Photo; p276t & c *Lumen* by Jenny Sabin Studio for The Museum of Modern Art and MoMA PS1's Young Architects Program 2017, on view at MoMA PS1 from June 29 to September 4, 2017. Images courtesy MoMA PS1. Photos by Pablo Enriquez, b Courtesy of The New Art Gallery Walsall, UK. Photo: Jonathan Shaw; p277l © Succession H. Matisse/ DACS 2018, photo © RMN-Grand Palais / Gérard Blot, r © Succession H. Matisse/ DACS 2018, photo: Allan Cash Picture Library/Alamy Stock Photo; p278t Fitzwilliam Museum, University of Cambridge/ Bridgeman Images, b © Anthony Green, courtesy of Chris Beetles Gallery, photo: Bridgeman Images; p279l The Israel Museum, Jerusalem, Israel/Gift of the British Friends of the Art Museums in Israel/Bridgeman Images, r Cultura Creative (RF)/Alamy Stock Photo; p280l Keystone Pictures USA/ Alamy Stock Photo, r © Succession Picasso/DACS, London 2018, photo: Agra Art, Warsaw/Bridgeman Images; p281l Wanida McHugh/Alamy Stock Photo, r Vladimir Tomovic/ Alamy Stock Photo; p282t frank_peters/Shutterstock.com, b © David Roberts; p283 LaModa/Alamy Stock Photo; p285l Ian Dagnall/Alamy Stock Photo, r Lordprice Collection/Alamy Stock Photo; p288l & r © Zeba Safdar; p289l & r © Anna-Maie Southern; p290t & b © Anna-Maie Southern; p291l & tr © Shannen McCusker, br © Natalie Percival; p293l © Harper Collins, r © Azra Iqbal; p294t Media-Mode.com, b WENN UK/Alamy Stock Photo; p295t Régis BOSSU/Sygma/Getty Images, b © The Estate of Eva Hesse, courtesy Hauser & Wirth; p297t CHRISTOPHE PETIT TESSON/EPA-EFE/REX/Shutterstock, b ZUMA Press, Inc./Alamy Stock Photo; p298t © Yinka Shonibare MBE. All Rights Reserved, DACS/Artimage 2018. Image courtesy National Gallery of Canada, Ottawa. Photo: Stephen White, bl © Sunna Yasin, br Josse Christophel/Alamy Stock Photo; p299 Model Ameera Hadrami, Photography Scott Taylor, courtesy Sunna Yasin; p300t © Succession Picasso/DACS, London 2018, photo Bridgeman Images, b Bridgeman Images; p301l © Yayoi Kusama, photo: Bridgeman Images, r Photo © Christie's Images/Bridgeman Images; p302 Danny Coope/Alamy Stock Photo; p303 © Richard Wilson, courtesy MDS Fine Art, photo: Guy Corbishley/Alamy Stock Photo; p304 © Mona Hatoum. Courtesy the artist and MdbK Leipzig (Photo: dotgain.info); p305 © Ana Maria Pacheco/Bridgeman Images, photo: David Burton/Alamy Stock Photo; p306 Chronicle/Alamy Stock Photo; p307t Brooklyn Museum of Art, New York/Designated Purchase Fund/Bridgeman Images, b © Anne Desmett/Bridgeman Images, photo: Bridgeman Images; p308 © Chris Ofili, Courtesy the artist and Victoria Miro, London/Venice; p309t © Faiza Shaikh/Bridgeman Images, photo: Bridgeman Images, b © Faiza Shaikh/Bridgeman Images, photo: Bridgeman Images; p310t © Alan Parsons, b © Anthony Green, courtesy Chris Beetles Gallery, photo: Bridgeman Images; p311t Dennis Hallinan/Alamy Stock Photo, b Justin Kase zsixz/Alamy Stock Photo; p312l Greg Vaughn/Alamy Stock Photo, r Horizons WWP/TRVL/Alamy Stock Photo; p313 Artokoloro Quint Lox Limited/Alamy Stock Photo; p314t courtesy Alan Parsons, b courtesy Saatchi Gallery, London; p315 © Alan Parsons; p316t Georgina198/ Shutterstock.com, b Rob Scott/Digital Camera Magazine/ Getty Images; p317 © Zineb Sedira. All Rights Reserved, DACS 2018, © Photo William Martin, Courtesy the artist and kamel mennour, Paris/London; p318 Simon Turner/Alamy Stock Photo; p319t VIEW Pictures Ltd/Alamy Stock Photo, b Barry Winiker/Getty Images; p320 Melanie Lemahieu/ Shutterstock.com; p321 SIHASAKPRACHUM/Shutterstock.com; p322 TonyV3112/Shutterstock.com; p323 Stephen Emerson/Alamy Stock Photo; p324 Gimas/Shutterstock.com; p325t Will Thomass/Shutterstock.com, b Dragon Images/Shutterstock.com; p326 Keith Homan/Shutterstock.com; p327 courtesy Robert Yellin Yakimono Gallery, Kyoto, Japan; p328 Art Directors & TRIP/Alamy Stock Photo; p330 robertharding/Alamy Stock Photo; p331 Dimitrios Kambouris/Getty Images for Harper's BAZAAR; p332 © Metro Trains Melbourne; p333 RosalreneBetancourt 7/ Alamy Stock Photo; p334 A7880S/Alamy Stock Vector; p336 CTK/Alamy Stock Photo; p337 ALPA PROD/ Shutterstock.com; p338–339 Simon Turner/Alamy Stock Photo; p348 Westend61 GmbH/Alamy Stock Photo; p353 SurfsUp/Shutterstock.com; p354–355 Sunny-s/ Shutterstock.com; p356–357 © Anna Buriak; p358 © Suki Fong; p359–360 © Thomas Bailey; p361–363 © Alison Page; p364 © Eloise Groves; p365t © Jackie German; p365b © Ashlea Philips; p366–367 © Mahnoor Abassi; p368t © Isabella Vanackere Castellano; p368bl © Blaze Chapman; p368br © Julia Vila Rosell; p369 © George Groves; p370t © Stefan-Marc Seymour; p370b © Jackie German; p371–372 © Christine Wiggil; p373 © Naomi Flowers; p374 © Jessica Bennett.